MANAGING PEOPLE AT WORK

CONCEPTS AND CASES IN INTERPERSONAL BEHAVIOR

MANAGING
PEOPLE
AT
WORK

CONCEPTS AND CASES IN INTERPERSONAL BEHAVIOR

O. Jeff Harris, Jr.

Professor of Management
Louisiana State University

A Wiley/Hamilton Publication
JOHN WILEY & SONS, INC.
Santa Barbara · New York · London · Sydney · Toronto

Library of Congress Cataloging in Publication Data

Harris, O. Jeff, Jr.
Managing people at work.

"A Wiley/Hamilton publication."
Includes bibliographies.
1.   Personnel management—United States.
2.   Personnel management.   I.   Title.
HF5549.2.U5H37   658.3   75-19272
ISBN 0-471-35410-4

Printed in the United States of America

10 9 8 7 6 5 4 3 2 1

to Carolyn

Preface

Today is an exciting time to be living, studying, and managing. It is also a challenging period in that new discoveries are being made, there are pressures for social, cultural, and economic changes, and the total environment seems dynamic. For students of management, this period is an enlightening one, as new theories are being forwarded, and research endeavors reveal previously hidden truths.

The changes, innovations, research findings, and theories that have been developed all have an impact on people at work. This book purposes to glean the important, relevant concepts about managing people (the theories, research findings, and innovations) and to present them in an actionable format. One of my chief ambitions in writing this book has been the desire to provide more direct links with management theory and application than has frequently been the case in the past. While the overview of the book is presented in Chapter 1, the design of the book was purposefully chosen to present management concepts and then to illustrate and provide opportunities to use the concepts in the many cases contained in the book. In particular, the cases at the beginning of each chapter were placed there to stimulate thought about the content that follows. The cases at the back of the book provide an opportunity to practice the concepts.

As I look back at the writing of the book, I recognize the tremendous amount of teamwork that is involved in putting the book together. I have come to realize even more fully the contributions of early and contemporary writers to management thought. The theory and research efforts of many forebearers and colleagues have provided the foundations of this book. I am particularly indebted to several of my colleagues at Louisiana State University for their immediate contributions and constructive criticisms. In particular Professors Raymond V. Lesikar, Herbert G. Hicks, Leon C. Megginson, and Edmund R. Gray served as sounding boards and innovators as the book was designed and written. Professor Wilmar Bernthal of the University of Colorado provided invaluable support through his comprehensive reviews of the book. I am also indebted to other reviewers supplied by Wiley/Hamilton for their helpful suggestions.

The editorial assistance of George C. Thomsen, Ronald Q. Lewton, and Judyl Mudfoot brought the book together in a more meaningful way. Gloria Armistead, Sara Jo Norris, Rhonda Alexander, and others put my longhand scribblings into typed words for the first draft of the book. Dorothy Langlois and Carolyn Harris, my wife, typed the final draft of the book in meticulous form. I am most grateful to each of these.

I have been blessed with excellent graduate assistants during the preparation of the book. Specifically, Richard Walcott, Ali Parsinia, David Hovey, Jr., Warren Reddin, and Richard Blizzard contributed to the book through their research efforts and their assistance in the development of some of the cases. Many other students, both graduate and undergraduate, have originated important ideas. All of my students in recent semesters have helped in the development of the book as I have discussed concepts and cases with them and have benefited from their feedback.

My family has played an important role in the completion of this book. In addition to typing parts of the final manuscript, Carolyn has served as a continuing source of support and encouragement. Larkin and Stephen, our young sons, have provided a pleasurable source of distraction and inspiration.

This has been a team effort in the truest sense. To each team member I am most grateful. To those of you who read and utilize this book, may it prove useful in your study of the exciting, expanding field of managing people at work!

O. Jeff Harris, Jr.

About the Author

O. Jeff Harris, Jr. is a professor of management at Louisiana State University in Baton Rouge. He has also taught at the University of Arkansas in Fayetteville and the University of Texas at Austin. Dr. Harris has instructed graduate and undergraduate courses in organizational behavior, interpersonal relations, manpower management, evolution of management thought, organizational theory, and organizational communication in his fifteen-year career.

A native of New Mexico, Professor Harris earned his Ph.D. in management from the University of Texas. He is an active member of the Academy of Management and also holds memberships in Beta Gamma Sigma, Sigma Iota Epsilon, and Delta Sigma Pi. He has written a number of articles that have appeared in professional journals and has edited a publication entitled *Current Concepts in Management*.

Many of the concepts for *Managing People at Work* are a direct result of the consulting and training activities conducted by Dr. Harris. The author is an active consultant having worked with managers in processing, petrochemical, service, government, medical, and retail fields extensively. In particular, Professor Harris has devoted much time to consulting in the fields of hospital and nursing home administration. One of the primary activities of these consulting efforts has been to conduct managerial training and development programs. It is in these programs that many of the ideas for this book have been developed and tested.

Contents

Chapter 1

Introduction

As the title suggests, this is a book about managing people at work. Attention is focused upon the attitudes, experiences, expectations, problems, needs, and changes in those who are a part of work-oriented organizations. Answers are sought for questions such as: Why do employees do the things they do while at work? Why do people work anyway? Are managers and nonmanagers alike or different in their work motivations and responsibilities? To whom do those who manage have obligations and responsibilities? How should managers go about performing their duties effectively and beneficially? What changes and trends are occurring today within and outside of organizations that have a bearing upon people at work? What future trends can be expected to have an effect upon managers and their responsibilities? The answers to some of these questions may be obvious, while other answers are exceedingly difficult to uncover.

Every endeavor is based upon certain assumptions, and this endeavor to analyze the management of people at work has its own set of underpinnings. The philosophy of this book and the materials presented here are a direct result of these assumptions. The assumptions are presented at this early stage as the foundation for further building. Assumptions about the nature of organizations, about the qualities and expectations of people who work, about the expectations and responsibilities of those who manage, and about what a book on managing those who work should be are discussed in the paragraphs that follow.

Assumptions about
Work Organizations

Some work, of course, is done by individuals independently in isolated circumstances. However, *the vast majority of all work in today's environment takes place within the context of a structured organization—a grouping of individuals into a unified, common effort.* The structuring may be a loosely knit one in which interrelationships are scarcely discernible, or the organizational pattern may be a highly formalized one in which authority relationships are defined in detail and prescribed worker behavior is unwaveringly expected. Frequently, the organizational grouping lies somewhere in between these two extremes.

The organization in which work occurs (regardless of whether it is informal or formal) *exists to accomplish goals.* In other words, every organization has a mission (or a set of missions). One goal of a public utility, for example, might be to provide an adequate source of energy to individuals and industrial and commercial consumers at a reasonable cost. One objective of a manufacturing concern would be to design and produce an item to satisfy the demands of a certain market. A hospital will have among its objectives the goal of providing a healing hand to the sick and infirm. The objectives of organizations will not all be the same, but each organization has its own reasons for existence. These reasons may remain relatively constant, but they are more likely to be modified over a period of time. Changing needs and new internal and external demands require modifications to occur.

As we shall see in later chapters, organizational objectives are likely to be multiple. That is to say, most organizations attempt to achieve several goals and to serve a number of publics simultaneously. While this book is written largely in the context of private business, the general assumptions about work organizations and people at work hold true also for nonprofit organizations.

Organizations typically consist of a combination of financial resources, materials, machines or equipment, and people. Each of these elements is critically important to the success of the organization. One of the most important, of course, is the people who make up the organization.

Assumptions about People at Work

The philosophy of this book centers upon a high regard for workers as individual human beings. Every individual is respected for what he is, what he needs, and what he wishes to become. Individuals in the work place exhibit similar behavior patterns and characteristics to a certain degree, but they also show many dissimilarities. *Each individual who works has his own set of needs, drives, goals, and experiences. Each individual has his own physical and psychological traits. Each human being is not only a product of his biological inheritance but also a result of interactions with his environment.* Family relationships, religious influences, racial backgrounds, educational accomplishments, the application of technological innovations, and a number of additional environmental-experiential influences affect the individual *as he works.* Among the environmental factors that influence work behavior are several organizational elements—defined authority relationships; organizational goals, procedures, and rules; informal interactions of workers; and the type and manner of supervision received by the employee, to cite a few examples.

In Chapters 7 and 10, the idea that *people come to work expecting specific things from their jobs and work careers* will be developed more fully. Workers agree to exchange their skills, abilities, and energies in return for the fulfillment of certain needs or expectations through the employing organization. This book is based upon the assumption that the employing organization has a responsibility to help individual workers achieve reasonable, legitimate expectations while at work whenever this is possible.

People, of course, are extremely important to the success of organizations. People provide the knowledge and much of the energy through which organizational objectives are accomplished.

Assumptions about Those Who Manage

Individuals who serve as managers or supervisors within organizations have a unique set of obligations and responsibilities. Managers are expected to make things happen—to aid in the achievement of organizational objectives, to coordinate the resources of the organization so that useful results are achieved. One of the major responsibilities of those who manage is *to work with other people* to get things done. At least, this would be a definition of managing from a traditional point of view. Inherent in such a definition is the belief that those who manage are directly accountable for the performance of those who are their "subordinates." In less traditional definitions, managers are said to have a responsibility for the behavior of other people, as managers must achieve coordination among team members or fellow work associates. Regardless of the point of view taken, managers have responsibilities for leading or influencing the behavior of other workers. This responsibility is an important differentiation between managers and nonmanagers. *Managers are responsible not only for their own behavior but also for the performance of other people.* Nonmanagers do not have accountability for others in their own job descriptions.

Managers, of course, are just as human as nonmanagers. Managers have personal goals, expectations, and value systems just as nonmanagers do. Managers also have their individual strengths and weaknesses. As we progress in this book, it sometimes will seem that the manager is a superhuman who makes no mistakes, has no personal feelings, has no problems, and experiences no difficulties. Even if such a utopian set of conditions would be desirable from the organization's point of view, there would be no realism in this position. As Chapter 8 shows, managers are human beings and are fallible and imperfect just as everyone else is. Managers, however, are exposed to different pressures in work organizations than are nonmanagers.

Through the years, there have been many different perceptions of what the role of the manager should be. Managers have been portrayed as taskmasters striving only to get more performance from people for the good of the organization; they have been shown as instruments to keep other people happy while they work; and they have been shown as self-satisfiers out to fulfill their own personal goals. This book is based upon the assumption that managers must be aware of organizational, employee, and self needs simultaneously. No one of these forces can be ignored. Managers must work to achieve a number of objectives for a number of individuals and groups concurrently. It is also assumed that achievement for organizations, the people in them, those who manage, and other groups is possible through a concerted effort. The manager can (and must) seek the achievement of goals for a number of individuals and groups.

Theorists in the field of management have frequently been accused of promoting one school of thought to the total exclusion of other legitimate schools or philosophies. Koontz, for example, in his classic manuscript entitled "The Management Theory Jungle,"[1] suggested that management has seen at least six schools of thought—the operational, empirical, human behavior, social system, decision theory, and mathematical schools—and that adherents to each school acted as if theirs was the only reasonable position. He went further to suggest that there were many valid points to consider from each school and that an integration of ideas and concepts was needed for a more complete, comprehensive school of management thought.

By the same token, management-leadership theory has undergone periods in which authoritative-task leadership (leadership centered in the hands of a few autocratic managers), participative leadership (leadership in which those being led interacted with their leaders to make decisions), free-rein leadership (where individual workers were given complete freedom for decision making, motivating, controlling, and so forth), and other leadership approaches have been promoted as the single, best management-leadership approach. The current position, and the one to which this book subscribes, is that the right type of leadership for the right situation is a function of a number of variables. Each leader has to be capable of analyzing the variables prevalent at a given point in time and then flexibly adjusting his managerial leadership approach to fit current needs and demands.

[1]See Harold Koontz, "The Management Theory Jungle," *Academy of Management Journal,* Volume 4, Number 3 (September 1961), pp. 174–188, or "Making Sense of Management Theory," *Harvard Business Review,* Volume 40, Number 4 (July–August 1962), p. 24ff., for more complete discussions of these management schools.

Chapters in this book that deal with managerial responsibilities (in Sections III and IV in particular) emphasize flexibility or adaptability in managerial performance. In the vernacular of today, this is the contingency approach to leadership.

Assumptions about the Goals of a Book on Managing People

Artists seldom see the same painting in the same way; orchestra conductors usually see a different interpretation in the same score; and economists frequently see different solutions to the same problem. Those who write books on management typically view the same territory from different perspectives. There are differences of opinion on what a book about managing people should include. This book is written with the belief that a book about managing people should be descriptive, theoretical, and practical. To explain further, such a book should describe something of the nature of people who work, the environment in which people work, the responsibilities of those who manage, the reactions of employees to other employees (including those who manage), the problems that exist at the work place, and trends within and outside of the work environment. A basic knowledge of these elements is a starting point for further managerial development.

A book on managing people also has to include theories of management—proposed methods and concepts for analyzing the behavior of people at work and for fulfilling the responsibilities managers have for working with people. It is important to describe as many theories of merit proposed by other authors as possible, to report on the results of the application of those theories whenever results are known, and to develop and present new theories and new concepts to further extend the body of knowledge concerning people at work and management's responsibilities toward them.

Within the philosophy of this book is the belief that we should talk about things not only as they are but also *as they should be*. We must purpose to do better, to explore new frontiers, and must not be complacent with things as they have been.

Theories and explanations of behavior and managerial performance must also be made actionable—must be interpreted in terms that can be applied and implemented. Theories of behavior and management may improve the general understanding of the subject matter if they are presented without making them actionable, but they have true value when predictors and guidelines for behavior can be drawn from them. A book about managing people needs to be practical, useful.

The Purposes of this Book

This book attempts to be true to the above-described philosophy of what a book on managing people should be. It describes characteristics, needs, and expectations of those who work (both managers and nonmanagers). It details the elements and factors in the experiential-environmental network that have a bearing upon worker behavior and managerial performance. It outlines managerial responsibilities as they have been exhibited by those who manage. It views current trends and future expectations.

The book goes further by presenting several theoretical concepts of worker behavior and managerial performance. The ideas of many other authors are drawn upon for these theories. Ideas of this author are included to expand or further develop the theoretical concepts.

The theories and descriptions are then interpreted into managerial action guidelines. Concepts are discussed in terms of their implications for the manager of today and the manager of tomorrow.

The Plan of the Book

Almost every chapter combines descriptive details, theory, and application. The chapters in Section I concentrate upon the individual at work and the experience-environment field around him. Included in this section are many of the factors that affect the behavior of people at work. A model of the interaction of personal, environmental, and experiential variables is developed.

Section II presents concepts concerning the needs and expectations of all workers (Chapter 7) and managers in particular (Chapter 8). Section III presents some major functions of managers as they fulfill their responsibilities. Because it is possible to identify some important responsibilities that all managers have, it is possible in this section to speak candidly of some central issues, to discuss important theories, and to provide actionable guidelines. Section IV identifies current trends, contemporary issues, and future directions for the managing of people at work.

With a few exceptions, each chapter in this book is introduced by a brief case containing problems related to the contents of the chapter. The cases are presented preceding the chapter to encourage thought about central issues and problem areas involved in the following subject matter. After the material in each chapter is presented, it is hoped that the reader will go back and consider the case again and answer the questions raised concerning it. Also, at the ends of most chapters are questions to stimulate further thought about the concepts discussed in the chapter.

In the concluding section of the book, a number of additional cases are provided so that the concepts in the various chapters can be further analyzed and applied. Each of these cases has concepts and problems drawn from more than one chapter in the book. Cases are used frequently in this book to provide a means of translating knowledge into action. Most of the cases provide excellent opportunities for role playing as well as for decision-making exercises.

Limitations of the Book

One of the limiting factors of a book such as this is the difficulty in selecting material to be included from the enormous reservoir of information available on the subjects of worker behavior and the management of people at work. Literally hundreds of books and thousands of articles have been written on topics related to the subject matter of this book. As a result, many important concepts have been included, while other valuable concepts may not have been included. It is impossible in one volume to say all that can be said. Also, the elusive nature of human behavior handicaps a book about managing people. The concepts included were selected for their unique contributions to the study of managing people and may or may not be representative of all the literature available.

The body of management knowledge and information is a constantly expanding field. Even as this book comes off the press, new discoveries are being unveiled. Every student of management must monitor new developments regularly just to stay abreast of the field.

There is another problem in writing a book of this nature that needs acknowledgement at this point. Much of the literature seems to talk about *man*kind, *man*power, chair*men*, and so forth. The pronoun *his* is common in today's language. When speaking of managers, it seems easy to say *his* responsibilities. When talking about a laborer, it seems convenient to say *his* behavior. The point is, tradition has emphasized that the work world is a *man's* world. Many women would argue, and rightfully so, that women are entitled to equal time and equal consideration.

All of this is stated to make this point: The author is painfully aware of the male-oriented terminology used in the literature *and sometimes in this book* to describe things that occur in the work environment. An attempt has been made to break this cycle, but the substitute words for *man*power, *his* (the worker's) behavior, and so forth have not been perfected in today's language. The development of neuter gender words is welcomed, and this author will be among the first to adopt them. As women readers will see as they read several chapters and cases in the book, the author is aware of problems uniquely facing women. I ask your patience as we develop more equal terminology and more equal footing for women and men in the work environment.

SECTION I

INFLUENCES ON HUMAN BEHAVIOR

"What caused him to do that?" "Do you know why she got so upset?" "Some days Joe is very efficient and on other days he can't do anything right. Can you explain his erratic behavior?" "Why is she against everything new?" Managers and nonmanagers alike find themselves puzzling over the actions and attitudes of fellow workers, subordinates, and superiors, as expressed in the statements above.

The search for predictable explanations of human behavior has been in process since the beginning of time. People have sought explanations of their own behavior and the behavior of others. Some observers have written off the pursuit of explanations as a hopeless task with too many unknowns and variables to make possible any understandable patterns of human behavior. Other students of behavior, while agreeing that unknowns may exist, have developed theories to explain and predict many facets of human behavior.

The position taken in this book is that human behavior *is* subject to a number of influences. Many of these can be identified and their effects analyzed and predicted. It is, of course, impossible to completely forecast what individuals will do or think, but it is possible to more adequately understand (and sometimes to influence) their behavior.

In this section of the book, we will explore many of the more pertinent explanations of human behavior and the effects of different behavioral influences upon worker behavior. Our concern will be to identify important concepts that explain and predict human behavior everywhere, and then our thoughts will turn more specifically to behavior within organizations.

In Chapter 2 explanations of human nature are discussed. The individual is the basic unit of all behavioral activity, and psychologists in particular have advanced a number of concepts to explain the actions of individual human beings. Our study will begin with several basic Freudian concepts and will progress through a number of additional theories of behavior and human personality.

In Chapter 3 we will focus attention upon social, cultural, economic, and other influences that affect human behavior as they shape the environment in which people live and work. This chapter shifts from the predominantly psychological concepts of Chapter 2 to a primarily sociological point of view. The effects of social institutions (the family, religion, education, unions, and government) upon individuals are considered. Other environmental-experiential influences—such as the economic network, peer groups, race, occupation, place of residence, and personal health—are explored to determine their contributions to interpersonal behavior.

Technology (Chapter 4) in the form of inventions, discoveries, and other creative ideas has not only influenced society in general, but has uniquely and pointedly influenced the behavior of people at work. The effects of technology upon managers and operatives are traced in this chapter. As we will see, technology has been a mixed blessing for many individuals. As students of management, we will strive to utilize the positive contributions of technology while overcoming the negative effects.

Chapter 5 is concerned with the formalized authority relationships in which people work. The first part of the chapter looks at cornerstones of organizations, the functions of the formal structure, the weaknesses of formalized work arrangements, and some different types of organizational groupings of people. The latter part provides guidelines for selecting the best type of formal structure to meet each organizational need. The chapter vividly portrays the behavioral influences formalized organizational relationships have upon people as they work together.

In Chapter 6, the informal organization and its effects upon employees are considered. Informal organizations work within the boundaries of formal organizations to accomplish many of the personal goals and objectives of the people involved. Sometimes the informal organization supports the formal organization; at other times it resists and combats the formal organization.

The individual, the environment-experience field, technology, the formal organization, and the informal organization are all a part of interpersonal organizational behavior. Some of the more significant effects of each behavioral factor are included in a model that is completed at the end of Chapter 6.

Chapter 2

The Basic Unit of Human Relations– the Individual

Two short cases to consider before reading chapter 2

SCOTT MOORE—THE GRADUATE WHO REFUSED TO MOVE

Scott Moore is a junior executive in the accounting department of the Gibraltar Paper Company, a small paper-processing company located in the northwestern United States. The paper company is the major industrial concern in the small college town (Williamsport) in which it is located. The national headquarters for the Gibraltar Company is in a large metropolitan center approximately 700 miles from this town.

Scott grew up and was educated (from elementary school through college) in Williamsport. He was an accounting major in college and was pleased to be able to secure a job in the accounting department at the paper mill when he received his B.B.A. some five years ago. The job Scott holds is a very routine job and, in many respects, involves mostly a process of bookkeeping rather than actual accounting. Scott readily recognizes that he is not using the accounting knowledge he acquired in college fully, nor is he making complete use of his other business administration training. Additional responsibility appears to be several years away, because the local plant is growing very slowly, and retirement will come only in fifteen or more years for the senior accounting personnel.

An official in the headquarters accounting office has recognized that the potential of Scott Moore has not been tapped and has offered him a more responsible, better-paying position in the accounting office at the headquarters. This, of course, would require Scott, his wife, and their two daughters to move from Williamsport. After one week of considering the opportunity, Scott refuses the transfer, saying that he is happy in his present position and prefers to remain in Williamsport.

The senior executive in the headquarters office is somewhat shocked at Scott's decision. The transfer not only offered additional responsibility and pay, but it also provided an avenue of definite promotions if Scott performed successfully. The senior executive expresses difficulty in understanding the logic of Scott's decision.

Questions about the Scott Moore case

1. What clues are available to explain the reasoning behind Scott Moore's decision to remain with his job in Williamsport?

2. What values and goals appear to be important to Scott?

3. What realities of human nature has the senior accounting executive at the head-quarters office apparently failed to recognize?

4. Does Scott's decision appear logical or illogical? Why?

MARK QUARTZ—THE GRADUATE WHO MOVED ACROSS THE COUNTRY

Mark Quartz is a recent college graduate with a major in finance and real estate. He was an honor graduate, compiling an outstanding academic record. Mark comes from an extremely wealthy family, one that owns a chain of hotels and restaurants throughout the United States. Mark's father has offered him an attractive starting position in the family business.

With his good academic record and his outstanding general background, Mark received several offers of employment. He has reviewed a number of alternatives and, to everyone's surprise, has announced that he plans to reject all offers except one—the opportunity to join the VISTA (Volunteers in Service to America) corps and spend the next two years working among the under-privileged children in a city a thousand miles away from his own family.

Questions about the Mark Quartz case

1. What motivations would cause Mark Quartz to make the decision he did?

2.   Is Mark's behavior normal or abnormal? Why?

3.   What realities of human nature does Mark's behavior illustrate?

4.   Was this decision easier or more difficult for Mark to make than it would be for other recent college graduates? Explain your answer.

Organizations are collections of individual human beings who have united to accomplish goals and objectives. The individual human being, therefore, is the basic unit upon which organizational interaction and behavior centers. In some ways, as will be discussed momentarily, individuals are very similar. In other ways, individuals differ significantly in their attitudes, needs, and actions.

Throughout the years, many attempts have been made to explain the behavior of individual human beings thoroughly and completely. In some situations, an effort has been made to predict individual behavior. Unfortunately, the nature of the individual human being makes the description and prediction of behavior rather elusive. What has evolved from the attempts to describe and predict behavior has been a group of theories of human behavior. A theory may be defined as a formulation of apparent relationships or underlying principles, that is, a set of explanations and speculations related to certain phenomena. No one theory of human behavior has gained acceptance as being totally inclusive or comprehensive, but several theories have gained prominence on the basis of their unique (and usually meaningful) contributions to the understanding of individual behavior. Some of the more significant theories of behavior are presented in the next several pages. These theories should be examined for the insight they can provide. Each theory has its own unique characteristics. Some theories have gained more acceptance than others. When the theories are related to each other, they tend to be complementary.

Following the presentation of this group of theories, some generalizations concerning the nature of man are drawn, and an integrating model is begun. This model is more fully developed in Chapters 3 through 6.

The Freudian Explanation of Behavior

The granddaddy of many behavioral theories is the one originated by Sigmund Freud as a result of his psychoanalytical explorations. Freud found that the human personality and its resulting actions are determined primarily by three structures within the human mind—the id, the ego, and the superego. These parts of the mind are responsible for originating human action or for modifying it.

The original, most basic system of the human personality in Freud's theory is the id. The id consists of everything psychological that is inherited and present at birth, including instincts.[1] The id is the foundation upon which the other parts of the personality are built. The id is the source of all psychic energy and furnishes the power for the operation of the ego and superego. The id cannot tolerate uncomfortable levels of tension within it and seeks to release tensions as quickly as possible when they arise. Whenever tensions develop, regardless of whether they originate internally or externally, the immediate reaction of the id is to discharge the tension and return to a normal level. This tension-release instinct as described by Freud has led into the well-known concept called the pleasure principle, which states that man seeks a pleasurable level of existence while avoiding pain.

The id has two methods for dealing with tensions that build up within it—the primary process and reflex actions. The primary process attempts to discharge a tension by forming a mental image of a desirable means of releasing the tension. For example, if the individual feels tension developing because of the need for food, the id would deal with this tension by creating a mental image of desirable food. The tension release would be only mental and temporary and would not satisfy the real need. Reflex actions such as sneezing, the blinking of eyes, and so forth might be capable of handling minor tensions but seldom effectively release major tensions. The id is incapable of resolving most tensions in a realistic, lasting manner. The search for a realistic release of tension is delegated to the section of the personality known as the ego.

The ego exists to provide the individual with a means of obtaining real solutions to needs and tensions. The ego has the ability to distinguish between mental images and actual sources of tension release, and it responds to real sources of tension reduction. This procedure of pursuing real sources of tension resolution is called the reality principle.

> The ego performs its task by: (1) observing accurately what exists in the external world (perceiving), (2) recording these experiences carefully (remembering), and (3) modifying the external world in such a way as to satisfy the instinctual wishes (acting). Failing this last, the ego must hold off the discharge of energy until such modification can be brought about or an appropriate substitute found.[2]

[1]Sigmund Freud, *An Outline of Psychoanalysis* (translated by J. Strachey), New York: W. W. Norton and Company, 1949, p. 14.

[2]C. N. Cofer and M. H. Appley, *Motivation: Theory and Research*, New York: John Wiley & Sons, Inc., 1966, p. 609, in which this Freudian concept is discussed.

The ego attempts to achieve the reality principle through the secondary process, the formulation and testing of alternate plans of need satisfaction and tension release (pleasure achievement and pain avoidance). The ego seeks a workable means of attaining need fulfillment.

> The ego is said to be the executive [part] of the personality because it controls the gateways to action, selects the features of the environment to which it will respond, and decides what instincts will be satisfied.[3]

When the ego finds a workable means of satisfying a need, the individual does not necessarily do what the ego recommends. The third part of the personality, the superego, may propose a modification or redirection of the action suggested by the ego. The superego is the moralistic segment of the human personality—the branch that concerns itself with directing the behavior of the individual in socially acceptable directions. The main concern of the superego is to determine whether an action proposed by the ego is right or wrong so that the individual will act in accordance with the moral standards and values of society.

The main input into the superego comes from parents or guardians (or those who surround the individual) as they interpret the values of society for the individual while he is a child. The values a child receives will continue to influence him as he becomes an adult. The "enforcers" that encourage the individual to see that his behavior conforms to social expectations are the ego-ideal and the conscience. The ego-ideal (the positive subsystem of the superego) makes the individual feel rewarded and satisfied when he acts in accordance with what he knows to be morally correct. The conscience is the negative factor that penalizes the individual and makes him feel guilty when his actions are contrary to social values. If the efforts of the superego are fruitful, the individual will do what is right as well as what is realistic. In other words, he will do what is morally correct as well as what is useful and real. If food is needed to resolve a tension, it will be earned rather than stolen. Figure 2.1 illustrates the interrelationships and interactions of the id, ego, and superego. The superego may not always be successful in influencing the ego to act as it prefers, but the attempt is made.

According to the diagram, an individual could become hungry and desire fulfillment of his need for food. Because the id, through the primary process and reflex actions, cannot deal with the need adequately, the problem is referred to the ego (Step 1). The ego considers alternatives that would result in real satisfaction through the procurement and consumption of food and selects a workable

---

[3]Calvin S. Hall and Gardner Lindzey, *Theories of Personality*, New York: John Wiley & Sons, Inc., 1957, p. 35.

FIGURE 2.1   Interactions of the id, ego, and superego

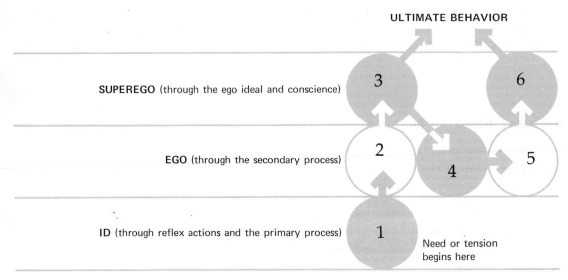

6   If the superego approves, the action is taken. If not, the superego may call upon the ego for another alternative, etc.

5   Other alternatives are considered, and another is recommended for consideration by the superego.

4   If unacceptable, the superego attempts to persuade the ego to reconsider its actions and to resubmit a new plan.

3   The superego approves or disapproves of the recommendation from the ego. If acceptable, action may be taken.

2   Real alternatives are considered as means for satisfying needs or releasing tensions. A workable solution is selected and sent to the superego for approval.

1   Reflex actions and the primary process try to deal with the tension. The primary process creates mental images that are unsatisfactory as permanent satisfiers of needs. The individual then turns to the ego for real solutions.

approach (Step 2), which is referred to the superego for approval. If the action is morally acceptable, the superego approves and the action may be taken (Step 3). If the action is morally unacceptable, the ego is encouraged to reconsider and recommend another, more acceptable action (Step 4). This process continues until an action that is both workable and moral is found (if the superego is listened to).

Some phases of the Freudian approach have come under attack by other writers, but the framework it provided has been widely considered and utilized.[4] In particular, the Freudian framework contributes by identifying the source of behavioral actions, the separate parts of the personality, the capacity of the individual to deal with reality, and the element of moral influence.

A Theory Based on Homeostasis

Another theory of human behavior is based upon homeostasis, a concept related to the desire of the organism to maintain a constant level of inner tissue conditions. The original concept of homeostasis was specifically related to conditions of oxygen, temperature, glucose, and other internal needs. The biological conception of homeostasis suggests that the organism wants and achieves biological equilibrium by anticipating potential disturbances and by perceiving and acquiring environmental objects (food, clothing, shelter, etc.) to minimize the effects of disturbances and tensions and to adjust to them. Ross Stagner[5] and other authors suggest also that the organism (the individual), while striving to preserve his inner tissue constancies (biological environment), strives to build a constant *physical environment* and a constant *social environment*. In other words, the human being desires constancy not only in his inner biological realm but also in his physical and social environments. Accordingly, the individual perceives the elements in his environments that may be disruptive to his equilibrium and attempts to minimize the effects of those disturbances.

To illustrate the desire for equilibrium and constancy in the physical environment, most individuals admit to being more comfortable in familiar settings. A familiar, comfortable environment for the college student needing a place to study may be the privacy of his own room with the coffee pot brewing and the stereo playing his favorite records. A comfortable environment for a small child may be a lighted room located near his parents. The homeostatic theory suggests that every human being will attempt to restore a comfortable environment if it is lost or is otherwise threatened.

At the same time, the individual prefers a reasonably constant social environment—familiar, acceptable people surrounding him. Individuals who are well-known acquaintances tend to be thought of as desirable and sustaining, while

---

[4]The author is indebted to Cofer and Appley, *op. cit.*, and to Hall and Lindzey, *op. cit.*, for a large amount of the interpretive data related to the Freudian theories.

[5]Ross Stagner, "Homeostasis as a Unifying Concept in Personality Theory," *Psychological Review*, Volume 58, Number 1 (1951), pp. 5–17.

strangers are associated with the disturbance of equilibrium, the thwarting of needs, and the creation of pain, discomfort, and insecurity. Perceptions of specific individuals may become organized as constants. Friends tend to be perceived as acceptable even when they possess bad characteristics, and strangers may be perceived as dangerous even though they possess good characteristics. ~~Constancy continues to be the most important factor~~. The environments are not completely static, but change gradually as a result of new experiences and new situations.

Occasionally, the desire to maintain constancy within one of the environments may cause conflict within the individual personality. If an individual is invited to go on a mountain-climbing expedition by a group of his friends, his biological constancies may suggest he refuse the opportunity to "break his neck" while his need for social environment constancy may encourage him to go on the expedition to avoid being ostracized and called a coward by his friends—and therefore lose his constant social environment.

The desire to maintain environmental constancies is not a complete description of human behavior. Stagner states that at the core of human behavior is the ego or self-image. The ego is the individual's perception of his own values, beliefs, and goals. The individual wishes to maintain a constant concept of his self-image as well as constant environments. In other words, the human organism seeks constancy for his own ego (self-image), for his inner biological needs, for his physical environment, and for his social environment (Figure 2.2). This drive

FIGURE 2.2   Areas where equilibrium and constancy are sought.

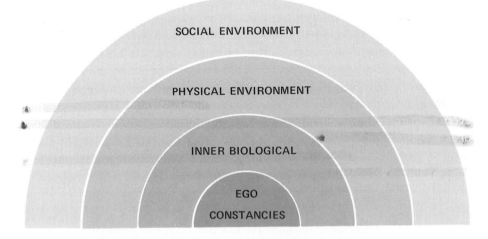

Source: Ross Stagner, "Homeostasis as a Unifying Concept in Personality Theory," *Psychological Review*, Volume 58, Number 1, January 1951, p. 12. Copyright 1951 by the American Psychological Association. Reprinted by permission.

toward equilibrium is a key factor in the explanation of human behavior from the homeostatic point of view.[6]

The concept of homeostasis makes a significant contribution to the development of a complete behavior model. In later chapters (such as those dealing with change and conflict), homeostasis will be helpful in explaining some of the events that occur between people.

The Sheldon Body Type-Temperament Model

A rather unique concept of behavioral determinants was explored by William Sheldon and his colleagues.[7] For many years, researchers had attempted to correlate anatomical-physiological traits and characteristics with manifested behavioral patterns but had gained little consensus or support from other researchers and theorists. In his extensive research, Sheldon identified some relationships between physiques or body types of individuals and personality temperaments. The Sheldon line of thinking promotes the position that human temperament and the resulting behavior tend to relate directly to the anatomical makeup of each individual—the bone structure, the muscular build, the shape of the chest, and other physical attributes. Because human body types change little in the mature adult, the behavioral temperament tends to remain relatively constant throughout life. Sheldon identified three specific body types and their related behavioral temperaments. The three body types (the endomorphic, mesomorphic, and ectomorphic) and the typical behavioral patterns for each type are described in Figure 2.3.

The tendency of most modern theorists of behavior is to treat anatomical traits and characteristics as one influencing factor out of many. In some theories, anatomical factors are even ignored. However, an individual's physical structure and condition do appear to have a bearing on how that individual is likely to behave. For example, if an individual has great strength and stamina, he or she may be able to engage in physical activities easily and successfully. The physically weak

---

[6]*Loc. cit.* For an additional set of concepts related to homeostatic theory, see Leon Festinger, *A Theory of Cognitive Dissonance*, Stanford, California: Stanford University Press, 1957.

[7]The original materials relating to the Sheldon theories were presented in William H. Sheldon *et al., The Varieties of Human Physique: An Introduction to Constitutional Psychology.* New York: Harper and Company, 1940, and in W. H. Sheldon and S. S. Stevens, *The Varieties of Temperament: A Psychology of Constitutional Differences*, New York: Harper and Company, 1942. Condensations of the Sheldon theory are found in Hall and Lindzey, *op. cit.,* pp. 336–375, and David J. Lawless, *Effective Management: Social Psychological Approach*, Englewood Cliffs, New Jersey: Prentice-Hall, Inc., 1972, pp. 59–60.

FIGURE 2.3   Sheldon body types and behavioral temperaments

ENDOMORPHY

Body Type—softness and spherical appearance; underdevelopment of bone and muscle; floats high in water; highly developed abdominal area.

Behavioral temperament—The endormorphic type of individual usually has a love for comfort, eats heavily, likes to be around people and desires affection. He shows a relaxed posture, reads slowly, is even-tempered, is tolerant of others, and is easy to get along with. He is somewhat complacent and prefers to be led rather than to lead.

MESOMORPHY

Body type—hard and rectangular physique with a predominance of bone and muscle; strong, tough, and injury-resistant body; well equipped for strenuous physical demands.

Behavioral temperament—The mesomorphic individual likes physical adventure and risk taking. He needs muscular and vigorous physical activity. He is aggressive and insensitive toward others. He tends to be noisy and courageous; he desires action, power, and domination. He is athletic and seeks outdoor activity.

ECTOMORPHY

Body type—linear and fragile; flat chest and delicate body; usually thin and light-muscled.

Behavioral temperament—The ectomorphic individual displays restraint, inhibition, and the desire for concealment. He tends to be distrustful of people. He works well in enclosed areas. He reacts overquickly, sleeps poorly, and prefers solitude when his mind is troubled. Also, he prefers not to attract attention to himself. Typically, he is anxious, ambitious, and dedicated.

Source: Adapted from David J. Lawless, *Effective Management, Social Psychological Approach,* © 1972. Reprinted by permission Prentice-Hall, Inc., Englewood Cliffs, New Jersey.

individual may recognize his limitations and direct his actions toward less strenuous, more reserved activities. The individual who is small in physical structure
may attempt to compensate for limited size by outbursts of energy and enthusiasm. In brief, physical factors do influence individual behavior, but the relationships between physical structure and behavior are not always clear.

Experiences of Success
and Failure

A fruitful exploration of individual behavior has been the investigation of the
effects of an individual's experiences as he interacts with his environment. Arthur
Combs and Donald Snygg have developed a theory of behavior emphasizing the
importance of success-failure experiences, which shape individual perception,
which in turn influences the individual's behavior pattern (see Figure 2.4).[8] If the
interaction between the individual and his environment is good, the individual
will normally experience success. If he is successful, the individual tends to have
a positive perception of himself. He sees himself as being liked, wanted, acceptable, able, and worthy. He sees himself as possessing dignity and integrity. He
feels that he belongs in the world and has something to contribute to it. In general,
he sees himself as capable of meeting challenges that he may encounter.

The positive regard the individual has for himself and others as a result of his
successful interaction with his environment affects his behavior in many ways.
Success seems to breed success, because the individual who has experienced
success develops an optimistic outlook and anticipates future success. This optimism tends to aid in the achievement of positive expectations. In addition, the

FIGURE 2.4   Relationship of perception to behavior

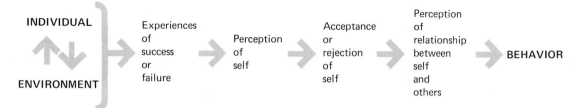

INDIVIDUAL

ENVIRONMENT

Experiences
of
success
or
failure

→ Perception
of
self

→ Acceptance
or
rejection
of
self

→ Perception
of
relationship
between
self
and
others

→ BEHAVIOR

[8]Arthur W. Combs and Donald Snygg, *Individual Behavior: A Perceptual Approach to Behavior*, Revised
Edition, New York: Harper and Brothers, 1959, p. 240ff.

positive outlook coupled with previous successes provides the individual with a reservoir of strength to draw upon when negative experiences are encountered.[9]
The successful personality, because of his experiences and perceptions:

1. Is open and ready for new experiences
2. Has the ability to admit and cope with the existence of unflattering things concerning himself
3. Can remain more objective in analyzing data because he feels less need to defend himself
4. Is capable of living with (being tolerant of) unsolvable problems
5. Is capable of experimentation and creativity because of his inner security and strength
6. Achieves a higher degree of independence from social and physical forces because of his individual success
7. Has a high regard for others[10]

In other words, the adequate personality (the one who has experienced success) has a high perception of himself and others, and this perception results in an open, positive set of activities and actions (Figure 2.5).

If, however, an experience results in failure, a whole new set of perceptions and behavioral patterns may result. The individual who, through his assessment of his own experiences, sees himself as unsuccessful eventually comes to see himself as unworthy, unwanted, unacceptable, and incapable. He has a low perception of himself; he has difficulty in accepting himself as he perceives himself; and he finds it difficult to identify with others because of his perceptions and experiences.[11]

FIGURE 2.5   Positive perception and its effects

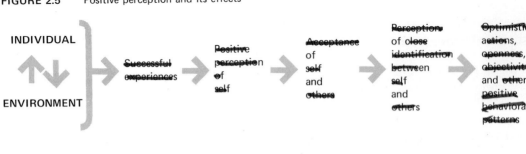

[9]Ibid., pp. 241–242.
[10]Ibid., pp. 243–257.
[11]Ibid., pp. 265–267.

FIGURE 2.6   Negative perception and its effects

The resulting behavior may be evidenced in several ways. Sometimes the individual who perceives himself as unsuccessful enters into a continuously belligerent, aggressive pattern in which he attempts to enhance himself and to overcome his negative perceptions. On other occasions, he may withdraw from interaction and may give up in despair. Sometimes the experiences and perceptions become so traumatic that the individual behaves neurotically or psychotically. Whatever the case may be, the level of self-confidence, self-acceptance, and interpersonal identification is very low, and the resulting behavior tends to be uneasy and disturbed (see Figure 2.6). In the brief coverage of the Combs-Snygg explanation of behavior above, the specific environmental and experiential factors influencing behavior have not been identified, but future discussions in this book will attempt to establish and clarify several of these elements. However, two main points can be drawn from the Combs-Snygg discussion: (1) the individual-environment interactions that result in successful or unsuccessful experiences have an influential effect on individual behavior, and (2) individual *perceptions of self, acceptance of self,* and *perception of identification between self and others* influence individual behavior.

Individual Initiative as a Behavioral Determinant

It would be easy to derive the position that man is primarily a victim of his environment and experiences and can exercise little initiative or control over his own fate if some of the completely environmental theories of behavior were adopted. However, in an attempt not to refute, but rather to build upon the experiential foundations of experience-environment theories, Carl Rogers and his associates have developed a behavioral theory that places emphasis on the individual as an initiating, creating, influential determinant of behavior within the environmental framework. From this point of view, the individual can and does

FIGURE 2.7   The self-concept

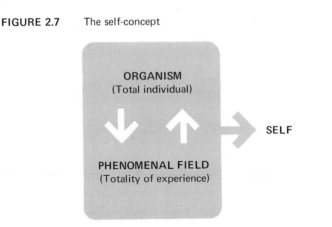

Source: Adapted from a discussion of the Carl Rogers self-concept in Calvin S. Hall and Gardner Lindzey, *Theories of Personality*, New York: John Wiley & Sons, 1957, p. 478.

effectively originate behavior in addition to interacting with his environment. At the same time, however, the environment does influence the individual.

In the Rogers explanation of behavior, there are three basic ingredients of the personality: (1) the organism, which is the total individual, (2) the phenomenal field, which is the totality of experience, and (3) the self, which is a pattern of perceptions, desires, and values that the individual possesses (see Figure 2.7). The self develops out of the interaction between the organism and the phenomenal field (experience).[12]

Because there are some basic similarities in the nature of human organisms and some similarities in the environment and experiences within which individuals live, there will be similarities in individual drives and values. However, because human beings are also unique organisms and because each individual experiences his own unique interactions with his environment, people will also differ in some of their needs and values. As the organism interacts with the experiential world, the unique values of the individual are established and the self emerges. The self may be revised as additional experience, learning, and maturation occur.

The individual self strives to actualize, maintain, and enhance itself. The individual behaves in ways that fulfill the goals of the self and are consistent with its ambitions. The self is not so miserly and inner-directed as might be expected, according to most self-actualization theorists. As Rogers has said, "the basic nature

[12]Hall and Lindzey, *op. cit.,* p. 478.

of the human being, when functioning fully, is constructive and trustworthy."[13] The self takes the initiative in improving conditions in its environment so that the values of the self can be attained. Therefore, individuals normally are active creators and initiators of experience rather than passive reactors to the pressures of the environment. The individual makes an impact on the environment and vice versa.

A Model of Personal Productivity

The theories presented previously have each attempted to describe fundamental patterns of people wherever they may be. Because it is the concern of this book to deal with people at work, models and theories that explain the behavior of people *at work* are of value and interest. Perhaps the most encompassing attempt to describe human behavior at work up to this point has been the model developed by Sutermeister. Rather than describing all forms of behavior, the Sutermeister model is directed specifically toward explaining the productivity of people (productivity is defined by Sutermeister as "the output per man per hour, quality considered").[14] While the model and its related theory attempt to explain only one human phenomenon at work, the contributing factors and the resulting interactions provide insight into individual behavior in the work organization.

As Sutermeister views productive behavior, there are at least thirty-two factor-areas that may contribute to individual action. The model developed (see Figure 2.8) begins with the inner circle and progresses to the outer rings. For example, productivity (1) is determined by technological development (2) and employees' job performance (3). Employees' job performance is a result of worker ability (4) and worker motivation (7). Worker ability is a derivative of individual knowledge (5) and individual skill (6). Motivation results from the effects of physical conditions (8), individuals' needs (9), and social conditions (12). Each of these factors may be traced to other causing or influencing factors.

Each of the factors in the model is subject to change with time. In particular, time is significant as it affects individuals' needs (9) and formal organization (13).[15] The model recognizes many of the influencing factors identified in the

---

[13]Carl R. Rogers, *The Concept of the Fully Functioning Person,* a mimeographed paper, 1955, quoted by Cofer and Appley, *op. cit.,* p. 666.

[14]Robert A Sutermeister, *People and Productivity,* Second Edition, New York: McGraw-Hill Book Company, 1969, p. 2.

[15]*Ibid.,* pp. 1–71.

FIGURE 2.8   Sutermeister model of influences on employee job performance and productivity

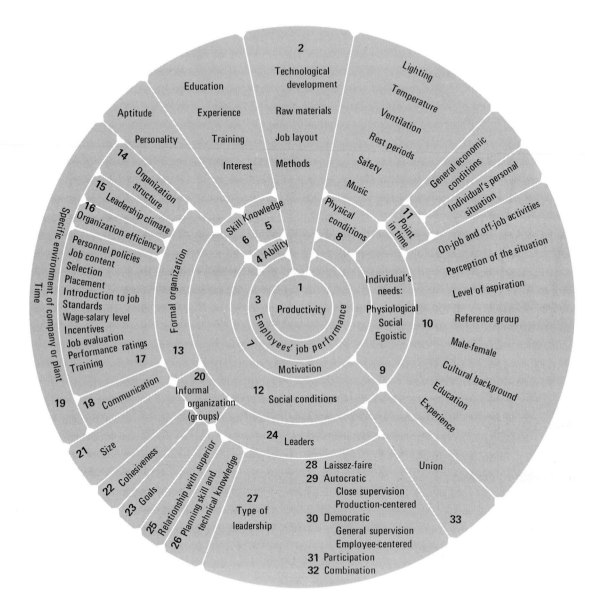

Source: Robert A. Sutermeister, *People and Productivity*, Second Edition, New York:
McGraw-Hill Book Company, 1969.

previous theories, and attempts to integrate them into a description of the final output of productive behavior.

An Integrative Model of Behavior

In an attempt to integrate, unify, and clarify the many theories and concepts of human behavior that have been presented (and some that have not), the author will now present a set of factors and relationships that he feels have come to the front as the most significant determinants of individual behavior of people at work. A broad outline of the integrating model is presented in this chapter. The model will be explained in more detail in the concluding pages of this chapter and in the next four chapters.

From Figure 2.9 it can be seen that the integrated model has drawn four important areas into the determination of the individual behavior of a worker—the individual himself (his characteristics, traits, goals, desires, abilities, and so forth); the external environment of the worker (particularly including off-the-job factors

FIGURE 2.9   Simplified model of worker behavior and its determinants

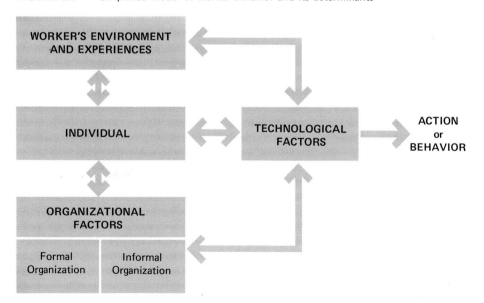

that may be important); organizational factors (including formal, structural factors and informal influences); and the effects of technological development.

The Individual and Human Nature

The ~~first ingredient~~ of ~~individual behavior~~ at ~~work~~ is the ~~single human being~~. Behavior is, after all, the actions of individual people. From behavioral theories, the following generalizations can be drawn concerning human nature, which affects the behavior of individuals generally (and people at work more specifically).

1. ~~Every individual is born with a set of basic needs, goals, drives~~, or ~~desires~~. There is by no means a common agreement upon all of the ~~innate drives~~ with which the individual comes into the world, but there is widespread recognition of some inherent needs. Perhaps the most universally accepted ~~inborn goal~~s are ~~those of physical maintenance~~ and ~~security (or safe~~ty). The release of all types of organismic tension is listed by some as a universal drive. ~~Social needs, self-actualization drives~~, and the need for hope are also mentioned prominently in some lists of inborn human needs. Whatever the list of needs may include, it is universally acceptable to think of the individual as a needing, goal-seeking entity.

2. ~~As a result of experience, training, and interaction, human needs may be modified and expanded.~~ Social needs and esteem (~~recognition~~ and ~~reputation needs~~) are particularly susceptible to modification and expansion.[16] Other needs may also be affected by environmental and experiential factors.

3. ~~Each individual is affected by the successes and failures he experiences~~. Pleasure (reward) is attractive and encourages behavior that promises the attainment of satisfaction, while pain (penalty) is unattractive and tends to discourage behavior that might result in further discomfort.

4. ~~Each individual seeks a constancy—a state of continuing equilibrium with his inner biological needs~~ and also with his external environments. Constant states provide ~~comfort and ease~~, while variations threaten danger and discomfort. ~~Normally, people prefer the familiar rather than the unknown.~~

5. ~~Human beings have the capacity to think, plan, and act rationally.~~ It is true that individual behavior does not always appear to be logical, calculated, or systematic, but the capacity to review alternatives and to decide in a structured manner is within the capabilities of the normal human being. The Freudian theory, the self-actualization theories, and other concepts of behavior stress the ability of people to think and act in a rational manner.

---

[16]For illustrations of the expansion and creation of new social motives and needs, see Murray Horowitz, "Psychological Needs as a Function of the Social Environment," in L. D. White, *The State of the Social Sciences,* Chicago: University of Chicago Press, 1956, pp. 162–183.

6.   While individuals may have the ability to act rationally, many of their actions are precipitated and controlled by their emotions—appeals to the senses of sight, sound, touch, etc. Many psychologists have come to believe that there is a degree of emotion connected with every human behavior. Emotional reactions were thought for a time to be completely disorganizing actions that caused an individual to behave illogically. However, emotion has come to be accepted as an organizing and facilitating action that may have constructive results also.[17]

7.   The behavior of each individual is related to the individual's physical traits and abilities. Size, sex, stamina, dexterity, color, and other physical characteristics will be influential in shaping an individual's behavior. Some of the effects may be a result of learned role functions, while other effects may be derived from real physiological strengths and limitations.

8.   Each individual is a unique personality differentiated from other individuals in some of his goals, drives, responses, experiences, or other behavioral factors. While some drives and desires may be universal, the interaction of the human organism with his environment produces differentiated human entities. Individuals have the capacity to initiate action as well as to react to the behavior of others.

9.   In general, each individual is empathetic toward the moral values of the culture and society in which he lives. This does not mean that the individual embraces each value suggested to him, but moral guidelines will tend to be considered as behavior is carried out.

10.   An individual's *perception* of himself, his experiences, and his relationship to other individuals has a significant effect on his behavior. The individual's assessment of these factors will influence his outlook and his approach to action.

Other generalizations can be drawn concerning individuals, human nature, and behavioral patterns, but those listed above represent some of the more universally acceptable conceptualizations of man.

These capacities for and influences on human behavior provide an important frame of reference in considering managerial action for people at work. These generalizations can be applied by the manager as he works with the employees in his own organization. Several subsequent chapters in this book (the chapters on leadership, motivation, change, and conflict, among others) will be directly related to the individual and his human characteristics and capacities.

Summary

Some details can now be added to the first phase of the proposed integrative model of human behavior. On the basis of discussion thus far, the model may be developed to the degree shown in Figure 2.10. The characteristics of the individual based upon the descriptions of human nature presented in this

[17]Combs and Snygg, *op. cit.*, p. 226.

FIGURE 2.10   Partially detailed model of worker behavior and its determinants

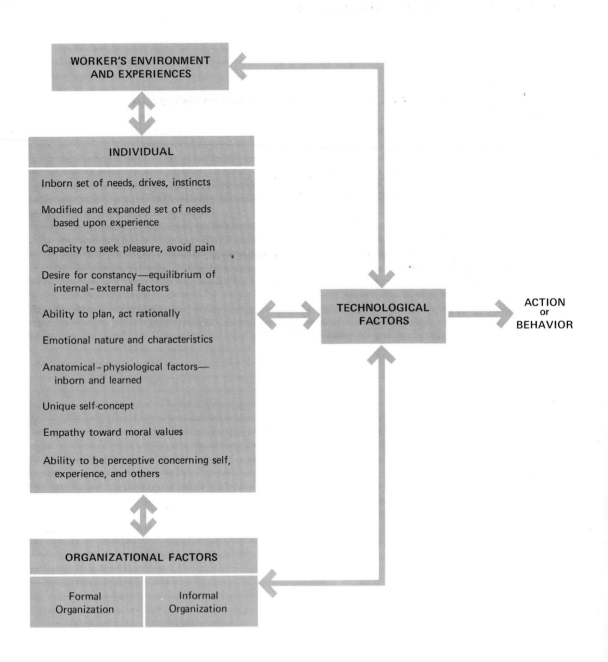

chapter can now be included. In the four chapters that immediately follow this one, other items will be added so that at the conclusion of Chapter 6, the model will have all of its components illustrated in some detail.

Questions to consider after reading Chapter 2

1.   What are the strengths and weaknesses of the theories reviewed in this chapter?

2.   There are some authors who reject the statement that people are basically needing, goal-seeking individuals. What defense could these authors give for their position? What arguments can be offered against their position?

3.   What specific physiological traits may have an influence upon individual behavior? Which physiological traits may be less important than some theories have tended to emphasize?

4.   Do you accept or reject the theory that people seek and prefer constant levels of self-image (ego), biological needs, and physical and social environments? Why or why not?

5.   The Combs-Snygg model suggests that successful behavior results in additional successful behavior and failing behavior tends to result in continuing unsuccessful behavior. Can you give examples that illustrate this chain of events?

6.   Some authors argue that every individual is totally a victim of his environment and circumstances. What evidence (if any) is available to support this position? What evidence is available to counter this position?

7.   While people have the capacity to think and act rationally, they do not always do so. What factors explain the sometimes lack of rationality in human behavior?

8.   "No two people are identical in their goals, drives, and ambitions." Why might this statement be true?

9.   Looking back at the cases at the beginning of the chapter, how do the theories presented in the chapter help to explain the behavior of the two young men? Relate specific theories to the actions of the two men.

The following cases at the back of the book contain problems related to Chapter 2:

Mark Williams

Stanley Lowell

Bentley Cantrell

Susan Swanson

Walt Gladberry

Abigail Spiegal and Trudy Pennington

Alan Purdy

Additional readings

Allport, Gordon W., *Pattern and Growth in Personality,* New York: Holt, Rinehart and Winston, 1961.

————, *Personality: A Psychological Interpretation,* New York: Holt, 1937.

Berne, Eric L., *Games People Play,* New York: Grove Press, Incorporated, 1964.

Berelson, Bernard, and Gary A. Steiner, *Human Behavior, An Inventory of Scientific Findings,* New York: Harcourt, Brace, and World, 1964, pp. 38–296.

Cattell, Raymond B., *The Scientific Analysis of Personality,* Baltimore: Penguin Books, 1965.

Combs, Arthur W., and Daniel W. Soper, "The Self, Its Derivative Terms, and Research," *Journal of Individual Psychology,* Volume 13, Number 2 (November 1957), pp. 134–144.

Herzberg, Frederick W., *Work and the Nature of Man,* Cleveland: The World Publishing Company, 1966, pp. 44–70.

Janis, Irving, editor, *Personality,* New York: Harcourt, Brace, and World, 1969.

Kelly, Joe, *Organizational Behavior,* Homewood, Illinois: Richard D. Irwin, Inc., and The Dorsey Press, 1969, pp. 145–201.

Lawless, David J., *Effective Management: Social Psychological Approach,* Englewood Cliffs, New Jersey: Prentice-Hall, Inc., 1972, pp. 51–77.

Maslow, Abraham, *Motivation and Personality,* Second Edition, New York: Harper & Row, Publishers, 1970.

Murphy, Gardner, *Personality: A Biosocial Approach to Origins and Structure,* New York: Harper, 1947.

Norbeck, Edward, Douglass Price-Williams, and William McCord, editors, *The Study of Personality,* New York: Holt, Rinehart and Winston, 1968.

Strecker, Edward A., Kenneth E. Appel, and John W. Appel, *Discovering Ourselves,* Third Edition, New York: The Macmillan Company, 1962.

Chapter 3

Environmental and Experiential Influences on Individual Behavior

A case to consider before reading chapter 3

WILL STEAKLEY—A ONCE-VALUED EMPLOYEE*

Established forty-five years ago, Alright Chemical Company was years ahead of its competitors in the treatment of its employees, especially in granting employee fringe benefits. It was one of the first companies in its area to grant fringe benefits comparable to those enjoyed by employees today. Even though this supplier of agricultural fertilizers ~~paid lower wages~~, it nevertheless enjoyed a ~~reputation~~ of ~~providing handsomely for its employee~~s. Although the stock ownership was ultimately made public, the company was originally founded by two brothers and has been operated for twenty-six years as a family-owned enterprise. After World War II, the tax structure made it advisable for the family to offer the company to public ownership, although sufficient control was maintained to continue the policy of paternalistic employee relations.

The sick leave policy at Alright Chemical is extremely liberal and in many ways is comparable to a guaranteed yearly salary. If an employee has been with the company for fifteen years or more, sick leave time becomes unlimited unless permanent disability forces the employee's retirement. In this event, the disabled employee is provided with a pension greater than that which could be justified by his longevity with the company.

Three years ago, a foreman in one of the control sections noticed that a fireman, Will Steakley, was continually losing time from work. With his good employment record and twenty-one years of service with the company, Steakley's occasional absences were overlooked and his pay was not docked. However,

*Adapted from *Human Resources: Cases and Concepts* by Leon C. Megginson, © 1968 by Harcourt Brace Jovanovich, Inc., and reprinted with their permission.

when his absences became more frequent and his job performance suffered noticeably, his foreman suggested that Will should see the company doctor. Steakley refused. He was then absent for ten consecutive days. Company procedures required the foreman to make a report of the absences to a special welfare committee. The committee then asked the company doctor to examine the employee, ascertain the seriousness of his illness, and estimate how much additional time would be lost.

Following his investigation, the doctor reported to the welfare committee that Steakley had received him "courteously but not enthusiastically." The employee was dressed and engaged in minor household chores though visibly in a weakened condition. He submitted to an examination; the doctor diagnosed a well-advanced case of tuberculosis. Because of the employee's condition, and for the protection of his exposed children, the doctor urged that the employee enter a sanitarium immediately. The man refused but gave no explanation for his unwillingness to do so.

When the welfare committee received the doctor's report, it asked Steakley's foreman to call on him. It was hoped that the foreman, because of his long acquaintance with the man, could convince him to submit to hospitalization.

When the foreman telephoned Steakley to seek permission to call at his home, the employee stated that he would prefer to come to the plant and see the foreman. When the sick employee arrived, the foreman took him to the welfare committee to discuss the situation.

The chairman of the committee explained to Steakley that the company had a great deal of interest in his well-being and, in addition to the humanitarian considerations, they felt that they had a large financial investment in him and would like to see him healthy and back at work. Steakley then revealed the fact that he belonged to a religious organization that prevented him from accepting medical help. He did not feel that he could violate his religious beliefs.

The situation eventually reached an impasse, although the chairman of the welfare committee endeavored to present the company's case while impressing on Steakley that no attempt was being made to influence his religious beliefs. Steakley was told he would continue to receive his salary for an indefinite period if he would consent to medical treatment and that the company would continue his pay for a considerable period even if he refused treatment. He was informed that in all fairness to the company, he could expect a forced retirement if, in the company's opinion, he became unable to work.

Upon hearing this information from the welfare committee, Steakley declared he would return to work the next week. The committee conferred privately with Steakley's foreman to see if the ill man could be utilized in a job of minimum contact with other personnel. A place was found for Steakley at the bagging scales instead of the control section, and he consented to report there. The meeting adjourned in an amicable manner.

Steakley, however, failed to report at the time he said he would, and several days later he called his old foreman and asked if he could meet with the welfare committee once more. He was told to report the following morning. Steakley met with the committee again and told them that after the previous meeting he realized he could not work at the bagging scales because the dust would give him a distressful cough.

Questions about the Will Steakley case

1.   Will Steakley was once a very valuable employee. Although the reasons may appear to be obvious, what factors resulted in Steakley's poor performance and lessening of value to Alright Chemical Company?

2   Why were the supervisors at Alright Chemical so slow in uncovering the reasons for Steakley's problems? How might the delay have been avoided?

3.   At the end of the case, no satisfactory solution had been found. What solution would you suggest? Please support your recommendations.

4.   Evaluate the company's employee policies and procedures that are shown in this case.

5.   In addition to the factors that caused Steakley's personal problems, what other personal and environmental influences affect employee behavior? Explain your answer.

The theories presented in Chapter 2 revealed several characteristics and capacities of the individual human being. The general thesis developed was that human beings have a number of inborn drives and abilities, but their behavior patterns also are directly influenced by factors in their environment and by experiences that result from interaction with other people and with the objects that surround them. It is the purpose of this chapter to identify important factors in an individual's environment and experiences and to show some of the purposes and effects of these surrounding influences. In the last sections of the chapter, the environmental and experiential influences upon worker behavior are reviewed specifically, and managerial responsibilities for recognizing and working with these influences are considered.

The analysis of environmental factors and personal experiences as they affect individuals is divided into two parts. First, the effects of social institutions upon personal behavior are examined. Then the impacts of some specific environmental and personal conditions upon individual behavior are reviewed.

Social Institutions—Their Nature and Functions

A social institution is a body of behavioral patterns designed to meet the central needs of the individuals composing the society or community. Social institutions provide direction and support to the lives of the human beings within the scope of their influence.[1] Institutions are functional in the sense that the daily activities of individuals are directly related to the activities of the institutions.

Some of the more common groupings of behavior patterns that have become known as institutions are the family, religion, education, the union, the government, and the economic network. Another social grouping that is not an institution as such but is strong in its capacity to influence is the peer group or friendship circle. These groupings will now be defined and their behavioral influences will be analyzed.

The Family.   In the strictest sense, the family has been defined as "a socially sanctioned grouping of persons united by kinship, marriage, or adoption ties, who generally share a common habitat and interact according to well-defined social roles. . . ."[2] The family performs a number of functions for the individuals who are members of a particular family unit. As the functions are performed, society at large is influenced by the actions of the family.

A partial list of the functions of the family unit as a social institution includes these:

1. Perpetuating and protecting the human race
2. Providing care and training for the young.
3. Nurturing and supporting the infirm, impoverished, elderly, or otherwise needy
4. Providing for and regulating sexual and parental drives

---

[1] Frances E. Merrill, *Society and Culture,* Third Edition, Englewood Cliffs, New Jersey: Prentice-Hall, Inc., 1965, pp. 357–358.

[2] Alvin L. Bertrand, *Basic Sociology,* Second Edition, New York: Appleton-Century-Crofts, 1973, p. 252.

5. Creating an intimate social circle for affection and companionship

6. Providing a basis of economic inheritance through private property rights

7. Establishing initial social status positions

8. Introducing the inexperienced to the socialization process—the process of relating to other people

9. Encouraging individuals to accept specific social roles

10. Creating a set of moral and ethical values

11. Stimulating life goals and ambitions[3]

The family as a basic societal unit has been recognized as a major influence in formulating and sustaining the behavior of individuals throughout the history of the world. While the structure and size of the family may vary, the functions performed by the unit are an integral determinant of behavior patterns. It is the family unit that nurtures the child when he comes into the world, helps him to mature, and supports him in his interactions with the outside world. The family unit of the employee normally has a significant influence upon his performance at work, as it shapes his mental and physical behavior patterns. The family unit determines many of the responsibilities, roles, value systems, and other factors that have a bearing upon the employee's attitude and ultimate performance.

Religion.   Another important factor influencing behavior is religion. **Religion** as a social institution may be described as "a unified system of beliefs and practices relative to sacred things, uniting into a single community all of those who adhere to those beliefs and practices."[4] Members of a religious group share common values and attitudes regarding supernatural powers and spiritual relationships. Quite often the form, manner, and subject of worship cherished by various religious groups vary, but the institutional functions performed by each unit have many similarities.

A partial list of the functions of religion as an institution would include these actions:

1. Providing spiritual guidance to the individual

2. Identifying a relationship between the individual and a Superior Being

3. Providing a meaning for life—the completion of a pattern of living

[3]See Merrill, *op. cit.,* pp. 405–426, Bertrand, *op. cit.,* pp. 251–273, and Melvin L. DeFleur, William V. D'Antonio, and Lois B. DeFleur, *Sociology: Human Society,* Glenview, Illinois: Scott, Foresman and Company, 1973, pp. 504–535, for more complete discussions of the functions of the institution known as the family.

[4]Emile Durkheim, *The Elementary Forms of Religious Life,* New York: The Free Press, 1947, p. 47.

4. Establishing a set of moral and ethical values

5. Providing a means to surmount or survive the crises of life—giving comfort and aid in difficult times

6. Providing a means of confronting death more confidently

7. Furnishing a frame of reference with which to interpret man's environment

8. Facilitating social cohesion and solidarity through the promotion of compassion, consideration, and concern for the welfare of others[5]

The functions of religion are numerous and invaluable. From the point of view of many religious groups, religion is the foundation for living. From a sociological perspective, many of the values and standards of behavior are derived from religion. Historically, an individual's religion has been an important influence upon the value he or she places on work. Religion has always played an important role in determining socially acceptable behavior through ethical values.

Education. In a formalized sense, **education** represents a behavioral pattern through which knowledge, skills, and concepts are transmitted to individuals through teaching mechanisms (human or otherwise). Educational systems are usually identified with schools but may also include less traditional methods of learning.

As a social institution, education aids in:

1. Systematically transmitting a cultural heritage from one generation to another

2. Creating an awareness of the proper role for the individual to play with respect to the many publics with whom he may have contact—friends, the government, his future employers, and so forth

3. Training individuals to perform practical roles through the acquisition of skills and technical knowledge

4. Providing a means of evaluating personal status dependent upon the level of formal organizational achievement

5. Promoting the acceptance of change and innovation

6. Imparting social and moral values[6]

7. Reducing prejudices and increasing tolerance and understanding among people[7]

The Union. Unions are the collective affiliations of individuals mutually joined together for the achievement of common goals and purposes. The union

[5]Merrill, *op. cit.*, pp. 376–377, Bertrand, *op. cit.*, pp. 275–291, and DeFleur, D'Antonio, and DeFleur, *op. cit.*, pp. 536–561, discuss the role of religion in detail.

[6]Merrill, *op. cit.*, p. 369, Bertrand, *op. cit.*, pp. 291–300, and DeFleur, D'Antonio, and DeFleur, *op. cit.*, pp. 562–595.

[7]Gordon W. Allport, *The Nature of Prejudice*, Boston: Addison-Wesley Publishing Company, 1954, pp. 79–80.

coexists with other forces that are often thought to be in opposition to it. Perhaps the most customary type of union is the labor union, which consists of a group of employees banded together for mutual benefit; but group affiliations of consumers, of members of a particular age group, and of members of a particular sex (the women's liberation movement, for example) may also occur.

Unions exist for the purposes of:

1. Providing the power of collective action
2. Serving as a force of resistance to externally oppressive forces
3. Providing the means to acquire possessions and conditions to meet the needs of individual members
4. Serving as a source of social interaction and social status
5. Making available an outlet for grievances and dissatisfactions
6. Establishing rules, standards, and guidelines for the behavior of members
7. Providing training and support for members
8. Serving as a mouthpiece for the desires and wishes of the collective membership

The Government.   A **government** may be defined as an agency or social structure designed to administer the affairs of the constituents of a state or territory. The citizens of a particular area may formulate their own government and elect administrative officials by common consent, or the government and its administrators may be determined through the exercise of power and force.

Perhaps the most universally accepted functions of a governing body are:

1. Incorporating norms and standards into laws and regulations
2. Enforcing laws and regulations
3. Mediating and resolving conflicts and disputes between individuals
4. Promoting the general welfare of individuals within the governed state (through health care, educational programs, communication and transportation systems, etc.)
5. Protecting individuals from external attacks

There are several indications that the government as an institutional body has increased the scope of its influence and operations to include other functions as well. In particular, it has been suggested that the government has acquired many humanitarian and instructional functions from the home, an increased number of economic functions from the financial and industrial world, and some interpersonal functions (increased control of marriage and divorce regulations, etc.) from religious institutions.[8]

[8]Merrill, *op. cit.*, pp. 366–375.

The Economic Network.   The **economic network** in a given society is the grouping of financial, commercial, and industrial factors into relationships that will provide for the physical subsistence of the society as well as performing other social functions. More specifically, the economic structure of a society exists to:

1. Provide for the production, processing, distribution, and consumption of goods and services necessary for human survival
2. Determine the monetary returns individuals may receive in exchange for the use of raw materials, mental effort, physical labor, financial holdings, or other contributions
3. Influence the distribution of wealth
4. Provide a distribution of labor so that the necessary work can be accomplished
5. Encourage individuals to cooperate collectively for achievement as well as to compete against each other for advancement
6. Provide a means of gaining or classifying levels of status and prestige through money and the symbolic powers of money
7. Place power in the hands of those possessing resources that are in demand

The Peer Group.   The **peer group** may include individuals either on the job or off the job who have interests, characteristics, or values in common. The social ties that unite friends and peer groups usually begin on an informal basis and tend to remain on that level unless unusual pressures are exerted (usually from external sources), which may cause the formalization of the group.

Peer groups exist to:

1. Establish, cultivate, and maintain uniform codes of conduct among participants of the socializing group
2. Encourage pleasurable interaction and affiliation for participants
3. Provide a source of recognition and status for individuals
4. Help and support individuals experiencing problems or difficulties
5. Serve as a means of communication and a source of information
6. Provide a means for resisting oppressive external forces

Personal and Environmental Conditions

In addition to the institutions and social groupings mentioned above, each individual encounters factors that affect his behavior patterns as he lives and works. The list of environmental and experiential factors influencing behavior is an almost inexhaustible one, and the cause-effect relationships are not always clearly documented. A few selected environmental or experiential influences are listed below with illustrations of the functions they serve in shaping behavior. The factors will include those of race or ethnic background, occupational standing, location of place of residence (urban or rural), and status of physical health.

The Experiential Elements of Race.   It can be effectively argued that race is an inherited factor and should have been discussed exclusively in the preceding chapter. However, there are many habits, customs, and behavior patterns that are a part of each individual's *experience* as he relates to others. These behavioral habits are a derivation of the individual's racial background primarily in terms of learned patterns rather than physically inherited functions of race. For example, race often functions to:

1.   Determine the language spoken by the individual (along with the influence of his nationality)
2.   Strongly influence the religious affiliations and involvements of the individual
3.   Create a separate set of behavior patterns to differentiate members of one race from those of another
4.   Provide a source for mutual affiliation and support
5.   Establish a common culture and set of traditions
6.   Unify group feelings of solidarity and uniqueness[9]

Occupational Standing.   Occupational standing refers to the type of job each worker performs to earn his livelihood and the associations related to it. Occupational divisions used by the United States government separate workers into four classifications: white-collar workers (professional and technical workers, managers, sales and clerical workers), blue-collar workers (craftsmen, operatives, and other nonfarm laborers), service workers (those who perform functions related to support, maintenance, and housekeeping), and agricultural workers. Occupational standing:

1.   Is a means by which prestige and status ranks are determined
2.   Influences the type of working conditions in which the employee may labor
3.   Is an influential determinant of the level of income received by the worker
4.   Is a determinant of the degree of ease or difficulty involved in gaining employment (based on skill requirements and on earning promotions)

[9]Brewton Berry, *Race and Ethnic Relations,* Third Edition, Boston: Houghton Mifflin and Company, 1965, p. 31.

5.   ~~Affects~~ the ~~level~~ of ~~satisfaction~~ a ~~worker gains~~ from his job

6.   ~~Determines~~ the ~~pattern~~ of ~~daily activities~~ for the ~~worker~~ and ~~his family~~ (in ~~terms~~ of ~~hours worked, hours free~~ for ~~recreation~~, and the ~~like~~)

7.   ~~Provides~~ a ~~career identity~~ for the ~~individual~~[10]

The ~~Effects~~ of ~~Place~~ of ~~Residence~~.   The place of residence (whether rural or urban) ~~sets~~ the ~~community environment~~ in which the individual and his family live, work, play, worship, spend their earnings, and engage in other activities. The place of residence:

1.   ~~Influences~~ the ~~amount~~ of ~~personal freedom~~ of ~~movement~~ and ~~action~~

2.   ~~Affixe~~s a ~~level~~ of ~~social~~ responsibility ~~toward~~ other ~~citizens~~

3.   ~~Establishe~~s the ~~availability~~ of ~~employment~~ through its ~~businesses~~ and in~~dustries~~

4.   ~~Determine~~s the ~~recreational patter~~ns of the ~~individual~~ on the ~~basis~~ of ~~available facilities~~

5.   ~~Determines~~ the ~~standard~~ of ~~living~~, based upon the ~~availability, cost~~, and ~~means~~ of ~~acquiring goods~~ and services

6.   ~~Establishe~~s ~~transportation~~ and ~~travel~~ patterns for the ~~individual~~

7.   ~~Influences~~ the ~~level~~ of c~~ooperation~~, competition, c~~onflict~~, or ~~assimilation~~ be~~tween individual~~s

~~Personal Health~~ as an Influencing Factor.   The status of an individual's physical health will:

1.   ~~Influen~~ce the ~~vigor~~ and ~~strength~~ he b~~rings~~ to his ~~work~~

2.   Be a ~~determinant~~ of ~~worker~~ longevity in ~~employment~~

3.   Be a ~~factor~~ in ~~earning~~ ad~~vancements~~ and ~~promotion~~ opportunities

4.   Possibly be a ~~determinant~~ in ~~setting~~ his ~~income level~~

5.   ~~Influen~~ce his ~~off-the-job~~ activities as well

Health is a variable that tends to be overlooked or underestimated. When all physical and mental facilities of the individual are functioning properly, most individuals tend to give very little thought to the proper care and maintenance of health. When illness or weaknesses occur, bodily limitations are recognized and

[10]See Walter L. Slocum, *Occupational Careers: A Sociological Perspective*, Chicago: Aldine Publishing Company, 1966, p. 277, and Richard H. Hall, *Occupations and the Social Structure*, Englewood Cliffs, New Jersey: Prentice-Hall, Inc., 1969, p. 393, for more complete discussions of the effects of occupational standing.

adjustments are required. The physical strength and stamina of employees are definite contributing factors to their operational abilities at work.

In addition to the environmental and experiential factors already mentioned, factors related to geographical location, climate, nationality, personal wealth or poverty, age and its related effects, and literally hundreds of other factors can also be considered because they influence the attitudes, capabilities, and performances of people at work.

Effects of Environment and Experience on Behavior at Work

From the material presented above, the importance of environmental factors and personal experience is obvious. Institutions and social groups interact with the individual and his personal conditions so that a unique set of experiences is developed (see Figure 3.1). As the individual relates his experience to his own personal drives and needs, his goals become more clearly formulated, his values are developed in more detail, his behavior tends to follow norms consistent with the more influential environmental factors, he receives his social status designations, and he perceives his role in relation to the elements in his environment.

If the effects of the environment and experience as they interact with the individual are considered in sociological terms (in terms of the scientific study of human social relationships and their consequences), the end result assumes additional meaning. Goal formulation, in a sociological sense, implies that the individual acts not only to achieve his own personal needs and ambitions but also to fulfill the wishes and demands of his social environment. Radical goals may be moderated as a result of social interaction, or passive ambitions may be kindled by the flames of social discontent.

If the values of the individual human being are defined as "a conception of what is desirable . . . an idea held by an individual but often shared with his friends and relations, which influences his choice of what to do and how to do it by defining what is worthwhile, precious, attractive, or suitable,"[11] the function of environment linked with experience becomes obvious. Environmental-experiential factors (through the family, religion, education, the peer group, and other sources) formulate a set of socially desirable values within the human mind. In Freudian terms, these values are fed into the superego. In the context of Rogers,

[11]Theodore Caplow, *Elementary Sociology,* Englewood Cliffs, New Jersey: Prentice-Hall, Inc., 1971, p. 20.

FIGURE 3.1   Interactions between the individual, his environment, and his personal conditions
               and circumstances

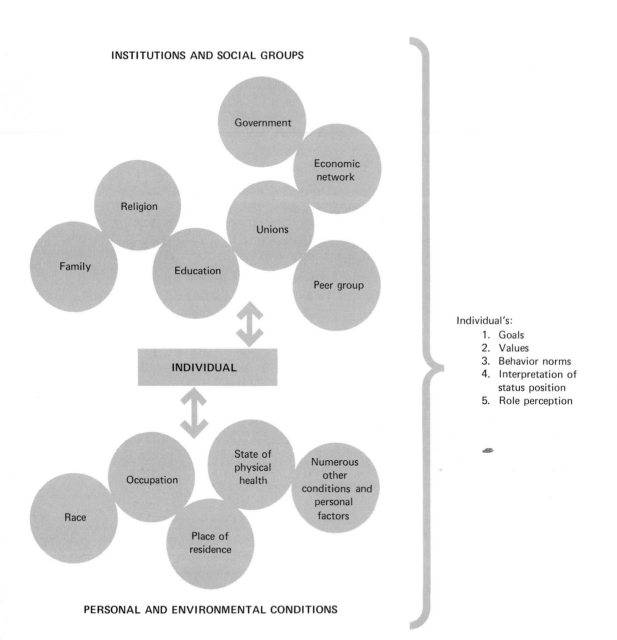

these concepts interact with the self. (Review the concepts presented in Chapter 2 for other discussions of individual capacities to absorb and develop value systems.) On the basis of individual-social-environmental encounters, the social conscience is developed.

From the goal structure, the value system, and the continuing interaction of the individual with other individuals and groups of people, a behavior code or a set of behavior norms is developed. A norm is defined as "a standard of conduct among a particular group which enables a person to determine in advance how his actions will be judged by other persons . . . it provides those other persons with criteria for approval and disapproval."[12] Each institution or social group with which an individual has contact may have unique norms or standards that it attempts to impose upon individuals within its domain. As a result, each individual may be forced to learn and adhere to a number of different behavior norms.

Through the individual's affiliation with groups in his environment and his own personal performance, the individual acquires a specific level of social status. Social status may be defined as the position, rank, or degree of power possessed by the individual in the total social system. Individuals who are given high rankings on the social ladder in comparison with other individuals and have a significant influence over the actions and behavior of others are said to have high social status. Those who rank low on the social scale and possess little influence are low in social status. Because social status is granted by others and is a function of social interaction, the social-environmental influences upon the individual are important behavioral determinants.

Environmental influences also affect the roles individuals play. A role is a pattern of behavior expected of an individual occupying a position of status within a social group. Role expectations are determined on the basis of the functions served by the individual and the power to act that he has been granted by the social group. Role perception, then, is the identification by the individual of the expectations held by himself and others for his behavior in the status position he uniquely possesses. Role perception involves the discovery by the individual of the social rights and responsibilities that uniquely belong to him. An accurate perception of the individual's role is gained only through a period of interaction with the social system that surrounds him.

Every individual who makes the decision to enter the work force and to offer his services and skills for employment takes with him a set of goals, values, behavior norms, status ranks, and role perceptions. These personal possessions will be

---

[12]*Ibid.,* p. 21.

a continuing influence on his behavior as he affiliates himself with a business organization or industrial enterprise. These goals, values, status factors, and role perceptions are derived from the interactions of each individual with his environment.

Entry into a position with a business organization will tend to bring an additional environment and new pressures and sources of influence upon the employee. Each business organization has its own set of goals, its own set of organizational objectives. The official philosophy of the organization and the unofficial actions of managers and workers will impose a new set of social values upon the worker. Company rules, regulations, and policies along with the informal behavior norms of the workers themselves will suggest new codes of conduct for the employee. The social system of the organization will delegate status and prestige using a system of its own. Role expectations will be extended in addition to the off-the-job expectations already perceived by the worker.

Responsibilities of the Manager

The manager sometimes finds himself hard pressed to interpret the actions of a particular employee or to identify the root of an interpersonal problem existing between workers. However, a clear understanding of the cause and effect relationships that evolve for the worker through his experiences with his environment (and his own personal conditions) can be a valuable tool for the manager as he attempts to work with his subordinates. An understanding of the influence of social groupings upon the formulation of personal goals, the establishment of a personal value system, the development of a pattern of behavior norms, the allocation of social status, and the perception of role responsibilities will also aid in administering the relationships of people.

The more a supervisor knows and understands the specific goals, values, norms, status levels, and role perceptions of each individual worker, the more adequately the supervisor will be able to motivate, support, and utilize the talents and abilities of the workers. For example, an individual worker who possesses a high level of skill, who has achieved a superior level of educational attainment, and whose parents have encouraged him to be an achiever usually possesses the capacity to be a highly productive performer and will not be satisfied with an insignificant job demanding little in the way of ability or effort. The supervisor who perceives the high goal, status, and norm expectations of this worker can utilize these expectations in a way that will be appealing and rewarding to the worker.

In general, *it is desirable to select and assign individuals to work tasks consistent with the values, norms, and roles their environmental-experiential backgrounds have prepared them for.* It would be unwise, for example, for a worker with strong religious training forbidding him to work on Sunday to be hired and placed in a position in which regular Sunday labor was an essential part of the job. The worker would be dissatisfied, and his job tenure might well turn out to be brief. In the same manner, it would be unwise to assign an individual to a job requiring a high level of self-confidence and self-motivation if the individual has a long history of failures and inadequacies in his personal background and has developed feelings of inferiority and guilt.

In addition, *the manager who perceives the off-the-job social standing of a worker and provides on-the-job opportunities to improve or sustain his social rank will normally have found an effective way to appeal to the energies and desires of the worker.* A worker with high off-the-job social influences and power will find it difficult to adjust to an organizational position in which his organizational social rank is minimal and which may even detract from his off-the-job social rank. He will, however, respond to opportunities that sustain or enhance the social status he already possesses. Whenever a manager can improve or enhance the social standing of a worker through job assignments, responsibilities, and rewards, the worker's reaction will usually be favorable.

In jobs in which a high level of social interaction is desirable between workers—where workers must communicate freely and must be highly cooperative—a knowledge of the environmental-experiential background of workers is also important. *If workers can be selected and placed together so that they can be compatible and amiable, they will be much more cooperative and productivity will be enhanced.* Unfortunately, compatibility is not necessarily a matter of selecting individuals with similar backgrounds, values, goals, and social standing, although such similarity may be helpful in unifying effort. Perhaps the most important characteristic in grouping workers for social interaction would be the discovery and placement of individuals together who have proved their ability to relate to or socialize with others. The ability to socialize might be defined as the capacity of individuals to learn and respond to the values, norms, and roles expected by the group.[13]

From this selected application, it can be seen that the individual is, in part, a product of his environment and experiences. The manager who is aware of the environments, experiences, and socialization abilities of individual workers can respond to the attitudes and behavior patterns of each individual more meaningfully and constructively.

[13]*Ibid.,* p. 23.

Summary

Individual behavior is a product of internal needs and desires and of environmental and experiential factors as well. This chapter has concerned itself with the functions and effects of several social groupings or institutions and selected personal conditions. The roles of family, religion, education, unions, the government, the economic network, and peer and friendship groups have been presented. The effects of personal conditions such as race, occupational standing, health, and place of residence have also been reviewed.

It has become obvious that the individual interacts with a number of environmental-experiential factors in ways that determine his personal goals, value system, behavior norms, social standing, and role perceptions. These factors influence both on-the-job and off-the-job behavior for workers. Astute managers recognize and utilize the perceived environmental-experiential factors of employees in their manner and methods of supervision.

On the basis of the materials presented in this chapter, details of the behavior model being developed can be added so that the model now appears as shown in Figure 3.2. The characteristics of the individual (human nature) and effects of the worker's environment and experience are now detailed in the model. In Chapter 4, technological factors will be described.

Questions to consider after reading Chapter 3

1.   Analyze the lists of contributions and effects of each environmental and experiential factor. Do you agree with the stated effects? Is each of the lists complete?

2.   What is a family unit?

3.   Is the environmental-experiential concept presented in this chapter compatible with the theories of individual behavior presented in the previous chapter? Why or why not?

4.   Can you identify any similarities between the effects of unions and peer groups? In what ways are the structures and effects of unions and peer groups different?

5.   It was mentioned that many believe the role of the government as a social institution is changing. Are there indications that the roles of the other social institutions are also changing? Please support your answer.

6.   In your own words, define the following terms: the socialization process, peer group, values, behavior norms, status, role, role perception.

7.   This chapter concludes that social institutions and personal experiences have influential effects upon the behavior of people at work. Give a tangible illustration of the effects of a worker's family upon the worker's behavior. Also, illustrate the effects of religion, education, unions, the government, the economic network, and peer groups on workers you know personally. Do you know of situations where racial, occupational, residential, and health factors have influenced worker behavior? Illustrate these also.

8.   Do any of the environmental-experiential factors seem to dominate and influence worker behavior more than other factors?

FIGURE 3.2   Partially detailed model of worker behavior and its determinants

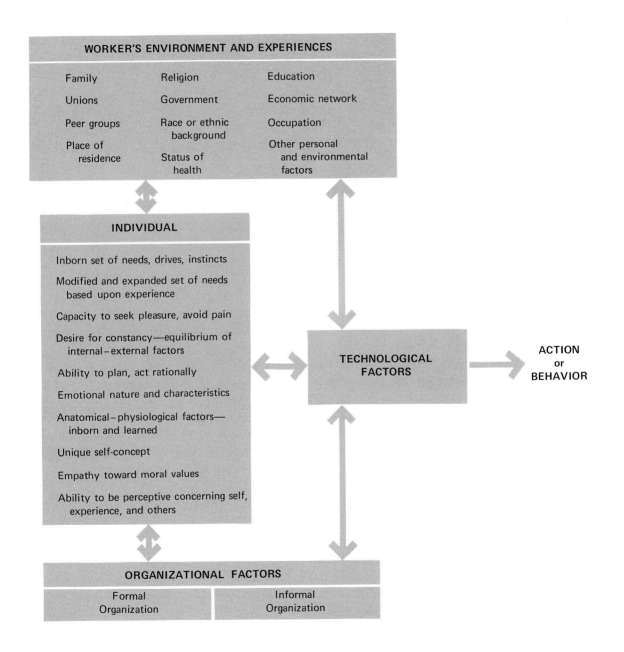

The following cases at the back of the book contain problems related to Chapter 3:

> Mark Williams
>
> Stanley Lowell
>
> Billy Snyder
>
> Susan Swanson
>
> Richard Jameson
>
> Abigail Spiegal and Trudy Pennington

Additional readings

Berger, Bennett M., *Working Class Suburb*, Berkeley: University of California Press, 1960.

Bertrand, Alvin L., editor, *Rural Sociology*, New York: McGraw-Hill Book Company, 1968.

Blood, Milton R., and Charles L. Hulin, "Alienation, Environmental Characteristics, and Worker Responses," *Journal of Applied Psychology*, Volume 51, Number 3 (June 1967), pp. 284–290.

Burke, Ronald J., "Effects of Organizational Experience on Managerial Attitudes and Beliefs: A Better Press for Managers," *Journal of Business Research*, Volume 1, Number 1 (Summer 1973), pp. 21–30.

Connor, John T., "The Political Environment for Business," in Peter F. Drucker, editor, *Preparing Tomorrow's Business Leaders Today*, Englewood Cliffs, New Jersey: Prentice-Hall, Inc., 1969, pp. 27–35.

Foss, Lawrence, "Managerial Strategy for the Future: Theory Z Management," *California Management Review*, Volume 15, Number 3 (Spring 1973), pp. 68–81.

Gibson, James L., and Stuart M. Klein, "Employee Attitudes as a Function of Age and Length of Service," *The Academy of Management Journal*, Volume 13, Number 4 (December 1970), pp. 411–416.

Goode, William J., *The Family*, Englewood Cliffs, New Jersey: Prentice-Hall, Inc., 1964.

Hertzler, J. O., *American Social Institutions*, Boston: Allyn and Bacon, Incorporated, 1961.

Kelley, Lane, and Clayton Reeser, "The Persistence of Culture as a Determinant of Differentiated Attitudes on the Part of American Managers of Japanese Ancestry," *The Academy of Management Journal*, Volume 16, Number 1 (March 1973), pp. 67–76.

Klein, Stuart M., and John R. Maher, "Educational Level, Attitudes, and Future Expectations among First-Level Management," *Personnel Psychology*, Volume 21, Number 1 (Spring 1968), pp. 43–53.

Miner, John B., *The Management of Ineffective Performance,* New York: McGraw-Hill Book Company, 1963, pp. 97–129, 179–214.

Osborne, Richard H., *The Biological and Social Meaning of Race,* San Francisco: W. H. Freeman and Company, 1971.

Sanders, Irwin T., *The Community,* Second Edition, New York: The Ronald Press Company, 1966.

Warren, Roland L., *The Community in America,* Second Edition, Chicago: Rand McNally and Company, 1972.

Williams, Robin M., Jr., *American Society,* Third Edition, New York: Alfred A. Knopf, 1970.

Chapter 4

The Impact of Technology

A case to consider before reading chapter 4

JOEL McCAMERON—THE UNHAPPY ASSEMBLY-LINE WORKER

Joel McCameron is a twenty-nine-year-old worker in an automobile assembly plant. Joel has worked in the same plant since he received his military service discharge nearly seven years ago. He is married and has a preschool-aged son. Joel works as a door-panel assembler. It is his job to select the proper color for the right front door of each car passing along the asembly line and to insert the panel and fasten it to the door frame. Joel has a very limited amount of time to perform his job before another automobile moves up the assembly line to be fitted.

Joel makes the following statements about his job and work career.

I despise what I'm doing. I think a monkey or a robot could do my job as well as I do it. There's absolutely no challenge to it, and the repetition is terrible. I actually miss thirty or more days of work each year, and my absences usually have nothing to do with illness. I just get up some mornings and can't make myself go to work.

I don't really have any good friends at work. You don't have much chance to talk to other people on the line. I've got to admit the pay is pretty good. That's the main reason I keep working there. I think my wife is a little embarrassed to tell people that she's married to an assembly-line robot.

Actually, I'm the black sheep of my family. Both of my brothers are in business for themselves and are doing pretty well. My wife's brother is a college graduate with a high-paying job with an insurance company.

I sure don't want my son to get caught in this kind of work. I'm going to see to it that he gets a good education so that he has more job choices than I've had. I'm looking around for another job myself, but I just can't find anything that pays well enough.

Questions about the Joel McCameron case

1.   Which of Joel McCameron's personal goals and objectives are being met while he works?

2.   Which of Joel McCameron's personal goals and objectives are not being provided for by his job?

3.   What additional job factors does Joel find unsatisfactory? Why?

4.   How many of today's workers share these same types of frustration with "Robot" McCameron?

5.   What can be done by perceptive supervisors and innovative companies to make jobs such as the one McCameron has more beneficial and rewarding for the worker?

6.   What factors limit the amount of improvement that can be provided for workers on jobs of this kind?

Technology is the harnessing of scientific and technical knowledge for the purpose of improving the state of the human race. In the context of the work organization, technology has also been defined as the creation of new outputs by the utilization of new inputs or by the restructuring of old inputs. Technology had its humble beginnings when the cave man tired of performing all of his labors strictly with his hands and felt restricted in the end results of his labors. He wanted to be able to achieve bigger and better things more effectively and more easily. Through the years, technology has built upon the advancements of previous eras until a rather complex and very productive application of scientific knowledge has been reached.

In reality, our current stage of technological development is a result of an evolution of innovations. The beginning period of development was known as the handicraft era and consisted of a long period of time in which work was rather simplistic, and people did most of their own work themselves. The earliest colonial settlers in the Americas lived in this period, for example. These people tilled the soil, built their houses, made their own clothes, developed their own rudimentary medicines, and performed other tasks utilizing their limited resources and knowledge. Most individuals had to become jacks-of-all-trades just to survive. Workers in the handicraft era suffered many frustrations as a result of the limitations under which they labored, but they received satisfaction through achieving things themselves and through the development and cultivation of skills. They had the opportunity to be somewhat self-sufficient and frequently labored under very challenging conditions.

Then came the mechanization era, in which new energy sources and methods of harnessing that energy were discovered. As one author has stated, the mechanization era was the period of time when "machines replaced man labor with machine labor."[1] A particularly pronounced effect of this era was the beginning of job specialization, in which most workers were assigned limited numbers of tasks in a constant, repetitive pattern. The machine removed some tedious, undesirable details from the duties of the typical worker while frequently replacing them with other unattractive working conditions. In many instances, for example, the work pace was dictated by the rate at which the machine worked and not by the pace the worker preferred. Some jobs required only limited skills. During this era, worker compensation and working conditions were not known for their excellence.

The mechanization era was followed by the assembly-line era—an era still in existence today. The assembly-line era was and is characterized by worker performance tied to a conveyor belt that moves in a continuing line. Each worker along the line performs a small task as a part of a larger assembly until a total product is put together. The advantages and disadvantages of working in assembly-line situations will be discussed momentarily.

The most recent era of technological development to affect business and industry has been the era of automation. Automation is an extension of the machine and assembly-line eras in that computers and other-control capabilities have been added to machines and assembly lines so that equipment and machinery perform a large percentage of the work in automated organizations, and computers regulate the pace and sequence of events. The human role in relation to automation is one of planning, programming, and maintaining the control and performance equipment upon which automation depends.

With this brief description of the four stages of technological development and evolution, it is now time to place technology within the framework of our model of organizational behavior and to discuss the contributions and effects of technology in more detail.

Technology has an impact upon almost everything that exists. The society and the economy of every civilization is influenced by technology. The business enterprises within each society feel direct influences from technology. The people at work (both operative personnel and managerial personnel) come under the influence of technological development. Technology has an impact upon the relationships between managers and labor unions. The effects of technological innovation

[1]Daniel A. Wren, *The Evolution of Management Thought,* New York: The Ronald Press Company, 1972, p. 485.

upon these groups and relationships will be reviewed more closely in the remainder of this chapter.

Effects on the Society
and the Economy

A ~~society~~ is a ~~large grouping~~ of ~~individuals who~~ are ~~related together~~ in ~~some way~~ to ~~form~~ a ~~community.~~ However loosely connected the society may be, the individuals who are a part of it have interests and ties in common. Within the society there exists an economic structure that controls the production, distribution, and consumption of the wealth of the society.

Technology affects a society and an economy in many ways. *One of the ~~primary purposes~~ of ~~technology~~ is to ~~provide new products~~ for ~~consumption~~ by the ~~individuals within the economy.~~*[2] In societies where technology has been allowed to progress more fully, the range of products available to the individual consumer is much wider, and the availability of processed goods and services is much more complete than in societies where technology has not been pursued to a high degree. This wider availability of processed goods illustrates another result of technology—*the ~~application~~ of ~~technological innovation~~ normally ~~results~~ in an ~~increased~~ capacity to ~~provide manufactured~~ products ~~to~~ the ~~individuals within~~ the ~~society.~~*[3] The increase in products and the wider availability of products is not limited to industrially processed goods alone, however. ~~Technology has~~ also had a ~~direct~~ impact ~~upon~~ the ~~production~~ of ~~greater varieties~~ and ~~quantities~~ of ~~agricultural products.~~[4]

~~Another~~ *effect* of ~~technological~~ applications to ~~industry~~ has been the ~~reduction~~ of ~~production costs, primarily through~~ a ~~decrease~~ in ~~labor costs.~~[5] Technology often provides less expensive, more efficient ways of producing goods and services. Lower labor costs have normally resulted in lower prices for goods and services made available to the consuming public.[6] Not to be overlooked, of course, is the fact that *technology ~~has~~ also made possible the ~~preservation~~ of ~~many~~ products and ~~their transportation~~ to ~~customers~~ in ~~previously remote~~ or ~~inconvenient places.~~* So it can be seen that technology

[2]Simon Marcson, editor, *Automation, Alienation, and Anomie*, New York: Harper & Row, Publishers, 1970, p. 4.

[3]Ben B. Seligman, *Most Notorious Victory: Man in the Age of Automation*, New York: The Macmillan Company, 1966, pp. 3–30.

[4]Seymour L. Wolfbein, "The Pace of Technological Change and the Factors Affecting It," in Marcson, *op. cit.*, p. 55.

[5]*Ibid.*, pp. 69–76.

[6]Seligman, *op. cit.*, pp. 29–30.

has made possible a much wider range of products, at more affordable prices, to a larger segment of society than has ever been known. As technology continues to advance, this trend will continue. New markets will be developed, and new consumption patterns will result.

Another socioeconomic effect of technological advancement has been its ~~impact upon~~ the ~~rate~~ of ~~employment~~ (and the related factors of distribution of wealth). The effects of technology upon employment have been the subject of considerable controversy. The earlier phases of industrialization in the American economy are typically regarded as having created more jobs for more people. The eras of mechanization and coordination attracted larger numbers of people into the work force and, as will be discussed later, had an effect on the skill levels of the workers. The effects of technology in the automation era have been viewed in both favorable and unfavorable lights in relation to the level of employment.

Some observers of the effects of technological change have expressed the belief that automation tends to create more jobs than it eliminates and that temporary displacement is the most serious negative effect of automation felt by the technically obsolete worker. In other words, some workers will lose their jobs because they are incapable of meeting new requirements; but these workers will be replaced by other, more capable workers. This position suggests that, in the long run, employment will be higher as a result of the use of automated techniques. In an optimistic outlook, the Joint Economic Committee of the Congress of the United States wrote that "automation, if used effectively, can reduce unemployment rather than add to it."[7]

Other writers, however, have taken a different view of the effects of technology upon employment. One author has suggested that in the future fewer people will be needed to perform the productive work of a society, because a single individual will be able to increase his output enough to do the work of several.[8] This increased individual productivity will have significant effects on unemployment, on the length of work days and work weeks, and on the leisure patterns of individuals. Seligman states that unemployment has an effect particularly upon unskilled and semiskilled workers but also among professional workers.[9] Rosenberg has stated more specifically that clerical workers, laborers, machine operators, inspectors, and payroll clerks are the ones whose jobs are being eliminated to the largest

---

[7]Joint Economic Committee, Congress of the United States, *Employment and Manpower Problems in the Cities*, Washington, D.C.: U.S. Government Printing Office, 1968, pp. 21–23.

[8]Leon C. Megginson, *Personnel: A Behavioral Approach to Administration*, Second Edition, Homewood, Illinois: Richard D. Irwin, Inc., 1972, p. 145.

[9]Seligman, *op. cit.*, pp. 194–215.

degree as a direct result of automation.[10] Because the work force is composed of such a mixture of workers (some in automated jobs, some in assembly-line jobs, and so forth), a completely accurate assessment of the effects of technology upon employment is extremely difficult.

Since technology possesses the ability to provide new products, increased production capacities and varieties, reduced costs and thus lower consumer prices, and the ability to alter the composition of the work force (in quantity and skill level), technology must be viewed as an innovator and modifier of human behavior. Technology creates new frontiers for human experience. Technology often runs ahead of the values of society, and it presses for the acceptance of new ways and new ideas. In many situations, social values view technological change in a favorable light and accept the innovations it offers. The introduction of television, for example, represented a technological innovation that was accepted and adopted into social patterns. In other situations, however, the values of society reject changes, and technology is not allowed to proceed according to its potential. New manufacturing methods, for example, are sometimes resisted because they appear to threaten the ecology of an area. Clean air and clean water may be preferred over a new or less expensive product. Of course, technology does not always produce these negative consequences.

Impact on Business
and Industry

Technology has greatly affected the scope and manner of operations within the business enterprise itself. In addition to creating new products and stimulating new marketing cycles, *technology has brought about additional innovations that have modified business operations.* Wolfbein lists at least nine other areas in which technology has influenced industrial operations. These areas of innovation include the introduction and utilization of electronic computers, the application of instrumentation and automation to process industries, the utilization of numerical control devices for tools and equipment, advances in communication technology, overall improvements in machinery, the mechanization of materials handling, new developments in metal processing, advances in the speed and ease of transportation, and improvements and efficiencies in power production.[11]

---

[10]Jerry M. Rosenberg, *Automation, Manpower, and Education,* New York: Random House, 1966, pp. 128–129.

[11]Wolfbein, *op. cit.,* pp. 55–59.

In a perceptive review and forecast of technological and mechanical impacts upon industry, Bright came up with an additional list of results, benefits, and problems springing out of technical innovations. His list of benefits was presented prior to the realization of some anticipated effects of technology, and many of the predicted effects have since become reality (see Figure 4.1).

When the impact of technology is viewed on the basis of improved products, methods, materials, economy, and efficiency, mechanization and automation appear to have had many positive effects. Of course, not all products, conditions, and effects of the industrial age resulting from technological innovation may be superior to those of the preindustrial era, but from an industrial point of view the advantages appear to overshadow the disadvantages.

Effects of Technological Change on People at Work

While an overview of the results of technological innovation upon the society as a whole is of definite importance, the main concern here is what happens to people at work as a result of technology. The innovations from technology have had a significant influence on the work environment, work relationships, work responsibilities, and the nature and number of jobs available. Several of the effects will now be considered.

The stages of technological impact upon industry and workers mentioned earlier are represented by four eras—the pretechnological handicraft era, the mechanization era, the assembly-line era, and the era of automation. The real impact of technology began to be felt by workers in the mechanization era and has continued through the automation era. In many respects, the effects of technology upon the worker have been viewed by observers as somewhat negative in the mechanization and assembly-line eras but somewhat improved with the advent of automation. As a result, the effects of technological change upon the worker are separated into two categories for consideration.

The Mechanization and Assembly-Line Eras.   The mechanization stage of development was largely the phase in which machine labor replaced human labor in performing many of the heavier, more strenuous tasks; the assembly-line era is the phase in which jobs become integrated more closely along conveyor belts and assembly lines. There were some positive benefits for the workers out of these developments. Workers were freed from some of the heavier, more unpleasant tasks; many working conditions were improved; and wages climbed

FIGURE 4.1   Significant areas of mechanical–technical progress

AREA OF MECHANIZATION	NATURE OF TASK
A. Functions where major advances are being made	
Work feeding	mechanized supply and removal of parts and materials at production machines
Materials handling	industrial trucks, cranes, conveyers move materials between machines, departments, and buildings and in shipping and receiving operations
Inspection, testing	automatic verification and control of dimensions, qualities, and operating characteristics
Assembly, operations	automatic assembly of product parts, taking into account variations in components and in models
Communications	two-way radio, closed-circuit television, tape recorders, documents, conveyers, telephones with conference circuit arrangements, facsimile devices, teletypewriter and telescriber, and many other devices and combinations thereof
Containerization	master shipping containers to move materials between shipping points; production containers adapted to feed foodstuffs, chemicals, fertilizers, and so on, into production equipment
Warehousing, shipping, receiving	mechanization of receipt, storage, inventory control, and documentation; order picking, packaging, and shipping
B. Design trends with far-reaching implications	
Program control	numerical control applied to machine tools, punched-tape typewriters; punched-card systems of machine control
Feedback control	control mechanisms used to sense environmental conditions and alter equipment performance
Compounding of equipment	production devices compressed so that fewer machines are needed
Integration of computer control and production equipment	data-processing machine systems initiate production work, control machines, analyze data on performance, determine and make process adjustments

MAJOR BENEFITS	SOME PROBLEMS AND DISADVANTAGES
large increase in equipment utilization, safety conditions improved, less fatigue and other worker benefits	risk of machine stoppage increased; cost increases likely in purchasing, inspection
indirect labor reduced, direct labor frequently relieved of handling work, improved safety, scrap reduction	commitment to mechanized system may reduce flexibility if improperly planned
more uniform testing, shorter testing time, lower labor requirements, reduced inspector training problem, improved product quality	possible high development cost, possible serious delays in event of malfunction
significant reductions in labor cost, shorter manufacturing cycle time	high degree of uniformity of parts required, long production runs necessary, larger inventories sometimes needed to justify setup cost
speed and accuracy in passing of information increased, faster material movement as a result, reductions in indirect labor and clerical force, shorter manufacturing	difficulty in designing an integrated, flexible, and comprehensive system; some training problems may arise
great economies in handling and packaging costs, reduced transportation time, greater product protection, faster discharge and loading	more careful analysis of shipping function and of purchasing-receiving-issuing cycle required, large financial commitment, relative inflexibility to changes
reduction in inventory stocks, faster customer service, lower storage space requirements, reduced labor cost	substantial additional capital required for distribution function, less flexibility, new order of executive skill required, economic justification dubious in many instances, still in development stage
less labor content, superior process control, faster response to manufacturing orders, reduced setup time, reduced operator skill requirement	cost, flexibility, and development problems in some cases; new "programmer" skill requirements
more uniformity, better quality, less waste, optimum process and product control, reduced operator skill requirements	same as for program control
less plant space needed, large cuts in work-in-process inventory, quicker handling of orders	less flexibility in product changes, maintenance more important because of stoppage danger
faster and more efficient production, lower inventories, better service to customers, optimum control of process costs and product characteristics, reduced skill	increased necessity of planning a business as an integrated system rather than as a series of functional activities; still largely in development stage

Source: James R. Bright, "Are We Falling Behind in Mechanization?", *Harvard Business Review*, Volume 38, Number 6 (November-December 1960), p. 96.

significantly. The workers, as consumers, also benefited from the general increase in productivity and the lowering of unit production costs.

The jobs performed by the typical worker in mechanized and assembly-line plants tended to become more specialized and repetitive in nature. The pace at which the worker performed and the freedom of movement of the worker were often restricted to the rate at which the machines and conveyor belts moved. Many workers found this more confining, less controllable work pattern unsatisfactory. When one researcher went to industrial workers employed under these conditions and asked the question, "If you could go back to the age of 15 and start over again, would you choose a different trade or occupation?" a majority of those employed in the industrial trades said yes. As many as 65 to 71 percent of the production workers in the leather, sawmill, oil refining, automotive, and steel and iron industries said that they would like to start their working careers again in other types of employment. Out of all factory workers surveyed, 59 percent indicated a preference for a different line of work. The workers who indicated the least desire to start again in a different occupation were those employed in the printing industry (36 percent desired a change)—an area where greater skill demands are placed upon the worker and more freedom and independence are allowed than is typical in other industries.[12]

In commenting on the dissatisfaction of many industrial workers with their jobs, Broom and Selznick have said that the most alienated of all workmen are those who labor on the assembly line. Reasons for this alienation include the factor that "his [the worker's] job denies him control and meaning, and the social atmosphere of the large assembly plant intensifies his sense of isolation."[13] Further, they stated that mechanization and the assembly line inhibit the activities of the informal work group and that job duties become meaningless and real responsibilities become few.

Other studies tend to substantiate these effects of technology as represented by mechanization and the assembly line. One study revealed that workers in assembly-line jobs have fewer opportunities to interact socially, and the number of people with whom interaction may occur is also decreased noticeably.[14] Another author sees the potential dissatisfaction for workers in mechanized and

[12]Robert Blauner, *Alienation and Freedom: The Manual Worker in Industry,* Chicago: University of Chicago Press, 1964, p. 202. Blauner quotes data from a Roper study taken for *Fortune* in 1947.

[13]Leonard Broom and Philip Selznick, *Sociology,* Third Edition, New York: Harper & Row, Publishers, 1963, p. 651.

[14]William A. Faunce, "Automation in the Automobile Industry: Some Consequences for In-Plant Social Structure," *American Sociological Review,* Volume 23, Number 4 (August 1958), pp. 401–407.

coordinated jobs because powerlessness, meaninglessness, isolation, and self-estrangement may occur. By definition, man is powerless "when he is an object controlled and manipulated by other persons or by an impersonal system and when he cannot assert himself as a subject to change or modify this domination."[15] Meaninglessness occurs when the individual's work responsibilities appear to have no relationship to broader goals and purposes of life; in other words, when there is no congruence between on-the-job results and personal goals. Isolation, of course, refers to individual separation from socially desirable contacts. Self-estrangement suggests that the individual is not actualizing his self goals and may be suffering loss of self-esteem. Powerlessness, meaninglessness, isolation, and self-estrangement are all possible under technological mechanization and coordination, although there is not an absolute relationship that forces this result.

Another damaging effect in these stages of technological innovation may be a reduction in the skills required of employees to perform their jobs.[16] The development of skills is a source of pride for the worker; as a result, jobs that require little or no skill are low-status jobs and do not foster personal pride and prestige.

While no modern-day consumer would desire to be without the benefits of technology as evidenced in mechanization and coordination, the negative effects of the developments upon the work force can be readily recognized. Society in general and management in particular have often been concerned about reducing many of the negative effects of these eras. Some gains have been made in overcoming or offsetting the undesirable effects, as will be seen in later chapters (Chapter 15, for example).

The Effects of Automation.   As the level of technological development has increased, machines and computers have become even more involved in productive performance. In those industries where automation has been accepted and utilized, a large percentage of the production and processing work is being performed by machines, and computers regulate and control the integrated machine activities. The role of workers in the highly automated industries tends to become one of monitoring, maintaining, adjusting, and repairing the equipment involved in the production process. The worker is responsible for keeping the process moving. The production process is heavily interrelated so that the need to avoid breakdowns in the equipment has a high priority.

[15]Blauner, *op. cit.,* p. 16.
[16]Wilbert E. Moore, *Industrial Relations and the Social Order,* New York: The Macmillan Company, 1951, pp. 512–515.

From many points of view, the ~~work life~~ of the ~~employee laboring~~ with ~~automation appears~~ to be ~~improved~~. Researchers have concluded that the consequences of automation for the worker include:

1. ~~Work~~ assignments that ~~are cleaner~~ and ~~lighter~~
2. ~~Increased demands~~ for ~~mental~~ and ~~mathematical~~ skill along with a concurrent ~~decrease in manual skill~~ demands
3. ~~Job~~ assignments that ~~increase rather~~ than ~~decrease employee responsibilities.~~
4. ~~Job responsibilities~~ that ~~encourage enlargement~~ rather than divisionalization of skills
5. ~~Work~~ relationships that ~~enhance~~ the ~~interdependence~~ of ~~employees~~ and ~~contribute~~ to the ~~integration~~ of the ~~organization~~
6. ~~Better communication~~ horizontally and vertically throughout the organization as a result of better consultation
7. ~~More interesting work~~ because of the variety of duties
8. ~~More pleasant working conditions~~ and ~~environments~~
9. ~~Higher pay~~
10. An ~~increased sense~~ of ~~job security~~
11. A ~~safer job~~ and ~~work atmosphere.~~
12. An ~~increased pride~~ in ~~work~~ because of the fine equipment being used
13. ~~Educational~~ and ~~experiential opportunities~~ valuable for personal development[17]

The advantages listed above are potential gains for the employee as a result of automation and are not absolutely assured, but several observations of the effects of automation have shown them to be predominately true. This does not suggest that automation is without negative effects. Automated work often may involve constant, steady, repetitive tasks that may become monotonous and may restrict the curiosity and initiative of the individual worker.[18] Some workers also seem to feel more uncertainties and insecurities as a result of having to work with automated equipment. Fears of an inadequate ability to meet required standards, fears of eventual job loss as a result of further automation, fears of possible reduced wages, fears of a lack of safety while working with machines, and a general contempt for imposed changes are some of the apprehensions workers may feel when

[17]Broom and Selznick, *op. cit.,* pp. 654–655, and James R. Bright, *Automation and Management,* Boston: Division of Research of the Graduate School of Business Administration, Harvard University, 1958, p. 211.

[18]Pierre Naville, "The Structure of Employment and Automation," *International Social Science Bulletin,* Volume 9, Numbers 1–4 (February 1957), pp. 16–30, as quoted by Rosenberg, *op. cit.,* p. 78.

automation occurs.[19] In general, however, the status of the average worker is felt to be improved where automation has taken place.

Effects of Technology upon the Manager

Technology has influenced the task of being a manager in many ways. Burack and Pati, for example, have made the following assessment of technology's impact.

> Increased ability to think in quantitative terms, ability to communicate in the "new way" to a new set of people about new things, ability to comprehend what advanced technology can or cannot do, and the aptitude to learn are some of the requirements which the supervisor considers in order to achieve his goals as well as the organizational goals of the company.[20]

Automation demands an alert, machinery-conscious supervisor of a higher caliber.

1. He must be acquainted with all the performance processes, since he directs a complete line rather than one department.
2. He must be conscious of a machinery-oriented production system. This means appreciating the need for preventive maintenance and having reasonable knowledge of each machine element.
3. He must be imaginative and resourceful, since downtime must be anticipated, minimized, and circumvented as much as possible.
4. He must be willing to accept change, since automation may mean a great revision of existing procedures as well as continuing change.[21]

The list above shows that the manager who supervises workers in organizations where mechanization, coordination, and automation have occurred must be a much more knowledgeable, astute individual than was true of the manager in less technologically developed times.

Beginning with the first-line supervisor, the level of technical competence must be sufficient to deal with mechanical problems that may develop and the corresponding manpower needs that may result. The supervisor must be capable of

---

[19]Bright, *op. cit.,* p. 203.

[20]Elmer H. Burack and Gopal C. Pati, "Technology and Managerial Obsolescence," *M.S.U. Business Topics,* Volume 18, Number 2 (Spring 1970), p. 53.

[21]Bright, *op. cit.,* p. 209.

dealing with the human needs and hostilities that may occur also. He must be capable of bridging two separate worlds—the world of the machine with its potential breakdowns or foul-ups and the world of humans with their weaknesses and sensitivities.[22]

Middle and upper-level managers have more demanded of them as a result of technological advances also. Technical knowledge, coordinative abilities, conceptual understanding of production and communication systems, and sound analytical and decision-making abilities are becoming increasingly important for higher-level managers. Educational requirements have increased for most managers who serve in middle and upper-level management capacities. Technological innovations have also precipitated an increase in the number of high-level staff specialists to assist managers in performing the statistical and technical requirements of their jobs.

This brief overview of the effects of technology upon the manager indicates that serving in a managerial capacity has become increasingly demanding in knowledge and abilities. The modern manager is forced to develop and cultivate new skills and to be aware of changing trends and demands as technology introduces them.

The Effect on Manpower Policies and Practices

As the development of machinery, assembly lines, and computers initiated new production methods and procedures, it became necessary to modify organizational policies and regulations regarding selection and hiring of workers, the provision of job training, the compensation of labor through wages and salaries, the handling of union relations, and other practices related to the work force. Manpower policies and practices differed somewhat in the mechanization and assembly-line eras from those needed in the automation era. In the earlier stages of the industrial movement, the recruitment and selection of workers was primarily a matter of attracting trainable, willing workers and placing them in organizational positions where their talents could be utilized to the fullest. There was a shortage of laborers in some jobs that called for the possession of a specific set of skills as a basis of employment, and these workers were competed for rather vigorously. Wages and salaries on the basis of seniority and merit were generally on the increase.

[22]Roy Fenstermaker, "Managing Technology: The Challenge of the Seventies," *Management Review,* Volume 58, Number 4 (April 1969), p. 38.

Wages were sometimes used as production incentives, as were several other techniques (many of them negatively oriented). Management-union relations were often competitive, with managers attempting to protect their right to manage and unions attempting to gain more control over the activities and welfare of their members. There were exceptions to these broad generalizations, but the tendency was for manpower policies to exist in a developmental, and sometimes explosive, atmosphere.

The Specific Effects of Automation.   In several areas, automation has brought about adjustments in organizational policies concerning manpower. Some of the effects have been minor; others have been far-reaching. One study has revealed that while the number of people being hired by automated companies has fluctuated very little following the implementation of automation, the selection procedures have intensified. Selection techniques are being developed and applied to identify the individual who possesses the necessary skills and to locate potential workers who have the aptitude to be trained to meet skill-level requirements. Automation normally has increased the employment standards for beginning positions.[23] Also, automation has encouraged many organizations to consider retraining present employees to meet the needs of new jobs rather than hiring completely new personnel.

The training of workers (both new and old) has been expanded significantly as a result of the needs of automation. New training techniques are being mixed with traditional approaches. In-house training is being interspersed with external professional help.[24]

Wage and salary programs have also been affected by the introduction of automation. In many instances, the use of monetary incentive techniques has been altered noticeably. The basis of monetary incentives is to reward the worker for his own personal effort—the extension of his efforts and abilities beyond the average level of performance. With automation, the typical worker does not control the pace at which he works; as a result, more effort on his part may not result in increased productivity. This condition has led Bright to state that piece rates and monetary incentive systems are out of place in automated organizations. He recommends straight hourly wages graded in brackets based upon helper, operator, and specialist categories.[25]

---

[23]Julius Rezler, "Automation and the Personnel Manager," *Advanced Management Journal*, Volume 32, Number 1 (January 1967), p. 78.

[24]*Ibid.*, p. 79.

[25]Bright, *op. cit.*, pp. 208–209.

To the surprise of some managers, union-management relations have not worsened appreciably in most organizations as a result of the application of automation. In fact, the cooperation between the two elements has sometimes improved. It is natural, of course, that some grievances and worker complaints have increased. Industrial relations administrators report that requests for attention to displacement procedures, increased wages for increased responsibilities, issues of job security, guarantees of former earnings, and other types of wage and work load grievances have been received more frequently.[26]

The labor movement is said to have numerous goals in protecting its members against the possible dangers of automation, including the enactment of agreements that would provide for:

1. Advance notification of the union and workers by management on a regular, scheduled basis of all innovations in machinery and methods of production

2. Restriction of the hiring of new employees to allow for the transfer of displaced employees to other jobs

3. Establishment of retraining programs to qualify existing employees for new jobs

4. Prescription of specific transfer rights of present employees to new jobs

5. Guarantee of seniority systems that would insure maximum security for long-service employees

6. Establishment of a joint labor-management development agency to promote introduction of new products and the development of new uses for old products

7. Declaration of a shorter work week to permit workers to share in the economy's output and to assure jobs for more workers

8. Guarantee of salaries and severance pay for workers laid off because of technological change

9. Provision of supplementary unemployment benefits

10. Creation of new pension plans[27]

Summary

The effects of technological innovation have been felt by every segment of the American community. The society at large (and its economy) has felt the results of new, more advanced knowledge. The scope

[26]Rezler, *op. cit.*, pp. 78–80.

[27]Rosenberg, *op. cit.*, p. 126, quoting the New York City Central Labor Counsel, *Unions Meet Automation,* Proceedings of the Conference on Automation, New York, November 29, 1960.

and manner of operation within the business enterprises of the nation have been modified by technology. The worker laboring within the business enterprise has seen his role and status altered significantly. The functions and requirements for managerial action have been made more complex and more challenging as a result of technological innovation. Manpower policies and procedures have been revised and management-union relations restructured as a result of demands that have accompanied the acceptance of technological change.

The consumer public probably would applaud most of the innovations that have resulted from new production techniques and methods. The worker within the business organization might, if asked, express mixed emotions concerning the implications and effects of mechanization, the assembly line, and automation upon his personal work life.

It can be said without question that technology is an innovating force providing avenues of change and demanding the alteration of existing behavior patterns as a result of interactions with other determinants of human behavior.

With the inclusion of these factors and attributes of technology, some details of the behavior model become more complete, as is shown in Figure 4.2 (next page). As can be seen, technology interacts with individuals and with environmental-experiential forces as well.

Questions to consider after reading Chapter 4

1.   The statement was made that "technology often runs ahead of society, and it presses for the acceptance of new ways and new ideas." What does this statement mean? If it is true, what causes it to be valid?

2.   Factory workers in particular have expressed a dissatisfaction with their jobs. What has technology done to contribute to this dissatisfaction?

3.   Many people expected automation to result in a significant worsening of management-union relations. Why has automation been less disruptive to management-union relations than many anticipated?

4.   Evaluate the goals of labor where automation is occurring. Which of these goals appear to be justifiable? Which of these may prove difficult for organizations to provide?

5.   What future directions do you foresee for technology? What will the emphases of the future be?

The following cases at the back of the book contain problems related to Chapter 4:

Susan Swanson

Grace Lanham

FIGURE 4.2   Partially detailed model of worker behavior and its determinants

WORKER'S ENVIRONMENT AND EXPERIENCES

Family	Religion	Education
Unions	Government	Economic network
Peer groups	Race or ethnic background	Occupation
Place of residence	Status of health	Other personal and environmental factors

INDIVIDUAL

Inborn set of needs, drives, instincts

Modified and expanded set of needs based upon experience

Capacity to seek pleasure, avoid pain

Desire for constancy—equilibrium of internal–external factors

Ability to plan, act rationally

Emotional nature and characteristics

Anatomical–physiological factors— inborn and learned

Unique self-concept

Empathy toward moral values

Ability to be perceptive concerning self, experience, and others

TECHNOLOGICAL FACTORS

Provide new products and services

Increase capacity to provide manufactured goods

Decrease labor costs

Affect the level of employment

Change many production and communication processes

Have a significant impact upon the lives of workers within the business enterprise

Demand more of managers

Alter manpower policies and practices

Modify union–management relations

ACTION or BEHAVIOR

ORGANIZATIONAL FACTORS

Formal Organization	Informal Organization

Additional readings

Boettinger, Henry M., "Technology in the Manager's Future," *Harvard Business Review,* Volume 48, Number 6 (November–December 1970), pp. 4–14, 165.

Bright, James R., "What Technology Means to Management," *Management Today*, July 1969, pp. 94–99, 150.

Davis, Keith, "Human Adjustment to Automation," *Advanced Management Journal*, Volume 29, Number 1 (January 1964), pp. 20–27.

Davis, Louis E., "Readying the Unready, Postindustrial Jobs," *California Management Review*, Volume 13, Number 4 (Summer 1971), pp. 27–36.

Diebold, John, "Automation—Perceiving the Magnitude of the Problem," *Advanced Managment Journal*, Volume 29, Number 2 (April 1964), pp. 29–33.

Drucker, Peter F., *Technology, Management, and Society*, New York: Harper & Row, Publishers, 1970.

Fried, Louis, "The Twilight of the Mechanical Technology," *California Management Review*, Volume 11, Number 4 (Summer 1969), pp. 63–68.

Haber, William, Louis A. Ferman, and James R. Hudson, *The Impact of Technological Change*, Kalamazoo, Michigan: The W. E. Upjohn Institute for Employment Research, 1963.

Hardin, William G., Jr., and Lloyd L. Byars, "Human Relations and Automation," *Advanced Management Journal*, Volume 35, Number 3 (July 1970), pp. 43–48.

Harvey, Edward, "Technology and the Structure of Organizations," *American Sociological Review*, Volume 33, Number 2 (April 1968), pp. 247–259.

Jackson, H. B., and J. S. Roucek, editors, *Automation and Society*, New York: Philosophical Library, 1959.

Keller, Robert T., "A Look at the Sociotechnical System," *California Management Review*, Volume 15, Number 1 (Fall 1972), pp. 86–91.

Lee, Hak Chong, "Organizational Impact of Computers," *Management Services*, Volume 4, Number 3 (May–June 1967), pp. 39–43.

Mann, Floyd C., and L. Richard Hoffman, *Automation and the Worker*, New York: Holt, 1960.

Maughn, John, "Are Technological Upheavals Inevitable," *Harvard Business Review*, Volume 47, Number 5 (September–October 1969), pp. 73–83.

Meissner, Martin, *Technology and the Worker: Technical Demands and Social Pressures in Industry*, San Francisco: Chandler Publishing Company, 1969.

Mesthene, Emmanuel, *Technological Change*, Cambridge, Massachusetts: Harvard University Press, 1970.

Rogers, Virgil M., "Automation and Tomorrow's World of Work," *Personnel Administration*, Volume 29, Number 4 (July–August 1966), pp. 23–33.

Swart, Carroll, and Richard A. Baldwin, "E D P Effects on Clerical Workers," *The Academy of Management Journal*, Volume 14, Number 4 (December 1971), pp. 497–512.

Thomas, O. P., "Technology and the Individual," *Personnel*, Volume 42, Number 5 (September–October 1965), pp. 8–15.

Chapter 5

The Formal Organization-Framework for Organizational Behavior

A case to consider before reading chapter 5

MANAGING IN THE COMMUNITY SERVICES OFFICE

Community Services is a local charitable and service organization supported entirely by public contributions of money and labor. The staff of the organization, although rather small, is well trained and quite capable. For the most part, the personnel are in their thirties and early forties. The paid staff is officed in a building donated to the organization several years ago. While the space is adequate in size, the floor plan is not well suited for the purpose for which it is being used.

The organizational structure of the paid personnel of Community Services is relatively simple. The three vice-presidents and the office manager report directly to the president (see Exhibit 1). Each of the vice-presidents has two or three field managers reporting to him. The field managers are responsible for working with community volunteers and for coordinating specific programs in the community. The field managers spend most of their time outside the offices and, therefore, have only a minimum of contact with office personnel. The office manager has four secretaries whom she is supposed to supervise. In addition, the office manager is expected to maintain the organization's set of financial records, to maintain all personnel files for the paid personnel, and to serve as personal secretary to the president.

Difficulties have arisen in the area of performance of duties by the office manager and the secretaries. The secretaries are officed in the extreme end of the building (see Exhibit II) away from the office manager, who can neither see nor hear them. The secretaries are supposed to do the secretarial and clerical work of the three vice-presidents and the field managers. Instead of giving the work to the office manager for allocation to the various secretaries as they are supposed to do, the officers of the organization individually take their work to the secretary of their own choosing and tell her to do it. This results in the secretaries being given assignments without consideration for projects in which they are currently involved or existing backlogs of work. This practice creates a situation in which the most efficient and capable worker, the woman who does the best work, is always swamped with responsibilities while the woman who is the slowest and least efficient often has unoccupied time on her hands. This situation frequently leads to friction among the secretaries.

A similar problem exists for the office manager. Because she has a ~~good command~~ of sh~~orthand~~ and is an ~~excellent typist,~~ one of the ~~vice-presidents— although ful~~ly a~~w~~are of the ~~office manager's heavy work~~ load and the fact that his work is supposed to be performed by one of the other women—often insists upon dictating a "confidential" letter to her (the office manager) and asking her to prepare it immediately. On one occasion, after repeated interruptions of this type, the office manager became irritated and asked the vice-president if it mat-

EXHIBIT I   Organization chart for community services

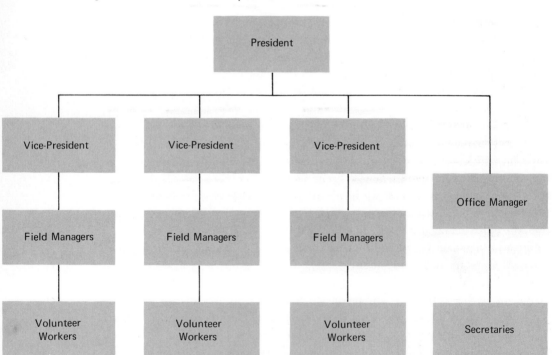

EXHIBIT II   Office Layout at Community Services

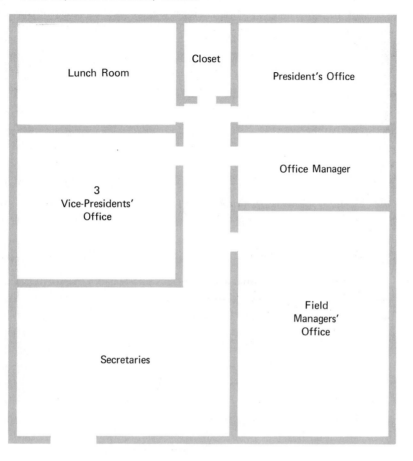

tered to him that she had other important responsibilities to fulfill. The vice-president said he was not concerned.

The office manager has one additional problem. She is supposed to be totally in charge of the secretaries and their performance. However, if one of the secretaries develops a problem, she more typically goes to the president for a solution. The president has not discouraged this practice but, to the contrary, seems to want the secretaries to come to him when they need help. This situation makes it even more difficult for the office manager to perform her supervisory duties adequately. The office manager is becoming increasingly frustrated in her work.

Questions about the Community Services case

1.   Does the organization chart for Community Services accurately reflect the structure of the organization? Why or why not?

2.   Organization charts ideally show the flow of authority from the top of the organization to its lowest level. Are the lines of authority clearly defined at Community Services? Explain your answer.

3.   What was the office manager's job description intended to be? In reality, what is her job description?

4.   Identify the organizational and administrative causes of problems that affect the office manager and the secretaries.

5.   What principles of sound managerial practice are not followed at Community Services?

6.   What actions should be taken to eliminate the problems faced by the office manager? by the secretaries?

It has been said that a **formal work organization** is a group of people working together cooperatively *under authority* toward goals and objectives that mutually benefit the participants and the organization. This statement implies that people who work together require a defined system or structure through which they can relate to each other and through which their efforts can be coordinated. Every organization has goals or purposes for its existence, and these goals can be achieved in a more suitable fashion if the behavior of the workers composing the organization can be predicted and integrated cooperatively. The formal organization structure attempts to give order and unity to the actions and efforts of those who work together.

The Organizing Process

The traditional approach to the structure of formal interpersonal relationships has been rather task-oriented, concentrating on the work to be accomplished by individuals who are a part of the organization. The traditional concept of the organizing process includes eight steps if the cycle is to be performed fully and completely.

1.   Determination of organizational goals. The traditional approach to formal organizations starts with the definition of a set of goals or purposes. Before work relationships can be arranged, management must decide what objectives will be strived for.

2.   Definition of work to be performed. After objectives are known, the task requirements necessary to achieve the stated goals must be determined. The amount of skill, effort, and knowledge required to reach the objectives must be determined.

3.   Division of tasks into job-sized units. Following the definition of total work requirements, the work must be divided into job-sized units so that the number of individuals needed to properly fulfill the tasks can be determined.

4.   Integrating jobs into departments or other work groups. Jobs to be performed by individuals are related together for purposes of direction, coordination, control, and mutual cooperation, and to take advantage of the appropriate amount of specialization and efficiency.

5.   Selection of personnel to fill jobs. As soon as jobs are defined and organizationally related, management must recruit and select individuals in the proper number with the appropriate skills to perform the necessary organizational tasks.

6.   Assignment of job tasks. Individuals selected to fill work positions are then assigned to the duties essential to the achievement of organizational goals.

7.   Granting of authority to performers. In addition to receiving job performance requirements, workers need the corresponding authority to carry out the duties of their jobs. Authority may be defined as the right to act, to direct, and to requisition resources needed to properly perform the job.

8.   Evaluation of worker performances. The organizational process normally includes the determination of superior-subordinate relationships for the facilitation of performance evaluation. The worker is held accountable for his actions and efforts in support of organizational goals.

In fulfilling each step of the organizational process, the practicing manager must find answers to a number of questions. As one question is answered, another must sequentially be considered until all questions have been answered. In fulfilling the organizational process, the following questions should be considered:

Step 1.   What is the goal we as an organization are striving for?

Step 2.   What work must be performed to achieve the goal?

Step 3.   How many people will be needed to perform the necessary work? (And what qualifications must they possess?)

Step 4.   How can the jobs (and people) best be grouped together for purposes of coordination and control?

Step 5.   Which individuals will best fill the positions that need staffing? In other words, which individuals have the skills and abilities needed to perform the work?

Step 6.   Do the people selected have a clear knowledge and understanding of their job responsibilities?

Step 7.   Do the individuals involved have the authority needed to perform their duties properly?

Step 8.   Are individuals performing their duties adequately so that the goals are being attained?

The cycle of organizing tasks, assigning individuals to jobs, and monitoring performance levels must be continued as goals and objectives are modified over a period of time.

Concepts of Organization Structure

The traditional school of thought (including its many branches—classical, bureaucratic, scientific management, etc.) has been responsible for more emphasis on the formal structuring of work assignments than any other approach or school. The traditional school has presented several fundamental concepts describing the essentials of a sound organizational structure. Included in the traditional concepts of structure are those dealing with the division of labor to achieve specialization, the establishment of a vertical authority structure for the organization, the creation of horizontal work relationships, the development of useful line-staff relationships, and the determination of workable spans of supervision or control. Each of these concepts has provided unique contributions to the organizational process.

Specialization.   Specialization in the development of organizational design affects Steps 3 and 4 of the organizational process. **Specialization** of job assignments (Step 3) refers to the delineation of jobs into work units whereby each individual assigned to a job is given concentrated duties and responsibilities requiring a specific set of skills and knowledge.

In the highly specialized job, the individual performs a limited number of tasks somewhat repetitively. A highly specialized job on an automobile production line might require the worker to tighten two screws on a car door as the door and the automobile move along the assembly line. The worker would be expected to perform his limited duties quickly and efficiently so that the line would be kept moving and the car in process could be passed along to another specialist to perform other duties. A less specialized arrangement might allow a worker to assemble the complete car door by himself. His job would demand a much larger set of skills and would require more effort on his part than would the more specialized arrangement.

Specialization may also occur as jobs are grouped (departmentalized). A group of jobs may be placed under the supervision of a single supervisor on the basis of similarity of skills and knowledge so that the department performs specialized tasks regularly.

Workers in a specialized department might all be operating machines similar in structure and performance rates. The skill demands of every job in the department will be almost identical and interchangeable. In a less specialized department, the jobs might be totally dissimilar, requiring one worker to operate a machine, another worker to handle electrical problems, another worker to labor over a drawing board, and other workers to perform other differentiated duties. Duties and responsibilities in the nonspecialized department tend to be differentiated.

When job specialization is accomplished, the worker tends to develop a high level of expertise in more narrow responsibilities. A high-level of efficiency and economy is possible. Training of new workers and retraining of older workers can be achieved more quickly as a result of the streamlined, simplified duties of specialized workers. There are some disadvantages, too, and these are discussed in other chapters. Departmental specialization tends to result in advantages and deficiencies similar to those that occur with job specialization.

Vertical Authority Structure.   The vertical authority structure, viewed from the traditional position, clearly defines superior-subordinate relationships from the top of the organization through the lowest levels. At the top of the structure the ultimate source of power is identified. The board of directors, the organization's owners, the general manager, or whoever is the supreme authority holds the highest position in the organizational hierarchy. The highest superior has subordinates who are directly accountable to him; his subordinates have their own subordinates; and so the hierarchy goes until the lowest level is reached (see Figure 5.1). On the basis of organizational hierarchy, the lines of authority from top to bottom are defined, and the formal channels of communication (downward, upward, *and across* the organization) are clarified.

There is a principle of management that is particularly important to the traditionalist in preserving the organizational hierarchy and in providing for proper superior-subordinate relationships. That principle, known as the unity-of-command principle, states that every subordinate should have only one superior to whom he is directly accountable and through whom orders and directions should flow. The unity-of-command concept helps every employee know to whom he should listen and who is available for consultation and guidance. The

FIGURE 5.1   Formal hierarchy

Connecting links represent
the line of authority and
formal communication

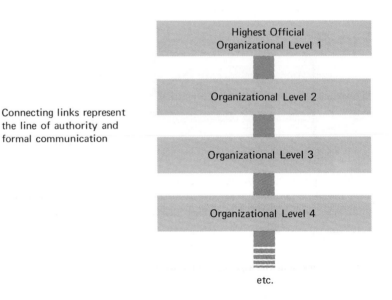

Highest Official
Organizational Level 1

Organizational Level 2

Organizational Level 3

Organizational Level 4

etc.

~~employee~~ is ~~not~~ ~~confused~~ by ~~guidelines~~ ~~coming~~ from ~~several~~ ~~sources~~; he must respond only to instructions from his immediate superior.

The vertical hierarchy serves another purpose as well. As authority patterns are established and hierarchical levels are determined, social status standings are influenced. Those individuals who rank at the top of the formal authority network tend to rank at the upper levels of the social status ladder. Those who serve in middle management positions normally are a little further down the social ranking scale. Those with no authority at all gravitate toward the bottom of the social ladder. There are, of course, a number of additional determinants of an individual's social status, but the amount of authority possessed has a significant influence upon the status achieved.

~~Horizontal Organizational Relationships.~~   Closely related to the development of the vertical hierarchy is the **horizontal structure** or the relationship between peers, colleagues, and fellow workers *across* the organization (see Figure 5.2). ~~Individuals located~~ on the ~~same horizontal~~ level ~~within~~ the ~~organization~~ ~~normally~~ ~~have~~ ~~no authority over~~ ~~each other~~, and they tend to be about ~~equal~~ in ~~terms~~ of the ~~amount~~ of ~~authority~~ and ~~formal influence~~ they have. They also tend to be ~~some~~-~~what~~ ~~equal~~ in ~~social~~ ~~status~~ insofar as formal authority possessed is a determinant of relative social standing.

FIGURE 5.2   Horizontal relationships

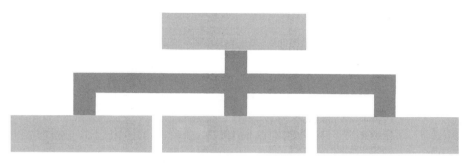

Peer groups such as those that come from similar horizontal levels tend to be the source of most work teams. In other words, a majority of the work that requires a coordinated effort is performed in teams composed mostly of peers or those on similar horizontal levels. As a result, the typical employee (manager or nonmanager) derives a great deal of work-oriented communication, support, assistance from his peers, *and* he also receives an appreciable amount of social interaction and support from those who are his equals or near equals in the horizontal framework of the organization.

Knowledge of the horizontal structure of an organization helps to clarify authority relationships, to understand communication patterns, and to discern more about social interactions and status networks.

Line and Staff Relationships.   Line and staff relationships are also put into context in the traditional organization structure. Line officers are individuals who have been placed in positions in the direct flow of authority within the organizational hierarchy. Staff specialists, assigned to support and service line officials, typically report to those whom they serve (see Figure 5.3). In the pure staff concept, the staff worker has no authority himself but is directly tied to the line official he serves. A marketing research specialist, for example, cannot take action on the basis of the findings of his surveys unless otherwise specified. Instead, he gives his reports to his superiors for their consideration and action.

Staff specialists serve their superiors by performing tasks for which the line officials lack specialized skill or knowledge or tasks the line officers do not have time to perform. The engineering specialist may recommend structural specifications for the line supervisor with a nontechnical background. The personnel officer may screen twenty job applicants as a service for a line official before recommending two or three of the better candidates for his closer consideration. Staff specialists perform many advisory and service duties.

FIGURE 5.3   Line-staff relationships

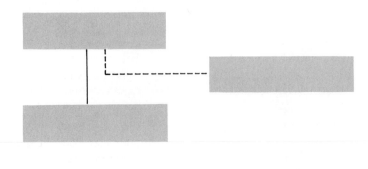

——— formal line authority

- - - - - staff connecting lines

~~Span of Supervision.~~ Formal organization structures also determine the breadth of a supervisor's responsibilities by indicating the number of individuals who are directly accountable to that supervisor. The **span of supervision** in each situation is important, because it determines the ~~amount~~ of ~~attention each super-visor can give~~ to ~~each subordinate,~~ and it affects ease in communicating, methods of decision making that can be used, and a number of other superior-subordinate relationships. Managers (in the traditional sense) are accountable for the performance of their subordinates, so it is important that the span of supervision be a workable one. Years of study have gone into the analysis of the proper number of subordinates a supervisor should have reporting to him. Some of the conclusions will be shown later in this chapter.

Functions of the Formal Organization Structure

Through attention to the structural factors just mentioned, a vehicle is created whereby organizational and personal goals can be attained in a better way than would be possible through uncoordinated action. A structured vehicle performs many functions for both the organization and the individuals who participate in the organization. If the ~~organizational process~~ is carried out properly and the organization structure is designed as it should be, several ~~results~~ should occur.

1.   Available ~~resources~~ (human and otherwise) will be ~~utilized~~ in the ~~most effec-tive way~~.

2.   Directional and operational goals and procedures will be determined clearly and energies devoted to their achievement.

3.   An orderly hierarchy in which people are related in a meaningful sequence will result. Individual responsibilities will be known clearly and the authority to act will be defined. Communication networks will be formulated and maintained.

4.   Workers will benefit from planned superior-subordinate relationships in which each worker receives essential support and direction.

5.   The activities of groups and individuals will become more rational, stable, and predictable.

6.   In some ways, a structured organization may make the treatment of individual workers more democratic, because patronage and favoritism tend to be reduced.[1]

7.   Responsibilities will be assigned to individuals in work loads that are reasonable. Individuals will be selected on the basis of ability to perform expected tasks. Simplification and specialization of job assignments will be possible in a more effective way.

The structuring of organizational activities and work relationships is not without its drawbacks, however. Very often the fixed relationships and lines of authority seem inflexible and difficult to adjust to meet changing needs. Individual creativity and originality may be stifled by the rather rigid determination of duties and responsibilities. Interpersonal communication may be slowed or stopped as a result of strict adherence to formal lines of communication. Workers may become less willing to assume unprescribed duties (those not formally a part of their original assignments). A spirit of cooperation is sometimes lost in jurisdictional disputes.[2]

Other dysfunctions of formalized organizations may include the fact that organizations tend to:

1.   Be nonadaptive and impersonal

2.   Fail to account for important differences in workers as human beings

3.   Emphasize organizational growth and self-perpetuation too much

4.   Produce anxiety in individual workers by pressuring too heavily for routine and conformity

5.   Be too costly in terms of time and human dignity in order to implement organizational rules and regulations.[3]

[1]Herbert G. Hicks and C. Ray Gullett, *Organizations: Theory and Behavior*, New York: McGraw-Hill Book Company, 1975, p. 138.

[2]For further discussion of the detrimental effects of formal organization structures, see Chris Argyris, "The Individual and Organization: Some Problems of Mutual Adjustment," *Administrative Science Quarterly*, Volume 2, Number 1 (June 1957), pp. 1–24.

[3]Hicks and Gullett, *op. cit.*, pp. 144–145, 149–150.

Most of these disadvantages occur in the administration of the organization rather than in the organization itself. Many of the organizational imperfections and administrative weaknesses can be reduced through careful planning and a concentrated effort by supervisors to be responsive to human problems created by formal structures.

Other Organizational Designs

The previous discussions have been based primarily upon a traditional organizational design that pictures the organization as a pyramid. Other forms of organizational design (some traditional and some not) have also been used. Occasionally the formal organization structure has been drawn as a wheel. In this scheme the top-level manager (ultimate source of authority) is placed at the hub of the wheel, with each progression outward on the wheel indicating the authority hierarchy and communication network (see Figure 5.4). This approach is little different from the pyramid approach except for the fact that it attempts to pictorially de-emphasize the ominous powers of the authority structure centered at the top and to portray the coordinative and cooperative aspects of management and supervision. The lines of authority and communication are basically the same as

FIGURE 5.4   Organization as a wheel

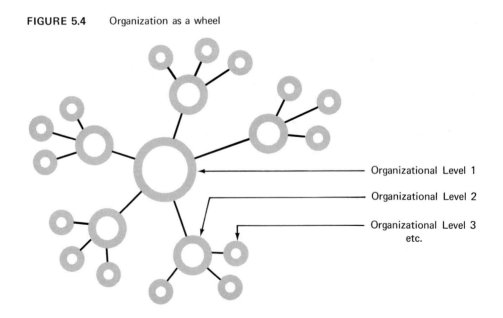

Organizational Level 1

Organizational Level 2

Organizational Level 3
etc.

FIGURE 5.5   Systems viewpoint of the organization and its structure

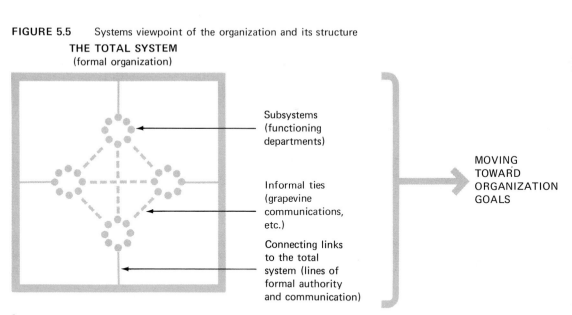

THE TOTAL SYSTEM
(formal organization)

Subsystems
(functioning
departments)

Informal ties
(grapevine
communications,
etc.)

Connecting links
to the total
system (lines of
formal authority
and communication)

MOVING
TOWARD
ORGANIZATION
GOALS

Source: Adapted in part from Lawrence J. Henderson, *Pareto's General Sociology*,
Cambridge: Harvard University Press, 1935, p. 14, and William G. Scott and Terrence W.
Mitchell, *Organization Theory*, Revised Edition, Homewood, Illinois, Richard D. Irwin, Inc.,
and The Dorsey Press, 1972, pp. 56-60.

in the pyramid. The manager in this structure becomes more of a communicator, coordinator, and integrator rather than the authority figure described by the pyramid.

Another description of the organization has shown it as a total system. In this approach, the formal structure is composed of a set of subsystems. Some authors look upon the subsystems as the departments in the organization. To others, the subsystems are the functions of the organization (purchasing, processing, selling, shipping, etc.). The emphasis of this approach is to describe the total content of an organization and to show its interacting relationships. As Scott and Mitchell see the thrust of the systems analysis of the organization, its goals as a system are to provide for stability, growth, and interaction.[4] In the model of a systems organization shown in Figure 5.5, each subsystem is related to the total system (formal organization) by formal lines of authority, and each subsystem is also related to other subsystems by an informal communication network. In this model the subsystems are the functioning departments of the total organization. The

---

[4]William G. Scott and Terence R. Mitchell, *Organization Theory: A Structural and Behavioral Analysis for Management*, Homewood, Illinois: Richard D. Irwin, Inc., 1972, p. 57.

use of the systems approach may be particularly helpful in considering the informal interaction of the working parts of the organization, but formal ties are also recognized.

The systems approach is especially helpful in creating an awareness of the influential and countervailing powers of the parts of an organization. This approach is a very useful way of discovering interrelationships of people and departments (and the subsequent effects). The analysis of the organization from this point of view incorporates the formal structure with informal aspects. The systems approach tends to complement more traditional approaches rather than to dispute them or detract from them.

Finding the Right Organization Structure

In the organizational process, the administrators in charge of designing the formal organization structure have many decisions to make that will directly influence the organization's successful operation while minimizing possible negative effects. Answers to a number of questions must be found. What should the organizational emphasis be—the accomplishment of organizational tasks or the achievement of personal employee goals? How much delegation of authority and organizational decentralization should be built into the structure? What span of supervision and control is proper? How much job specialization should be practiced in the arrangement of job assignments? How can worker originality and initiative be encouraged rather than discouraged? How can flexibility be provided for? How can interpersonal communication be kept appropriately active and open? Answers to these questions are considered in the following pages.

Task Accomplishment or Personal Satisfaction?   The question of organizational emphasis appears to suggest that an organization has a choice between maximizing productivity, profits, and other task-oriented goals, or it has the choice of fulfilling the goals and objectives of its employees. No combination is suggested in the wording of the question. It is true that many organizations have been developed primarily with the single purpose of task accomplishment; and at the opposite extreme, many authors have discussed organizations as primarily sources of employee fulfillment. However, the current attitude toward organizational accomplishment is that the structuring of work relationships should be planned so that task purposes and individual attainment can both be realized simultaneously.

The decision can be based not on which one of these goals to emphasize but on how both types of goals can be achieved best in an integrated effort. Such a commitment to strive for both types of goals involves the administrative desire to achieve these goals and the belief that they can be accomplished.

How Much Delegation and Decentralization?   The ~~delegation of authority~~ is the ~~delivery by one individual to another~~ of the ~~right to act~~, to ~~make decisions~~, ~~to requisition resources~~, and to ~~perform other tasks~~ in order to fulfill job responsibilities. Authority, in the traditional sense, is handed down from superior to subordinate. Most managers would answer the question concerning the proper degree of authority delegation by saying that the amount of authority delegated should be equal to the amount of responsibility assumed. In other words, an individual should be supplied with the authority needed to make it possible for him to fulfill his organizational obligations. A survey of the obligations and responsibilities of each performing individual should make possible the identification of his needs for power through formal authority. This survey may begin with a review of the individual's job description, but it will need to consider informal responsibilities as well as formal ones. Once the responsibilities are identified, the appropriate authority (in a formal sense) can be extended to the individual by his superiors.

Even when organizations have been designed to achieve proper delegation, personal factors within the superior and his subordinate may interfere with this delegation.[5] Some personal factors that may hinder the delegation of authority are shown in Figure 5.6.

In addition to providing the necessary delegation of authority so that individuals can perform their jobs satisfactorily, managers also must decide whether they will keep most planning, decision-making, and controlling activities within their own responsibilities and rights or whether they will encourage subordinates to show their own initiative in these areas. Whether to decentralize or to centralize becomes the critical issue.

~~Decentralization~~ is the ~~pushing downward~~ of ~~authority~~ and ~~responsibility to~~ the ~~lowest level~~ in the organization where the necessary information and competence are available. Normally, it is thought of as the delegation of authority to perform complete tasks into the hands of groups of people who will work together (departments). ~~Centralization~~ is the ~~opposite action~~: Authority and responsibility

---

[5]William H. Newman, Charles E. Summer, and E. Kirby Warren, *The Process of Management,* Third Edition, Englewood Cliffs, New Jersey: Prentice-Hall, Inc., 1972, p. 49.

FIGURE 5.6   Personal obstacles to effective delegation

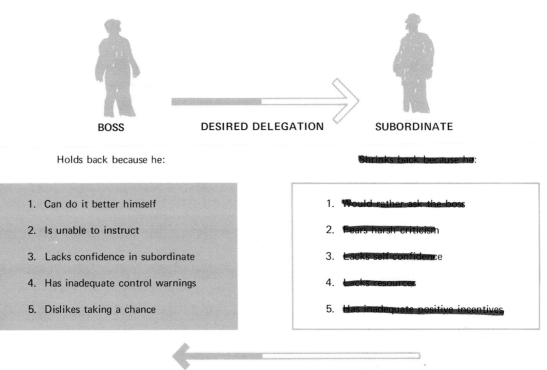

BOSS   DESIRED DELEGATION   SUBORDINATE

Holds back because he: Shrinks back because he:

Can do it better himself		Would rather ask the boss
1. Can do it better himself	1. Would rather ask the boss
2. Is unable to instruct	2. Fears harsh criticism
3. Lacks confidence in subordinate	3. Lacks self-confidence
4. Has inadequate control warnings	4. Lacks resources
5. Dislikes taking a chance	5. Has inadequate positive incentives

Source: William H. Newman, Charles E. Summer, and E. Kirby Warren, *The Process of Management,* Third Edition, Englewood Cliffs, New Jersey: Prentice-Hall, Incorporated, 1972, p. 49.

are tightly held by officials in the upper levels of the organization and are not delegated.

Several questions and their appropriate answers may be helpful in making the decision whether to remain centralized or to extend decentralization.

1. How much coordination is needed between units or individuals?
The more coordination that is needed, the more likely will be the need for centralization. If only limited coordination is needed, decentralization is possible.

2. Where can planning best be accomplished?
If planning must be performed by individuals possessing a broad overview of the entire organization, centralization may be needed. If, however, planning needs to be oriented to local, more specialized functions and duties, decentralization may be best.

3. Are rigid controls necessary?
If strict performance standards are essential, centralization usually is the preferable structure. If tight performance controls are not required, decentralization is more likely to be possible.

4. Are the individuals who would potentially be a part of the decentralized unit capable of self-direction, self-motivation, and self-control?
The more capable subordinates are of handling authority, the more authority they may be given.

5. Are the individuals who are to be decentralized willing to assume the self-generating responsibilities of decentralization?
The attitude of the individuals receiving decentralized authority must be favorable toward the delegation if it is to be successful.

6. "Will initiative and morale be significantly improved by decentralization?"[6]
Decentralization normally improves the initiative and morale of the receiving unit (the decentralized one), but what will be the effect on other levels? Ideally, the response to decentralization will be favorable from all quarters.

The appropriate degree of centralization-decentralization will be dependent upon the answers to these questions. Obviously, both the centralization and decentralization of authority have advantages and disadvantages. The strengths and weaknesses of the two approaches are summarized in Figure 5.7.

What is the Proper Span of Supervision?   How many people can one supervisor lead, motivate, and control adequately? This organizational question has intrigued and perplexed administrators for many years. Attempts at determining an absolute ratio of superior to subordinates have proved extremely difficult. The contemporary position concerning spans of supervision and control is based upon a flexible formula that states that the proper span of supervision for superior-subordinates is a function of a number of variables. One author, drawing upon studies of the Lockheed Missile and Space Company, has stated that seven variables must be considered in making the decision of how many subordinates to place directly beneath one manager. These factors include:

1. The similarity or dissimilarity of functions performed by the individuals being supervised
2. The geographical or physical nearness of the workers to each other
3. The level of complexity or simplicity of the functions being performed (and the resultant skill requirements)
4. The amount and degree of continuing attention the supervisor must exhibit toward each subordinate

[6]*Ibid.,* p. 55.

FIGURE 5.7   Strengths and weaknesses of centralized and decentralized organization structures

STRENGTHS	WEAKNESSES
Centralized Organization	
Assures uniformity of standards and policies among organizational units	Floods communication lines to a few individuals at the top of organization
Allows use of outstanding talent in managers by the whole organization rather than a single unit	Makes great demands on a few managers rather than spreading responsibility
Decisions are uniform	Personalizes decisions to the judgments of a few key decision-makers
Helps eliminate duplication of effort and activity	Forces top managers to possess a broad view that may be beyond their capacity
	Gives vast amounts of power to a few individuals
	Reduces sense of participation for all but a few people
Decentralized Organization	
Reduces total responsibility to more manageable units	Lack of uniformity of standards and policies among organizational units
Helps develop more personnel in decision-making process	Capable managers are not always available or willing to participate in decision making
Shortens lines of communication	Creates problems of coordination between separate organizational units
Places decision making close to situations affected by decisions	Interunit rivalry can interfere with the total organization's operations
Allows more people to use skills and talents in decisions	Requires training programs that may be time-consuming and costly
Disperses power among many persons	

Source: Fred G. Carvell, *Human Relations in Business*, Second Edition, New York: The Macmillan Company, 1975, p. 356.

5.   The effort required to coordinate and correlate the actions of subordinates

6.   The importance and complexity of future programs and objectives and the time required to review and establish them

7.   The amount of support and help the superior receives from line and staff assistants[7]

Other authors have added that spans of control should also be established after considering:

1.   The level of cohesiveness of the workers

2.   The degree of member consensus and identification with common goals

3.   The amount of job satisfaction derived by subordinates from their jobs

4.   Existing levels of performance and productivity[8]

Spans can be narrowed or widened according to the assessment of needs specified by analysis of these variables.

A series of studies has been conducted in which the spans of supervision and the number of **hierarchical levels** (steps from the bottom to the top) of organizations have been analyzed to determine the most effective combinations. These analyses have centered around the impact of "tall" and "flat" organizations. A tall structure is one in which spans of supervision are narrow (each supervisor directs the activities of, for example, only three or four people) and the hierarchical levels are numerous (there may be seven or eight rungs on the organizational ladder). The tall organization structure makes close supervision possible and allows the supervisor to communicate with his immediate subordinates on a more constant basis.

With the flat organization, the span of supervision is large (perhaps as many as thirty or forty people) and there are few ladders in the formal organizational hierarchy. There may be only three or four steps from the top of the organization to the bottom. Supervisors in flat organizations, of necessity, must be more generalized or delegative in their styles than is true in tall organizations. Upward and downward communications are less restricted in flat structures. Self-motivation and self-control are more essential in flat organizations if these organizations are

[7]Harold Stieglitz, *Organization Planning,* New York: National Industrial Conference Board, 1966, p. 15.

[8]Robert J. House and John B. Miner, "Merging Management Theory: The Interaction Between Span of Control and Group Size," *Administrative Science Quarterly,* Volume 14, Number 3 (September 1969), p. 461.

FIGURE 5.8   Organizational designs of tall and flat structures

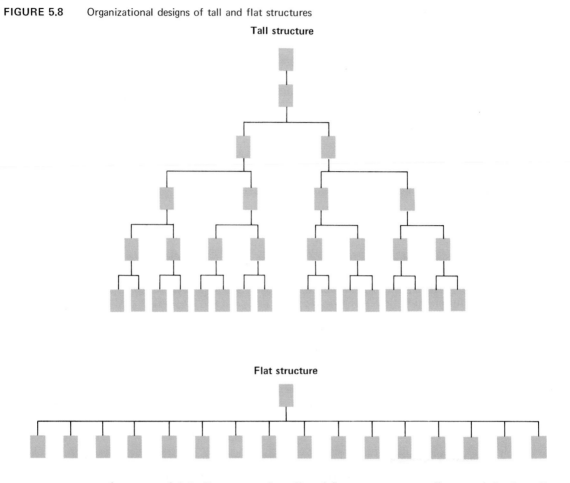

Tall structure

Flat structure

to be successful. In Figure 5.8, the tall and flat structures are illustrated. In the tall structure shown in the illustration, the span of supervision never exceeds two, but the hierarchical levels reach five stages. The flat structure has a wide span of supervision, and the number of hierarchical levels is held to a minimum.

Worthy, in his studies of the Sears organization, has suggested that tall organization structures may have many disadvantages that create supervisory problems and interpersonal difficulties.[9] Tall structures, he suggests, often result in overspecialization and overfunctionalization of activities and job assignments. Individuals in tall structures tend to work under close, constant supervision and may be

[9]James C. Worthy, "Organizational Structure and Employee Morale," *American Sociological Review*, Volume 15, Number 2 (April 1950), pp. 169–179.

exposed to undue pressure from the formal hierarchy. ~~Superior-subordinate~~ ~~relation~~s are ~~strain~~ed as a ~~result~~ of ~~intense~~ ~~supervision~~ and ~~control~~. Donnelly, Gibson, and Ivancevich extend the Worthy study by saying that the implication of Worthy's analysis is that organizations with fewer levels and wider spans of control (and supervision) yield a less complex organizational system. The ~~wide~~ ~~span~~ of ~~supervision~~ ~~forc~~es ~~management~~ to ~~delegate~~ ~~authority~~. In addition to delegation, the flattening technique (widening span of supervision and control) ~~re-~~ ~~quires~~ a ~~better-trained~~ ~~management team~~, ~~shortens~~ communication ~~networks~~, and also reduces the administrative distance between levels of management.[10]

Porter and Lawler, in their study of flat and tall structures, reached some additional conclusions. They analyzed the results of tall and flat structures in relation to organizational size and suggested that:

1. In companies ~~employing fewer than 5,000 people~~, *managerial satisfactions* seemed somewhat greater in the ~~flat structures.~~

2. In companies with ~~5,000 employees or more~~, *greater managerial need satisfaction* is perceived to occur in ~~tall structures.~~

3. However, the desire for need satisfaction and the organization's ability to fulfill it seem to vary according to the type of psychological need involved. ~~Tall structures~~ seem more suited to providing for ~~security~~ and ~~social satisfactions~~; ~~flat structures~~ are advantageous in fulfilling ~~self-actualization~~ needs; and the two structures are about equally effective in meeting ~~esteem~~ and ~~autonomy~~ needs.

4. The effects of a tall or a flat structure do not appear to be as simple as the Worthy study seems to suggest.[11]

Carzo and Yanouzas, in their recent studies, discovered fewer training differences (improvements in learning curves) between tall and flat structures than might be anticipated. Subjects (groups of people) who worked in tall structures showed better overall performance, as measured by profits and rate of return on sales revenue, than groups operating in flat structures.[12]

These mixed results concerning tall and flat structures further illustrate the need for selection and adaptation of the appropriate structure to meet the many needs and demands of an organization. Consideration of organizational goals, administrative requirements, employee abilities and desires, performance and

[10]James H. Donnelly, Jr., James L. Gibson, and John M. Ivancevich, *Fundamentals of Management*, Austin, Texas: Business Publications, Incorporated, 1971, p. 224.

[11]Lyman W. Porter and Edward E. Lawler, "The Effects of Tall versus Flat Organization Structures on Managerial Job Satisfaction," *Personnel Psychology*, Volume 17 (Summer 1964), pp. 135–148.

[12]Rocco Carzo, Jr., and John N. Yanouzas, "Effects of Flat and Tall Organization Structures," *Administrative Science Quarterly*, Volume 14, Number 2 (June 1969), p. 184 ff.

production demands, size of the organization, competitive forces, economic conditions, and many other elements go into the determination of the right organizational design for a specific organizational situation.

How Much Specialization?   Specialization is an organizational technique in which individuals or departments are directed to concentrate skills and efforts toward the performance of a limited number of responsibilities. Often, the limited duties are performed regularly and repetitively. From the individual worker's point of view, specialization makes the learning of job routines easier and allows the worker to become an expert in his work. On an organizational basis, specialization allows for utilization of the distinctive abilities of individual workers. Specialization in departments makes coordination of activities easier, facilitates the development and implementation of essential controls, encourages the efficient productiveness of work effort, speeds along the training process, and results in other advantages.

High degrees of specialization in work assignments, however, may result in negative effects upon the worker. It often appears that ~~too much job specialization makes work monotonous~~, and the ~~worker tends to~~ enjoy little ~~pride~~ of ~~accomplishment~~. Narrow specialization may also affect a person's opportunity for growth.[13] Personal development is aided by the acquisition of new knowledge and new experiences. In a study reviewed in detail in Chapter 11, it was also revealed that highly specialized jobs that resulted in short job cycles, limited numbers of tasks, and restricted freedom of movement tended to result in lower levels of performance than did jobs with longer cycles and greater flexibility.[14]

Therefore, the answer to the question concerning the desirable level of specialization is a variable one. Job assignments and departmentalization should be structured to gain efficiency and to expedite the fulfillment of operative and managerial duties. The degree of specialization should not reach the point of strict regimentation in which no variety of activities and responsibilities is permitted. Some freedom and flexibility in personal and departmental functions is desirable.

How Can Flexibility Be Provided?   As the formal organization structure is designed, it naturally builds in lines of authority, establishes responsibility, and determines patterns of accountability. The establishment of these working relationships gives support and guidance to each worker who assumes a role within the organization, but the formal structure also places upon the worker a number

---

[13]Newman, Summer, and Warren, *op. cit.*, p. 176.

[14]Melvin Sorcher and Herbert H. Meyer, "Motivating Factory Workers," *Personnel*, Volume 45, Number 1 (January–February 1968), pp. 22–28.

of requirements, restrictions, and pressures. The formal structure requests behavior that adheres to the demands it makes of the worker. Workers are given job descriptions, work rules, and organizational policies and are expected to conform to the standards required. As a result of the structural standards, flexibility, originality, and initiative are often stifled. Individuals may become fearful of taking any action that has not been clearly made a part of their jurisdiction in their own job description. The worker may also become unwilling to handle any nonroutine assignments and may cease any original thinking and planning. He may become personally passive and may be totally dependent upon his superiors for the initiation of actions. As such, the worker may become almost a robot.

> The plight of Benjamin Armstrong, who is a junior loan officer at International Bank and Trust Company, is a good illustration of the stifling of personal initiative, creativity, and flexibility. Ben has been in his current job for almost three years now (he's been with the bank a total of eight years). At first he was delighted to be promoted to his present position, because promotions at IBTC come slowly. But he now finds himself dissatisfied with the position. He works under a strict set of rules and guidelines, which may be understandable, to a limited degree at least, in a financially-oriented situation. However, Ben's job is basically one of seeing that loan application requests are filled out properly. He makes no decisions on the requests and passes them along to a senior officer who reviews the applications and advances them to another individual for final approval. Ben feels that his duties have been too narrowly defined, but he also feels no obligation to do more than his job description permits. In fact, he would be fearful of attempting any original activities. He knows that his superiors would not approve any actions initiated by him. Ben is capable of doing much more than he is allowed to do.

To avoid unnecessary rigidity and passive worker attitudes, it would be prudent to attempt to avoid overstructuring work relationships whenever possible. The practice of delegation and decentralization of authority (when conditions merit these approaches) may provide workers with greater freedom and may encourage more personal initiative. As policies, rules, and regulations are being developed, only the really essential ones should be spelled out, so that guidelines do not become unduly prohibitive.

Beyond the realm of strictly structural matters, the leadership techniques of supervisory personnel will influence flexibility and initiative. Supervisors may find it necessary to deliberately provide subordinates with "breathing room." The use of general supervision, in which the manager lays down broad guidelines without spelling out operational procedures in minute detail, may be useful in freeing up overly controlled workers. If initiative, creativity, and willingness to assume responsibility are desirable from individual subordinates, their bosses will need to encourage and reward these actions. The recognition and rewarding of desirable actions is conducive to the continuation of those actions.

How Can Communication Be Kept Flexible?   Formal channels of communication coincide with lines of authority. An important principle of management called the ~~bypassing principle~~ states that communication between individuals in vertical positions in the organizational hierarchy should pass through each rung of the ladder without omission as a message is moved upward or downward. ~~No manager~~ or ~~supervisor~~ in the ~~vertical chain should~~ be ~~bypassed as~~ the ~~communi-qué moves on its way~~. In addition, when messages need to be conveyed on a horizontal basis, they should move upward vertically from the sender to a point where the sender and receiver have a common superior, then the message can move downward vertically to the receiver. Again, no steps should be bypassed in the flow of the communication. Figure 5.9 illustrates the proper flow of formal communication and shows some possible violations of the bypassing principle.

Strict observance of the formal communication network has many advantages in that each supervisor has a good knowledge of the messages his subordinates are sending and receiving. This is helpful, because the supervisor is accountable

FIGURE 5.9   Proper and improper flows of formal communication

Vertical Communication Channel   **Horizontal Communicational Channel**

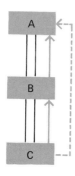
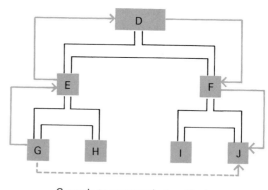

C wishes to communicate with A   G needs to communicate with J

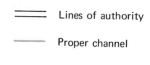

—————— Lines of authority

—————— Proper channel

– – – – – Improper channel

for the actions of his subordinates. However, the process may become cumbersome and slow and may be detrimental to the adequacy of communication. Supervisors may spend most of their time just handling messages flowing through them. Message recipients may receive information more slowly or not at all because of time lags and bottlenecks along the way.

To avoid the slowness and inflexibility of some formal networks, emergency systems can be established whereby senders can move swiftly and directly to receivers so long as they notify the appropriate superiors after the emergency, giving them the basic message content. Reporting procedures may be established in which individuals send duplicate messages to appropriate hierarchical authorities as well as to the ultimate recipients.

Many managers are also operating on the basis of the exception principle, which states that subordinates should communicate to their superiors only the highlights of their actions and the critical and unusual problems they encounter. Highly routine communications and actions no longer are required to proceed through immediate superiors. This approach is a departure from strict formalization, but is workable in many instances.

Summary

The formal organization is a vehicle for joining together individuals and their efforts so that goals and objectives can be accomplished. Traditionally, most organizations have been designed in the form of a pyramid with the ultimate authority source resting at the top. Authority is spread downward to a widening base of people. Most organizational structures specify hierarchical lines of authority, formal channels of communication, spans of supervision and control, levels of job and departmental specialization, and line-staff relationships.

The development of the proper structural design for the organization is an extremely important factor in facilitating the achievement of organizational goals as well as personal objectives. In designing the structure, consideration must be directed to developing authority, control, coordination, and communication relationships that will be effective and useful. Questions must be answered concerning the appropriate degree of authority delegation and decentralization, the right amount of specialization, and the proper spans of control.

A well-designed structure provides the guidance, consistency, and control essential to achieving a productive, unified effort. Of course, the danger of overstructuring or improperly structuring relationships is always a possibility. Care in providing for flexibility and encouraging originality and individual initiative is an important consideration whenever this type of behavior is desirable.

The proper structure would normally be the one in which both organizational and individual (personal) achievement are maximized. The proper degree of delegation and decentralization provides the needed authority to individual performers while supplying the necessary amount of control. Spans of supervision are supportive without being too restrictive. The level of specialization (both individual and group) allows for efficiency and effectiveness in performance without stifling creativity and initia-

FIGURE 5.10   Partially detailed model of worker behavior and its determinants

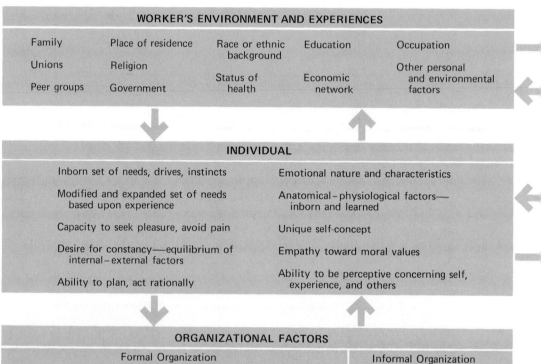

tive. Flexibility is provided for and undue rigidity avoided. Channels of communication are made available that preserve important superior-subordinate relationships without sacrificing speed and accessibility. The correct structural design for a specific organization is a product of a number of variables and may be modified to meet changing needs. Figure 5.10 relates the effects of formal organization to the influences of other factors upon people at work.

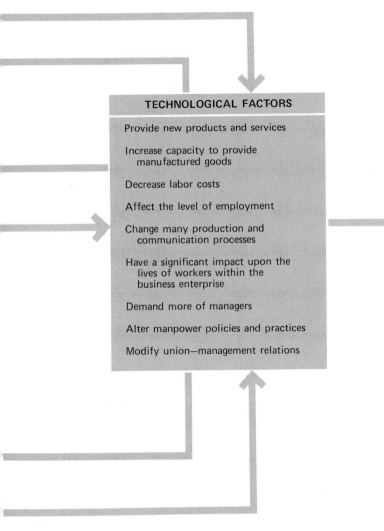

TECHNOLOGICAL FACTORS

Provide new products and services

Increase capacity to provide
  manufactured goods

Decrease labor costs

Affect the level of employment

Change many production and
  communication processes

Have a significant impact upon the
  lives of workers within the
  business enterprise

Demand more of managers

Alter manpower policies and practices

Modify union—management relations

ACTION
or
BEHAVIOR

Questions to consider after reading Chapter 5

1.   It has been said that formal organizations exist to make the behavior of employees more predictable. What is the meaning of this statement?

2.   In what ways does the formal organization structure help the manager to perform his job? How does it help the nonmanager?

3.   Line and staff relationships are a frequent source of organizational conflict. As you look at the roles, responsibilities, and rights of line and staff positions, what factors would seem to be conducive to conflict?

4.   Staff specialists have frequently been given line authority over certain matters (quality control, production scheduling, and so forth). In this capacity, they give orders to employees simultaneously with line managers. What potential problems are created by giving functional authority to these specialists? Is it possible to avoid these problems? If so, how?

5.   Is the wheel structure an improvement over the pyramid form? Why or why not?

6.   Evaluate in detail the merits of looking at an organization structure as a system. Besides the systems structure shown in the chapter, can you think of other ways of showing an organization as a system? What other subsystems and connecting links may exist?

7.   Why is it that many employees have more responsibility than they have authority? What administrative actions can be taken to overcome this?

8.   What is the difference between delegation of authority and decentralization?

9.   Someone has said that decentralized organizations are more beneficial to employees than are centralized organizations. Why would anyone make such a statement? Do you agree or disagree with the statement? Please explain your position.

10.   Some authors have stated that there is a specific number of people that can be properly supervised by one manager, that is, there is an optimum number of people who can be included in a span of supervision. Some, for example, fix the optimum span of supervision at seven. What are the dangers in establishing an optimum number for a span of supervision?

11.   Would you prefer to work in a tall organization or a flat one? Why?

12.   What explanations seem plausible for the research finding that tall organizations provide more security and social satisfaction while flat ones provide more self-actualization?

13.   Illustrate and explain a job situation that is too structured and overly controlled. What steps could be taken to provide the right amount of structuring?

14.   Can you identify other steps that can be taken to keep organizations flexible, adaptive, and serviceable?

15.   Please go back to the case at the beginning of the chapter and answer the questions concerning the case in light of information discussed in the chapter.

The following cases at the back of the book contain problems related to Chapter 5:

Ben Stockton

Earl Fornette

Bentley Cantrell

Billy Snyder

Kurt Browning

Grace Lanham

Bill Caden

Abigail Spiegal and Trudy Pennington

Alan Purdy

Additional readings

Barnard, Chester I., *The Functions of the Executive,* Cambridge, Massachusetts: Harvard University Press, 1947.

Blau, Peter M., "A Formal Theory of Differentiation in Organizations," *American Sociological Review,* Volume 35, Number 2 (April 1970), pp. 201–218.

———, and W. Richard Scott, *Formal Organizations,* San Francisco: Chandler Publishing Company, 1962, pp. 1–115.

Brown, Philip J., and Robert T. Golembiewski, "The Line-Staff Concept Revisited: An Empirical Study of Organizational Image, *The Academy of Management Journal,* Volume 17, Number 3 (September 1974), pp. 406–417.

Dale, Ernest, *Planning and Developing the Company Organization Structure,* New York: American Management Association, 1952.

Galbraith, Jay R., "Matrix Organization Designs," *Business Horizons,* Volume 14, Number 1 (February 1971), pp. 29–40.

Gazell, James A., "Authority-Flow Theory and the Impact of Chester I. Barnard," *California Management Review,* Volume 13, Number 1 (Fall 1970), pp. 68–74.

Hicks, Herbert G., *The Management of Organizations,* Second Edition, New York: McGraw-Hill Book Company, 1972, pp. 386–412.

House, Robert J., "Role Conflict and Multiple Authority in Complex Organization," *California Management Review,* Volume 12, Number 4 (Summer 1970), pp. 53–60.

Likert, Rensis L., *New Patterns of Management,* New York: McGraw-Hill Book Company, 1961.

Lorsch, Jay W., and Paul R. Lawrence, *Studies in Organization Design*, Homewood, Illinois: Richard D. Irwin, Inc., 1970.

March, James G., and Herbert A. Simon, *Organizations*, New York: John Wiley & Sons, Inc., 1958.

Mooney, James D., *The Principles of Organization*, New York: Harper and Brothers, 1947.

Negandhi, Anant R., and Bernard C. Reimann, "Correlates of Decentralization: Closed and Open Systems Perspectives," *The Academy of Management Journal*, Volume 16, Number 4 (December 1973), pp. 570–582.

Newman, Derek, *Organization Design*, London: Edward Arnold, Limited, 1973.

Newman, William H., "Overcoming Obstacles to Effective Delegation," *Management Review*, Volume 45, Number 1 (January 1956), pp. 36–41.

Pfiffner, John M., and Frank P. Sherwood, *Administrative Organization*, Englewood Cliffs, New Jersey: Prentice-Hall, Inc., 1960.

Porter, Lyman W., and Edward E. Lawler, III, "Properties of Organization Structure in Relation to Job Attitudes and Job Behavior," *Psychological Bulletin*, Volume 64, Number 1 (1965), pp. 23–51.

Richetto, Gary M., "Organizations Circa 1990: Demise of the Pyramid," *Personnel Journal*, Volume 49, Number 7 (July 1970), pp. 598–603.

Schell, Erwin H., *Technique of Executive Control*, New York: McGraw-Hill Book Company, 1957, pp. 76–97.

Shartle, Carroll L., *Executive Performance and Leadership*, Englewood Cliffs, New Jersey: Prentice-Hall, Inc., 1956, pp. 34–73.

Shetty, Y. K., and Howard M. Carlisle, "A Contingency Model of Organization Design," *California Management Review*, Volume 15, Number 1 (Fall 1972), pp. 38–45.

Simon, Herbert A., *Administrative Behavior*, Second Edition, New York: The Macmillan Company, 1957.

——, "On the Concept of Organizational Goal," *Administrative Science Quarterly*, Volume 9, Number 1 (June 1964), pp. 1–22.

Thompson, James D., *Organizations in Action*, New York: McGraw-Hill Book Company, 1967.

Thompson, Victor A., *Modern Organization*, New York: Alfred A. Knopf, 1961.

Urwick, Lyndall, *The Elements of Supervision*, New York: Harper & Row, Publishers, 1943.

Chapter 6

The Informal
Work Group

A case to consider before reading chapter 6

THE THREE CUSTODIANS

~~Edwin Armitage~~ is ~~superintendent~~ of ~~maintenance~~ and ~~sanitation~~ at Audio Electronics Corporation, a company manufacturing and distributing electronic and sound equipment for a variety of functions. In his duties as superintendent, Mr. Armitage ~~supervises~~ the ~~maintenance~~ and ~~repair~~ of ~~mechanical~~ ~~equipment~~ ~~involved~~ in the ~~production process~~ and ~~oversees~~ janitorial and ~~custodial work~~. The production shift at Audio runs from 8 A.M. to 4:30 P.M. five days a week. All of the ~~maintenance~~ and ~~repair people~~ work the ~~day shift~~ (except in emergency situations) and are in constant contact with Mr. Armitage. ~~Also working during~~ the ~~day shift~~ are ~~three custodians~~; each of the ~~custodians~~ is ~~assigned to~~ one of the ~~production~~ buildings (there are three such buildings) to perform house-keeping activities that make it possible to avoid accidents and to keep the production process moving. These men perform duties similar to those of an orderly. The three custodians also work under the direct supervision of Mr. Armitage.

The more ~~thorough cleaning~~ functions (sweeping, mopping, waxing, etc.) are performed after the production lines are closed. At ~~4:30 P.M.~~ ~~three men arrive~~ and begin the clean-up process to prepare the work facilities for the next production day. These ~~men work independently~~; each one is responsible for cleaning one of the three production buildings. Mr. Armitage speaks with the men briefly at the beginning of their shift and then departs for his home. He does not see the men again until the next afternoon as they return to work. At 12:30 each night, the men are checked out by the security guard at the front gate. In the past, as can be seen, ~~Mr. Armitage~~ has ~~supervised~~ the ~~night cus-~~ ~~todians very loosely~~.

In recent weeks, Mr. Armitage has begun ~~receiving complaints~~ about poor janitorial performance. Most of the complaints have come from workers arriving to begin their day's work. Some floors have been left unswept, glass coverings have been left grimy, and other custodial duties have been ignored. The complaints have been increasing in number. In addition, Armitage has received word from supervisors who have been working after hours that the night custodians are spending a large amount of time together drinking coffee instead of working. One supervisor told Armitage that he knew of at least two hours spent by the custodians one night in which they "drank coffee, ate sandwiches, and laughed a lot." Rumors have also gotten back to Armitage that indicate the men may be napping on the job in the late evenings when no one else is around.

Because of the rumors and complaints, Armitage has begun dropping in on the custodians occasionally in the early evenings. However, on each evening when he has visited the men, they have each been busily working in their own separate buildings and everything has appeared quite normal. When he asks the men about the reasons for failing to do parts of their job, they have said that they need more help because there is too much work for them to do.

As Mr. Armitage arrived for work this morning, he was met by one of the production foremen, who wanted to talk to him. The foreman said:

Edwin, I think there's something you should know. You remember when you came out to the plant last Thursday night to talk with the custodians? They were all loafing around in the building where I was working (late). They got a call from someone, and I suspect it was the security guard at the gate. He must have told them you were coming, because two of the men started running like crazy toward their own buildings, and the janitor in our building sure got himself busy in a hurry. By the time you got to where they work, the custodians all appeared to be very busy. I think the fellows are trying to put something over on you.

Questions about the case of the Three Custodians

1. What type of work relationship appears to be developing among the night custodians?

2. What role does the night security guard appear to be serving for the work group?

3. Are there any explanations for the development of the informal work group? If so, what are the possible explanations?

4. For what additional reasons do some work groups informally bind themselves together?

5. What approach should Mr. Armitage take in dealing with the night custodians and security guard? Is there a way in which the informal ties can be used to the company's advantage?

6. Should one of the production supervisors working late have taken any action toward the custodians when the supervisors caught them loafing and cutting up?

The formal organization structure provides the framework through which objectives and goals can be accomplished. Formal relationships are defined by the structural design, and responsibility, authority, and accountability concepts are implemented. The formal organizational structure, however, shows only the officially planned relationships between groups and individuals working together. The planned relationships are initiated by managers in the upper levels of the organization and are designated through their authority.

In reality, the formal structure shows only one set of relationships between people working together. Other relationships exist that, for lack of a better term, are usually called informal work groups or informal organizations. The informal relationships coexist with the formal ones but are not bound by the formal lines of authority, nor are they forced to support and seek formally prescribed goals and objectives.[1] Informal relationships are initiated by the workers themselves to serve the needs of workers.

A look at a formal organization structure and some of the informal groupings active within it may help us understand the two systems and to clarify the purposes and characteristics of the informal organization. The formal organization chart for the United Manufacturing Company shown in Figure 6.1 is only a partial chart designed to show the formal location of office and secretarial personnel within the total structure. Only the formal channels connecting the office managers and secretaries with the lines of authority and communication are shown in this chart. Other personnel and authority relationships are omitted.

As can be seen in the formal structure, the company general manager has his own private executive secretary (Secretary I), and the manager of production has a private secretary (Secretary J). However, in the departments of sales and marketing, accounting services, and personnel, a secretarial pool has been created in each department to serve all managers and supervisors working in these departments. An office manager supervises the activities of each pool. There are no private, personal secretaries in these three departments. The formal chain of command and authority relationships are clearly defined in the chart.

[1]See Fred E. Katz, "Explaining Informal Work Groups in Complex Organizations: The Case for Autonomy in Structure," *Administrative Science Quarterly*, Volume 10, Number 2 (September 1965), pp. 204–223, for a more complete discussion of the differences between formal and informal organizations.

GURE 6.1   Location of office and secretarial personnel in the formal organization structure

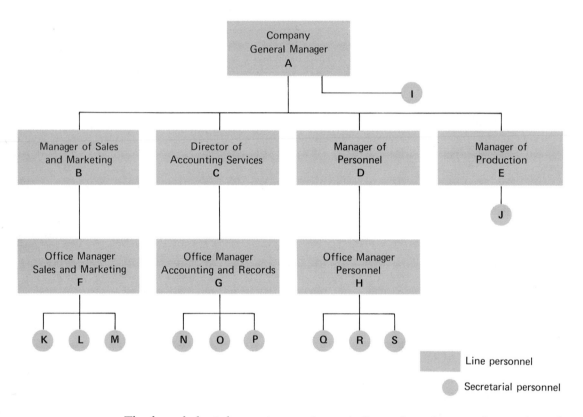

The formal chart does not recognize or indicate the existence of a number of informal groups that interact within the context of the formal structure. In many cases, the social ties, loyalties, communication systems, and behavior norms of the informal groups appear to be more influential than those of the formal structure. The visible informal groups that exist on a fairly continuous basis are identified in Figure 6.2.

The list of informal groups includes only those groups of which office and secretarial personnel are a part. The brief explanation of the content of each of the groupings given below attempts to provide some rationale for associations and ties that have developed.

The group including D, E, and H. D (manager of personnel) and E (production manager) normally might not include someone of lower organizational status and responsibility in their informal associations. However, Office Manager H happens to be the only male office manager in the company. He works regularly with the

FIGURE 6.2   Informal organizational relationships among office and secretarial personnel

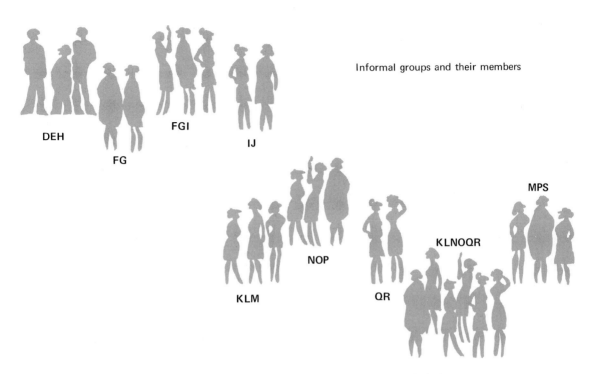

Informal groups and their members

personnel and production managers on a number of projects. He is included in their informal group because of his social acceptability as well as the frequency of his contact with these men.

The group including F and G. These two female office managers share many common interests and problems. They seem to need mutual support in dealing with the problems in their own departments. Office Manager H would be acceptable for membership in their group, but he has shown little interest in affiliating with them since he is a member of the DEH group.

The FGI group. This group is composed of the two women office managers and the general manager's executive secretary. The group is a high-status "club" as a result of the fact that two of its members are the only women managers in the company, and the other member is strategically located immediately beneath the top-level boss as his chief assistant. These women have both on-the-job and off-the-job interests in common.

The IJ group. These women are the only secretaries who work directly for only one boss. They perform a wider range of duties for their superiors than do the women working in the secretarial pools. They enjoy more freedom than do the other secretaries. They often "swap out" work when one is rushed and the other has little to do.

The KLM, NOP, and QR groups. These groups have been formed in the respective secretarial pools because the members are together constantly, share many common interests, and perform related duties. The women in these groups are at the bottom of the authority hierarchy. Secretary S is not included in the informal group with Q and R because she is an individualist who seems to prefer her own privacy over affiliation with them. She is considerably older than Q and R and has a set of personal values that does not concur with the other secretaries' interests. The women do not include their bosses in their informal ties because they are somewhat skeptical of their authority. They are not convinced that the office managers continually act in their best interests.

Group KLNOQR. The secretaries who compose this group come from the secretarial pools, share many common interests, and take their coffee break at the same time together each day. Their informal group is active not only in the company cafeteria; they also spend time on the phone gossiping with each other during work hours.

Group MPS. The women in this group stay in their work departments while the others are out to coffee, then go to coffee together when the other women have returned. Like the KLNOQR group, they share common interests, responsibilities, and coffee break hours. Secretary S, who is normally a loner, does participate in this informal group in a moderate way.

The existence of these informal groups reveals something of the nature of their development and perpetuation. Informal organizations develop automatically as individuals come in contact with each other. Ties or relationships are established (in addition to formal ties) that are expected to be mutually beneficial. *Similarities of interests,*[2] *frequency of contact, mutual desires for affiliation,*[3] and a *willingness to observe the rules and behavior guidelines established by the group* are all factors influencing the formation of the group. *Members must be acceptable to their fellow members,* and *each individual must accept membership* along with its advantages and demands. In the informal groups illustrated in the United Manufacturing Company case, Secretary S was not a part of the QR group because she did not conform to the expectations of Q and R and because she preferred to go her own separate way. Office Manager H could have been a part of the FG group, but he chose not to be.

Functions of Informal Organizations

The informal organization exists to fulfill specific needs of the group and its members. Already mentioned was the need for social affiliation. Informal organiza-

[2]Carroll E. Izard, "Personality Similarity and Friendship," *Journal of Abnormal Psychology,* Volume 61, Number 1, pp. 50–51.

[3]Stanley Schachter, *The Psychology of Affiliation,* Stanford, California: Stanford University Press, 1959.

tions are a primary source for the formation and furtherance of social ties.[4] Informal organizations also *provide* members with ~~useful information and knowledge~~ (~~through the grapevine~~), which may supplement or complement formal communication.[5] The informal organization may also be a ~~source of protection~~ against ~~threatening,~~ oppressive ~~forces~~. For example, the group may bind itself together to oppose a dangerously autocratic boss or to fight an unacceptable performance standard imposed by an unsympathetic time-and-motion-study man. Because there is strength in the unified actions of several, the group may collectively take stands no individual acting independently would be brave enough to take.[6] The informal group may seek to *~~further~~ preserve ~~important~~ values by ~~demanding~~ conformity to ~~group standards~~ by the ~~members themselves~~*. Penalties for nonconformity may range from verbal scoldings to removal from membership in the informal group.

Another important action of the informal organization is its involvement in helping its members *to ~~find~~ solutions to ~~mutual~~ and ~~personal~~ problems*. As was shown in the United Company illustration, the informal pact between Office Manager F and Office Manager G existed specifically to provide the two with a mutual exchange of ideas and assistance. Also, the informal ties between Secretary I and Secretary J revealed a concern for mutual help and support when job demands became too great.

The informal organization does, therefore, serve a number of purposes for those individuals who desire membership and are accepted into the group's ranks.

Characteristics and Activities

Several things are noteworthy concerning the composition and behavior of the informal organization. As was mentioned previously, the informal organization *has its own goals, objectives, and authority patterns, and these factors may or may not coincide with those of the formal structure.*[7] The design and actions of the informal organiza-

---

[4]See Donald F. Roy, "Banana Time, Job Satisfaction and Informal Interaction," *Human Organization,* Volume 18, Number 4 (1960), pp. 158–168, for an example of the social relationships that develop between people at work.

[5]David G. Bowers and Stanley E. Seashore, "Peer Leadership within Groups," *Personnel Administration,* Volume 30, Number 5 (September–October 1967), pp. 45–50.

[6]Bowers and Seashore, *loc. cit.,* stress the importance of the support the informal group gives to its members in times of stress and pressure. Schachter, *loc. cit.,* discovered that the need for affiliation and support from fellow informal group members increases in importance as oppression and anxiety increase.

[7]Katz, *op. cit.,* p. 206, and Keith Davis, "Grapevine Communications among Lower and Middle Managers," *Personnel Journal,* Volume 48, Number 4, p. 269, illustrate the role of the informal organization in affiliating with or working against the formal organization.

FIGURE 6.3   Illustration of overlapping membership in informal groups at United Manufacturing Company

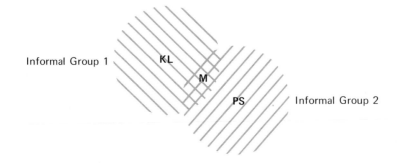

Secretary **M** belongs to these two informal groups simultaneously

tion have the capacity to be either supportive or detrimental to the goals of the formal organization. Since the informal organization exists to provide rewards, protection, and the preservation of other values for its members, formal and informal goals may be complementary if the members of the informal organization perceive benefits from working in a unified way with the formal structure. If, however, it seems more beneficial to work in opposition to the formal structure, the informal group has the capacity to do so.

Membership in an informal group is a selective process in which individuals are granted membership primarily on the basis of commonality of interests and willingness to be cooperative and to conform. *Individuals may have overlapping memberships in a number of informal groups,* depending upon the frequency of contacts, the mutual interests shared, and other factors. In the United Manufacturing Company illustration, several of the people were members of at least two informal groupings, and some had the potential for belonging to even more (see Figure 6.3).

Informal groups select individuals to serve as leaders. The selected leaders are granted authority by the members to make decisions, take action, seek conformity, or take other actions that seem appropriate. The leaders are selected on the basis of their ability to perform for the informal group and usually are not individuals possessing a great amount of formal authority. In other words, their authority to serve as leaders is granted to them by their fellow members to fill a need.[8] The leaders are expected to act in a way that achieves the goals of the group and protects its values. Informal leaders often are selected on the basis of respect, admiration, and the ability to perform advantageously for the benefit of the group.

[8]This concept of authority coincides with the "consent" theory of authority discussed by William G. Scott and Terence R. Mitchell, *Organization Theory,* Homewood, Illinois: Richard D. Irwin, Inc., 1972, pp. 218–219.

Quite often, *a group may select numerous individuals to serve in specific leadership capacities.* Leader A, for example, may be accepted as the production leader—the individual who sets and regulates the work pace (production standards, time standards, etc.) to which all members are expected to conform. Leader B may be expected to serve as the leader in charge of social and personal satisfaction; he is in charge of making work relationships pleasant and happy. Leader C may be selected as the public relations leader; it is his role to represent the group in all verbal contacts with outsiders—supervisor, inspectors, and public visitors. Other leaders may be selected to serve in additional capacities. Many of these roles, of course, may be combined and assigned to a single individual.

Each informal group characteristically establishes group behavior standards or norms to which it expects its members to conform. These standards are designed to achieve the goals of the group and to preserve and protect its values.[9] If, for example, the goals of the group are to provide a pleasant, enjoyable work pace for its members (to resist pressures for too much work or to fight back against rigid work controls), the group may establish maximum and minimum **production standards.** The standards may take the form of units produced, sales quotas achieved, time required to do a certain job, and so forth. In order to remain a member in good standing, every worker must adhere to the production guidelines. If a group working on an assembly-line job sets a maximum of 100 units assembled per day and a minimum of 75 units per day, anyone who consistently exceeds 100 units will be ostracized and eventually removed from the group if he fails to modify his behavior. He is a threat to the values of the rest of the group. If a worker frequently goes below the minimum 75 units, he will be pushed by the group to improve his performance to avoid penalties to himself (and perhaps to the whole group).

The informal group may also establish behavior norms in other areas. **Reaction norms,** which may be defined as prescribed ways of acting when outsiders are around, may also be outlined. If a "big boss" (an influential and authoritative manager) is near, every worker is expected to look busy to avoid getting into trouble. If a time-and-motion-study man is around, everyone is expected to perform at a somewhat slower pace so that unreasonable time standards can be avoided. If a threatening company inspector is on the premises, everything is to be made shipshape for his review. Through these actions, desirable conditions can be insured and penalties avoided.

The group can also establish norms and patterns to enhance its social interaction and affiliation desires. Members may adopt dress and appearance codes to show unity and affiliation. Members of an informal group on a construction crew

[9]Bowers and Seashore, *loc. cit.*

may start wearing metal helmets of a certain color to identify and distinguish themselves from other workers. A group of women may show their common affiliation through similarities of hair styles. The wearing of coats and ties may be begun by informal group members in a sales force to provide group identification and to build up status and prestige.

An especially important means of achieving many of the goals and objectives of the informal organization is the *development of its own communication network.* The informal network is commonly known as the **grapevine** and is uninhibited by the formal communication networks. Messages are spread by the grapevine to members by word of mouth or by other symbolic means. Anything that seems to have interest or value may be transmitted through the informal network. Seldom does the grapevine network operate in a rigidly defined pattern. Information may originate anywhere in the system and will be spread in a sometimes unpredictable manner. It has been suggested, however, that the cluster approach is the most frequently observable manner by which grapevine messages are passed along.[10] With the **cluster approach,** a message is communicated by an originator to two or three individuals, who in turn each pass the message along to two or three others, who do the same thing. The result is a sort of "ripple in the brook" effect as the message is spread (see Figure 6.4).

Grapevine messages tend to be passed along rapidly and more selectively than many people expect. The grapevine may withhold or retard the giving of information to some individuals.[11] The basis of withholding grapevine information may be the fact that the excluded individual lacks acceptable standing with the informal organization. The communication avoidance may also be a problem of lack of physical proximity (nearness) when messages are being passed along. For example, workers who labor in isolated areas often find themselves ignored or communicated to more slowly than workers in more exposed positions.

The informal organization acts similarly to a social fraternity in the sense that it develops secret codes through which it may communicate. To the outsider or the uninformed, the codes will have little significance. To the informal group members, however, the symbols have important meaning.

A college student employed in a manufacturing concern on a part-time basis reported that the work group in his department protected itself from outsiders by a novel system in which a certain worker who sat near the workroom's entrance was appointed the "warning" leader. It was his job to keep an eye on the door for the coming of individuals who might be threatening to the welfare of the group.

---

[10]Keith Davis, "Management Communication and the Grapevine," *Harvard Business Review,* Volume 31, Number 5 (September–October 1953), p. 45.

[11]*Ibid.,* p. 46.

FIGURE 6.4   Cluster pattern of grapevine communications

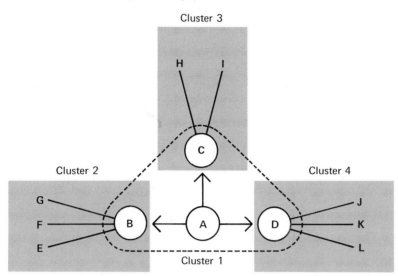

Source: Adapted from Keith Davis, "Management Communication and the Grapevine," *Harvard Business Review*, Volume 31, Number 5 (September-October 1953), p. 45.

If he spotted someone approaching who appeared to be dangerous, it was the warner's job to step on a foot pedal that released a blast of steam through a boiler valve. The steam blast was a warning to the other workers to be cautious because a possible enemy was entering. The warning system became even more sophisticated: One "toot" on the boiler meant the foreman was coming in; two "toots" meant that a production expediter was in view; and so forth.

The returning prisoners of war from the Vietnam conflict apparently developed their own communication symbols. One of the first men released referred to the times in which the group's morale would get low. He said that someone would then begin humming the melody to "California, Here I Come." The tune, which was unknown to their captors, reminded the men that someday their imprisonment would be over, and they would be returning home. The pleasant thought gave the men the encouragement needed to get through a bad time, and morale perked up accordingly.

Both of these illustrations show the importance of grapevine communications to the individuals involved.

The level of cohesiveness appears to vary significantly among informal work groups. Some groups seem to be tightly bound together for mutual support. Conformity to group standards or behavior norms tends to be high among these groups. Other groups appear to have only limited control and conformity. Several factors enter into the determination of group cohesiveness. Cohesiveness seems to be higher when a majority of the following conditions are present:

1.   The members have a broad general agreement concerning the goals and objectives the informal formation will serve.

2.   There is a significant amount of communication and interaction among the participating members.

3.   There is a satisfactory level of homogeneity in social status and social background among the members.

4.   Members are allowed to participate fully and directly in the determination of group standards.

5.   The size of the group is sufficient for interaction but is not too large to stymie personal attention. Normally, the optimum size of an informal organization is from four to seven members.[12]

6.   The members have a high regard for their fellow members.

7.   The members feel a strong need for the mutual benefits and protection the group appears to offer.

8.   The group is experiencing success in the achievement of its goals and in the protection of important values.[13]

The level of cohesiveness appears to have a direct influence upon the behavior of the members of each informal group. In groups, for example, where cohesiveness is high, members appear to be more attentive to each other, adherence to group goals is at a high level, pressure on violators of group goals is strong, and individual members find a strong sense of security and release from tensions as a result of their group affiliations.[14]

One additional characteristic of the informal group is noteworthy—the actions and existence of the group are not completely controllable by the use of formal authority methods. Informal relationships develop and act within the formal organization but tend to remain somewhat independent.[15] This aloofness provides many interesting challenges to formal managers and leaders.

[12]Edgar F. Huse and James L. Bowditch, *Behavior in Organizations: A System Approach to Managing,* Reading, Massachusetts: Addison-Wesley Publishing Company, 1973, pp. 123–124.

[13]See Barnard Berelson and Gary A. Steiner, *Human Behavior: An Inventory of Scientific Findings,* New York: Harcourt, Brace, and World, 1964, pp. 331–339, or Philip B. Applewhite, *Organizational Behavior,* Englewood Cliffs, New Jersey: Prentice-Hall, Inc., 1965, pp. 41–45, and Huse and Bowditch, *loc. cit.,* for further discussion of groups cohesiveness.

[14]Dorwin Cartwright and Alvin Zander, *Group Dynamics,* Evanston, Illinois: Row, Peterson, and Company, 1960, p. 89, includes a discussion of these and other effects of high-cohesion groups.

[15]Donald F. Roy, "Efficiency and the Fix: Informal Intergroup Relations in a Piecework Machine Shop," in S. M. Lipset and N. J. Smelser, editors, *Sociology: The Progress of a Decade,* Englewood Cliffs, New Jersey: Prentice-Hall, Inc., 1961, pp. 378–390.

Management's Relationship to the Informal Organization

As has been discussed, the informal organization has goals, objectives, and methods of operation designed to benefit its members. These functions may or may not be beneficial to the formal organization, and they are not completely within the control of the formal structure. In this rather confusing state of affairs, a justifiable question seems to be, How should the manager with formally designated responsibility and authority go about the task of confronting the informal organization and working with it?

One concept to keep in mind concerning the informal organization is that it serves many useful purposes for its members. It usually provides a satisfactory amount of social affiliation and interaction. It provides information to workers rapidly and, in many cases, accurately. The informal organization is capable of controlling or influencing the behavior of its members if their actions become so far out of line with formal organizational expectations that they tend to create problems and dangers for the informal group. In many cases, the informal group even works to support and achieve formal goals and objectives that are in harmony with informal ones. Since the informal group is capable of performing for its members many positive, constructive tasks that are desirable from the formal point of view, *the group should be permitted and encouraged to perform these supportive functions.* In meeting personal and group needs, and in regulating worker behavior constructively, the informal organization can be a very helpful auxiliary to the formal manager.

There are situations, however, in which the actions of the informal group are in opposition to formal goals and objectives, and the behavior of individual members is detrimental to constructive organizational achievement. If the workers have established lower production standards than is reasonable, if coffee break times are being abused collectively, if legitimate supervisory instructions are being ignored, etc., the managerial task of working with the informal group becomes more complex.

The goal of every manager should be to unify the actions and efforts of the informal organization with those of the formal organization whenever possible. In addition, the manager usually desires to replace attitudes of hostility with those of trust and confidence. The existence of a set of positive conditions helps to unify the efforts and actions of formal and informal structures and to make them mutually more beneficial. In general, the two systems pull together more favorably if:

1.   The workers have a high level of confidence in their boss (or bosses) and believe that he consistently considers their needs and desires as he makes decisions.

This kind of confidence tends to build over a period of time as a manager's actions are discerned to be fair, considerate, and favorably oriented toward the worker. Usually, the more positive leadership styles (such as those of participative or free-rein leadership) build confidence more than do negatively oriented styles (autocratic leadership, etc.).

2.   The workers know, understand, and accept the objectives of the formal organization. This condition calls for the communication of formal objectives to workers in clear, simplified terminology. If the objectives are reasonable and consistent with the values of the informal group, there will be general support of the goals. If the goals appear unreasonable, the workers may not support them. Normally, acceptance of reasonable goals can be attained, however.

3.   The workers are allowed some participation in the determination of formal goals, objectives, and policies. This condition does not mean that every worker must be involved in every decision, but it does mean that some type of representation in matters that affect the worker will increase his confidence in and acceptance of the decision or plan. Participation tends to increase confidence and support for the decision reached and reduces antagonism or mistrust. Workers tend to support decisions they help make.

4.   The workers are kept informed regularly and accurately concerning facts and policies of interest to them. Workers receive the information needed through formal channels so that speculative (and often false) rumors become unnecessary.

5.   The formal leaders (managers) listen for and seek out the feelings and sentiments of the workers.

When it is difficult for a formal manager to listen to every worker, to get participation from everyone, and to send messages directly to everyone, the identification and utilization of the informal leaders as representatives of the group may be effective. These leaders usually feel a great amount of responsibility for the well-being of their fellow members and perform conscientiously for them. The informal leader can serve in a capacity that will be beneficial for the group he represents and can at the same time be of assistance to the formal manager through participation in decision making and the communicating upward of important messages.

Attention to the Informal Organization—a Strength or a Weakness?   Not everyone has been willing to be attentive to the needs and demands of the informal work group. Some managers with a traditionally autocratic orientation have argued that the recognition and handling of the demands of the informal organization show a weakness on the part of management. This line of thinking suggests that formal managers, by their right of authority, can force conformity upon the informal group and its members. As a result, when a manager "caters" to the pressures and influences of the group, he is abdicating his own right to command and control.

A more perceptive review of the manager's role in relation to the informal organization reveals that giving recognition and attention to it indicates perceptive, realistic management rather than weak administration. The realistic point of view recognizes that informal organizations do exist, that they cannot be completely controlled, and that they can serve constructive as well as negative purposes so far as the formal structure is concerned. When the manager attempts to integrate the efforts of the formal and informal organizations, he strengthens the probabilities of successful action.

Summary

Informal organizations exist within the confines of the formal authority structure. The informal organization consists of a group of people who relate to each other spontaneously for purposes of mutual benefit and achievement. The interactions that occur informally are not prescribed by the formal structure, nor can they be completely controlled by formal authority.

The informal group sometimes acts in support of formal goals and objectives, but it is equally capable of opposing formal guidelines. The group provides many services for its members in good standing, often filling in where formal organizations are negligent.

The perceptive manager seeks to recognize the characteristics, functions, and activities of the informal organization and then tries to integrate these factors with the functions and activities of the formal structure.

Figure 6.5 shows where these factors of the informal organization fit into the model of worker behavior.

Questions to consider after reading Chapter 6

1. It was stated that the formal manager cannot control the activities of the informal organization. Evaluate and discuss this statement.

2. Some authors have said that the formal manager cannot destroy the informal organization by attempting to physically disperse its members. Why might this statement be true?

3. Does it appear likely that most managers are aware of the specific activities and standards established by informal groups working beneath them?

4. How can a formal manager come to recognize who the informal leaders are? What signs may indicate who the informal leaders are?

FIGURE 6.5   Model of worker behavior and its determinants

WORKER'S ENVIRONMENT AND EXPERIENCES

Family	Place of residence	Race or ethnic background	Education	Occupation
Unions	Religion			Other personal and environmental factors
Peer groups	Government	Status of health	Economic network	

INDIVIDUAL

Inborn set of needs, drives, instincts	Emotional nature and characteristics
Modified and expanded set of needs based upon experience	Anatomical–physiological factors— inborn and learned
Capacity to seek pleasure, avoid pain	Unique self-concept
Desire for constancy—equilibrium of internal–external factors	Empathy toward moral values
Ability to plan, act rationally	Ability to be perceptive concerning self, experience, and others

ORGANIZATIONAL FACTORS

Formal Organization		Informal Organization
Outlines organizational objectives	May structure line-staff relationships	Determines some social relationships
Provides the basis for defining jobs, determining departmentalization	Determines spans of supervision	Provides information and other communications
Determines the degree of specialization that will be utilized	Utilizes organizational resources effectively	Is a source of protection
	Provides guidance and control for employees	Protects important values
Influences social status		Demands conformity
Affixes authority-responsibility relationships	Provides formal communication networks	Helps individuals with problems
	Makes work environment more rational, stable, secure	Sets behavior norms
Outlines a horizontal authority hierarchy and vertical work relationships	Has other positive and negative effects	Selects leaders
		Provides cohesiveness

TECHNOLOGICAL FACTORS

Provide new products and services

Increase capacity to provide
  manufactured goods

Decrease labor costs

Affect the level of employment

Change many production and
  communication processes

Have a significant impact upon the
  lives of workers within the
  business enterprise

Demand more of managers

Alter manpower policies and practices

Modify union—management relations

ACTION
or
BEHAVIOR

5. Why is the autocratic, task-oriented manager more likely to stimulate the development of a strong, resistant informal grouping among his subordinates than would a
participative, employee-oriented manager?

6. Is it possible for a formal manager to be an informal leader? Why or why not?

7. Please discuss in more detail how formal organizations and informal organizations
can be unified or encouraged to support each other more fully.

**The following cases at the back of the book
contain problems related to Chapter 6:**

> Ben Stockton
>
> Mark Williams
>
> Stanley Lowell
>
> Earl Fornette
>
> Kurt Browning
>
> ~~Grace Lanham~~
>
> Abigail Spiegal and Trudy Pennington
>
> Alan Purdy

Additional readings

Collins, B. E., and B. H. Raven, "Group Structure: Attraction, Coalitions, Communication, and Power," in Gardner Lindzey and E. Aronson, editors, *The Handbook of Social
Psychology,* Volume 4, Menlo Park, California: Addison-Wesley Publishing Company,
1966, pp. 102–204.

Festinger, Leon, "Informal Social Communication," *Psychological Review,* Volume 57,
Number 5 (September 1950), pp. 271–282.

Freedman, Jonathan L., J. Merrill Carlsmith, and David O. Sears, *Social Psychology,*
Englewood Cliffs, New Jersey: Prentice-Hall, Inc., 1970, pp. 221–335.

Garfinkel, Harold, "Studies of the Routine Grounds of Evenplay Activities," *Social
Problems,* Volume 11, Number 3 (Winter 1964), pp. 225–250.

Golembiewski, Robert T., "Small Groups and Large Organizations," in James G. March,
editor, *Handbook of Organizations,* Chicago: Rand McNally and Company, 1968, pp. 87–141.

Graham, Gerald H., "Interpersonal Attraction as a Basis of Informal Organization,"
The Academy of Management Journal, Volume 14, Number 4 (December 1971), pp. 483–495.

Hershey, Robert, "The Grapevine—Here to Stay But Not Beyond Control," *Personnel,* Volume 43, Number 1 (January–February 1966), pp. 62–66.

Muti, Richard S., "The Informal Group—What It Is and How It Can Be Controlled," *Personnel Journal,* Volume 47, Number 8 (August 1968), pp. 563–571.

Roy, Donald, "Quota Restriction and Goldbricking in a Machine Shop," *American Journal of Sociology,* Volume 57, Number 5 (March 1952), pp. 427–442.

Sayles, Leonard R., *Behavior of Industrial Work Groups,* New York: John Wiley & Sons, Inc., 1958.

Sommer, Robert, "Small Group Ecology," *Psychological Bulletin,* Volume 67, Number 2 (1967), pp. 145–152.

Warren, Donald I., "Social Relations of Peers in a Formal Organization Setting," *Administrative Science Quarterly,* Volume 11, Number 3 (December 1966), pp. 440–478.

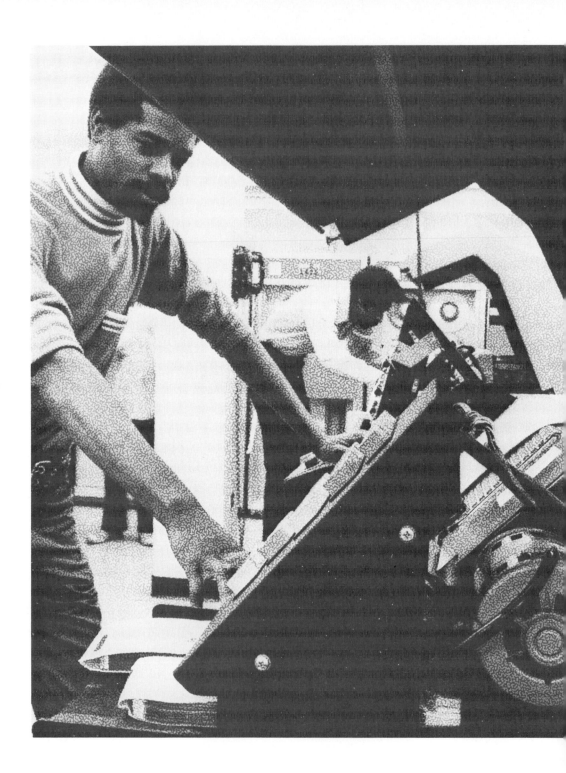

SECTION II

THE
EXPECTATIONS
OF
PEOPLE
AT
WORK

As Section I indicated, the behavior of people at work is influenced by a number of factors. Some of these influences are internal, while others come from external sources. Each individual is a unique being. When the individual enters the work force, he takes this step with specific ideas and expectations about his work career. The individual employee has definite goals in mind as he affiliates himself with a work organization. Sometimes the goals and motivations are overt and tangible. At other times, however, the personal objectives may be covert and less immediately identifiable.

In Chapter 7, several assumptions about the needs and expectations of employees are considered. Eight types of needs frequently exhibited by workers are presented. Ways in which organizations can go about meeting the expectations of employees are discussed. Because workers' expectations are not always readily apparent, some managerial techniques for identifying needs and expectations of employees are also included. Individual needs are changeable and dynamic—they tend not to remain constant over long periods of time. The chapter talks about the changing urgencies of people's needs. Ideas about why and how needs change are included.

Those who serve as managers have unique responsibilities and are subjected to pressures somewhat different from those of nonmanagers. Chapter 8 looks at the responsibilities, expectations, and pressures of those who serve in managerial capacities. The expectations of managers are compared to those of workers who have no responsibilities for the activities of other people. Because managers frequently find themselves in positions with conflicting roles, methods for living with conflicts are also discussed.

Chapter 7

What the Worker Expects from His Job

A case to consider before reading chapter 7

CRAIG SAVOY — A MANAGER WHO HAS EVERYTHING HE EVER WANTED

Craig Savoy is a district sales manager for the Diamond Refrigeration Company. He supervises sales activities in an eighteen-county area in a southeastern state for the Diamond Company, a manufacturer and distributor of commercial and residential heating and air-conditioning equipment.

Savoy has been ~~with Diamond since~~ he ~~graduated~~ from ~~college twenty-five years ago~~. He is now ~~forty-seven years of age.~~ Savoy came from what many people might call an impoverished background. His father was a coal miner as his father before him had been. The Savoy family was large, and ~~Craig's parents had to struggle financial~~ly to support their nine children. ~~Craig~~ was the ~~only one~~ of the ~~children to go~~ to ~~college~~. Through sheer determination and superior intelligence, he worked his way through school.

Savoy recently made the following statements in a conversation with his boss, Lowell Gifford, who is the director of sales for Diamond in its southeastern territory.

Lowell, this company has been good to me. When I came to work here twenty-five years ago, all I was looking for was a steady job, a good income, and an opportunity to make a place for myself in the community. As you know, I was just a poor boy from the hills when I started out. Not in my wildest dreams did I anticipate earning in excess of $30,000 the way I am today. Dorothy [Savoy's wife] and I have been able to raise and educate our children with relative ease. When Toni [the youngest child of the family] got married last month, Dorothy and I felt a sense of pride in what we had been able to do for our children. I'm most grateful for the opportunities this company has afforded me.

Diamond has even provided opportunities for community service and recognition beyond my expectations. When I was elected president of the Lions Club in town, this was a gratifying experience. My opportunity to serve on the Board of Education was also a rewarding experience. And I've had other similar responsibilities and honors.

I guess you could say that my problem today is that I'm looking for new frontiers for myself. I've got a good income, several opportunities for community service have been mine, and I've achieved a certain degree of civic recognition. Those things are fine, but I need something else to challenge me.

Now I seem to be lacking in motivation. My sales records don't show it yet, but they soon will, I'm afraid. I don't enjoy my work as much as I once did. I've lost the drive I once had. I'm satisfied with mediocre performance from myself and my subordinates more readily than I should be. I just don't know what the future holds for me.

Questions about the Craig Savoy case

1. Mr. Savoy has largely identified his problem already. What is the cause of his increasing lack of interest in his work?

2. What goals was Mr. Savoy formerly seeking from his work career? Why did he previously show so much enthusiasm for his job?

3. As Savoy's boss, what actions should Lowell Gifford take?

4. What principles of need fulfillment and motivation does this case suggest?

5. After you have read the chapter, review and analyze the implications of this case again.

Since Adam and Eve were directed in the Garden of Eden to earn their living by the "sweat of the brow," man has found labor essential to the maintenance of his own welfare. Today's worker is no exception. Consider for a moment the following assumptions concerning the motivations behind today's workers and their decisions about jobs.

1. The worker in the American society today affiliates himself with a specific business organization with the expectation that certain personal goals and objectives will be fulfilled as a result of that affiliation. Wages for securing food, clothing, and shelter normally are among his expectations, but he may be seeking many other additional achievements.

2.   The individual worker chooses to accept a specific job with a particular organization because he believes that position and company will provide him a higher level of fulfillment of his needs and expectations than would other jobs and other organizations.

3.   The organization employing the skills and services of a worker has a responsibility to fulfill the reasonable goals and needs of that worker.

The first assumption appears to be universally true. People work to attain their own personal economic, social, and psychological objectives. The pursuit of these goals through work is both practical and traditional.

The choices available to the worker in deciding which job to take (the second assumption) are not always as abundant as he might prefer, but normally some choice is possible. Choices may be limited as a result of economic depression or recession, regional oversupplies of labor, or job skill requirements the potential laborer is unable to satisfy. While the presence of these factors makes the job selection much more limited, the normal situation provides each worker with more than one choice for his job selection decision. It is assumed that the worker will decide upon the job that promises him either the immediate or the long-range achievement he is seeking, or both.

The employment agreement is a type of contract whereby the worker agrees to exchange his efforts and knowledge for certain monetary and nonmonetary reimbursements. The employing organization needs the skills and efforts of the worker, and the worker needs things the organization can provide.

A study by Kotter[1] supports the idea that employers and employees enter into a psychological contract when an employee is hired. Employers and subordinates come to an agreement on what each expects of the other as they work together in the organization. Kotter's study concludes that:

1.   When the expectations of the employing organization match those of the new employee, the employee will be more productive in his first year of employment, he will be more satisfied with his work, and he will tend to stay with the organization for a longer period of time than if there were a number of mismatches in the expectations of the two.

2.   Individuals and organizations who get more than they want or expect from each other may be as dissatisfied as those who get less than they expect.

3.   The more clearly individual employees and employers understand their own expectations, the more likely they are to reach a good match in their expectations of each other.

[1]John Paul Kotter, "The Psychological Contract, Managing the Joining Up Process," *California Management Review*, Volume 15, Number 3 (Spring 1973), pp. 91–99.

4. Verbal discussions between prospective employees and employers about their expectations of each other enhance the probability of a good match in the employment agreement and subsequent interactions.[2]

The degree to which the organization is responsible for providing need fulfillment (mentioned in the third assumption) is not universally agreed upon, but many employers recognize that a responsibility does exist.

Some writers have argued that workers in today's labor force expect less need fulfillment from their work affiliations than was true of workers in previous years. While this argument may be true for some workers, the more limited expectations of these workers are frequently not of their own choosing. In reality, workers who have come to expect little from their jobs usually have been deprived of the fulfillment of many of their needs and goals by their employing companies so often that they have reduced their expectations. Company size, technological advancement, managerial philosophy, or other factors may be contributing reasons for the reduction in personal fulfillment by these companies. Where workers have been deprived of intracompany sources of need satisfaction, they have had to turn to external sources. Workers especially have had to go outside their business organizations more often to find satisfaction of some of their social and psychological goals.

While the means to fulfillment may vary, individuals continue to seek fulfillment of their basic needs and expectations. Officials in most organizations are concerned about providing for the fulfillment of the needs and interests of their employees. Where the needs and desires of workers are considered and some attainment is provided for, worker response is normally positive and appreciative.

What Are Human Needs?

Every human being has needs and goals, whether he has rationally recognized them or not. A human need is a personal, unfilled vacancy that determines and organizes all mental processes and all behavior in the direction of its attainment. Needs are goals, known or unknown, that cause the individual to seek their satisfactory fulfillment. Each human being possesses many of these needs, and those who enter the labor force bring their needs with them as they come to work.

Every person who works with others (especially those in managerial positions) should attempt to identify his own personal needs and the needs and expectations of those with whom he labors. As the manager recognizes his own goals, he becomes more capable of directing his efforts to their fullest satisfaction. As each

[2]*Loc. cit.*

manager discerns the needs of his subordinates, he is in a better position to provide improved assistance and a more personal means of supervision for his subordinates.

What are the basic human needs that call for attention? Among the millions of people now living there exists a ~~set of needs~~ that may vary in intensity but are nevertheless quite common. The needs included for discussion here are those for ~~physical maintena~~nce, ~~security~~, ~~affiliati~~on, ~~competence~~, ~~reputatio~~n, ~~power~~, ~~achievement~~, and ~~hope~~. This is by no means a comprehensive list of all human needs, but the needs selected do represent factors often exhibited by individuals at work.[3] It is important to remember that people at work possess these needs and expect to attain at least a part of them while they work.

The ~~Physical Maintenance Need.~~   Every human being has a **physical mainte-nance need**—~~the need for biological surviva~~l. Adequate f~~oo~~d, ~~wate~~r, ~~oxyge~~n, and shelter are essential if life is to continue. The small child may be unaware of the cause of these needs, but he learns rather instinctively to attempt to satisfy them. At first, the infant is wholly dependent upon the adults around him to provide for his needs. As the individual matures, he comes to recognize his needs in a more rational way and to accept or reject the different choices of fulfillment available to him. Personal, cultural, and environmental factors may aid him in his decisions.

How Organizations Fulfill Physical Maintenance Needs. In today's society, most workers depend upon their employing companies to provide them with the means whereby they can obtain the necessary resources to satisfy the physical main-tenance needs of themselves and any dependents they may be supporting. Normally, this means that most workers expect to receive wages or salaries adequate to maintain physical needs. As mature adults, workers must then select the means to utilize the funds in providing for their physical maintenance.

In the American economy, there was once a day when the managers of some business organizations made decisions for their employees concerning how they should feed, clothe, and shelter themselves and their families. This era, of course, was known as the era of ~~paternalism~~. Paternalism is still a predominant management style in many areas of the world, but its effectiveness is waning in the more

---

[3]For other lists of human needs, see A. H. Maslow, *Motivation and Personality,* New York: Harper and Brothers, 1954, pp. 80–92; H. R. Murray et al., *Explorations in Personality,* New York: Oxford Press, 1938, pp. 152–226; Fredrick Herzberg, *Work and the Nature of Man,* Cleveland: The World Publishing Company, 1966, pp. 44–45; and Raymond B. Cattell, *Personality: A Systematic, Theoretical, and Factual Study,* New York: McGraw–Hill Book Company, 1950, pp. 179–205.

advanced industrial societies. In the United States, most of today's managers have moved away from this degree of managing the personal financial affairs of their subordinates and now view their duties in this area as primarily a responsibility to pay a reasonable wage. Most workers have the knowledge and the desire to manage their own personal finances themselves.

As a work organization structures its pay schedule, its scale should be arranged so that the lowest-paid full-time worker in the organization is paid at a rate that allows the worker (assuming an average-sized family) *at least* to provide for the physical maintenance needs of himself and his family. Most companies and organizations choose to go far beyond this for their lowest-level workers. The concept suggested here is based on the belief that every worker who devotes himself to a full-time job should receive compensation to allow fulfillment of this basic need. The actual wage that is required to do this may vary with the cost of living in the community in which he lives. In effect, what this suggests is that every organization needs to establish at least a minimum-standard-of-living wage necessary to provide adequately for all full-time employees. Most organizations will want to establish a foundation wage well above the minimum-standard-of-living figure.

The Need for Security.   The human need for security is partially related to physical maintenance needs, but the need encompasses other areas, too. Each individual has a need to feel safe, secure, and protected from anything that might harm him. The individual may fear factors that could do him bodily harm, or his concerns may be over the possibilities of mental anguish and distress.

Insecurity is one of the realities of life. As long as there are people and factors independent of an individual's control, security will be challenged. No individual can be completely secure in an environment that contains the potential (if not the actuality) of air and water pollution, that depends on mechanical transportation (which is subject to failure), that is governed by political leaders with widely differing ideologies, and where economic conditions tend to fluctuate spasmodically. These and many other social, technological, political, and economic factors pose threats to personal security.

It is normal for every individual to seek to protect himself and his family from as many elements of insecurity as he possibly can. The average individual buys life and medical insurance for himself and his family, purchases seat belts for his car, votes for his political candidates, opens bank savings accounts, and chooses his friends in a manner that reinforces his security values and improves his chances for attaining them.

How Needs for Security Can Be Fulfilled. While workers cannot expect to achieve complete security, several actions on the part of their supervisors and employing companies can foster a higher degree of security. Often workers feel insecure concerning the anticipated actions of their supervisors. The more trust a worker feels toward his superior, the more security he gains. Trust of superiors comes about primarily through consistent, fair, and concerned attention from the superior. On the opposite side, if the supervisor is dogmatic, arbitrary, and inconsistent, his subordinates will feel highly insecure.

Workers tend to feel economic insecurities in the face of potential health problems, possible loss of employment, future retirement, and many other possible difficulties. Most business organizations now provide some form of medical and hospitalization insurance, disability compensation, pension plan, social security contribution, and other programs to offset workers' economic insecurities. While the utilization of the seniority method may carry many undesirable attributes, the use of length of service as a criterion in making decisions concerning job layoffs gives long-term employees additional job security. Companies that use only the safest equipment and implement policies that encourage safe practices are aiding the physical security of their workers. These suggestions show that managers and their organizations can plan for and provide workers with improved levels of security.

The Need for Affiliation. Every human being has an **affiliation need,** a need for interpersonal relations with others. This need has been defined as the need for belonging, for association, for acceptance by one's fellowman or the need for giving and receiving friendship and love.[4] The affiliation need is characterized by its reciprocal nature of giving and receiving attention.

The affiliation need is apparently an inherent one, since even newborn babies respond to affiliation and tend to vegetate without it. Affiliation skills are cultivated, and means of satisfaction may be influenced by cultural and social factors. The child derives his affiliation satisfaction at first primarily from family members. As he grows older, peer groups and friends become the major source of fulfillment. When the adult joins a business organization, he usually focuses some of his social expectations upon co-workers and colleagues.

The worker expects to identify with other workers on the basis of common interests and goals. He expects to give friendly support to his peers when needed and to receive support in turn when he needs it. He expects to be accepted for what he is rather than to be rejected for what he is not. When the worker attains social satisfaction, he is fulfilling an important desire.

Achievement of affiliation needs not only provides benefits for the worker, but it also results in gains for the employing organization. Studies have shown, for

[4]Maslow, *op. cit.*, p. 90.

example, that absenteeism and turnover among employees tend to decrease as workers develop affiliations with their co-workers. Productivity often is high and production costs are low where affiliate groups develop, become cohesive, and establish organizationally supportive norms.[5] Most people enjoy having some contact with others rather than being isolated and will respond positively when given the opportunity. There are, of course, some individuals who prefer independence and aloofness, but they appear to be a minority.

How Affiliation Can Be Encouraged. No worker can be forced into social affiliations at his work place if he does not choose to relate to his fellow workers beyond the demands of the job, but workers can be provided with opportunities to satisfy their affiliation needs. Where there is flexibility in work stations, the stations can be placed together to improve the possibility of conversations and social interaction for the workers staffing those stations. Work breaks can sometimes be scheduled to provide several employees with the opportunity to get better acquainted. Organizationwide and departmental picnics and banquets are sometimes planned to enhance the social affiliations of the workers. Job assignments are frequently made to teams of workers rather than to separate individuals as a means of encouraging social development.

Most of the actions presented above are calculated efforts on the part of managers. Very often, the workers themselves take the initiative and find their own ways of social affiliation. Some of these actions were reviewed in Chapter 6. Employee-initiated affiliations may be even more enduring and meaningful than those precipitated by managerial efforts.

The Need for Competence.   The **competence need** is the desire human beings have to be adequate or capable of performing tasks and assignments. Interpreted in terms of the work place, this means that the typical worker has the need to feel (and be) capable of performing the duties and responsibilities expected of him. The average human being desires to be a success rather than a failure in his work performance. Satisfaction comes when the worker feels adequate to fulfill the tasks requested of him and believes himself capable of continuing this adequacy. In a recent study now being prepared for publication, this author has discovered that from a sample of college seniors, the desire to perform competently was the most important wish this young group had for their future work

[5]See Raymond H. Van Zelst, "Sociometrically Selected Work Teams Increase Production," *Personnel Psychology,* Volume 5, Number 3 (Autumn 1952), pp. 175–185, and John R. P. French, Arthur Kornhauser, and Alfred Marrow, "Conflict and Cooperation in Industry," in Schuyler D. Hoslett, editor, *Human Factors in Management,* Revised Edition, New York: Harper and Brothers, 1951, p. 187, for further discussions of the effects of affiliation.

careers. They wanted to feel competent and capable at their work more than anything else. The importance of competency is often overlooked by a manager, but the need usually is a strong one.

Nonsupervisors seek competence as they use materials, equipment, and their own physical resources to meet performance standards under time and quality pressures. Supervisors seek competency as they direct the efforts of their subordinates to useful achievement. In almost every situation, competency involves self-judgment—judgment that evaluates one's own performance and reaches a favorable conclusion. Outside judgments (from supervisors, colleagues, etc.) may also influence the feeling of competency.

One author has said:

> The competent individual feels potent and worthy of being taken seriously by others. ~~The person who lacks the attitude of competence may not dare to hope or achieve.~~ The competent person may experience conflict, disappointment, and frustration, but he is not likely to think of himself as bored or defeated.[6]

Obviously, individuals who have a feeling of competence approach situations differently from those who feel incompetent.

Providing for Attainment of Competency. Perhaps the best way for a worker to develop a feeling of being competent is to actually perform job assignments capably and adequately. With successful performance, the individual develops confidence in his own abilities and comes to regard himself positively.

Supervisors can help their subordinates to develop a feeling of competency by properly assessing the capabilities of each employee and ~~giving the worker job assignments within the boundaries of his ability to perform. Feelings of futility and frustration result when employees are given tasks beyond their capabilities~~. Supervisors also can be helpful by providing the necessary training, communication, and material assistance needed by the worker to increase his ability to perform.

Feedback on successful performance is also helpful to the attainment of competence. Each worker benefits if he has some means of measuring his performance level to determine his adequacy and to point out inadequacies.

As is true of most of the other need fulfillments, supervisors and managers cannot do everything for the worker in order to meet this need. The worker must exert some effort on his own, and he must possess a certain level of ability before competency can be attained.

---

[6]Perry A. Constas, "Alienation, Counseling Implications, and Management Therapy," *Personnel Journal*, Volume 52, Number 5 (May 1973), p. 351.

The Reputation Need   In many ways the **reputation need** is an ~~extension of~~ ~~both the affiliation and competence needs~~, for the ~~reputation need calls~~ for the ~~recognition~~ of an ~~individual's competency by others~~. Maslow defined the reputation need as a ~~desire for status, recognition,~~ and ~~deserved respect~~ from one's colleagues. The implication is that an individual is not satisfied with the fact that he has recognized his own competency, but he wishes others to realize this and respond to him with admiration.[7]

Workers, like all people, seek praise and recognition when they have performed well. When a supervisor makes the statement, "I don't see why I should have to commend a worker for doing his job well when I'm paying him $4.00 an hour to do it," the supervisor shows that he is out of touch with the realities of this need. Reputation is sought in addition to the satisfaction of other needs, including those satisfied primarily by money.

A by-product of fulfillment of the reputation need is status. As an esteemed reputation is acquired, status very often is an outward form of calling attention to this accomplishment. In a realistic sense, ~~status is an earned distinction~~ that provides the individual with unique recognition—something above the ordinary, the commonplace. Earned status calls for symbols to portray the status and requests further recognition on the part of those who see the status symbols. Attempts by some business organizations and some political philosophies to destroy status positions and status symbols have been basically unsuccessful. Where one symbol has been removed, another symbol has risen to take its place.

When channeled properly, the desire for a good reputation and high esteem (and status also) can be a very useful drive. Of course, it is imperative that all workers be given the opportunity to achieve this goal when their actions deserve recognition.

Providing Workers with Fulfillment of the Reputation Need. One of the simplest, most helpful ways of fulfilling the reputation need is for supervisors to identify and commend good performance whenever it is given. Most workers respond enthusiastically to praise. Praise can be given easily and can mean much to a worker; yet, it is interesting to note that many managers realize that they do not use praise as often as it is earned.

Promotions and salary increases based upon merit are other forms of managerial response to the needs of workers for esteem and recognition. Techniques such as employee-of-the-week awards, the giving of watches or pins for service rendered, and so forth are other ways of extending symbols of esteem. These techniques do not appear very sophisticated, but they are rewards that provide

[7]Maslow, *op. cit.,* p. 90.

recognition and enhance reputations. There are, of course, many status symbols (a private office, a large desk, a reserved place in the company parking lot) that provide esteem and reputation recognition. Many workers are self-conscious about their esteem ambitions, but the need continues to surface. Managers have an abundance of ways to provide for this need.

In providing recognition rewards and status achievement, it is important that opportunities to attain rewards and status are made known to all employees. Equitable reward systems provide everyone with equal opportunities to attain the benefits. The giving of rewards and recognition is something that should be earned by the recipient to satisfy his reputation and competence needs.

The Need for Power.   Power is the capacity to influence or control the objects and forces in one's environment. On a personal basis, power describes the ability of an individual to be dominant over or control the utilization of physical objects and the actions of other people. While power may make possible the fulfillment of other personal goals and objectives, many individuals seem to seek power primarily for the sake of being dominant and forceful. The need for power does not appear to be of the same intensity in all individuals—power is a chief concern of many and has a less interest for others.

It has been observed that power is an important need of many politicians and may be a vital part of the makeup of many supervisors and managers. There is little doubt that many administrators climb the organizational ladder in search of power, often at the sacrifice of other goals (such as those of affiliation).

Power, of course, may be achieved through acquisition of factors other than formal authority. A worker can gain power through persuasive abilities over an informal work group. Other workers gain power by virtue of strategic positions in which they exercise control over work flow processes or have direct access to financial resources. Again, it is important to remember that some workers appear more interested in the possession of power than do others.

Fulfilling the Need for Power. Managers face one of their greatest challenges in properly providing those workers who have a desire for power with opportunities for fulfillment in the work organization. A major element of the problem is the fact that not all individuals who desire power have the credentials and qualifications for handling it. Managers must assess not only the needs of their subordinates for power, but also they must assess the worker's ability to use it. Where ability seems commensurate with responsibility, the delegation of authority is an appropriate response for fulfillment. In defining the power need, it was pointed out that power includes dominance of both people and things. Where promotions to authority positions over people may be inappropriate, control of equipment or machinery may sometimes be sufficient. ~~The possession of formal authority is a satisfier of the power need for many workers; the possession of informal authority may satisfy other workers.~~

The Achievement Need.   The **achievement need** is the ~~human desire to accomplish a feat or task through the individual's efforts in the face of opposition and challenge~~. McClelland indicates that the achievement need involves an emotional risk in which pleasure is sought with the realization that pain is an immediate threat.[8] The achievement need differs from the competence need in that the competence need is satisfied by the ability to cope with routine situations while the achievement need is fulfilled primarily with the confrontation and mastery of extraordinary situations. Individuals with a desire to blaze new frontiers in a pioneering spirit may be responding to their need for achievement. Highly innovative, creative individuals may be motivated by the desire to do things no one else has done before. The Wall Street financier who states that he "thrives on a crisis" is indicating his desire to confront challenge and overcome it.

Providing the Opportunity for Achievement. Recognizing those individuals who have definite interests in achievement at a specific point in time and providing them with opportunities for fulfillment is another of the more demanding tasks faced by supervisors. The ~~achievement-oriented work~~er often ~~reveals himself by his willingness to assume responsibility~~ and ~~his desire to be innovative~~ and ~~to take risks~~. As each manager discovers this desire on the part of one of his subordinates, he has the opportunity to encourage the worker's initiative and to provide conditions that present a challenge. Managers can sometimes provide the desired challenge through greater delegation of decision-making duties. In other cases, workers are given assignments where high-risk performances are involved. Wherever workers are encouraged to be innovative through the existence of reward structures, achievement is being encouraged.

It is highly important that workers' desires and abilities be compatible with the risk-taking and creativity demands of the jobs they hold. The worker with high-level needs for achievement will thrive on challenge, while a less achievement-oriented worker may feel nothing but anxiety and frustration while working in a high-risk job.

The Need for Hope.   The **need for hope** is the human desire to ~~believe in the possibility that the future will bring conditions or circumstances that will coincide~~

[8]David C. McClelland, "The Business Drive and National Achievement," *Harvard Business Review,* Volume 40, Number 4 (July–August 1962), p. 104.

with the individual's values and expectations better than those now existing. The usual desire is for "things" to be better tomorrow than they are today. Hope is optimism based upon perceived opportunities for improvement or expectations that conditions and circumstances will improve. Without hope of improvement, the psychologically, socially, or economically depressed individual becomes increasingly listless, distressed, and sometimes even violent.

People at work are no different from other humans in their need for hope. They respond with optimism if hope is possible and may even tolerate deplorable conditions for a time if improvement is in view. On the other hand, those who work in less than ideal conditions become either passive or hostile if hope is denied them. The hope-oriented person will seek methods to bring the world more in line with his desires even if only remotely possible.

Encouraging Hope. Hope would, of course, be unnecessary if all conditions were perfect, but perfection is rarely achieved. Because hope is partially an intangible state of mind, managers must first provide an environment where optimism can exist. Workers acquire a spirit of optimism when they experience improvements in areas that have previously been unsatisfactory. While workers may normally be reluctant to accept change, change may be welcomed when existing conditions are intolerable.

When workers have confidence that their superiors are sincerely interested in the workers' personal welfare, they more readily feel that improvement is a real possibility. Workers are prone to believe that their bosses will therefore act in their best interests.

Perceptive managers have discovered that listening agencies such as grievance committees or other appeal boards serve an important role in encouraging hope. Workers often respond to the opportunity to present their feelings and concerns to a fair grievance committee if they know the grievance committee has a sympathetic ear and also the power to act when improvement is possible. The promise of improvement is not enough to continue the desire for hope. Hope will be furthered only if tangible evidence exists to show that previous concerns have sometimes been fulfilled and that resources are available to provide real fulfillment in the future.

The Changing Nature of Human Needs

Some authors, Abraham Maslow among them, have pointed out that while people may have many needs, the urgency of their fulfillment may vary with the state of their previous attainment. In fact, ~~Maslow developed~~ a ~~need hierarch~~y progressing through ~~five need level~~s beginning with ~~physiological need~~s and moving upward through s~~ecurity, lower, esteem,~~ and ~~self-actualization needs~~. The thesis of the hierarchy was that the ~~most basic human~~ urgency is the fulfillment of ~~physiologica~~l (p~~hysical maintenance) need~~s. When these needs are adequately provided for, the human organism turns to desiring the acquisition of security. When this has been acquired to a reasonable degree, the new concern is for social achievement until this has been acquired adequately, and so forth on up the ladder. Of course, each need is not completely exclusive of other needs, but the individual's concentration of interests is seen as variable and changing.[9] This progressive pattern of need fulfillment may be true in the achievement of all types of needs. As satisfaction in one area is obtained, interest moves to another focus.

The effect of progressive need fulfillment is to suggest that while all individuals are need-oriented and their needs have some common bases, not every individual feels the same needs at a given point in time. Individual needs will vary with previous accomplishments, present conditions, and future potentialities.

Recent studies have tended to support the position that needs do, indeed, vary on the basis of what the individual has already experienced, what an individual's responsibilities are, and on other factors. In a Department of Labor study, for example, it was discovered that the composite goal hierarchy for American employees put "interesting work" above all other goals. "Enough information to get the job done" was second in importance (see Figure 7.1 for other rankings).[10] In the composite figures, more than 50 percent of the employees were white-collar personnel (professional, technical, managerial, clerical, and sales workers). Distinct differences in the job expectations of the composite worker and blue-collar workers became evident in the analysis performed by Fein.[11] "Good pay" and "job security" appear to be more important for blue-collar workers than for white-collar employees. On the other hand, "interesting work" and "enough authority" appeared particularly to be of lesser importance to most blue-collar workers than was true of the composite.

In an international study of employees in seven occupational levels performed by Hofstede (including employees from sixteen different countries), clear differences were shown in the goals being sought by the different classifications of

[9]Maslow, *op. cit.*, pp. 80–92.

[10]Neil Q. Herrick, "Who's Unhappy at Work and Why," *Manpower*, U.S. Department of Labor, January 1972, p. 5.

[11]Mitchell Fein, "The Real Needs and Goals of Blue Collar Workers," *The Conference Board Record*, Volume 10, Number 2 (February 1973), pp. 26–33.

FIGURE 7.1   Order of importance of working condition factors for composite worker and blue collar worker

Working condition factor	Composite worker ranking	Blue-collar worker ranking		
		Factory worker	Construction worker	Miscellaneous and truck drivers
The work is interesting	1	7.5	5	3
Receive enough information to get the job done	2	2	4	5
Receive enough help and equipment to get the job done	3	1	6	1.5
Good pay	4	4	1	1.5
Enough authority to do the job	5	11	12	6.5
Friendly and helpful co-workers	6	5	3	4
Work where the results are visible	7	9	11	8
Good level of job security	8	3	2	6.5
Opportunity to develop special abilities	9.5	13	16	9
Job where responsibilities are clearly defined	9.5	6	7	10

Source: Mitchell Fein, "The Real Needs and Goals of Blue Collar Workers," *The Conference Board Record*, Volume 10, Number 2 (February 1973), p. 28.

workers (see Figure 7.2).[12] The professionals in the Hofstede study exhibited urgent needs for self-actualization and esteem (achievement and reputation). Managers had self-actualization, esteem, and social needs. Technicians had a mixture of self-actualization, esteem, social, security, and physiological needs. Clerical workers were most concerned about social needs, and unskilled workers sought the basis of security and physiological needs.

[12]Geert H. Hofstede, "The Color of Collars," *Columbia Journal of World Business,* Volume 7, Number 5 (September–October 1972), p. 78.

FIGURE 7.2   Ratings of goals by various worker groups

Goals ranked in Need Hierarchy	Professionals (research laboratories)	Professionals (branch offices)	Managers	Technicians (branch offices)	Technicians (manufacturing plants)	Clerical workers (branch offices)	Unskilled workers (manufacturing plants)
HIGH:							
Self-actualization and esteem needs:							
challenge	1	2	1	3	3		
training	3	1	2	1			
autonomy	2	3					
up-to-dateness	4	4		4			
use of skills							
MIDDLE:							
Social needs:							
cooperation			3–4			1	
manager			3–4		4	2	
friendly department						3	
efficient department						4	
LOW:							
Security and physiological needs:							
security				2	1		2
earnings					2		3
benefits							4
physical conditions							1

Source: Geert H. Hofstede, "The Color of Collars," *Columbia Journal of World Business*, Volume 7, Number 5 (September 1972), p. 78. Reprinted with permission of the *Columbia Journal of World Business*. Copyright © 1972 by the Trustees of Columbia University in the City of New York.

Obviously, it would be a mistake to conclude that every employee's needs and expectations are identical to those of other employees. Differences appear by occupation, and it should be expected that differences occur within individuals. On the basis of the Hofstede study in particular, a hierarchy seems to appear based upon the organizational level of the employee. Perhaps certain needs are met as the individual climbs the organizational hierarchy, and other needs become more urgent.

The Role of the Manager and Need Fulfillment

The last of the three assumptions at the beginning of this chapter stated that the business organization has a responsibility to provide fulfillment of the reasonable needs of its employees. This fulfillment is accomplished largely through the actions of managers and supervisors as they sense the needs of their subordinates, evaluate the legitimacy of their demands, and provide opportunities for their attainment. Managers face many decisions as they attempt to provide workers with personal fulfillment. Many questions must be answered. How can a supervisor know just what a worker's current needs are? Of a worker's present needs, which are legitimately the responsibility of the manager or the company? How does a supervisor provide the worker with the opportunity for need fulfillment? Answers to the last question already have been attempted in this chapter. Answers to the first two will be considered in the following sections.

Discovering the Current Needs of Workers. It was stated earlier that a worker's needs tend to change. While a worker may seek fulfillment of a certain need today, that same need may be completely satisfied or resolved tomorrow. Even needs that exist over long periods of time may vary in the intensity with which they are expressed. Also, the needs of one worker may not be indicative of the needs of other workers. As a result, the supervisor must individually (and continually) analyze the needs and expectations of each individual worker to determine what that worker currently needs and desires.

The perceptive supervisor looks for all available clues to a worker's needs. Observation of a worker's interest and response patterns may reveal the current interests of each worker. Workers have a way of frequently voicing their dissatisfactions, but sometimes they reveal only the symptoms of their needs and not the actual needs themselves. Astute managers listen to discern both what their subordinates are saying and what they are not saying.

Straightforward conversations between superiors and their subordinates sometimes will reveal the needs and desires of the subordinates. In other cases, non-
directed interviewing (discussed in Chapter 17) may be necessary to uncover the
real needs of workers. Some of the more innovative companies are asking workers
to put their goals and interests down in writing. In some cases, workers are being
asked to rate items from a list of job factors and work conditions as a means of
discovering worker interests. In other cases, workers are given open-ended invi-
tations to express their interests, goals, and ambitions. Regardless of the techniques chosen to identify workers' needs, the investigation must be a continuing
one based upon the concept of changing expectations over a period of time.

Whatever techniques are used, a supervisor's empathy for each of his subordinates goes far in helping to discover the subordinate's needs. The more the supervisor can project himself into the shoes of each of his subordinates, the more he
will be able to understand and help them. The challenge of discerning workers'
needs and interests is a demanding and rewarding process.

Determining Management's Responsibilities.   Managers are frequently faced
with the problem of deciding just how far they can go in providing need fulfillment for individual subordinates. Unfortunately, there is no clear-cut formula for
determining the extent of company-management involvement. A part of the
consideration of managerial responsibility toward need fulfillment is of necessity
practical; the other aspect to be considered is a philosophical one.

A practical consideration in deciding how far to go in meeting workers' needs
involves the determination of the costs of need fulfillment in relation to the benefits that will be received. Most business organizations possess limited resources.
Before workers' needs can be met, managers must assess the cost (in money, in
human effort, in time, etc.) and must evaluate the organization's ability to withstand the cost. Then the cost must be weighed against the benefits the company
will receive.

The effects on organizational matters and worker behavior must also be considered as a practical aspect of need fulfillment. Management needs answers to
questions such as these:

1. How will worker performance be affected by need satisfaction opportunities?
2. How will other workers react toward the need attainment of their fellow
workers?
3. Will authority relationships be enhanced or hindered by need fulfillment?

Managers also must come to grips with the philosophical side of need fulfillment for workers. An answer must be found to the question of the moral or

human responsibility the company and its managers bear for employees. Today's managers seem to vary widely in attitudes toward this issue. Managers in some organizations project a desire to fulfill as many needs as is physically possible; other managers feel an obligation to provide for only the most elementary expectations. The more typical position appears to lie somewhere in the middle.

Summary

Individuals have needs. Individuals who are a part of the work force take their needs and wants with them to work. Workers expect their employing organization to provide some level of need fulfillment. Organizations normally shoulder the responsibility for meeting the legitimate expectations of their employees. Perceptive managers look for clues that may reveal an individual worker's goals and desires and seek ways to provide fulfillment of these needs. The usual response from the worker who receives opportunities for need fulfillment is a positive and appreciative reaction.

Questions to consider after reading Chapter 7

1.   To what extent are companies and supervisors responsible for the fulfillment of each of the workers' needs?

2.   In considering each of the needs listed in this chapter, are there any legitimate reasons for management to avoid trying to fulfill these needs?

3.   What risks, if any, are involved in encouraging workers to affiliate with each other?

4.   What additional goals does the acquisition of power help to achieve besides dominance and control over objects and people? Which goal achievements does the possession of power seem to hinder?

5.   Can you think of real situations that support the statement that an individual's needs change over a period of time?

6.   Does it appear to be true that what one person needs and expects from his work is not necessarily the same as what another worker needs and expects? Support your answer.

7.   What additional ways do managers have for fulfilling the needs of workers?

The following cases at the back of the book contain problems related to Chapter 7:

> Mark Williams
> Stanley Lowell

H. Gerald Pretzler

Edith Capp and Janet Turner

Bentley Cantrell

Billy Snyder

Kurt Browning

Susan Swanson

Bill Caden

Richard Jameson

Walt Gladberry

Abigail Spiegal and Trudy Pennington

Additional readings

Centers, Richard, and Daphne E. Bugenthal, "Intrinsic and Extrensic Job Motivations among Different Aspects of the Working Population," *Journal of Applied Psychology*, Volume 50, Number 3 (June 1966), pp. 193–197.

Chung, Kae H., "A Markow Chain Model of Human Needs: An Extension of Maslow's Need Theory," *The Academy of Management Journal*, Volume 12, Number 1 (July 1969), pp. 223–234.

Ginzberg, Eli, *The Development of Human Resources*, New York: McGraw-Hill Book Company, 1966, pp. 22–43.

Hall, Douglas T., and Khalil E. Nougaim, "An Examination of Maslow's Need Hierarchy in an Organizational Setting, *Administrative Science Quarterly*, Volume 3, Number 1 (1968), pp. 12–35.

Miller, Neal E., "Learnable Drives and Rewards," in S. S. Stephens, editor, *Handbook of Experimental Psychology*, New York: John Wiley & Sons, Inc., 1951, pp. 435–472.

Ronan, W. W., "Relative Importance of Job Characteristics," *Journal of Applied Psychology*, Volume 54, Number 2 (April 1970), pp. 192–200.

Schachter, Stanley, *The Psychology of Affiliation*, Stanford, California: Stanford University Press, 1959.

Steiner, Gary A., editor, *The Creative Organization*, Chicago: University of Chicago Press, 1965.

Sutermeister, Robert A., "Employee Performance and Employee Need Satisfaction— Which Comes First?" *California Management Review*, Volume 13, Number 4 (Summer 1971), pp. 43–47.

Chapter 8

What the Manager Expects from His Work

A case to consider before reading chapter 8

BUDDY MIRRA—PERSONNEL MANAGER IN A TIGHT SPOT

Buddy Mirra was hired about eighteen months ago by Frank Kennedy, owner and president of Kennedy Oil Company, to become the organization's new personnel manager. Kennedy hired Buddy primarily to be a recruiter. Mr. Kennedy believes that the success of his company in the future is dependent upon how well it entices college graduates with the appropriate technical qualifications to affiliate themselves with the company. In particular, Mr. Kennedy feels that the organization needs engineers and chemists. Mirra was selected for his job because he was college recruiter for another large industrial corporation. Buddy, however, has experienced very little success in his new position, and he has begun to feel that his job is somewhat in jeopardy.

To understand Mirra's dilemma, it is necessary to understand more about Frank Kennedy and the background of Kennedy Oil. Mr. Kennedy entered the oil-drilling business at the age of eighteen in 1930. He started as a roughneck on a rig owned by Harvey Trussel, who had been in the business since the days when oil was first produced in profitable quantities. After several years of working as a driller, Mr. Kennedy won the drilling rig from Mr. Trussel in a game of poker. From that time forward, Mr. Kennedy has worked long hours to build his company into one of the best independent oilfield service companies in the business. He has experienced a large amount of success.

Through the years, Mr. Kennedy has relied upon the skills and abilities of people who have risen through the ranks to fill management positions. He realizes now, however, that if he is to attain his ambition of making his company the biggest and best one around, he must hire people for managerial positions who are already skilled executives and trained technicians. As a result, he hired

Buddy and commissioned him to go out and bring in well-qualified college graduates to provide the new blood he feels is necessary.

Buddy has encountered ~~three problem~~s in particular in his effort to live up to Mr. Kennedy's expectations. ~~First~~, the ~~present employee~~s are ~~demanding~~ that ~~they be given~~ the ~~new jobs~~ that are opening up as the company's operations are ~~expanded~~. The ~~existing~~ employees feel that their ~~experience~~ and ~~tenure qualify them~~ for the new positions, and any ~~newcomers~~ (whether they are college graduates or unskilled laborers) ~~should start~~ at the ~~bottom~~ and work their way up. In situations ~~where outsiders have been hired~~ and placed in important ~~positi~~ons in the past few months, the ~~oldtimer~~s have been ~~rebellious~~ and ~~hostile~~ toward them and toward Mirra.

~~Second~~, while Mr. Kennedy wants competent, technically qualified college graduates to be hired, ~~he too~~ believes they ~~should begin~~ their ~~careers~~ with the company by ~~serving as roughne~~cks and in other similar capacities for several months or years before they are given additional responsibility. This ~~unglamorous~~ prospect for the immediate future has kept most of the good employment prospects from seriously considering employment with Kennedy.

~~Third~~, Kennedy Oil has always ~~prided itself on being a family company~~. When the ~~son~~ or ~~daughter~~ of a ~~Kennedy~~ employee has reached the ~~age~~ of employment, Kennedy Oil has always ~~attempted~~ to provide an employment opportunity for them. This has been an attractive fringe benefit for most workers. The ~~new emphasis~~ of ~~hiring~~ technically ~~qualified~~ personnel runs counter to ~~this older policy~~. Many of the children of present employees are not technically trained to meet the new specifications and requirements. The offspring of current senior employees are disappointed when they are refused jobs because of their lack of qualifications, and their relatives who are already Kennedy employees have become angry at Mirra's unwillingness to hire employees' descendants.

Buddy Mirra wants to do his job well, but he appears to be facing great obstacles.

Questions about the Buddy Mirra case

1. What personal goals, expectations, and desires does Buddy Mirra have for his job? How well are these being fulfilled?

2. What personal goals has Frank Kennedy formulated for himself and his company?

3.   What are the pressures Buddy Mirra is feeling as he attempts to do his job? What are the underlying causes of these pressures?

4.   What kind of support and assistance should Mirra be receiving from Mr. Kennedy? from existing company employees? from other individuals? How much support is he now receiving from each of these?

5.   What steps could Buddy Mirra take to enlist support and assistance from these individuals and groups? In other words, what do you suggest that he do to get their cooperation and help?

6.   What can be done to resolve the differences in opinions and expectations at Kennedy Oil?

7.   Buddy Mirra as an individual is the center of much criticism when in reality he is only attempting to implement the new policies of Kennedy Oil. Why is he the focus of criticism?

8.   What actions should Buddy Mirra have taken when he first went to work for Kennedy?

In the previous chapter, the needs and expectations of individuals in general were identified and means to fulfill them were illustrated. The point was made that no two individuals have identical needs at a specific point in time. One factor in particular that may influence the level of needs and expectations of workers is the type of organizational responsibility the worker possesses. More precisely, a distinguishing factor between workers' expectations may be whether or not an individual works in a managerial or a nonmanagerial capacity.

For purposes of distinguishing between managers and nonmanagers, managers are those individuals in organizations who are responsible for utilizing and coordinating available resources to accomplish organizational objectives. Specifically, managers are responsible for achieving organizational goals through people. The manager is held accountable for his own performance as well as the performance of those who are his subordinates. He has a responsibility to see that the behavior of his subordinates is supportive of the organization rather than detrimental to it. The nonmanager, on the other hand, is accountable to his superior only for his own actions and normally is not expected to coordinate and control the actions of others.

Managers and nonmanagers, of course, have many common needs and expectations that the work environment is expected to fulfill. Since both are human beings, each of the typical human needs may require attention at some point in the individual's work career. Each of the assumptions made in the previous chapter would appear to be especially true for managers. Individuals who are managers work with the expectation of need fulfillment. Choices of jobs are based on the ability of the work situation to fulfill expectations and needs. (Perhaps this is even more true for managers than it is for other workers because job choices often are more abundant for those at managerial levels.) Organizations bear the same responsibilities for fulfillment of the needs of managers as they bear for other workers.

It has been pointed out that if there is any difference between the needs of managers and nonmanagers, the difference is in the existing level of urgency. For example, McClelland, in his studies of the achievement need, has concluded that ~~managers tend to exhibit a greater degree of the need for achievement than do those who are nonmanagers.~~[1] Herzberg, Mausner, and Snyderman have said that individuals who successfully assume the responsibilities of managership may be rewarded through recognition, advancement, achievement, and other kinds of more advanced fulfillment.[2] One of the studies in the previous chapter showed managers to be more concerned about self-actualization, esteem, and social needs than were clerical and unskilled workers.[3] Statements such as these suggest that individuals who are willing to assume the risks of being managers do so with the expectation of accomplishing personal need fulfillment. As some needs are fulfilled, other needs come to the forefront. The manager has opportunities to satisfy needs for achievement, recognition, power, hope (and others) in ways not always possible for nonmanagers.

If the manager has opportunities unavailable to the nonmanager, he also has burdens and pressures that differ significantly from those placed upon the nonmanager. The very nature of the manager's role brings inherent pressures. Scott[4] has said that every manager lives with pressures to produce successfully, to adapt to the demands of change, to live with great uncertainties in a hostile environment, to conform to the demands of others, to perform conflicting roles, and sometimes to survive in a socially ostracized position. Managers are expected to be people of action who can successfully make decisions in the face of sometimes inadequate

[1]David C. McClelland, "The Business Drive and National Achievement," *Harvard Business Review*, Volume 40, Number 4 (July–August 1962), p. 103.

[2]Frederick Herzberg, Bernard Mausner, and Barbara Snyderman, *The Motivation To Work*, Second Edition, New York: John Wiley & Sons, Inc., 1959, p. 80.

[3]Geert H. Hofstede, "The Color of Collars," *Columbia Journal of World Business*, Volume 7, Number 5 (September–October 1972), p. 78.

[4]William G. Scott, *Organization Theory: A Behavioral Analysis for Management*, Homewood, Illinois: Richard D. Irwin, Inc., 1967, pp. 369–371.

information, who can be appropriately rigid or appropriately adaptive when necessary, who can be cognizant of the feelings of others while subordinating their own feelings. In other words, the manager is expected to be a sort of super-person who can "do all, know all, and withstand all" whenever called upon. The heavy demands under which many managers work shape their actions and expectations.

A Pressure Viewpoint of Management

If there are any misgivings concerning the pressures under which managers exist and act, a look at pressure forces that demand attention in the performance of the most simple as well as the more complex management tasks will quickly put those doubts to rest. A look at almost any managerial action taken will reveal that the individual manager has to consult with the demands of a number of pressure sources before acting.

Suppose, for example, that John Q. Smith, who is a production foreman in a manufacturing concern, has been authorized to find a qualified applicant to fill a job opening. On the surface such action might appear to be a simple one—but in reality, the decision often is complex. Various groups and pressure sources may demand that Foreman Smith take different factors into consideration. Sometimes the special considerations are complementary, but many times the demands are contradictory. In the decision to choose the right employee from the applicants available, John Smith may receive separate guidelines from at least eight different sources. The company owners, the union, the government, the formal organization structure, the informal organization, competitive forces, social customs, and the personal values of the supervisor himself may contribute demands or expectations in the decision-making process.

To illustrate, the ownership of the organization, usually manifested by the policies of the board of directors, may encourage John to look for an applicant who will work efficiently at the least possible cost. The union may insist that the new employee should be a member in good standing within its ranks, or at least he should be capable and willing to join the union when hired. The government will encourage the choice of an individual on an equal opportunity basis. In some cases, the government may encourage or demand the hiring of an individual from a "minority" group (through programs such as the Manpower Development and Training Act, the Philadelphia Plan, etc.).

The formal structure of John's company (as interpreted for John by his superior) will suggest that an employee be hired who will abide by the rules and regulations of the organization and who will contribute constructively to the organization. The members of the informal organization (work group) may make it clear that they expect John to hire someone who will conform to their behavior norms and will be nonthreatening to their group values. The pressures from competition will influence the supply of applicants available and may even suggest traits the individual must possess if competition is to be outdistanced in performance.

Social customs and traditions will suggest to John that the status quo be preserved in the hiring decision. If the position now open has traditionally been filled by a male worker of southern European descent (for example), any departure from previous hiring patterns will be resisted by whatever social pressures may be available. In addition, John will have his own values of what an employee should be in terms of ability, integrity, motivation to work, and other characteristics.

The listed pressures are only some of the possible sources and demands any supervisor may face in making decisions. Figure 8.1 restates the demands list above and suggests other possible expectations from some of the pressure sources. While the pressures mentioned are related to only one area of managerial decision making, the concept may be applied to all supervisory actions. *Almost every act of a supervisor will receive numerous outside pressures and directives.*

Managerial Action in the Face of Pressure

On several occasions this author has asked groups of managers and students of management to identify decisions made by managers acting strictly on the individual manager's sole judgment and desires. Few decision actions are normally identifiable. The question next arises, How do managers perform their duties with so many pressures pushing and pulling in different directions?

Perhaps this can best be answered by saying that managers usually find it necessary to determine the pressure sources, evaluate the legitimacy of their demands, determine the priorities of each decision-making situation, and evaluate the capability of available alternatives to meet the needs of the situation. Many managers formally or informally find the use of the decision matrix to be a helpful technique in coping with the many variables of decision making.

The decision matrix involves the performance of the following steps. The usual procedure is for the manager to list the pressures and influences he feels have a bearing upon a decision he must make (Step 1 in Figure 8.2). The manager then decides if the pressure sources have something to contribute to the necessary decision or if the factor deserves attention. Those pressures deserving further attention are then surveyed for guidelines they may suggest and demands they may impose (Step 2). Following the identifications of the various guidelines, the relative importance of the factors (pressures) is determined and a weighted score is established that shows the projected values of each component as a total part of a possible score (Step 3). The weighted potential score and each of its components are established by the decision-maker or by a team of evaluators using whatever criteria are available to them. Sometimes the relative weightings of each factor are determined through a scientific evaluation by a team concentrating on multiple considerations. In other cases the category values are a result of a simple, arbitrary decision on the part of the manager. The process of value determination can be as complex or as simple as is desired.

As soon as relative weightings have been established for all of the pressure factors, the evaluation (Step 4) is performed to determine which of the alternatives has the best position in comparison with other available alternatives. In the hiring situation mentioned earlier as an illustration, the alternatives will vary to fit needs (ways to utilize available resources, choices of plant locations, individuals deserving promotions, etc.). Sometimes the evaluation reveals that one of the alternatives would result in some effect that would immediately prohibit further consideration of the alternative as an acceptable source of action. In Figure 8.2 this fact is illustrated in Alternative A, which is a decision that would result in violation of a government regulation. This result would consequently remove this alternative from consideration as a reasonable choice.

All other things being equal, the alternative with the highest total score (Step 5) would be the choice most satisfactory to the demands and pressures of all factors considered. Not every managerial decision goes through this formalized evaluation process, but most multifactor managerial decisions made under pressure require a similar procedure.

Meeting the Needs and Expectations of Managers

Managers are human beings with needs and desires that seek fulfillment. Some of the manager's needs are different from those of nonmanagers. Because of their unique organization roles, they are recipients of pressure from many sources and need help and assistance in meeting the demands of their roles. How can the

FIGURE 8.1   Pressure sources and their guidelines concerning which individual John Q. Smith should hire as a new employee

PRESSURE SOURCE	DEMANDS AND EXPECTATIONS
Company ownership	Wants a productive performer Wants an economical, efficient worker
Union	May demand that previously laid off workers be rehired before new employees are hired Prefers that a member in good standing be hired before nonunion personnel are considered Any applicant considered should be capable and willing to affiliate with the union
Government	Hiring must be done without preference being shown to any individual on the basis of race, religion, sex, or other factors covered by civil rights legislation In some cases preferential treatment may be encouraged for the hiring of a worker from a special minority group Veterans may be considered to have the right to return to jobs held prior to entering the service Techniques for selection and placement of the worker must be fair and unbiased

PRESSURE SOURCE	DEMANDS AND EXPECTATIONS
Formal organization structure (as interpreted by the supervisor's own boss)	Employee hired should be qualified and willing to perform constructively

Candidate chosen should be capable of developing as a loyal, dedicated employee

Potential to live by the rules and regulations of the organization should be considered in screening applicants |
| **Informal organization** | Preferably, the employee hired should possess goals, values, and attitudes consistent with those possessed by members in good standing within the existing informal organization

Potential nonconformists to group values and "rate-busters" should be rejected |
| **Competitive forces** | Capable, qualified personnel may be in limited supply where competition for needed skills is high

Monetary cost factors may be "bid up" over competitive wages and salaries |
| **Social customs and traditions** | Encourage the continuation of hiring patterns consistent with generally acceptable social values

May suggest that certain jobs be reserved for members of a specific sex, ethnic background, age, etc.

May encourage selected changes if they are in keeping with the "social responsibility" of the organization |
| **Personal values of the decision-maker** | May have conceptualization of the traits actually needed to perform the job in question in terms of skills, training, knowledge, and other attributes

May be influenced by personal biases such as attitudes toward grooming, courtesy, or other personal attributes of the applicants |

FIGURE 8.2   Example of the use of the ~~decision matrix~~ in decision-making under pressure

STEP 1 Pressure source	STEP 2 Guidelines from that source	STEP 3 Weighted value assigned to each pressure*	STEP 4 Scores assigned to each alternative		
			Alternative A	Alternative B	Alternative C
Company ownership	See Figure 8.1 for illustrations of guidelines on a possible decision	30	25	30	20
Union	"	50	20	30	30
Government	"	50	Prohibitive**	50	50
Formal organization	"	30	25	25	20
Informal organization	"	20	25	25	10
Competitive factors	"	20	20	20	20
Social customs and traditions	"	30	30	25	30
Personal values of the decision-maker	"	20	15	15	10
Total points scored (Step 5)			Prohibitive**	220***	190

*The weighted scores possible are determined by the decision-maker(s) in advance of the evaluation of possible alternatives.
**Prohibitive because the choice of this alternative would violate a government regulation.
***Alternative B has received the most points and would appear to be the best choice.

needs of managers be met, and what individuals can help to meet them? The sources of need fulfillment for the manager seem to lie in his superiors, his colleagues and fellow workers, his subordinates, staff personnel working on his behalf, and certain members of the general public. Some of the fulfillment roles of each of these groups are discussed next.

Superiors as Sources of Need Fulfillment.   In terms of the personal needs and expectations of supervisory personnel, the superiors of the supervisors ordinarily hold the keys to their fulfillment and attainment. Superiors must be sensitive to the current needs of managers working under their jurisdiction and should seek to provide avenues of attainment whenever possible. The manager deserves rewards, recognition, praise, the feeling of competency and achievement, the opportunity for hope, and the fulfillment of other needs as they make themselves felt. Like other individuals, the manager is entitled to treatment with dignity and respect. Because managers seem especially interested in the satisfaction of psychological needs, including those of achievement, recognition, power, hope, and self-fulfillment, those who manage managers need to be especially alert to opportunities whereby these needs can be provided for.

Because managers are expected to perform and to achieve under pressure, they also have needs for support and assistance from their superiors in ways that will enhance their job responsibility performance. It is important that every supervisor should know what his superior expects of him. Training in how to perform to meet expectations is also vital. Guidance in learning organizational decision-making criteria is helpful. Once decisions are made, the support of superiors is invaluable. Without this support, the manager's role will be extremely difficult to perform.

The manager is aided by feedback from his superior on the superior's assessment of his performance. Also helpful is the assistance superiors can give concerning the identification of pressure sources and the determination of a priority of demands from the pressure sources. Information on government expectations, union contract specifications, and any other useful communication from his superior is normally welcomed by the operating manager. The superior can be of inestimable assistance to his subordinate manager if he is a good practitioner of the behavior he expects of his subordinates. He can show subordinates much through his own examples of sound action.

Peers as Sources of Need Fulfillment.   One of the most underestimated sources of assistance and support managers have is the help that can be gained through the mutual interaction and sustenance of peer groups—other managers with similar amounts of authority and responsibility. Through mutual support and cooperation, the personal needs for greater security, affiliation, competence, and achievement are especially fortified by managers who sustain each other. One of the most obvious means of assistance and satisfaction lies in the fulfillment of affiliation needs by the manager's peers. Affiliation is most likely to occur between individuals with common interests and common values. Managers working at similar levels with related responsibilities share much in common. As a result, they can support and relate to each other in beneficial and socially rewarding ways.

Mentioned earlier in this chapter was the fact that many managers suffer pressures of aloneness and ostracism from subordinates (and sometimes from superiors) because their actions are not understood or empathized with. As a result, the understanding and acceptance received from colleagues becomes extremely valuable to the typical manager—and the mutual acceptance is given because of the mutual interests and problems peer-level managers share.

The better-trained, more knowledgeable managers can help the lesser-prepared ones; the more-experienced can be of assistance to the newer-managers; the discouraged managers can be given a brighter outlook by the optimistic supervisors; and so the list of peer interaction benefits goes.

Assistance by Subordinates in Meeting a Manager's Needs.   Frequently, the manager seems to look to subordinates only in a limited way for the satisfaction of personal needs. Subordinates usually are considered dependent upon their bosses rather than personally helpful to them. Some managers, for example, have little desire to relate to their subordinates in a socially affiliated way. In fact, some insist upon maintaining a social distance between themselves and those they supervise. Subordinates by their mere existence, however, serve to make possible the fulfillment of the power need as the manager controls and regulates the activities of his subordinates.

The traditional positions of management thought have always suggested that managers, because of their formal authority, are entitled to obedience and adherence to demands they make of their subordinates. Behavioral positions on manager-subordinate relationships, however, suggest that managers must earn the respect and obedience of subordinates before they can expect their workers to follow them. Regardless of the position on authority accepted, it is undeniable that managers must get performance from people if goals and objectives for which managers are accountable are to be achieved. As a result, cooperation and positive effort are contributions that managers greatly desire from their subordinates.

In addition, fulfillment of the role of the manager is facilitated when subordinates are willing and capable of communicating upward the facts and feelings they have at their command. Managerial decisions and actions will be greatly improved by upward communication, and manpower management will be handled more satisfactorily. Subordinates can have a significant impact upon the success and accomplishments of their superior through their efforts to support their superior.

Staff Specialists as a Means of Managerial Support.   Staff specialists and individuals who serve in technically specialized positions make their greatest contributions toward the facilitation of job performance through the services they provide to the manager. They make the manager's job more simplified and manageable. Individuals filling these positions usually aid the manager by (1) providing expertise and knowledge in some area where the manager needs special assistance (such as in research, statistical analysis, manpower training, etc.) or (2) performing tasks the manager lacks the time or facilities to perform. Staff specialists are particularly helpful to managers in the collection and provision of pertinent information upon which decisions can be based. The benefits that can accrue to managers through the proper utilization of staff assistance can be extremely important, yet these are overlooked by many managers.

It should be noted that not all managers view staff specialists as a means of support and assistance. Some managers are prone to consider staff personnel as threats to their own authority. Staff experts who serve as auditors, critics, or policemen are not always thought of as helpers by line personnel. Many jurisdictional problems may develop if the role of staff personnel is ill-defined or improperly executed.

Other Sources of Managerial Fulfillment.   It is possible that any public with which a manager has contact may be a source of reward and fulfillment. If a manager, as an illustration, has frequent contact with the customers his organization serves, he may develop satisfaction as he helps the customer find products suited to the customer's need. Social affiliations may also develop.

One of the primary sources of satisfaction, of course, is the family and friends of the manager. While these satisfactions are primarily off-the-job fulfillments, they have a significant influence on the level of personal fulfillment the manager achieves. All of the personal needs listed in Chapter 7 may be attended to in part by off-the-job contacts. Family and friends both provide gratification and share in absorbing problems and difficulties. There is an old story that the frustrated businessman goes home and fusses at his wife who in turn spanks their child; the child then whips the family dog, who turns around and subdues the family cat. Unhappiness is shared with family and friends, but happiness may be provided by them also. The potential sources of fulfillment are, indeed, as numerous as the contacts a manager may have.

Summary

The manager is a human being, like other workers, and has personal needs requiring fulfillment just like anyone else. In addition, a manager is exposed to heavy influences and pressures as a result of the responsibilities of his job. The manager is expected to live with pressures to produce, pressures to adapt to the demands for change, pressures to make decisions in the face of uncertainty in a hostile environment, pressures to conform to the demands of others, pressures to perform seemingly conflicting roles, and sometimes even pressures of social ostracism.

The needs and expectations of managers can, however, be met if the manager receives the proper support and cooperation from his superiors, colleagues, subordinates, staff assistants and technical specialists, family and friends, and others with whom he has contact.

Questions to consider after reading Chapter 8

1. Investigate the statement that managers' needs are often higher-level needs (on the need hierarchy) than are the needs of nonmanagers.

2. What additional sources of pressure besides those mentioned in the chapter do managers face?

3. What kinds of managerial decisions (if any) are made by managers acting strictly on their own initiative without pressures from external sources?

4. In the chapter, pressure sources were suggested for a recruiting and hiring decision. If a manager is facing a decision setting up a wage and salary structure, what would these same groups suggest to him?

5. How much social distance (if any) should a manager keep between himself and his subordinates?

6. If a manager is not getting the support he needs from his superiors, what can he do to get their help? How can he go about getting the needed support of colleagues, subordinates, staff personnel, and other individuals?

7. What are some typical ways in which superiors fail to support their subordinate managers properly?

8. In the face of all the pressures, why do managers keep on managing?

The following cases at the back of the book contain problems related to Chapter 8:

> Ben Stockton
>
> Earl Fornette
>
> Bentley Cantrell

Kurt Browning

Grace Lanham

Bill Caden

Abigail Spiegal and Trudy Pennington

Alan Purdy

Additional readings

Berlew, David E., and Douglas T. Hall, "The Socialization of Managers: Effects of Expectations on Performance," *Administrative Science Quarterly,* Volume 11, Number 1 (September 1966), pp. 207–223.

Bursk, Edward, editor, *Challenge to Leadership: Managing in a Changing World,* New York: The Free Press, 1973.

Curcuru, Edward H., and James H. Healey, "The Multiple Roles of the Manager," *Business Horizons,* Volume 15, Number 4 (August 1972), pp. 15–24.

Elbing, Alvar O., "The Value Issue of Business: The Responsibility of the Business-man," *The Academy of Management Journal,* Volume 13, Number 1 (March 1970), pp. 79–89.

Filley, Alan C., and Robert J. House, "Management and the Future," *Business Horizons,* Volume 13, Number 2 (April 1970), p. 7ff.

Mayer, Raymond R., "Management's Social Responsibility: Profit Maximization," *Advanced Management Journal,* Volume 35, Number 1 (January 1970), pp. 53–60.

Porter, Lyman W., "Job Attitudes in Management, Perceived Deficiencies in Need Fulfillment as a Function of Job Level," *Journal of Applied Psychology,* Volume 46, Number 6 (1962), pp. 375–384.

Richman, Barry, "New Paths to Social Responsibility," *California Management Review,* Volume 15, Number 3 (Spring 1973), pp. 20–36.

Steiner, George A., "Should Business Adopt the Social Audit?" *Conference Board Record,* Volume 7, Number 9 (September 1970), pp. 41–45.

———, "Social Policies for Business," *California Management Review,* Volume 15, Number 2 (Winter 1972), pp. 17–24.

SECTION III

MANAGERIAL RESPONSIBILITIES AND CHALLENGES

It is, of course, impossible to predict every managerial responsibility and to discuss methods and techniques for fulfilling all obligations, but it is possible to identify several major managerial duties and to discuss opportunities and problems that each may involve. The purpose of Section III, therefore, is to analyze and discuss some important responsibilities of those who manage people at work. The concepts included in this section are based upon the foundations of the previous two sections.

Specifically, it is assumed in this section that those who serve as managers must have leadership abilities and must be capable of working with and through others to accomplish organizational objectives. There are, of course, several techniques available for fulfilling the leadership role, but the one approach with the greatest promise is the contingency (adaptive) approach (see Chapter 9). Managers also have responsibilities for seeing that the motives an employee has are channeled toward goals that will be rewarding for the individual and productive for the organization. Positive incentives and reinforcements are more pleasant to work with, but negative motivational techniques sometimes are necessary (see Chapter 10). Money and morale each has an impact upon worker behavior in its own unique way (Chapter 11).

No organization can be successful without the proper amount and type of communication between organizational members. Chapter 12 discusses the role of communication, the types of communication needed in organizations, managerial responsibilities toward communication, problems people have in communicating, and ways to improve people-to-people interchanges.

Because organizations and the people in them are goal-oriented, managers have a responsibility for seeing that performance is directed toward achieving objectives effectively and efficiently. Chapter 13 discusses the prerequisites for satisfactorily achieving goals and management's role in the pursuit of goals. Chapter 14 presents a plan of discipline whereby the efforts of organization members can be encouraged to be constructive rather than destructive toward the achievement of objectives.

Perfect performance from employees is a practical impossibility. Most employees, however, are capable of performing so that their behavior is useful and beneficial to all concerned. Occasionally, individuals behave in ways that create problems for themselves, their fellow workers, and their employer. Chapter 15 considers the causes of worker problems, the organizational impact, and managerial responsibilities toward the problem workers. Chapter 16 analyzes three personnel problems that are of increasing importance—the problem of the alcoholic worker, the drug abuser, and the organizational thief. Chapter 17 discusses counseling responsibilities and techniques that may be useful in discovering and preventing problems as well as in providing for healthy employees and productive work environments.

Interpersonal conflict frequently arises within organizations and may handicap performance. Chapter 18 presents a philosophy toward conflict and some managerial actions that may succeed in transforming conflict from a threatening event into a productive encounter. Chapter 19 confronts the issue of getting people to work together effectively and cooperatively (an integrative effort that is becoming increasingly important).

New ideas, new technological developments, social and environmental influences, and a number of additional factors call upon organizations and the people within them to make changes and adjustments. Employee behavior is often difficult to modify. Resistance to change frequently becomes a severe problem. Chapter 20 presents several concepts of resistance to change and discusses ways whereby change can be implemented more successfully. Chapter 21 introduces concepts of training and organizational development, which are also oriented toward achieving change in individual and group behavior.

Chapters 9 through 21 treat a number of the more important managerial responsibilities and provide guidelines for the student of management and the practicing manager to consider.

Chapter 9

The Role of
Leadership in the
Organization

A case to consider before reading chapter 9

TED GUNDERSON—THE CONSTRUCTION SUPERVISOR

Ted Gunderson is a ~~general supervisor~~ for a large custom house-building concern. The company he works for is known for its quality work; most of the homes it builds are large, expensive, and uniquely designed. It is Ted's job to oversee the construction of five or six houses being built at the same time. He moves from one building site to another during each work day checking on progress. A ~~foreman~~ is in ~~charge of each house;~~ the foreman ~~spends all of his time at one site~~ and ~~works directly with~~ the ~~crew~~ there. The foreman of each job reports directly to Ted. Ted, in turn, is accountable to the owner-manager of the company.

Ted came up through the ranks to get to his present job. He started work as a carpenter's helper, worked for several years as a carpenter, spent three years as a foreman, and was recently promoted to the job of general supervisor.

Ted describes his job in the following manner.

As I view my job, I think my primary duty is to see that each foreman has the materials, equipment, and personnel needed to do his job. The foreman and I consult together on what is reasonable in terms of work schedules. The rest of the responsibility is completely in the hands of the foreman. He runs the whole construction job. He has a completely free hand to do things as he wishes. I try to interfere as little as possible. ~~That's the way I preferred things when I was a foreman, and that's the way that seems best to~~ me.

~~Ralph Cannister~~, one of the foremen working under Gunderson, ~~has been with the company as long as he has.~~ He has been a ~~foreman for about five years~~

himself. **These are his comments concerning Gunderson's supervisory abilities and actions.**

~~Ted is an excellent boss to work~~ for. He lets you run the show completely on your own. He doesn't bug you all the time like some bosses I've had in the past. He just puts you in charge of a crew and tells you to get the job done. That suits me fine.

Rudy Grantham, another of the foremen working under Gunderson, was ~~recently promoted to the job of foreman~~ to fill the vacancy Gunderson himself left. Grantham came up through the ranks like Gunderson. He has a different reaction toward the supervisory skills of Gunderson.

~~Frankly, I don't think too much~~ of Mr. Gunderson. He comes out on the construction site for a few minutes, and then he's gone and I don't see him for the rest of the day. Some days he doesn't come out at all. ~~I don't think he's interested in me~~. He's never available when I need him. I'm getting along all right with the boys working for me, but ~~I am having some trouble coordinating all of the work~~ and in ~~doing the paperwork. I've never had to do some of these things before~~. Mr. Gunderson just is no help to me personally.

Questions about the Ted Gunderson case

1. What leadership style is Ted Gunderson using? *free rein*

2. Why does this style seem to be working with Ralph Cannister? *his experience*

3. Why does this style seem to be unsatisfactory for Rudy Grantham? *inexperience*

4. How does a supervisor discover the type of leadership and supervision needed by each subordinate? *experience, desire of subs. knowledge — motivation goals*

5. What is deceptive about a supervisor giving his subordinates the same kind of leadership that he himself likes to receive?

Gunderson is not adaptive

In Biblical days, the children of Israel needed someone to guide them out of their bondage, and Moses stepped forward to lead them in their journey to the promised land. In the Great Depression the American people needed someone to restore their confidence and to provide a method of combatting the economic crisis they were facing, and Franklin D. Roosevelt became a leader to accomplish these tasks. In World War II, the British people were suffering severe losses and appeared to be unsuccessfully combatting their foes when Winston Churchill came to the forefront and guided the British efforts to victory. In a like manner, modern-day leaders have taken their places in guiding the thoughts and efforts of people to the achievement of common goals.

People working together in business organizations also have a need for ~~leaders—individuals who will be instrumental in guiding the efforts of groups of workers to the achievement of goals and objectives~~. The objectives may not be as far-reaching as those mentioned above, and the actions of the leaders may not be so dramatic, but the successful performance of the leadership role is essential to the survival of the business enterprise. Goods and services have to be provided, products and customers need to be united, and worker efforts require integration and coordination. The leader guides the actions of others in accomplishing these tasks.

There is by no means a universal concept of the role of the leader in an organization. Bowers and Seashore have said simply that "leadership is organizationally useful behavior by one member of an organizational family toward another member or members of that same organizational family."[1] This definition could apply to leaders serving in formal capacities or informal roles. In the eyes of others, accomplishing the leadership function is a matter of pushing or prodding people until they do what the leader-supervisor wishes them to do. This, of course, applies primarily to formal leaders. To others, leadership means encouraging and stimulating action from workers by involving them in planning and decision-making activities. And to still others, leadership is primarily a matter of removing barriers so that subordinates can act with freedom and independence. While the definitions of the leadership role vary widely, there is a general acceptance of the concept that someone is needed to serve as an agent for guiding and encouraging people to work together usefully.

Responsibilities of the Leader-Supervisor

While it is true that the approaches to leadership by different individuals may vary, there are some basic responsibilities that are frequently suggested as the

[1]David G. Bowers and Stanley E. Seashore, "Predicting Organizational Effectiveness with a Four-Factor Theory of Leadership," *Administrative Science Quarterly*, Volume 11, Number 2 (September 1966), p. 240.

more important duties leader-supervisors must perform. Most listings of leadership reponsibilities stress the leader's ~~obligation to attain organizational goal~~s and to ~~give attention to the needs of the individuals who are his subordinates~~. Kahn, for example, is both organization- and worker-oriented in his list of leadership functions. He states that the ~~leader serves best~~ when he:

1. Provides direct need satisfaction for his followers
2. Structures the path to goal attainment (In doing this, the leader provides the subordinate with cues toward filling personal needs while attaining organizational goals.)
3. Removes barriers to goal attainment
4. Modifies employee goals so that their personal goals can also be organizationally useful[2]

Miljus spells out leadership responsibilities in more detail. He lists the leader's responsibilities as those of:

1. ~~Determining realistic performance objective~~s (in terms of quantity, quality, safety, etc.)
2. ~~Providing workers with the necessary resources to perform their tasks~~
3. ~~Communicating to workers what is specifically expected of them~~
4. ~~Providing an adequate reward structure to encourage performance~~
5. ~~Delegating authority where needed and inviting participation where possible~~
6. ~~Removing barriers and stumbling blocks to effective performance~~
7. ~~Appraising performance and communicating the results of evaluations~~
8. ~~Showing personal consideration for the employee~~[3]

These actions again present the dual responsibility the leader has for the organization and for subordinates. These lists are by no means comprehensive, but they do suggest some of the most basic duties of the leader.

The Authority for Leadership

If a leader is to effectively achieve the goals expected of him, he must have authority to act in a way that will stimulate a positive response from those with

[2]R. L. Kahn, "Human Relations on the Shop Floor," in Edward M. Hugh-Jones, editor, *Human Relations and Modern Management,* Amsterdam, Holland: North-Holland Publishing Company, 1958, pp. 61–73.
[3]Robert C. Miljus, "Effective Leadership and the Motivation of Human Resources," *Personnel Journal,* Volume 49, Number 1 (January 1970), pp. 37–40.

FIGURE 9.1   How top-down authority works

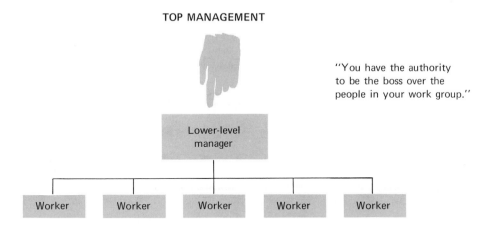

TOP MANAGEMENT

"You have the authority
to be the boss over the
people in your work group."

Lower-level
manager

Worker   Worker   Worker   Worker   Worker

whom he will work in reaching goals. The ~~authority for leadership~~ is the ~~right to take action or to induce behavior from those being led~~. There are at least two schools of thought about the sources of authority for leadership action.

The traditional position concerning the selection of leaders and the granting of authority for leadership has been that the leadership role is given to individuals thought to be capable and willing to serve in that capacity in a way that would achieve a productive response from their subordinates. Actual decisions concerning who will receive formal authority to serve as leaders are made by line officials in the organizational hierarchy. The source of all authority rests at the top of the organization in the hands of the board of directors, the president, the general manager, or whatever the top position may be. From this source, authority is delegated downward progressively to leaders filling whatever positions are essential to achieve the necessary performance.

On the basis of this theory, the leader-supervisor receives the authority to function as a leader by authorization from his own immediate superior, who in turn has received his authority from a leader one step higher in the organizational hierarchy. This ~~concept of leadership authority~~ is ~~known~~ as the ~~top-down authority concept~~.[4] (See Figure 9.1)

The other major concept of leadership authority is based upon the ~~acceptance theory~~ and is primarily a part of the behavioral philosophy of management. This

[4]William G. Scott and Terence R. Mitchell, *Organization Theory: A Structural and Behavioral Analysis,* Homewood, Illinois: Richard D. Irwin, Inc., and The Dorsey Press, 1972, p. 218.

theory states that leaders are selected (accepted) *by those who will be their followers.* Only when an individual is accepted as their leader and is given the right to guide will his followers become his subordinates and respond to him as their leader. The followers grant the authority because they have personal respect for or admiration of the individual or because the individual appears to represent values important to them.[5]

According to the acceptance theory, workers recognize a need for the guidance and support that can be provided through leadership. The workers then review the possible candidates for leadership and grant the authority to the chosen individual so that he can function in a leadership capacity. According to this approach, the source of authority lies at the bottom of the work group rather than at the top of the organization structure. On this basis, the approach to leadership authority has sometimes become known as the bottom-up theory. (See Figure 9.2.)

Although the two theories of authority appear to be contradictory, they need not be. Top-down authority is necessary if the proper level of coordination and control is to be achieved. At least a degree of centralized authority is appropriate to attain the necessary planning and decision making to help the organization operate cohesively. The formal authority structure, utilizing formally appointed leaders, helps to achieve the necessary unity. Formally appointed leaders work with their subordinates in a way that enhances a unified, constructive effort.

From a leadership-followership point of view, however, the formal leader's task can be accomplished much more easily if he has the acceptance and support of those he leads. When subordinates respond to their leader out of respect, admiration, or through other positive motivations, they follow him willingly and cooperatively. Superior-subordinate relations are more congenial and harmonious. The directives of the leader are responded to voluntarily rather than out of

FIGURE 9.2   How bottom-up authority works

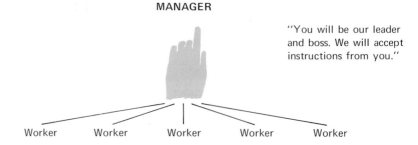

MANAGER

"You will be our leader and boss. We will accept instructions from you."

Worker   Worker   Worker   Worker   Worker

[5]For a discussion of the bottom-up "consent" theory of authority, see Chester I. Barnard, *The Functions of the Executive*, Cambridge, Massachusetts: Harvard University Press, 1939, pp. 161–184.

fear of his formal authority. ~~Leaders who have formal authority become more effective when their subordinates respond to them voluntarily under their own motivation.~~[6]

Criteria for Selecting the Leader

While keeping in mind the two concepts of leadership authority, managers who are high in the managerial hierarchy must make decisions concerning who will be the actual recipients of formal leadership authority. From the candidates available in the organization (and sometimes including those outside the organization), selections must be made and formal authority given to the individuals chosen to be the leaders. The question now arises, What criteria should be used in determining who will be given the authority to serve in a formal leadership capacity?

From the list of responsibilities leaders should perform, it is evident that the leader must at least be qualified to guide others to organizational achievement and must also be a capable handler of interpersonal relations. This author will shortly present a theory of leadership based on the concept of adaptability—~~the need for the leader to be capable of sizing up individual situations and providing the leadership called for by each situation.~~ The demands called for in this adaptive approach will further expand the necessary qualifications of leadership.

Qualities of Leaders.   For a time, the identification of potential leaders was based upon the concept that there was an identifiable set of traits that every good leader possessed. This approach has now been modified. As Scott and Mitchell have said, "in general across a number of situations, traits do not consistently distinguish the leaders from the followers or the good leaders from the poor ones."[7] While no set of *absolute* traits may be identifiable, it is reasonable to assume that individuals who possess abilities to lead others toward organizational achievement and sound interpersonal interaction, and who also have the ability to be situationally adaptive, may benefit from certain attributes helpful to them in performing their leadership roles.

---

[6]See Scott and Mitchell, *op. cit.,* pp. 211–223, George C. Homans, "Effort, Supervision, and Productivity," in Robert Dubin et al.; *Leadership and Productivity,* San Francisco: Chandler Publishing Company, 1965, pp. 51–67, and Max Weber, *The Theory of Social and Economic Organization* (edited by Talcott Parsons), New York: Oxford University Press, 1947, pp. 328–329, for further discussions on the sources of authority within organizations.

[7]Scott and Mitchell, *op. cit.,* p. 228.

A partial list of helpful (although not absolutely required) attributes of a leader might include the willingness of the leader to assume responsibility for achievement, the ability to be perceptive and empathetic, the ability to be objective, the ability to place a proper priority on duties and activities, and the ability to communicate effectively with others.

Willingness To Assume Responsibility. When the leader accepts responsibility for goal achievement, he agrees to be held accountable by his superiors for the performance of his followers. The leader, to a degree, becomes the extension of his superior to a lower level. When the leader-supervisor accepts responsibility for leadership, he assumes the possible risk of failure if he does not achieve the expected results through his subordinates. The leader exposes himself to pressures from the subordinates, from informal groups, sometimes from unions, and from many other sources. Most leaders also find the role of leader a very demanding one in terms of the time, effort, and knowledge required to fulfill the role effectively. Leader-supervisors who take their roles seriously usually discover their work to be more energy-consuming than do people working in nonleader roles.

Because the leadership role demands so much, it is helpful if the individual filling the role wants this responsibility. Not everyone is interested in such a responsibility. Fortunately, some individuals are willing to accept leadership roles. Usually, individuals expect to fulfill certain personal goals while serving as leaders. The personal goals of achievement, recognition, and power are particularly stimulated by the opportunity to assume positions of leadership. Where such rewards are possible, the leadership role becomes stimulating and satisfying. There is little doubt that some leaders serve in such a capacity unwillingly, but when the leader seriously wants out of his role he can usually find a way to be relieved of this responsibility.

The Ability To Be Perceptive. **Perception** entails the ability to observe or discover the realities of one's environment. Leaders in organizations need to be cognizant of the objectives and goals of the total organization so that they can work to support those goals. Each leader needs to be perceptive or empathetic toward his subordinate-followers so that he can discern their strengths, weaknesses, and ambitions and can give them the attention they deserve. The leader also needs to be perceptive introspectively (toward himself) so that he can know his own strengths, weaknesses, and goals and can give proper consideration to them. The ability to distinguish between that which is true and that which is false in the organization, in subordinates, and in one's self is particularly important in the adaptive leadership concept, which follows later in this chapter.

The Ability To Be Objective. **Objectivity** is the ability to look at issues and problems rationally, impersonally, and without bias. Objectivity is an extension of perceptiveness. Where perceptivity creates an awareness of facts, events, and other realities, objectivity helps the leader to minimize emotional and personal factors that might obscure reality. While the leader needs to be personally empathetic, he also needs to be able to keep emotional, nonrational considerations in perspective. Objectivity is a vital aspect of analytical decision making. Objectivity also helps to insure a fair, consistent course of action from the leader.

The Ability To Establish Proper Priorities. The really skillful leader is the one who is capable of sorting out the chaff to get to the real kernel of grain—in other words, he has the ability to see what is important and what is not. When decisions are necessary, the gifted leader knows which alternatives are worthy of consideration and which are not. When supervisory action is at stake, the priority-oriented leader gives attention to the critical, most meaningful areas. He is not distracted by surface issues but pierces the heart of the matter.

Katz[8] stresses the point that the more effective leader is the one who recognizes that his first priority is leadership. This leader plans, supports, and provides for the followers under his jurisdiction before he spends much of his time performing nonleadership activities.

Certainly, all leaders do not possess equally the ability to give order to issues that confront them. Those who have a high degree of this ability are usually considered better equipped to be leaders.

The Ability To Communicate. The ability to convey and receive information in a useful manner is a capacity often taken for granted. However, if the leader is to effectively accomplish any of the goals outlined above, he will benefit from the ability to send and receive messages clearly and distinctly. Many of the advantages and problems of communicating adequately will be reviewed in a subsequent chapter. Good communicators seem to find all responsibilities easier to perform (those of planning, organizing, controlling, and especially those involving leading), because they can relate to others more easily and can better utilize available data.[9]

[8]Daniel Katz, Nathan Maccoby, and Nancy C. Morse, *Productivity, Supervision, and Morale in an Office Situation,* Detroit: Darel Press, Inc., 1950, p. 35.

[9]See Arthur H. Kuriloff, "Identifying Leadership Potential for Management," *Personnel Administration,* Volume 30, Number 6 (November–December 1967), pp. 3–5, 27–29, and J. R. Joyce, "The Search for Leaders," *Personnel Journal,* Volume 49, Number 4 (April 1970), pp. 308–311, for additional suggestions of appropriate leadership qualifications.

Applying the Qualification Criteria.   After the qualities of leadership are classified, the qualifications must be matched with the available candidates. The first attribute, the willingness to serve in a leadership capacity, has to be indicated by the individual being considered for the assignment. The potential leader faces the task of viewing the responsibilities, risks, and rewards and indicating to his superiors if he is willing to assume a leadership role if it is offered to him.

The other qualities (perceptiveness, objectivity, ability to establish priorities, and ability to communicate) are more difficult to identify. A part of the identification process involves observation of the potential leader's behavior habits in fulfilling other assignments and his interactions with colleagues. If he has the ability to communicate well with his present superiors, colleagues, and subordinates (if he has any), perhaps he will be capable of doing the same in a new leadership position. Similar clues are sought for the other desired qualities.

Managers in many organizations attempt to determine the capabilities of new leaders by giving them leadership responsibilities on a progressively increasing basis. Small amounts of responsibility are assigned and authority given. If the neophyte responds capably, the responsibility and authority are increased. Whatever techniques are used to identify potentially sound leaders, no absolute certainty can be reached concerning the individual's potential until he is fully performing the duties of the leader and shows himself to be capable and willing.

Leadership Styles

When responsibility for leadership has been assigned and authority has been given, it becomes the leader's task to achieve and accomplish by working with and through his followers. Leaders have exhibited many different approaches as they fulfill their responsibilities in leader-follower relations. The customary approach to the analysis of leader behavior is to classify the various types of leadership into styles. The styles vary on the basis of the duties the leader feels he alone must perform, the responsibilities the leader expects his followers to accept, and the philosophical commitment of the leader to the development and fulfillment of subordinates' expectations. Many terms have been used to define leadership styles but perhaps the most meaningful approach has been to describe the three most basic styles as those of the autocratic leader, the participative leader, and the free-rein leader.[10]

[10]There are many other approaches to the classification of leadership styles—some of them more simple and others more complex. Keith Davis, *Human Behavior at Work*, Fourth Edition, New York: McGraw-Hill Book Company, 1972, pp. 497–498, has four theories of leadership behavior—autocratic, custodial, supportive, and collegial. Robert Tannenbaum and Warren H. Schmidt, "How To Choose

The Autocratic Leader.   An **autocratic** leader, assumes all responsibility for decision making, for initiating action, and for directing, motivating, and controlling his subordinates. Decision and guidance activities are centralized in the hands of the leader. The autocratic leader may decide that he is the only individual who is competent and capable of making important decisions, he may feel that his subordinates are incapable or unwilling to guide themselves, or he may have other reasons for assuming a strong position of guidance and control. The response requested from the subordinates by the autocratic leader is obedience and adherence to his decisions. The autocrat watches the performance levels of his subordinates in hopes of eliminating deviations from his directives if they occur.

The Participative Leader.   When a leader utilized the **participative** style, he practices leadership by consultation. The leader does not delegate away his right to make final decisions and to give specific directives to his subordinates, but he does seek out their thoughts and opinions on many decisions that affect them. If he is to be effective as a participative leader, he seriously listens to and reviews the thoughts of his subordinates and accepts their contributions wherever possible and practical. The participative leader cultivates the decision-making abilities of his subordinates so their thoughts will be increasingly useful and mature. The subordinates are also encouraged to increase their abilities to exercise self-control and are urged to assume greater responsibility for guiding their own efforts. The leader becomes more supportive in his contact with his subordinates rather than being dictatorial. Final authority on matters of importance, however, continues to reside in the hands of the leader.

The Free-Rein Leader.   Under the **free-rein** style of leadership, the leader delegates authority for decision making into the hands of the subordinates rather completely. The leader in effect says to his followers, "Here's a job to do. I don't care how you do it so long as it gets done satisfactorily." This leader expects his subordinates to assume responsibility for their own motivation, guidance, and control. Except for the stating of a minimum number of ground rules, leadership under this approach provides a very limited amount of contact and support for the

a Leadership Pattern," *Harvard Business Review,* Volume 36, Number 2 (March–April 1958), pp. 95–101, discuss leaders according to boss-centeredness and subordinate-centeredness. Robert R. Blake and Jane S. Mouton, *The Managerial Grid,* Houston: Gulf Publishing Company, 1971, 340 pp., identify leaders on the basis of production and people orientations. Robert C. Albrook, "Participative Management: Time for a Second Look," *Fortune,* Volume 75, Number 5 (May 1967), pp. 166–170, 197–200, and Rensis Likert, *The Human Organization,* New York: McGraw-Hill Book Company, 1967, pp. 13–46, use four styles—exploitive-authoritative, benevolent-authoritative, consultative, and participative.

followers. Obviously, the ~~subordinate has to be highly qualified~~ and ~~capable~~ if ~~this approach is to have a successful end result~~.

Of course, there are various degrees of leadership in between these styles. The styles discussed (see Figure 9.3) are three of the more distinctly defined positions.

There was a time when some authors and managers would single out one of these leadership styles and promote this style as the panacea for all supervisory needs. Most noteworthy was the emphasis upon participative management, but the autocratic style also has had a number of advocates promoting it as an exclusively effective technique. There have even been some occasional promoters of the free-rein style as the singularly most fruitful approach. More recent trends, however, emphasize the need for adaptation and flexibility in the use of leadership styles in opposition to the cultivation of one exclusive style.[11] It is felt that in our dynamic society rarely are two managers completely identical in their thoughts and preferences; seldom are two workers identical in their abilities and needs; and almost never are two business organizations identical in their goals and objectives. As a result, it is normally recommended that the manager consider a number of factors in determining what leadership style is appropriate in a specific situation. In other words, one leadership style will be more effective if certain situational factors prevail, while another style may be more useful if the factors change.

The Choice of a Leadership Style

If a leader is to be adaptive and flexible, he must be able to recognize situational variables and to combine the variables into a package that will be helpful in making decisions on appropriate leadership styles.[12] Several authors have outlined factors they felt were major determinants in the leadership style selection process and have attempted to break down factors into specific considerations. Perhaps the five authors who have been most helpful in identifying the variables

---

[11]See, for example, Tannenbaum and Schmidt, *op. cit.,* pp. 95–101, Fred E. Fiedler, "Style or Circumstance: The Leadership Enigma," *Psychology Today,* Volume 2, Number 10 (March 1969), pp. 38–43, or Fremont E. Kast and James E. Rosenzweig, *Contingency Views of Organization and Management,* Chicago: Science Research Associates, Incorporated, 1973, p. x, for discussion of situational, contingency approaches.

[12]Much of the adaptive model of leadership discussed in the following paragraphs was originally developed in an article by O. Jeff Harris entitled "Adaptive Leadership—The Answer to Today's Leadership Needs," which appeared in O. Jeff Harris, editor, *Current Concepts in Management,* Baton Rouge: Louisiana State University Bureau of Business Research, July 1972, pp. 31–40.

FIGURE 9.3   Autocratic, participative and free-rein leadership styles

AUTOCRATIC LEADER

"Look, I'm the boss around
here. I'll make the decisions,
and I'll tell you what I want
you to do. You'd better
do your job because I'll be
watching your every move."

PARTICIPATIVE LEADER

"I'm sure you understand that
the final responsibility for making
a decision is mine, but you
can help me by giving your
ideas and feelings. I'll let you
help in the implementation of the
decision once it has been made."

FREE-REIN LEADER

"Here's a job for you to do.
Do it any way you want to so
long as it gets done. I'll
only expect to hear from you
when you are experiencing
unusually difficult problems."

have been Tannenbaum, Schmidt,[13] Fiedler,[14] Albrook,[15] and Likert.[16] Tannenbaum and Schmidt indicate the choice of styles is dependent upon three sets of

[13]Tannenbaum and Schmidt, *op. cit.,* pp. 95–101.

[14]Fred E. Fiedler, *A Theory of Leadership Effectiveness,* New York: McGraw-Hill Book Company, 1967.

[15]Albrook, *op. cit.,* pp. 167–170, 197–200.

[16]Likert, *op. cit.,* pp. 13–46.

forces—forces within the leader himself, forces within the subordinates, and forces in the situation. Fiedler divides the important factors influencing the effectiveness of leadership styles into three other categories—the relations between the leader and his followers, the degree of task structure of the organization, and the degree of power possessed by the leader over his subordinates. Albrook and Likert expand the above concepts using additional variables.

In attempting to provide a set of criteria to be used by leader-supervisors in making decisions about the right leadership style to meet each situation, the author has attempted to combine the Tannenbaum-Schmidt, Fiedler, Albrook, and Likert concepts with his own. The result is a list of four major factors—factors in the organization, factors in the leader-supervisor, factors in the subordinates, and factors in the task situation. The factors chosen represent four significant influences upon the appropriateness of a leadership style. Factors within the organization provide the framework for all supervisory action. Factors within the leader-supervisor recognize the effects of the leader's own abilities, attitudes, and goals upon superior-subordinate relations. Factors within the subordinates reflect the needs of the subordinates for large or small amounts of direction and control. Factors in the task situation explore the effects of job complexity and the time element upon leadership decisions. The four major factors are shown in Figure 9.4, and a list of questions probing for clues to the proper choice is shown beneath each factor. The three leadership styles are then tested against the questions to find the conditions under which that leadership style is most appropriate, other things being equal.

To illustrate the appropriate adaptation of the right leadership style to the right situation, a review of the factors shown in Figure 9.4 indicates that autocratic leadership is the correct style when there is a set of conditions in which the subordinates lack knowledge of company goals and objectives, where the company endorses fear and punishment as acceptable disciplinary techniques, where the workers are inexperienced and somewhat lacking in training, where the leader prefers to be active and dominant in decision making, and where there is little room for error in the final performance. These conditions, other things being equal, would suggest the appropriateness of rather strong, autocratic leadership to provide the needed force, direction, and control.

Participative leadership might be more appropriate under conditions in which the company has communicated its goals and objectives to the subordinates and the subordinates have accepted them, where the company practices the use of rewards and involvement as the primary means of motivation and control, where the leader-supervisor truly desires to hear the ideas of others before making decisions, where the leader wishes to develop analytical and self-control abilities in his subordinates, where workers are reasonably knowledgeable and experienced, where subordinates desire involvement in matters that affect them, and where the time for task completion allows for participation. If other conditions are relatively neutral, these conditions would suggest the appropriateness of the participative style in meeting existing demands.

The free-rein style of leadership would seem to be most appropriate under conditions in which company goals have been thoroughly communicated and are highly acceptable to the subordinates; in fact, the company's goals and the subordinates' goals need to be highly compatible. In addition, free-rein leadership is most appropriate when the leader desires to delegate decision-making fully, when the leader has a high degree of confidence in the abilities of his subordinates, when the subordinates themselves are well trained and highly knowledgeable concerning their jobs and are willing to assume responsibility for decision-making and self-control, when the subordinates have a high need for independence, when the subordinates derive large amounts of personal satisfaction from their work, and where performance demands allow some room for error if mistakes occur in the rather decentralized arrangement. Under these conditions, where workers are highly competent and self-motivated and organizational conditions are nearly ideal, free-rein leadership may be utilized most successfully.

If the individual leader-supervisor is to be proficient in his application of leadership styles, he must be well informed on organizational policies, plans, and structures that influence his choice of styles. The adaptive leader must practice introspection to discern his own inclinations, desires, and motivations. He must also be keenly empathetic to the needs, desires, abilities, and knowledge of the subordinates under his leadership. The leader must also be able to size up task situation factors that might influence a subordinate's need for leadership.

The use of adaptive leadership becomes a demanding yet interesting challenge to the conscientious leader. Adaptive leadership demands much from the leader both perceptively and actively, but the results of his efforts are beneficial to himself, his subordinates, and his company. Each human aspect of the organization receives the proper amount of attention and guidance when adaptive leadership is practiced.

The Problem of Consistency.   In applying adaptive leadership, the leader often finds it necessary to change his approach in dealing with certain of his followers. This shift in leadership approaches ordinarily is effective in accomplishing its purposes, but the use of this flexible approach may sometimes cause confusion and misunderstanding. Worker A may feel that his leader is erratic when he autocratically supervises him in an emergency situation, then later in the same

FIGURE 9.4   Factors and primary determinants in selection of appropriate leadership style

FACTORS IN SELECTION OF A LEADERSHIP STYLE	LEADERSHIP STYLE		
	AUTOCRATIC LEADERSHIP	PARTICIPATIVE LEADERSHIP	FREE-REIN LEADERSHIP
FACTORS IN THE ORGANIZATION			
1. How clearly are organizational goals defined?	Clear definition helpful	Clear definition a requisite	Clear definition a requisite
2. How thoroughly have goals been communicated to subordinates?	May or may not have been communicated	Must be communicated rather thoroughly	Must be communicated thoroughly and completely
3. How adequate are formal communication channels? Are both upward and downward channels provided for?	Downward channels definitely provided for	Two-way communication provided for and encouraged	Two-way communication provided for but used infrequently
4. Does company philosophy support the predominant use of: a. fear b. threats c. punishment d. rewards e. involvement	Mostly a, b, and c are encouraged	Mostly d and e are used	d, e, and sometimes c are used
5. How wide is the normal span of supervision and control?	Usually narrow	Must be moderately narrow	Can be wide

FACTORS IN SELECTION OF A LEADERSHIP STYLE	LEADERSHIP STYLE		
	AUTOCRATIC LEADERSHIP	PARTICIPATIVE LEADERSHIP	FREE-REIN LEADERSHIP
FACTORS IN THE LEADER-MANAGER			
1. What are the leader's inclinations in terms of communicating to, listening to, and empathizing with subordinates?	Tends to be somewhat self-centered	Keenly aware of and interested in them	Tends to observe only highlights and trouble spots
2. What are leader's attitudes toward involvement in decision making?	Prefers own decisions to decisions of others	Wants ideas from others before deciding	Prefers to let others make decisions on their own
3. What degree of confidence and trust does he have in the abilities and knowledge of his subordinates?	Has a questionable amount	Has a reasonably high degree	Has a high degree
4. How knowledgeable is the leader concerning decisions that are necessary and tasks that must be performed?	Must be highly knowledgeable	May be moderately to highly knowledgeable	May or may not be knowledgeable
5. How important to the leader is the development of analytical skills and self-control abilities in the subordinates?	Unimportant	Important	Highly important

(Continued)

FIGURE 9.4   Factors and primary determinants in selection of appropriate leadership style (Continued)

FACTORS IN SELECTION OF A LEADERSHIP STYLE	LEADERSHIP STYLE		
	AUTOCRATIC LEADERSHIP	PARTICIPATIVE LEADERSHIP	FREE-REIN LEADERSHIP
FACTORS IN SUBORDINATES			
1. To what degree do subordinates accept the goals of the company, and how loyal are they to these goals?	Accepted to a questionable degree in both areas	Some degree of acceptance and loyalty evidenced	High degree of acceptance and loyalty essential
2. Do the subordinates have a relatively high need for independence?	No, they prefer dependence	At least moderately, yes	Yes
3. Are subordinates willing to assume responsibility for decision making and self-control?	May not be willing	Should be at least moderately	Must be willing
4. How much personal satisfaction do workers derive from the performance of their jobs?	Questionable degree	Moderate to high degree	High degree
5. Are subordinates well trained, knowledgeable, and experienced at their work?	Usually not	Yes, from a moderate to high degree	Yes, they must be of necessity
6. Have subordinates shared in decision-making and control processes previously?	Probably not much	Probably, to some degree	Yes, they should be well acquainted with decision-making and control responsibilities
7. Are subordinates' personal goals and objectives compatible with those of the organization?	Questionably so	Normally necessary	Yes, essential
8. Do subordinates have mutually positive respect for each other?	May or may not	Yes, very helpful	Yes, vitally important

FACTORS IN SELECTION OF A LEADERSHIP STYLE	LEADERSHIP STYLE		
	AUTOCRATIC LEADERSHIP	PARTICIPATIVE LEADERSHIP	FREE-REIN LEADERSHIP
FACTORS IN THE TASK SITUATION			
1. How much room for error is there in the task to be accomplished?	Little or none	Limited to moderate amount	Moderate amount
2. How much time is available for making decisions and completing tasks?	Very little	Moderate to large amount	
3. How important are new ideas and innovations to the successful task completion?	Unimportant	Important	Very important

Source: Adapted in part from Robert C. Albrook, "Participative Management: Time for a Second Look," *Fortune*, Volume 75, Number 5 (May 1967), pp. 166-170, Rensis Likert, *The Human Organization*, New York: McGraw–Hill, Inc., 1967, pp. 13-46, and Robert Tannenbaum and Warren H. Schmidt, "How to Choose a Leadership Pattern," *Harvard Business Review*, Volume 36, Number 2 (March–April 1958), pp. 95-101.

day gives the worker a free hand to do as he pleases on a less urgent project. Also, Worker B may feel that he is being treated unfairly when he sees his boss give a free rein to one of the worker's colleagues, Worker C, then spells out in detail what Worker B must do in performing his own tasks.

Changes in leadership style when dealing with one specific employee usually are a result of changes in the task situation. The factors involved in the leader, the subordinate, and the organizational setting tend to remain more constant. Task situation changes may result from modifications in the tolerance of errors, the amount of time available to act, or the need for creative thinking. If the task situation changes, the leader might be well advised to inform his follower of the change before modifying his leadership style. For example, when Supervisor A finds it necessary to retract the freedom he has given to one of his subordinates because of a time urgency, it would be helpful if he informed the subordinate by saying, "John, you know I normally would have discussed this with you before taking action. But I had to tell our customer what we could do for him while I was talking to him on the phone. I had to make a decision before talking with you." Most subordinates will accept changes in leadership exercised toward them if the modifications are explained adequately and appear to be reasonable.

The use of different leadership styles *simultaneously* toward different subordinates is a more difficult problem to handle. Supposedly, the change is not made necessary by organizational factors or leader-supervisor factors. Those remain fairly constant. If there is a need for a variation of the leadership style applied to two different subordinates, factors in the task situation and the subordinate usually account for the style change. If Leader-Supervisor B has less confidence in the abilities of Worker D and the project must be completed without error, he may become highly autocratic. If on the other hand, he has a high confidence in Worker E and the performance level is flexible, he may open up his style.

Some workers recognize the leadership they are receiving as the kind of leadership they need in order to get their work done. In these situations, the difference in leadership style applied to them (as opposed to the leadership received by other workers) may be quite acceptable. However, if a worker feels he is being treated unfairly or is being discriminated against by the unequal leadership actions of his superior, concern or resentment may develop.

If a worker is unhappy because he feels that his boss is more autocratic with him than with other workers, the leader should sense this and help the subordinate to understand the reasons for the difference in treatment. If the difference is related to task situation factors, the communication of this fact may resolve the feeling. If the reason for the difference is a factor within the subordinate, the leader may be able to point out that the employee who is given more freedom of move- ment has won his freedom on the basis of long years of experience, concentrated effort to develop skills, or other factors of merit. The worker in question can be encouraged to devote his efforts in the same way if he wishes to attain greater autonomy himself. A typical leadership reaction in this situation might be, "John has performed this task so many times that he can almost do it in his sleep. He doesn't need my assistance. As you repeat the job, you'll be the same way, and I'll not stick so close to you either."

If the worker, on the other hand, feels neglected because his superior does not give him as much attention and help as the superior gives to others, the leader- supervisor may be able to point out that he has felt the worker capable of directing himself. Assurance should be given that the supervisor is interested in the worker and stands ready to help when needed.

Other problems may also develop in the application of leadership techniques, but with effort the problems can be overcome. Leadership techniques and styles properly applied are a major factor in the success or failure of organizational achievement. Adaptive leadership is an invaluable aid in the accomplishment of organizational objectives.

Summary

In every organization it is necessary that some individuals assume the roles of leadership. There is by no means a consensus on what the leader's roles and duties may be, but there is agreement that someone needs to be responsible for guiding and encouraging people to work together usefully.

Not all leaders are formally appointed leaders (see Chapter 6 for a discussion of informal leaders), but those who are perform a number of tasks in the fulfillment of their obligations to their employer, their subordinates, and other groups to whom they may have responsibilities. While it is difficult to pinpoint specific traits that effective leaders possess, it is possible to say that effective leaders normally are willing to serve as leaders; are perceptive toward others, environmental influences, and themselves; have the ability to be objective; are capable of establishing priorities appropriately; and have the ability to communicate successfully with others.

Several styles or approaches are utilized by those who serve in formal leadership capacities. Three leadership styles frequently used are the autocratic, participative, and free-rein approaches. Autocratic leadership tends to be centralized and somewhat leader-centered. Participative leadership is leadership by consultation in which the leader involves his subordinates in planning, decision making, and other activities without delegating away his own authority. Free-rein leadership is a rather complete dele- gation of authority into the hands of the subordinates so that they must plan, motivate, control, and otherwise be responsible for their own actions.

The current emphasis in organizational leadership is a flexible, adaptive approach in which the leader adjusts his style according to a number of factors. The effective leader becomes autocratic, participative, or free-rein based upon factors in the organization, in himself, in the subordinates, and in the task situation. Leadership becomes a matter of finding the right approach for each situation and then performing the role that is appropriate with that approach.

Problems exist, of course, in the implementation of adaptive leadership, but with effort the difficulties can be overcome. Adaptive leadership is an invaluable aid in the accomplishment of organizational and personal objectives.

Questions to consider after reading Chapter 9

1. Why are some seemingly capable individuals unwilling to assume leadership responsibilities?

2. In addition to the responsibilities of the leader listed in this chapter, what other responsibilities may leaders have?

3. Can individuals who desire to become leaders develop their perceptivity, objectivity, and ability to set priorities so that they have an improved chance of receiving leadership responsibilities? If you answer yes, discuss how these attributes can be developed. If you answer no, defend your position.

4. To what degree is it possible to achieve objectivity? What are the major stumbling blocks that stand in the way of reaching greater objectivity?

5. What do your own preferences and abilities reveal your favorite leadership style to be?

6. To which of the questions in Figure 9.4 would answers be difficult to provide? Where might the leader search in looking for these answers?

7. How can an appropriate level of consistency be achieved in the face of a need for adaptability and flexibility?

**All of the cases at the back of the book contain materials
related to Chapter 10. In particular
these cases are closely related:**

> Ben Stockton
>
> Mark Williams
>
> Stanley Lowell
>
> H. Gerald Pretzler

Edith Capp and Janet Turner

Earl Fornette

Bentley Cantrell

Susan Swanson

Grace Lanham

Bill Caden

Walt Gladberry

Additional readings

Argyris, Chris, "The CEO's Behavior: Key to Organizational Development," *Harvard Business Review,* Volume 51, Number 2 (March–April 1973), pp. 55–64.

Bavelas, Alex, "Leadership: Man and Functions," *Administrative Science Quarterly,* Vol-4, Number 4 (March 1960), pp. 491–498.

Beer, Michael, *Leadership, Employee Needs, and Motivation,* Columbus: Bureau of Business Research, Ohio State University, Monograph Number 129, 1966.

Bennis, Warren G., "The Revisionist Theory of Leadership," *Harvard Business Review,* Volume 39, Number 1 (January–February 1961), pp. 26–28.

Carson, John J., "A Neglected Element of Political Leadership," *Personnel Administration,* Volume 34, Number 3 (May–June 1971), pp. 39–43.

Day, Robert C., and Robert L. Hamblin, "Some Effects of Close and Primitive Styles of Supervision," *American Journal of Sociology,* Volume 69, Number 5 (March 1964), pp. 499–510.

Dubin, Robert, *Leadership and Productivity,* San Francisco: Chandler Publishing Company, 1965.

Fiedler, Fred E., "Engineer the Job to Fit the Manager," *Harvard Business Review,* Volume 43, Number 5 (September–October 1965), pp. 115–122.

George, Norman, and Thomas J. Van Der Embse, "Six Propositions for Managerial Leadership," *Business Horizons,* Volume 14, Number 6 (December 1971), pp. 33–43.

Graen, George, Kenneth Alvares, and James Arris, "Contingency Model of Leadership Effectiveness: Antecedent and Evidential Results," *Psychological Bulletin,* Volume 74, Number 4 (October 1970), pp. 285–296.

Greiner, Larry E., "What Managers Think of Participative Leadership," *Harvard Business Review,* Volume 51, Number 2 (March–April 1973), pp. 111–117.

Hill, Walter, "A Situational Approach to Leadership Effectiveness," *Journal of Applied Psychology,* Volume 53, Number 6 (December 1969), pp. 513–517.

Hollander, Edwin P., "Style, Structure, and Setting in Organizational Leadership," *Administrative Science Quarterly*, Volume 16, Number 1 (March 1971), pp. 1–9.

———, and James W. Julian, "Contemporary Trends in the Analysis of Leadership Processes," in W. E. Scott and L. L. Cummings, editors, *Readings in Organizational Behavior and Human Performance*, Revised Edition, Homewood, Illinois: Richard D. Irwin, Inc., 1973, pp. 432–440.

House, Robert J., "A Path Goal Theory of Leader Effectiveness," *Administrative Science Quarterly*, Volume 16, Number 3 (September 1971), pp. 321–338.

Korman, A. K., "Consideration, Initiative, Structure, and Organizational Criteria—A Review," *Personnel Psychology*, Volume 19, Number 4 (Winter 1966), pp. 349–361.

Lowin, Aaron, William J. Hrapchak, and Michael J. Kavanagh, "Consideration and Initiating Structure: An Experimental Investigation of Leadership Traits," *Administrative Science Quarterly*, Volume 14, Number 2 (June 1969), pp. 238–252.

McCurdy, Harold G., and Harbert W. Beer, "Democratic versus Authoritarian: A Further Investigation of Group Problem-Solving," *Journal of Personality*, Volume 22, Number 2 (1953), pp. 258–269.

McMurray, Robert N., "The Case for Benevolent Autocracy," *Harvard Business Review*, Volume 36, Number 1 (January–February 1958), pp. 82–90.

Mullen, James H., "Differential Leadership Modes and Productivity in a Large Organization," *The Academy of Management Journal*, Volume 8, Number 2 (June 1965), pp. 107–126.

Powell, Reed M., and John L. Schlacter, "Participative Management—A Panacea?" *The Academy of Management Journal*, Volume 14, Number 2 (June 1971), pp. 165–173.

Rowland, Kendrith M., and William E. Scott, "Psychological Attributes of Effective Leadership in a Formal Organization," *Personnel Psychology*, Volume 21, Number 3 (Autumn 1968), pp. 365–378.

Sadler, Phillip, "Leadership Style, Confidence in Management, and Job Satisfaction," *Journal of Applied Behavioral Science*, Volume 6, Number 1 (March 1970), pp. 3–20.

Sales, S. M., "Supervisory Style and Productivity: Review and Theory," *Personnel Psychology*, Volume 19, Number 3 (Autumn 1966), pp. 275–285.

Schoenfield, Erwin, "Authoritarian Management: A Reviewing Concept," *Personnel*, Volume 36, Number 1 (January–February 1959), pp. 21–24.

Sorcher, Melvin, "Motivation, Participation, and Myth," *Personnel Administration*, Volume 34, Number 5 (September–October 1971), pp. 20–24.

Stogdill, Ralph M., "Personal Factors Associated With Leadership: A Survey of the Literature," *Journal of Psychology*, Volume 25, First Half (January 1948), pp. 35–71.

Tannenbaum, Robert, and Fred Massarik, "Leadership: A Frame of Reference," *Management Science*, Volume 4, Number 1 (October 1957), pp. 1–19.

Vroom, Victor H., and Floyd C. Mann, "Leader Authoritarianism and Employee Attitudes," *Personnel Psychology,* Volume 13, Number 2 (Summer 1960), pp. 125–139.

Yukl, Gary, "Toward a Behavioral Theory of Leadership," *Organizational Behavior and Human Performance,* Volume 6, Number 4 (July 1971), pp. 414–440.

Chapter 10

Motivating the Worker

A case to consider before reading chapter 10

BRENT TEMPLETON—THE UNINSPIRED DRAFTSMAN

Brent Templeton works as a draftsman for a large industrial equipment man-ufacturer. He has been with the company for more than ~~seven years~~ and is ~~well respected~~ for his ~~abilities~~. In a recent conversation with one of his friends, Brent revealed the following thoughts about his work.

I really shouldn't complain about my job, I guess. The ~~money~~ is ~~good~~. The working ~~conditions~~ are ~~excellent~~. I have ~~good friends~~ who work with me, and that's important. While retirement is a long way off, I'm putting aside funds to help me live comfortably then. I'm also setting aside money to put our children through college when the time comes.

My problem is this: I just ~~don't see~~ anything ~~different~~ in the ~~future~~. I have already reached the top rung on the pay-scale ladder for draftsmen. Except for cost-of-living adjustments, my income will never be much greater than it now is. More importantly, I've reached the top level for promotions that a draftsman can achieve. To get into a higher-level design or engineering job, the company requires that you must be a college graduate. Since I don't have a college degree, I have no real hope of advancing. Even if I could go back to college to get a degree, it would take years for me to get one. I must support my family, so I can spare neither the time nor the money that would be necessary to get a degree.

As I view the alternatives available, I just don't see many within the company it-self. Perhaps what I should do is get involved in something off the job that would be stimulating. One of the boys' clubs in town needs someone to teach the kids how to do carpentry and woodwork, and I'm pretty good at those things; so I may volunteer to work in that program.

I guess it's not really important that I be all fired up about my work with this company. Just so long as I do my job and stay out of trouble, that's all that's really important, isn't it?

Questions about the Brent Templeton case

1. On the basis of material from Chapter 7, which of Brent Templeton's needs are being fulfilled by his employing organization?

2. Which of Brent's needs, goals, or expectations are not being met by his employer? Why is this particularly discouraging to Brent?

3. Is it important that an employee be "fired up" about his work, or is it enough to expect him to do his job and stay out of trouble?

4. What steps could Brent's employer take that would result in a change of attitude and improve his inspiration to perform?

5. What concepts concerning motivation does this case illustrate? Please be specific.

6. With a partner, role play this case with one person playing Brent's role and the other acting out the role of Brent's boss. Seek to identify the causes of the problems that have developed and the possible solutions.

When a manager accepts the responsibility for serving in a supervisory capacity, he agrees to strive toward goal achievement by working with and through his superiors, subordinates, and fellow workers. A major part of his responsibility becomes that of stimulating his subordinates to perform their own duties and responsibilities usefully and constructively. The function of stimulating others toward productive performance is called the motivational process. The motivational pattern has also been defined as the process of arousing action, sustaining the activity in progress, and regulating the pattern of activity.[1] Thus, the motivational process attracts and initiates action *and also* serves as a factor in the continuation of activity until objectives have been attained.

The modern conceptualization of motivation also includes another function of the motivational process—that of rewarding the employee for his efforts so that his own personal goals are fulfilled as he works toward the attainment of the organization's objectives. This position is the basic thesis of McGregor's Theory Y concept, in which it is stated that "the essential task of management is to arrange organizational conditions and methods of operation so that people can achieve their own goals best by directing their own efforts toward organizational objectives."[2] In essence, successful supervisors will be those who integrate the goal-

---

[1]Paul T. Young, *Motivation and Emotion*, New York: John Wiley & Sons, Inc., 1961, pp. 17–19.

[2]Douglas M. McGregor, "The Human Side of Enterprise," *Management Review*, Volume 46, Number 11 (November 1957), p. 89.

oriented actions of individual workers with the pursuit of organizational goals.[3] The implication of these statements is that workers will apply their efforts and abilities toward organizationally useful performance if they can foresee benefits that can be gained by expending their efforts, and the employing organization will be benefitted correspondingly.

The motivational models presented in this chapter are related to what is usually called the expectancy school of thought. Expectancy theory is based primarily upon the premise that people behave as they do in response to their "expectations" or anticipations about the future.[4] The assumption is made that people will expend effort if a positive, valuable reward can be expected as an end result, but little constructive behavior will be exhibited for unattractive, irrelevant rewards. In other words, people respond to opportunities that have reward, utility, or reinforcement value. People have preferences and desires about the future that affect what they will and will not do as organizational performers.[5]

A major factor of the motivational process, therefore, becomes the one of providing opportunities for personal need fulfillment (reward opportunities) to each worker in a way that encourages him to work productively for the organization. A beginning point of the motivational process is the determination of organizational goals to be accomplished. Then the motivational process becomes personalized as it reviews the desires, goals, and needs of individuals in search of personal motives that can be appealed to in stimulating individual energies for productive uses. Personal, human motives are internalized goals within individuals. As Berelson and Steiner state, "a motive is an *inner* state that energizes, activates, or moves . . . and directs or channels behavior toward goals."[6] Environmental factors influence the development and expression of motives, but the motive (or need) is centered within the individual human being.

The simple thesis of motivation, then, is that a worker is motivated by opportunities to achieve and satisfy unfilled needs. Within the individual exists the desire to fulfill these unsatisfied needs, and this desire becomes the force that initiates or excites action. When the individual sees an opportunity to achieve that which is important to him, he is attracted to the opportunity. The perceived opportunity is called an **incentive.** Incentives are visible opportunities that appear

[3]John B. Miner, "Bridging the Gulf in Organizational Performance," *Harvard Business Review,* Volume 46, Number 4 (July–August 1968), p. 103.

[4]Lyman W. Porter and Edward E. Lawler, III, *Managerial Attitudes and Performance,* Homewood, Illinois: Richard D. Irwin, Inc., 1968, p. 9.

[5]*Ibid.,* p. 10.

[6]Bernard Berelson and Gary A. Steiner, *Human Behavior: An Inventory of Scientific Findings,* New York: Harcourt, Brace and World, 1964, p. 240.

to offer the worker the fulfillment of specific drives, needs, or goals (motives). Where the motive determines the need for action within the individual, the incentive provides a means for attainment and encourages and sustains action until fulfillment is achieved.

The relationship between an incentive and a motive is very similar to the relationship between a magnet and a metallic object. The metallic object lies ready to be drawn into the field of action but becomes activated only as the magnet comes within range and attracts or draws the metal toward it. The motive seeks a means to accomplish need fulfillment, and the incentive appeals to the motive and attempts to mobilize it into action by promising the attainment of the urgent need (see Figure 10.1).

FIGURE 10.1   Magnetic effect of the incentive

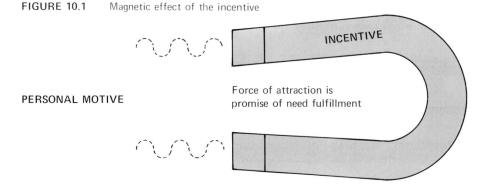

PERSONAL MOTIVE

Force of attraction is
promise of need fulfillment

INCENTIVE

Result: Effort expended to achieve the promised need fulfillment

Just as a magnet must be directed toward the metal object, so the incentive must be directed so that it appeals precisely to the personal motive. The incentive, in fact, must be tailored to the motive. If the urgent motive of an individual is, for example, the need for power, an incentive in the form of better working conditions will not draw out the desired action. However, if the promised reward is a promotion with increased authority, the individual can be expected to respond with the appropriate effort to earn the promises of the incentive (see Figure 10.2).

As the power-oriented individual may respond to the opportunity to gain more power, so may the friendship-starved individual be appealed to by the opportunity to attain social interaction. Other motives (such as the needs discussed in Chapter 7) create the same need-action sequence.

As an additional reminder of materials presented in Chapter 7, it should be recalled that the importance of specific human needs changes over a period of

FIGURE 10.2   Effects of a desirable incentive upon personal motive

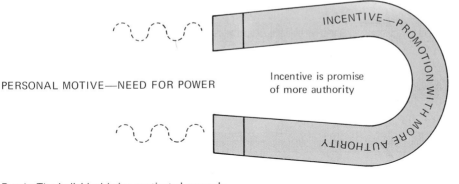

PERSONAL MOTIVE—NEED FOR POWER

Incentive is promise
of more authority

Result: The individual being motivated expends
          the effort required in an attempt to gain
          the promised reward (more authority)

time. An urgent motive today may not be important tomorrow. Carried further, this means that an incentive that has appeal at one point in time may lose its appeal, and other incentives may need to be discovered to appeal to newly important motives.[7]

Not only are motives dynamic and constantly changing within individuals, but they also vary between individuals. In other words, what motivates one individual at a given point in time may not be the motive of another individual at the same time. Motives differ with the needs of each individual.

A Motivational Model

The managerial implications of the motivational process suggest that supervisors must identify the specific motives individual workers possess (their drives, needs, and desires) and must provide opportunities (incentives) that encourage action to fulfill those motives. The incentives offered must be aligned with the motives of the specific worker if they are to induce action from him.[8]

[7]Abraham H. Maslow, *Motivation and Personality*, New York: Harper and Brothers, 1954, pp. 104–105.

[8]See William J. Roche and Neil L. MacKinnon, "Motivating People with Meaningful Work," *Harvard Business Review*, Volume 48, Number 3 (May–June 1970), pp. 97–110, for an excellent discussion of methods that prepare supervisors to utilize incentives that are meaningful for their subordinates.

As a springboard for a model of motivation, Vroom suggests that after a worker's motives are identified, any incentives that will effectively attract attention and effort from him must promise sufficient future rewards and must appear to be reasonably attainable.[9] The Vroom formula states that valence (anticipated worth) multiplied times expectancy (probability of attainment) equals the motivational effectiveness of a particular incentive as a stimulator of action. Using the basic concepts of the Vroom model and another motivational model developed by Porter and Lawler,[10] the author has developed a comprehensive model of the motivational process.[11] The model describes the chain of events that must occur if action stimulated by incentives is to be attained and needs are to be fulfilled satisfactorily. Also, the model provides clues concerning the responsibilities managers have toward helping to motivate their subordinates.

The initial factor in any motivational process is the motive for action—the reason, the desire, the inadequately filled need. Without the motive, there can be no motivational process. Motives cause individuals to reach out, to seek fulfillment, to begin action. As is shown by the arrows in Figure 10.3, motives initially may be satisfied in many ways. The eventual course of behavior is not immediately determined by the mere existence of the motive itself. Several courses of action may be possible. The individual with an unfilled need is normally ready to consider available methods whereby his goals and desires can be achieved.

The incentive enters the motivational process as Phase 2. The incentive is the magnetic force that catches the attention of the individual because it promises rewards and achievement that may satisfy his desires and motives (the same basic sequence as in Figure 10.2). If the incentive provided is relevant to the motive, it will catch the attention of the individual. However, if the incentive offered seems to provide no means of fulfilling the needs of the individual, it will be perceived accordingly and will attract little attention.

If the incentive appears to offer a means for satisfying the motive, the individual begins to consider the value of the incentive as a means of achieving his motives.

---

[9]Victor H. Vroom, *Work and Motivation,* New York: John Wiley & Sons, Inc., 1964, pp. 81–87.

[10]Porter and Lawler, *op. cit.,* p. 165.

[11]There are numerous other motivational models in addition to the models selected for discussion in this book. A cross-section of other models might include the motivation-hygiene model introduced by Frederick Herzberg, Bernard Mausner, and Barbara Snyderman, *The Motivation To Work,* Second Edition, New York: John Wiley & Sons, Inc., 1959, 157 pp., the path-goal model presented by Martin G. Evans, "Leadership and Motivation: A Core Concept," *The Academy of Management Journal,* Volume 13, Number 1 (March 1970), pp. 91–102, and the integrative theory presented by Kae H. Chung, "Toward a General Theory of Motivation and Performance," *California Management Review,* Volume 11, Number 3 (Spring 1969), pp. 81–88.

FIGURE 10.3   Positive motivational model

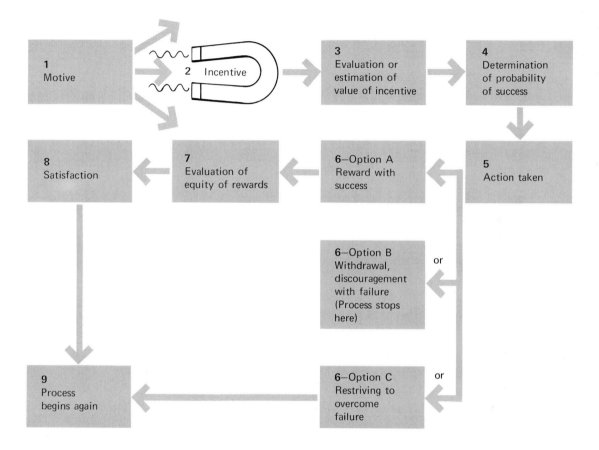

Source: Parts of the model are adapted from Lyman W. Porter and Edward E. Lawler, III,
Managerial Attitudes and Performance, Homewood, Illinois: Richard D. Irwin, Inc., 1968, p. 165.

The chief consideration at this point (Phase 3) centers on the degree of satisfaction
that would result if effort is expended to perform, if the performance is successful,
and if the reward promised by the incentive is received. The value promised by a
particular incentive is considered on the basis of two criteria: (1) To what degree
will the unfilled need be satisfied, and (2) will the reward (if attained as promised)
be equal to or greater than the effort required to perform successfully and to earn

the promised reward?[12] The review of these criteria, of course, is a rather subjective one. Previous experience, existing urgencies, and future needs are all surveyed in an attempt to determine potential satisfaction levels. The relevance of the incentive to the felt need is considered. The demands of the job in terms of mental and physical effort are reviewed. If the promise of reward (value) is perceived to be acceptable, the motivational process moves to another pre-action phase—the probability that the individual can perform in such a way that he can successfully earn the reward promised (Phase 4).

The probability of successful performance is reviewed by the individual in several ways. As a potential performer, the worker surveys his own knowledge and skills to determine if he believes himself capable of performance that will help him to earn the anticipated reward. The worker analyzes the resources at his command (including the appropriate machinery, materials, etc.) to determine the availability and adequacy of these in helping him do his work. The individual also considers the amount and type of support he can expect from his superiors, his colleagues (peers), his subordinates, and other personnel on whom he may be dependent. He questions whether or not they will be willing and able to assist him in this performance effort if he decides to respond to the attraction of the incentive (see Figure 10.4).

Other factors also enter into the assessment of the probability of success. The worker reviews the time available for his performance in an effort to judge if it is sufficient. In addition, he considers the intent and sincerity of the agent offering the incentive as a means of motive fulfillment. Is the agent (who usually is his own superior) genuinely interested in having the worker achieve success in his performance so that the reward can be earned? These and other factors help the individual worker determine if he has a reasonable chance to perform in a way that would make possible the earning of the reward promised by the incentive.

If the value of the benefits offered by the incentive and the probability of successful performance appear to be positive, the worker usually decides to take action (expend effort) in order to achieve the promised rewards. Action on the part of the worker (Phase 5 of the model) is a voluntary step entered into with optimism and a sense of expectation. An action-result relationship is anticipated in which the adequate performance of the worker is expected to result in need fulfillment.

Quite often, theorists discussing the motivation process stop their analysis with the action being taken by the worker. However, post-action events are extremely

[12]Edgar F. Huse and James L. Bowditch, *Behavior in Organizations, A Systems Approach to Managing,* Reading, Massachusetts: Addison-Wesley Publishing Company, 1973, p. 74, state that the degree of motivation will be a result of the reward promised minus the cost involved in earning the reward.

FIGURE 10.4   Evaluating probabilities of successful performance

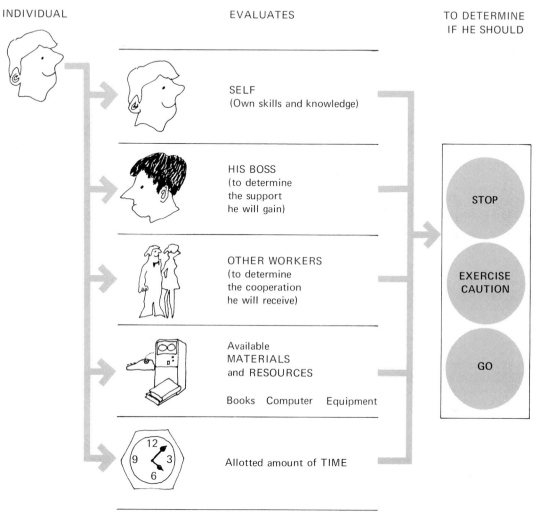

INDIVIDUAL   EVALUATES   TO DETERMINE
                                                                                  IF HE SHOULD

SELF
(Own skills and knowledge)

HIS BOSS
(to determine
the support
he will gain)

STOP

OTHER WORKERS
(to determine
the cooperation
he will receive)

EXERCISE
CAUTION

Available
MATERIALS
and RESOURCES

Books   Computer   Equipment

GO

Allotted amount of TIME

etc.

important if immediate satisfaction is to be gained by the worker and future receptivity to incentives is to be provided. When the worker performs in the manner required by the incentive pact, he should receive the promised reward (Phase 6—Option A). As he receives the anticipated reward, his motives are potentially fulfilled and his confidence in future motive-incentive situations is reinforced. If he performs adequately but does not receive the promised reward, he will become skeptical of incentive offerings in the future as well as being disappointed at the failure to earn rewards immediately.

If, on the other hand, the worker fails to perform adequately and does not earn the reward expected, the effects are less certain. Sometimes the worker who fails in his performance becomes bitter and antagonistic toward external factors he feels caused him to fail. The worker may lose confidence in himself. In most situations, future motivation-incentive situations will be viewed more critically and the value and probability factors will need to have strongly positive scores before action will be taken to attain their rewards (Phase 6—Option B).[13]

~~In some situations, however, failure makes the worker even more determined to succeed.~~ In these reactions, the worker reassesses the motives, incentives, values, and probability of success factors and *restrives* or puts forth additional effort to perform satisfactorily in order to gain the rewards needed to fulfill his basic motives and goals (Phase 6—Option C). Through additional effort, performance deserving the reward may be achieved and the reward may be received.

When performance is successful and rewards are received, motive fulfillment or satisfaction (Phase 8) does not always occur immediately. The individual assesses the equity of the rewards that have been passed along to him (Phase 7). He ~~evaluates~~ the ~~rewards received~~ on the basis of justice and fair treatment according to: (1) the ~~rewards originally offered~~, (2) the ~~effort required to earn the~~ ~~rewards~~, and (3) the ~~rewards received by others for similar effort and actions~~. If he perceives the reward to be just and equitable, his acceptance of the reward will be gratification and satisfaction. If he perceives inequities, the effects of the rewards may be reduced. If all phases of the process have been completely successful, satisfaction of needs and expectations (motives) is finally attained (Phase 8). The motivational process then starts anew (Phase 9). The assessment of motives must be made again and incentives must be renewed to fulfill existing motives. ~~In a healthy work environment~~, the ~~motivational process is a continuous cycle~~.

The detailed breakdown of this motivational process makes the total cycle appear lengthy and laborious. While the progression is calculated, the process may actually move rapidly. Some phases may occur almost subconsciously and without a large amount of mental or physical effort.

Studies Related to Positive Motivation.   The model of positive motivation just presented is consistent with the findings of Greene, who states that effort will be expended only if the motivation-reward structure meets the following criteria:

---

[13]Note the relationship of these concepts to the ideas of Combs and Snygg presented in Chapter 2. Successful behavior tends to breed confidence and continuing success. Unsuccessful performance may result in a lack of confidence and corresponding belligerence, or it may result in an effort to overcome, to restrive.

1.   The reward to be attained has value to the employee. There is a consistency between the employee's needs and wants and the reward offered.

2.   The magnitude of the reward is significant to the employee. The benefits to be attained by gaining the reward are of more than just passing importance to the worker.

3.   The worker has confidence in his ability to perform well enough to earn the reward. He must feel that the task to be accomplished is not too difficult and the obstacles in view can be overcome.

4.   The rewards to be given must actually reflect the contributions of the individual performer. It must be possible to link the employee's individual performance to the rewards he receives.[14]

No other study of expectancy theory has been done that can be directly related to the positive model of motivation presented in this chapter. However, the studies performed by Kuhn, Slocum, and Chase[15] and Cherrington, Reitz, and Scott[16] provide information concerning other expectancy theories.

The Role of the Supervisor.   The motivational process presented in Figure 10.3 is a positively based model and suggests that the primary source of motivation is internal (within the worker himself). The supervisor and his company have only limited influence upon the creation of the original motives and needs of the worker. If managers have only limited control over the development and existence of employee motives, what is the manager's role in the motivational process?

The manager's role in the motivational process is directly related to each phase of progress in the motivation model (shown in Figure 10.3). First, the motives and needs of the worker must be assessed to determine the existence of needs and the intensity of the drives to fulfill them. Each individual must be analyzed separately to discover his own unique motives. All available techniques may be enlisted in attempting to uncover the urgent goals of each worker. Observation, interview, written attitude survey, assessment of previous goal achievement, and other possible sources of need information may be reviewed. The task of identifying existing needs is often complex and difficult, as shown in an old, but classic study performed by the Labor Relations Institute.[17]

[14]Charles N. Greene, "The Satisfaction-Performance Controversy," *Business Horizons*, Volume 15, Number 5 (October 1972), pp. 31–41.

[15]David G. Kuhn, John W. Slocum, Jr., and Richard B. Chase, "Does Job Performance Affect Employee Satisfaction?" *Personnel Journal*, Volume 50, Number 6 (June 1971), pp. 455–459, 485.

[16]David J. Cherrington, H. Joseph Reitz, and William E. Scott, Jr., "Effects of Contingent and Noncontingent Reward on the Relationship between Satisfaction and Task Performance," *Journal of Applied Psychology*, Volume 55, Number 6 (December 1971), pp. 531–536.

[17]"Do You Know What Your Workers Want?" *Foreman Facts*, New York: Labor Relations Institute, 1946, pp. 3–4.

In the L.R.I. survey (Figure 10.5), each member of a large group of workers was asked to rank ten items in terms of their importance to him (the individual worker) as he performed his job. The supervisors over the workers were also asked to rank the factors as they thought their subordinates would rank them. A review of the two separate rankings shows that the order of importance of the factors for the workers was considerably different from the rankings anticipated by their supervisors. While the listings should not be considered descriptive of all workers, they do have a significance for the specific time in which the survey was made.

As can be seen, the two rankings varied widely in the importance given to each factor. There are two possible explanations for the variations between the worker and the supervisory ratings. It is possible that the supervisors and other manage-

FIGURE 10.5   Worker and supervisory rankings of desires and expectations of workers

Expectation or desire	Workers' rankings	Supervisors' rankings of what they expected workers to say
Feel appreciation of work done	1	8
Feeling "in" on things	2	10
Sympathetic help on personal problems	3	9
Job security	4	2
Good wages	5	1
"Work that keeps you interested"	6	5
Promotion and growth opportunities	7	3
Personal loyalty of supervisors to workers	8	6
Good working conditions	9	4
Tactful disciplining	10	7

Source: "Do You Know Your Workers' Wants?", *Foreman Facts*, New York: Labor Relations Institute, 1946, pp. 3-4.

rial personnel had perceptively discovered previous worker desires for good wages and job security and had adequately provided for fulfillment of these desires to the point that they were no longer of top priority to the workers. In other words, money and job security may have been important at one time but have decreased in urgency because of earlier attainment. Other factors, therefore, may have advanced themselves as new desires with a higher priority.

The other possible explanation for the inconsistencies could lie in the lack of perceptiveness of the supervisors at the time of the survey (or previously) for the true feelings and interests of their subordinates. Neither of these explanations, however, alters the reality that ~~supervisors who do not know the motives or needs of their subordinates are seriously handicapped in providing incentives that will effectively stimulate interest and action from their workers~~. The motivational process will be only randomly successful unless the needs and interests of the individual worker are perceived correctly.

After motives have been identified, incentives that will be appealing and stimulating must be decided upon and offered. This is primarily a process of matching needs to possible means of fulfillment. The worker may play an active role by indicating incentives that would be attractive to him, but supervisors also have responsibilities in the selection and provision of incentives. The manager-supervisor should make an effort to select and provide incentives that will be adequately rewarding to the worker if his performance satisfactorily earns the reward. The supervisor also must consider whether or not the incentive will attract and sustain the type of effort from the subordinate that will help the organization attain its objectives. Also, the supervisor must discern the cost to the organization of providing the incentive (to determine if the results to the company are justifiable in relation to the expenditure). Incentives offered to workers must be attractive, realistic, and worthwhile, for all parties involved.

Determination of the potential value of an incentive offered (Phase 3) is primarily an activity of the worker himself, but the manager-supervisor can help the worker make the assessment. The supervisor can communicate the reward terms as fully as possible by showing the worker what he will earn if he performs capably and successfully. For example, if a job promotion awaits successful performance, the promotion and its benefits can be discussed. If a wage increase is the impending reward, a breakdown of the reward benefits into dollar earnings may be helpful in the assessment of value. Sometimes the manager may find it necessary to help the worker see the need fulfillment possible in less obvious situations. If, for example, a worker has a desire for recognition and a strengthened reputation, his boss may assist him in discovering the recognition attainable if he performs a certain task successfully. As the supervisor does this, he helps the

individual see the relevance of the incentive to his personal motives. *The supervisor's assistance must be informational and supportive rather than manipulative if his role
is to accomplish positive results.*[18] The supervisor should never be involved in creating
or promising false values to his subordinates. The supervisor's job is to match the
genuine needs of the worker with real opportunities to fulfill these needs within
the organization. The supervisor must consider personal, social, and organizational factors as he provides incentive opportunities. It is not the supervisor's
purpose to trick the worker into doing something against the worker's own will.
~~True motivation fulfills personal needs while achieving organizational goals.~~

The job of matching employee needs with incentives that may be attractive
and encourage better performance may be a difficult challenge for the supervisor.
Frequently, the incentives available are limited in number and in variety. When
this is the case, it is imperative that organizational decision-makers in the upper
hierarchies provide as many alternative incentive patterns as possible for use by
supervisors. This means that upper levels of management must plan for flexibility
in the incentive approaches that are to be available, and they must communicate
the variety of alternatives to the managers who must apply them. Upper-level
managers will, of course, be instrumental in training lower-level managers in
how to discuss employee needs and to offer useful incentives. The supervisor
working with the employee (regardless of the organizational level) is the one who
finally implements the incentive plan.

The supervisor can be of major assistance to a subordinate as the worker attempts to measure the probabilities of success in earning a reward through his
performance (Phase 4). The worker usually questions his own capacity to perform,
the availability of sufficient help from his fellow workers, and the existence of a
favorable work environment. The supervisor should encourage the worker to do
things that are *within his capability to achieve.* Incentives with performance demands
beyond the abilities of the worker will lead only to frustration. Capable workers
sometimes also need reassurance from others before they are willing to take
action.

Managers can help their subordinates in the motivational process by supporting
them with their own actions and by providing the necessary training, physical
resources, equipment, policy support, and a cooperative work atmosphere. Some
management theorists have taken the position that when a worker fails at the
performance of duties assigned to him, his failure is partially the fault of his
superior, who may have given him the wrong kind of assignments and support.
Not everyone accepts this statement, but in many cases it may be applicable.

[18]See, for example, the article by Frank M. Sterner, "Motivate—Don't Manipulate," *Personnel
Journal,* Volume 48, Number 8 (August 1969), pp. 623–627.

Taking action (Phase 5) has been prepared for by each of the previous steps. The next managerial action comes following performance. The supervisor (sometimes with the help of the performer) evaluates the actions of the worker to determine if the performance is sufficient to earn the promised reward. If the worker deserves the reward, it should be given promptly to reinforce and encourage future performance (Phase 6—Option A).[19] If performance is insufficient or inadequate, the supervisor should be concerned about the failure and should attempt to identify the causes of the inadequacy. If the manager-supervisor has the knowledge and authority to correct organization conditions that may have contributed to the failure, he should make an effort to correct them. He should communicate his support to the worker and should try to encourage him to restrive and to be receptive to future incentive situations. The supervisor's intent when failure occurs should be to get Phase 6—Option C into action rather than Option B.

Managerial actions are helpful in getting a positive reaction concerning the feeling of reward equity (Phase 7) if rewards are given as described and promised, with equal and fair treatment for everyone. Satisfaction (Phase 8) then occurs spontaneously, and the motivational cycle begins again (Phase 9).

While the total motivational process is oriented toward motive fulfillment of the individual worker, the actions of the worker's supervisor determine to a large degree whether or not the process will be rewarding to the individual and useful to the organization.

A Negative Motivational Model

The motivational model presented above is primarily based on positive motives and constructive rewards. The implication of the model is that people want improvement over existing conditions (fulfillment of existing needs) and are willing to direct their efforts and actions toward organizationally useful behavior if they visualize means to fulfill existing needs. However, there are times when motivational techniques that are negatively based as opposed to positively oriented appear among the actions of some managers.[20] The use of negative motivation, therefore, deserves investigation.

The negative motivational process is primarily the inducement of the desired behavior or performance from a subordinate through the use of fear. The fundamental assumption behind the negative motivational process is that people are

[19]Berelson and Steiner, op. cit., p. 141.

[20]Negative motivation is somewhat similar to the Theory X approach to leadership or the "stick" approach sometimes referred to in motivational literature.

protective by nature—they wish to preserve and protect what they already have, to maintain the status quo in terms of their existing possessions and previous achievements. Thus, the worker's basic motives include the protection and preservation of his previous attainments so that already fulfilled needs are not jeopardized by future action (see Figure 10.6). The effect of this protectiveness is to maintain and hold secure rather than to enrich and fulfill.

The incentives of negative motivation (Phase 2) are threats to reduce or restrict existing levels of attainment and satisfaction. If a worker is earning a good wage presently and is achieving personal goal satisfaction from it, the negative approach

FIGURE 10.6   Model of negative motivation

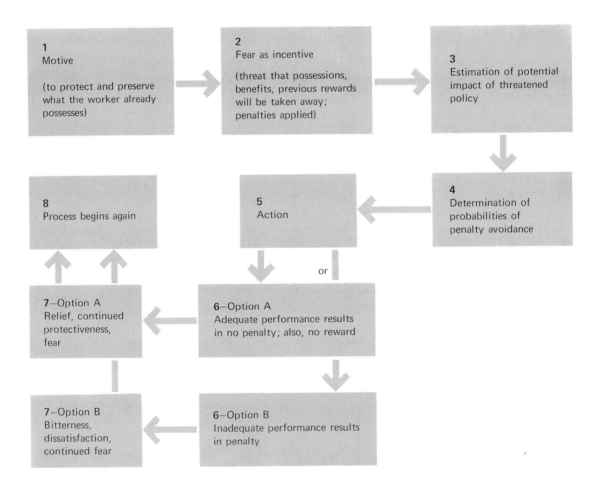

threatens to reduce his income level if a certain performance action is not achieved or maintained by the worker. If the worker presently enjoys respect and admiration, the negative motivational approach may threaten to destroy or reduce his reputation if a certain performance is not adhered to. Other motive-need categories may be threatened in a similar manner. The threatened penalties are analyzed in terms of the potential discomfort and pain they will cause (Phase 3). The more punishment and suffering that is anticipated, the more urgent will be the desire to avoid the threatened penalty. The penalty must be avoidable, however, if the individual is to be enticed into an attempt to avoid its predicted effects. As a result, the worker must be convinced that he has the ability to perform successfully to avoid the penalty, and he must also have confidence in the support he will receive from his superiors, peers, and subordinates (Phase 4).

Action is taken (Phase 5) with the specific purpose of performing adequately to avoid receiving the penalty that threatens the worker's goal of keeping secure what he already possesses. The action often takes place with apprehension and resentment. If the individual's performance meets the standard imposed upon him, the penalty is avoided (Phase 6—Option A). If performance falls below the behavior expected, the penalty occurs (Phase 6—Option B) and the worker loses something he values (wages, prestige, security, the opportunity for achievement or advancement, etc.).

The effect of penalty avoidance (Phase 7—Option A) is temporary relief but a continued protectiveness and a fear that the threat of penalties will be a reality sometime in the future. The results of receiving a penalty (Phase 7—Option B) may include disappointment, bitterness, dissatisfaction, and continued fear. Psychologists have stated that if the negative motivational approach is to have success in the long run, penalties and threats of penalties must be constantly present to reinforce the fear. Otherwise, the negative motivational process will be condemned to failure.[21] Also, the worker must feel a dependency on the organization so that he cannot readily escape from the threat by leaving (or sabotaging) the organization.

The Role of the Supervisor.   The role of the manager-supervisor in the negative motivational process begins with the discovery of the worker's motives. From the negative viewpoint, these motives are achievements, values, or possessions the worker is seeking to protect and preserve. The supervisor suggests the possible

---

[21]For helpful discussions of the use of fear as a conditioning factor, see Gregory A. Kimble, *Hilgard and Marquis' Conditioning and Learning,* Second Edition, New York: Appleton-Century-Crofts, 1961, pp. 263–280, or Berelson and Stein, *op. cit.,* pp. 137–157.

penalty (applies the incentive) and outlines the specific performance that is expected if the penalty is to be avoided. If he wishes to impress the individual with the seriousness of the penalty, he may emphasize the potential effects of the penalty upon the factors the worker is attempting to maintain. He also helps the worker to realize that penalties can be avoided by acceptable performance. After the action is taken, the supervisor is a primary participant in the evaluation of performance. He judges the action to determine if it meets expectations or falls below them. Penalties are meted out or withheld depending upon his assessment of the performance. For maximum effectiveness, necessary penalties are applied rather rigidly as threatened. The process then begins again.

The negative motivational approach has been the center of a large amount of controversy. Traditionalists have taken the position that the "stick" approach is essential with some individuals in specific situations. Behavioralists have often called the approach "old-fashioned," "brutal," and "unnecessary." This author takes the position that positive motivation is infinitely more desirable, pleasant, and usually more effective. It is possible, however, that conditions may call for the use of negative motivational techniques. From an idealistic point of view, the negative approach should be utilized only temporarily with the goal of shifting to the positive approach as a central factor in future planning.

Summary

Managers perform many tasks as they fulfill leadership roles. One of the most important managerial duties is that of discerning employee motives and providing opportunities to fulfill needs and to be rewarded for productive performance. Expectancy theories of motivation suggest that the most effective motivational methods are those that focus on achievement of future rewards rather than those that concentrate on past rewards and satisfactions. A basic thesis of expectancy theory states that people will respond to work opportunities that promise rewards that are of significant value to them and are within the probability of attainment. Probability of attainment implies that the employee can perform well enough to successfully earn the reward he values.

The positive motivational model developed in this chapter embraces the expectancy concept that employees will respond to opportunities that promise rewards they personally value and believe they can attain through expending their efforts. When employees respond and perform successfully they must, of course, be rewarded promptly and adequately if positive motivation is to work effectively. If employees fail to perform adequately, they should be encouraged to restrive and should be given appropriate supervisory assistance to achieve future successes. When rewards are given to successful performers, they must be fair, equitable, and in keeping with promised incentives. When satisfaction is achieved for an employee, the motivational process begins again. New incentives may be necessary for newly activated motives. The concept of positive motivation is a pleasant, satisfying situation for the parties involved.

Occasionally some individuals seem to respond to threats and fear more than to opportunities to attain rewards. Negative motivation threatens to take something away from the employee if he fails to perform adequately. The employee who values whatever is being threatened (wages, a promotion, and so forth) and believes he can perform well enough to avoid the penalty may take action to perform and overcome the threat. Good performance should result in no penalty being assessed and temporary relief on the employee's part. Inadequate performance normally results in the threat's being fulfilled, and the employee feels bitterness and dissatisfaction. Negative motivational techniques are not enjoyable methods of getting work accomplished and, as a result, usually give way to positive motivational techniques whenever possible.

From an organizational point of view, motivation has as one of its major purposes the accomplishment of performance goals in line with organizational objectives. From a personal point of view, motivational techniques are an important means of providing individual workers with the fulfillment of important needs. The next chapter will consider some specific incentives and other factors that may contribute to or detract from worker performances and motive fulfillment.

Questions to consider after reading Chapter 10

1.   When a manager attempts to motivate a worker so that the worker will be more productive, is the manager manipulating the worker to do something that the worker doesn't want to do?

2.   Is it true that the satisfied worker often is not a very productive worker? Why or why not?

3.   In this chapter it was stated that motives are within individuals. Can management have any effect upon the development of these motives?

4.   How can a manager who wishes to apply the positive motivational model discover the need-motives of his workers?

5.   Discuss in detail a manager's role in helping a worker determine the value of an incentive. Also, discuss a manager's role in helping an employee determine the possibility of successful performance in order to earn a reward.

6.   If a worker fails to perform successfully and therefore does not earn a reward, what can the manager do to help the worker decide to restrive rather than to withdraw?

7.   Would the negative motivational model be applicable to most workers under typical working conditions? In other words, will the average worker respond favorably to negative motivation?

8.   What is the theory behind negative motivation? Are the assumptions upon which negative motivation is based valid?

All of the cases at the back of the book contain problems related to Chapter 10. In particular, the following cases have motivational problems or illustrations:

Ben Stockton

Mark Williams

Stanley Lowell

H. Gerald Pretzler

Edith Capp and Janet Turner

Earl Fornette

Bentley Cantrell

Billy Snyder

Grace Lanham

Bill Caden

Richard Jameson

Walt Gladberry

Abigail Spiegal and Trudy Pennington

Additional reading

Brayfield, A. H., and H. F. Rothe, "An Index of Job Satisfaction," *Journal of Applied Psychology,* Volume 35, Number 5 (October 1951), pp. 307–311.

Evans, Martin G., "Leadership and Motivation: A Core Concept," *The Academy of Management Journal,* Volume 13, Number 1 (March 1970), pp. 91–102.

Johnson, LeRoy, "Toward A Y System," *California Management Review,* Volume 15 Number 1 (Fall 1972), pp. 22–29.

Katz, Daniel, "Motivational Basis of Organizational Behavior," *Behavioral Science,* Volume 9, Number 2 (April 1964), pp. 131–146.

Kunin, Theodore, "The Construction of a New Type of Attitude Measure," *Personnel Psychology,* Volume 8, Number 1 (Spring 1955), pp. 65–77.

Roberts, Karlene H., Gordon A. Walter, and Raymond E. Miles, "A Factor Analytic Study of Job Satisfaction Items Designed To Measure Maslow Need Categories," *Personnel Psychology,* Volume 24, Number 2 (Summer 1971), pp. 205–220.

———, and Frederick Savage, "Twenty Questions: Utilizing Job Satisfaction Measures," *California Management Review,* Volume 15, Number 3 (Spring 1973), pp. 82–90.

Sutermeister, Robert A., "Employee Performance and Employee Need Satisfaction—Which Comes First?" *California Management Review,* Volume 13, Number 4 (Summer 1971), pp. 43–47.

Viteles, Morris S., *Motivation and Morale in Industry,* New York: W. W. Norton and Company, 1953, pp. 271–290, 394–413.

For additional readings relating to this chapter, please see the lists following chapters 2, 7, and 11.

Chapter 11

Money, Morale, and other Influences on Worker Behavior

A case to consider before
reading chapter II

NEW MANAGEMENT AT GARDEN-RITE

The Garden-Rite Company, located in a large western city, is a wholly-owned subsidiary of the Mayfair Company. The Garden-Rite Company manufactures and distributes equipment and machinery for use by individuals who cultivate vegetables and fruits on a limited scale (mostly for noncommercial production). The company also manufactures machinery and equipment for lawn care.

The management of the parent firm, the Mayfair Company, recently became concerned about decreasing profit ratios at Garden-Rite and decided that the subsidiary needed a new management team to make some changes and to implement a more strenuous, vigorous management plan. The general manager, production manager, and sales manager of Garden-Rite were all replaced with men transferred from other Mayfair operations. The replacements all have a reputation for being aggressive, demanding managers.

Shortly after their arrival on the new assignment three months ago, the new managers sent memoranda to department heads and workers stating some policy changes that were being instituted. The introductory remarks accompanying the new policies indicated the three managers' belief that unless the changes were accepted and implemented promptly, the Garden-Rite Company's future was in serious jeopardy. One of the major policy changes included in the memorandum indicated that there would be a shift in worker pay plans from an hourly rate, on which all production workers' salaries had previously been based, to a modified piece-rate plan whereby each worker would receive a small weekly base salary, and the remainder of his income would be determined strictly by his own production performance. Policies outlining new disciplinary programs in which more severe penalties would be applied for performance errors and acts of negligence were also indicated. Each worker was told that he could expect closer supervision in the future and should anticipate being held directly accountable for failures and inadequacies.

The immediate reaction of most workers (and their immediate supervisors) was one of shock and insecurity. As the weeks have passed by, it has become apparent that the new managers are standing behind the stated policies. The new wage plans have been implemented, with a resulting slight decrease in the wages of a majority of the workers. Penalties for performance violations have been more numerous and more severe. The number of worker discharges has increased. Supervisors have been pressured to watch their subordinates more closely.

At first, productivity took an abrupt jump upward, but in the past few weeks it has settled into a pattern at approximately the same level it was in the pre-change days. While the effect on productivity has been minimal, the impact on morale has been disastrous. Cooperation between workers and supervisors has disintegrated. Bitterness and dissension have become commonplace. Worker actions have become careless and indifferent.

Questions about the Garden-Rite case

1. What motivational philosophy was the new management team pursuing with its new policies and methods? Was this philosophy correct or incorrect under the existing conditions?

2. In what ways did the approach used to introduce the policy changes contribute to the resentment that developed? What steps might have been taken by the new management team to reduce the resentment and hostility to its more stringent policies?

3. The majority of the workers' earnings decreased as a result of the change in the method of payment. In reality, most of the workers could have earned more by exerting more personal effort. Why didn't the workers extend more effort so that they could earn more money?

4. Under what conditions will workers perform more effectively in order to earn more money? In other words, when is money an effective motivator?

5. What is morale? What specific factors caused the morale of the workers to decrease in this case?

6. Should the company's management be concerned about the decrease in morale? Why or why not?

7. Now that productivity still remains at an unsatisfactory level and morale has decreased greatly, what steps can be taken to correct the situation?

8.   Go back to the beginning of the case. If you had been a manager with the Mayfair Company and were concerned about implementing changes to improve performance at the Garden-Rite Company, what actions would you have suggested?

9.   Could this case be used as an argument against autocratic management and close supervision? Why or why not?

10.   What role did the informal organization probably play in the way the change was resisted? Why? What constructive role could the informal organization have played if the change had been handled properly?

If the motivational process is functioning properly, the end result should be worker performance that is both productive for the organization and rewarding to the individual worker. Several factors appear capable of encouraging performance that is mutually beneficial to the organization and to the individual. Some of these factors are directly identifiable as incentives in the motivational model presented in Chapter 10. Other factors are primarily conditions or relationships that may influence performance and personal fulfillment. In this chapter, several of the more important influencing factors are considered and their implications analyzed.

Money as a Motivating Force

Perhaps the most analyzed incentive is that of money. The fact that money is easily identifiable and quantifiable has caused much attention to be directed toward it. Attitudes toward money as a motivator seem to vary widely. Some attitudes are represented by the statement, "People will do anything for money." This, of course, is an extreme position, but some managers have operated on the assumption that money is the only real value workers desire from their jobs, and that the workers will be willing to perform almost any task (regardless of the danger or undesirability of it) if the wage for doing it is adequate. The opposite extreme of attitudes toward money as a motivator is that it may have been effective at one time in the American economy, but it no longer is influential because the economic well-being of most individuals has reached a point of sufficiency. In other words, the need level of the average worker has progressed beyond the point at which money can help to satisfy.

Neither of these positions is completely adequate. According to the motivational model presented in the previous chapter, an incentive may effectively stimulate action if it appears to promise a value important and relevant to the worker and if the incentive seems to be reasonably attainable.[1] If money is offered as the incentive and is made attainable, the issue for the worker becomes one of deciding whether the needs that can be fulfilled by money are of pertinent value. Will money do the things needed and desired by the potential performer? Are the values equal to or greater than the effort required to earn the reward? If the answer is yes (if the values are considered worthwhile), money can serve as a useful incentive.

Money often is looked upon primarily as a means of fulfilling the most basic needs of man—his physical maintenance and security needs. Certainly money helps provide many things to fulfill these needs. Food, clothing, shelter, transportation, insurance, pension plans, education, and other physical maintenance and security factors are made available through the purchasing power provided by monetary income—salaries and wages. Where these needs are urgent and vital, the opportunity to earn money is important.

In a study conducted by the author, a group of upperclassmen nearing graduation at a major university was asked to rank ten items they hoped to obtain through the first full-time job they would have following graduation.[2] A good monetary income (take-home pay) was the number one item in the ranking of importance of the ten items available. (See Figure 11.1 for the complete list and rankings of other items.) In discussions with the students, it was brought out that many of them were on very limited budgets while working on their college educations. Also, many of the students were married or soon would be. Purchasing power was needed by almost everyone to aid in the acquisition of the basics of living as well as to provide some desirable luxuries. The opportunity to earn money, therefore, was a powerful motivator for the young people as a result of what it could buy. Typically, the more youthful part of the work force finds money to be an attractive incentive because it offers the means to purchase important items. Quite often, younger workers find many of the payroll deductions for pension items and other deferred benefits something of a hindrance to the attainment of more immediate monetary needs.

Other age segments of the work force may be equally interested in the purchasing power of money. Many workers nearing retirement age have a serious interest in money as a means of providing economic security as well as physical maintenance in the years of retirement, when income will be limited. The middle-

---

[1]See N. R. F. Maier and L. R. Hoffman, "Financial Incentives and Group Decision in Motivating Change," *Journal of Social Psychology,* Volume 64, Second Half (December 1964), pp. 369–378, for additional ideas concerning the importance of money when the worker's needs are intense.

[2]O. Jeff Harris, "Young People in Today's Labor Force," *Louisiana Business Review,* Volume 35, Number 6 (June 1971), pp. 4–6, 9.

FIGURE 11.1   Student rankings of ten job-related factors

OVERALL RANK ORDER	FACTOR
1	Job provides a good income
2	Job provides opportunities to develop abilities and knowledge
3	Job allows freedom and independence of action
4	Job with friendly work environment
5	Job with boss who is fair
6	Job allows experimentation and encourages new ideas
7	Job provides contact with other people
8	Job has good retirement benefits
9	Job provides good physical working conditions
10	Job allows profit-sharing participation

Source: O. Jeff Harris, "Young People in Today's Labor Force," *Louisiana Business Review*, Volume 35, Number 6 (June 1971), p. 5.

aged to older worker who has children in college and must provide significant financial support for them while they complete their education finds money an attractive reward. To each of these individuals, the opportunity to earn more money serves as a positive incentive at work.

The points presented above illustrate the value and attractiveness of money to many workers. In the face of these facts, it cannot reasonably be argued that the American economy has become so affluent that money is no longer an important incentive for at least some members of the work force. Whenever basic needs remain unfilled, money has potential as a motivator.

In many ways, money also has potential as a means of fulfillment for several of the higher-level needs. For example, increased monetary earnings as a reward for increased performance (in either quantity or quality) serve as a form of feedback to the worker. If the worker performs well, the monetary reward in the form of increased earnings informs him of his success. As such, the monetary reward may appeal to the worker's desires for achievement and competency. Money becomes a tangible gauge of achievement and accomplishment.

The reality of this statement opens up many doors to motivation and answers some of the critics who have limited the effectiveness of money as an incentive. The motivation-hygiene conceptualization presented by Herzberg, for example, has frequently been interpreted as one of the most effective arguments for playing down the importance of money as a stimulus to action. In his motivational model, Herzberg states that there are some factors that stimulate people to higher levels of performance, including opportunities for advancement, the opportunity to assume more meaningful organizational responsibility, intrinsic job satisfactions, recognition for good performance, and opportunities for achievement. These are known as motivators or **satisfiers.** There are also some factors that he believes fail to stimulate and motivate, including working conditions, supervision and interpersonal relations, wages and salaries, the technical supervision received, and company policy and administration. He calls these **dissatisfiers** or hygienic factors.[3] One way of interpreting dissatisfiers would be to say that they are needs that have already been fulfilled. As a result, the dissatisfier has lost its motivational attraction.

If money is a genuine gauge of achievement and is a meaningful form of recognition, *it can then be classified as a motivator* (satisfier) *rather than as a dissatisfier.* As Belcher states:

> To regard Herzberg's theory as disproving pay as a motivator may be something of a misinterpretation of the theory itself. Rather, it can be argued that whether pay is an achievement or a maintenance factor depends on how pay is determined. If pay is geared to achievement and serves as a recognition of achievement, it would seem to be an achievement factor and thus a motivator. It is when pay is unrelated to performance that it serves purely as a maintenance factor (dissatisfier).[4]

Merit increases, bonuses based upon performance, and other forms of monetary recognition for achievement are genuine motivators. However, basic pay, cost-of-living increases, and other wage increases unrelated to an individual's own productivity typically may fall into the maintenance or dissatisfier categories.

The power need, defined earlier as the need to control or to be dominant, often is increased by additional earnings, as money allows a worker to increase his

[3]Frederick Herzberg, Bernard Mausner, and Barbara Snyderman, *The Motivation to Work*, Second Edition, New York: John Wiley & Sons, Inc., 1959.
[4]David W. Belcher, "Ominous Trends in Wage and Salary Administration," *Personnel*, Volume 41, Number 5 (September–October 1964), p. 44

holdings and enlarge the domain over which he can be influential. ~~Monetary~~ ~~rewards also build status and reputation, as wages, salaries, and bonuses are used~~ ~~as a form of social comparison~~.

Money *does* appear to have potential as an incentive beyond the elementary procurement of necessities. Alert managers can identify opportunities in which money may be appealing and can utilize these opportunities as stimulators of action.[5]

Workers will normally respond to monetary incentives, however, only to a certain point. Beyond that point, money becomes ineffective as an inciter of action. There are at least two possible explanations for the ineffectiveness of money as a motivator when that point is reached. It may be that an individual's needs have reached a phase in which only nonmonetary rewards can be visualized as possessing the immediately needed values. In other words, money is not foreseen as having the ability to satisfy an urgent need. A worker, for example, may have a pressing desire to be placed in a work position that requires a fuller utilization of his skills and abilities. This worker may find the offer of more money as a reward for keeping his old, unchallenging position an unacceptable proposal.

The second limiting situation is the one in which the demands (personal cost) required to earn additional money are of greater value than the value of the monetary rewards if they are achieved. To state it another way, the worker may respond to money as a motivator if he believes the benefits will be greater than the expenditures required of him. If the benefits perceived are less than the personal cost, he will not respond to money as an incentive any further (see Figure 11.2). In

FIGURE 11.2   Relationship between perceived personal cost and perceived value of obtained monetary rewards

IF	Perceived personal cost (in terms of effort, sacrifice, unpleasant work demands, etc.)	GREATER THAN	The perceived value of the monetary reward	→	The response to money as an incentive is reduced or eliminated
IF	Perceived personal cost	LESS THAN	The perceived value of the monetary reward	→	The attraction to opportunity to earn more money is enhanced

[5]Other discussions of the potential motivational forces of money may be found in Burt K. Scanlon, "Is Money Still the Motivator?" *Personnel Administrator,* Volume 15, Number 4 (July–August 1970), pp. 8–11, and Saul W. Gellerman, "Motivating Men with Money," *Fortune,* Volume 77, Number 3 (March 1968), p. 144 ff.

effect, a breakeven point is reached in which additional monetary earnings become marginal or even undesirable because of the effort and conditions demanded to earn the added income. In economic terms, it has been said that "a man will work up to the point where the marginal utility of the income he derives from his work equals the marginal disutility he incurs in the effort to acquire it."[6] (See Figure 11.3.)

The perceived personal value of money is considered in terms of the expectations the individual worker holds for potential earnings as a means of providing fulfillment of needs. These expectations have been covered earlier in this chapter. Perceived personal cost of earning additional money can be analyzed in several ways. For example, additional income often calls for harder work effort if the earnings are to be attained. A worker laboring on a piece-rate system has to do more work to get more money. A worker may be willing to put out some additional effort for more money, but seldom does he maximize his earnings, because the demands are too great. Maximization of earnings under a piece-rate plan often calls for more physical and mental effort than the worker believes is justifiable. Also, maximization of earnings might cause the worker to divert his attention from other activities that may be important to him, such as the maintenance of friendly relationships with other workers and the preservation of his role in

FIGURE 11.3   Breakeven analysis of perceived monetary value and perceived personal cost

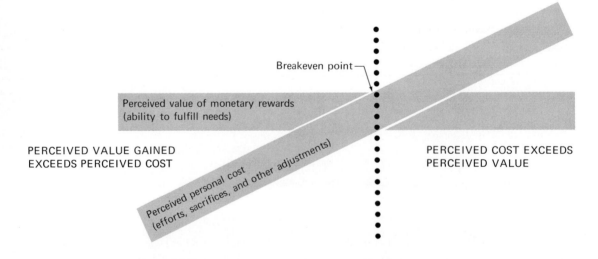

Breakeven point

Perceived value of monetary rewards
(ability to fulfill needs)

PERCEIVED VALUE GAINED
EXCEEDS PERCEIVED COST

Perceived personal cost
(efforts, sacrifices, and other adjustments)

PERCEIVED COST EXCEEDS
PERCEIVED VALUE

[6]Alfred Marshall, quoted in John R. Hicks, *The Theory of Wages*, London: Macmillan and Company, Limited, 1932, p. 96.

existing informal organizations. In these situations, the benefits of earning more money seem to be less than the costs.

An excellent illustration of the diminishing rewards received from earning more money is the observable trend of many workers to reject the opportunity to work overtime in their jobs at twice the pay (in some cases at triple the pay) that they receive in a normal time period. According to one source, workers are refusing to work overtime because they prefer leisure time over additional earnings.[7] Working overtime may be disruptive to family and personal routines. Monotonous jobs and declining loyalty to the company also are listed as contributing factors to disinterest in overtime. Regular wages are considered at least sufficient without the need for additional effort to gain increased earnings.

Personal cost is not always directly related to additional effort required to do a job. In some cases, the cost may be figured in terms of sacrificing something already obtained in order to gain more money. Many workers, for example, decide to turn down higher-paying jobs in other communities because they would be forced to give up social contacts they already have with friends and relatives where they now live. To these workers, the cost of sacrificing personal relationships is greater than the monetary benefits promised.

It can be safely said that some people will be attracted by the opportunity to earn more money and will be willing to direct their efforts accordingly. From the examples shown above, however, it is obvious that most people will not do just anything to get more money.

Monetary Incentive Plans.   Plans used to provide incentives through the use of money may take many forms. Some of the better-known approaches are piece-rate incentives, bonuses, profit sharing, and merit raises. Each of these approaches may be modified in assorted ways. The piece rate, for example, may be paid on the basis of straight monetary rewards for units processed or sold, or the rate of reward may be accelerated or decreased with the increasing number of units handled. Instead of using units handled as a basis of measuring the deserved reward, some "piece-rate" plans pay rewards on the basis of time saved. The employee is rewarded on the basis of his ability to perform a task in less than the standard time allotted to perform the task.

Research findings have shown that piece-rate incentive plans and related approaches tend to increase worker productivity above the level attained through straight salary payment plans. Estimates of increased productivity range from 20

<hr>

[7]"More Factory Workers Give Firms Headaches by Spurning Overtime," *Wall Street Journal,* August 28, 1972, pp. 1, 11.

percent to 60 percent or more.[8] There have been situations where workers have resisted piece-rate incentives, and this trend has been reversed. However, the overall trend still has been observed. Labor costs also tend to be reduced as a result of the use of incentive techniques. On the average, labor costs go down from 10 to 25 percent after monetary incentive techniques are introduced.[9] Incentive plans have been used more frequently in manufacturing organizations, but their usage has spread to almost every type of organizational operation.

In their original form, most incentive plans were based upon individual effort, but in more recent years group incentive plans have been devised whereby several members of a work team coordinate their efforts and are rewarded on the basis of their collective performances. One of the better-known group incentive plans is the Canadian-originated Scanlon plan, which pays the members a bonus on the basis of savings in labor costs. A unique worker suggestion system is normally built into the Scanlon plan in which the workers formulate their own methods of saving cost and effort and are rewarded as their ideas successfully result in labor cost savings.[10] Another well-known plan encouraging group effort is the one devised at Lincoln Electric Company (Cleveland, Ohio).[11] This method is primarily a merit rating system with group cooperation as a part of the total evaluation and reward device. The Scanlon and Lincoln plans are but two of the many incentive techniques that may be applied to group action.

The bonus plan is often quite similar to the piece-rate method in that the worker is normally assigned a task and, if he successfully performs his job, he is rewarded. The main differentiation between most bonus plans and piece-rate methods is that the time period for bonus plans often runs longer and the performance expected is more general in nature. Sometimes, for example, companies pay only annual year-end performance bonuses based upon overall performance criteria.

Profit sharing usually involves the determination of an organization's profits at the end of a fiscal time period (usually annually) and the distribution of a percentage of the profits to workers qualified to share in the earnings. The percentage

[8]See Edward E. Lawler, *Pay and Organizational Effectiveness, A Psychological View,* New York: McGraw-Hill Book Company, 1971, and John D. Dale, "Wage Incentives and Productivity," reported in "Increase Productivity 50 Per Cent in One Year with Sound Wage Incentives," *Management Methods,* Volume 15, Number 5 (February 1959), pp. 38–42, for further discussions of increased productivity through wage incentive methods.

[9]Leon C. Megginson, *Personnel: A Behavioral Approach to Administration,* Revised Edition, Homewood, Illinois: Richard D. Irwin, Inc., 1972, p. 455.

[10]Fred G. Lesieur and Elbridge S. Puckett, "The Scanlon Plan Has Proved Itself," *Harvard Business Review,* Volume 47, Number 5 (September–October 1969), pp. 109–118.

[11]James F. Lincoln, *Incentive Management,* Cleveland: The Lincoln Electric Company, 1951.

to be shared by the workers is often predetermined at the beginning of the work period and is communicated to the workers so that they have some knowledge of their potential gains.[12] Workers sometimes are required to work a certain number of years and develop some seniority before they may participate in the profit sharing. The theory behind profit sharing, simply stated, is that management feels its workers will fulfill their responsibilities more diligently if they realize that their efforts may result in higher profits, which will be returned to the workers through profit sharing.

The merit raise recognizes good performance over a period of time by providing a permanent increase in the basic salary or wage classification of the worker. Merit increases are usually strong positive motivators because, in addition to providing the worker with more purchasing power through increased money, the earned increase fulfills recognition or reputation needs and gives the worker a feeling of competency and achievement. Merit increases represent an excellent illustration of the use of positive motivation.

These and other monetary incentive plans will not be effective without careful planning and implementation. In fact, several authors have suggested a list of requisites that monetary incentive plans should meet if the incentive method is to be attractive to the worker and at the same time administratively sound. Some of the more important requisites are:

1. The reward provided for the worker should be related to his performance contributions in terms of his own productivity, effort, skill, etc.

2. The individual's (or group's if the group method is used) contributions and efforts must be clearly identifiable if rewards are to be given for specific performance.

3. Increased monetary earnings must have the potential to satisfy the existing needs of the worker if the worker is to be attracted by them. In other words, the monetary incentive offered must be relative to current or visible future needs.

4. The reward offered as the incentive must meet government regulations regarding compensation. The level of reward and the frequency of it, for example, must meet minimum wage guidelines. (Some sales commission incentives have had to be redesigned to assure salesmen of at least a regular minimum wage.)

5. The incentive plan should be easily understood by the workers so that they can calculate personal cost and personal benefit factors readily.

6. The incentive plan should provide for rewards to follow quickly after the performance that justifies the reward.

7. The incentive plan must be within the financial and budgetary capacity of the organization. It must be compatible with the financial resources available, in other words. (Some companies have had to revoke commitments to incentive plans as a

[12]Megginson, *op. cit.*, pp. 461–462.

result of lack of financial resources, with disastrous effects on worker morale and worker performance.)

8.   The incentive plan should minimize friction between workers. Ideally, the plan encourages workers to support each other rather than to be noncooperative.

9.   The incentive plan should include some guaranteed protection for the worker who is hindered in his work performance by conditions beyond his control. If the worker has an assignment to carry out and is willing and qualified to perform but is kept from his performance by other forces (such as a breakdown on the assembly line, shortage of inventory elsewhere in the plant, etc.), his earnings should not be completely jeopardized if he is working on an incentive-performance basis. The worker is entitled to at least some kind of minimum earnings in this situation.[13]

Each incentive method must be weighed to determine its ability to meet the criteria outlined above. Some piece-rate methods meet most of the suggested requirements successfully. Others do not. Bonuses paid after a performance period often fail to meet criterion 6—in many cases there is a time lag between the performance and the reward. This is especially true with annual performance bonuses. The cause-effect relationship may become muddled and confused, and the desired reinforcement effect can be lost.

Profit-sharing programs also suffer weaknesses at times, particularly in meeting criteria 1, 2, 5, and 6. Often a worker sees little relationship between his own efforts and the rewards he receives. He also feels that there are many things affecting profits that are outside his realm of control. It may be noted that in Figure 11.1, the opportunity for profit sharing was ranked last in the student preference poll. While many students (and probably workers too) desire to increase their purchasing power and monetary standing, profit sharing is looked upon somewhat skeptically as an unreliable avenue of improvement. Merit wage increases may measure up to the criteria fairly adequately if handled properly.

There are nonmonetary incentives and conditions that are conducive to encouraging performance in addition to monetary ones, and they will be discussed next.

Nonmonetary Incentives

An incentive can be anything that attracts a worker's attention and stimulates him to act. While monetary incentives often appear central, many factors unre-

---

[13]For a more complete discussion of important requisites of monetary incentive plans, see Walter D. Scott, Robert C. Clothier, and William R. Spriegel, *Personnel Management*, Fifth Edition, New York: McGraw-Hill Book Company, 1954, p. 374, and Charles W. Brennan, *Wage Administration*, Revised Edition, Homewood, Illinois: Richard D. Irwin, Inc., 1963, pp. 225–228, 448–450.

lated to money can serve as attention-getters and encouragers of action. The need-motives for affiliation, power, and recognition (see Chapter 7 for a more detailed discussion of these needs) in particular can be appealed to by nonmonetary incentives. Other need-motives may also be fulfilled through nonmonetary means.

A worker, for example, with strong affiliation desires may respond readily to job assignments that provide him with opportunities to relate to socially attractive and satisfying individuals or groups. The opportunity to communicate with and relate to others is a factor many workers emphasize and seek. Particularly attractive are affiliation opportunities that allow an individual to increase his own social status as he relates to others. The key to the executive washroom, while often joked about, is extremely important to some individuals because it symbolizes achievement of high status.

A worker with high-level desires for power may respond readily to an opportunity whereby he can gain leadership and administrative responsibilities. The power-seeking individual may be stimulated by participative or free-rein leadership from his superior because these styles provide the potential of more involvement in the decision-making process. The use of job enlargement may provide added incentive to some workers because they feel capable of controlling wider sets of activities than they previously did.

Workers interested in enhancing their reputations and receiving recognition in the eyes of others may respond to verbal praise or to publicized awards (such as being named employee of the month). Employees proud of their long service are attracted by awards recognizing their seniority. Workers in safety-minded organizations are often attracted by competition for awards for the best safety performance records. Individuals proud of past accomplishments may feel recognized and rewarded if their superiors extend opportunities for participation in more complex and more important job assignments. The opportunity to participate in the formulation of policies may serve as a reputation-reward opportunity for the recognition-oriented individual.

In short, managers can look to many nonmonetary areas for effective, meaningful incentives that will appeal to most of the need-motives of the average worker. In several cases, these nonmonetary factors will stimulate even more attention than would monetary factors.

Morale—Its Determinants and Effects

One of the more evasive, controversial topics concerning worker behavior is that of worker morale. There has been no universal position taken concerning the effects of morale on worker performance, nor has there even been a completely comprehensive definition of what it is. A helpful approach to the analysis of **morale** is to view it as the workers' perceptions of the existing state of their well-being—in other words, the workers' degree of satisfaction with organizational conditions and circumstances. Morale is said to be "high" when conditions and circumstances appear to be favorable and "low" when conditions are unfavorable.

The above definition has two levels of impact. First, morale is a group feeling—a group assessment of conditions. Morale is esprit de corps. Secondly, however, morale also relates to the individual worker and his own perceptions of the existing state of well-being in the organization as it pertains to him. Group morale and the morale of single individuals are interrelated but not necessarily identical. They have an effect on each other. It is conceivable that an individual's own personal perception of existing conditions as they relate to himself may be high, and the group's perception of conditions may be low, or vice versa, but more usually the two share common feelings.

The findings of Roach[14] reinforce the concept of the worker's attitudes toward the satisfactory or unsatisfactory nature of existing factors. Roach determined that twelve factors influence the level of morale: general worker attitudes toward the company; general worker attitudes toward supervision being received; the level of satisfaction with job standards; the level of consideration the supervisor shows his subordinates; the work load and work pressure level; the treatment of individuals by management; the level of worker pride in the company and its activities; the level of worker satisfaction with salaries; worker reactions to the formal communication network in the organization; intrinsic job satisfaction levels of the workers; worker satisfaction with the progress and opportunities for further progression; and worker attitudes toward fellow workers. The more favorably these *were perceived,* the higher was the level of morale.

Applewhite reduces the number of factors influencing the level of morale to five.[15] He states that the components of morale are: the image of the company in the employee's mind; the general quality of supervision received by the employee; the financial satisfaction or material rewards granted to the worker; the friendliness of fellow employees and their ability to work together without friction; and the level of intrinsic job satisfaction.[16]

---

[14]Darrell E. Roach, "Dimensions of Employee Morale," *Personnel Psychology,* Volume 11, Number 3 (Autumn 1958), pp. 419–431.

[15]Philip B. Applewhite, *Organizational Behavior,* Englewood Cliffs, New Jersey: Prentice-Hall, Inc., 1965, p. 25.

[16]For an excellent summary of findings on morale, see Albert R. Martin, "Morale and Productivity: A Review of the Literature," *Public Personnel Review,* Volume 30, Number 1 (January 1969), pp. 42–45.

Perceived reactions to several criteria, therefore, seem important in the determination of levels of worker morale. This author sees three major categories of perception as the ~~critical determinants of the level of morale:~~ (1) the ~~workers'~~ ~~perceptions of the status of organizational factors over which they have no control~~; (2) ~~the workers' perception of the level of satisfaction attained from rewards~~ ~~previously granted to them~~; and (3) the ~~workers' perception of future opportu-~~ ~~nities and conditions whereby additional rewards can be gained.~~ These three basic factors form an organizational climate and determine the perception of well-being at a given moment.

The first of these perceptions includes many factors over which the individual worker sees himself as having little or no influence. The type of supervision the worker receives, the cooperative (or uncooperative) spirit of the employee's fellow workers, the company's policies and attitudes toward its workers, the status of working conditions, and other factors often seem to be largely out of the control of the individual employee. If these factors are perceived to be favorable to the worker, morale will tend to be higher than if the factors seem unfavorable.

The second perception relates to the worker's reaction to rewards received in the past. If the rewards are considered fair and the satisfaction received from them sufficient, morale will tend to be higher than if the perceptions are in the opposite direction.

The third perception has a similar effect. If the worker looks to the future and perceives opportunities for satisfaction and for attainment in the rewards and conditions that lie ahead, morale will tend to be high. If, however, the rewards and opportunities for the future appear to be bleak, morale will tend to be dampened.

The Effects of Morale.   Since morale manifests itself in the attitudes of workers, it is important to review the results of high morale (high perceived satisfaction) and low morale (low perceived satisfaction). One of the most unpredictable effects of the level of morale is its impact upon worker productivity. The studies performed by Katz[17] and Vroom[18] showed no consistent relationships between a specific level of morale and the productive performance of workers. Productivity sometimes is high with high morale, but at other times may be low even when morale is high, and vice versa.

[17]Daniel Katz et al., *Productivity, Supervision, and Morale in an Office Situation,* Ann Arbor: University of Michigan Institute of Social Research, 1950, pp. 48–63, and Daniel Katz et al., *Productivity, Supervision, and Morale among Railroad Workers,* Ann Arbor: University of Michigan Institute of Social Research, 1951, p. 35.

[18]Victor H. Vroom, *Work and Motivation,* New York: John Wiley & Sons, Inc., 1964. p. 26.

This author believes that a possible clue to the relation between productivity and the level of morale may be in a consideration of the three perceptions that affect morale levels. Perception 1 (the worker's perception of the state of factors out of his control) will not encourage better future performance because the worker's behavior will not alter the factors anyway. Perception 2 (the worker's attitude toward past rewards) has been shown by many authors to be ineffective in encouraging good performance in the future.[19] Past rewards seem to have little effect upon future productivity. The worker often looks at the past reward as something that he had the right to receive, and no longer finds the past gain a stimulating, motivating influence. He may be appreciative of previous earnings, but his attention turns to current needs and goals.

Therefore, the major factor that does appear to affect future performance and productivity is the perceived opportunity to gain future rewards through performance (Perception 3). If the opportunity to gain future rewards is present, the possibility exists that this morale factor may influence the worker to strive for increased productivity. The fact remains, however, that no consistent relationship appears to exist between the level of morale and the level of worker productivity.

If worker perceptions lead to a state of high morale, other positive effects may result, and most of these actions are voluntary. With high morale, workers tend to exhibit a willingness to cooperate; employees tend to be more satisfied with existing conditions; employees tend to be more willing to observe company rules; laborers are careful in handling company property and equipment; workers show a loyalty and respect toward their company; people work together harmoniously; and individuals do their jobs without grumbling. High morale also tends to coincide with reduced absenteeism, tardiness, and employee turnover.[20]

Of course, if morale is low, many of the effects will be just the opposite of the effects stated above. The material in Figure 11.4 shows the relationships among perceptions, the level of morale, and the effects of each type of morale.

From the list of benefits accruing from high morale, it can be seen that there are many advantages to be gained from the existence of high morale levels among workers. The benefits suggest to the manager that high morale is worth striving for in order to achieve the many other positive effects even if the positive impact upon productivity is unpredictable. Since morale is determined largely by

[19]See Leonard R. Sayles and George Strauss, *Human Behavior in Organizations,* Englewood Cliffs, New Jersey: Prentice-Hall, Inc., 1967, pp. 143–146, for a good discussion of the effects of past rewards on future performance.

[20]See William J. McLarney, *Management Training,* Fourth Edition, Homewood, Illinois: Richard D. Irwin, Inc., 1964, pp. 592–602, for a discussion of morale.

FIGURE 11.4   Relationships among worker perceptions, levels of morale, and effects of morale

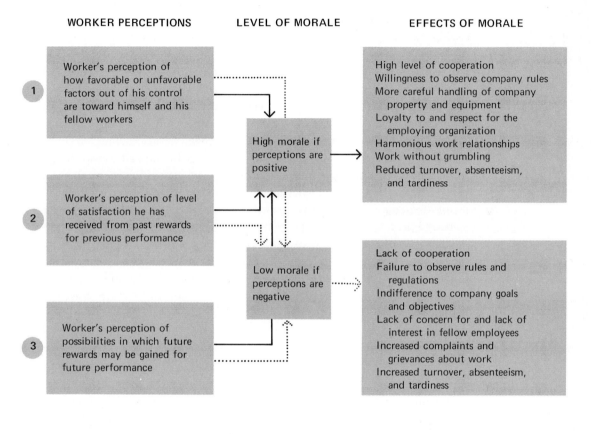

workers' perceptions and attitudes, managers can work on the conditions that define these perceptions so that they will be positively oriented.

For example, managers can concentrate on supervisory styles, company policies, working conditions, and other factors external to and out of the control of the worker to see that such factors are employee-oriented. Leadership styles that support the worker and encourage him may be applied. Policies and conditions that benefit the worker can be established. Communication networks to keep the worker informed can be initiated. Particularly important following the establishment of these employee-oriented programs, however, is the communication of their benefits to the worker himself so that his perception becomes positive as he sees action being taken that is favorable to him.

Perhaps little can be done to remind the worker of positive rewards for past performance, but the manager can help each subordinate to see the opportunities for future rewards through the worker's own performance. Rewards must be consistent, equitable, and known in advance if the perceptions of them are to be positive.

Since morale is, in part at least, a group process, the informal organization and its leaders may have a large impact upon the perceptions and attitudes of members of the group. If informal norms and attitudes are aligned with formal goals, the level of morale is more likely to be high. Manager-supervisors must be sensitive to the attitudes of members of the informal organizations of workers and must cultivate a cooperative attitude.

Managers who are concerned about the welfare of their subordinates, establish policies and take active steps beneficial to the workers, and communicate the positive concern they have for their employees may succeed in encouraging high morale and in gaining the benefits that accompany it.

Other Factors Influencing Worker Behavior

In addition to the studies of worker behavior that have concentrated upon incentives and morale, several studies have reviewed other work conditions and human interaction factors that influence worker performance. One of the more interesting studies in recent years was one conducted by Sorcher and Meyer[21] at General Electric. These psychologists identified six job-related factors that distinguished between the company's more productive and less productive work groups in several of the organization's manufacturing plants. The factors having a relationship to worker performance and the effects of each factor were:

1. The amount of job training possessed by the workers in each work group. The better-trained work groups tended to be better performers than the lesser-trained groups.

[21]Melvin Sorcher and Herbert H. Meyer, "Motivating Factory Workers," *Personnel*, Volume 45, Number 1 (January-February 1968), pp. 22-28.

2.   The degree of goal definition. The better-performing work groups knew what their goals and responsibilities were while the poorer-performing groups had vague notions of their goals and responsibilities.

3.   The level of performance feedback. The groups in which performance feedback was regular were higher in productive motivation and output quality than were the less-informed groups.

4.   The neatness-cleanliness of work areas. The more productive work groups tended to have neater work areas than did the lower-performing groups.

5.   The amount of social facilitation or social distraction. Quality of workmanship was highest in groups where conversation and social interaction were very easy because there was little noise or distance between work stations, or where interaction was impossible.

6.   The repetitiveness of work. Work with short job cycles, limited numbers of tasks, and restricted freedom of movement tended to result in the lowest levels of performance.

The conclusions from this study suggested that to improve worker performance, organizations should: provide more than a minimum of training for employees; create specific performance goals for workers to strive for; provide performance feedback on a regular and frequent basis; encourage neat, orderly work areas; arrange work stations so that conversation (and interaction) between employees is either easy or impossible; increase the number of operations performed by each employee whenever possible; structure jobs so that workers can at least occasionally move about the work area; and explore ways to assign greater responsibility to each individual. These suggestions appear to be sound advice in almost any setting.

Summary

Monetary and nonmonetary incentives can have a direct influence on worker performance if the need-motives of the individual are closely related to the rewards the incentives offer to provide. Astute managers perceive the needs of their subordinates and offer attractive incentives advantageous to the worker and the organization. The effects of morale, on the other hand, are not always predictable. High morale is normally beneficial but does not always result in higher worker productivity. There are a number of work conditions and job factors that also have a bearing on worker behavior.

Questions to consider after reading Chapter 11

1.   Why would anyone make the statement, "People will do anything for money"?

2.   It has been said that the effectiveness of money as an incentive is related to the age

of the worker. Why has this relationship been suggested? How valid is the stated relationship?

3.   Why did the prospective college graduates rank the top items in Figure 11.1 as high as they did? Why were the lower factors rated so low?

4.   What are the manager's responsibilities (if any) in helping his workers to determine the personal cost and personal benefits of monetary incentives?

5.   Analyze piece-rate incentives, bonuses, profit sharing, and merit raises more closely to determine which of the monetary incentive requisites each one meets or fails to meet.

6.   Eight human needs were listed in Chapter 7. Which of these needs can be fulfilled by nonmonetary incentives? Discuss which nonmonetary incentives have the potential for fulfilling these need-motives specifically.

7.   Define the term "morale" in your own words.

8.   If morale is related to a worker's perception of specific conditions, what is management's role in improving morale?

9.   Why is it sometimes difficult to improve morale?

10.   Some managers seem to view morale as the most important indicator of whether or not they have been successful as managers. What causes a manager to consider morale to be so important? Is this a sound managerial position?

11.   Excluding money and morale, what other factors legitimately affect worker productivity?

The following cases at the back of the book contain problems related to Chapter 11:

> Stanley Lowell
>
> Earl Fornette
>
> Bentley Cantrell
>
> Billy Snyder
>
> Kurt Browning
>
> Susan Swanson
>
> Grace Lanham

Additional readings

Adams, J. Stacey, "Wage Inequities, Productivity, and Work Quality," *Industrial Relations,* Volume 3, Number 1 (October 1963), pp. 9–16.

Atchison, T. J., and D. W. Belcher, "Equity, Rewards, and Compensation Administration," *Personnel Administration*, Volume 34, Number 2 (March–April 1971), pp. 32–36.

Brennan, Charles W., *Wage Administration*, Revised Edition, Homewood, Illinois: Richard D. Irwin, Inc., 1963.

Chung, Kae H., "Incentive Theory and Research," *Personnel Administration*, Volume 35, Number 1 (January–February 1972), pp. 31–40.

Crandall, Richard E., "De-Emphasized Wage Incentives," *Harvard Business Review*, Volume 40, Number 2 (March–April 1972), pp. 113–116.

Deardon, John, "How To Make Incentive Plans Work," *Harvard Business Review*, Volume 50, Number 4 (July–August 1972), pp. 117–124.

Ennis, Ruth, "Poor Employee Morale? Supervisors Must Pitch In," *Administrative Management*, Volume 32, Number 8 (August 1971), p. 52.

Evans, Martin A., and Larry Molinari, "Equity, Piece-Rate, Overpayment, and Job Security: Some Effects Upon Performance," *Journal of Applied Psychology*, Volume 54, Number 2 (April 1970), pp. 105–114.

Felton, Thomas C., "Incentive Grievance Bargaining," *The Personnel Administrator*, Volume 14, Number 4 (July–August 1969), pp. 2–15.

Gellerman, Saul W., "Facts and Fallacies about Employee Morale," *Supervisory Management*, Volume 15, Number 10 (October 1970), pp. 4–6.

———, "Motivating Men with Money," *Fortune*, Volume 77, Number 3 (March 1968), pp. 144–146.

Haire, Mason, Edwin E. Ghiselli, and Lyman W. Porter, "Psychological Research on Pay," *Industrial Relations*, Volume 3, Number 1 (October 1963), pp. 3–8.

Hicks, John R., *The Theory of Wages*, London: Macmillan and Company, Limited, 1932.

Houston, Bryon, "Let's Put More Esprit in de Corporation," *Harvard Business Review*, Volume 34, Number 6 (November–December 1971), pp. 48–51.

Howell, Margaret A., "Time Off as a Reward for Productivity," *Personnel Administration*, Volume 34, Number 6 (November–December 1971), pp. 48–51.

Kofka, Vincent W., "A Motivation System That Works Both Ways," *Personnel*, Volume 49, Number 4 (July–August 1972), pp. 61–66.

Lincoln, James F., *Incentive Management*, Cleveland: Lincoln Electric Company, 1951.

Mahoney, Thomas A., "Compensation Preference of Managers," *Industrial Relations*, Volume 3, Number 3 (May 1964), pp. 135–144.

Mayfield, Harold, "The Many Effects of Morale," *Supervisory Management*, Volume 15, Number 11 (November 1970), pp. 14–15.

Opsahl, Robert L., and Marvin D. Dunnette, "The Role of Financial Compensation in Industrial Motivation," *Psychological Bulletin*, Volume 66, Number 2 (August 1966), pp. 94–118.

Patton, Arch, "Why Incentive Plans Fail," *Harvard Business Review,* Volume 50, Number 3 (May–June 1972), pp. 58–66.

Pogalies, Joan L., "Incentive Programs that Work," *The Personnel Administrator,* Volume 17, Number 6 (November–December 1972), pp. 28–29.

Powell, Reed M., and John L. Schlacter, "Participative Management—A Panacea?" *The Academy of Management Journal,* Volume 14, Number 2 (June 1971), pp. 165–173.

Roethlisberger, Fritz J., *Management and Morale,* Cambridge, Massachusetts: Harvard University Press, 1941.

Ross, Timothy L., and Gardner M. Jones, "An Approach to Increased Productivity: The Scanlon Plan," *Financial Executive,* Volume 40, Number 2 (February 1972), pp. 23–29.

Sirota, David, and Alan D. Wolfson, "Work Measurement and Worker Morale," *Business Horizons,* Volume 15, Number 4 (August 1972), pp. 43–48.

Sloan, Stanley, and David E. Schrieber, "Incentives: Are They Relevant? Obsolete? Misunderstood?" *Personnel Administrator,* Volume 33, Number 1 (January–February 1970), pp. 52–57.

Sullivan, John F., "Indirect Compensation: The Years Ahead," *California Management Review,* Volume 15, Number 2 (Winter 1972), pp. 65–75.

Svetlik, Bryan, Erich Prien, and Gerald Barrett, "Relationships between Job Difficulty, Employee's Attitude toward His Job, and Supervisory Ratings of the Employee's Supervisor," *Journal of Applied Psychology,* Volume 48, Number 5 (October 1964), pp. 320–324.

Traum, Richard, "Manpower Bank and Reward Systems for Professionals," *Personnel,* Volume 50, Number 4 (July–August 1973), pp. 19–29.

Wulfsberg, Arthur H., "A Growth-Oriented Incentive Compensation," *Personnel Journal,* Volume 50, Number 10 (October 1971), pp. 759–769.

Chapter 12

Communicating Concepts and Knowledge

A case to consider before reading chapter 12

COMMUNICATING POLICIES AT CENTRAL FOOD

Central Food Processing Corporation is a young, diversified processor and distributor of agricultural products for human consumption. The company has been in business only two years. The company purchases raw food materials, processes them to fit the needs of the consumer, packages the finished products for the customer's convenience, and distributes the products to wholesalers and retailers.

At the beginning, the organization was small and had only a limited number of personnel. The management of the corporation did not feel it was necessary to draft a long list of detailed policies and procedures because most policies could be spread by word of mouth when necessary. Also, it was felt that there would be more flexibility in handling policies if they were oral rather than written. However, with the tremendous growth in the company in the two-year period, it is now felt that more written policies are necessary. In accordance with this plan, new statements of policy are periodically distributed in memorandum form to all supervisory personnel. The supervisors are expected to inform their subordinates of the policy through whatever means they feel is appropriate. A few days ago, the company issued the following statement of policy concerning disciplinary action.

Disciplinary action shall be taken by supervisors for just cause whenever necessary. Each supervisor shall be certain to establish that the worker to be disciplined has actually committed an offense worthy of a penalty before the penalty is applied. Whenever possible, four steps shall be followed in disciplining a worker. First, the worker shall be given an oral warning following the first commission of a mistake. Second, if the poor behavior continues, the worker shall be given a written

249

warning that future errors will result in the application of serious penalties. Third, if no improvement in performance is evidenced, a penalty such as a disciplinary layoff without pay will be implemented. Finally, if no change in behavior is exhibited, discharge will occur. All of the preliminary steps may be bypassed in the case of serious offenses such as fighting or actions that endanger the health and safety of other workers.

The company director of personnel is curious to know the reactions of supervisors and their subordinates to the new policy statement; so he circulates through the plant interviewing different people to see what they think of the policy. He gets a variety of reactions. From one supervisor, he hears:

I think this is what we've needed for a long time. This new policy gives me the authority to knuckle down on some guys that have been getting away with murder. I try to run a tight ship. I want my workers to know who is the boss. With this policy in effect, I'm going to give some people written warnings in the next day or two. I should be able to discharge some poor workers pretty soon.

Another supervisor has these comments:

The policy statement doesn't give me much help. From what it says, I don't really know when I'm supposed to give a written warning or when I'm supposed to deal out a penalty. And I don't know how severe a penalty should be. This only seems to complicate my job. I could use some help in interpreting the policy, but nobody has offered any.

A worker (a nonsupervisor) with a history of work infractions (for which he already been disciplined) has this to say:

Well, I haven't actually seen the policy statement, but my boss said that I'd better be on my toes from here on because he had the company's okay to fire me if I did anything wrong again. I feel like I'm pretty well under the gun. I'm kinda shook up about it all.

Another worker (a nonsupervisor) with a good work record (and in another department) makes this statement:

I've read the statement and it seems fine to me. As long as I do my job, I've got nothing to be afraid of. I've got a good boss, one who treats me well. I personally feel the policy is a protection for me.

The director of personnel is struck by the diversity of reactions to the new policy statement. It appears to him as if the four individuals interviewed have been looking at four different policy statements instead of the single one issued by his office.

Questions about the Central Food case

1.   To what factors do you attribute the different reactions to the policy statement? Take each individual who was interviewed and analyze the causes for his reaction.

2.   Analyze the way in which policy statements were introduced to the workers. What problem areas exist in the communication methods?

3.   What steps could the company take to improve its methods of communicating important matters such as policy statements?

4.   Someone has said that distortion of communication messages is likely to occur when there are middlemen who relay messages from one individual to another individual. What situation in this case supports this statement?

5.   What lessons can be learned about interpersonal communications from this case?

Providing the proper leadership, determining the appropriate incentives to appeal to employees' motives, and giving careful attention to workers' morale are essential responsibilities for every manager. Another important duty of every manager is to see that there is a good exchange of ideas, information, and knowledge between all individuals who must work together.

One of the most vital activities in an organization is the communication of ideas between individuals as they interrelate with each other. When people communicate with each other, they are exchanging messages upon which action can be taken. **Communication** has sometimes been defined as the transferring of a mental concept from the brain of one individual to the brain of another. Communication, of course, may occur between two people anywhere. The main concern in a book such as this is the transfer of mental concepts between people in the work environment.

The Functions of Communication

Proper interpersonal communication has many purposes to accomplish in the work-oriented organization. Thayer divides the functions of communication into four specific categories: the ~~information functio~~n, the ~~command and instructive~~ ~~function~~, the ~~influence and persuasion function~~, and the ~~integrative function~~.[1] The ~~information functio~~n serves to ~~provide knowledge~~ to the ~~individuals needing~~ ~~it for guidance in their actions~~. The information function also fulfills workers' desires for awareness of things that affect them. McLarney suggests that "employees are hungry for information about anything that is related to their job."

> They want to know about the company—its background and present organization. They want to know what its products are—how they're made and where they go. They want to know what the company's policies are—especially new policies—as they affect themselves and their fellow workers. They want to know the reasons for changes in methods, and to have information about new products—and they want this information in advance. They want to know what is expected of them and how they are measuring up. They want to know how their jobs fit into the scheme of things, and what their chances for advancement are. They want to know what the outlook is for the business, and what the prospects are for steady work. They want to know about the company's income, and about its profits and losses. Should circumstances make layoffs necessary, they want to know as far in advance as possible, the reasons and how the individuals are affected.[2]

The ~~command and instructive function~~s serve to ~~make~~ the ~~employee aware~~ of ~~his obligations~~ to the ~~formal organization~~ and to provide him with additional guidance and assistance on how to perform his duties adequately.[3] Most of this type of communication appears to flow downward in the organization. The ~~influence and persuasion function~~ is sometimes known as the ~~motivational func-~~ ~~tion~~ because its ~~main purpose~~ is to ~~encourage~~ the ~~appropriate individuals to per-~~ ~~form~~ or to ~~exhibit~~ a ~~certain behavior~~. Messages communicated are used to convince individuals that their actions can be personally or organizationally beneficial, or perhaps both.[4]

The ~~integrative function~~ of communication refers to the fact that the ~~communi-~~ ~~cation~~ of ~~messages and ideas~~, ~~if handled properly~~, ~~should help~~ to ~~relate~~ the ~~activities~~ of the ~~workers~~ so that ~~their efforts complement rather than detract from~~ ~~each other~~. Work efforts are unified rather than fragmented as a result of properly integrative communication.[5]

---

[1]Lee Thayer, *Communication and Communication Systems,* Homewood, Illinois: Richard D. Irwin, Inc., 1968, pp. 187, 205, 220, 239.

[2]William J. McLarney, *Management Training,* Fourth Edition, Homewood, Illinois: Richard D. Irwin, Inc., 1964, p. 600, quoting from *Employee Communications for Better Understanding,* New York: National Association of Manufacturers, July 1951, pp. 8, 9–11.

[3]Thayer, *op. cit.,* p. 205.

[4]*Ibid.,* p. 226.

[5]*Ibid.,* p. 239.

If the functions of ~~communication~~ are to be accomplished, communication within the organization must be a t~~hree-directional~~ matter. ~~Communication must occur~~ adequately from the ~~top-down~~ (~~downward communication~~), from the ~~bottom-up~~ (~~upward communication~~), and ~~across the organization~~ (~~horizontal communicatio~~n) between peers and colleagues working at similar levels. Downward communication serves all four functions; upward communication particularly provides operational information needed by those high in the organizational hierarchy (the information function) and also facilitates the achievement of integrated activities. Horizontal communication is important for all purposes, but it especially assists in the performance of informational and integrative functions.

One of the responsibilities of managerial personnel is to create and sustain channels of communication so that messages will flow in every direction as needed. Normally, the o~~rganization structure defines the path through which communications should flow~~. If the formally prescribed channels are not working, other channels must be substituted. Barriers to communication must be removed. Conditions conducive to a free interchange of ideas must be encouraged.

The Communication Process

There are many phases to the communication process. The communication model in Figure 12.1 illustrates the many steps in the complete process. The sender begins the communication process as he realizes the need to convey a message to someone else. He has some information, guidelines, motivational material, or coordinative concepts that may be important to the receiver. As the sender plans the issuance of his message, he considers the knowledge that the receiver has of the subject matter to be communicated, the working conditions under which the receiver labors, the job responsibilities the receiver possesses, and other background information.

The sender analyzes the receiver to determine the meaning that the message will have for him as he receives and interprets it. People communicate through symbols (words, gestures, expressions, etc.). As a result, the sender must anticipate the meaning a symbol may have for his receiver and choose the symbol that will best be interpreted as the sender intends. Thus, he looks for clues that will help him gauge the receiver's interpretation; then he sends along the appropriate symbol. The s~~election of the proper symbol is often called the~~ **encoding** ~~process~~.

After the symbol is selected, it is sent along to the receiver. The burden of interpretation and action then is placed upon the receiver. He takes the message and attempts to discover its meaning by analyzing the sender and his intent by looking at the sender's role, knowledge, experience, and authority. The receiver

FIGURE 12.1   Model of purposeful communication

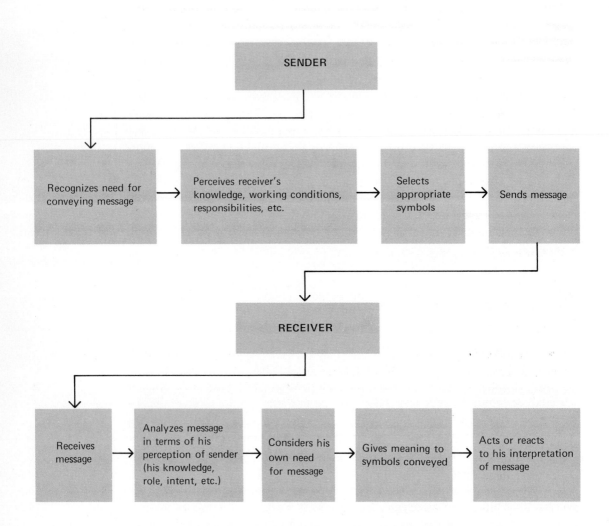

Source: This model is an adaptation of models from many sources. For further discussion of communication models, see Raymond V. Lesikar, *Business Communication: Theory and Application*, Revised Edition, Homewood, Illinois: Richard D. Irwin, Inc., 1972, pp. 18-27; or Lee Thayer, *Communication and Communication Systems*, Homewood, Illinois: Richard D. Irwin, Inc., 1968, pp. 122-123.

also considers his own need for the message and its significance for him. He then places his own meaning on the symbols conveyed and acts or reacts to the message as he has interpreted it.

Improving the Understanding of Messages.   Managers bear a heavy load of responsibility for improving of the level of understanding when they exchange messages and ideas with their subordinates, colleagues, and superiors. As a matter of fact, the sender of messages and ideas, whatever his role in the organization, is a key to the successful exchange and interpretation of messages. If the supervisor-manager is the sender of messages, he must carefully prepare and convey the message so that it will be received and interpreted as he intended it to be. Only with correct interpretation will the message be useful. The manager must also help his subordinates know how to communicate to others so that messages the subordinates send will be understood and reacted to properly.

Problems in Conveying the Meaning Intended.   As the sender communicates a message, he may encounter several difficulties in insuring that the receiver gets the message he intended and assesses the meaning he had hoped for. Some of the problems are perceptual and psychological; other difficulties occur primarily because of the situation.

The Problem of Filtering.   Objectivity in receiving and interpreting messages is often difficult to achieve. Receivers have a tendency to hear what they wish to hear in messages directed toward them. The filtering of messages occurs both in what the receiver is willing to acknowledge receiving and in the interpretation given to the message.[6] Messages that are consistent with the receiver's self-image and provide useful knowledge may be received and interpreted carefully. Messages that threaten his self-image or negatively affect his desires and expectations may either be ignored or interpreted in a less threatening way.

The Problem of Distortion.   Distortion is another form of message misinterpretation. Distortion is less of an intentional manipulation of messages than is filtering. Instead, **distortion** is the improper assessment of meanings that may result from misleading circumstances or conditions. Distortion frequently occurs, for example, when a communiqué must go through several intermediaries in order to reach the intended recipient. Anyone who has played the parlor game called "gossip"

---

[6]For an excellent review of the way in which filters develop, see Raymond V. Lesikar, *Business Communication*, Revised Edition, Homewood, Illinois: Richard D. Irwin, Inc., 1972, pp. 43–54.

understands the possibilities of distortion. As a message is passed through a long chain of individuals, the content and order of the message undergoes a transformation. The hearing problem is especially compounded when the message is received out of context. Distance between the sender and receiver normally results in such difficulties.

Distortion may also occur when the receiver is distracted from the intended message by other **noises** (symbols without significant form or value). Numerous communiqués frequently descend upon the employee as he works. Sometimes messages and rumors are cascaded upon the recipient from all directions—superiors, subordinates, and colleagues. Frequently one source sends out too many messages—some of the messages sent may even appear to be contradictory. Overcommunication may be as much a problem (resulting in distortion) as other sources of difficulty.

Sayles and Strauss say that another form of distortion is exaggeration.[7] With **exaggeration,** the message is received and then overstated or overreacted to. The message is interpreted to mean more than it really does. Often this results from the perception of the large amount of authority carried by the sender of the message—particularly a high-level official. Exaggeration tends especially to be a problem of downward communication.

Timing as a Problem.   On occasion, the stumbling block to the proper interpretation of messages is the fact that the message reaches the receiver at a time when he is not ready to utilize the message (it is premature), or the message is too late to be helpful, or the message is received at a time when the receiver is preoccupied with other matters and, therefore, misinterprets the meaning. The difficulties of receiving messages before or after they are needed are fairly obvious. The more unique problem, however, is the one of sending a message when the receiver has other thoughts on his mind. If, for example, a worker is feeling insecure about his job because he has heard rumors of an impending layoff of a large number of workers, he may conclude that his boss's request for data concerning what he has done to improve himself and his performance the past year is a request for data to find some grounds for dismissing him. His boss, in fact, may have been looking for data on which to consider him for a promotion, but the timing caused the worker to misinterpret his intent. Communicators must make an attempt to time messages sent so that the receiver can more accurately interpret their meaning.

[7]Leonard R. Sayles and George Strauss, *Human Behavior in Organizations,* Englewood Cliffs, New Jersey: Prentice-Hall, Inc., 1966, p. 363.

Inconsistent Actions and Messages.   The interpretation of messages by the receiver is significantly influenced by his perception of and attitude toward the sender. If the sender is consistent in his actions, the receiver will find the development of his set of perceptions and attitudes toward the sender much easier to develop than if the sender constantly says one thing and does something different. If the sender appears steady, competent, and knowledgeable, the receiver may learn to respect the information fed his way and to place high value on receiving it. If the sender appears flighty, erratic, and uncertain, the receiver will come to be apprehensive toward messages received. Even more important may be the consistency of information passed along by the sender. If his information is regularly useful and dependable, the receiver learns to give trusting attention to it. If the messages are variable and sometimes inadequate, skepticism develops rapidly. The level of confidence in the sender as a result of consistent actions and messages, therefore, has its own impact upon message interpretation.

The Receiver's State of Mind   Running through all of the barriers mentioned above is the perception the receiver holds of the sender and vice versa. One of the overall determining factors of the success of communications is the state of mind of those involved. If the participants' minds are free of bias, optimistic, and forward-looking, the communication and interpretation of messages is more likely to be objective and accurate. If, on the other hand, the minds of the participants are anxious, emotional, and predispositioned, communications and interpretations will probably be biased, subjective, and sometimes unrealistic.

Anxiety, as many psychologists call the latter state of mind, tends to be detrimental in either the sender or the receiver. If the sender is in a state of anxiety, he either tends to overcommunicate (often including a lot of unnecessary information) or he remains silent when he should be communicating. If the receiver is in an apprehensive state, he tends toward overreaction and distortion or toward a biased reaction. He may even fail to listen because of his tensions or mental strains. His mind may be closed to useful receiving and interpretation.

Overcoming Problems of Message Interpretation.   The sender of a message has at least partial control over the communication process. As a result, there are several actions on his part that may improve interpretation of and reaction to the messages he sends.[8] Following is a list of suggestions to be considered by senders in the communication process.

[8]One of the pioneer works in the field of communicating clearly is one by Rudolph Flesch entitled *The Art of Plain Talk,* New York: Harper & Row, Publishers, 1946.

1.   The ~~sender should attempt to remove biases and tensions that may cloud his own mind~~.
While it may be impossible to remove them completely, identification and acknowledgement of the existence of personal biases and tensions goes a long way in managing the effects they will have. At least they may be compensated for or overcome.

2.   *Before communicating, the* ~~communicator should attempt to determine what the real need~~
~~for communication is.~~ What reasons does the sender have for sending messages, asking
for actions and reactions, or requesting return information? What are the receiver's
needs for communication? Once the need has been determined, it is wise to *send*
only necessary communication and refrain from sending nonpurposeful messages. This will
help check massive flows of communications that can result in distortion and
insensitivity.

3.   *It is* ~~desirable to learn as much about the receiver as possible before communicating with~~
~~him~~. This will help in determining how the receiver is likely to interpret or react
to the message he receives. In addition to looking for clues concerning his communication needs, the sender should look for signals relating to the receiver's state
of mind, his background, his previous experiences, his organizational authority and
responsibilities, his own perception of himself, and anything else that might indicate
how he will decode and utilize messages. The sender should empathize with the
receiver as completely as possible.

4.   *In issuing the message,* ~~it is important to have the receiver's attention so that he will be~~
~~sensitive to what is being sent to him.~~ If he is preoccupied with other thoughts or the
noise level is high, the receiver may fail to "hear" the message sent his way.

5.   *The* ~~sender should communicate as directly with the intended receiver as is practical~~.
While it is not always possible to give the message directly to the person intended,
the fewer go-betweens involved, the more the chances of distortion or other forms
of misinterpretation are reduced.

6.   *The* ~~use of symbols~~ (words, gestures, etc.) ~~that are simple and uncomplicated is helpful~~.
The more complex the communication symbols are, the more likely is the misinterpretation of their intended meaning.

7.   ~~Repetition of messages may be helpful in conveying the intended thoughts~~. Often a single
transmission of an idea may not be received or decoded properly. A second or third
statement of the message may assist the receiver in his understanding and use of
the concept. Communicators are frequently reluctant to repeat themselves because
they feel repetition is either unnecessary or insulting to the receiver. However, after
a communiqué fails, the sender is often aware that a second or third repetition
would have been useful.

8.   ~~Also desirable is consistency in actions and in communication of thought~~s. The receiver
can learn to perceive and react to consistent messages from a consistent sender
more readily than to fluctuating messages from an unpredictable sender.

9.   ~~Messages should be timed~~ *so that they are r~~eceived when~~ they are ~~needed~~, and are not
misconstrued as a result of other thoughts on the receiver's mind.* The sender must put
himself in the receiver's place (empathize with him) if the timing of messages is to
be handled properly.

The receiver has a responsibility to put messages into the context in which they were intended. The receiver should also attempt to be aware of his own biases, to recognize his need for a message sent to him and the needs of the sender, to size up the sender through the process of empathizing with him, and to "listen" for all intended meanings in messages. The receiver must be aware of his own biases and of the conditions existing in his environment as he interprets the message. Out of respect for the sender, an acknowledgement and reaction to the message would be desirable.

Creating Conditions for Effective Communication

The previous section emphasized sender-receiver relationships and the communication process in general. It is important to recognize that the environment within the formal organization structure will also have an effect upon the successful transmission of concepts and ideas from the appropriate sender(s) to the appropriate receiver(s).

For example, how clearly defined the channel of formal communication is will influence the ease and accuracy of formal communication. In Chapter 5, it was pointed out that the formal hierarchy with its accompanying lines of authority determines to a large degree how communication channels are to move. If the employees of an organization are clearly aware of superior-subordinate relationships and horizontal networks, the employees will know with whom they should communicate directly and what communication needs and expectations the receivers will have. If lines of authority and channels of communication are not known, an abundance of miscommunication, excessive communication, or lack of communication will occur. Difficulties with lines of authority and communication are most likely to occur when organization structures are altered frequently or when organizations are established and grow without the proper determination of authority relationships.

The spans of control for supervisors and the number of intervening levels in the organizational authority hierarchy from top to bottom also influence the success or failure of organizational communication. Wide spans of supervision tend to restrict the amount of time a supervisor can spend with each of his subordinates and may result in hurried communication on the part of both superior and subordinate. Communication tends to become more impersonal if the interests of supervisors are spread too widely. Subordinates who work for bosses with many subordinates may feel that their boss has no direct, personal interest in communicating with them.

On the other hand, the chances of upward-downward distortion are decreased with flat structures (see Chapter 5), because messages flow through fewer hierarchical levels in getting from the top of the organization to the bottom or vice versa. Tall organization structures provide more workable spans of supervision in terms of fewer subordinates for one supervisor to communicate with and listen to. However, the possibility of upward-downward distortion increases as the number of hierarchical levels increases.

As individuals perform their individual responsibilities, those who are physically within range of easy communication will encounter fewer barriers than those who are beyond the range of instant, immediate contact. Ease of communication is usually enhanced as physical distance is reduced.

From a communication point of view, it is obvious that the exchange of information and knowledge will be improved when organizational authority and communication networks are clear, when the spans of supervision and the number of intervening levels in the authority network provide for personalized, direct communication between individuals in the appropriate manner, and when physical distance problems are overcome or compensated for.

Encouraging Upward Communication.   The initiative for downward communication is primarily in the hands of the supervisor in charge of a group of people and their activities. The supervisor knows that he is responsible for their actions and that someone will be holding him accountable for their performance. As a result, he is encouraged to communicate downward information needed by his subordinates.

Encouraging subordinates to communicate upward is more difficult because much of the initiative in this direction is in the hands of the subordinate, and he must feel a special need and a certain amount of confidence and security before he will communicate effectively to his superiors. There are several circumstances in which a subordinate is reluctant to communicate upward or may even "manipulate" what he tells his boss.

1.   The subordinate will be hesitant to send upward any messages that may result in negative, punitive actions toward the subordinate by his superiors. Messages the subordinate feels his boss will not be happy about will tend to be suppressed or slowed down. The subordinate will be tempted to distort or rearrange negative

information about himself to reduce the probabilities of negative action toward himself.[9] As Gemmill states:

> If a subordinate believes that disclosure of his feelings, opinions, or difficulties may lead a superior to block or hinder the attainment of a personal goal, he will conceal or distort it.[10]

2.   The subordinate who feels that his superior is autocratic, unsympathetic, and task-oriented will develop a distrust for his superior that may cause him to withhold useful information. The more trust and confidence the subordinate has in his superior, on the other hand, the more likely he will be to give the boss messages freely and openly.[11]

3.   The subordinate who feels that his job is of little importance and the information he possesses is probably nonvital will not be likely to communicate messages to his superior. There appears to be a direct relationship between one's feeling of importance and responsibility and one's willingness to communicate upward.[12]

4.   Subordinates keep their superiors better informed when the subordinates know what will be done with their work, when they share common references with their superiors, and when the superior is easily available to the subordinate.[13]

5.   The subordinate's perception of his boss's attitude toward him (the amount of interest the boss has in him, etc.) and the open-mindedness of the boss will affect upward communication. If the superior regularly shows a desire for messages from his subordinates, practices an open-door policy, and provides feedback on information received, upward communication will be enhanced.[14]

The implications of these conditions are clear for the supervisor who needs and wants upward communication.

1.   The supervisor must make known his need for messages from his subordinates and his interest in hearing from them.

---

[9]For a more complete analysis of upward communication problems, see William M. Pride and O. Jeff Harris, "Psychological Barriers to the Upward Flow of Communication," *Atlanta Economic Review*, Volume 21, Number 3 (March 1971), pp. 30–32.

[10]Gary Gemmill, "Managing Upward Communication," *Personnel Journal*, Volume 49, Number 2 (February 1970), pp. 107–110.

[11]Pride and Harris, *op. cit.*, pp. 30–32.

[12]*Loc. cit.*

[13]Marshall H. Brenner and Norman B. Sigband, "Organizational Communication—An Analysis Based upon Empirical Data," *The Academy of Management Journal*, Volume 16, Number 2 (June 1973), pp. 323–325.

[14]Pride and Harris, *op. cit.*, pp. 30–32, and Ronald J. Burke and Douglas S. Wilcox, "Effects of Different Patterns and Degrees of Openness in Superior-Subordinate Communication on Subordinate Job Satisfaction," *The Academy of Management Journal*, Volume 12, Number 3 (September 1969), pp. 319–326.

2.   The supervisor should reward his subordinates for their upward communication efforts when this is possible.

3.   The supervisor should cultivate a relationship of mutual understanding and respect between himself and his subordinates. Through his own actions, he can gain the trust and respect that will encourage his subordinates to communicate more fully. Regular feedback on subordinates' messages will also encourage more open communication.

4.   Superiors should emphasize to subordinates the positive uses made of their messages as well as the negative uses.

5.   Supervisors can delegate authority and encourage subordinates to feel responsible for specific action performances. The importance of upward communication will normally be felt under these conditions.

6.   If upward communication is still below desired levels, other steps may be necessary in order to gain needed information. Formal questionnaires, reports, and other information sources may be called for.

Very little analysis has been done in the past concerning the problems involved in horizontal (cross) communication. Supervisors and subordinates both should be aware of the needs of their colleagues and should attempt to send and receive messages accurately and usefully. A spirit of cooperation greatly facilitates the effectiveness of cross communication.

Problems of the Communication Grapevine.   In Chapter 6, the informal communication network (the grapevine) was discussed and several of its effects were identified. As was pointed out, the grapevine can make many positive contributions to the organization, because it does tend to convey messages rapidly, and it often accurately supplements the workings of formal communication channels. Grapevine communication may flow three-directionally within the organization, but its pattern is normally more unpredictable than is the formal pattern. Much of the flow of messages is uncontrollable by the formal authority structure.

While many of the contributions of the grapevine are useful, supervisors must be aware of possible problems and difficulties, and they should take preventive or corrective action. Informal communication channels are noted for spreading incorrect rumors or false information. It now appears that grapevines are more accurate than originally thought. Davis, for example, states that grapevine information is normally correct 75 to 95 percent of the time.[15] The 5 to 25 percent of the time that rumors are erroneous, however, is a bothersome problem. "Once a

[15]Keith Davis, "The Care and Cultivation of the Corporate Grapevine," *Duns Review,* Volume 102, Number 1 (July 1973), p. 47.

rumor is known and accepted, employees tend to distort future happenings to conform to the rumor."[16]

Grapevines tend to act rapidly and selectively (see Chapter 6). This means that some people get grapevine information while others do not. Superiors and subordinates alike may discover that they are being left out of the informal network, often to their own personal disadvantage. Grapevines, therefore, cannot be depended upon to disseminate messages faithfully throughout organizations in the place of formal communiqués.

The messages spread by the grapevine may be in support of the formal organization and its goals, or the messages may be antagonistic. A large number of variables determines whether the messages of the grapevine will support or work against the formal organization.

Because problems and difficulties are sometimes associated with grapevines, formally appointed managers need to ask themselves several questions concerning the grapevine patterns and habits in their own organizations. Some questions appropriate for each manager to consider would include the following:

1.   Am I (as a manager) included in grapevine information or am I being completely bypassed? This question is significant because it is, in part, a gauge of the confidence and acceptability rating of the manager in the eyes of his superiors, subordinates, and peers. If a manager discovers that he is completely isolated, he will need to work toward gaining the respect and confidence of those around him so that he will receive important messages. No manager, of course, will be able to overcome completely the authority barrier of being a supervisor. However, supervisors who talk with individuals about matters other than official business can cultivate the grapevine more effectively and can be included in grapevine communications more frequently.[17]

2.   Are individuals who need information being left out of the grapevine without their knowledge? Where the answer to this question is yes (and it often is), formally appointed supervisors will need to issue messages of significant importance in ways that will reach the parties needing the information. In other words, important messages should either be issued formally, monitored to see that they reach all appropriate individuals, or both.

3.   Is the information being spread accurate in content? Because the answer is normally yes, there typically may be no cause for concern. However, to avoid the danger of inaccuracies and to counter false rumors, several actions may be necessary. If managers decide to utilize informal networks to spread information, messages should be given to individuals who have the respect and confidence of both the sender and prospective receivers. Messages should be given to several respected messengers throughout the grapevine so that distortion will be less likely to occur.

[16]*Loc. cit.*
[17]*Ibid.,* p. 45.

When false rumors are spread, formal networks should immediately send out the correct information with the appropriate supporting evidence. Sources of incorrect information should be traced, and individuals sending such information should be asked to take part in the correctional process. When false rumors tend to occur frequently, managers may need to question whether or not they are giving out enough meaningful information to all individuals who need the messages. Because people tend to rumor about things of personal concern, rumors may indicate specific informational needs that are not being met.

4. Is the grapevine typically supportive of or antagonistic toward the formal organization? The answer to this question may be a revelation of the general feelings and sentiments of informal organizations toward the formal organization. If grapevines normally remain on a positive plane, formal organization-informal organization relations are usually good. If the informal grapevine continually acts in a manner derogatory to the formal, relationships between the two need careful attention.

Formal managers should never expect to completely control the workings of informal grapevines, but they can learn to sense the activities and effects of grapevines. Managers can learn when additional formal actions and personal efforts are needed to make formal and informal relationships mutually beneficial. Trouble spots can be identified and corrective action taken more quickly.

Other Communication Problems.   Communication problems not specifically identified above may arise as a result of differences in perceptions, physical distances, psychological and emotional barriers, and other factors. A problem-solving approach is essential in the handling of each problem as it arises. Specific underlying causes must be identified, alternative solutions considered, decisions made on courses of action, solutions implemented, and follow-up analyses conducted to determine continuing communication needs. The manager-supervisor, as a result of his position and responsibilities, is primarily responsible for the successful resolution of communication problems and the proper activity of communication networks. This does not mean that other parties may be excused from concern about communication exchanges, but it does establish the ultimate responsibility.

Summary

Communication is the exchange of ideas or concepts for purposes of information, command and instruction, influence and persuasion, or integration. Without some type of communication, no organization will exist long. Without accurate, meaningful communication, no organization will be successful.

Managers bear a heavy responsibility for the creation of a proper environment for communication and for establishing and maintaining the necessary organizational communication channels. Senders and receivers both bear a responsibility for the successful interpretation and understanding of messages communicated. Communication barriers exist in abundance, but most of the problems they present can be overcome with proper attention and effort.

Questions to consider after reading Chapter 12

1.   In the chapter, the comment was made that employees desire large amounts of information about their employing organization, economic and competitive influences that affect their employer, and a host of additional information. Do you think this statement reflects the interests of the majority of today's workers? Why or why not?

2.   How does the upward flow of communications help to achieve the integrative function of communication?

3.   Is the sender more responsible for the successful exchange of an idea through the communication process than the receiver? Explain your answer in detail.

4.   Someone has said that words have no meanings in themselves. What does this statement mean?

5.   In most organizations, downward communications are given more attention and emphasis than are upward communications. If this trend continues to be true over a long period of time in one specific organization, what will the effect be? Why are downward communications usually handled more effectively than upward communications?

6.   Anxiety and other personal factors can be barriers to effective communication. What can the concerned manager do to overcome this problem?

7.   What communication barriers do large organizations present that are less of a problem with smaller organizations? Why?

All of the cases at the back of the book contain problems related to Chapter 12. The following cases in particular contain communication problems or concepts:

> Ben Stockton
>
> Mark Williams
>
> Stanley Lowell
>
> H. Gerald Pretzler

Edith Capp and Janet Turner

Bentley Cantrell

Kurt Browning

Grace Lanham

Bill Caden

Walt Gladberry

Abigail Spiegal and Trudy Pennington

Alan Purdy

Additional readings

Abbatiello, Aurelius A., and Robert T. Bidstrup, "Listening and Understanding," *Personnel Journal,* Volume 48, Number 8 (August 1969), pp. 593–596.

Bavelas, Alex, "Communication Patterns in Task-Oriented Groups," *Journal of the Acoustical Society of America,* Volume 22 (1950), pp. 725–730, reprinted in Dorwin Cartwright and Alvin F. Zander, editors, *Group Dynamics: Research and Theory,* Second Edition, New York: Row, Peterson, and Company, 1960, pp. 669–682.

Bormann, Ernest G., et al., *Interpersonal Communication in the Modern Organization,* Englewood Cliffs, New Jersey: Prentice-Hall, Inc., 1969.

Fenn, Margaret, and George Head, "Upward Communication: The Subordinates' Viewpoint," *California Management Review,* Volume 7, Number 4 (Summer 1965), pp. 75–80.

Gemmill, Gary, "Managing Upward Communication," *Personnel Journal,* Volume 49, Number 2 (February 1970), pp. 107–110.

Geneen, Harold S., "The Human Element in Communication," *California Management Review,* Volume 9, Number 2 (Winter 1966), pp. 3–8.

Haney, William V., "A Comparative Study of Unilateral and Bilateral Communication," *The Academy of Management Journal,* Volume 7, Number 2 (June 1964), pp. 128–136.

Huseman, Richard C., Cal M. Logue, and Dwight L. Freshley, *Readings in Interpersonal and Organizational Communication,* Boston: Holbrook Press, Incorporated, 1969.

Leavitt, Harold J., "Some Effects of Certain Communication Patterns on Group Performance," *Journal of Abnormal and Social Psychology,* Volume 46, Number 1 (January 1951), pp. 38–50.

Jackson, Jay M., "The Organization and Its Communications Problem," *Advanced Management,* Volume 24, Number 2 (February 1959), pp. 17–20.

Redding, W. Charles, and George A. Sanborn, editors, *Business and Industrial Communication,* New York: Harper & Row, Publishers, 1964.

Strenski, James B., "The Two-Way Communication—A Management Necessity," *Personnel Journal,* Volume 49, Number 1 (January 1970), pp. 29–31.

Vardaman, George T., and Carroll C. Halterman, *Managerial Control through Communication,* New York: John Wiley & Sons, Inc., 1968.

Chapter 13

Controlling Worker Performance

A case to consider before reading chapter 13

CHAIRMAN STEELE AND HIS EVALUATION SYSTEM

The Department of Elementary Education in the College of Education at State University is headed by Irving Steele, a recognized expert in the field of early educational instruction. Professor Steele administers his department vigorously and with enthusiasm. He prides himself on being student-oriented. He meets regularly with students to discuss their problems and interests. He also maintains a constant check on the faculty members in his department to determine if they are providing the type of instruction their students (who are prospective teachers) can benefit from.

One of Chairman Steele's techniques for evaluating the performance of instructors is to use a student evaluation. Late in the spring semester, each student in the Department of Elementary Education comes into Chairman Steele's office and fills out an evaluation form on each professor with whom he has studied during the year. Each student is asked to evaluate his professors using criteria such as how well prepared for lectures the professor is, the neatness of the professor's appearance, the promptness with which the professor begins his classes, his knowledge of the subject matter, and so forth. The student is assured that all information given by him will be kept strictly confidential. Professor Steele honors this promise very carefully. He never reveals the content of any student's evaluation of a professor. In fact, most professors have never even seen a copy of the evaluation questionnaire. Many of the professors are not even aware of all of the criteria used in the survey.

After the questionnaires have been completed by all students, Professor Steele tabulates the results and uses the data in making several decisions. The student evaluation is a major determinant of which professors will have their contracts renewed, which ones will receive tenure and promotions, and who will get salary increases. This is the major source of feedback to the professor in the department. In other words, if a professor receives a promotion, he assumes that he scored well on the student evaluations. If he gets no increase or loses his contract, he knows that he must have scored poorly in the eyes of the students.

There is one other form of feedback to the professors—the annual training day seminar Chairman Steele holds before the fall semester. When this is held each year in August, Professor Steele leads the instructors in a review of concepts and ideas he believes might be helpful in improving the quality of education within the department. The instructors who attend these training seminars normally assume that many of the topics selected were a result of findings generated by the student evaluations.

Questions about the Chairman Steele case

1.   What goals and objectives does Professor Steele have in mind when he uses the student evaluations?

2.   What mistakes is Professor Steele making that tend to jeopardize the probabilities of achieving what he would like to achieve with the evaluations?

3.   What are the effects of the student evaluations on the attitudes of professors who are performing their jobs well? What are the effects on the attitudes and behavior of professors who are performing their jobs poorly?

4.   How could the evaluations have been improved for better results?

5.·   What are some additional ways in which Professor Steele could have evaluated and controlled the performance of the instructors in his department?

6.   What lessons are to be learned from the problems in this case?

7.   After you have read the following chapter, please come back and review the case again.

When someone prepares to go on a long trip by automobile, several things happen. Normally a specific destination is selected and a time of arrival is projected. If the travel schedule is a tight one demanding strict adherence, intermediate checkpoints are determined that will act as gauges of progress along the way. The travel vehicle is readied for the trip, and other necessary resources are selected and prepared for the journey. If other people are involved, information is exchanged and, sometimes, assignments are given to them.

Once the journey is under way, travelers regularly monitor the travel vehicle, the fuel supply, the time schedule, and other essential items to determine if everything is operating smoothly and if the destination will be reached on schedule. If one of the essential elements of the trip varies from the plan or malfunctions, immediate attention is given to returning operations to normal.

Going on a long automobile trip is analogous to the activities within organizations. Every organizational unit begins with a destination, a mission (or set of missions) toward which it is striving. These missions will be different for each organization, but they are important determinants of the focus of organizational energies. A clear definition of organizational objectives is extremely important, since the individual plan is designed to achieve these objectives or fulfill the mission.

When objectives are well defined, appropriate organizational structures for accomplishing goals are selected, resources are gathered and analyzed, and performance assignments are given. Organizational performance checkpoints are established in support of long-range objectives so that short-term operations and activities can be monitored to determine if satisfactory progress is being made in the pursuit of the organization's targets. The efforts of individuals who are a part of the organization are important determinants of the success or failure of the organization in achieving its objectives. If inadequacies in performance are spotted that might hinder the organization's progress or keep it from reaching its objectives, immediate attention is given to correcting the difficulty.

The materials in this chapter are concerned with the control processes of the organization, processes that monitor and influence worker behavior to encourage successful performance so that objectives are attained. Because this book emphasizes the human resources of organizations, this chapter concentrates chiefly upon the control and direction of human effort toward the achievement of an organization's missions. The utilization of financial and material resources are not of immediate concern here, although they, of course, are important. Much of the control process is a part of a larger, interrelated program, which will now be discussed.

The *total* manpower planning, organizing, and controlling process is a multiphased one that, as discussed in Chapter 5, normally contains as many as eight steps. The point of origin of the manpower utilization process begins with the determination and delineation of objectives. The step-by-step sequencing of events is repeated below because it provides the foundation upon which the control process is built.

1. ~~Determinatio~~n of the ~~organization's~~ goals and ~~objectiv~~es.

2. ~~Determination~~ of the ~~amount~~ of ~~work to be done~~ in order ~~to achieve~~ defined ~~goals~~ and ~~objecti~~ves. In other words, a definition of the amount of production, sales, distribution, financing, and accounting work, etc. that must be performed in order for goals to be achieved.

3. ~~Fragmentation of total work~~ to be ~~done into job-sized units~~, which can be performed by individual workers.

4. ~~Grouping of job~~s into ~~department~~s for administrative purposes.

5. ~~Selection~~ and ~~training~~ of ~~individua~~ls ~~to perform~~ the ~~jobs~~ defined.

6. ~~Assignment of~~ ~~tasks~~ to ~~individuals~~ along with the corresponding authority to act.

7. ~~Granting authori~~ty ~~to performers~~ so that they can perform their jobs.

8. ~~Review of the performan~~ce of ~~individuals~~ to determine if the obligations and demands of the jobs are being fulfilled. Following the evaluation, correctional actions and performance adjustments are implemented.

The Control Process

The process outlined above emphasizes procedures for planning and organizing manpower to accomplish organizational goals and objectives. At the same time, the seeds from which manpower control grows are presented. Manpower control is concerned with the exacting of a specific type of performance from individuals so that the defined organizational goals are reached satisfactorily. Deviations from the necessary level of performance should be discovered and corrected quickly as a result of proper control measures. The control process is in part a matter of *monitoring* the actions of individuals to facilitate conformity to prescribed goals and objectives.

The performance-monitoring process is often outlined in a procedural manner for ease of implementation. The evaluation procedures draw upon the stated objectives and goals of the organization to identify the contributions expected of each individual worker. Larger goals are interpreted into standards of performance for the individual worker. Regularly, or at stated intervals, the actual performance of the worker is compared against the required standards to determine if the worker's actions are contributing satisfactorily so that overall objectives can be attained. The results of the performance evaluation are communicated to the appropriate individuals (the worker, the worker's boss, quality control specialists, inventory control officials, etc.). If corrective action is needed in order to align worker performance with required standards, the appropriate steps are taken to improve performance. Retraining and additional guidance may be required. If performance is determined to have been in line with the requested standards, the worker's performance is commended. Rewards or penalties appropriate to the performance level are applied. If the monitoring approach is followed, the **performance evaluation** includes:

Try to obtain a behavior change

Step 1.   ~~Determination~~ of ~~organizational goals~~ and ~~objectives.~~

Step 2.   ~~Delineation of performance standard~~s for an individual worker's per- *(Establish)* formance.

Step 3.   ~~Comparison of actual performance~~ of a worker ~~against expected~~ standards of performance.

Step 4.   ~~Communication of finding~~s of the evaluation to the appropriate individuals. *decide how to achieve correct*

Step 5.   ~~Corrective action~~ (for inadequate performance) and ~~commendative action~~ *behavior* (for adequate performance).

Step 6.   ~~Application~~ of a~~ppropri~~ate rewards or ~~penalties.~~

Actually, the control process performs many other services in addition to its monitoring duties. The well-designed and implemented control process *integrates and coordinates* the efforts of individuals so that they become mutually supportive. Through the design of the control plan, individuals working together on cooperative tasks have their jobs structured so that they fit together in a compatible time sequence. Concepts similar to the **PERT** (Program Evaluation and Review Technique), originally developed by the U.S. Navy for planning and controlling the Polaris Missile, are illustrative of the integration and coordination function. If seven tasks, for example, must be performed by a number of individuals in order to complete a project through a collective effort, a time sequence is established and followed. In Figure 13.1, seven tasks with differing completing times are integrated so that all tasks will be accomplished by the time the longest continuous set of tasks (tasks A to B to E to G) is completed. The longest time sequence (known as the critical path) sets the control schedule and the rate at which all work must be done to be completed as a team. Each individual must perform his share of the tasks within the time allotted for the total assignment to be completed correctly. The PERT design determines time and other performance expectations for employees and coordinates their efforts effectively.

The process illustrated in Figure 13.1 in reality is much more complicated than the illustration shows, because there are typically many more activities happening simultaneously, and not all events are completed together. However, the principle of coordination and integration is appropriately established.

FIGURE 13.1   Simplified illustration of PERT

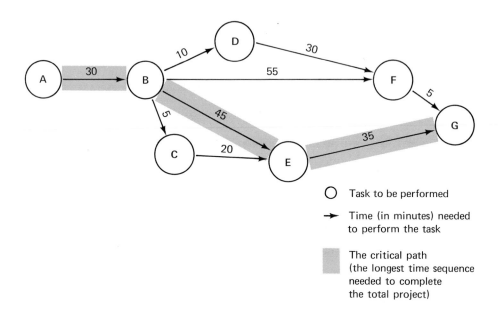

○   Task to be performed

→   Time (in minutes) needed
    to perform the task

▨   The critical path
    (the longest time sequence
    needed to complete
    the total project)

The control process also provides for the mutual *protection* of each individual involved. Because an individual is judged on the basis of his own performance, he is not held directly accountable for the performances of other individuals unless, of course, the other individuals work beneath him in a superior-subordinate relationship. However, where teamwork is called for, there may be an increased sense of accountability for the performances of fellow team members. Another form of personal protection also comes when performance standards include safety and security factors. When these standards are enforced, all workers benefit from the protective value.

The control process makes possible a more regular flow of performance feedback to the worker. In Chapter 7, the natural human needs for security, competency, achievement, and recognition were identified. Human beings appear to have a natural desire to know how they are progressing in terms of goals set for or by them. The communication of performance achievement in the form of evaluation feedback helps to satisfy these needs, especially if the feedback received suggests that the worker is achieving good results. Feedback, however, is necessary even if results are below standard. The discovery of substandard performance provides an alarm signal that calls for improvement so that expected standards can be achieved. If a worker is below standard in his performance, information about how to improve his performance is usually welcomed. As a result, performance evaluation and control usually facilitate instructional and correctional activities.

In addition, the ~~well-implemented evaluation process makes possible a more just and equitable method of distributing rewards and penalties.~~ Expected performance is known by all workers in advance, and rewards and penalties are handed out on the basis of deserved merit. If an individual wishes to attain a reward, he knows what he must do to earn it. Promotion and salary increases can be given on the basis of earned rewards. If a worker wishes to avoid a penalty, he knows what actions to take to escape it.

As can be seen, the control process not only provides organizational benefits; the workers benefit also.

Implementing the Evaluation Process

Determining Organizational Goals.   Because the evaluation process is based on adherence to organizational goals and objectives, a clear statement of organizational purposes is critical to the successful implementation of this control method. Many organizations state their objectives in terms of the fulfillment of goals to the various publics served by the organization. As a result, organizations may have objectives categorized on the basis of responsibilities to the stockholders (owners), the customers, the employees, the government, the community, and society at large. Objectives are often declared for both the immediate and long-range future.

The stated goals may be concerned with desired achievements in the realm of production, sales, distribution, customer service, research, industry position, leadership position in regard to technological innovation, social responsibility, business ethics, product development, employee development, and any other pertinent guidelines. A sample statement of organizational objectives might read:

> It is the objective of the ABC Corporation to fulfill the goals and expectations of the publics served by this corporation to the fullest degree possible. The following publics are identified as being within the scope of the organization's responsibilities, and the goals and objectives of the organization toward each public are stated.

To the stockholders:

1. It shall be the goal of the managers and workers of this organization to attempt to enhance and improve profit ratios so that returns on investment will be maximized.

2.   The organization shall be administered and performance encouraged so that efficiency and effectiveness of operations shall be achieved.

3.   Effort shall be made to increase sales volumes and product outreach.

4.   Continuous planning shall be performed so that the organization will maintain the ability to adjust and adapt to new demands.

To the customers:

1.   Every effort shall be made to provide products and services of superior quality at the lowest possible price.

2.   Products and services will be developed and modified on a continuing basis so that the latest technological advances are built into corporate products.

3.   Advertising and marketing approaches will attempt to inform customers accurately and honestly of the qualities and merits of company products and services.

4.   Sales representatives will be encouraged to seek information from customers that will reveal the customers' needs and desires so that products and services can be tailored to their demands.

To the employees:

1.   The Corporation shall attempt to foster harmony and to provide working conditions that are pleasant and desirable.

2.   The organization shall compensate, reward, encourage, inform, train and develop, and properly assign all workers so that their lives and work shall be meaningful and with dignity, satisfaction, and purpose both on and off the job.

3.   Opportunities for employment and promotions shall be based upon merit; discriminatory actions will be avoided.

To the government:

1.   Every effort shall be made to cooperate with the government in projects of benefit to the community and the economy.

2.   Government laws and regulations will be abided by and enforced vigorously.

To the community and society in general:

1.   The Corporation shall make a concerted effort to be a good citizen in each community with which it has contact.

2.   The Corporation will exercise all available safeguards to improve the environments in the locations in which it does business.

3.   The Corporation will attempt to fortify and reinforce the economies on which it may have an effect.

Organizational goals and objectives sometimes sound idealistic, but reasonable goals provide direction to the efforts and action of the people working within the organization. Long-range, general goals are interpreted in short-range operational goals for the immediate future.

Establishing Performance Standards.   From the overall organizational goals, individual performance guidelines and standards are drawn. Each worker's job description is developed and a set of performance standards is outlined. The individual standards ideally are in direct support of the overall goals. If, for example, the organization's goals for a one-year period include (1) increased sales of $100,000, (2) introduction of company products to at least 1,000 new commercial customers, and (3) the adaptation of company products to meet the needs of the customer more directly, each of the company's salesmen should find these goals reflected in his own performance standards for the year. Salesman A may discover that his objectives for the year are: (1) to increase his sales volume by $10,000, (2) to introduce the company's products to 100 new commercial customers, and (3) to collect information concerning customers' needs and report the information to the research and development department. If the salesman performs the designated assignments, stated organizational goals can be reached (assuming that other workers do their share also).

Not all objectives and standards can be stated as easily as those just mentioned. Standards relating to sales, production, and profit goals can normally be stated in terms of quantity and quality expectations rather easily. However, standards for service, research, social responsibility, business ethics, and employee development may be more difficult to clarify and may result in more subjective statements and interpretations.

Most of the effects of clearly stated objectives and standards are beneficial ones, but negative effects may also result. In particular, standards that have been developed in detail are sometimes considered by the worker to be a statement of restrictions rather than a statement of guidelines. In other words, a worker may interpret his duties as strictly those outlined in his job description and performance standards and may refuse to exercise initiative in areas not directly outlined. Where originality and creativity are desirable, this rigid presentation and interpretation of job standards may be unnecessarily restrictive.

Performing the Evaluation. The ~~third pha~~se of the ~~evaluation process~~ is the ~~comparison of performance standards to the actual performance of each worke~~r to determine if the worker is operating at an acceptable level so that goals and objectives are being met. If work standards have been defined in clear terms, the evaluation can be conducted more easily. If the standards are based upon subjective concepts, however, the evaluation will require interpretation and will involve personal judgments and less clear-cut decisions.

There is no universal agreement concerning which individual(s) should conduct the evaluation of a specific worker's performance. It has been said that any worker whose performance is subject to regular inspection should be provided with the ways and means to maintain an independent check (self-evaluation) of his work. This statement suggests that *the performer himself* should regularly be in a position to evaluate his own performance before his boss, or anyone else in a position of authority, reviews his performance, so that all details are in order when others review his work. Regardless of the timing of the evaluation, the worker himself should find self-evaluation a developmental experience. It has frequently been observed that an individual worker tends to be more critical of his own performance than are most outside reviewers.

~~T~~raditionally, *the immediate supervisor* of the worker whose performance is to be evaluated ~~is~~ also a ~~pa~~rt of the ~~evaluation team~~. The theory behind the supervisor's participation in the review process is based upon the fact that the supervisor, as the worker's boss, delegates the authority for action to the worker and in the final analysis is accountable for the worker's performance. In addition to the authority-accountability factor, the supervisor is normally more knowledgeable than anyone (except the worker himself) concerning the actions and efforts of the worker because of the frequent interactions that typically occur between the two.

Where unique types of performance are involved, specialists may be called on to review and interpret performance. A financial analyst may be called in to review the work of a highly specialized accountant; a quality control expert may be used to evaluate an intricate production performance; and so forth. Workers are sometimes reluctant to allow unknown outsiders to become involved in the evaluation of their performance, but highly specialized tasks and standards may necessitate this action.

In a ~~trend~~ that appears to be ~~increasing,~~ the ~~publics served by a worke~~r frequently ~~are being consulted to determine if the service needed is actually being received~~. For example, the consumer is being asked to evaluate the performance of product designers and salesmen. Citizens of the community are being polled to determine the degree of satisfaction with the policies and actions of executives concerning social responsibility and business ethics. The government on its own initiative often provides feedback concerning the performance of supervisors and personnel specialists in the area of equal treatment for all employees and other areas of managerial action.

If the worker being evaluated is a supervisor, his subordinates often are asked to evaluate the supervisor's actions toward them. The supervisor's performance in matters such as training, clarifying duties, applying disciplinary action, and providing capable leadership may be analyzed in this manner. Some supervisors are reluctant to endorse this approach because they feel that the evaluation may become a popularity poll rather than a genuine indication of the strengths and weaknesses of their performance. Subordinates also may be reluctant to supply negative data about their superiors out of the fear that their boss might find out what was said and a feeling of resentment might develop.

The fellow workers and colleagues of a worker may also be questioned concerning a fellow employee's performance, but the results of this action are normally minimal. If the esprit de corps of the work group is high and loyalty is significant, negative information will seldom be brought out on any worker who is a part of the work team. If, on the other hand, there is little loyalty among workers, performance reports about fellow workers may be unjustifiably negative and vindictive. In either case, the resulting evaluation will tend to be biased.

Communicating Evaluation Findings.   Regardless of which individuals perform the evaluations, the data gathered and the interpretations of them must be conveyed to the performer and to whatever additional parties may need the information. The information must be communicated to the performer, his superior, trainers, and other individuals who may be involved in improving inadequate performance. Individuals who control the reward and penalty structures must also receive the information so that the appropriate response may be given. Controllers and other managerial personnel must have the information for the purpose of coordinating individual efforts with organizational needs.

Acting Upon Evaluation Results.   If, in the evaluation process, it is discovered that work performance is below the established standards, steps are taken to improve performance in the future. Additional training and guidance are provided in keeping with the needs and demands of the job. If the standards have been achieved, the worker is commended for his efforts. In order to reinforce and support good performance, rewards may be given. Sometimes penalties are applied in an attempt to discourage poor performance and to stimulate improvement. The use of positive and negative motivational techniques may be effectively applied to influence worker performance.

Other Traditional Controls.   Performance standards as they have just been discussed are usually created for the purpose of giving specific guidance to the individual worker. In addition to these tailored goals and objectives, organizations establish policies, rules, and regulations that apply to the behavior of all workers. These performance guidelines may be stated in broad terms or they may be minutely spelled out. The intent of policies, rules, and regulations is to condition and control the actions of all workers to whom the guidelines are applied so that organizational and personal goals may be achieved more fully.

Worker Reactions to Control Techniques

The point was made earlier that the end result of the application of the control process should be not only improved organizational achievement, but also better guidance, protection, feedback, and rewards for the workers themselves. While a worker may readily see the benefits of the control process, there are often some dissatisfactions with the application of control measures. One group of authors has said that worker dissatisfaction with change is based upon: (1) the worker's lack of acceptance of the organizational goal he is expected to work toward; (2) the worker's feeling that performance standards are unnecessarily high or rigid; (3) the worker's belief that measuring devices are inadequate or inappropriate; (4) the worker's general dislike for unpleasant details related to conducting the evaluation; (5) the worker's disdain for unqualified, illegitimate evaluators and controllers; and (6) the fact that organizational controls often are at odds with personal and informal group goals.[1]

Trends in the Control Process

In recent years, there has been a distinct trend among control programs to encourage more involvement from the workers themselves, and the emphasis in the evaluation has been placed primarily on performance rather than personalities. These trends perhaps have been a natural response to the negative reactions sometimes evidenced by workers toward the control process. Worker confidence normally is increased when the worker participates in the planning phases of the control process, is included in the process of applying standards to his own performance, and may initiate his own program of correction and improvement.

[1]William H. Newman, Charles E. Summer, and E. Kirby Warren, *The Process of Management,* Third Edition, Englewood Cliffs, New Jersey: Prentice-Hall, Inc., 1972, pp. 624–630.

An outgrowth of this emphasis on worker involvement in the control process has been the program called ~~managing by objectives~~. The thrust of this approach is to place the responsibility for performance standard determination and performance evaluation upon the worker himself. There are at least five distinct phases in the managing-by-objectives process.

1. At an early stage, the worker and his boss discuss the organization's goals and objectives. At this time, the worker's job description is discussed, and the two agree on the content of the job and the relative importance of the major duties. Together, they determine what the worker is to be held accountable for.

2. The worker, after some time for consideration, determines performance targets for each of his responsibilities in a specified time period.

3. The worker and his supervisor meet to review and finalize the standards the worker has set for himself. The targets may be modified or revised if necessary.

4. Checkpoints are established for the evaluation of progress. Ways of measuring performance are specified, and the worker monitors his performance regularly.

5. At predetermined time intervals, the worker and his boss meet to discuss performance progress, to determine corrections needed, and to modify future standards where changes are called for.[2]

The managing-by-objectives technique may not always be practical, but it does provide the mechanism to overcome much of the resistance workers may feel toward control techniques.

In addition, there is an increasing trend toward a concept known as ~~management by exception~~. Simply stated, this means that ~~supervisors are to become concerned only with worker performance that deviates in an exceptional way from expected norms and standards~~. Workers are watched less closely when performance goals are being met or where deviations are minor. This more generalized type of supervision and control gives attention where attention is needed and tends to remove unnecessary pressures from the workers.

Summary

Organizations exist to attain goals and objectives through a unified effort. Some form of control is needed to facilitate the achievement of organizational purposes. Control devices in the form of performance evaluations, policies, rules, and regulations may be implemented to aid in the guidance of worker performance in the support of goal attainment. The control process (through performance

[2]Alva F. Kindall and James Gatza, "Positive Program for Performance Appraisal," *Harvard Business Review,* Volume 41, Number 6 (November–December 1963), p. 157, contains a good description of this process.

evaluation) serves to monitor the efforts of individuals, to integrate and coordinate worker efforts into a cooperative endeavor, to provide protection and feedback to the individual worker, to provide a means of correcting or commending the efforts of individuals, and to provide an equitable and consistent basis of distributing rewards and penalties.

The performance evaluation process includes: (1) a clear definition of organizational goals; (2) the delineation of individual performance responsibilities and standards in keeping with organizational goals; (3) the evaluation of individual performance by comparing actual performance against expected standards; (4) the communication of evaluation results to the individuals needing the information; (5) the implementation of corrective action or commendative procedures; and (6) the application of the appropriate rewards or procedures.

While a number of people may be included in the evaluation and control process, the performer and his boss normally are essential participants. Current control approaches appear to be encouraging an increased amount of worker involvement in self-evaluation and control procedures.

Questions to consider after reading Chapter 13

1.   Many employees are of the opinion that the control process is for their employer's benefit and offers nothing for them. What points can be made to offset this position?

2.   Several individuals and groups were mentioned in the chapter as possible participants in the evaluation process. What problems may result if peers evaluate one of their colleagues? If subordinates evaluate one of their superiors? If those being served evaluate the performer?

3.   Why do many supervisors have a dislike for performing the control process on their own subordinates?

4.   Managing by objectives has not caught on as rapidly as many predicted when the idea was first developed. What reasons may possibly contribute to the reluctance of some managers to utilize management by objectives?

5.   In addition to the control techniques mentioned in the chapter, what other techniques are being applied in today's organizations? What are the strengths and weaknesses of these techniques?

The following cases at the back of the book contain problems related to Chapter 13:

> Ben Stockton
>
> Mark Williams
>
> H. Gerald Pretzler
>
> Edith Capp and Janet Turner

Earl Fornette

Bentley Cantrell

Billy Snyder

Kurt Browning

Susan Swanson

Grace Lanham

Richard Jameson

Walt Gladberry

Abigail Spiegal and Trudy Pennington

Alan Purdy

Additional readings

Burke, Ronald J., and Douglas S. Wilcox, "Characteristics of Effective Employee Performance Review and Development Interviews," *Personnel Psychology,* Volume 22, Number 3 (Autumn 1969), pp. 291–305.

Carroll, Stephen J., Jr., and Henry L. Tosi, Jr., *Management by Objectives,* New York: The Macmillan Company, 1973.

Howell, R. A., "A Fresh Look at Management by Objectives," *Business Horizons,* Volume 10, Number 3 (Fall 1967), pp. 51–58.

Jerome, William T., III, *Executive Control—The Catalyst,* New York: John Wiley & Sons, Inc., 1967.

Koontz, Harold, "Making Managerial Appraisal Effective," *California Management Review,* Volume 15, Number 2 (Winter 1972), pp. 46–55.

Lopez, Felix M., Jr., *Evaluating Employee Performance,* Chicago: Public Personnel Association, 1968.

Luthans, Fred, *Organizational Behavior,* New York: McGraw-Hill Book Company, 1973, pp. 256–279.

McGregor, Douglas, "An Uneasy Look at Performance Appraisal," *Harvard Business Review,* Volume 37, Number 3 (May–June 1957), pp. 89–94.

Meyer, Herbert H., Emmanual Kay, and John R. P. French, Jr., "Split Roles in Performance Appraisal," *Harvard Business Review,* Volume 43, Number 1 (January–February 1965), pp. 123–129.

Murdick, Robert G., "Management Control: Concepts and Practice," *Advanced Management Journal,* Volume 35, Number 1 (January 1970), pp. 48–52.

Odiorne, George S., *Management by Objectives,* New York: Pittman Publishing Company, 1965.

Patton, Arch, "How To Appraise Executive Performance," *Harvard Business Review,* Volume 38, Number 1 (January–February 1960), pp. 63–70.

Tosi, Henry L., John R. Rizzo, and Stephen J. Carroll, "Setting Goals in Management by Objectives," *California Management Review,* Volume 12, Number 4 (Summer 1970), pp. 70–78.

Wallace, William H., "Performance Appraisal for Nonself-directed Personnel," *Personnel Journal,* Volume 50, Number 7 (July 1971), pp. 521–527.

Winstanley, N. B., "Performance Appraisal: Another Pollution Problem?" *The Conference Board Record,* Volume 9, Number 9 (September 1972), pp. 59–63.

Chapter 14

When Disciplinary Action Becomes Necessary

A case to consider before reading chapter 14

MARINELL CLAYTON—THE FULL-TIME NURSE WHO SELDOM IS

Patrick Osborne is the owner-manager of Rest Manor Nursing Home, a facility for elderly or infirm patients who require constant care including medical treatment. The home is located in a small community of about 5,000 residents and is somewhat isolated from major cities and population centers. In addition to Rest Manor, the town has a full-service hospital, a small medical clinic, and several doctors' offices that require staffing by nurses. As a result, trained nurses are in heavy demand in the small community. It is especially difficult to hire and keep good registered nurses.

Rest Manor is small by most nursing home standards; it contains twenty-eight beds, which remain filled constantly. Mr. Osborne indicates that he has a waiting list of applicants wishing to enter the facility whenever a vacancy occurs. One of the state laws regulating nursing homes requires the presence of a qualified registered nurse at all times. Practical nurses, orderlies, and other assistants may be used for treatment, service, and other care purposes, but an R.N. must constantly be present and in charge of nursing care.

Osborne has been able to hire three registered nurses who each work an eight-hour shift five days a week. On weekends, two nurses from a local doctor's office and a semiretired nurse fill in while the regular nurses have their time off. This arrangement has been the best one Mr. Osborne has been able to organize, because of the shortage of registered nurses. He has tried to attract nurses from other communities to come in to work, but has been unable to do so. Seemingly, there are no other qualified nurses locally who are willing to work.

This arrangement might be reasonably satisfactory except for the fact that one of the regular registered nurses, Marinell Clayton, is creating a problem.

Marinell works the 3 P.M. to 11 P.M. shift Monday through Friday. She is a woman in her late forties, is married, and has three grown children. Her husband is self-employed as a clock and watch repairman.

Mrs. Clayton is an excellent nurse when she is present and working. She is extremely considerate of the patients; they all respond to her favorably and with admiration. The workers Marinell supervises indicate that she treats them fairly and helps them whenever they need it. The problem is—Marinell has a habit of taking off from work a day or two almost every other week to accompany her husband on some trip he is taking.

Because Mr. Clayton is self-employed, he sets his own work days and hours. He is an avid sportsman and takes off a few days regularly to hunt, fish, or travel some distance to see a special sporting event. His wife could seldom go with him while their children were at home, but now that the children are grown, he wants Marinell to go with him whenever possible. Because she shares his interests, she usually goes with him. This practice requires her frequently to stay away from work on a Friday (or sometimes a Monday) so that she can be away for a long weekend.

Marinell doesn't ask for a day off before she leaves. She just tells Mr. Osborne she won't be in the next day because Robert (her husband) wants her to go with him. She never asks to be paid for the days she is away. She explains that money is not too important now to her. Robert and she have an adequate income and just want to enjoy themselves. In addition, she feels that her job is secure because Mr. Osborne can't find anyone to replace her and because he wouldn't fire her under any circumstances. She also believes that the other nurses can fill in adequately for her when she's out of town. She has frankly stated that if she can't go places with Robert when he asks her, she'll give up her job to make it possible.

Her absences, however, upset the work schedules and attention given to the patients. One of the other registered nurses has to fill in extra hours in her place, or the shift goes along without a registered nurse. The operating license of the nursing home is being placed in jeopardy by her actions.

Questions about the Marinell Clayton case

1.   What alternatives does Mr. Osborne have?

2.   What potential do positive control and disciplinary approaches have as solutions to the problem?

3.   What negative control devices are worth considering (if any)? What specific actions can be taken here?

4.   In the past, Mr. Osborne has been very flexible concerning absenteeism and tardiness among workers. He gives each worker a two-week annual paid vacation and one week of paid sick leave. What rules and regulations are needed to cover absenteeism and tardiness at Rest Manor?

5.   If an organization has rules and regulations concerning absenteeism or other types of worker behavior, can the rules and regulations be ignored in special cases?

6.   In what way (if any) is the positive motivational process (discussed in Chapter 10) a factor in this case?

7.   Role play the conversation that might occur between Mr. Osborne and Mrs. Clayton about this problem.

It was suggested in the previous chapter that in many instances, the worker accepts the responsibility for regulating his own behavior so that his performance is organizationally beneficial and productive. Self-control and self-discipline are always preferable to control or discipline imposed by another force, but sometimes it becomes necessary for a supervisor to influence the behavior of his workers through the use of managerially initiated control and discipline.

Discipline is often defined as the process of training a worker so that he can develop self-control and so that he can become more effective in his work. The purpose of the supervisorily imposed disciplinary process is the development and furtherance of the type of performance from the individual worker that will be conducive to the achievement of organization goals. The ideal disciplinary approach exacts a specific response from the performer not only in the short run but also over a longer period of time.

In many respects, the disciplining of a worker is related to the **conditioning process:** It is desirable for the worker to act a certain way when a specific set of conditions prevail, and the worker is encouraged to perform accordingly. Both positive rewards and negative penalties may be used to encourage the desired behavior. The positive and negative motivational models presented in Chapter 10 can be useful in reinforcing the intent of disciplinary action to control or moderate actions.

The term "discipline" often connotes the giving of rewards or punishment after the fact, when in reality discipline in its proper context should be visualized as the development of the ability to analyze situations, to determine what is the

correct behavior, and to decide to act favorably *in advance* of the receiving of specific rewards or penalties. The worker eventually should become goal-oriented
voluntarily and under his own power. He becomes "disciplined" to do what is
best rather than to do something that would be incorrect or "wrong."

The well-disciplined individual is the one who cannot only discuss what is
right and wrong, but who also has his own emotions, feelings, and desires so well
under control that he can perform the appropriate action even when it seems
against his own personal wishes. Ideally, no worker would ever be called upon to
sacrifice important moral values for the benefit of the organization, but workers
sometimes do find disciplining necessary in order to follow the course charted by
organizational planners. Rules, regulations, procedures, and guidelines are a
necessity in any organization. Adherence to these controls may require discipline
on the part of the worker. Psychologists have indicated that disciplining is an
essential part of living and working and does not have to be viewed with total
skepticism.

A Philosophy of Discipline

Before the discussion becomes involved in the details of a disciplinary program,
the development of a philosophy of disciplining is important. Perhaps an analogy
to the philosophy behind an entirely different managerial activity will be helpful
in establishing the positive frame of reference desirable as a foundation for disciplining. While the setting involved in the analogy is totally different from a situation requiring employee disciplining, the philosophy is illustrated.

Wayne Housey is the credit and collections manager for Landmark Department
Store, a major retail establishment in a large metropolitan area. Landmark handles
all of its own credit and collections. Whenever Wayne or one of his assistants
receives an application for credit, he reviews the credit record of the applicant to
determine if the applicant has an acceptable history of meeting his financial obligations. Other data, such as monthly income and indebtedness outstanding, are
also considered before the decision is made on whether or not to extend credit to
the customer. When a decision is made to allow the credit requested, Wayne and
his assistants are indicating that they have confidence that the customer is willing
and able to meet the financial obligations the credit extension involves. As the credit
is extended, Wayne discusses the conditions (dates of payment, interest rates,
and so forth) with the creditor to be certain that the obligations are understood.

When the customer makes a purchase using his credit, the purchase is recorded.
A statement is sent at the appropriate time (at the end of the month) which reminds
the customer that it is now time for him to make a payment on his account. The de-

partment store (through its credit manager) has confidence that the customer *will* meet his obligation and that only a simple reminder (usually an impersonal bill) is all that is necessary to secure the payment.

If, for some reason, the customer fails to pay his indebtedness, Wayne sends another brief statement the next month restating the obligation. The statement is handled very positively; it is still expected that the customer will pay his account.

If no response is received on the basis of the reminders, the collection procedure progresses to the "should pay" stage, in which Wayne sends a note discussing the terms of the original agreement and suggesting that the customer "should pay" his account in order to protect his credit rating, or out of a sense of fair play, or some other line of logic. The assumption behind this phase is that the customer is still a valued customer—one whom the store wishes to keep as a customer. It is also expected that the customer will respond to logic, reason, and the desire to act fairly and honorably. Perhaps more than one "should pay" letter may be issued over a period of time.

If the customer fails to respond to the appeal to reason and honesty, Wayne eventually decides that the customer has no intention of living up to his obligation. The customer is no longer welcomed as a credit risk. In order to get action, a letter threatening to take steps harmful to the customer (through a legal suit, the loss of all credit privileges, etc.) will be issued. Continued contact is not considered desirable if the customer is unwilling to meet his obligation. The threat of action is made and exercised if necessary.

The philosophy behind Wayne Housey's approach to collecting his company's credit statements is that *qualified* people who are *knowledgeable concerning their responsibilities* normally will fulfill their obligations willingly. Housey's role primarily is one of selecting qualified people and reminding them of their obligations at the appropriate time. Only when individuals do not fulfill their obligations does the role change. If the conditions back of nonpayment appear to be beyond the control of the creditor, Housey is helpful in attempting to find agreeable terms and adjustments. If the creditor, however, shows that he has no desire to meet his obligations and fails to respond to reason and logic, the procedure moves to a negative, threatening stage. The customer is urged to action through fear of what might happen to him or to his credit rating if he does not assume responsibility for his obligations.

The similarity between this case and the proper handling of disciplining is dramatic. Individuals selected and placed in jobs ideally are chosen because they are qualified to perform adequately—they have the skills and abilities required to do the job. Their supervisor instructs them in their duties so that there is a clear understanding of the job demands. Organizational rules, regulations, and procedures are spelled out and the reward and penalty system is clarified in advance. Understanding and acceptance of goals and expectations from the beginning is extremely important; it is these factors that the worker must discipline himself to observe or to work toward. If training is needed in order to help the worker live up to expectations, this should be provided as a part of the disciplinary program.

If a worker is to be disciplined to his obligations and to requirements and demands, he must be given regular feedback concerning the strengths and weaknesses of his performance. His supervisor, and other qualified personnel, need to help him discover his progress and assist him in overcoming difficulties he may encounter. Rewards should be given whenever possible for the individual's success in performing in a way that satisfactorily adheres to requirements and expectations.

Normally, when a worker's performance falls below the standards expected of him, he will catch his own errors and correct himself. If this does not occur, a gentle reminder from his supervisor usually receives a positive response, and the inadequate behavior is corrected. If, for some reason, the worker does not immediately correct inadequacies in his performance, other constructive reminders may be appropriate. If there is still no noticeable response to the oral reminders, the disciplinary process may enter a phase very similar to the "should pay" stage in the collection process. The supervisor may need to explain to the worker the importance of his actions and may need to review the worker's understanding of his own obligations. If the employee is willing to perform satisfactorily but is being hindered by other factors, the supervisor may be able to help him overcome obstacles to his performance. At this stage of the disciplinary program, good will prevails and the supervisor's intent is to help the worker meet his obligations and continue his employment.

If, however, the worker shows no intention of living up to the obligations he accepted when he agreed to take the job, the negative phase of the process begins. The worker may receive a warning that penalties will be applied if he does not fulfill his job responsibilities. The penalties may vary depending upon the nature and degree of his lack of fulfillment of his responsibilities.

If a worker fails to exercise self-control and self-discipline, the phases of the disciplinary process proceed progressively.

First, the worker receives one or more gentle reminders of the performance obligations he has accepted and the feedback that his performance needs correction.

Second, if the worker needs help in correcting his actions, his supervisor provides the appropriate assistance.

Third, if the worker still fails to respond and to fulfill his responsibilities, he may be made aware of the positive contributions his performance can make to the organization and the benefits that will come to him personally from performing satisfactorily. Sometimes a written warning is given at this stage to clarify the seriousness of the problem and to notify whatever unions may be involved.

Eventually, if the worker shows no desire to improve or to perform adequately, penalties will be threatened and applied. A disciplinary approach, therefore, can be conducted on a very positive, constructive level. It is assumed that workers will live up to goals and standards if they are known and accepted. The performance evaluation and control procedures are kept on a positive plane unless the actions and intent of the worker call for negative action. Disciplining is much more than the application of penalties. It is the training and regulating of behavior (preferably through self-control) so that worker performance contributes to organizational and personal achievement.

Making Decisions about Disciplining

A task managers often find difficult to perform is the one that involves calling attention to a worker's failures and shortcomings, applying penalties, and seeking corrective action. If not handled skillfully, the process of constructive criticism can be distasteful to all parties involved. There are some procedures and conditions that help make the process of criticism and correction more pleasant and more effective. The success of constructive disciplining is dependent upon who does the disciplining, when the corrective action is taken, and how constructive criticism is given to the performer. These factors are explored in the next few paragraphs.

Who Should Discipline?   As was stated earlier, the best form of discipline is self-discipline. The performer himself is the key to disciplinary success in this approach. If external disciplinary action is needed, the immediate superior of the worker requiring disciplining is usually in the best position to provide correctional comments and to suggest future courses of action. The supervisor is formally responsible for the actions of those who work under him. As a result, he should be knowledgeable concerning the level of performance required and the individual worker's actions in meeting specified standards. The working relationship between a superior and his subordinate should be close enough so that communications between the two flow easily. Criticism from a respected immediate

supervisor is usually more palatable to a subordinate than criticism from a specialist or an outsider whom the subordinate knows to a limited degree if at all.

When Is Corrective Action Appropriate?   Another dilemma the manager
must face concerns when to take corrective action if a worker makes a mistake
and when to remain silent. Some managers operate on the assumption that a
worker should be corrected at the first hint of a mistake, while other managers
prefer to postpone action until a deliberate pattern of errors can be identified. In
clarifying the appropriate time for disciplining to occur, it seems advisable to
apply corrective and/or punitive action only *after the facts indicate that the individual
in question has performed unsatisfactorily and has failed to take the initiative in correcting
his own behavior.* Disciplinary action before the facts have been gathered may
result in incorrectly disciplining individuals who neither deserve disciplining nor
are remotely responsible for organizational failures. Careless disciplining can do
more harm than good.

Some managers use the additional guideline for disciplining that the likelihood
of the error being committed again must be present before discipline and criticism
can be justified. The feeling behind this is that workers do not need to be conditioned to avoid events and actions that are not likely to occur again. However,
not everyone agrees that the possibility of repetitive occurrence is a valid criterion
for determining when to discipline and when to withhold discipline.

McGregor, in the development of the "hot stove" approach to disciplining,
suggested that criticism and penalties should occur: (1) immediately following the
commission of an erroneous or insufficient act; (2) with advance warning in the
sense that the worker knows what is expected and what the action will be toward
him if he does not live up to expectations; (3) consistently against all individuals
who commit the same shortcoming under the same conditions; and (4) impersonally in that personalities are not criticized, but the deed or action receives the
corrective or punitive attention.[1] The immediacy of action (following the identification of the facts of performance inadequacies, of course) is desirable to relate
the undesirable behavior to the penalty or to the need for correction. The need
for advance warning makes certain that goals and penalties have been communicated before any action is begun. The need for consistency of action in disciplining
is designed to provide fair treatment and to avoid favoritism to certain individuals.
The need for impersonality of correctional action removes the subjective, more
emotional element of discipline so that corrective action can be handled objec-

---

[1]Leonard R. Sayles and George Strauss, in *Human Behavior in Organizations*, Englewood Cliffs,
New Jersey: Prentice-Hall, Inc., 1966, p. 329, state that the "hot stove" rule originated with Douglas
McGregor.

tively and constructively. Except for a few conditions, these guidelines have merit in deciding when the manager should initiate correctional disciplining.

Conducting the Correctional Interview.   When it has been established that a worker needs correctional assistance and constructive criticism, the manager is confronted with the task of discussing the worker's behavior with him. The purpose of the discussion is the achievement of improved performance, and it concentrates primarily upon future needs and future behavior. Several factors and conditions can help to transform the session from a potentially negative and subjective review of a worker's shortcomings into a constructive, objective analysis that can result in improved performance.

1.   First, it is extremely helpful if the supervisor-worker conversation concerning performance needs and inadequacies can take place in a private, confidential environment. Privacy tends to remove the threat of making individual imperfection a matter of public record. Workers tend to respond to constructive criticism that is confidentially given more favorably than to public criticism. Resentment and resistance build when a supervisor broadcasts the deficiencies of one of his subordinates to the co-workers and subordinates of the faulty worker.

2.   Before any criticism is given, the manager determines if the worker understands the duties and expectations the job involves. If goals and standards are not understood, the correctional process must clarify them.

3.   Any criticism that occurs dwells upon performance standards and the worker's inability to meet those standards. Criticism concentrates upon the job to be done and avoids personal references and accusations. Instead of saying to a worker, "You must not want to do what's right because your performance is always lacking," a much better approach would be to say, "Your job makes these contributions and requires these actions. . . . You seem to be having some difficulty with this area. . . . What can be done to correct the problem?"

4.   The initiative for identifying and correcting problem areas is given to the worker himself as much as possible.

5.   Constructive criticism searches for tangible steps that can provide solutions for improvement. The worker is not criticized and penalized and then left to flounder around aimlessly. Instead, positive steps for improvement are considered and implemented.

6.   The tone of constructive criticism is forward-looking rather than dwelling upon past actions. The damage from yesterday's mistakes has been done, but tomorrow's errors can be avoided. Any good coach, for example, will tell his athletes that if a mistake is made, the offender should recognize his mistake, determine how he can correct it, then forget about it or put it out of his mind. The same situation is true with the worker and his superior. When a problem is identified and a solution is found, the mistake should not be continually brought to mind. In other words, the error should be forgotten after a positive plan of action is developed.

7.   Constructive evaluations include praise and affirmative recognition of good performance as well as criticism and penalties for inadequate performance. ~~Recognition~~ of a~~dequate performance frequently~~ is ~~overlooked~~ but is imp~~ortant to the performer~~.

8.   When ~~penalties are involved~~, they are ~~applied objectively and are explaine~~d. ~~Methods~~ and ~~means~~ for a~~voiding future penalties are reviewed~~.

The utilization of these concepts will help to make criticism and correction constructive rather than destructive.[2]

Determining Penalties.   Where a system of penalties has been devised to enforce adherence to standards, rules and regulations, decisions have to be made concerning the severity of the penalty justifiable in a given situation. If an action sequence has been designated (oral warning, to written warning, to disciplinary layoff, to discharge), the decision may be simplified. However, other factors must be considered, such as the length of time since the last offense, the intent of the offender (Was his action willfully negligent or was he attempting to do what was right and failed?), the seriousness of the worker's offense, and the organization's previous practices in handling similar cases. The factors must all be considered before the appropriate penalty is determined. Consistency of action is an extremely important guideline in determining and applying penalties. Without consistency, charges of unfairness and favoritism will inevitably arise.

Discipline without Punishment

One company has developed an approach to disciplinary action that has eliminated all direct penalties (except discharge) in an attempt to capitalize on worker self-control and to emphasize positive supervision rather than negative leadership. In the process of de-emphasizing the threat of penalties, the organization has developed six policies and procedures.[3]

1.   No disciplinary demotions, suspensions, or other forms of punishment will henceforth be applied.

2.   In case of unsatisfactory work performance (e.g., carelessness in handling materials, inattention to duty) or breach of discipline (e.g., overstaying rest or lunch periods, unnecessary absenteeism, disregard of safety, failure to carry out the foreman's instructions), the following steps will be followed:

[2]For an excellent discussion of the art of constructive criticism, see George Weinberg, *The Action Approach*, New York: The World Publishing Company, 1969.

[3]John Huberman, "Discipline without Punishment," *Harvard Business Review*, Volume 42, Number 4 (July–August 1964), pp. 65–67.

Step One: The foreman will offer the worker a casual and friendly reminder on the job.

Step Two: Should another incident arise within four to six weeks of Step One, the foreman will again correct it casually on the job but will later call the individual to his office for a serious but friendly chat. He will explain the need for and purpose of the rule(s); make sure the person understands the explanation; and express his confidence that the person will henceforth decide to abide by them. He will also listen to any reasonable excuse the employee may bring up. If he decides that the transgression was unintentional or based on misunderstanding, the matter is closed.

Step Three: In case of further incidents within about six weeks, Step Two is repeated with some variation. First, the shift foreman is also present at the discussion; secondly, the employee's attention is directed to the possibility that he may dislike the work the organization has to offer, or he may find the relatively strict industrial discipline distasteful. In such case, would it be better to look for some other job or line of work? (Vocational counseling is available through the personnel office.) The foreman then expresses his hope that the employee will, in fact, decide that he likes the work and the company and will adapt himself to the requirements. This conversation is confirmed in a letter to the employee's home.

Step Four: The employee who perpetrates another incident of poor workmanship or breach of discipline within six to eight weeks of Step Three is called off the floor into the foreman's office, again in the presence of the shift foreman. There he is directed to go home for the rest of the shift and consider seriously whether he does or does not wish to abide by company standards. He is informed that he will receive full pay for the time as a last expression of the company's hope that he will wish to stay and abide by the rules. He is also told that another occurrence of trouble within reasonable time will lead—regretfully—to termination.

3.   If another incident should occur within reasonable time, the employee's services are terminated.

4.   In case several incidents happen at unusually close intervals, Step Two or Step Three may be skipped.

5.   If no further incident occurs within six to eight weeks of any one step (except Step Four), such step is cleared from the employee's record. Should another incident happen at a later time, the last step will be repeated. Considerable time—in the range of a year—would have to elapse without incident before Step Four is cleared from the records.

6.   In case of discovery of criminal behavior or in-plant fighting, termination results without preliminary steps. Such behavior is taken as conclusive evidence of lack of adequate self-respect and discipline even if it happens only once.

When a worker is sent home (Step Four) for his unsatisfactory performance, he receives pay for the remainder of the shift day. If he comes back to work, it is assumed that he is committing himself to perform satisfactorily in the future. This approach has shown signs of effectiveness in many situations where it has been used.

Disciplinary Action from Other Sources

In addition to self-discipline and supervisory discipline, a worker may be subject to control and discipline from other sources. The informal work group disciplines its members (sometimes very rigidly) to gain conformity to behavior norms it has developed. Failure to adhere to group-imposed guidelines may result in penalties that are most undesirable to the worker. Especially harmful are sanctions such as social ostracism and loss of social affiliation.

The union has been granted the formal right to discipline its members for failure to conform to legally established union guidelines. As a result, an individual worker may be subject to his own disciplining and the disciplining of his superiors, his informal colleagues, and his union (if he belongs to one). The behavior demanded by each of these different forces may or may not concur, which, of course, may create a role conflict for the worker.

Summary

Discipline is the process of training and regulating the behavior of a worker so that the worker's actions will be organizationally and personally beneficial and productive. Self-control and self-discipline are preferable to externally imposed discipline, but supervisors sometimes of necessity must become involved in applying discipline to workers.

A positive frame of reference is desirable in activating the disciplinary process. Unless a worker exhibits poor intentions and a lack of willingness to cooperate, a system of rewards and reminders may be sufficient to condition or sustain positive response. If negative disciplining becomes necessary, it should follow a progression from gentle to severe penalties for inadequate actions.

The performer and his superior play key roles in the disciplinary process. Through careful selection of the time, place, and reward or penalty, disciplinary action can be conducted in a constructive, objective manner.

Questions to consider after reading Chapter 14

1. Compare and contrast the purposes of disciplinary action with those of the motivational process.

2. To many people, disciplining means applying penalties and nothing more. In what ways is this attitude toward disciplinary action erroneous? How can this attitude be corrected?

3. How can discipline be beneficial to the worker?

4. Review and evaluate the eight suggestions for conducting the correctional interview. Which may be difficult to adhere to?

5.   Why is it that so many supervisors find performance evaluations and correctional interviews distasteful?

6.   Why is it usually held that the immediate superior of the worker needing discipline should be the one to apply disciplinary action if the worker himself fails to exercise self-discipline?

7.   If disciplinary action is needed but is not applied, what results can be expected?

The following cases at the back of the book contain problems related to Chapter 14:

Ben Stockton

Mark Williams

H. Gerald Pretzler

Edith Capp and Janet Turner

Bentley Cantrell

Billy Snyder

Richard Jameson

Walt Gladberry

Abigail Spiegal and Trudy Pennington

Alan Purdy

Additional readings

Black, James M., *Positive Discipline,* New York: American Management Association, 1970.

Boise, William B., "Supervisors' Attitudes toward Disciplinary Actions," *Personnel Administration,* Volume 28, Number 3 (May–June 1965), pp. 24–27.

Booker, Gene S., "Behavioral Aspects of Disciplinary Action," *Personnel Journal,* Volume 48, Number 7 (July 1969), pp. 525–529.

"Employee Discipline: Problems and Policies," *Management Review,* Volume 49, Number 10 (October 1960), pp. 49–52.

Gragg, Charles J., "Whose Fault Was It?", *Harvard Business Review,* Volume 42, Number 1 (January–February 1964), pp. 107–110.

Handsaker, Morrison, "Arbitration of Discipline Cases," *Personnel Journal,* Volume 46, Number 3 (March 1967), pp. 153–156.

Jones, Dallas L., "Supervisor and the Disciplinary Process in a Unionized Setting," *Personnel Administration,* Volume 26, Number 1 (January–February 1963), pp. 42–46.

See Chapter 13 for additional readings related to this topic.

Chapter 15

Coping with Problem Employees

A case to consider before reading chapter 15

MADSEN QUALITY DRUG STORE

Howard Madsen, a registered pharmacist, is owner-manager of the largest drug store in a small town where farming and the local state university are the largest industries. Madsen opened the drug store nearly fifteen years ago, beginning first strictly as a pharmacy and adding new lines and services until the store has become almost a department store. Additional services now range from a soda fountain to sales of household items, hobby supplies, office supplies, and many other products. Madsen actively manages all phases of the store's operations. In addition he has an assistant manager who helps supervise all nonpharmacy sales and services and a middle-aged woman who is in charge of the soda fountain. Madsen also employs two other pharmacists, three cashiers, eight sales clerks, four soda jerks, and a bookkeeper. Some of these are part-time, but most are full-time permanent employees.

Mr. Madsen has a good friend who teaches business administration courses at the local university. In a recent conversation between the two men, Madsen discussed his business philosophy and revealed a problem he was having with one of his part-time employees. The following monologue reveals what Madsen told his professor friend.

At our drug store, we emphasize customer service. We do everything within our power to provide the customer with the best products available and the best service available at a reasonable price. We select the merchandise that we sell on the basis of what we feel the customer will want and on the basis of our previous experiences with the reliability of the product. We don't sell products that we feel we can't guarantee, because we stand behind what we sell.

We attempt to select our employees as best we can on the basis of their ability to give considerate, informed assistance to customers. As you know, we have a relatively small store and don't have a large staff. We don't have the time, means, or money to put each employee through a formal training program on courteous salesmanship. Instead we give each employee coaching and other supervisory assistance to show him the proper way to open a sales contact, to considerately provide product information, to close the sales contact considerately, and to provide other customer courtesies.

We've been rather successful over the years at hiring the right people and developing their sales and service abilities and attitudes, I think. We pay good, fair wages to everyone. At least we're comparable to similar businesses in this area. The money is not outstanding, but it's pretty good. We pay a straight salary to all full-time employees and hourly wages to part-timers.

I don't think I'm boasting too much when I say that we've had good employer-employee relations and haven't lost a full-time employee in over five years. The part-timers we've lost have all had firm reasons for leaving. Some have completed their college education and moved; some of the women have gotten married and have quit working to take care of their families.

We feel we've kept good people because we attempt to give each one personal consideration. For example, we're very flexible on giving time off for personal reasons. We get to know each employee pretty well. We encourage everyone to have confidence in and concern for his fellow workers. We seem to have a good team spirit.

Right now we've got a problem that's unusual to us. Last summer we hired a young man just out of a four-year tour of duty in the service. We had known him casually before he went in. His parents and other family members live here, and we've known them for years. They are honest, hard-working people.

The young man is a handsome, well-groomed fellow. He went into the service immediately upon graduation from high school. When he got out of the service, he wanted to start to college. He decided to stay with his parents and go to the university here. He asked us for a part-time job to earn some extra money to supplement what he's getting from the G.I. Bill. We needed some part-time help, and his credentials looked good (he had done well in the service); so we hired him.

The problems we have with him are twofold. First, he's not very considerate and helpful to our customers. Almost from the first Edwin failed to show an interest in the customer. When a customer requested a certain item, and we had a variety of goods that might do the job, Edwin wouldn't show the customer the variety. He still won't, for that matter. Instead he seems to decide upon the product that he thinks is best and pushes that item without showing the variety and letting the customer select what he wants. Some customers find this very irritating.

Just yesterday, we almost lost a big sale because of Edwin's attitude. We had a customer who was interested in buying a 35 mm camera. Edwin pulled out a camera that he happened to like and gave the customer the hard sell on it. He ignored the customer's questions about other cameras and hardly would show any of the others. The customer was becoming disgusted and was about ready to leave when I came up and got others out and started talking about each of them. We made the sale.

Word has gotten back to me through friends who are our customers that Edwin's attitude has actually run some business away. My friends tell me that Edwin is too curt and unfriendly. I've tried to coach Edwin on how to improve his approach, and

Len Steele (the assistant manager) has tried also. We haven't given up yet, but we're not much encouraged.

Our second problem is Edwin's lack of cooperation with fellow workers. He's been somewhat of an antagonistic loner since joining the Madsen family. He has no really close friends here. He makes frequent comments and requests that have not endeared him to the other employees. For example, he keeps poking fun at Mrs. O'Reilly (the soda fountain manager) because he doesn't like the way she wears her hair all rolled up in a knot. He has also asked me confidential questions about other employees—questions such as how much money they are making and what my plans are for them. Sometimes they've overheard these questions and were infuriated by his nosiness. And another example—he's been attempting to date Louise Atkinson, a part-time cashier. She's engaged to be married next month, and has come to me requesting that I do something to get him to leave her alone. These are a few tangible illustrations of the problems I have with him.

I'm planning to give Edwin a little more time before I decide what to do. Right now I'm not sure how to help him develop into a useful worker.

Questions about the Madsen Drug Store case

1.   **What are the goals and objectives of Madsen Quality Drug Store?**

2.   **What do Edwin's objectives appear to be?**

3.   **What organizational and supervisory deficiencies have contributed to the problems that have developed?**

4.   **What other factors appear to contribute to Edwin's problems?**

5.   **Complaints about Edwin's behavior have come from a number of sources. Which ones should Mr. Madsen be concerned about? Why?**

6.   **What course of action should Mr. Madsen take now to cope with the problems that have already developed? Role play discussions that might take place between Mr. Madsen and Edwin.**

7.   **What lessons should Mr. Madsen have learned from this experience that will be helpful to him in the future?**

"Nobody's perfect." How often has this been given by an individual as an excuse for his poor behavior? As we look at the meaning of the statement more closely, most of us will readily admit our own flaws and shortcomings, and we can easily point to the weaknesses and inadequacies in other individuals. Perfection can be found only in the Divine and not in the human.

As the statement regarding perfection is applied to employees in the labor force, it is obviously true. No worker is without faults. The manager who expects perfection in the performance and behavior of his subordinates will be surprised to discover some areas of performance in which workers fall short of those expectations. Even though no worker is perfect, some workers exhibit overall performance that is satisfactory and adequate while other workers deviate from the expected level of performance to the point they become what is known as a "problem worker."

A ~~problem worker,~~ then, is an ~~individual whose behavior at work is inadequate or improper in relation to the needs and expectations of the organization and the other individuals who are a part of the organization.~~ His behavior is such that he hinders the progress of the organization, handicaps the performance of his fellow workers, and may even eliminate the possibility of achieving his own objectives. The most obvious performance inadequacy is identifiable as poor job productivity—the failure to meet sales goals or production goals specified in terms of quantity, quality, and so forth. There are, however, other clues that, when they are exhibited regularly, indicate serious problems. Other authors, for example, have suggested that hostility, indecisiveness, inappropriate responses, and destructiveness are signals of improper employee behavior that can become problematic.[1]

~~Hostility~~ is an act of ~~ill will~~ or ~~unfriendliness~~ exhibited by a worker toward superiors, subordinates, or peers.

~~Indecisiveness~~ represents the ~~inability~~ of the worker ~~to formulate a position,~~ to take a stand, or to agree on an appropriate course of action. Some workers, under stress, have severe difficulty in making decisions. Workers may also be lacking in self-confidence and, as a result, may be unable to finalize a decision.

~~Inappropriate responses,~~ simply stated, are ~~actions that are improper or are poorly timed.~~ The problem worker may be passive when he is expected to be dynamic. The chronic alcoholic gets drunk when his skills are needed for the completion of a crucial project, and so forth.

~~Destructiveness~~ is the term used to express the fact that the actions of some problem workers are such that they ~~tend to destroy themselves or others through their misdeeds or promiscuities.~~ The destruction may be physical, emotional, or organizational—any of these domains may suffer because of the acts of destruction.[2]

Chronic absenteeism may also be an indicator of a worker with problems, as may poor attitudes and low personal morale.

[1]Mortimer R. Feinberg and John R. Tarrant, "Dealing with Subordinates' Personal Problems," *Management Review*, Volume 59, Number 6 (June 1970), pp. 52–54.
[2]*Loc. cit.*

When a worker begins to exhibit symptoms of a problem on a regular basis, the level of management concern starts to mount. The problems of the worker become the problems of the organization when his difficulties begin to affect organizational performance. Managers normally become involved with the problems of workers when they reach the magnitude that the continued existence of the problem is detrimental to the achievement of organizational goals. Managers, of course, should also be concerned about the welfare of the worker who has the problem. Everyone gains when a worker's problems are eliminated.

The problems of workers originate from a number of sources. In this chapter, workers' problems created by organizational factors (on-the-job or around-the-job problems) are considered and worker problems resulting from off-the-job causes are also reviewed. Several alternative courses of action are considered. In the chapter that follows, three very severe problems will be emphasized—the problems of alcoholism, drug abuse, and theft—and solutions will be explored.

The beginning point for dealing with any problem is the attempt to diagnose the causes of the problem. In dealing with the problems of workers, this may be accomplished in several ways. As Sirota and Wolfson have stated, employees are the best source of information about their own problems.[3] Personal counseling in which the worker with a problem is encouraged to reveal the source of his difficulties is a much used technique (as is discussed in Chapter 17). More often than not, personal counseling seems to be used only after problems have already arisen and have become serious. However, it would also appear important to utilize routine, regular counseling to identify potential problems and to "nip them in the bud" before they have a chance to develop.

In addition to formal counseling sessions, any expression of communication (formal or informal) from each worker may reveal clues that show causes of problems and potential danger areas. It is important for supervisors to chat regularly with their subordinates to learn what they are thinking about and what their interests and concerns are.[4]

Ideally, much of the counseling and the routine conversations described above can be performed by the regular supervisory personnel of the organization. However, if the usual supervisors do not have the necessary skills and attitudes or cannot identify the problems and develop the necessary solutions, the task may need handling by professionally trained troubleshooters (who may be staff personnel or outside consultants).

---

[3]David Sirota and Alan D. Wolfson, "Pragmatic Approach to People Problems," *Harvard Business Review,* Volume 51, Number 1 (January–February 1973), p. 123.
   [4]*Loc. cit.*

Causes of Employee Problems

If the sources of worker problems can be identified, solutions usually become visible almost simultaneously. In many situations problems are generated by actions and decisions made by the employing organization itself. For example, many worker problems originate with the *nature of the jobs* workers are asked to perform. It has been shown that *jobs that are highly repetitive* and *involve very short job time cycles* often result in lowered productivity (as opposed to jobs with less repetition and fairly lengthy time cycles).[5] Jobs that provide the worker with *little freedom of movement* and very *limited opportunities to be innovative* and think with originality may also decrease productivity and increase the frustrations and mental barriers to superior performance.[6]

Job assignments that *disrupt social ties* and *isolate workers* from the benefits of socialization reduce the opportunities for fulfillment of affiliation and recognition needs and result in other social maladjustments.[7]

The *type of supervision* received by workers may also create problems. If a worker needs support and assistance from his boss but receives neither, he will be less productive and less satisfied. If a worker needs little supervision but a significant amount of freedom (and authority) to act and receives close, dominant supervision instead, the worker will experience some difficulties.

The relationship between working conditions and worker problems is not always clear-cut, but *working conditions* obviously may have a bearing upon the level of a worker's performance and the status of his well-being. Poor working conditions (those that distract, restrict, or inhibit the performance of the worker) will result in problems for the individual employee and the organization. Poor working conditions may include inappropriate levels of noise, temperatures, lighting, ventilation, safety devices, or any other threat to individual productivity and security. Workers, for example, seem to do their most creative, innovative work in environments that are cooler and more refreshing to the mind and body.

Inadequate reward structures in the form of poor wages, lack of recognition, and limited promotion opportunities tend to lead to worker frustration and to indifference toward organizational goals and objectives. As was discussed in earlier chapters, workers have goals and expectations of their jobs, and when these are

[5]Melvin Sorcher and Herbert H. Meyer, "Motivating Factory Employees," *Personnel*, Volume 45, Number 1 (January–February 1968), p. 25.

[6]Gerald I. Susman, "Process Design, Automation, and Worker Alienation," *Industrial Relations*, Volume 11, Number 1 (February 1972), p. 35.

[7]Paul G. Adams, III, and John W. Slocum, Jr., "Work Groups and Employee Satisfaction," *Personnel Administration*, Volume 34, Number 2 (March–April 1971), p. 38.

thwarted, worker attitudes tend to disintegrate. Not all workers show equal interest in the rewards just mentioned, but every worker has his own set of needs.
Workers who are allowed little or no goal achievement will tend to become
impassive and indifferent over a period of time.

As the organization creates conditions that (1) are inconsistent with the needs
and expectations of the worker, (2) are unnecessarily restrictive, (3) are limited in
reward structure, or (4) otherwise inhibit the actions and development of workers,
problems will develop. The effect will be to encourage the development of poor
attitudes and sometimes poor performance, aggression, hostility, indecisiveness,
inappropriate responses, destructiveness, absenteeism, and other behaviors that
may become problematic.

Solutions to Job-Related Problems

Organizations have taken many different approaches to the problems that have
their source in on-the-job or around-the-job factors. Several actions will now be
mentioned. Each problem, of course, has its own set of potential solutions.

Many of the jobs characterized by repetition and short time cycles for performance have been structured in that manner to take advantage of specialization
and to coincide with mechanical innovations such as assembly lines and automation. In many cases, specialization and mechanical innovations have been useful
in increasing productivity and reducing training costs and learning time. At the
same time, however, these emphases have taken a toll on the positive attitudes of
many workers toward their jobs. Many workers view their jobs as activities requiring little skill, hardly any thought, and permitting little freedom or exercise
of authority. As was mentioned in an earlier chapter, many workers have come to
see themselves as robots that can be maneuvered at the command of a superior or
the conveyor belt.

Just what percentage of today's work force finds itself entangled in overly
specialized, heavily routinized jobs, resulting in loss of pride and personal involvement along with increased boredom and monotony, is not completely clear. Studies by Sheppard and Herrick suggest that almost 50 percent of the work force is
employed in oversimplified, undemanding jobs.[8] At the same time, the well-
known American pollster George Gallup states that fewer workers are finding

[8]Harold L. Sheppard and Neil Q. Herrick, *Where Have All the Robots Gone?* New York: Free Press,
1972, pp. 43–74.

their jobs boring and monotonous, while an increasing number of workers indicate satisfaction with their jobs as they are now composed.[9] In a similar poll conducted by a popular family magazine, it was discovered that 91 percent of working men and 84 percent of working women are satisfied with their jobs and do not find them undemanding or too routine and monotonous.[10]

Whether or not the existence of short-cycle, repetitive jobs is universal, there are many situations in which these types of jobs prevail and result in problems of worker attitude and behavior. Jobs that are too specialized or undemanding lend themselves to improvement through techniques called job enrichment. **Job enrichment** may be defined as the application of changes and innovations to jobs so that they will become more meaningful and rewarding to the incumbents holding the positions. The acts of enrichment enhance the performer's potential satisfaction as a worker and may also improve the probabilities of better performance. Job enrichment takes many forms as it combats the factors that degrade work.

One form of job enrichment is known as **job enlargement.** Job enlargement is particularly effective in enriching jobs that are too specialized or routine, because it allows a worker to perform a wide number of related tasks instead of only one or two repetitive, short-cycle tasks. The nature of some products is such that a whole unit can be assembled by an individual or a group of individuals instead of utilizing the customary assembly-line technique. The production of a whole unit not only broadens the tasks an individual performs, but it also increases his responsibilities and provides a new sense of accomplishment.[11] Many organizations have noticed an increase in pride of workmanship where workers are allowed to perform whole tasks by themselves or in small groups.[12]

In some situations, jobs are enriched by allowing employees both to perform and inspect their own work. This adds a new dimension to the work and often results in more careful performance and a higher level of job interest. Some types of work are now coming out with labels indicating who constructed the item or who did the work to prepare it for the customer. For example, a piece of clothing might be sold with a label stating, "This shirt was tailored by Rosemary Cooper.

[9]The results of this Gallup poll are discussed in "The Job Blahs: Who Wants To Work?" *Newsweek*, Volume 81, Number 13 (March 26, 1973), pp. 80–82.

[10]Thomas C. Sorensen, "Do Americans Like Their Jobs?" *Parade*, June 3, 1973, p. 15.

[11]See David Sirota, "Job Enrichment—Another Management Fad," *Conference Board Record*, Volume 10, Number 4 (April 1973), pp. 40–45, Richard N. Ford, "Job Enrichment Lessons from AT and T," *Harvard Business Review*, Volume 51, Number 1 (January–February 1973), pp. 96–106, and "G.M. Zeroes in on Employee Discontent," *Business Week*, Number 2279 (May 12, 1973), pp. 140–144 for additional discussions of job enrichment.

[12]Irving Bluestone, "A Good Paying Job Can Be Deadly," *U.S. News and World Report*, Volume 73, Number 3 (July 17, 1972), p. 53.

FIGURE 15.1   Proposed technique for increasing pride of workmanship: affixing worker's name to product

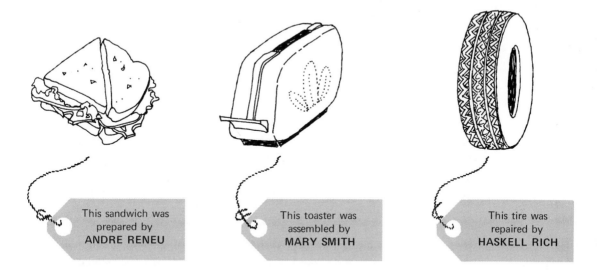

This sandwich was
prepared by
ANDRE RENEU

This toaster was
assembled by
MARY SMITH

This tire was
repaired by
HASKELL RICH

She hopes you enjoy wearing it. If you have any problems with the shirt, please refer it back to Rosemary. Thank you." (See Figure 15.1.) Many workers find this combination of recognition and responsibility very appealing. This technique is particularly useful with manufacturing jobs, but the same principle applies to other jobs—managerial, clerical, sales, and the like.

Great delegation and decentralization of authority make many jobs more challenging and more rewarding. Many workers respond positively when they are given more freedom to make decisions concerning their own actions and are allowed to exercise increased amounts of self-control. To make work more meaningful through delegation and decentralization, Roche and MacKinnon suggest that a technique similar to management by objectives be applied. When this approach is applied, the supervisor works with his subordinate to:

1. Identify problems and set standards
2. Establish challenging personal goals that will be motivational
3. Conduct regular self-evaluations that will ward off failures
4. Pursue areas of growth and development
5. Be innovative and use new methods[13]

Workers, of course, will differ in their abilities to be self-governing.

[13]William J. Roche and Neil MacKinnon, "Motivating People with Meaningful Work," *Harvard Business Review,* Volume 48, Number 3 (May–June 1970), pp. 97–110.

Workers are frequently combined into work teams to provide opportunities and satisfactions that otherwise might be unavailable. Work teams normally are given assignments toward which the individual members are expected to contribute in a collective, cooperative spirit. Teamwork provides members with socialization opportunities that might be denied them in more isolated assignments. Work teams are often delegated the authority and responsibility for self-governance and thereby provide team members with the rewards and satisfactions of self-control. The level of morale among workers frequently is increased when individuals are encouraged to engage in teamwork. Productivity may be increased appreciably when workers labor together in autonomous or semi-autonomous teams. In one General Foods plant, for example, team-oriented task groups produced 20 to 30 percent more than did a comparable number of people working individually in a more conventionally designed plant.[14]

Job rotation is also an often-used method of avoiding monotony and increasing the skills of workers (and providing the workers with a higher level of satisfaction). Jobs in which a high degree of repetition (or other undesirable factors) is necessary may be passed around so that no single individual is required to perform one task continuously. Repetition that might be unbearable otherwise becomes more palatable if there are breaks in the pattern of performance. Regular rotational patterns usually remain in related families of jobs (a worker may move from operating a machine to assembling a part, to maintaining equipment, and back to operating the machine), but some companies have recently ventured to greater extremes with widely differing types of jobs included in the rotation. It has been reported that in one plant workers rotate (within teams) from office jobs, to processing jobs, to shipping jobs before they begin the rotational cycle over again. Workers in this unusual rotation are said to enjoy the change, and their performance maintains a high level. Production costs are down, productivity is up, absenteeism has been cut, and theft and property abuse have almost declined to zero.[15]

Other forms of worker involvement and delegation may be similarly used to achieve more meaningful work for employees and higher levels of performance for the organization. Where the problem-precipitating causes lie more in the type of supervision received by the worker rather than within the content of the worker's job, the obvious solution is to retrain and instruct the supervisor in methods that will improve his ability to lead and manage. Some observers feel that the greatest obstacle to be overcome in supervisors' performances that have a negative effect upon their subordinates is the problem of a closed mind—of pre-

[14]"The Job Blahs, Who Wants to Work?" *op. cit.,* p. 84.

[15]"The Drive To Make Dull Jobs More Interesting," *U.S. News and World Report,* Volume 73, Number 3 (July 17, 1972), p. 53.

conceived concepts of what workers need or require to perform well and in a self-rewarding way. The emphasis of a contingency leadership training program (contingency leadership was discussed in Chapter 9) is on improving the supervisor's ability to adjust and adapt to different situations and different workers.

Problems involving poor working conditions, improper wage structures, inadequate reward and promotional systems, and so forth, can only be corrected by identifying the causes and taking corrective action. The possible causes of these problems are too complicated and too diverse to handle in a precise manner in this chapter. The chapters dealing with motivation may provide assistance in improving improper wage and reward structures.

It is appropriate to note that not all on-the-job and around-the-job factors that are deficient can be corrected. Some jobs require repetitious specialization. Some tasks must be performed in less-than-satisfactory circumstances. Faulty supervisory attitudes cannot always be altered. Where unsatisfactory conditions cannot be corrected, many organizations have found it necessary to admit the undesirable circumstances and point out to the workers that the organization stands ready to correct the problem when a feasible alternative becomes available. Workers often are willing to tolerate undesirable conditions if they know their superiors are concerned about their welfare and have done everything within their power to alleviate the problem.

Sometimes, organizations that must contend with undesirable conditions that cannot be corrected attempt to counter the poor worker attitudes that may develop by compensating or substituting for them in other ways. Workers who must labor in dangerous or excessively hot working conditions are paid a compensatory bonus. Workers who perform unchallenging, unrewarding tasks are given additional leave time, and so forth. These steps are taken to soften the impact of otherwise undesirable situations.

It must be remembered that the thesis of this chapter to this point is based on the assumption that the organization itself is at fault in some way that results in poor attitudes or poor performance from the worker. Because the organization creates the problem, it is in the best position to provide the necessary corrective action. All of the difficulties of problem workers, of course, do not originate with the organization. Workers frequently bring their own problems with them as they come to work.

Dealing with Off-the-Job Problems

The problems of workers that originate from off-the-job sources can have the same type of effect as those that originate with or around the job. Workers may be indifferent to their jobs, may show hostilities toward fellow workers, may exhibit inappropriate responses, may be uncooperative and unproductive, or may perform in other negative ways because things are not going well in their personal lives. Health problems, financial difficulties, family troubles, educational shortcomings, and similar sources of stress all may result in inadequate performance at work. Occasionally a worker can be heard to say, "When I come to work, I leave my personal problems at home." While a worker may attempt to separate his personal life from his work career, he can never completely do so. The two most certainly will affect each other.

Personal problems of workers are the most difficult source of employee difficulties for the supervisor to diagnose correctly. If a worker is exhibiting a problem through his behavior, the supervisor typically surveys all of the possible organizational causes of the problem before going further in his actions. If the symptoms point toward personal problems, the supervisor must proceed with caution in attempting to identify and solve the problem.

A supervisor should be careful never to pry into the personal life of a worker strictly for the sake of satisfying the supervisor's personal curiosity. The investigation of the personal problems of a worker should be initiated only for the purpose of helping the worker meet the demands of his job and, if possible, to give him the encouragement he needs in facing his private difficulties. The supervisor may play several roles as he works with the employee to resolve his problems. If the worker has not recognized that he has a problem or is creating one organizationally, the supervisor must help him to come to this realization. If the worker cannot develop and implement solutions that would eliminate his hindrance of organizational achievement, his supervisor can serve as a catalyst in uncovering the appropriate remedies. If the worker seems to lack motivation to take corrective steps, the supervisor may help him to see the realities of his failure to act (the consequences both for himself and for the organization). The supervisor can always provide an extremely valuable service for the problem worker by functioning as a confidant and listener if the worker needs someone to whom he can express his problems. The supervisor, however, may find himself in a situation of role conflict as he serves as confidant and boss simultaneously; so he must be cognizant of the difficulties of this dual role and plan his actions accordingly. It is situations like this in which the employee has been unable to see the problems he has and to develop solutions to those problems, that a professional counselor is particularly helpful. He is in a position removed from the authority structure. He has only a single role to play—that of counselor. As a result, he may be able to work more openly and objectively to help the problem employee identify problem causes and solutions.

The more the worker can recognize his own problems, identify the best solutions to his difficulties, and see the benefits of eliminating his own problems without too much pressure from his superiors, the more unlikely will be the possibilities of resentment and resistance toward interference from outside forces. The philosophy which states that people accept what they create and originate and may be indifferent or even hostile toward what they consider the personal interferences of others into their own personal affairs appears to be quite correct.

Supervisors can legitimately seek correction of worker behavior when that behavior is interfering with organizational accomplishment. However, the supervisor can go no further with off-the-job problems than to point out the problems a worker is causing, identify the type of behavior needed to perform satisfactorily (clarify performance needs), and show the benefits that would accrue if the action is taken. The worker must decide for himself if he will respond to suggestions or directives from his superiors and attempt to alter his performance accordingly. In giving suggestions for correcting behavior, the supervisor must concern himself only with what is needed for on-the-job behavior. He can never afford to give specific advice to a worker on how to resolve personal problems such as those involving marital or financial difficulties, for example. These important judgments are the right and responsibility only of the worker himself. Legal suits have been filed and won by individuals who have claimed that they were given advice on how to solve a personal problem, and when the advice was followed, negative results were experienced.

The author remembers reading about a legal judgment decided in favor of a widow who stated that her husband had once been given financial advice by one of his superiors on where to invest his savings for security and for excellent dividends. After the worker invested his money in the advised institution, the institution went bankrupt and the man lost his fortune. Following the man's death, his wife went to court saying that the advice of her late husband's employer had deprived her of money she had a right to receive. The court held in her favor and rewarded her the damages incurred.

This example is given to illustrate just one of many reasons why it is dangerous to give specific advice to a worker concerning how he should go about alleviating a personal problem. The supervisor can be helpful, however, by working with the subordinate to discuss the alternative courses of action available to him and by being empathetic as his problems are expressed.

If a worker has a problem for which no solution can be initiated by the worker, the role of the supervisor may be to facilitate and support the worker in making adjustments to meet the irreconcilable problem. If a worker's poor health makes it impossible for him to work eight hours a day in a physically demanding position, the supervisor may be able to assist in the location of a less demanding job. If the worker has a family problem that requires his presence at home during certain hours of the day (to take care of members of his family who need his help), a flexible schedule may be arranged for him.

When a worker has a problem and is unwilling to take steps to correct or eliminate his problem, the organization may have no alternative except to remove the worker from his position of responsibility.

Summary

While it would be unrealistic to expect every worker to be flawless in his performance, it is reasonable to expect regular behavior to be productive and useful. Employees whose performance becomes problematic deserve attention, as their behavior hurts themselves, their fellow employees, and the organization to which they belong.

The problems of many employees originate within the organization—overly specialized job assignments, jobs that are restrictive and unimaginative, work assignments that disrupt or forbid pleasant social relationships among employees, supervision that is ill-suited to employees' needs, inadequate working conditions, and insufficient reward structures, for example. Many worker problems caused by the employing organization can, of course, be corrected, and the problem worker's performance may then show the desired response. Job enrichment techniques, corrections in motivational programs, the application of adaptive leadership techniques, and other organizational adjustments may eliminate the causes of many problems. On-the-job factors that cause problems but cannot be corrected must be recognized, admitted, and compensated for whenever possible.

Problem behavior by employees with causes in personal, off-the-job factors must be handled quite differently. When an employee's off-the-job problems begin to affect his work performance, his supervisor has a responsibility to be concerned. Ideally, the problem employee will discover and correct his own problems. If he does not take the initiative, however, he may need assistance from his organizational superiors. Supervisory personnel can play invaluable roles as they counsel with employees concerning personal problems. As conversations between problem workers and their superiors are related to work performance, job requirements can be emphasized, the inadequate behavior can be pointed out, and the employee can be encouraged to take corrective action. If the employee wishes to improve and needs help, his boss can assist him in finding the appropriate course of action. Improved performance should be recognized and rewarded appropriately. Failure to correct problematic behavior will call for additional counseling and may lead to disciplinary action.

The next chapter will discuss some severe worker problems and possible solutions. A subsequent chapter will then discuss some ways in which counseling may be helpful in working through employees' problems.

Questions to consider after reading Chapter 15

1. In the chapter it was stated that nobody is perfect. Does this mean that no manager should ever expect perfection in the performances of his subordinates?

2.   Several clues to the identification of the problem worker were given. What additional clues might be added to the list?

3.   What are the factors that limit an organization's ability to correct problems that it creates? In particular, what may limit an organization's ability to implement job enrichment techniques?

4.   A few illustrations were given of compensation by organizations for conditions that could not be corrected. What forms of compensation in addition to money and leave time may appropriately reimburse individuals for poor organizational conditions that result in problems?

5.   What are the differences between on-the-job, off-the-job, and around-the-job problems? What are the differences in the way these problems are treated?

6.   Consider the statement made by some workers that they leave their personal problems at home when they come to work. Does anyone have the capacity to do this?

7.   Do organizations deliberately create conditions that cause the problems mentioned in this chapter?

The following cases at the back of the book contain problems related to Chapter 15:

> Ben Stockton
>
> Mark Williams
>
> Stanley Lowell
>
> Edith Capp and Janet Turner
>
> Earl Fornette
>
> Billy Snyder
>
> Susan Swanson
>
> Grace Lanham
>
> Bill Caden
>
> Richard Jameson
>
> Abigail Spiegal and Trudy Pennington
>
> Alan Purdy

Additional readings

Clifford, J. B., "Job Enlargement," *Personnel Administration,* Volume 35, Number 1 (January 1972), pp. 42–45.

Foulkes, Fred K., *Creating More Meaningful Work,* New York: American Management Association, 1969.

Grote, Richard C., "Implementing Job Enrichment," *California Management Review,* Volume 15, Number 1 (Fall 1972), pp. 16–21.

Hulin, Charles L., and Milton R. Blood, "Job Enlargement, Individual Differences, and Worker Responses," *Psychological Bulletin,* Volume 69, Number 1 (January 1968), pp. 41–55.

Maher, John R., editor, *New Perspectives in Job Enrichment,* New York: Van Nostrand Reinhold Company, 1971.

Paul, William J., et al., "Job Enrichment Pays Off," *Harvard Business Review,* Volume 47, Number 2 (March–April 1969), pp. 61–78.

Reif, William E., and Fred Luthans, "Does Job Enrichment Really Pay Off?" *California Management Review,* Volume 15, Number 1 (Fall 1972), pp. 30–37.

Sirota, David, and Alan D. Wolfson, "Job Enrichment: Surmounting the Obstacles," *Personnel,* Volume 49, Number 4 (July–August 1971), pp. 8–19.

————, "Job Enrichment: What Are the Obstacles?" *Personnel,* Volume 49, Number 3 (May–June 1972), pp. 8–17.

Chapter 16

Chronic Worker Problems— Alcoholism, Drug Abuse, and Theft

A case to consider before reading chapter 16

THE DEMISE OF BOB BROWN

Bob Brown was employed by the Chaffee Oil Company as an engineer in its southwestern district. His work in the ten years he had been with Chaffee had been satisfactory although not particularly outstanding. He was known as a congenial, extroverted worker. He had been bypassed once for a promotion to the position of area engineer when the incumbent was killed in an automobile accident. An organization chart of the district, including Brown's position, is provided in Exhibit I.

The functions of the district manager and the assistant district manager are those of making major decisions concerning large expenditures or major policy changes. The chief engineer is responsible for major decisions in matters concerning engineering and the various technical aspects of oil production. Also, part of his responsibility is the evaluation and deployment of the engineering personnel and the coordination of the entire engineering staff. The staff engineer serves as an advisor to the chief engineer. The area engineers are responsible for specific geographical territories. They are supported by a staff of engineers. The size of this staff depends upon the number of wells for which the area engineer is responsible. Each staff of engineers is in turn supported by an adequate number of engineer technicians.

The distinction between the engineers and engineer technicians is an important factor in the case being considered. An engineer is a very technically oriented employee usually holding a degree in petroleum engineering or a related engineering field. His responsibilities are numerous and varied, and he essentially does very demanding engineering work requiring all of the knowledge he has acquired as a result of his educational background and his work experience. The majority of his time is spent in the office.

EXHIBIT I Organization chart of southwestern district of Chaffee Oil Company

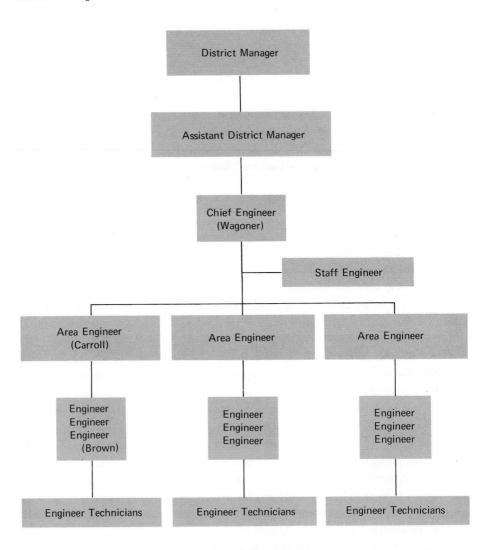

The principal responsibility of the engineer technician is to serve as a go-between from the field to the office. He gathers data and supervises tests in the field and communicates with field personnel. Because his duties are less technically demanding, they carry lower status value than do those of the engineer. The typical engineer technician usually has some college experience but doesn't have a degree. Occasionally a technician may be a college graduate who holds a degree in a field not related to petroleum engineering. The engineer technician receives significantly less pay than the engineer.

Early last year, Bob Brown's attitude underwent a dramatic change. Instead of being outgoing and carefree, he became withdrawn and unsociable. He seemed unconcerned about his responsibilities as an engineer, and his work became less than satisfactory. His area engineer, Wiley Carroll, noticed the change in behavior and performance but took no immediate actions to identify the causes. Instead, Carroll's reaction primarily was to criticize the reports produced by Bob and to show his displeasure verbally whenever Bob made mistakes. Mr. Carroll took the position that "Bob had better shape up or we're going to punish him."

The situation failed to improve. Bob's performance and general demeanor grew steadily worse. He began coming to work with hangovers. He frequently missed a day or two of work. The entire district office became aware of his condition. Mr. Carroll still made no attempt to discover the causes of Bob's changed behavior. He continued to issue threats concerning Bob's sub-par work. Finally, Mr. Carroll confronted Bob in the hallway one Monday morning as Bob was coming to work two hours late. A shouting scene resulted that attracted the attention of most of the office. An hour later, Bob was called to the office of the chief engineer, Mr. Wagoner. He was informed by Wagoner that his performance as an engineer wasn't meeting the standards of the company and that he was being demoted to an engineer technician with the resulting decrease in salary.

Wagoner's action was taken after hearing only Carroll's side of the story. Bob was never given the opportunity to present his version. The result of the demotion and verbal chastisement was an attitude of bitterness by Bob toward his superiors, co-workers, and the company in general. He believed himself a victim of a grave injustice. The decrease in salary plus the personal problems he was experiencing were a serious handicap to him. He suffered a substantial loss of status and professional pride. He felt that his career as an engineer was virtually ruined.

What no one bothered to discover was the cause of Bob's deteriorating attitude and performance. If the truth had been revealed, it would have been discovered that Bob's wife had filed for a divorce after almost twelve years of marriage. The separation was a very trying emotional one, with bitter fighting occurring over the custody of the couple's only child. In addition, Bob was confronted with severe financial problems as the family's property was being divided.

Questions about the Bob Brown case

1. Critique Mr. Carroll's performance as Bob Brown's supervisor. What mistakes did he make?

2. Also evaluate Mr. Wagoner's actions.

3. What will the long-range effects of his superiors' actions be upon Bob Brown? upon his fellow workers?

4. What responsibilities, if any, does a company such as Chaffee Oil have toward its employees? Discuss in detail.

5. What actions should have been taken by Brown's boss, Mr. Carroll, immediately following Brown's change in behavior? Outline in detail.

6. What kind of personal counseling should have taken place to identify the underlying causes of Brown's poor performance? Who should have conducted this counseling?

7. Role play the counseling session between Carroll (or others) and Brown as it should have occurred.

8. Evaluate the control and disciplinary approach used in this case. In what ways did it meet or fail to meet sound control and disciplinary criteria?

9. Suppose that Mr. Carroll finally discovers the true causes of Brown's problems after he has already been demoted (one of Brown's co-workers discovers the truth and tells Carroll). What actions should Carroll take, since the demotion has already occurred?

10. How could the oil company have helped Bob Brown if it had given attention to his personal problems earlier?

In the previous chapter, a number of worker problems were reviewed and possible solutions were suggested. Many of the problems had their beginnings in specific on-the-job or off-the-job factors. There are three particularly chronic problems with some workers that deserve separate attention, and these are the problems of alcoholism, drug abuse, and theft and other dishonest acts of employees. These three areas are the source of many managerial headaches.

The Problems of Alcoholism

Many managers regard alcoholism and the problem drinker as the number one personnel problem in business and industry today. It is estimated that there are approximately nine million alcoholics in the United States and that approximately one-half of all alcoholics are currently employed in some type of work capacity.[1] An ~~alcoholic~~ is technically defined as a "~~person who consumes large amounts of alcohol over a considerable length of time, and whose addiction causes chronic, increasing incapacitation~~."[2] There are, in addition, a number of ~~problem drinkers~~—drinkers who may not be addicted to alcohol but ~~whose behavior as a result of alcohol causes trouble for themselves and for others~~. If the estimates given above are accurate, more than ~~5 percent~~ of the total ~~labor force are alcoholics or problem drinkers~~. The problems of alcoholism do not belong solely to blue-collar workers as some might believe, but a number of managerial and white-collar workers are included also.

When the cost of the problem drinker is counted in dollars and cents, American business incurs losses in excess of ten billion dollars annually as a result of alcoholism.[3] The losses are encountered in several ways. Absenteeism and tardiness for the heavy drinker tend to be fifteen to sixteen times more frequent than for the nondrinker or minimal drinker. The heavy drinker is involved in four times more accidents than is the nondrinker. Problem drinkers tend to work more slowly, do work of a poorer quality, make more bad decisions, and forget safety regulations more frequently than do workers who have no alcohol problems.[4]

The monetary costs, the internal strife, the effects on morale—any one of these items alone would be enough to justify a concentrated effort to erase the problem. However, as strange as it may appear, most of the nation's employers have been involved in only a minimal way in any effort to seriously help the alcoholic worker and to remedy the work organization's resulting problems. Some have estimated that only about 300 companies have active programs to deal with alcoholism and drug abuse.[5] The reasons for the lack of significant programs in these areas are numerous. Managers in many organizations seem to ignore the existence of such problems. Others feel that the nature of alcohol problems is such that only hospitals and medical units should be working with the heavy drinker. Some managers think that the development of alcoholism programs would create a bad public relations image—it would acknowledge to the whole world that a bad situation exists within the organization. Still other employers believe that working

---

[1]Marion Sadler and James F. Horst, "Company-Union Programs for Alcoholics," *Harvard Business Review*, Volume 50, Number 5 (September–October 1972), p. 22.

[2]*Ibid.*, p. 23.

[3]This figure has been supported from several sources. One article, for example, that quoted this figure was "Rising Toll of Alcoholism: New Steps To Combat It," *U.S. News and World Report*, Volume 75, Number 18 (October 29, 1973), pp. 45–48.

[4]Sadler and Horst, *op. cit.*, p. 23.

[5]*Ibid.*, p. 22.

with an employee on his alcohol problems would be an invasion of the employee's private life. Some managers have already given up on the problem and have said that alcohol difficulties cannot be overcome.[6]

Those administrators who feel that alcohol problems cannot be solved or even improved may not be aware of the fact that the success ratio for alleviating the problems of alcoholism is in the 60 to 70 percent range for workers who accept treatment.[7] There *are* problems, however, with the application of programs of treatment and rehabilitation. The worker with an alcohol (or drug) problem frequently is very difficult to identify. Workers with poor health, lack of motivation, or other personal problems may exhibit many of the identical symptoms shown by the problem drinker. Even when it is established that alcohol is the source of the difficulty, many workers are unwilling to admit their problem and to seek assistance in combating it.

While there are many barriers to the successful resolution of a worker's chronic alcohol problems, executives in many organizations are willing to invest time and money to help the employee come to grips with his problem. There may be some humanitarian purposes behind such a rehabilitation program, but there are also benefits for the organization. A trained, otherwise competent worker is difficult to replace. New workers have to be recruited, trained, oriented to company operations, and given expensive cultivation before they can become useful, productive workers. If a problem drinker can be helped to overcome his infirmity, both he and his employer will have benefited. Some of the more successful approaches to dealing with the alcoholic or problem drinker will be considered following the discussion of drugs and the worker.

The Problems of Drug Abuse

The use of drugs in an excessive manner by workers has become almost as much a problem as has alcoholism. A survey conducted for the National Industrial Conference Board in 1971 revealed that 53 percent of the companies participating had already experienced problems of drug abuse among their employees.[8] A 1970 study showed an even higher incidence of drug abuse problems among com-

[6]*Ibid.*, p. 23.

[7]*Loc. cit.*

[8]"The Drug Problem in Business," *The Conference Board Record*, Volume 8, Number 3 (March 1971), pp. 6–15.

panies (90 percent of the eighty companies surveyed).[9] Estimates indicate that the cost of drug abuse to industry probably exceeds eight billion dollars a year.[10] Some of the cost is a result of the same types of problems that occur with alcohol and the worker—problems of absenteeism, poor performance, and other factors that influence productivity. Higher insurance rates and a much higher incidence of theft seem to parallel the abusive use of drugs by employees.[11]

From every indication, the evidence of drug abuse in the work force is steadily increasing. Frequently cited explanations for the increase in drug use by workers include:

1. The increasing number of ~~young people~~ entering the work force who have grown up in somewhat of a "drug culture"

2. A number of ~~military veterans~~ and others who have lived abroad and became dependent upon drugs while living there

3. An ~~increase in~~ the ~~usage of drugs among middle class workers~~ (drug abuse formerly was primarily a lower class worker problem)

4. The increase in the number of ~~disadvantaged workers being hired~~ who have long been subjected to cultural environments where drug usage was acceptable[12]

While drug abuse is far from being the norm for the average worker, it has worked its way into more and more cultures and social classes and, as a result, is no longer the isolated problem that it once was. An unfortunate aspect of drug abuse in business frequently is the tie-in it stimulates with criminal actions. In the study performed by Levy, for example, he discovered that most workers who used drugs regularly (most of them were using heroin) were inclined to engage in criminal actions while at work. ~~More than 90 percent of all drug abusers possessed and used the drugs while at work. Over 50 percent of the drug abusers sold drugs to other workers on the work premises~~ (another criminal offense). ~~More than 40 percent of the workers using drugs admitted that they had stolen goods and materials from their employer and had sold them for personal profit.~~ In excess of ~~30 percent of the workers on drugs indicated that they had stolen cash or checks from their employer or fellow employees.~~ Several other criminal actions while at

---

[9]From the findings of a study conducted by the Research Institute of America and published by the New York Chamber of Commerce in 1970, quoted by Stephen J. Levy, "Drug Abuse in Business: Telling It Like It Is," *Personnel*, Volume 49, Number 5 (September–October 1972), p. 8.

[10]"The Rising Problem of Drugs on the Job." *Time Magazine*, June 29, 1970, p. 71.

[11]Levy, *op. cit.*, p. 8.

[12]Harold M. F. Rush, "Combating Employee Drug Abuse," *The Conference Board Record*, Volume 8, Number 11 (November 1971), p. 58.

work were also admitted.[13] While workers with alcohol problems seldom try to entice their fellow workers to join them in their heavy drinking, most drug users attempt to get one or more of their colleagues to join them in the use of drugs.

Supervisors seldom identify that the source of a drug abuser's problem is, in fact, drugs. While a drug addict may have symptoms such as dilated eyes, shaky coordination, and impaired depth perception, he is usually able to camouflage his symptoms under the guise of being too tired from overwork, lack of sleep, a personal problem, or even too much alcohol. An alcohol alibi such as having a hangover from too much drinking the night before usually is more acceptable to the worker's superior than one based on a drug-related explanation.[14]

As can be seen, the detection of a worker with a drug problem may be even more difficult than the discovery of the problem drinker. Regular physical examinations (including urine tests) have been required in some organizations with the hope of discovering the drug abuser, but these exams have proved to be somewhat unreliable. Undercover agents or informants placed among workers are often suggested as the best means of identifying the drug abuser.[15]

Dealing with Alcohol and Drug Problems

Obviously, the preferred way to solve the unpleasantness that results from problem drinking or drug usage would be to keep them from getting a start among employees. One preventive method used is to avoid hiring workers who already are experiencing problems. In many organizations, extensive screening occurs before a prospective employee is hired. Every applicant who is seriously being considered for a job may be given a thorough physical examination. In addition, the previous work record, educational records, and behavioral habits of the prospect are carefully scrutinized to uncover possible signs of alcohol or drug difficulties.

Another preventive measure used by many organizations is the implementation of educational programs to impress upon employees the dangers of excessive alcohol or drug usage. Seminars, films, speakers, booklets, and other techniques are used to point out the dangers and difficulties that can be felt by the worker and his family should addiction or heavy usage develop. Company policies on

---

[13]*Ibid.*, pp. 11, 12.

[14]*Ibid.*, p. 14.

[15]"The Rising Problem of Drugs on the Job," *op. cit.*, p. 70.

heavy usage are sometimes presented as an additional means of dissuading workers from the use of addictive substances.

Managerial personnel are being encouraged to set the right example for their subordinates by avoiding the use of drugs or by avoiding heavy drinking that might lead to problems. To illustrate this last problem, it has been noticed in many organizations that afternoon performance (particularly among executives) is at a much lower level than morning performance. One of the contributing factors has been traced to the cocktails indulged in by executives during the lunch hour. Senior executives who have set the pace in the lunch hour imbibing have been encouraged to cease or limit their drinking during the between-work-hours period. Their example serves to encourage others toward more moderate habits also.

If the techniques of screening, educating, and example setting do not eliminate problem drinkers and drug users, more active programs may be necessary to seek out the worker with the problem, eliminate or correct the problem, or remove the worker from the organization if the problem is severe and the solution is impossible to discover. ~~It is important that the employing organization have a positive philosophy toward alcoholism and the problem drinker~~. It is also essential for the organizational attitudes to be developed into policies and communicated to all personnel. General Motors, for example, makes it a regular practice to give a statement of policy on alcoholism to its employees. The statement is issued in a handbook and includes the following comments:

> 1. Alcoholism is recognized as a highly complex disease which is treatable. . . . Alcoholism is defined as a disease in which an employe's consumption of any alcoholic beverage definitely and repeatedly interferes with his job performance and/or his health.
>
> 2. Employe alcoholism becomes a concern when it interferes with the employe's job performance. To drink or not to drink socially is the prerogative of the employe. The social stigma often associated with alcoholism has no basis in fact. A realistic recognition of this illness will encourage employes to take advantage of available treatment. Employes with this illness will receive the same consideration and referral for treatment that is presently extended to all employes having other illnesses.
>
> 3. Every effort should be made to identify the disease in its early stages, to work with and assist the employe, and to encourage him to obtain treatment without delay.
>
> 4. Early identification of the alcoholic employe should be based entirely on evidence of poor job performance and other related factors. The immediate supervisor should refer such an employe to the plant medical director or his designated representative for further evaluation.

5.   A medically qualified individual will be available to consult with the employe about the nature of alcoholism and whether or not treatment is indicated. Medical records of employes will be maintained in a confidential manner.

6.   The decision to undertake treatment is the responsibility of the individual. . . . The medical department is available to provide referral assistance if desired. Where a leave of absence for treatment is necessary, a sick leave will be granted and the employe will be eligible for company insurance benefits.

7.   The employe should be assured that if he brings his illness under control and his job performance becomes satisfactory, his job security will not be jeopardized solely by his decision to seek treatment. However, he should also be advised that he may expect no special privileges or exemptions from standard personnel administration practices. Failure to obtain treatment and to improve in performance will result in a review of the employee's situation according to policies and rules.

8.   Considerate and careful follow-up is vital for effective employe rehabilitation or continuance of corrective action, whichever is appropriate.[16]

This program provides a positive, tangible approach to the problems of alcoholism. It conveys the attitude and the support the organization expects and provides. It clarifies the role of the employee and his supervisor. Using this set of guidelines and others drawn from additional organizations, it is now possible to outline supervisory responsibilities for problem drinkers (and drug abusers). From an organizational point of view, *the initial phase of the alcohol or drug abuse program is the identification of the individual who has the problem.* Because the symptoms are often obscured or are similar to symptoms of other problems, identification may be difficult. Occasionally a worker will voluntarily seek help in overcoming his addiction or his behavior, but this worker is the exception rather than the rule.

The key to the identification of the problem worker (whatever his problem is) is the worker's immediate superior. In some alcohol and drug abuse programs, the supervisor is expected to identify the symptoms of the specific problem (drowsiness, alcohol on the worker's breath, etc.) and make a judgment concerning the nature of the worker's problem. The supervisor may also be responsible for determining what correctional course should be followed. Not everyone agrees that the supervisor (even with some training) is the best individual to make judgments concerning symptoms and correctional methods where alcohol and drug abuse are concerned. One author states that companies that expect supervisors to be diagnosticians of alcohol or drug abuse manage to reach only about 15 percent of the real problem workers in their companies.[17]

[16]"Some Facts About the G.M. Employe Alcoholism Recovery Program," *General Motors Personnel Bulletin,* 1974, pp. 6–8.

[17]James S. Ray, "Drug Abuse in Business: Part of a Larger Problem," *Personnel,* Volume 49, Number 5 (September–October 1972), p. 15.

Instead of putting the supervisor on the spot to diagnose the cause of a worker's poor performance, some companies (Western Electric and Kennecott Copper Corporation, for example) ask the supervisor to watch the total performance of each worker. When a worker falls down in productivity, absenteeism, or other performance areas, the supervisor is asked to take the normal leadership steps (motivation, disciplinary action, etc.) to encourage a change in the behavior of the worker. If the employee fails to respond to the supervisor's efforts, the supervisor then is requested to refer the worker to a specialist who will try to diagnose the problem and aid in the determination of a course of improvement. The specialist may be an individual trained in health care or counseling. Under this method, everyone with a continuing problem is given attention from an expert helper. Serious problems such as alcoholism and drug abuse stand a better chance of being identified and corrected.

Identification of the problem is only the initial step. Following the discovery of the problem, *the worker must be willing to admit that he does, indeed, have a problem and must indicate a desire to take action to overcome the impediment to his performance and behavior.* As was mentioned earlier, the success ratio for conquering alcohol problems is high when the worker wishes to succeed. Unfortunately, the ratio of success for drug abuse is less promising, but success is sometimes achieved.

Because some workers have such a difficult time recognizing and admitting their problems, some organizations force the issue by identifying the symptoms and threatening them with the loss of something important unless they seek treatment. As one company's director of alcohol recovery programs said,

> You have to find something that they [the alcoholics] love more than drinking, and that isn't easy. Once you find it, you have to threaten to take it away unless they seek treatment.[18]

For many workers, the thing that persuades them to seek help is the threat of the loss of their job. When this becomes a reality, assistance finally may be sought.

If the worker makes a commitment to do his part in fighting his problem, and the organization believes the prospects of success to be promising and fruitful, a course of action is plotted for the worker. In less severe cases, the employee may continue working while he undergoes therapy. In other, more chronic situations, it may be decided that the worker must undergo hospitalization or treatment outside the boundaries of the organization. *In the therapy phase of the rehabilitation program, the organization plays an*

---

[18]Nicholas Pace, Director of the employer alcoholism-recovery program of General Motors, as quoted in "Rising Toll of Alcoholism: New Steps To Combat It," *op. cit.,* p. 47.

important supporting role. If the employee continues to work while receiving treatment, he may need special encouragement and understanding. If the employee is receiving treatment while hospitalized, he will need financial backing for himself and his family. Some organizations carefully provide the support needed for the worker with a problem, and these are the companies that have the greatest probabilities of success in rehabilitation programs.[19]

In summary, the correctional or rehabilitation program for the problem drinker or drug abuser follows this pattern:

1.   The worker with a ~~problem is identified~~ through the symptoms he exhibits.

2.   The nature of the ~~problem~~ (whether it is alcohol, drugs, or something else) is ~~clarified by the worker, by his supervisor, by a specialist, or by a combination of these working together.~~

3.   ~~If the worker recognizes his problem~~ and asks for help, the ~~organization helps outline a rehabilitation plan~~ whereby he may overcome his problem. It is important that the worker commit himself to doing his share, or the progress of rehabilitation is not likely to be successful.

4.   The ~~organization lends its support~~ to the success of a worker's fight with ~~encouragement~~ and ~~understanding~~ and ~~through financial backing~~ where necessary. The organization makes a commitment to the worker to help him through his difficulty.

The program described above is the one used by many of the more progressive organizations. Other organizations take a harder line and choose to discharge the worker without helping him, while still others ignore the problem as if it did not exist. Neither of those approaches comes to grips with the problem as it really exists, and therefore little improvement can be expected through them.

Employee Dishonesty and Theft

Another chronic problem in organizations is the action of the dishonest employee who acquires company cash or merchandise and willfully uses them for his own purposes. The type of theft may take many forms—padding an expense account, pocketing money from the cash register, taking home office supplies for personal use, removing company products for the purpose of reselling them, and many other techniques. Estimates of the cost of employee theft range up to as

---

[19]"The Rising Problem of Drugs on the Job," *op. cit.,* p. 71.

high as ten billion dollars annually, but there is little way to keep track of the actual cost. One expert on the subject has said that the cost of theft from organizations is passed along to the customer to the tune of 15 percent of the cost of the merchandise being purchased. In other words, if employees did not steal from their employers, the cost of purchasing most goods could be reduced by that percentage.[20]

Acts of theft by employees are manifestations of selfishness at the expense of the employing organization. Workers who engage in dishonest actions at work subordinate the interests of the organization and their honest co-workers to their own personal interests. The president of one theft control agency has said:

> Most workers who steal do so because opportunity beckons, and they think it's coming to them. They feel they're being underpaid; so they'll just take something to even the score.[21]

Very often, the dishonest employee feels very little loyalty to his employer and feels little responsibility to deal fairly with his bosses. Theft may even become a game among workers who contrive ways of getting things from their employer.

Sometimes the actions of the management of the employing organization seem to encourage theft among employees. Supervisors who are dishonest themselves encourage their subordinates to follow in their footsteps. The design of buildings and plant facilities may contribute to the convenience and ease with which theft or other forms of dishonesty occur. While most organizations have policies designed to severely discipline (usually to discharge) the worker caught engaging in dishonest activities, these policies are seldom applied. Managers or skilled employees are often thought to be too valuable to discipline. Poor publicity growing out of the organization's admission that it has dishonest employees is another excuse given to justify lack of disciplinary action. An organization's failure to apply disciplinary actions prescribed in stated policies and regulations appears to open the door to further dishonesty. As the chief of the Pinkerton Agency states:

> We urge that the employer prosecute the dishonest employee. Our experience shows that most unpunished employees sooner or later repeat their crimes.[22]

[20]Norman Jaspan, "Why Employees Steal," *The Office,* Volume 76, Number 3 (September 1972), p. 58.

[21]Ira Lipman, President of Guardsmark, quoted by Mort Weisinger in "$10 Billion a Year Employee Thievery is Big Business," *Parade,* December 9, 1973, p. 27.

[22]Henry C. Neville of the Pinkerton Agency, quoted by Mort Weisinger, *ibid.,* p. 27.

More frequently than not, when solutions are suggested for dealing with the problem of theft through employee dishonesty, they concentrate on the negative, punitive type of actions; and these definitely have value as a discouragement to stealing. Rules that threaten to discharge a worker (or otherwise penalize him) if he is caught engaging in acts of theft are a deterrent to further actions *if they are applied.*

~~Organizational efforts to eliminate opportunities for theft may be effective in discouraging theft also~~. Television monitoring devices, frequent patrols by security officers, and other techniques for watching employees reduce opportunities to steal. Requiring employees to wear standardized, no-pockets uniforms may be a viable deterrent in some manufacturing concerns. Implementing policies where all checks and expense accounts must be signed or approved by more than one individual may reduce the temptation to cheat the organization out of funds. The use of polygraph examinations at regular intervals may keep some workers on their toes. The location of the employees' parking lot some distance away from the building in a supervised area may eliminate the carrying of some merchandise away from the premises.

It should be noted that preventive measures such as television monitoring, polygraph examinations, and the use of undercover agents are not warmly received by most employees. Even the honest employees who have no intentions of stealing from their employer tend to regard the constant checking as an insult to their integrity. Work under circumstances where there is a lack of mutual confidence and trust may negatively affect morale.

Regardless of the number of monitoring actions and precautionary measures a company has available to it and the efforts it makes to decrease the opportunities for dishonesty, some theft will continue to occur. An additional technique to discourage dishonesty—one with much promise—is the creation of the desire within each employee to want to do his best for the organization rather than to do something that could be harmful to it. Instead of acting in a selfish, dishonest way, the employee with a positive regard for his employer will feel that his actions should be mutually beneficial to himself and the organization. A few ~~techniques for formulating a positive attitude within the worker~~ to encourage honesty are mentioned below.

1.   The ~~decentralization of authori~~ty or the ~~delegation downward~~ of responsibility for decision making and control has the effect of helping the worker see his importance to the organization. A worker who feels that his actions can make a difference in the success of the organization and feels that he will be adequately rewarded for his loyal performance usually will respond in a positive manner. In one of the

studies mentioned in the previous chapter, it was noted that one company experienced a great deal of success when it divided up workers into work teams and gave each team authority to regulate and control itself and its members. The team was held accountable for its performance and rewarded when excellence occurred. One of the by-products of this action was a marked reduction in theft. Workers felt responsible for their actions and realized that honesty was beneficial to themselves as individuals, to their fellow team members, and to the total organization.[23]

2.   As a way of reinforcing the point, it is ~~important~~ for ~~workers~~ to be ~~adequately rewarded for their good performance~~. Rewards for constructive effort create a desire to earn further rewards. At the same time, adequate compensation for performance reduces the need for stealing from the employer.

3.   The ~~example of an honest boss~~ who does not cheat on the company is an inspiration to his subordinates to deal honestly and fairly themselves. Subordinates are inclined to follow the lead of a supervisor with integrity.

4.   In addition, any other action that makes the worker feel it is important that he act honestly for his benefit and for the organization's will be a positive force in creating a desire to avoid engaging in theft.

Summary

Most organizations, regardless of their size, can expect to encounter chronic employee problems related to alcoholism, drug abuse, or employee dishonesty. If these problems are to be overcome, their sources must be identified and courses of action plotted for their improvement. Managers must be committed to programs of prevention, rehabilitation, and elimination if success is to be attained. Particularly in the cases of alcoholism and drug abuse, the worker with the problem must also commit himself to a program of rehabilitation if the problem is to be corrected. Employers must be more willing to admit the possibility of such problems among employees and must be more courageous in engaging in improvement campaigns.

Questions to consider after reading Chapter 16

1.   Why is it difficult for individuals with chronic alcohol or drug problems to admit that they have such a problem?

2.   Many organizations do nothing about alcohol or drug problems among workers because they feel that giving attention to these problems in their organizations would

[23]"The Drive To Make Dull Jobs More Interesting," *U.S. News and World Report*, Volume 73, Number 3 (July 17, 1972), p. 53.

hurt the organization's image in the community. Is this a realistic concern? What can be done to overcome this feeling?

3.　In what ways (if any) do organizations contribute to the development of alcohol, drug, and theft problems among employees?

4.　In addition to the rehabilitation programs mentioned in the chapter, what additional programs are sometimes used?

5.　The rehabilitation ratio for drug abusers is much lower than that for problem drinkers. Should the probability of successful rehabilitation have an effect upon what an employer is willing to do to help problem employees? Why or why not?

6.　If the business organization does not assume the responsiblity for helping employees with the problems described in this chapter, who should assume this responsibility?

7.　Should applications from "rehabilitated" employees be given the same consideration when new employees are being hired that is given to applicants with no previous problems on their work records? In other words, should a prospective employee with a record of alcoholism, drug abuse, or theft be given consideration equally with those who have no record of misdeeds even if he appears to have overcome his problem?

8.　What actions not mentioned in the chapter can be taken to discourage theft?

In addition to the case that appears with this chapter, the Danny Tabor case at the beginning of Chapter 17 contains problems related to this chapter.

Additional readings

Bitter, William, Jr., "Drug Abuses—An Employment Problem," *Personnel Journal,* Volume 50, Number 11 (November 1971), pp. 858–860.

Eaton, Merrill T., "Alcohol, Drugs, and Personnel Practices," *Personnel Journal,* Volume 50, Number 10 (October 1971), pp. 754–758.

Habbe, Stephen, "Controlling the Alcohol Problem: Not by Management Alone," *The Conference Board Record,* Volume 10, Number 4 (April 1973), pp. 31–33.

Jones, Dean C., "Employee Theft in Organizations," *Advanced Management Journal,* Volume 37, Number 3 (July 1972), pp. 59–63.

Morris, Joseph, "The Unions Look at Alcohol and Drug Dependency," *International Labour Review,* Volume 106, Number 4 (October 1972), pp. 335–346.

Peterson, James E., "Insight: A Management Program of Help for Troubled People," *Labor Law Journal,* Volume 23, Number 8 (August 1972), pp. 492–495.

Rush, Harold M. F., and James K. Brown, "The Drug Problem in Business," *The Conference Board Record,* Volume 8, Number 3 (March 1971), pp. 6–15.

Chapter 17

Counseling with Employees

A case to consider before reading chapter 17

DANNY TABOR—THE SALESMAN WHO WON'T ADMIT HIS PROBLEMS

Bruce Clover began Commerical Security, Incorporated, three years ago on a very small capital investment he was able to scrape together from personal savings and a loan from the bank. He saw an opportunity for a company that provides television cameras and monitoring devices, alarm systems, and other security equipment for banks, commercial enterprises, and industrial firms. The security equipment leased or sold by Commercial Security assists businesses in protecting themselves against thefts, burglaries, and robberies on their premises.

Bruce began his business as a two-man operation. Bruce did all of the sales contact work himself, designed the security systems to meet the needs of each customer, and kept all records. He hired a technician to install the systems (and help with their design) and to service and maintain all equipment. Business has been good and the demands of the work have grown until Bruce has had to add six additional employees in his home office. He now serves as the general manager; his original helper now manages installation and customer service. Bruce has hired a sales manager, an additional salesman, two installation and service technicians, a systems design specialist, and a secretary-bookkeeper.

As soon as Bruce got the home office operating efficiently, he decided that it was time to open a branch office in a nearby city that had an excellent market potential. Bruce decided that at the beginning he would drive to the branch office each week and spend one or two days managing the business personally. In addition, he felt that a salesman, an installation-service technician, and a secretary-bookkeeper would be necessary to complete the branch office staff. Any specialized help could be supplied by the main office as necessary. Also, telephone communications would make possible other contact as needed. Everyone would report directly to Bruce until the branch office grew big enough to hire a full-time manager. In Bruce's absence, each employee was to be self-controlling.

The branch office has been in operation for more than a year, and business there has been excellent also. An assistant service technician has been added to the staff to meet the heavy volume of installation and maintenance demands. The original salesman resigned about two months ago to take another job, and Bruce hired a replacement, Danny Tabor, to be the new salesman. Danny came well recommended as a salesman from a music and electronic equipment company. He is in his thirties, has been a salesman since high school graduation, and indicated a strong interest in security systems when he was hired. He has been at Commercial Security for five weeks now.

When Bruce hired Danny, it was agreed that Danny would be on a straight salary for eight weeks until he learned the business and developed a clientele of customers. At the end of the eight weeks, Danny will be placed on a commission earnings basis. During the eight-week training program, Bruce is meeting with Danny at least once a week to help him get acquainted with customers and to learn how to uncover prospects.

Bruce is now quite worried about Danny's performance. Danny regularly has been late for their weekly meetings—often an hour or more late. He has reported very few new sales agreements each of the five weeks of his employment. The secretary-bookkeeper reports that she sees very little of Danny—he spends very little time in his office and appears to be staying at his home an unusually large amount of time. Bruce has begun to suspect that he is getting very little in return for the straight salary he has paid the past five weeks. He has asked Danny about his work and has gotten unenthusiastic answers such as, "It's taking me a while to learn things, but I eventually will get the hang of things," or, "It's taking me more time than I expected to begin to show any good results." When Bruce has asked what specific problems Danny has experienced, his only response has been, "Oh, nothing in particular. Just the problems any new employee experiences." Danny will not be any more specific.

What Bruce has not been able to uncover is the fact that Danny has been working only a few hours a week on his new job. In addition to the time they have spent together (Bruce and Danny), Danny has averaged only eight to ten hours a week at his work. The main reasons for his lack of work lie in health problems. Danny's wife, in particular, has been very ill for the past two months. She suffers frequent dizzy spells and faints unexpectedly. Because they have no relatives living near them, Danny must stay with her except for the time their school-aged child is home to help. In addition, Danny himself has been sick for the last few days and it now appears that he may have a diabetic condition. He also has had dental problems since he began his employment with Commercial Security. He needs the money from his job badly, but he has not felt well, and he needs to be at home to care for his wife.

Bruce has another meeting with Danny scheduled for tomorrow morning. He has decided that he must get more information from Danny (remember, he doesn't know anything about the health problems) so that he can help Danny with his job and so that he can protect Commercial Security's investment in his training. His previous inquiries have been unsuccessful, but Bruce feels that it is imperative that he get more information from Danny.

Questions about the Danny Tabor case

1.   Why is Danny unwilling to tell Bruce what his real problems are?

2.   Is it possible for Bruce to get more helpful information directly from Danny himself concerning his progress, his problems, and his goals? If so, how can he help Danny discuss his concerns more openly? How can supervisors help their subordinates to be more open and complete in their communications?

3.   Evaluate the way Bruce has handled Danny and his new assignment up to this time. What has Bruce handled well? What has he done poorly?

4.   Evaluate the branch office arrangement Bruce has devised. What are its strengths and weaknesses?

5.   Suppose that through counseling Danny finally tells Bruce about his family health problems. What should Bruce do then?

Counseling is a concentrated form of interpersonal communication. With most types of counseling, the interchange of ideas between the parties involved (the counselors and the counselees) is directed toward a problem or a need that requires in-depth attention. Counseling may have obvious benefits in dealing with problems such as those discussed in the two previous chapters.

To be more specific, counseling may serve at least four functions. Counseling, in the context of work organizations, is corrective or remedial if it identifies conditions, attitudes, or behavior patterns that precipitate problems *and* if it

advances a set of actions that results in improved performance. Counseling is
therapeutic if it diagnoses personal or organizational ills and prescribes and
applies "medicine" to the wounds so that some form of normalcy results. Counseling of this type can help the individual or the organization to become whole
again. Tensions can be released and anxieties may be vented. Counseling may be
primarily a means of *conveying information* and exchanging ideas—informational
counseling may serve more to prevent problems than to diagnose those already
in existence.

Counseling may also be **developmental** in nature, helping individuals to more
fully utilize their capabilities and to more completely achieve their own potential.
Developmental counseling may accelerate the growth of an individual so that he
achieves higher levels of efficiency or productivity more rapidly than would
otherwise be the case.[1] This type of assistance, when given to an employee,
helps him to determine his existing capabilities, to establish goals for future
development, to determine if the goals he has in mind are realistically compatible
with his existing abilities and his aptitude to develop, and to work out a plan of
action through which realistic development can occur.[2]

To illustrate how developmental counseling works, let's suppose that Lester
Cunningham, a young college graduate, wishes to advance into a managerial
position with his employing organization. He sits down with his superior, and
they review his present skills and abilities in comparison with the abilities he
will need in order to achieve his goals. They analyze his present skills by looking
at his operative, interpersonal, and decision-making abilities. These skills are
defined in more detail in Chapter 21, but it is important to note that operative
skills are the technical requirements people need in the fulfillment of their job
tasks. Interpersonal skills are the abilities individuals need in order to relate
effectively to other individuals. Decision-making skills, of course, refer to the
ability to gather facts, review alternatives, and make effective selections of courses
of action.

To complete the illustration, Lester and his boss analyze his strengths and
weaknesses in the three areas (see Figure 17.1). Together they attempt to help
him verbalize his goals and ambitions. Then the two view his goals in the light of
what additional skills and knowledge Lester will need to achieve his goals. If they
determine that his aptitudes and motivations are realistic, they may plot a course
of training and development for him. If the goals are unrealistic, this will also be

[1]John J. Pietrofesa, George E. Leonard, and William Van Hoose, *The Authentic Counselor,* Chicago:
Rand McNally and Company, 1971, p. 4.
[2]See M. I. Gould, "Counseling for Self-Development," *Personnel Journal,* Volume 49, Number 3
(March 1970), pp. 226–234, for a more detailed discussion of developmental counseling.

FIGURE 17.1   Existing skills compared to required skills in developmental counseling

	AREAS OF SKILLS AND ABILITIES		
	Technical skills and abilities	Human relations skills and abilities	Analytical abilities
Goal position skills and abilities	●●●	●●●●●	●●●
Skills and abilities already possessed by counselee	● ●	● ●●	●
Skills and abilities that must be developed to achieve counselee's goals	●	● ●	● ●

Source: This chart is a modification of one developed by M.I. Gould, "Counseling for Self-Development," *Personnel Journal*, Volume 49, Number 3 (March 1970), p. 230.

acknowledged, a substitute set of more realistic goals will be defined, and a course of development toward those goals will be charted.

If counseling serves its purposes well, everyone will benefit. Counselors will gather needed information, counselees will be helped, and organizational goals will be achieved more effectively.

Schuh and Hakel suggest that for the individual, counseling can result in:

1. Greater stability of employment (reduced absenteeism and turnover)
2. Improved ability to relate with people in positions of authority
3. Development of better, more friendly co-worker relationships
4. Improved personal mood and disposition
5. Reduction of anxieties

6. ~~Improved ability to communicate with others~~
7. ~~Increased willingness to assume responsibility for decision-making and activity~~
8. ~~Elimination of feelings of aloneness~~[3]

The personal value of these advantages is obvious, but they may also be translated into organizational advantages. Counseling may reduce absenteeism, turnover, lack of cooperation between workers, interpersonal anxieties, poor communication patterns, and may otherwise result in improvement for the organization.

Who Should Handle Counseling

The question of who should perform the counseling duties within an organization may have several answers. It is obvious that psychological problems, deep-seated personality difficulties, and some personal matters may require the attention of well-trained psychiatrists or psychologists if the needed help is to be provided. Many organizations have hired full-time counselors with the qualifications to handle the more profound problems of individual employees. Other organizations have chosen to pay a retainer to trained counselors so that they can be available to help workers when their skills are needed. Some organizations have sent a few employees to counselor training programs so that they can come back to the organization and handle many of the counseling needs. These individuals are often placed in staff positions or are otherwise placed so their services will be available to people throughout the organization.

The truth of the matter is, however, that professional counselors and psychiatrists have not been utilized in any great numbers for organizational counseling purposes.[4] Perhaps managers in most organizations have never fully appreciated the services available through these counseling experts, or perhaps some have thought the expense involved in having specialists available could not be justified on a cost-benefit basis. At any rate, the counseling duties in the majority of today's organizations typically are channeled into the hands of line managers. Supervisors are expected to handle the corrective, informational, developmental, and to some extent, therapeutic needs of their subordinates through counseling or other appropriate actions.

From many points of observation, the manager himself may be better suited than anyone else to communicate with his immediate subordinates and to counsel

---

[3]Allen J. Schuh and Milton D. Hakel, "The Counselor in Organizations: A Look to the Future," *Personnel Journal,* Volume 51, Number 5 (May 1972), p. 358.

[4]Joseph P. Zima, "Counseling Concepts for Supervisors," *Personnel Journal,* Volume 50, Number 6 (June 1971), p. 482.

with them properly. An employee's own boss is in a position to know more about the employee's abilities, strengths, weaknesses, ambitions, and needs than most outsiders or staff specialists would be, because the supervisor and his subordinate work together regularly and communicate on a wide range of matters. Supervisors also may have the authority to take action on organizational conditions that are creating employee problems. Supervisory counselors may help activate organizational opportunities that could help an individual develop his abilities and fulfil goals and ambitions.

Perhaps the main handicap in having supervisors counsel their own subordinates is the fact that subordinates may wish to avoid revealing some of their personal problems, feelings, and ambitions to their superiors. Subordinates may feel threatened by the authority of their superiors, and they may be afraid to confide in them. This reluctance to open up and discuss freely with one's superior may seriously impede managerial attempts at counseling.

The fact remains that in more cases than not, the manager himself will find it appropriate to counsel with his own subordinates. In view of this basic reality, the comments and suggestions in this chapter concentrate particularly on the manager and his role as a counselor.

Conditions for Effective Counseling

Many types of counseling may occur on a spontaneous basis, and this is often a desirable way of coping with problems or plotting courses of change. Other counseling sessions, however, are planned in advance and are instigated deliberately and methodically. In either counseling situation, there are conditions that are conducive to a higher degree of success and effectiveness. Some of the conditions are environmental; others are within the participants.

In the first place, the location (setting) for the counseling discussion is of vital importance to the type of interaction that will occur. Ideally, when a superior and one of his subordinates are talking together in a counseling session, the location should be a room that will be nonthreatening to the counselee and one that is private, free of noise, and removed from potential distractions.[5] The manager's office may not be the best place for the discussion to be held because the conversation will be taking place on his own ground, in a setting he tends to dominate. The supervisor's authority role may present itself as a significant barrier if counseling is attempted in *his* office as *he* sits behind *his* desk in *his* own comfortable chair while the subordinate squirms in a hard chair on the other side of the desk.

[5]Alfred Benjamin, *The Helping Interview*, Boston: Houghton Mifflin Company, 1969, p. 3.

A ~~conference room where both~~ the ~~counselor~~ and the ~~counselee sit as equals across a table may be more conducive~~ to an open exchange of ideas. Any additional environmental conditions that might help to overcome authority barriers would be desirable.

The ~~interruption-free atmosphere~~ in which counseling can occur should be emphasized. In the ideal setting, conversations should take place in an area free of interference from phone calls, knocks on the door, or other distractions. Another intruder may be the time clock. Serious counseling sessions should be held when both the counselor and the counselee have the necessary amount of time to give full, complete attention to the issue before them. These and other ideal environmental factors, while not always possible to achieve, aid the counselor and the counselee as they endeavor to achieve their common goals.

Perhaps even more important than environmental factors are the ~~attitudes~~, ~~perceptions~~, and ~~abilities of the participants themselves~~. It is especially important that the counselor have a positive outlook on the potential usefulness of counseling and the abilities of the counselee to contribute meaningfully as counseling takes place. In a National Defense Education Act study, for example, it was discovered that "~~good" counselors have a set of values and perception~~s that differ from less effective counselors. Study results showed that:

1. In general perception orientation, good counselors are more likely to perceive:
    a. from an internal view rather than an external one
    b. in terms of people rather than things
2. In their perceptions of other people, good counselors see others as:
    a. able rather than unable
    b. dependable rather than undependable
    c. friendly rather than unfriendly
    d. worthy rather than unworthy
3. In their perceptions of themselves, good counselors perceive themselves as:
    a. identifying with people rather than being apart from them
    b. having enough rather than wanting
    c. self-revealing rather than self-concealing
4. In their perceptions of goals and purposes as counselors, they perceive their goals to be:
    a. freeing rather than controlling
    b. unselfish rather than self-serving
    c. concerned with larger rather than smaller meanings[6]

[6]A. W. Combs, et al., *Florida Studies in the Helping Professions*, Monograph Number 37, Gainesville: University of Florida, 1969, pp. 21–27.

In a few moments, we will be looking at techniques of counseling. One of those techniques (the one that will be given the most emphasis) stresses *the value of allowing the counselee to identify his own problems or goals and arrive at his own action conclusions.* If this approach is to be used, it has been suggested that the ~~counselor's attitude toward those being counseled~~ (his subordinates, for example) should include:

1.   A belief that the individual is responsible for himself and is mature enough to keep that responsibility.

2.   A belief that a person is capable of solving his own problems once he recognizes them.

3.   A belief that people want to be understood, not judged. True feelings can only be expressed by developing a permissive atmosphere.

4.   A belief that the individual is important, hence, the creation of a feeling of acceptance.

5.   A deep-seated respect for the feelings of the subordinate (counselee). Disagreement and argument will not enhance this respect. Only by trying to understand the individual's feelings can a mutual respect be created.[7]

The ~~preparation for counseling is also important,~~ particularly from the counselor's point of view. He must prepare his mind so that his attitude is one of desiring to be helpful. The counselor's desire to be of service is a key ingredient to the success of counseling.[8] Rogers has suggested some soul searching should go on within the mind of the counselor as he prepares to enter into any counseling relationship. He suggests that the counselor ask himself:

1.   Can I be in some way, which will be perceived by the other person (counselee), trustworthy, dependable, or consistent in some deep sense?

2.   Can I be expressive enough as a person that what I am will be communicated unambiguously?

3.   Can I let myself experience positive attitudes toward this other person—attitudes of warmth, caring, liking, interest, respect?

4.   Can I be strong enough as a person to be separate from the other (the counselee)?

5.   Am I secure enough as a person to permit him (the counselee) his separateness?

6.   Can I let myself enter freely into the world of his feelings and personal meanings and see things as he does?

7.   Can I receive him as he is? Can I communicate this attitude?

[7]I. L. Heckmann, Jr., and S. G. Huneryager, editors, *Human Relations in Management,* Cincinnati: South-Western Publishing Company, 1960, pp. 508–509.

[8]Benjamin, *op. cit.,* p. 5.

8. Can I act with sufficient sensitivity in the relationship that my behavior will not be perceived as a threat?

9. Can I free him from the threat of external evaluation?

10. Can I meet this other individual as a person who is in the process of *becoming,* or will I be bound by his past and by my past?[9]

These guidelines help the counselor to enter into discussions with an attitude of helpfulness and progressiveness. As we read through them, they appear rather idealistic, but they are the essence of sincere counseling.

Up to this point our discussions have concentrated on external conditions and conditions internal to the counselor, but it is important to realize that the success of counseling efforts is heavily dependent upon the attitudes and perceptions of the counselee (subordinate) as well. The more objective he can be, the more secure he feels in himself, the more confidence he has in the counselor, the more skilled he is as a communicator, and the more he desires to improve himself and the organization, the more likely it is that the counseling session will succeed in achieving worthy objectives.

Two Types of Counseling

Directive Counseling.   While there are many approaches to counseling, the two most discussed styles differ distinctly. They are known as the directive and nondirective approaches. **Directive counseling** is a structured interaction controlled and propelled by the counselor. If the purpose of the counseling is corrective or remedial in nature, the counselor pointedly asks (or tells) the counselee what the problem is, asks (or tells) the counselee what the alternatives are, and asks (or tells) the counselee the course of action to be taken for improvement. If the counseling session is for developmental purposes, the counselor leads (again through asking or telling) the counselee into what his goals are or should be, helps to determine what skill requirements will be necessary to reach those goals, leads in the analysis of the capabilities of the individual to develop those skills, and charts a course of action. If the counseling purpose is therapeutic, the counselor guides in the diagnosis of weaknesses and the prescription of solutions. If the purpose is to provide information to the counselee or to gather information from him, straightforward communication results with little superfluous material included.

[9]Carl R. Rogers, "The Characteristics of a Helping Relationship," *Personnel and Guidance Journal,* Volume 37, Number 1 (September 1958), pp. 6–16.

Directive counseling may include a large amount of advice giving, admonishment, exhortation (motivational pep talks on how and why the counselee should improve or change his behavior), explanation, and reassurance (the giving of encouragement).[10]

As can be seen, directive counseling is counselor-centered to a large degree. It is he who activates and controls the thought processes of the interaction. If he is unusually skillful, he may succeed in drawing the counselee into the discussion verbally, but he seldom is successful at involving the counselee wholeheartedly in the quest for solutions or development. Instead, it has often been observed that counseling that is too direct and too forceful may tend to choke off involvement and may even push the counselee into a defensive, protective position.

These comments should not be taken as a complete rejection of the use of directive counseling in every situation, because there are places in which forceful leadership is required to compel individuals to think and act. There are times when individuals (counselees) are incapable of discovering problems, objectives, and courses of action on their own. There are also situations in which time permits the use of only direct, to-the-point counseling. The directive technique may be the answer to these needs.

Directive counseling may be the only technique that supervisors who tend toward an authoritative leadership style will adopt. Nondirective techniques may be out of character with their other actions and may result in role inconsistencies. Bosses who have greater flexibility or who are frequently more participative or free-rein in their actions, however, may also utilize the nondirective approach.

Nondirective Counseling.   Nondirective counseling is counselee-centered. When this technique is used, the counselor plays a supportive role. The counselor is present primarily to listen and to help the counselee verbalize his thoughts. The counselee is encouraged to lead the interaction so that it will fit his needs and will represent his ideas. The counselor adopts the philosophy that the counselee is responsible for himself, is capable of solving his own problems, wants to be understood, is an important human being, and has feelings that deserve to be respected.

In the pure form of nondirective counseling, the counselor does not diagnose the employee's problems. The counselor does not offer solutions to the employee's problems. The counselor does not give advice.[11] In his role as a supportive listener, the counselor reflects the counselee's thoughts back to him, attempts to increase his perspective, and helps him to explore thoughts he may not have

[10]Heckmann and Huneryager, op. cit., pp. 505–506.

[11]See William A. Ruch, "The Why and How of Nondirective Interviewing," Supervisory Management, Volume 18, Number 1 (January 1973), pp. 13–19, for some additional thoughts on this.

considered previously. Although nondirective counseling is not closely structured, the counselor would like to *help* the counselee:

1. See where he currently is—what his problems are, what his attitudes are, what his capabilities are
2. Determine what he needs or wishes to achieve—what his objectives are or should be, what solutions are available to resolve problem areas
3. Discover specific actions to achieve those objectives or solutions

The counselor using the nondirective technique helps the counselee to accomplish these purposes in a number of ways. *Before the counseling begins,* the counselor tries to arrange environmental and personal conditions so that they will facilitate the counseling interaction. He concerns himself with arranging the place, the interruption-free atmosphere, the necessary time for consultation, and especially his own mental preparedness so that he will be totally ready to support and assist the counselee in his counseling journey.

The nondirective interview has basically three parts—an initiation phase, an exploration or development phase, and a closing phase.[12] In the initiation phase, the counselor's role is mostly one of trying to help the counselee feel at ease and to establish rapport between them so that a good discussion can occur. Together they briefly explore their previous relationship and their mutual interests. The counselor wants the counselee to know that he cares about him and is interested in his growth and welfare. If the counselee has initiated the interaction himself, the initiation phase may be extremely brief, because he is probably ready to get on with whatever is on his mind.

When the exploratory and developmental phase of the nondirective counseling interview is reached, the counselor's role becomes even more supportive and less dominant. The counselor explores with the counselee matters that seem pertinent. The subjects have not been predetermined but are introduced by the counselee as he is encouraged (by the counselor) to talk.

The counselor cannot fulfill his role as a good listener unless the counselee is saying something. If the employee is not talking, the counselor may extend an **interested invitation** to him to talk about whatever is on his mind. This can be done in the form of a soft question: "After working here for six months, how do you feel about your job?" "What thoughts do you have about the new work routine?" "You mentioned some concerns you had about your future when we talked last month. Have you had any further impressions of the future?" These questions indicate that the counselor has an interest in the counselee, and they open the door for him to bring his thoughts out into the open.

[12]Benjamin, *op. cit.,* p. 19.

~~Probes~~ are slightly ~~more direct questions used to stimulate discussion and obtain more information~~: "I'd like to know more about your thinking on this subject." "What did you have in mind when you said that?" "What do you think causes that?" "Is there anything else that may be affecting this situation?"[13] The counselor must be careful to word probes so that they are not too pointed, do not put the employee on the defensive, and do not reveal any biases on his (the counselor's) part. Probes serve to motivate the counselee to communicate more fully so that he enlarges, clarifies, or explains reasons behind what he has previously said.[14] Probes also invite attention to areas not previously identified or explored.

Another extremely effective technique for encouraging the further revelation of ideas is the **restatement** by the counselor of points already made by the counselee in an attempt to encourage in-depth consideration of the thoughts. As Benjamin states, the restatement tells the counselee:

> I am listening to you very carefully, so carefully, in fact, that I can restate what you have said. I am doing so now because it may help you to hear yourself through me. I am restating what you have said so that you may absorb it and consider its impact, if any, on you. For the time being, I am keeping myself out of it.[15]

If an employee tells his boss, "I can hardly wait until I get old enough to retire— this job has gotten to be a regular monster," the boss as a counselor might use restatement by saying, "You say your job has gotten to be a monster." When a worker tells his superior, "I don't feel this job utilizes my abilities and knowledge fully," the boss could reflectively restate, "Your job doesn't utilize your abilities and knowledge fully." The restatement usually provides the necessary amount of encouragement to bring important ideas above the surface.

If ideas have been explored fully and the counselee has identified his problem or goals, all angles have been considered, and solutions discerned or conclusions reached to the mutual satisfaction of the counselor and the counselee, the counselor can help the counselee to close the immediate conversation gracefully. There is no established formula for winding down a counseling interaction. The counselor should attempt to keep the relationship an easy, open one. If a concluding summarization of facts and resolutions is appropriate, the counselor can see that this is accomplished. Interest in the counselee's progress can be promised, and the counselor can emphasize his desire to give continuing support and assistance. For another view of how to conduct the nondirective counseling session, note the suggestions of Heckmann and Huneryager (Figure 17.2).

---

[13]Zima, *op. cit.*, p. 484.

[14]*Interviewer's Manual*, Ann Arbor: Institute for Social Research, The University of Michigan, Survey Research Center, 1969, p. 51.

[15]Benjamin, *op. cit.*, pp. 113–114.

FIGURE 17.2   Steps to remember in conducting a nondirective counseling session

> 1.   **Be prepared.**

If you, either as a professional counselor or as a supervisor of some type, are aware that a particular individual is coming in later in the day to discuss a problem, it is always wise to ~~know as much about the individual as possible.~~ In most companies, handy reference can be made to a person's personnel folder. If the employee appears unannounced and no advance preparation is possible, it is always best to be prepared for such happenings by a periodic review of your subordinates. In this way some knowledge of your people is always with you.

> 2.   **Put the counselee at ease.**

There are many ways for achieving this. Hold the interview in comfortable surroundings where you can both sit and relax. People are always willing to talk more fully in surroundings conducive to personal comfort.

> 3.   **Establish rapport.**

This refers to establishing a friendly, rather intimate relationship between yourself and the counselee. Let the counselee know that you want to listen to him, that what he says will be held in the strictest confidence. In Himler's words, there must be "a mutual feeling of friendliness and sympathetic unity." You must convey to the individual that you want to share his problem with him and aid him in deciding on a definite course of action.

> 4.   **Don't argue or admonish.**

If you start either one of these, immediately the counselee will assume a defensive position. If he senses that he is in any way wrong, he will become even more emotional than he was at the start of the interview. This only defeats the purpose of the interview. If he becomes defensive in attitude, issues become hazy and more involved.

5.   Don't display authority.

      Avoid exerting any authority before this individual, not only organizational authority but intellectual authority as well. People resent social subordination, so do not command or confuse. Talk with the counselee, not to him. Seek to understand and be understood.

6.   Listen carefully.

      This is essential to nondirective interviewing. Listen critically for negative and positive feelings. Don't interrupt. Encourage the counselee to speak fully and openly without fear. *Echo his statements back to him* by careful questioning, by facial expressions, and by body movements. And remember to listen with eyes as well as ears. Seek to understand through good listening.

7.   Don't advise.

      Try to avoid giving the counselee advice even though he may emotionally ask: "But what should I do?" Keep encouraging him to speak; in this way emotions are cleared away. Sooner or later he will offer his own advice. Seize upon this and encourage more probing. You can answer some questions about company policies and procedures, perhaps, but offer as little as possible direct advice for solving his problem. Keep him talking so self-awareness and insight can begin occurring.

8.   Help clarify positive courses of action.

      When the counselee does start making positive suggestions, encourage him to continue to go further and to recognize the consequences of his behavior. An occasional suggestion might help when he reaches this stage. Let him know that you agree when he gets on the right track; help him, again by questioning, to see various alternatives for solving his problem, but let him make his own choice.

Source: I. L. Heckmann, Jr., and S. G. Huneryager, *Human Relations in Management,* Cincinnati: South-Western Publishing Company, 1960, pp. 508-509.

Applying Contingency Theory to Counseling

Obviously each of the types of counseling (directive and nondirective) has its merits and demerits. Each has occasions or situations in which it is most useful. The same concepts that were applied to the selection of leadership styles in Chapter 9 (the discussion of contingency leadership) are appropriate for the selection of counseling techniques. While Figure 17.3 fills in the important details, we can generalize by saying that a combination of variables based upon organizational conditions; counselor preferences, attitudes, and abilities; counselee attitudes and abilities; and task situations may influence the choice of the proper counseling technique as the vehicle for accomplishing organizational-personal goals. Directive counseling usually is more appropriate when the end result of counseling is already known and the means to achieve it are easily visible. The nondirective approach works best when the desired end result is not known from the beginning and the intermediate steps to success are still open to debate. There are, of course, a number of additional considerations.

Most supervisory personnel who attempt to perform counseling may find it difficult to adhere to a pure form of nondirective counseling because it may appear awkward and may have a tendency to drift and ramble. However, if the effort is made to listen rather than dominate the conversation, to be open rather than to be overly restrictive, and to be helpful instead of forceful, a form of nondirective counseling can be achieved. Most experienced counselors believe that nondirective counseling will provide many longer lasting results for the counselee and his employer than directive counseling will. Nondirective counseling will be a particularly natural style for those who serve in staff positions, because the role of the staff specialist usually coincides precisely with the role of the nondirective counselor. Few adjustments may be necessary for the staff specialist, because he may already be cast in a helping role.

The Ethics of Counseling

Because counseling often probes into the ambitions, attitudes, and personal problems of individual employees, questions are frequently raised concerning how ethical it is for the manager-counselor to pry into the personal matters of individuals. The position is often expressed that counseling results in an invasion into the privacy of personal lives—into areas where managers have no right to delve. In many cases this is probably a valid issue.

Managers who serve as counselors to their subordinates have the right to be concerned only with behavior and attitudes that affect the employee's level of performance at work—how well he is contributing to the organization, whether or not he is carrying his fair share of the load, whether he is preparing himself adequately for future responsibilities, and so forth. As was stated earlier, managers have the right only to help individual employees see their organizational needs, responsibilities, and problems and to focus on the consequences of their actions (or misdeeds). If personal attitudes or personal needs are the source of concern discovered through counseling, the ethical manager's role is to listen, to reflect, and to support but *not* to enforce or command. The manager-counselor may even find it necessary to caution the counselee about going too far in unveiling private details of his life that he may wish to remain secret. Most manager-counselors are not trained psychiatrists and cannot skillfully handle some psychological or particularly personal problems that employees may reveal in counseling. The role of being a confidential listener to what the employee *wants* to tell about himself is about as far as (sometimes further than) most managers wish to go.

Another important ethical consideration should be the confidential nature of ideas exchanged and feelings communicated during counseling. Information given in confidence should be kept in confidence. When important personal information is to be communicated to other individuals (up the chain of command, for example), the counselor should inform the counselee concerning who will receive such information *before* the information is obtained. Counselees who are informed in this manner can screen out information they do not wish to have conveyed to others. Counselors do indeed have a heavy burden of responsibility for the ethical use of data collected during counseling sessions.

Summary

It would be a miscalculation to assume that counseling is the key that opens the door to all personal problem-solving and developmental tasks managers face. Counseling only provides a mechanism whereby attitudes, interests, objectives, problems, and causing factors can be brought to the surface. Skillful counseling can unlock some doors, identify some attitudes, present some alternative courses of action, and help individuals outline programs of development when the counseling is handled properly.

While a number of conditions must prevail for counseling to be successful, the counselor can go a long way in securing this success through adequate preparation in advance of the counseling interaction. The counselor's own attitude is important. The more the counselor is counselee-oriented, the more helpful he will be when actual counseling takes place. Both directive and nondirective counseling have their place in the fulfillment of organizational and personal goals. However, nondirective counseling, in particular, offers an unusual number of advantages. The choice of a particular technique for a particular situation may be aided by the use of a contingency decision framework.

FIGURE 17.3   Factors in selection of a counseling approach

FACTOR VARIABLE	COUNSELING METHOD	
	DIRECTIVE	NONDIRECTIVE
FACTORS IN THE ORGANIZATION		
1. Is the organization concerned about achieving organizational goals, helping employees to achieve their own goals, or both?	Tends to be more organizationally oriented, although not always planned that way	Fits best in organizations that are both performance *and* people oriented
2. What kinds of communication networks are maintained within the organization?	Works more easily in organizations with stronger downward communication channels	Good two-way communication systems helpful
3. What kind of spans of supervision and control exist?	May be applied with either wide or narrow spans	Because a large amount of time is involved and personal rapport is important, narrow spans of supervision make application easier
FACTORS IN THE MANAGER—COUNSELOR		
1. For what purposes does the manager—counselor view the use of counseling?	As a means of increasing control over the subordinate, as an important method of achieving an organizational goal	As a means of helping the individual involved and the organization simultaneously
2. How important is it to the supervisor that his own authority position be maintained?	The counselor who constantly prefers this approach tends to regard the maintenance of his authority position as very important	The counselor using this approach normally feels fairly secure in his own authority and tends to be unconcerned about threats to it
3. What attitude does the manager-counselor have toward his subordinates (counselees)?	Typically has a limited amount of confidence and trust in the counselee's abilities and intentions, tends to be somewhat insensitive to the feelings of the counselee	Holds a high assessment of the abilities and intentions of his counselees, believes people are capable of identifying their own goals and supplying their own solutions, is sensitive to the feelings and attitudes of others
4. How well trained is the counselor as a discussion leader? as a listener?	Usually a capable, forceful leader; listening skills not required in this approach	Must be a particularly capable listener; it is helpful if he is skilled at helping others to talk

FACTOR VARIABLE	COUNSELING METHOD	
	DIRECTIVE	NONDIRECTIVE
FACTORS IN THE COUNSELEE		
1. Is the counselee self-motivating and self-controlling, or is external pressure necessary to get him moving and keep him on the right track?	Since this approach does not require self-motivation and self-control, it is usually assumed that the employee needs external pressures	It normally is assumed that the employee is self-motivating and self-controlling
2. Is the counselee articulate, knowledgeable, and otherwise capable of identifying problems and goals and finding desirable courses of self-action?	Need not be particularly articulate, knowledgeable, or capable; may be offended by this approach if he is	It is helpful if the counselee is articulate, knowledgeable, and capable
3. Does the counselee need and want a degree of independence and self-determination, or would he prefer to let others lead?	Works best when the counselee would prefer to let others make decisions	Usually is more satisfactory when the counselee wants a degree of independence and self-determination
FACTORS IN THE TASK SITUATION		
1. How well defined are the counseling session's objectives? How much room for variation and individual initiative in the end result is there?	Normally most useful when the desired end result is known, the means to achieve it are available, and little or no variations are desired	Most useful when the end result is not completely known in advance and individual initiative is highly desirable in uncovering the end *and* the means to achieve it
2. How much time is available for counseling and consultation?	Since objectives are more clearly stated and methods to achieve them are more prescribed, this approach can move more quickly to completion	Normally unfolds slowly, deliberately; as a result, significant amounts of time are required

Finally, the ethical responsibilities of the manager-counselor must also be recognized and observed. Counselors should go no further than they have a right to go. The confidentiality of information exchanged is also of primary importance.

Questions to consider after reading Chapter 17

1.   In what ways may counseling for corrective (remedial) and therapeutic purposes be different?

2.   What problems may exist for the manager-counselor in formal, planned counseling sessions that might not exist in informal, unplanned, spontaneous counseling? What problems may develop for the manager-counselor in unplanned, spontaneous counseling that might not occur in planned counseling?

3.   One of the conditions for optimum counseling is said to be a desire on the part of the counselee to improve himself and the organization. Do employees universally wish to improve themselves and to rid themselves and their employers of problems? Explain your answer.

4.   Why is the nondirective counseling technique recommended so much more than the directive approach by most of the experts?

5.   What should the counselor do if he tries all of the techniques mentioned in the chapter to get the counselee to talk (under nondirective counseling) and the counselee refuses to respond?

6.   When nondirective counseling reaches the stage where alternative solutions are being reviewed, what should the counselor do if the counselee asks him for his opinion concerning which course of action to take?

7.   How can a counselor learn to listen more and talk less in counseling sessions?

8.   Role play a situation in which a worker has a problem that is keeping him from his peak performance (because of lack of interest in his job, personal problems at home, and so forth). How would the directive counseling technique go about dealing with the employee? the nondirective technique?

9.   Please go back and consider the case at the beginning of the chapter and apply the concepts discussed in the chapter. Role play the case using directive and nondirective techniques.

The following cases at the back of the book contain problems which relate to Chapter 17:

Ben Stockton

Mark Williams

Stanley Lowell

H. Gerald Pretzler

Edith Capp and Janet Turner

Bentley Cantrell

Billy Snyder

Kurt Browning

Susan Swanson

Grace Lanham

Billy Caden

Richard Jameson

Walt Gladberry

Abigail Spiegal and Trudy Pennington

Alan Purdy

Additional readings

Banaka, William H., *Training in Depth Interviewing,* New York: Harper & Row, Publishers, 1971.

Constas, Perry A., "Alienation Counseling Implications and Management Therapy," *Personnel Journal,* Volume 52, Number 5 (May 1973), pp. 349–356.

Dickson, William J., and Fritz J. Roethlisberger, *Counseling in an Organization,* Boston: Harvard University Press, 1966.

Grote, Richard C., "Make the Most of Counseling Sessions," *Supervisory Management,* Volume 16, Number 9 (September 1971), pp. 7–10.

Kolb, David A., and Richard E. Boyatzis, "On the Dynamics of the Helping Relationship," in David A. Kolb, Irwin M. Rubin, and James M. McIntyre, editors, *Organizational Psychology,* Second Edition, Englewood Cliffs, New Jersey: Prentice-Hall, Inc., 1974, pp. 371–387.

Lopez, Felix M., Jr., *Personnel Interviewing,* New York: McGraw-Hill Book Company, 1965.

Rogers, Carl R., *Client-Centered Therapy,* Boston: Houghton Mifflin Company, 1951.

———, "The Interpersonal Relationship: The Core of Guidance," *Harvard Educational Review,* Volume 32, Number 4 (Fall 1962), pp. 416–429.

Snyder, William U., *Casebook of Nondirective Counseling,* Boston: Houghton Mifflin Company, 1947.

Chapter 18

Managing Conflict

A case to consider before reading chapter 18

ELIZABETH REYNOLDS–THE MOST WANTED SECRETARY

Aaron Slade is a regional sales manager for World-International Airlines. He administers a wide range of responsibilities and has three district sales managers (in the same office) who cover smaller territories within the region to help him fulfill his duties. One of the district sales managers, James Calton, has reached retirement age and will begin his retirement at the beginning of next month. The retirement of this district manager has created something of a crisis between the two remaining district managers in a rather unique way. Each of the managers wants Calton's personal secretary to become his own secretary.

Mr. Calton's secretary, Elizabeth Reynolds, is a long-time employee of World-International and knows its operations from the inside out. She is exceptionally knowledgeable, capable, and skilled as an executive secretary. Ms. Reynolds has been an employee of World-International for almost twenty-five years. The past eighteen years she was Mr. Calton's secretary; so she is totally familiar with the responsibilities and functions of a district sales manager's office. Her vast knowledge of the duties of the district manager's office and her superior abilities create the keen demand for her skills. As a result, a clash has developed between Charles McGrath and Merwin Powell, who are the remaining DSM's.

Both McGrath and Powell have demanded of Don Bright, the regional personnel director, that Ms. Reynolds be assigned to them as personal secretary upon Calton's retirement. McGrath has told Bright that he should be entitled to Ms. Reynolds's assistance for the following reasons:

1. He (McGrath) has the longest seniority with World-International both in years of total service and in rank. McGrath has been with World-International for twenty

years and has been a district sales manager for nine years. Powell has been with the organization only fourteen years and has been a district sales manager for only three years.

2.   He is out of town almost constantly and needs someone in his office who can handle matters competently in his absence. His present secretary has made a number of mistakes and appears incapable of performing well in his absence.

3.   He has spoken with Ms. Reynolds about making the move to his office, and she has indicated her willingness to do so.

Mr. Powell has argued his case before Mr. Bright too. He states that:

1.   He requested Ms. Reynolds be transferred to his office at an early date, several days before McGrath made his request.

2.   His secretary resigned a few weeks ago to move to a different city; therefore, he has no secretary while McGrath already has one.

3.   Ms. Reynolds could be of invaluable assistance to him (because of her knowledge and experience) as he formulates new plans for the district that he supervises. He, too, is out of town a large percentage of the time.

Both McGrath and Powell have been rigid in their demands and hostility seems to be developing. Bright has been unable to resolve the problem, and there is no precedent upon which he can base a decision. He has no authority over either McGrath or Powell. When vacancies have occurred in secretarial positions in the past, it has been Bright's responsibility to screen applicants and forward qualified prospects to the manager in need of replacement personnel. Mr. Bright has been searching for an appropriate replacement for Mr. Powell's secretary for nearly a month and has sent two candidates to his office. However, Powell is adamant in his wish to have Ms. Reynolds as his secretary. Mr. Bright also realizes that he must find a personal secretary for the new district sales manager as soon as one is appointed.

Because Bright lacks the authority to decide which DSM will have Ms. Reynolds as his secretary, he has requested that the regional sales manager (Aaron Slade) step in and handle the situation, and the RSM has accepted this responsibility.

Questions about the Elizabeth Reynolds case

1.   As Mr. Slade (the RSM) assumes responsibility for resolving the differences between the two DSM's, what should his goals include? Please be specific.

2.   What are the specific, underlying causes of the conflict that is developing. In other words, what's to blame for this situation?

3.   The hostilities between McGrath and Powell have already begun to develop. What should Mr. Slade do to resolve these hostilities?

4.   In your opinion, which DSM has the best claim to Ms. Reynolds' assistance? Why?

5.   Who should make the decision on where to assign Ms. Reynolds? Why?

6.   What concepts does this case illustrate concerning conflict and its development?

7.   Does Ms. Reynolds have any rights in the matter? What about her preferences? Is she merely the object of the decision, or is she an integral part of it?

A major thesis of this book stresses that one of the primary purposes behind the existence of organizations is the coordination and integration of the efforts of a number of people so that mutual goals and objectives can be attained. As people work together, tensions sometimes develop that may result in dissension and hostility. The causes of these tensions may be simple and petty or, at other times, complex and serious. This author does not subscribe to the theory advanced by some writers that conflict (in a hostile sense) between people working together is totally inevitable and unavoidable nor that conflict is necessarily bad. It is true that a certain amount of tension and disagreement is normal. The focus of attention in this chapter is on conflict between people (interpersonal conflict), but many of the concepts discussed may also be applied to intergroup and inter-organizational conflict.

The predominant attitude of many managers toward conflict arising between workers has, over the years, been one of fear and disdain. The feeling has prevailed that conflict can result only in bad things happening—lack of cooperation, confusion, harsh treatment, and disunity. While it is true that negative results may occur, there has been an increased acceptance of the idea that conflict in many situations can be channeled into useful and productive results. The difference between successful and unsuccessful results from conflict is partially a product of the leadership skills and abilities of the supervisors involved, but it is also a result of the causes of conflict and the proper identification and treatment of the problem areas.

Management's Goals When Conflict Arises

If conflict is to be managed positively and constructively, those who manage need a set of goals and objectives to strive toward. While the following goals may not always be attained, they provide a helpful set of guidelines to pursue. When conflict arises, managers and supervisors who are in positions to influence and affect the attitudes and actions of those in disagreement may find it helpful to:

1. ~~Attempt to identify the causes and feelings of the parties involved in conflict~~. Conflict may be symptomatic of more deep-seated problems that may need attention and corrective action. The underlying causes of conflict, if left unattended, may fester and develop into even deeper, more severe problems. Resolution of conflict that deals only with surface tensions and not with actual causes can be considered only a temporary treatment of conflict. A more thorough approach to conflict is to identify and deal with the *causes* of conflict rather than the surface tensions.

2. ~~Provide a redirection of the tensions and hostilities~~. These words were chosen carefully to avoid the statement, "~~provide for a release of tensions~~," because it has been discovered that people are often more highly motivated when a "healthy" amount of tension prevails.[1] If an individual feels strongly enough about something, it would be more helpful to channel his interests and feelings in a positive direction rather than simply to release his feelings and emotions. In other words, when a tension is felt, the channeling of that tension toward the discovery and resolution of the problem rather than toward the simple venting of emotions may be a productive endeavor.[2]

3. ~~Achieve an integration of ideas~~ from the conflicting parties rather than a compromise solution. It was Mary Parker Follett who first suggested that decisions involving more than one person do not have to be reached on the basis of pure compromise in which each party states a position; then the two extremes are conceded to a purely middle-ground position between the two poles. The middle-ground position tends not to represent the most satisfactory resolution of conflict but simply the most expedient solution. In place of the compromise position, conflict is best resolved with a solution that is *best for the organization and for the parties who are involved.* By integrating the ideas of the conflicting parties, the *best* ideas and concepts are utilized rather than the most easily agreed upon ideas.[3]

4. ~~Achieve unity through a "meeting of the minds" between the parties in conflict~~. This desired result of the proper handling of conflict is not absolutely essential, but it is helpful. Through unity, the efforts and interests of individuals can be coordinated, and cooperation tends to progress.

5. ~~Accomplish solutions that are real and can be supported~~ by the parties in disagreement. Artificial, temporary solutions are quickly recognized by individuals and will not be respected or supported. Only genuine resolutions of conflict that attend to the causes of problems will be supported by those affected.

[1]Joseph A. Litterer, "Managing Conflict in Organizations," *Proceedings of the Eighth Annual Midwest Management Conference,* Carbondale, Illinois: Southern Illinois University Bureau of Business Research, 1965, p. 27.

[2]See the previous article by Litterer for further discussion of this.

[3]Mary Parker Follett, *Dynamic Administration: The Collected Papers of Mary Parker Follett* (edited by Henry C. Metcalf and L. Urwick), New York: Harper and Brothers, Publishers, 1940, pp. 30–49.

The Sources of Conflict

Throughout the statements of goals and objectives for handling conflict, the need for identifying the causes of conflict was stressed as an essential part of the proper resolution of conflict. The sources of interpersonal conflict are numerous and varied, but problems tend to group themselves into three general categories—problems based upon individual differences, difficulties resulting from perceptual differences, and issues arising out of functional difficulties and differences within the organization.

Individual Differences.   As has often been observed, no two people are identical. The *temperaments* of individuals vary. Some individuals are aggressive; others are passive. Some individuals are extroverted; others prefer to be introspective and self-centered. Some people are highly ambitious and upward bound, while others seek primarily to preserve and protect what they already have. One worker may seek a work situation that maximizes the possibility of social interaction, while another worker will prefer isolation. One individual will prefer independence in decision making, while another will seek out the opinions and ideas of others before acting. One worker may be able to withstand criticism and difficulty with a high degree of tolerance, while another may react emotionally at the slightest personal challenge.

The attitudes and actions of individuals also differ on the basis of *background* factors involving dissimilarities in educational, cultural, social, ethnic, and other similar factors (see Chapter 3 for a more complete discussion of this). The differences that occur because of variations in workers' backgrounds tend to influence the philosophical values of the worker. An individual's philosophy provides a set of guidelines or principles by which his life is conducted. Because people's backgrounds are different, their philosophies will tend to be different. Differences in philosophies (which determine action guidelines) will have a direct bearing on individual behavior and may be a significant cause of interpersonal conflict when incongruent philosophies interact.

Conflict based upon personal differences (personality and philosophy) is often the most difficult type of conflict to manage because of its embedded and ingrained nature. Specific causes and effects may be obscured by inherited and environmental influences.

Perceptual Differences.   **Individual perception** is the conscious awareness of occurrences, events, or happenings in one's surroundings. As most people view the ~~activities in their environment~~, there is a ~~tendency to classify those events as either supportive and beneficial or threatening and derogatory~~. The perceptions workers have of the events that surround them in their work environment have a direct, important bearing upon the development or avoidance of conflict. When a ~~worker views something~~ in ~~his environment~~ that ~~appears~~ to be ~~supportive~~ or ~~favorable to him~~, that ~~occurrence will be accepted~~, but ~~when an event~~ ~~appears~~ to ~~be threaten~~ing, he has an a~~lmost instinctive reaction to fight back~~, ~~to resist~~, to ~~attempt to master or overpower the threatening force~~. It matters not whether the perception is accurate or inaccurate. If the action or force is perceived to be threatening, the tensions and resistances will build. There are, of course, many events that potentially may cause perceptions of threatening situations with the resulting tensions and antagonisms. Some illustrative ~~examples of perceptions leading to possible conflict~~ include perceptions of:

1. ~~Loss of authority~~. If a worker sees the actions of another as a threat to his freedom and his right to act and make decisions, this perception will usually result in increased tensions and potential hostilities. Jurisdictional disputes often take place on these very grounds.

2. ~~Role conflict~~. A worker perceives the expectations and demands that others make of him as incompatible, and some (or all) of the attempted influences of individuals who are perceived to be involved in the overlapping demands may be resisted. If, for example, a supervisor feels that his boss and his subordinates are making incompatible, irreconcilable demands of him, he may resist and resent the sources of the contradictory demands.

3. ~~Unequal or unfair treatment~~. If a worker feels that he is receiving treatment that discriminates against him in favor of someone else, this negative perception usually will result in tensions toward the discriminator and sometimes against the worker who is considered to be favored by the action. Jealousy, in particular, precipitates conflict between individuals. In addition to the feelings of unequal treatment, the threatening actions of another worker may be perceived in a derogatory manner. When a worker senses that he has been penalized unfairly, rewarded improperly, or acted against arbitrarily without opportunity for a hearing, resentment or hostility may build.

4. ~~Status incongruities~~. Every worker has a perception of his position in relation to social standing, esteem, and reputation in the eyes of others. When the actions of others are perceived as a threat to his perceptions of himself, the actions and the sources of these actions will be censored and fought against.

5. ~~Goal differences~~. The worker has a set of personal goals toward which he is striving. As he encounters actions of others that he perceives will hinder the achievement of these goals, tensions and resistance will mount toward the source of opposing goals.

There are many other sources of potential perceptual difficulties. Some of the perceptions are realistic and are truly perceived as impending dangers. Other perceptions are unwarranted and are not based upon fact. Misunderstandings and miscommunications may be the source of many of the erroneous perceptions. Again, however, it must be remembered that perceptions do not have to be accurate to be influential.

Organizational and Functional Differences.   Conflict sometimes is encouraged by the actions, constraints, and demands of the organization and the responsibilities (functions) to be performed by the worker. Every worker is expected to be a performer and an achiever. Each worker who realizes his responsibilities and recognizes his accountability almost automatically begins to experience the development of tensions in connection with the fulfillment of his duties. Conflict may result when the resources allocated to the worker seem inadequate to do the job. Competition may be fostered between workers to obtain scarce resources.

Conflict between workers may result when individuals are placed on a win-lose competitive basis for rewards (such as salary increases or promotions). When a worker recognizes that his success is gained at the expense of another worker, the potential for interpersonal conflict is present.

Conflict may be encouraged by the functional duties of the workers. A production foreman who is being pressured by his supervisor (the production superintendent) to produce more units of the company's product may not concur with the quality control manager's zeal for higher quality if the emphasis on higher quality means a sacrifice in units produced. Goal incompatibility can be a very real problem between workers on a purely functional, accountability basis.

There may be other organizational-functional causes of conflict besides those mentioned above. For the most part, the pressures for performance and achievement set off the reactions resulting in conflict when organizational forces are involved. This recognition leads to another important observation: *Conflict often arises when a worker sincerely is attempting to do his best*—when he is trying to perform to meet the worthy expectations he and others have established. Conflict does not necessarily result because a worker wishes to be disruptive and destructive. Quite to the contrary, many individuals enter into conflict as a result of the pursuit of goals considered valuable and important. The recognition by managers of this important concept may cast a new light on the handling of some types of conflict. Over the years, a number of suggestions have been made for avoiding unnecessary conflict and directing it toward a constructive resolution if it has already arisen.

Most of the solutions mentioned have practical applications, but a few will be questioned as they are presented below.

Dealing with Conflict

The first objective, suggested earlier, for situations in which conflict arises is to discover the sources or causes of the conflict. This action is vitally important in order to identify trouble areas that require attention, and it is equally important as an indicator of the pressures and urgencies individual workers feel.

When underlying causes have been identified, action can begin to redirect, reduce, or release tensions that have developed. If conditions that have caused unnecessary tensions can be corrected, such action would be appropriate. Tensions that develop between individuals on the basis of personal differences (personality, philosophy, etc.) are very difficult to redirect or release because of the inbred, immovable nature of much of this conflict. Some have suggested that the least complicated method of dealing with conflict having a personal cause is to separate or create a buffer between the interacting parties. While this approach may temporarily reduce existing tensions, its long-range value is questionable because underlying causes are ignored and the pursuit of a lasting solution is merely postponed. Other techniques that have been suggested include the use of personal counseling, including the help of psychologists or psychiatrists if the sources of conflict are beyond the scope of supervisory assistance. Sensitivity training has also been used as a means of coping with interpersonal conflict. Sensitivity training is designed to help the individual develop a better understanding of his own outlook and to help him relate to other individuals more effectively.

If the source of the conflict is primarily a perceptual problem, there are two possible directions corrective action might take. If the worker's perceptions are accurately based upon an actual loss of authority, a real role conflict, unequal or unfair treatment, and so forth, the corrective action may be to modify the conditions or the behavior of others to correct the source of the conflict. If, for some reason, the practice causing the conflict cannot be corrected, the worker has to be helped to face the reality of the situation. In some cases, the worker may be compensated for the injustice he is receiving or has received. An important outlet for the worker is a grievance or appeal device such as a grievance committee that has the authority to hear individual complaints and to take corrective or compensatory action when appropriate.[4]

[4]William G. Scott, *The Management of Conflict*, Homewood, Illinois: Richard D. Irwin, Inc., 1965, contains an excellent review of workers' rights to appeal unjust actions.

If the source of conflict is discovered to be erroneous perceptions (the worker thinks events are occurring that jeopardize him but he's wrong), the usual course of action includes steps to correct the faulty view. Reality has to be communicated and reinforced.

Some organizational-functional sources of conflict cannot be eliminated completely, but an emphasis on mutual understanding and good intraorganizational communication may soften some of the tensions. Team effort can replace some of the individualistic efforts that tend to separate rather than unify workers. The use of win-lose situations of competition can be abolished in favor of competition that rewards winners but does not punish those who lose.

Thus far, the discussion about means and methods of handling conflict has considered only the identification of underlying causes and some fundamental techniques for dealing with tensions. Many of the tension-related approaches have been geared primarily toward release rather than redirection. Also, the previous discussions have not really considered the achievement of the three additional objectives—the integration of conflicting ideas, the development of unity and a "meeting of the minds," and the accomplishment of a resolution that can be supported by all parties involved in a disagreement. Through a deliberate effort on the part of supervisory personnel and the conflicting parties, it is possible to achieve all of the goals set for the proper resolution of conflict. One means of accomplishing all of the desired objectives is the application of the team approach to the resolution of conflict. Among the foremost advocates of the team approach to problem solving are psychologists Robert R. Blake and Jane S. Mouton. They have developed what they call the **Managerial Grid**®, which provides a means whereby all managers can be evaluated on the basis of the way their actions and efforts emphasize two basic criteria—the achievement of organizational tasks and the satisfaction of the personal goals of people at work.[5] The Grid not only provides a basis for the evaluation of a manager's performance, but it also provides a description of five typical approaches to the completion of managerial duties and presents a set of ideals (through its 9,9 approach) toward which the conscientious manager can aspire.

The Managerial Grid. While the main concern of this chapter is to find ways of channeling conflict, whenever possible, into productive and fulfilling uses, a brief review of the total concept of the Managerial Grid may be helpful. From the overview, specific guidelines for the utilization of approaches to handling conflict will be drawn.

[5]Robert R. Blake and Jane S. Mouton, *The Managerial Grid,* Houston: Gulf Publishing Company, 1964.

FIGURE 18.1   The Managerial Grid

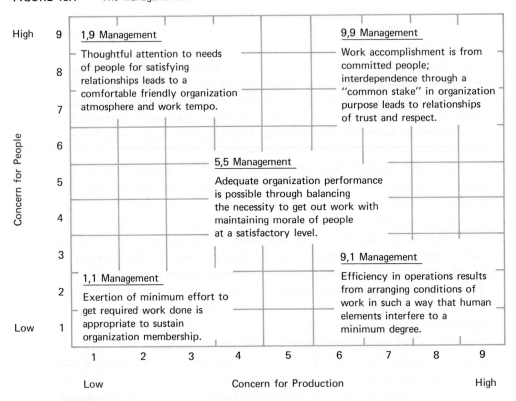

Source: Robert R. Blake and Jane S. Mouton, *The Managerial Grid*, Houston: Gulf
Publishing Company, 1964, p. 10.

The basic thesis of the Grid is that managerial actions can be viewed on the
basis of the priorities each manager places upon the achievement of organizational tasks and the achievement of the personal goals of the workers. Two scales
are drawn to provide a means of classifying managerial emphases. Managerial
effort may range from the 1,1 manager who attempts to achieve little for the organization or the people in it, to the 9,9 manager who seeks to maximize both
organizational achievement and personal fulfillment for workers (see Figure 18.1).

A brief description of the philosophy behind each of the managerial styles on
the Grid would appear like this:

1,1 *Management*: High production and sound relationships are in conflict and
the supervisor's job is to not get involved in the struggle. He has a low concern for
either production or people, however. He tends to stay neutral and to see to it that

rules and procedures established in the past are carried out. He shows no initiative and expects none from others.

9,1   *Management:* He has a high concern for people. A supervisor's major responsibility is to see to it that production goals are achieved by assuming the task of planning, directing, and controlling all work. The achievement of the personal goals of the workers is relatively unimportant. The 9,1 manager drives himself and his subordinates toward performance.

1,9   *Management:* He has a low concern for production and a high concern for people. A supervisor's major responsibility is to see that harmonious relationships between people are established and that the work atmosphere is secure and pleasant. The achievement of organizational goals is a secondary matter.

5,5   *Management:* He has a moderate concern for production and the needs of people. The major responsibility of the supervisor is to find a middle ground so that a reasonable degree of production can be achieved without destroying morale. No maximization of personal or organizational goals is attempted.

9,9   *Management:* Production results from the integration of task and human requirements. Good relationships and high production are *both* attainable and the supervisor's major responsibility is to attain effective production through participation and involvement of people and their ideas. The way to maximize achievement is to provide for personal fulfillment while pursuing organizational goals.[6]

On the basis of these philosophies and managerial positions, five unique approaches to handling conflict can be drawn. If, for example, an individual finds himself in conflict *with a superior or a colleague* over whom he has no formal authority, the Grid suggests that the following positions tend to be taken by the individual embracing the respective Grid style.

1,1   *Management:* Keeps his mouth shut and doesn't express any dissent. Neutrality continues to be his important aim. He keeps a low profile. He is outwardly, at least, compliant with his boss and makes no demands on peers.

9,1   *Management:* Takes a win-lose approach and fights to win his own points as long as possible. He believes the cause is important and his position is correct; he fights to win his position. He has a closed mind toward the other party's position.

1,9   *Management:* Avoids conflict by conforming to the thinking of his boss or peers. He seeks knowledge of the boss's position and never "goes out on the limb" against the boss. He never gives the boss any information that would be upsetting. He wants his boss to be pleased and happy.

5,5   *Management:* He concentrates on compromises and tentative statements . . . . To his boss or peers he may state "we could do this . . . or we could do this . . . ."

9,9   *Management:* Confronts conflict directly. Feelings and facts are communicated so that there is a basis for understanding and working through the conflict.[7]

[6]*Ibid.,* pp. 85–101, 18–56, 57–84, 110–141, and 142–191.
[7]*Ibid.,* pp. 93–95, 29–35, 66–70, 121–126, and 162–166.

The approach to be used in handling conflict may be altered somewhat if a supervisor perceives conflict between two subordinates or between a subordinate and himself. In these situations, the supervisor can utilize the authority of his own position to influence the resolution of conflict if he desires to involve himself in that manner. Not every Grid style would utilize formal authority as a means of resolving conflict, as can be seen in the following statements. When conflict arises *between two of the supervisor's subordinates or between himself and a subordinate*, the:

1,1   *Management:* Just doesn't get involved. He usually is able to completely avoid issues which might give rise to conflict by not discussing them with subordinates.

9,1   *Management:* Suppresses by the use of authority. He fears the disruptive effects of conflict on organizational achievement and beats down the impending threats he perceives.

1,9   *Management:* Smoothes over conflict. He attempts to encourage people to relax and forget about their troubles. He suggests that some troubles have a way of disappearing or resolving themselves. People are encouraged to "count their blessings" and be happy with what they already have.

5,5   *Management:* He "splits up" parties in conflict and keeps them separated. He talks with each party individually, discusses their position, and blends or compromises their ideas to reach a solution. He then attempts to get acceptance of the compromise even though each party tends to be only moderately satisfied with a compromise.

9,9   *Management:* Confronts conflict directly and works it through at the time it arises. Conflict is accepted so that the clash of ideas and people can generate creative solutions to problems. Those involved are brought together to work through differences.[8]

The 9,9 manager faces conflict by bringing the parties in conflict together (this is the only approach in which the parties are brought together). He stresses the importance of both (or all) parties to the organization and attempts to emphasize the desirability of mutual cooperation and understanding. He indicates a genuine interest in the parties individually and collectively. He attempts to inspire the participants to communicate fully the causes of the disagreement and the tensions felt in relation to the conflict. He encourages the individuals to present and review all feasible alternative solutions to their problems. *The emphasis is placed upon reaching a decision that will be most beneficial to the individuals in conflict and to the organization as an entity.* If the individuals seem to be sliding into a situation of pure compromise, he raises questions and issues to stimulate a more complete review of facts and decision. *The alternatives presented and the decision reached should be the*

---

[8]*Ibid.*, pp. 93–94, 29–33, 66–69, 121–125, and 162–165.

agreed upon choice of the parties originally in conflict. Only on this basis will the parties support the ultimate outcome. The role of the manager is one primarily of coordination and stimulation. In many ways, ~~the 9,9 approach parallels the nondirective counseling approach discussed in Chapter 17.~~

The approach selected from the Grid styles for dealing with conflict may be determined by factors in addition to the philosophical desires of the manager. The decision concerning the approach to use may be similar to the overall choice of leadership style discussed in Chapter 9 in connection with adaptive leadership. The choice of approaches will be dependent upon forces within the leader, within the subordinates, within the organization, and within the task situation. While the 9,9 approach to the resolution of conflict has the potential for accomplishing all of the objectives outlined earlier in this chapter, it also requires skill and commitment to this approach from the manager. It consumes a large amount of time in its execution. It demands maturity, patience, and tolerance from participants. Some situations of tension may not concur with these conditions, and some other approach to conflict resolution that approximates this effort has the potential for discovering the real sources of conflict, redirecting tensions to a constructive outlet, integrating opposing viewpoints in the best interests of individuals and the organization, developing unity and cooperation, and achieving a resolution capable of full support from the parties involved. It is a goal worth striving toward.

Summary

Conflicts and tensions may develop between people working together. While conflict should not normally be encouraged, neither should its consequences be treated entirely with fear and dread. The tensions resulting from many types of conflict can be channeled and redirected toward constructive, productive results. Worthy managerial objectives for the resolution of conflict include: clear identification of the underlying causes and sources of conflict; redirection of the tensions toward productive accomplishment; integration of the ideas of parties in conflict to achieve solutions in the best interest of the individuals and the organization; a unity of cooperative spirits and attitudes; and a solution that can be wholeheartedly supported by the parties previously in conflict.

There are many approaches to the handling of conflict. The ultimate choice concerning which approach to use will be dependent upon factors within the leader, the workers themselves, the organization, and the task situation. Only a team approach that directly involves the parties in conflict has the potential for full conflict resolution.

Conflict demands attention because sources of tension left unattended tend to smolder or fester until larger explosions erupt.

Questions to consider after reading Chapter 18

1.   Why is it that so many managers and employees are afraid of conflict and attempt to avoid it at all costs?

2.   Some authors have said that interpersonal and intergroup conflict will inevitably result whenever people must work together. Do you agree with this statement? Why or why not?

3.   Is it ever wise to avoid getting the causes of conflict out in the open? Is it ever useful to avoid the issues conflict presents?

4.   Is it possible to predict when background differences of individuals will be likely to result in conflict? If you answer yes, explain how this may be done.

5.   Is it ever desirable to handle conflict in the 9,1 manner? The 1,9 way? The 5,5 approach? Support your answers.

6.   Role play a situation in which conflict develops between a production manager and a sales manager over production requirements for the next month. The sales manager wants more units produced than the production manager believes is reasonable. How would a 9,9 general manager handle this conflict?

7.   Look again at the case that preceded this chapter. How might the conflict that developed have been handled most effectively? Role play the situation as a 1,1; 1,9; 9,1; 5,5; and 9,9 type of regional sales manager might handle the situation.

The following cases at the back of the book contain problems related to Chapter 18:

Mark Williams

Stanley Lowell

Edith Capp and Janet Turner

Earl Fornette

Bentley Cantrell

Kurt Browning

Richard Jameson

Alan Purdy

Additional readings

Burke, Ronald J., "Methods of Resolving Conflict," *Personnel Administration*, Volume 32, Number 4 (July–August 1969), pp. 48–55.

Kelly, Joe, "Make Conflict Work for You," *Harvard Business Review*, Volume 48, Number 4 (July–August 1970), pp. 103–113.

Litterer, Joseph A., "Conflict in Organizations: A Re-examination," *The Academy of Management Journal*, Volume 11, Number 3 (September 1968), pp. 78–86.

Miner, John B., *The Management Process*, New York: The Macmillan Company, 1973, pp. 391–427.

Pondy, Louis R., "Organizational Conflicts: Concepts and Models," *Administrative Science Quarterly*, Volume 12, Number 2 (September 1967), pp. 296–320.

————, "Varieties of Organizational Conflict," *Administrative Science Quarterly*, Volume 14, Number 4 (December 1969), pp. 499–505.

Scott, William G., *The Management of Conflict*, Homewood, Illinois: Richard D. Irwin, Inc., 1965.

Sherif, Muzafer, "Subordinate Goals in the Redirection of Intergroup Conflict," *American Journal of Sociology*, Volume 63, Number 4 (January 1958), pp. 349–358.

Stagner, Ross, *The Dimensions of Human Conflict*, Detroit: Wayne State University Press, 1967.

William, Fredrik P., and Raymond L. Read, "Contemporary Approaches to the Control of Organizational Conflict," North Texas State University *Business Studies*, Volume 8, Number 2 (Fall 1969), pp. 78–84.

Chapter 19

Team Effort

A case to consider before reading chapter 19

ARLIN O'KEEFE-THE DIRECTOR WHO WANTS A GROUP DECISION

Arlin O'Keefe is director of the eastern district of the State Highway Department. He has under his jurisdiction all of the highways and state-maintained roads in a twelve-county region, and he reports directly to the deputy director of the State Highway Department. It is Mr. O'Keefe's responsibility to see that roads in his district are maintained satisfactorily, and it is also his duty to make decisions concerning the construction of new roads, bridges, and other highway structures in his district.

To make his job more manageable, Mr. O'Keefe has divided his district into three subdistricts composed of four counties each. He has put one of his assistants in charge of each subdistrict and has given them the title of assistant district director. Each assistant director is responsible for supervising the construction and maintenance activities in his own subdistrict.

One of O'Keefe's major responsibilities is the determination of priorities for new construction projects. The state derives all of its funds for highway construction from gasoline taxes. The annual income from gasoline taxes is forecast at the beginning of each year, and the anticipated resources are allocated to the four districts within the state on a fairly equal basis. It is then the responsibility of the district director to allocate the resources given to his district to the projects of most urgent importance. There is never enough money to do all of the things that are needed. This year, for example, Mr. O'Keefe has been told that his district will receive $16 million and he knows of four major projects of urgent importance that would cost $34 million if all were undertaken at once. There are a number of minor projects to consider also, and a contingency fund for emergency projects in the sum of $300,000 is customarily set aside each year.

The large number of costly, important projects and the limited availability of resources mean that some difficult decisions must be reached concerning which projects to approve for this coming year and which ones to postpone for some future year.

To aid him in his annual priority allocation decision, Mr. O'Keefe calls in his subdistrict directors and his district research assistant to work with him as a decision-making team. They meet each year in the last week of January to make their priority decisions. It is nearing time for this year's decisions, and Tom Wittman (Subdistrict A), Marlin Schell (Subdistrict B), Roy Regis (subdistrict C), and Dale Edwards (district research) will soon be called in for the conference. Mr. O'Keefe observes that of the four major projects under consideration this year, two are in Wittman's subdistrict (an $8 million project and a $9 million project); one is in Schell's subdistrict (a $9 million project); and one is in Regis' subdistrict (an $8 million project). The smaller projects are scattered throughout all three subdistricts.

Mr. O'Keefe has experienced some difficulties in past years in getting these men to work together smoothly. Tom Wittman is the oldest man in the group and has more seniority with the Highway Department. He sometimes attempts to use his seniority to influence others to think the way he wants them to and to accept his position on issues. He is willing to make concessions at times, but he attempts to manipulate the group to follow his own line of logic. Roy Regis frequently has a very closed mind and fights for projects within his own subdistrict without much regard for the welfare of the other subdistricts. Marlin Schell, on the other hand, is a team player and usually tries to remain objective in the decision-making process. Dale Edwards seldom does anything more than supply information and provide supportive material for consideration in making decisions.

In spite of these difficulties, Mr. O'Keefe feels that a group decision on the priority for allocating funds is essential; so he is preparing to use team decision making this year. He hopes to be able to overcome the difficulties that have occurred with this group in previous years.

Questions about the Arlin O'Keefe case

1. Why does Mr. O'Keefe prefer to have a group decision rather than to make the decision himself? What are the advantages of a group decision in the case?

2. What are the disadvantages of group decision making in the highway department situation?

3.   What preliminary steps can Mr. O'Keefe take prior to group meetings to smooth the way for more productive, more objective group discussions?

4.   What actions should Mr. O'Keefe perform during group discussions to help encourage open-minded, fair, objective consideration of issues confronting the group?

Most of my time each day is spent in meetings with other executives and employees in which plans are made and organizational strategies are outlined.

We seldom make decisions by individual action in our company anymore. Several people are involved in each decision.

Our production process has become so interrelated that our employees must now work together as a team instead of working as individuals.

The most important training a young executive could receive today would be training on how to lead groups to work together to achieve goals [spoken by an older manager].

These comments from managers in different types of industries help point out the importance of group efforts and teamwork in today's organizations. An increasing number of organizational functions (design, production, sales, distribution, and so forth) are being handled by teams. Planning and decision-making responsibilities are being given to teams more frequently rather than centralizing these responsibilities in the hands of individuals who can act independently.

There may be many explanations for the emergence of teamwork as a dominant influence in today's organizations. In an era of increasingly complex organizations (resulting from mergers, diversification programs, technological innovations, population growth patterns, economic developments, etc.), the importance of coordination and the integration of effort have progressed to new heights. Emphasis on teamwork and group dynamics has served to unify and tie together management or organizational activities that otherwise might have the tendency to pursue their own self-interests.

Team decision making has increased in usage as a means for collecting all essential information, for widening the perspective of decisions, and for unifying the efforts of individuals. As we shall see in a few moments, many managers believe that teamwork in decision making enlists the commitment of the participants to support the resulting plans. Teamwork, because it allows participation in important decisions, is also a means of fulfilling many personal goals and objectives of employees (such as the desire for power or achievement).

The type of **teamwork** we are talking about in this chapter is a structured set of relationships (as opposed to informal work groups) in which employees are assigned responsibilities to perform together, and authority relationships are clarified, to a degree at least, at the beginning. Teams are typically formulated in organizations to serve two functions: (1) problem-solving and decision-making and (2) operational performance. Problem-solving and decision-making teams are bodies formulated to review policies, plans, procedures, or areas of difficulty; consider alternate courses of action; and formulate solutions or plans on the basis of the group's findings. This type of team may be temporary in nature, formulated to solve a unique problem or reach a special decision, or it may be constituted on a more permanent basis to continually review and decide issues.

In the same manner, operational teams may be special task forces designed to integrate effort for the accomplishment of an extraordinary task, or they may be permanent teams that perform together for months or years at a time. An illustration of a temporary operational team might be formation by a real estate firm of a special promotional team to advertise and sell tracts of land in a new industrial subdivision. When the special task is accomplished, the temporary unit may be dissolved. A more continuous operational group might be illustrated by a team of assembly-line workers who perform together day after day to assemble television sets. Each member of this group contributes his part to the task completion, and the group collectively fulfills its responsibilities repetitively and continuously.

Characteristics of Formalized Teams

Problem-solving, decision-making, and operational teams that have been formally appointed have several attributes that are assigned to them or emerge as functions are performed. Teams have central goals and objectives, role differentiation of members, value systems, standards or norms of behavior, levels of power and influence, and degrees of cohesiveness.[1] Team objectives or goals are, in part, predetermined. Each team, as it is formed, is normally given some specific objectives or goals it is expected to achieve. A problem-solving group is charged with the responsibility for finding an answer to a trouble area. A production team may be directed to be prolific in quantity and high in quality.

In the pursuit of the team's objectives, several other patterns develop. The roles of the various members of the group become defined and differentiated. Roles in groups may be defined as the rights, duties, status, and prestige assigned to individual team members. To a degree, some aspects of role differentiation are determined by organizational elements—who has the most formal authority, who

---

[1]Clovis R. Shepherd, *Small Groups: Some Sociological Perspectives,* San Francisco: Chandler Publishing Company, 1964, p. 25.

FIGURE 19.1   Content and process roles of decision-making, problem-solving teams

CONTENT ROLES

Initiator—makes suggestions

Information-seeker—asks questions

Blocker—objects to other people's suggestions for action

Expert—knows the facts

Destructive critic—tears other people's ideas apart

PROCESS ROLES

Summarizer—summarizes where the group stands

Task-setter—tries to get the group to move on, emphasizes what still has to be done

Decision-announcer—announces decisions after the group has reached agreement

Traffic cop—decides who talks when

Encourager—encourages others to contribute

Mediator—tries to narrow differences

Playboy—kids around (and sometimes reduces excess tension)

Source: Leonard R. Sayles and George Strauss, *Human Behavior in Organizations*, Englewood Cliffs, New Jersey: Prentice Hall, Inc., 1966, p. 283.

has been assigned as the formal team leader, and so forth. In addition, the team affixes its own role expectations upon its members as the team works to fulfill its responsibilities. In speaking of problem-solving teams in particular, Sayles and Strauss say that team members come to play several roles.[2] Some of the roles they describe include **task** (content) roles and **process** roles (how the group progresses toward its objectives). These roles are listed in Figure 19.1. Sayles and Strauss, in

[2]Leonard R. Sayles and George Strauss, *Human Behavior in Organizations*, Englewood Cliffs, New Jersey: Prentice-Hall, Inc., 1966, p. 283.

addition, state that the roles individuals play may vary from time to time. Not all of the roles that emerge among members of teams are constructive ones, from the organization's point of view.[3]

Group values may be defined as a system of group judgments through which priorities are established and importance (worth) is given to activities and materials within the realm of the group's control As the members of a group interact, values are formulated, usually on the basis of what is most beneficial for the group and its members. Using the priority system defined by group values, behavior patterns (norms) are formulated that will support these values, and individual members are expected to align their behavior with these norms.

As interaction among team members continues, some individuals become more influential or powerful as they lead and control the patterns of group efforts and opinions. A level of cohesiveness develops among the team members (see Chapter 6 for a more complete discussion of group cohesiveness). Some temporary teams may not develop elaborate definitions of role relationships, value systems, behavior norms, power-influence patterns, and cohesiveness because the length of interaction may be too brief to allow this.

Groups for Decision Making and Problem Solving

Groups formulated for the purpose of problem solving and decision making deserve special attention, because their activities are particularly important and because information relating to this team effort is more readily available than is true of operational teams. Decision-making teams have been the center of a great amount of controversy. The next several paragraphs will attempt to put some of this controversy into perspective.

Advantages and Disadvantages.   Team decision making and problem solving have been ridiculed as an escape from responsible individual management action, a source of agitation, and a folly resulting in confusion and lack of direction. Some have said that no one feels responsible for decisions made by teams. Are these statements true or are they based on misconceptions and misinformation? In reality, group decision making has a number of strengths and more than a few weaknesses.

[3]*Loc. cit.*

In reviewing the positive points concerning team effort for problem solving and decision making, research has shown that:

1.   Team decision making usually results in the ~~accumulation of a wider variety of facts and knowledge~~ than does individual decision making. Individuals working together as a team ~~tend to supplement and complement each other's knowledge~~ as issues are being considered.

2.   Team interaction tends to result in the consideration of a ~~greater number of alternatives before decisions are made~~. The nature of groups and their membership usually results in a broadened perspective for analysis and action.[4]

3.   Recommendations advanced through group ~~problem solving have a higher level of accuracy than do most individual solutions and recommendations.~~ Team members tend to correct false assumptions and inaccuracies in the thinking of some individual members.[5]

4.   Individuals who participate in team problem solving and decision making are ~~more likely to accept the resulting decision~~ (than if it had been made by one individual) and will feel more responsibility toward its successful implementation. In other words, people support what they help create.[6] When the group comes to a decision that represents a high degree of group consensus, individual members will be particularly diligent in their support and execution of it.[7] Even individuals who are not a direct part of the decision-making team will tend to look more favorably upon a decision if their views were represented by a team member in the deliberations. If team members report group decisions favorably to other employees, the nonparticipants will tend to adopt a favorable attitude toward the decision.

5.   Group decision making results in employees who are better informed, more knowledgeable concerning the decisions reached. The participants in the deliberation process are personally aware of problems, alternatives considered, and decision constraints, because they have been personally involved in confronting them while reaching the decisions. This knowledge can be shared with other employees to result in a well-informed group of workers in general.[8]

[4]These findings are based upon conclusions drawn by Norman R. F. Maier, "Assets and Liabilities in Group Problem Solving: The Need for an Integrative Function," *Psychological Review,* Volume 47, Number 4 (July 1967), pp. 239–240.

[5]David R. Hampton, Charles E. Summer, and Ross A. Webber, *Organizational Behavior and the Practice of Management,* Revised Edition, Glenview, Illinois: Scott, Foresman and Company, 1973, p. 285; Irving Lorge, David Fox, Joel Davitz, and Marlin Brenner, "A Survey of Studies Contrasting the Quality of Group Performance and Individual Performance 1920–1957," *Psychological Bulletin,* Volume 55, Number 6 (November 1958), pp. 353–357; and Charles R. Holloman and Hal W. Hendrick, "Adequacy of Group Decisions as a Function of the Decision-Making Process," *Academy of Management Journal,* Volume 15, Number 2 (June 1972), p. 182.

[6]Maier, *op. cit.,* p. 240.

[7]Edith B. Bennett, "Discussion, Decision, Commitment, and Consensus in Group Decision," *Human Relations,* Volume 8, Number 3 (1955), pp. 251–273.

[8]Maier, *op. cit.,* p. 240–241.

6.   The participants in the group interaction come to ~~develop rapport toward each other.~~ Goals, ambitions, interests, and concerns are revealed, and a better understanding is achieved. This may be useful in improving communications among peer-level individuals as well as individuals who are differentiated within the vertical hierarchy of organizations.

In brief, the positive effects of group decision making and problem solving are ~~better decisions~~ (or solutions), ~~greater support and cooperation~~ in the implementation of decisions, and ~~better communication~~ and ~~understanding of decisions~~ and ~~personalities involved in teams~~. Team decision making has its drawbacks also:

1.   Group decision making tends to ~~work more slowly~~ than decision-making processes involving single individuals.[9]

2.   Because team decisions are slower to process and involve several individuals, the ~~decisions reached become expensive ones~~. Where one employee might be able to reach a decision working alone in twenty minutes, a group of five might take one hour. The salaries of the five individuals and the longer time period involved make the group decision a much more costly one (at least in terms of immediate expenses).

3.   Group efforts ~~frequently result in compromise decisions that are not always the most useful~~, most beneficial decisions. Decision team members often are more concerned about being good team members than they are about the quality of the final decision. As a result, groups tend to settle on the first generally agreeable solution rather than seeking the best possible solution. Majority opinions also tend to be accepted regardless of whether or not they are logical and scientifically sound.[10]

4.   Group interaction is often conducive to domination by one of the members of the team.

'This may result because one of the team members is in a higher position of authority [in the authority hierarchy] than are other members or it may occur when some individual simply participates more, is more persuasive, or is more stubborn than anyone else. As a result, others concede to his domination. This domination may destroy many of the positive effects of group decision-making.'[11]

The remainder of the group (those dominated) may become passive and indifferent toward the team's responsibilities. Original contributions to team deliberations cease and support for decisions reached becomes minimal.

5.   Conflict and disharmony may result if group actions are not handled properly. Because no two individuals think totally alike, group interactions may result in the airing of different feelings and different opinions. Individuals may begin to compete

[9]Hampton, Summer, and Webber, *op. cit.*, p. 285.
[10]Maier, *op. cit.*, p. 241.
[11]*Loc. cit.*

with each other to "win" their point of view rather than to find the best decision.[12] This, of course, can result in the failure of the team's actions to be as useful as they should be. The disruptive effects may be deep-seated and enduring.

6. While it does not have to be the case, too much dependence upon group decision making can hinder management's ability to act. In organizations in which teams are utilized for almost every type of decision, individuals who serve in managerial capacities may have almost no authority. If a manager encounters a problem that needs an immediate answer, he may not be able to provide it if team decision making has pre-empted this right. Teams might have to agonize over whether to buy two dollars worth of pencils and a dollar's worth of paper clips if organizations refer all decisions to teams. It is possible for organizations to vest too much power and responsibility in the hands of teams.

In addition to these weaknesses or dangers of group decision making, there is at least one mixed blessing. Groups usually are more willing to take risks in their decisions than are individuals acting independently.[13] Groups often are more daring in their actions than individuals, which may mean that more opportunities are seized. Some of the opportunities may prove to be advantageous, while others may result in losses and failures.

Conditions for Successful Team Interactions. When decision-making and problem-solving groups work together successfully, it is more than a chance happening. There are circumstances and conditions that aid in the successful achievement of group decisions and results. Many of the factors are related to the type of leadership exhibited by individuals in the group, and these elements will be considered momentarily. There are also many other factors that influence a group's effectiveness.

1. It is important for participants in group interaction to have a common goal. Team members need a unity of direction if they are to pull together. The goals should be universally known by the members of the group and acceptable to them.

2. It is extremely helpful if the participants share not only a common purpose but also a fairly homogeneous set of *personal values* and *goals*. Hare states that groups composed of individuals with more homogeneous values and ambitions "show more positive responses to each other, are more favorable in their perceptions, are more involved in the task, and have greater satisfaction with their work."[14]

[12]L. Richard Hoffman and Norman R. F. Maier, "Quality and Acceptance of Problem Solutions by Members of Homogeneous and Heterogeneous Groups," *Journal of Abnormal and Social Psychology*, Volume 69, Number 3 (September 1964), pp. 264–271.

[13]Michael A. Wallach, Nathan Krogan, Daryl J. Bem, "Group Influence on Individual Risk Taking," *Journal of Abnormal and Social Psychology*, Volume 65, Number 2 (August 1962), pp. 75–86.

[14]A. Paul Hare, *Handbook of Small Group Research*, New York: The Free Press, 1962, p. 254.

Deutsch indicates that groups whose members have similar interests and ambitions will also feel a stronger responsibility to accomplish tasks and to help each other, will communicate with each other more effectively, and will have more mutual respect for each other.[15]

3.   It is also important that the individual participants be able to perceive personal benefits that will accrue to them if the group performs its responsibilities successfully. Hampton et al. state that "in general, both the effectiveness of the group and the satisfaction of its members are increased when the members see their personal goals as being advanced by the group's success."[16]

4.   The more productive teams normally are those whose members are relatively equal in formal authority. One group of authors refers to co-equal peers by calling them "hierarchically undifferentiated individuals."[17] Because everyone in one of these groups is similar in formal authority, it becomes easier for them to cooperate. Also, there are fewer opportunities for a formally superior individual to dominate and control the group and its actions.

5.   If participating members enter into their responsibilities with an open mind, the probability of a better interaction between members will also be increased. Open-mindedness means that individuals are receptive to the views of other individuals and will listen to other points of view with the possibility of accepting those views if they are reasonable. This, of course, does not imply that the participants cannot enter into team discussions without ideas of their own, but it does mean that they may be willing to accept the ideas of others if those ideas are sound. A state of open-mindedness cannot be created instantly within individuals, but managers (leaders) of group interactions can attempt to create an atmosphere in which objectivity is sought and personal biases and prejudices are minimized.

Those who serve in positions of leadership particularly must have an open, receptive mind as idea interchanges progress. If a leader begins group interactions with preconceived ideas of what a team's position and end results should be, the leader will tend to manipulate and shape the direction of activities in a way that may restrict the successful functioning of the group. If he does have prejudgments of what the team should do, the leader should bring them out in the open as early as possible in the interaction so that all participants are aware of them.

6.   The size of the group appears to have a direct bearing upon the successful performance of the group. The most effective groups typically are those small enough to allow a good interchange of ideas and large enough to provide enough diversity of ideas to stimulate creativity. In Slater's studies, he discerned that teams

[15]Morton Deutsch, "The Effects of Cooperation and Competition upon the Work Process," in Dorwin Cartwright and Alvin Zander, editors, *Group Dynamics: Research and Theory*, New York: Harper & Row, Publishers, 1953, pp. 319–353.

[16]Hampton, Summer, and Webber, *op. cit.*, p. 289.

[17]Edwin M. Bridges, Wayne F. Doyle, and David F. Mahan, "Effects of Hierarchical Differentiation on Group Productivity, Efficiency, and Risk Taking," *Administrative Science Quarterly*, Volume 13, Number 2 (September 1968), pp. 305–319.

composed of five members are about the ideal size.[18] A group of this size is most effective for task achievement and for fulfilling the personal goals of the participants, he suggests.

In some additional remarks concerning the conditions under which group decision making is most effective, Berelson and Steiner have stated that team efforts are superior to individual efforts only when:

1. Individual members subordinate their own self-interests to those of the group

2. Individual self needs expressed are satisfied during the course of group interactions

3. There is a generally pleasant atmosphere, and the participants recognize the need for unified action

4. The group's problem-solving activity is understandable, orderly, and focused on one issue at a time

5. Facts are available and used

6. The participants are warm and friendly toward each other

7. The chairman (leader), through much solution proposing, aids the group in penetrating its agenda problems[19]

Hall and Williams suggest that previous research has shown that decision-making groups will perform more effectively when:

1. Democratic or "participative" leadership is employed so that:

    a. the interpersonal climate will be relatively free of power-based constraints

    b. all members feel that they share equally in opportunities for influencing the group effort

    c. there is an opportunity for "emergent" leadership based upon expertise and group needs

2. Flexible patterns of communication are used so that:

    a. all members are able to participate equally and at will

    b. minority opinions are encouraged and, consequently, are more likely to be voiced

3. A cooperative "problem-solving" approach to discussion is employed rather than a competitive "win-lose" approach, so that:

    a. disagreements may be viewed as substantive rather than affective and, therefore, will be tolerated

[18]Philip E. Slater, "Contrasting Correlates of Group Size," *Sociometry*, Volume 21, Number 2 (June 1958), pp. 129–139.

[19]Bernard Berelson and George Steiner, *Human Behavior: An Inventory of Scientific Findings*, New York: Harcourt Brace Jovanovich, 1964, p. 335.

b. individual members become more sensitive to the ideas and reactions of others

4. Members deal more openly and candidly with one another so that:

a. "hidden agendas" or personal needs do not distort the handling of the task

b. feelings of resistance or doubt can be discussed and resolved at the time they are experienced rather than remaining as latent barriers to commitment

5. Decision techniques which favor a sharing of responsibility via a protection of individual rights are used, rather than techniques which place the responsibility clearly in the hands of but a portion of the group membership so that:

a. all share equally the burden of performing the necessary task and social-maintenance functions required by the above actions

b. all members feel a sense of responsibility for group success[20]

While not everyone may agree with the absolute importance of all of these factors, it becomes obvious that the success of group effort is heavily influenced by those who serve in leadership capacities within the group.

The Leader and Team Performance

~~Every group functions better if some individual(s) performs in the role of group~~ ~~leader~~(s). The leader may be formally appointed to his role, or he may emerge from the participants to fill the need for leadership. There may, in fact, be more than one leader in each group.[21]

Many of the leadership characteristics mentioned in earlier chapters are pertinent to leadership in problem-solving and decision-making task forces. Group leaders must have the confidence and respect of the other participants if they are to fully contribute to the group process. It will be helpful for the leader to be skilled in the application of situational, contingency leadership. At times, the group leader will need to be forceful and aggressive in order to activate participants' interest and involvement. At other times, the leader will need to be silent and observant when the group is working well without additional stimulation. The leader must be well acquainted with the task before the group and the

[20]Reproduced by special permission from "Group Dynamics Training and Improved Decision Making," *The Journal of Applied Behavioral Science*, Jay Hall and Martha S. Williams, pp. 39–68, © January–February 1970, published by the NTL Institute for Applied Behavioral Science.

[21]Alan C. Filley, "Committee Management: Guidelines for Social Science Research," *California Management Review*, Volume 13, Number 1 (Fall 1970), pp. 17–18.

objectives toward which it is striving. It is the team leader's responsibility to rally the participants together toward fulfillment of the group's responsibilities.[22]

One of the dangers of group interaction mentioned earlier was the fact that not everyone may think alike and that antagonism and dissension can result if participants are allowed to take win-lose positions and in-fighting and competition occur. Skilled leaders of team efforts must be able to sense potential sources of conflict and disagreement and attempt to channel participants with conflicting views in a positive, constructive direction. The more successful leader has the ability to find mutual interests among a group and to emphasize those goals so that the separate interests of individuals will not be allowed to dominate. The capable leader will also have the ability to protect participants who hold minority views that have merit so that majority rule does not beat down valuable ideas that may initially be lacking in support.[23]

The successful group leader will do whatever he can to create the proper conditions for group interaction—a common goal, homogeneous personal values, an adequate reward structure, similar authority and status, conditions for objectivity and open-mindedness, satisfactory group size, and other helpful conditions.

If leaders are appointed or selected in advance of team interactions convened to deal with specific problems or decisions, group leaders can take several preliminary steps to enhance the probability of successful team interaction. If the leader is selected prior to assembling the problem-solving team (sometimes known as the conference group, task force, or simply as a project committee), the leader can take the following actions before the group is called together for its deliberations:

1.   If the problem or responsibility of the team is known in advance, the leader can attempt to clarify the team's responsibilities and define problem areas more clearly. If the problem or tasks are not known at the outset, he can review symptoms and attempt to focus on problems, goals, and needs.

2.   The leader can collect all pertinent data available, and he can encourage others to seek relevant information before the group begins its interactions.

3.   If the membership of the group has not been determined already, the leader can be influential in seeing that members are selected who not only have common interests in the task and homogeneous value systems (where this is desirable) but who also have knowledge and expertise that would help the group in the pursuit of its responsibilities.

4.   The leader should begin his preconference solicitation of participation by making all pertinent facts available to team members along with other thought-provoking stimulations. Before meetings occur, he should convey agendas to the

[22]See Filley, *ibid.*, pp. 13–21, for additional discussions of group leadership needs.
[23]Maier, *op. cit.*, pp. 241–247.

participants so their thoughts can be concentrated upon areas of importance. The agenda may be as tight or as loose as the situation demands.

5.   The leader can make necessary arrangements for the interactions to occur—adequate time for deliberation, a satisfactory (distraction-free) meeting place, and so forth.

These preliminary steps, if handled properly, can go far in making the team deliberations a success or a failure. Once the preliminaries are provided for, team members can be called together for activities to begin. When the group is assembled, there are several actions someone must initiate. The leader should see that this is achieved. The amount of his own personal involvement will be dependent upon what other members do or fail to do. Some of these activities include the following actions.

1.   Most group interactions will profit from a brief period of social introduction and development. Some time for establishing rapport, exchanging values, and allowing affiliative patterns to develop will be beneficial not only to the satisfaction of individual needs but also to the accomplishment of group goals. While the time devoted to this endeavor should be restricted, members will work more effectively if they can relate to each other more readily.

2.   Early in the interaction, the leader should make certain that all participants are aware of the team's responsibilities and objectives. Team members will want to know if their decision is to be final or if they are simply making a recommendation for someone else to consider. Any pertinent data that has not been communicated should be given out, and information possessed by the participating members should be solicited.

3.   The leader should encourage a participative discussion in which problems and their underlying causes are identified and defined. Once areas of difficulty are made known, alternative solutions should be established and reviewed. From the available alternatives, a course of action (decision) should be reached.

4.   While the interaction is taking place *and* following the group's performance, the leader should be concerned with seeing that participants are rewarded for their contributions and constructive involvement.

5.   Because participants in team efforts usually want to know how their decisions and efforts materialize, the leader should indicate that feedback will be coming to them whenever it becomes available. Support for the action of the team should also be sought.

After the group has completed its performance responsibilities, the results of its efforts should be communicated to the appropriate managerial authorities for action and implementation. Individuals in positions of team leadership should attempt to continue to provide feedback to team members concerning the effects and results achieved through the group's actions. If the team has monitoring and reevaluation responsibilities, the leader may need to guide the group in completing these duties. In Figure 19.2, these leadership duties are briefly summarized.

These leadership actions are in keeping with accepted problem-solving techniques, which state that problem areas should be defined, all pertinent data collected, reasonable alternatives stated, alternatives reviewed, and a course of action chosen. In achieving these decision-making steps, the group leader must give special attention to involving the individual members in the process. He must provide everyone with the opportunity to contribute input into the deliberations while not allowing individuals to dominate the discussions. Again, the role of the leader will vary with the qualifications and actions of the individual participants. In some situations, group leaders may be, of necessity, active and forceful, while at other times they may be only supportive and servants of group interactions.

Maier suggests that in most situations the leader may not have to be domineering, but instead his function can be to receive information, facilitate communication between individuals, relay messages, and integrate the incoming responses so that a single, unified response occurs.[24]

Operational Teams

While decision-making and problem-solving teams were selected for special attention in this chapter, many of the same characteristics, problems, advantages, and leadership responsibilities mentioned apply to operational teams as well. Operational teams have their own sets of objectives—to perform certain organizational functions (usually on a continuing basis). Role differentiation occurs among team members. In addition to the interaction roles mentioned in the discussion of decision-making teams, operational team members develop functional roles as a part of their organizational responsibilities. The receptionist takes phone calls for the other workers, schedules appointments, and routes mail in his or her role as the team public relations contact in an office group. The set-up worker in the assembly team regulates team production patterns as he brings together tools and equipment needed by other team members. Organizational responsibilities heavily influence individual team roles in operational groups.

Operational teams also have their own value systems, behavior norm patterns, power and influence sources, and degrees of cohesiveness. Some of these patterns

[24]*Ibid.*, p. 246.

FIGURE 19.2   Leadership responsibilities in the team decision-making and problem-solving session

BEFORE SESSION BEGINS	1. Review facts and symptoms; clarify problems, goals, and objectives 2. Encourage the collection of all pertinent data 3. Assist in the selection of team participants who have an interest in the problem (task) and are qualified to contribute 4. Stimulate thought, provide information, and submit an interaction agenda to participants if possible 5. Make the appropriate physical arrangements
DURING SESSION	1. Encourage a period of social introduction and development 2. Help participants to become aware of group responsibilities and of pertinent information related to the fulfillment of responsibilities 3. Lead the group in discussing problems, discovering and reviewing alternative solutions, and selecting the best available course of action 4. See that individuals are rewarded for positive contributions 5. Promise feedback and enlist the support of all participants
AFTER SESSION	1. Communicate the results of group performance to all appropriate individuals and see that ideas are acted upon 2. Lead in monitoring and evaluating the results of group efforts and continue to provide feedback to participants

are founded in formal organizational guidelines, while others originate through informal organizations.

Operational teams are usually designed as a part of the formal organization. Unlike many problem-solving teams, most operational teams have a formal hierarchy with authority relationships already defined. Members of the operational team include a superior (in some cases more than one) and several operational personnel. In a sense, most formal departments or work groups are operational teams. The workers (team members) exist to achieve a common purpose, and they can achieve their goals more effectively and efficiently by working together. Some operational groups must work more closely with each other because of the interrelated nature of their duties—assembly-line teams, research groups, etc.

Individuals who serve in leadership capacities with operational groups have an additional concern not present with temporary decision-making and problem-solving groups, because most operational teams work together on a more-or-less permanent basis. These teams do not interact for a couple of hours and then disperse for hours or days at a time. Instead, the individual members coexist with each other day after day. These more continuous relationships call for the developing of a deeper understanding, a higher level of tolerance, and a higher degree of lasting cooperation than is true of many temporary task forces. Leaders and followers alike in these groups have mutual obligations toward each other that are essential if the team is to be successful.

In the Managerial Grid concept discussed in the previous chapter, the team leader has unique responsibilities and must embrace a special philosophy if he is to create a cooperative, productive work environment. According to the Managerial Grid, the more effective team leader must be committed to the philosophy that good performance results from the integration of task and human requirements. Good interpersonal relationships and high performance are both attainable. Team members can attain their own goals and organizational goals simultaneously. Employees will support and attain organizational goals when they help to determine goals and procedures.[25]

The effective team leader, according to the Grid, is the one who gets high levels of performance by encouraging participation and involvement in the team membership. The leader encourages deliberation and debate by team members when group decisions are necessary. He wants individuals who are interested and

[25]Edwin W. Mumma, Martha S. Williams, and John L. Jackson, *Human Relations in Business: A Laboratory Manual for Instructors*, Austin, Texas: College of Business Administration, 1964, pp. 138–142.

capable to be involved in making decisions that influence their own destiny. The leader gives full, special attention to interpersonal problems that develop. He confronts conflict directly by bringing the parties who are in disagreement together to work through their problems (see Chapter 18 for a more complete discussion of this). He encourages members to be creative and innovative in structuring their goals and planning for future performance. Open, full communication of all pertinent data is encouraged. This approach to leadership fosters a feeling of responsibility, cooperation, and mutual benefit from operational team effort.

Summary

There is an increasing trend toward interrelated team task performance. Groups function regularly for purposes of decision making, problem solving, and operational performance. Groups that interact tend to develop many similar features—group objectives, role differentiations, value systems, behavior norms, levels of power and influence, and degrees of cohesiveness. Group interactions for decision making and problem solving have many positive effects. Often better decisions result, participants are more prone to support the group's decision, better interpersonal relations and personal satisfaction develop, and other positive dividends are felt. Group decision making is expensive and time consuming, tends toward compromise too often, is easily dominated, often results in competition rather than coordination, and can undermine managerial authority if not handled properly.

Groups usually function much more successfully when group participants have common goals to strive toward, when the consequences of their decision are clearly understood, when personal values and goals are compatible, when personal benefits may result from the common effort, when no one individual dominates the group's efforts, when the size of the group encourages good involvement, when the group's members are open-minded toward alternatives, and when other supportive conditions prevail.

Group leaders play important roles in the success of group interactions. The leaders must be particularly sensitive to the needs and abilities of the participants, to the objective of the group, and to potential problem areas that confront the work team. Where decision-making conferences are involved, leaders serve important functions in preparing for interactions and following up interactions as well as contributing to the interactions themselves.

Operational teams normally function together for more lengthy periods of time and require perceptive, dynamic managers who can guide the group's efforts toward personal and organizational attainment simultaneously.

Questions to consider after reading Chapter 19

1.   Why do many managers who are highly traditional in their philosophies oppose the use of teams for decision making and problem solving?

2.   Is it possible to go too far in the use of teams and groups for decisions, problem solving, and operational matters? Support your answer.

3.   What kinds of organizational decisions are groups best equipped to handle? What kinds of organizational decisions can individuals handle more effectively?

4.   What explanations can be given for the tendencies of groups to compromise or reach quick decisions without thoroughly considering issues pertinent to a problem?

5.   Evaluate a group effort you are acquainted with. Who played each of the content and process roles mentioned in the chapter?

6.   It was stated that individuals with a large amount of formal authority sometimes dominate team efforts. How can this problem be avoided?

7.   How is a spirit of cooperation developed among operational team members?

8.   What can be done about individual team members who fail to carry their share of a group's work responsibilities?

9.   Go back and analyze the case at the beginning of this chapter. How can the decision-making team and its leader improve their performance?

The following cases at the back of the book contain problems related to Chapter 19:

> Ben Stockton
>
> Mark Williams
>
> Stanley Lowell
>
> Edith Capp and Janet Turner
>
> Grace Lanham
>
> Richard Jameson

Additional readings

Argyris, Chris, *Management and Organizational Development,* New York: McGraw-Hill Book Company, 1971.

Bass, Bernard M., "Group Effectiveness," in Robert Cathcart and Larry Samovar, editors, *Small Group Communication,* Dubuque, Iowa: William C. Brown Company, 1970, pp. 7–18.

Blake, Robert R., and Jane S. Mouton, *Group Dynamics—Key to Decision Making,* Houston: Gulf Publishing Company, 1961.

Bonner, Hubert, *Group Dynamics—Principles and Applications,* New York: The Ronald Press Company, 1959.

Bucklow, Maxine, "A New Role for the Work Group," *Administrative Science Quarterly,* Volume 2, Number 1 (June 1966), pp. 59–78.

Cartwright, Dorwin, and Alvin D. Zander, editors, *Group Dynamics: Research and Theory,* Second Edition, Evanston, Illinois: Row, Peterson, and Company, 1960.

Crockett, William J., "Team Building—One Approach to Organizational Development," *Journal of Applied Behavioral Science,* Volume 6, Number 3 (July–August 1970), pp. 291–306.

Cummings, Larry L., George P. Huber, and Eugene Arendt, "Effects of Size and Spacial Arrangements on Group Decision Making," *The Academy of Management Journal,* Volume 17, Number 3 (September 1974), pp. 460–475.

Delbecq, Andre L., "World within the Span of Control," *Business Horizons,* Volume 11, Number 4 (August 1968), pp. 47–56.

House, Robert J., and John B. Miner, "Merging Management and Behavioral Theory: The Interaction between Group Size and Span of Control," *Administrative Science Quarterly,* Volume 14, Number 3 (September 1969), pp. 451–464.

Kelley, Harold H., and John W. Thibaut, "Experimental Studies of Group Problem Solving and Process," in Gardner Lindzey, editor, *Handbook of Social Psychology,* Volume 2, Cambridge, Massachusetts: Addison-Wesley Publishing Company, 1954, pp. 737–785.

Kemp, C. Grafton, *Perspectives on the Group Process,* Boston: Houghton Mifflin Company, 1964.

Lippitt, Ronald, and Dorwin Cartwright, "Group Dynamics and the Individual," *International Journal of Group Psychotherapy,* Volume 7, Number 1 (January 1957), pp. 86–102.

McGrath, Joseph E., and Irwin Altman, *Small Group Research,* New York: Holt, Rinehart and Winston, 1966.

Olmsted, Michael, *The Small Group,* New York: Random House, 1959.

Phillips, Gerald M., and Eugene C. Erickson, *Interpersonal Dynamics in the Small Group,* New York: Random House, 1970.

Schachter, Stanley, et al., "An Experimental Study of Cohesiveness and Productivity," *Human Relations,* Volume 4, Number 3 (1951), pp. 229–238.

Thomas, Edwin J., and Clinton F. Fink, "Effects of Group Size," *Psychological Bulletin,* Volume 6, Number 4 (1963), pp. 371–384.

Chapter 20

Managing Change and Innovation within the Organization

A case to consider before
reading chapter 20

CARLTON LANDRY–THE DIRECTOR WHO CAME FROM HEADQUARTERS

The Forestry, Game, and Fish Department was created many years ago in a western state to regulate and control the use of state-owned lands (mostly forests) and to provide for the development and control of fish and game within the state. The staff of the department includes a headquarters group composed of approximately forty people who live and work in the state capital. The headquarters personnel are primarily concerned with planning, policy making, and overall supervision of the programs of the department. In addition, the state is divided into three regions for direct enforcement and implementation of the department's policies. Each division is supervised by a regional director, an assistant regional director, and a number of functional supervisors. There are one to two hundred employees within each region with most of the personnel serving in capacities of wardens or technicians.

There tends to be very little movement from one region to another insofar as personnel are concerned. Most people spend their entire work careers in the same region in which they first began their employment. There are no agency regulations against interregional transfers, but most employees prefer to continue working in familiar areas rather than moving to geographically different locations. Transfers occur only occasionally and are usually initiated by the worker desiring the change.

The regional director for Region III is Marshall DeBrannon. He is reaching retirement age, and a successor for his position must be found. The assistant regional director, Thurman Jacobs, would normally be considered the prime candidate for the position, but he has asked for a transfer to the headquarters office. Jacobs' wife recently died, and his two married daughters and their families live in the capital city. As a result, Jacobs asked for the transfer so that he can be near his family. The transfer has been granted.

With Jacobs out of the running, the candidate from within Region III with the greatest opportunity to become director is Paul Ferriday. Ferriday has been with the Forestry Department for over twenty-five years, serving most of that time as a supervisor in the fish and game control section. Ferriday is considered a prime candidate for two reasons. First, seniority has always been one of the most influential bases for making promotion decisions, and Ferriday has more supervisory seniority than anyone else within the region. Second, Ferriday appears to want the job more than anyone else and has been campaigning informally to succeed DeBrannon since it was learned that Jacobs did not want the job.

Most employees of Region III are willing to concede that Ferriday is entitled to the job on the basis of his seniority even though they have had their own personal differences with him. Ferriday is considered by his fellow workers to be conscientious, ambitious, and diligent. However, many workers think he tends to overexert his authority to let people know that he is the boss in his section. He often uses negative disciplinary action on his subordinates for very minor mistakes or misdeeds. He also does not secure cooperation from his staff and his subordinates. In spite of his shortcomings, most of the people in Region III seem to prefer him as their next director, and many have written letters in support of his candidacy to the state-wide director of the department.

One month before DeBrannon's official retirement, it was announced that the new director of Region III would be Carlton Landry, a supervisor in the staff at the headquarters office. Landry, who is forty-two years of age, has been with the department for fifteen years. He began his work in one of the offices in Region I, where he worked for three years before his transfer to headquarters, where he has since served continuously. The people in Region III are only casually acquainted with Landry through his infrequent visits in his staff capacity with the headquarters office.

The personnel in Region III for the most part were informed of their new director's appointment through the weekly newsletter issued by the headquarters office. The article in the newsletter described the qualifications of Landry in glowing terms. Landry holds a master's degree in forest conservation and has participated in a number of interstate and national programs for the conservation and development of forestry resources. He is also described as a good leader and team player. The article states that he is an innovator and has pioneered in the use of computers and other technological innovations for the development of forestry management. The write-up stresses that this last quality in particular was considered in appointing him to be the director of Region III. The same article also states that Paul Ferriday has been appointed to serve as assistant director of the region.

Unlike most of his fellow workers, Ferriday was notified of his appointment as assistant director by a telephone call from the state director one day before the public announcement was made. He was bitterly disappointed that he was not given the appointment of the directorship. Even before Landry came to the division, Ferriday began to complain about the way he was being mistreated. He made comments to other workers in the division such as, "Look what they've done to me. After working twenty-five years in the division, they didn't promote me to head the division. Instead, they promoted some outsider. We've been cheated! That's the thanks you get for years of hard work."

When DeBrannon stepped down and Landry officially took over the reins, he found Ferriday and most other regional employees uncooperative and somewhat unfriendly toward him. He had hoped to get voluntary support from his subordinates, but it now appears that only firm directives will evoke any kind of meaningful response from the workers in the department. At the end of his first month in office, Landry is quite concerned about the resistance he is encountering in his new position.

Questions about the Carlton Landry case

1.   Perhaps the reasons seem obvious, but what specific factors have caused Ferriday's hostility and uncooperative attitude toward his new boss?

2.   Why have many of the other employees in Region III responded so indifferently to Landry as their superior? What values does he appear to threaten?

3.   In what ways are organizational objectives apparently different from the objectives of some employees?

4.   How much consideration should be given to seniority in making important decisions such as those involving promotions?

5.   How are the workings of an informal organization evidenced in this case?

6.   The changing of directors was poorly received by Ferriday and other workers. How might the decision to put Landry (or anyone else) in as director have gained better acceptance and support?

7.   Evaluate the way in which workers were informed of their new boss.

8.   What actions should Landry take as the new director in order to gain support and acceptance? What actions (if any) should be taken toward Ferriday?

Change within an organization calls for a modification of the relationships, responsibilities, or behavior of individuals who are members of the organization. While not every change may require a significant amount of adjustment, change is a daily event in most work environments. To illustrate the frequency and variety of changes that occur in work groups, consider the following change situations.

EMPLOYEE A is asked to cooperate with a newly formed decision-making team instead of acting independently in making decisions about the future of a specific product.

EMPLOYEE B (who is a supervisor) is asked to try a new method of counseling with his subordinates in an attempt to improve organizational communications.

EMPLOYEE C is instructed to accept a new job description that requires him to increase his responsibilities and increase the rate of his daily performance.

EMPLOYEE D is told that, beginning the following week, he is being transferred to a new department.

EMPLOYEES E, F, and G are informed that their present boss is being transferred and a new superior is being brought in.

The employees of a small branch store are informed that their store is being consolidated with the main store and that all personnel will be transferred to the larger store.

Each of these changes requires adjustments and modifications in habits, procedures, and working relationships. As can be seen from the examples, the types of organizational changes that may occur are numerous. Changes may occur in organizational objectives, in organizational authority relationships, in the methods of performance and operation, in the interpersonal relationships of personnel, in the work environment, and in other intraorganizational factors.[1]

Why Change Is Necessary

The intentions of *planned* change that has its beginning within the organization are usually positive; that is, changes are made with the purpose of achieving

[1]For a more complete discussion of the types of change that may occur within organizations see Edgar G. Williams, "Changing Systems and Behavior: People's Perspectives on Prospective Changes," *Business Horizons*, Volume 12, Number 4 (August 1969), p. 54, and Arnold S. Judson, *A Manager's Guide to Making Changes*, London: John Wiley and Sons, Limited, 1966, pp. 7-8.

something that might otherwise be unattainable. Organizations make changes in order to reach new frontiers or to progress more directly toward a set of planned goals and objectives. One author has suggested that managers should institute changes when necessary:

1. To improve the means for satisfying somebody's economic wants
2. To increase profitability
3. To promote human work for human beings
4. To contribute to individual satisfaction and social well-being[2]

If change is planned within the context of these purposes, customers, stockholders, employees, and the public at large potentially may benefit from the results of change. All groups may benefit simultaneously. However, there are times when change may appear to benefit one group at the expense of another.

There are also times when change is called for as a result of factors *external* to the organization. The external factors may be a result of economic, technological, legal, or social influences.

An illustration of an economic influence from an external source would be the supply-demand problem of energy resources first noted seriously in the United States in 1973. The energy shortage forced many automobile manufacturers to alter their production patterns to emphasize smaller, more economical vehicles while de-emphasizing larger automobiles with higher consumption levels. The shortage-related changes resulted in redesign of job routines for many engineers, production workers, salesmen, and mechanics. A number of employees lost their jobs because of the reduced demand for larger automobiles, and many other workers were transferred. Other economic influences that might be instrumental in creating organizational change could be the existence of competitive forces in the marketplace, other supply-demand factors, monetary inflationary-deflationary trends, the prosperity-depression cycle, and the status of international trade.

While technology was discussed in an earlier chapter, a quick example of the effects of technology as a causal factor for change might be the availability of computers to monitor and control production processes. This computerization potential has forced employees to revise their skills, has reorganized the socialization patterns within organizations, has displaced some workers, and has resulted in numerous additional modifications. Technology has created new products, processes, procedures, and personnel requirements. Of course, the decision of whether or not to take advantage of technological innovations may be in part

[2]Williams, *op. cit.*, p. 53.

a voluntary one, but the desire to be competitive and progressive may leave little choice to most organizations.

An illustration of an organizational change with a legal origin might be the Occupational Health and Safety Act passed in 1970, which required a more rigid utilization of safety equipment by employees in manufacturing industries. The new law required employees to wear or use safety equipment and to work with more caution for their own protection and the safety of fellow workers. This law forced a new set of rules and operational procedures upon employees and employers. Other legislation such as equal rights, training and manpower development, antitrust, and tax laws have also had a significant impact upon organizations and behavior within organizations.

An illustration of an organizational change with a social origin might be the revision of an organization's wage policy to provide equal wages for equal performance regardless of the sex of the individual. The women's liberation movement and other social change agents may cause organizations to adjust and adopt policies and procedures in keeping with the evolution of new social values. Some of the changes are translated into laws before they become organizational regulations. Changing social values can have an impact upon almost every phase of an organization's operations.

The Effects of Change
upon Employees

It has already been mentioned that most change that begins internally within the organization has positive, progressive intentions in mind and, in fact, may be necessary for the survival of the organization. Also mentioned was the fact that external forces may pressure for organizational changes to occur. Therefore, it seems inevitable, and often desirable, that changes should take place within organizations.

When change does occur, what is its impact upon the members (employees) of the organization? Change, of course, demands that adjustments and modifications must occur. Judson suggests that these adjustments must be made in three different ways for every employee—in behavioral patterns, in psychological outlook, and in social adaptation. Behavioral adjustments are defined as "the objective alterations that must be done by those doing the work to the physical routines by which the work is performed."[3] Behavioral patterns must be adapted

---

[3]Judson, *op. cit.,* p. 10.

to fit new regulations, procedures, and methods of operation. New patterns of communication, cooperation, and interaction may also be necessitated by change.

The ~~psychological effect~~ of change might be defined as the ~~attitude developed by the individual employee toward change based upon his own ability to cope with its demand~~s. If a worker perceives himself as capable of adjusting to change without an overwhelming degree of personal sacrifice *and* if he views the end result of the change as largely beneficial, he may psychologically adopt a positive attitude toward the change. If, on the other hand, the employee feels incapable and insecure and fails to see many personal benefits forthcoming from the change, his psychological attitude may be negative and in opposition to the change. Judson further suggests that there is a range of attitudes usually representative of workers reacting to change that runs from open, complete acceptance of change to active resistance to it (see Figure 20.1). These attitudes, of course, result in behavioral

FIGURE 20.1   ~~Range of attitudes toward change and resulting behavior~~

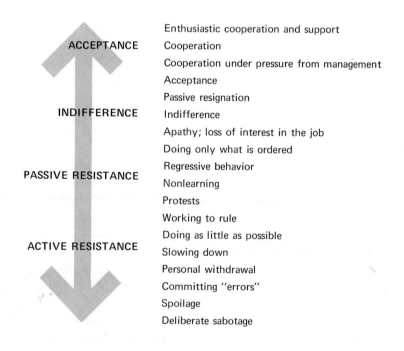

ACCEPTANCE	Enthusiastic cooperation and support
	Cooperation
	Cooperation under pressure from management
	Acceptance
	Passive resignation
INDIFFERENCE	Indifference
	Apathy; loss of interest in the job
	Doing only what is ordered
PASSIVE RESISTANCE	Regressive behavior
	Nonlearning
	Protests
	Working to rule
	Doing as little as possible
ACTIVE RESISTANCE	Slowing down
	Personal withdrawal
	Committing "errors"
	Spoilage
	Deliberate sabotage

Source: Arnold S. Judson, *A Manager's Guide to Making Changes*, London: John Wiley & Sons, Limited, 1966, p. 41.

patterns that may attempt to enhance the outcome of change, try to impede the progress of change, or take a neutral, more passive position toward it.

The social adaptations change calls for involve alterations in the relationships between individual employees, their superiors, their colleagues, their subordinates, the informal groups to which they may belong, and new employees with whom they may come in contact. Change often affects the degree of social interaction between individuals. Change may also have an impact upon roles, status, cohesiveness, and patterns of identification and acceptance between people. Change seldom leaves social patterns totally uninterrupted when it occurs.

In addition to the categories already described, change may also result in new reward systems for employees, new job freedoms and constraints, new authority structures, new action-time boundaries, and new working environments.

When Resistance to Change Occurs

If all changes, regardless of their origins, were accepted and implemented enthusiastically by the managers and other employees of every organization, it would be unnecessary to include this chapter. There would be no problems of concern to the manager involving the development of a strategy for change. However, change often results in resistance, and negative employee reactions may doom the success of programs of change if not handled properly.

Why do employees sometimes resist changes within their employing organization? A number of explanations have been given for the development of attitudes and behavior patterns of resistance to change. The tension-release theories of human behavior, such as the Freudian model described in Chapter 2, suggest that change causes tensions to develop within the individual. Until these tensions have been removed or properly directed, discomfort will continue to be present. Tensions may occur as a result of the pressures from uncertainty, insecurity, or from other concerns. The ultimate goal of tension-release models of behavior would be to avoid the tensions caused by change through erecting barriers to protect the individual from change or to minimize the time period between the creation of the tension (caused by change) and the restoration of the situation back to more "normal" circumstances (see Figure 20.2).

Behavior models based upon the concept of homeostasis (also discussed in Chapter 2) appear to coincide with the tension-release models in that a state of equilibrium is sought by the individual in matters that relate to the preservation of the self-image, biological factors, physical surroundings, social environment, and

FIGURE 20.2   Tensions and reactions to tensions caused by change

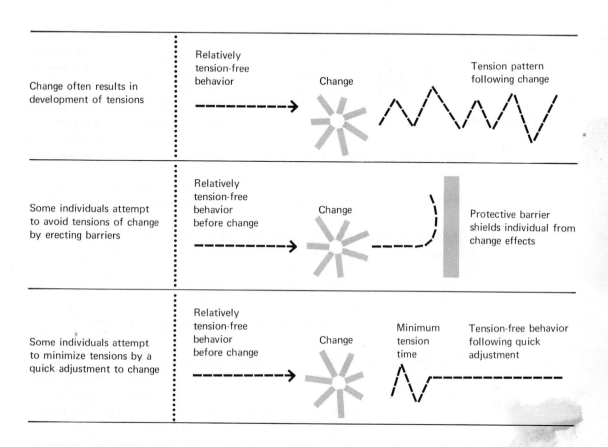

other conditions that are familar and comfortable. Changes that represent threats to the equilibrium attained by the individual will not be readily accepted. Employees anticipating change will also seek methods to stabilize the effects of change.

Success-failure models, such as the Combs-Snygg model presented in Chapter 2, suggest that the acceptance or rejection of change will be heavily dependent upon the previous experiences of the individual when change has occurred. If an individual has been called upon to adapt to change in the past and has successfully adapted and benefited from the adaptation, he will greet new requests for change with a spirit of optimism and openness (see Figure 20.3). However, when an individual encounters change, fails to cope with it successfully, and receives

FIGURE 20.3   Acceptance of change based upon previous success

penalties and few benefits, his receptivity to change in the future will be considerably diminished. He may openly resist change when he is confronted with it (Figure 20.4).

The success-failure explanation of reactions to change is in keeping with the McGregor Theory Y approach to change, which states that people become resistant or passive in their behavior depending upon their previous experiences (successes and failures) rather than as a result of inherent human characteristics of resistance.[4] Positive experiences tend to result in openness and optimism toward change; negative experiences result in skepticism and resistance.

Fear Theories of Change.   In capturing a thread of unity from all of the previously described theories of resistance to change and adding a new dimension as well, it is clear that a large part of employees' resistance to organizational change lies in the element of fear—employees are *afraid* that change will result in the loss of something important to them. The anticipated loss suggests that a vacuum will be created in an area of personal value. One author has suggested that most of these fears are not based upon fictional imaginations, but in fact usually result in real losses.

All change—promotion, transfer, demotion, reorganization, merger, retirement and most other managerial actions—produces loss. Despite the fact that change is necessary and is often for the better, the new always displaces the old, and, at some level of consciousness, individuals experience the threat of this displacement or loss.[5]

---

[4]Douglas McGregor, "The Human Side of Enterprise," *Management Review,* Volume 50, Number 11 (November 1957), p. 88.

[5]Harry Levinson, "Easing the Pain of Personal Loss," *Harvard Business Review,* Volume 50, Number 5 (September–October 1972), p. 81.

Levinson goes further to say that personal losses because of change usually result in at least four areas of deprivation: the loss of love, the loss of support, the loss of sensory input, and the loss of the capacity to act.[6]

The loss of love is defined as the decrease in the sense of being valued and revered by others—people fear the loss of social esteem and respect. The loss of support is another way of saying that the individual can no longer depend upon old relationships, affiliations, superiors, subordinates, methods of operation, skills, and theories that have carried him through past experiences. Instead, replacements must be found that can be trusted and utilized for support.

The loss of sensory input means that an individual (as a result of change) no longer gets the kind of information he needs to fulfill his responsibilities adequately, or he gets information he is not prepared to interpret (sense and utilize)—he has lost his skill or sensitivity to perceive and react to some of the things that communicate around him. The loss of the capacity to act is the loss of the ability to influence, control, or have power over individuals and things in one's environment. As a result, the individual becomes more of a victim and less of a master of his own fate.[7] Any of the losses may or may not be permanent, but a period of adjustment and adaptation is necessary just the same. As a result, change is resisted because these losses are anticipated and the demands of the period of adjustment are avoided whenever possible.

Another way of looking at fears that develop because of the demands of change is simply to consider change as a threat to the personal needs and ambitions of the employee. Change may undermine the fulfillment of any or all human needs—physical maintenance, security, affiliation, social esteem (recognition and reputation), competence, power, achievement, and hope. When a new superior comes

FIGURE 20.4   Rejection of change based upon previous failures

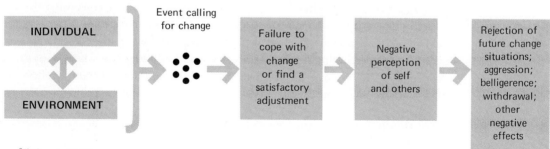

[6]*Ibid.*, pp. 81–83.
[7]*Loc. cit.*

on the scene, for example, an employee may immediately become concerned about the protection of his needs for security, social esteem, competence, and power. When a worker is asked to modify a job routine, he may instantly be afraid that he may suffer losses of security, affiliation, competency, power, and achievement as a direct result of the demands change presents. Some fears connected with the demands change may call for are only imaginary, while others are unmistakably real. ~~The important fact, however, is that change is often resisted because of the anticipated threatening effects employees believe will result~~.

The Initiator of Change.   Another important factor in the acceptance or rejection of change is the employee's attitude toward the individual(s) deciding that the change is necessary and introducing the change. If the change agent is respected, and the employee has confidence that he will act in the employee's best interests in deciding upon and implementing change, the employee may be more disposed to cooperate with the requested change. If, on the other hand, the employee lacks confidence and trust in the instigator of change, the resistance to change may be much greater.

The Necessity of Change.   The author believes that there is another dimension to resistance to change, and that is the *magnitude of the necessity for the change.* If an organizational change *must* take place for the survival of the organization itself, workers will accept and implement change with less reluctance. If economic developments or competitive factors, for example, demand that a modification in work precedures must occur for a processor to continue in business, the adjustment may be made without too much foot-dragging. Workers have been known to volunteer to work longer hours for less pay so that their employing organizations could continue operations.[8]

If organizational alterations appear unnecessary, employee receptivity is not likely to be very high. If a manager, for example, asks his subordinates to stop taking the customary coffee break without supplying a good reason for the requested change, the subordinates typically will be nonreceptive to the request and will resist at great length. In this situation, the workers believe that the underlying forces necessitating the change are not really important, and they treat them accordingly. The required adjustments appear unnecessary and nonbeneficial to them. If there is an important reason, however, acceptance may result quickly.

[8]See Dougles T. Hall and Roger Mansfield, "Organizational Stress and Individual Response to External Stress," *Administrative Science Quarterly,* Volume 16, Number 4 (December 1971), pp. 533–547, for an interesting analysis of employees' receptivity to change resulting from forces external to the organization.

Management's Goals for Change

It is undeniable that change affects the people who work together within an organization. As change is being considered, the management of the organization must determine what their goals and objectives are in bringing about modifications and alterations. Some worthy objectives for change within organizations from a management point of view may include the following.

Strive to make changes and alterations that are universally beneficial whenever this is possible. In other words, a change that results in gains for the organization, its owners, its employees, the public being served, and the community at large would be highly desirable.

Initiate changes in such a way that employees are receptive to them and will be willing to give them a fair trial. Strive for acceptance and support of changes on the part of those who will be responsible for their successful completion.

Anticipate the effects of change upon organizational members and, whenever possible, make adjustments for the impending effects. Attempt to minimize personal losses and fears that may develop as change approaches.

Managerial Guidelines

With the managerial objectives of beneficial achievement, employee acceptance and support, and minimization of fears and personal losses in mind, it is appropriate to consider tangible actions managers can take to accomplish these objectives. Several actions offer positive results.

In the first place, it would seem essential to investigate overall organizational objectives to be certain that objectives sincerely support the philosophy of providing positive benefits for the organization, its owners, its employees, its customers, and the community in general. Unless organizational objectives specify the pursuit of mutually beneficial results, changes may fall short of providing fulfillment for everyone.

If objectives are outlined in a collectively advantageous manner, changes and innovations can be considered on the basis of whether or not they will contribute effectively to the reasonable fulfillment of responsibilities for all publics (owners, employees, customers, and so forth). Changes that do not have the interests of all publics in mind may be dismissed *if the option lies within the organization.* Externally forced changes cannot, of course, be treated in the same manner. However, when external factors make change necessary, care can be observed to try to share the reasons for the change with those affected, and to channel the modifications so that they can be useful to everyone. Carrying this thesis one step further, it can be said that only changes that promise desirable results should be implemented except in most unusual circumstances. Changes that offer minimal opportunities for success and desirable results normally will not be given serious consideration because the adverse effects of adaptation to change will often overshadow the attainable merits.

A particularly helpful managerial action in considering change is to allow and encourage employee participation in deciding whether or not the change should be made and how it should be made if a decision to change is reached. Early participation by employees affected by the change accomplishes a number of purposes. Change decisions that have overwhelmingly negative consequences on employees can be identified and eliminated or revised. Participation helps the new method or procedure to become the brainchild of the workers themselves, and they will support the change when it occurs. Participation aids in the full disclosure of the causes of change, its consequences, and its implications so that uncertainties concerning it are avoided. Participation in the change process is one of the most useful tools of management for the successful introduction and implementation of change.[9]

When a change has officially been decided upon, early planning for the change and notification of those affected usually is helpful. An organization that knows a year in advance that it will be necessary to transfer several employees to new jobs can take the necessary steps to provide the reorientation, training, equipment realignment, social adjustment, and other actions necessary to be ready for the transfer when it finally happens. Employees appreciate advance notifications of changes that affect them personally so that they can begin to make physical, psychological, and social readjustments. Of course, not all changes give an advance warning signal, but when it is possible to sense a change in advance and communicate that fact, employees can prepare themselves more satisfactorily.

The adoption of organizational policies that provide protection and support for employees may add stability to the work force when faced with change. A wage policy that guarantees that employees cannot be forced by any changing circumstance to accept jobs with lower pay scales within the organization removes some of the economic threat of change. A policy of utilizing seniority as the basis

[9]John R. P. French, Jr. et al., "Employee Participation in a Program of Industrial Change," *Personnel*, Volume 35, Number 3 (November–December 1958), pp. 16-29. See also Hall and Mansfield, *op. cit.*, pp. 533-547, and Kenneth C. Scheflen, Edward E. Lawler, and J. Richard Hackman, "Long-Term Impact of Employee Participation in the Development of Pay Incentive Plans: A Field Experiment Revisited," *Journal of Applied Psychology*, Volume 55, Number 3 (June 1971), pp. 182-186, for other discussions of the importance of participation in change.

for making decisions on layoffs, position bidding and bumping, and in other important areas gives security to the more established employees. A policy of providing adequate severance pay when an employee in good standing must be released from the organization also cushions economic fears. Informal policies of preserving status and upgrading positions when change occurs encourage workers to be more receptive to future change. A policy of retraining employees whose skills have become obsolete lends encouragement when technology forces change. Most policies that provide protection from fears of loss will improve attitudes toward impending changes.

Many steps can be taken to overcome or soften fears of loss of social rapport and affiliation. Whole groups of employees often are allowed to adjust to a change together so that social realignment will be as limited as is possible. Workers may be allowed to interact with future co-workers for long periods of time in advance of their actual working together so that affiliations can be made and fears overcome before the situation becomes binding.

Judson suggests that an effective technique for overcoming fears is the use of the **tentative approach.** This technique is basically the establishment of a trial period of change in which employees are asked to work under the new requirements or conditions without actually accepting the change and committing themselves to abide by its new demands. Judson suggests several advantages to the use of the tentative, trial approach.

1. Those involved are able to test their reactions to the new situation before committing themselves irrevocably.

2. Those involved are able to acquire more facts on which to base their attitudes and behavior toward the change.

3. Those involved with strong preconceptions are in a better position to regard the change with greater objectivity. Consequently, they could review their preconceptions and perhaps modify some of them.

4. Those involved are less likely to regard the change as a threat.

5. Management is better able to evaluate the method of change and make any necessary modifications before carrying it out more fully.[10]

The tentative approach has a way of defusing potentially explosive rejection of change. Most individuals approaching a change on this basis discover that they are capable of the adjustment; often they discover that the consequences are better than anticipated. There are, of course, some instances when a change is rejected after a trial, and management must be prepared to deal with that eventuality.

[10]Judson, *op. cit.,* p. 118.

As was mentioned earlier, the individual(s) selected to introduce change and to enlist employee cooperation will also have an effect upon the level of worker acceptance. Selection of individuals as change agents who are respected and who have the confidence of other workers, improves the probabilities of successful reactions and adjustments to change.

When the employees of an organization lose something as a result of change that cannot be prevented (loss of wages, loss of desirable social climate, loss of freedom, and so forth), an effort can be made to substitute something else for the loss. The salesman who is transferred from a prime sales territory to one with less potential may receive an upward adjustment in his commission ratio. The employee who is placed in an isolated, confining work position may be given shorter work hours or more coffee breaks to offset the restrictive environment. The manager who gives up his private office to another manager may receive other status symbols (preferred parking space, a fancy job title, etc.) to partially offset the losses he has sustained. It is true that not every loss can be compensated for, but efforts to do so often provide fruitful results.

Management should not overlook other sources of assistance in implementing change and getting its acceptance. Labor unions, for example, frequently work with managers in organizations to implement change when the change promises benefits to employees. Informal work groups within the formal organization may encourage members to give favorable responses to change when the benefits of change are communicated and understood. Influential individuals both within and outside organizations may be persuasive in leading individuals to respond favorably to change. Government agencies sometimes provide financial and advisory assistance in implementing organizational change.

This list of actions to enhance the positive side of organizational change and to minimize the negative consequences of change is by no means comprehensive. The list does show, however, that many negative reactions to change can be prevented or adjusted to if careful consideration is given to the benefits and negative consequences of change and care and planning are included in its implementation. To summarize the suggested techniques, change can be facilitated by:

1. Defining organizational objectives that provide benefits for all parties related to the organization—the owners, employees, customers, and citizens of the community at large

2. Choosing to make changes (whenever possible) that optimize the mutual benefits for all of these publics

3. Allowing and encouraging participation by the employees to be affected by change in the decision-making and implementation stages of change

4.   Utilizing advance planning, notification, and communication of change and its anticipated effects

5.   Adopting organizational policies that provide maximum amounts of encouragement and support for organizational members when change occurs

6.   Considering a number of methods of facilitating the social adaptation demanded by change and utilizing the appropriate methods

7.   Utilizing the tentative trial technique whenever feasible

8.   Carefully selecting respected, valued individuals to serve as change agents (introducers of change)

9.   Compensating or substituting for personal losses that are unavoidable

Some Anecdotes Involving Change

Closing a Branch Office.   The author remembers a report issued a number of years ago concerning the closing of a branch office of an engineering consulting firm that was handled in a superb fashion. The branch office was located hundreds of miles away from headquarters. The reason for the closure has been forgotten by this author, but a decision was made to close the branch more than a year in advance of the planned closing date. There were no positions open at the headquarters office or in other branch offices of the organization; so the change in effect meant that most of the personnel at the office being phased out would be out of a job when the shutdown time came.

As soon as the decision became final, the manager of the branch office was authorized to tell the personnel what was about to happen, why it was occurring, and when it would take place. (The personnel of the staff included mostly engineers, technicians, and secretarial personnel.) The manager extended a number of assurances to the staff. He told them that the company would initiate a placement service whereby employees' data sheets would be distributed to prospective employers of the employees' choice. An office would be opened within the branch office to allow recruiting representatives of other organizations to interview the employees concerning new jobs. Other placement assistance would be given as needed. Appropriate severance pay would be provided for any employees who had not secured a job (if they were actively seeking one).

When the time came to close the office, every employee had received at least three offers from other employers, and most employees were able to move to higher-paying, attractive positions. Not only were the displaced employees grateful for the interest and support of their old employer, but employees of the firm who worked at headquarters or in other branches had a greater respect for their employer and a higher level of security in the knowledge that their organization was sincerely concerned about the welfare of its employees.

A New Chief Executive Takes Office.   In another situation of change, an organization selected a new chief executive to take over the leadership of the organization following the death of the former head, who had served in that capacity for over thirty years. The new leader came from outside the organization and was uneasy about being accepted and given an opportunity to exercise influence in directing the organization. He feared that sentiment for the previous executive and his policies might stifle his effectiveness.

When the new chief took over his responsibilities, he convened the supervisory personnel of the organization in a series of meetings to gather information from them. In the first meeting, he had the supervisors fill out a questionaire concerning what directions they would like to see their organization go and what attributes they would prefer to see exhibited by their chief executive. The new leader then led the group in a period of listing and discussing all of the good things they could identify about the organization—all of its strengths. The supervisors gave their thoughts and the chief executive gave his.

At the next session, the executive asked the supervisors to name and discuss all of the bad points or weaknesses of the organization they could think of. Again, the new leader gave his thoughts on weaknesses. Together, they discussed why these weaknesses existed.

In another meeting, the leader asked his supervisory personnel to brainstorm and discuss with him future courses of action the organization should take. The discussion was an open one without domination from any one individual. Through this series of three meetings, a great amount of communication and understanding began to develop between the new executive and his subordinates. Instead of resisting the ideas and suggestions of their new boss, the employees gave him an opportunity to lead them. The period of transition from the old executive to the new one turned out to be a relatively smooth one.

Summary

From an organizational point of view, change calls for modifications in the attitudes and behavior of the organization's members. Change frequently results from internal plans to improve the performance of the organization and to benefit organizational members and others. Change also may be a result of external influences, including economic, technological, and social factors.

Employees in organizations where changes occur are called upon to make several behavioral, psycho-logical, and social adaptations. Worker reactions to these demands range from hearty acceptance to active resistance. The tension-release, homeostasis, and success-failure theories discussed first in Chapter 2 provide explanations for the resistance and rejection of change that frequently occur. Fear often prevails when change is introduced. The individuals who serve as change agents also play a part in getting acceptance or rejection of change. The nature of change (whether it is really necessary or only a luxury) may also influence the reactions organizational members exhibit toward change.

It should be the purpose of every manager to maximize the positive effects of change and to minimize the negative consequences upon organizational members. If the guidelines suggested in this chapter are implemented, the results of change normally will be beneficial to employees and to the organization simultaneously.

Questions to consider after reading Chapter 20

1.   Why is it that so often change seems to benefit one individual or group at the expense of another?

2.   Evaluate the statement that change that seems unavoidable is normally accepted more readily than change made when options are available. Is this statement valid?

3.   Which types of adjustments are made most easily—the behavioral, the psychological, or the social?

4.   Consider your own observations of change. Can you cite situations where change was handled adequately because individuals had successful previous experiences with change? Can you also recall instances where individuals have rejected change because of previous bad experiences?

5.   "Changes should never be made unless there is a reasonable certainty that benefits will definitely result." Is this statement valid? Why or why not?

6.   What problems exist with giving workers advance notice of impending changes?

7.   "Preventive measures are always better than actions taken after problems develop." What is the meaning of this statement? Does it apply to the management of change?

8.   Is it possible to forecast the effects of change? Please explain.

9.   Please go back to the case at the beginning of the chapter and analyze it according to the concepts presented in the chapter.

The following cases at the back of the book contain problems related to Chapter 20:

Ben Stockton

Mark Williams

Stanley Lowell

Edith Capp and Janet Turner

Bentley Cantrell

Kurt Browning

Bill Caden

Walt Gladberry

Additional readings

Dalton, Gene W., "Influence and Organizational Change, " in David A. Kolb, Irwin M. Rubin, and James M. McIntyre, editors, *Organizational Psychology: A Book of Readings,* Second Edition, Englewood Cliffs, New Jersey: Prentice-Hall Inc., 1974, pp. 401–424.

Glueck, William F., "Organization Change in Business and Government," *Academy of Management Journal,* Volume 12, Number 4 (December 1969), pp. 439-449.

Greenfield, T. Barr, "Organizations as Social Inventions: Rethinking Assumptions about Change," *Journal of Applied Behavioral Science,* Volume 9, Number 5 (September–October 1973), pp. 551–574.

Greiner, Larry E., "Patterns of Organizational Change," *Harvard Business Review,* Volume 45, Number 3 (May–June 1967), pp. 119–122.

Lake, Dale G., "Concepts of Change and Innovation in 1966," *Journal of Applied Behavioral Science,* Volume 4, Number 1 (January, February, March 1968), pp. 3–24.

Lawrence, Paul R., "How to Deal with Resistance to Change," *Harvard Business Review,* Volume 47, Number 1 (January 1969), p. 4ff.

Lewin, Kurt, "Group Decision and Social," in T. M. Newcomb and E. L. Hartley, editors, *Readings in Social Psychology,* New York: Holt, Rinehart and Winston, 1958.

Ronken, Harriet O., and Paul R. Lawrence, *Administering Change: A Case Study of Human Relations in the Factory,* Boston: Harvard University Press, 1952.

Seashore, Stanley E., and David G. Bowers, *Changing the Structure and Functioning of an Organization,* Ann Arbor: University of Michigan, Survey Research Center Monograph Number 33, 1963.

Trumbo, Don A., "Individual and Group Correlates of Attitudes toward Work-Related Change, *Journal of Applied Psychology,* Volume 45, Number 5 (October 1961), pp. 338–344.

Wilson, J. Q., "Innovation in Organization: Notes toward a Theory," in J. D. Thompson, editor, *Approaches to Organizational Design,* Pittsburgh: University of Pittsburgh Press, 1966, pp. 195–218.

Chapter 21

Training and Organizational Development

A case to consider before reading chapter 21

GARY HARBIN AND HIS COLLEGE-TRAINED FOREMEN

A professor of management has been employed by an automobile assembly plant to help instigate a program of training in human relations that it is hoped will result in improved attitudes, better interpersonal relations, and a higher level of performance within the plant. One of the professor's first tasks is to interview the divisional and departmental supervisors in the plant to sample their opinions of the training needs of the foremen and other employees who have supervisory responsibilities.

One of the professor's interviews is with an older departmental supervisor, Gary Harbin, who is in charge of one phase of the car body assembly. The supervisor came up through the ranks, and his formal education includes a high school diploma, but nothing beyond that. In the early part of the conversation between the two men, the supervisor expresses his dissatisfaction with the company's rather new policy of hiring college graduates for jobs as foremen instead of bringing workers up from the ranks.

Harbin feels that the young college graduates who are hired to become foremen don't know how to handle people very well. He thinks that the company's three-month training program (before assignment as a foreman) adequately prepares the college graduate for the technical aspects of job performance but does little to provide the necessary supervisory training.

The three-month training program is primarily an indoctrination program in which the college graduate becomes familiar with the technical aspects of operations and company policies and regulations. Each college graduate spends one month becoming acquainted with the operational aspects of the plant. He then is assigned to a foreman for two months as his assistant. Following this apprenticeship period, the new, college-trained employee is assigned to a job as a foreman in one of the departments in the plant. He reports directly to the departmental supervisor. Normally, each foreman has from ten to twenty-five subordinates.

Additional dialogue between the professor and the older departmental supervisor (Harbin) is shown below.

PROFESSOR: You say you're not pleased with the way most of the college graduates your company is hiring go about handling people. Can you give one illustration of what you consider the problem?

HARBIN: Sure. The main problem with these young, "educated" supervisors is the fact that they all think they know everything. They boss the workers around and tell them every move that they should make. If the truth is known, some of the operators bossed by these young foremen know more about their work than these college guys do. And another thing, you can't tell these young fellows a thing. You try to point their mistakes out to them, and they get mad and huff around for days. Most of them are just a bunch of prima donnas.

PROFESSOR: Describe for me how you would like your young, educated supervisors to perform.

HARBIN: Well, that's a difficult question to answer. I haven't given much thought to how they should act because I've had to spend so much time trying to correct their mistakes. I guess you could say that I would like for them to be better listeners—both to me and to their subordinates. They need to be able to receive instructions and information more readily than they now do. And they need to be more considerate of their subordinates and superiors. They don't seem to care about anyone but themselves.

              I would also like to see them be a little more humble about the knowledge and educational achievement. They go around wearing their college diploma on their sleeves, and that just doesn't work in a place like this where a lot of the people don't even have high school diplomas.

              Also, I would like for them to learn how to motivate their subordinates to do their work more conscientiously. In a plant like this, we often have problems with workers being careless and indifferent to their jobs. I wish these young fellows could inspire their workers to take their jobs more seriously.

PROFESSOR: What do you feel are the keys to better motivation and more efficient performance?

HARBIN: Well, first every worker has to know his job—what he's expected to do and how to do it. I also think you have to pay a worker well to keep him motivated. I think you have to give each worker verbal encouragement as he progresses in his job. You have to be careful not to nag him too much. As he develops his knowledge and skills, you should leave him alone and let him do his job without a lot of interference.

PROFESSOR: What do you do to help your supervisors become more skilled in handling people the way you would like for them to?

HARBIN: By the time I get them, most of them know the technical aspects of automobile assembly; so I spend a couple of hours with them the first day they are in my department laying down the law on what I expect them to do. I tell them that I'll be watching them and will be making suggestions and giving them advice whenever I see it is necessary.

                 I give them a little pamphlet that I found in some trade journal entitled "How To Supervise Effectively." I give them a few days to read the booklet, then we talk over the contents together.

                 Most of the remainder of my help comes in day-to-day suggestions and criticisms. I coach and correct each of them a great deal.

PROFESSOR: Do you give them regular feedback on their performance?

HARBIN: You bet I do. For example, just this morning I had to call two new foremen in and chew them out good for the slipshod way they were supervising. You can bet they won't forget what I told them.

Questions about the Gary Harbin case

1.   Why is Gary Harbin opposed to the policy of hiring college graduates and training them to become foremen? Are these reasonable, valid objections?

2.   What training techniques is the departmental supervisor currently using on the new, "educated" foremen in his department? Evaluate these techniques.

3.   What objectives does Harbin have in mind for the training program he has devised for his new foremen? Are these sound supervisory training objectives? What other objectives would be appropriate?

4.   Why may it be difficult to improve the human relations actions of the foremen under the existing conditions?

5.   Evaluate the motivational philosophy Harbin now adheres to. What parts of it are acceptable, and which may be questionable?

6.   Can workers, such as these young foremen, really be trained in a way that will improve their human relations attitudes and abilities?

7.   What conclusions and recommendations should the professor be able to advance to the company on the basis of this one interview?

8.   What training technique might be employed for better human relations actions that is not now being used?

Most managers find themselves faced with the need not only to be good practitioners of sound interpersonal relations techniques (such as those described in earlier chapters in this book) but also to help others become good practitioners. Managers, regardless of their level in the organizational hierarchy, would prefer for their subordinates to communicate effectively, to work well as team members, to respect the needs and wishes of others, and to be otherwise effective in their interpersonal relations. Managers who are formal superiors of other managers (a middle-level manager over a first-line supervisor, for example) desire competency from their subordinate supervisors in the application of essential leadership, motivation, communication, disciplining, group dynamics, counseling, and problem-solving techniques (to name but a few areas).

As organizations have grown in size, they have become more complex in functional operations and often have become increasingly impersonal. The importance of good interpersonal relations has increased. As the processes of decision making and performance have become group-oriented in many organizations, sound interaction between individuals and groups has become imperative. While some workers (both managers and nonmanagers) are already reasonably capable of interacting well with their superiors, peers, and subordinates, not everyone is equally well prepared. Most workers have a need for improvement in the skills, attitudes, and behavior they exhibit in relating to others. In fact, almost every organizational member can benefit from well-designed training in interpersonal relations.

Training of any kind should have as its objective the redirection or improvement of behavior so that the performance of the trainee becomes more useful and productive for himself and for the organization of which he is a part. Training normally concentrates on the improvement of either operative skills (the basic skills related to the successful completion of a task), interpersonal skills (how to relate satisfactorily to others), decision-making skills (how to arrive at the most satisfactory courses of action), or a combination of these. The primary concern of our discussions now is for the improvement of interpersonal skills, although many of the points discussed may have equal applicability to the development of the other types of skills.

Analysis of Training Needs

Effective training is tied to the achievement of predetermined goals.[1] Certain types of performance are necessary to help the organization reach its objectives, and training assists by providing organizational members with the tools to get the

[1]George S. Odiorne, *Training by Objectives*, New York: The Macmillan Company, 1970, pp. 98–106.

job done. It has been suggested that the determination of the training needs in an organization must contain three types of analyses—organizational analysis, operations analysis, and man analysis.[2] ~~Organizational analysis~~ centers primarily upon the ~~determination of the organization's goal~~s, its resources, and the allocation of the resources as they relate to organizational goals. The analysis of organizational objectives establishes the framework in which training needs can be defined more clearly. ~~Operations analysis~~ "focuses on the ~~task or job regardless of the employee performing the job.~~"[3] This analysis includes the determination of what the worker must do—the specific behavior required—if the job is to be performed effectively. The concentration here is upon the task at hand and not on the individual performing the task.

Once the required behavior for each job becomes known, the man analysis can occur. ~~Man analysis~~ reviews the knowledge, attitudes, and skills of the incumbent in each position and determines what knowledge, attitudes, or skills he must acquire and what alterations in his behavior he must make if he is to contribute satisfactorily to the attainment of organizational objectives.[4] In effect, the analysis process raises three questions:

1.   Where is the organization going (in terms of ~~objectives~~)?

2.   What behavior (~~performance~~) is necessary from each job incumbent if he is to contribute effectively to the achievement of the organization's objectives?

3.   Is each incumbent adequately prepared in knowledge, attitudes, and skills to perform his role effectively? If he is not, what training will be necessary for him to be adequately prepared?

The description of training needs on the basis of the operations analysis reveals the desirable abilities and competencies each managerial incumbent must have in terms of leadership, motivation, communication, group dynamics, conflict resolution, change implementation, and the many other attributes reviewed earlier, in addition to a number of technical and decision-making skills. These needs are discovered not only by analyzing the activities involved in the job, but also by creatively projecting optimum performance requirements. These requirements may be discovered by a review of the literature to discern what areas may have the potential for improvement.[5] A review of the concepts presented in earlier

[2]William McGehee and Paul W. Thayer, *Training in Business and Industry,* New York: John Wiley & Sons, Inc., 1961, pp. 25–26.

[3]*Ibid.,* p. 26.

[4]*Loc. cit.*

[5]*Ibid.,* p. 70.

FIGURE 21.1   Sequence for training and reinforcement

Identification of training needs (through organizational, operations, and man analysis) → Selection of training methods → Creation of desire to train and to change behavior → Application of training techniques → Performance → Rewards and feedback

chapters of this book, for example, might be helpful in the operations analysis phase of some training programs.

An analysis of the past performance records of the prospective trainee may provide many clues to specific interpersonal skills that may need development. In addition, tests of these skills through the handling of posed cases, incidents, and direct questioning may also reveal training needs.[6] Observation by his superiors and self-analysis by the trainee may identify other training needs. Armed with the knowledge of each trainee's specific training needs, programs of improvement can be developed that are tailored to these unique needs. The training program then follows a general sequence aimed at supplying the trainee with the opportunity to develop his skills and abilities. This sequence is shown in Figure 21.1.

After training needs have been identified, training methods (lectures, group conferences, case analysis, etc.) are chosen according to their ability to supply the needed training. The trainee is then stimulated to undertake the appropriate training. If the trainee is willing to be trained, he participates in the training program. Through the training program, new knowledge and skills are acquired. If the training program is carried to its proper completion, the trainee is rewarded for his performance in keeping with his post-training behavior. The trainee also receives detailed feedback on the level of his performance and the continuing adjustments his performance may require. The support and guidance given after the formal training program has been completed are extremely vital to the continued usage by the trainee of newly acquired abilities.

Creating a Desire for Training

In reviewing the various phases of training, the selection and application of training methods will be temporarily bypassed so that we can concentrate on the creation of the desire for training. It has been suggested that since training is primarily a matter of changing behavior, there are three ways of interesting people in changing their behavior.

[6]*Ibid.,* p. 125.

1. People will respond to programs involving changed behavior if they ~~believe~~ that the ~~resulting modification is in their own interest~~, that they will ~~receive personal benefits~~ as a result of their new behavior.

2. Trainees will change their behavior if they ~~become aware of better ways of performing~~ (more productive or otherwise more satisfactory ways) and ~~gain experience~~ in the new pattern of behavior so that it becomes their normal manner of operation.

3. A trainee may change his behavior in compliance with the forced demands of his superiors or others with more power than the trainee possesses. In this situation, the change is a result of demands for conformity rather than the acknowledgement of a better or personally more gratifying way of performing.[7]

From these general strategies of change have come several principles or concepts of training. For example, it has been stated that:

1. Trainees in work organizations tend to be most responsive to training programs when they feel the need to learn. In other words, the trainee will be more eager to learn if training promises answers to problems or needs he has as an employee. The individual who perceives training as the solution to problems will be more willing to enter into a training program than will the individual who is satisfied with (and complacent about) his present performance abilities.[8]

2. ~~Learning~~ is ~~more effective when there is reinforcement~~ in the form of rewards and punishments.[9]

3. In the long run, ~~rewards tend to be more effective for changing behavio~~r and increasing one's learning ~~than are punishments~~.[10]

4. ~~Rewar~~ds for the application of learned behavior are ~~most useful when they quickly follow~~ the ~~desired performance~~.[11]

[7]Robert Chin and Kenneth D. Benne, "General Strategies for Effecting Changes in Human System," in Warren G. Bennis, Kenneth D. Benne, and Robert Chin, *The Planning of Change*, Second Edition, New York: Holt, Rinehart and Winston, 1969, pp. 32–59, call these strategies of changing behavior the empirical-rational, the normative-reeducative, and the power-coercive strategies for change.

[8]See Bernard M. Bass and James A. Vaughn, *Training in Industry: The Management of Learning*, Belmont, California: Wadsworth Publishing Company, Incorporated, 1966, p. 56, for a more complete discussion of this.

[9]Burrhust F. Skinner, *The Behavior of Organisms*, New York: D. Appleton Century Company, Incorporated, 1938, pp. 228–231.

[10]Richard B. Bugelski, *The Psychology of Learning*, New York: Holt and Company, Incorporated, 1956, pp. 250–255, or Harold J. Leavitt, *Managerial Psychology*, Chicago: University of Chicago Press, 1958, pp. 167–170.

[11]Douglas H. Fryer, Mortimer R. Feinberg, and Sheldon S. Zalkind, *Developing People in Industry*, New York: Harper and Brothers, 1956, p. 95, and Murray Sidman, "Operant Techniques," in Arthur J. Bachrach, editor, *Experimental Foundations of Clinical Psychology*, New York: Basic Books, Incorporated, 1962, pp. 173–174.

5.   The ~~larger the reward for good performance~~ following the implementation of
learned behavior, the ~~greater will be the reinforcement~~ (strengthening) of the new
behavior.[12]

6.   ~~Negative reinforcement~~ through the ~~application of penalti~~es and ~~criticism may
have a disruptive effect upon the learning experience~~ of the trainee in some cases.
Workers who already feel a lack of competence or self-confidence may show less
improvement in their performance—for example, if they receive heavy criticism
or punishment following inadequate performance.[13] In general, negative reinforcement tends to be less predictable in its effects than positive reinforcement.

7.   ~~Training~~ that requests the trainee to make ~~changes in his values, attitudes, and
social beliefs~~ (as interpersonal skill training tends to do) usually achieves better
results if the ~~trainee is encouraged to participate, discuss, and discover new, desirable behavior norms~~. Involvement is usually an extremely important factor in the
successful completion of behavioral training programs.[14]

8.   The development of ~~new behavior norms and skills is facilitated through
practice and repetiti~~on.

These training concepts tend to support the assumptions stated earlier relating
to changes in behavior. Trainees are attracted to rewards and other forms of
positive reinforcement because they are considered beneficial. As was stated
many years ago, individuals do the things that give pleasure and avoid things
that give pain. After an action, if a satisfier is received, the action will be repeated.
If no satisfaction is received, the action will not be repeated.[15] Also, the more
we perform (or practice) an action in a specific way, the more it becomes a natural
behavior pattern or norm for us. We may also be forced into the performance of
prescribed actions through penalties and the fear of punishments, but this method
of training (and changing behavior) is less predictable than reward systems and
normative reeducation techniques.

Another ~~very important facet of training is providing the trainee with feedback
on the progress he is making~~ in utilizing the training he has received. While the
receiving of rewards and penalties may be a form of feedback, the trainee will
benefit from more specific information about strengths and weaknesses in his
performance. Only with specific, tangible feedback can the trainee adjust his
performance to fit the behavioral needs of his job. As Miller has stated:

[12]Clark Hull, *Principles of Behavior,* New York: Appleton-Century-Crofts, 1963, pp. 131–133.
[13]Emanual Kay, John R. P. French, and Herbert H. Meyer, *A Study of the Performance Appraisal
Interview,* Behavioral Research Service, New York, General Electric Company, 1962.
[14]Bass and Vaughn, *op. cit.* p. 54.
[15]See Edward L. Thorndike, *Human Learning,* New York: The Century Company, 1931, for a
discussion of several pertinent points.

. . . if a person with the required abilities is to improve his performance, he must (1) know what aspect of his performance is not up to par, (2) know precisely what corrective actions he must take to improve his performance. . . .[16]

Knowledge of the results of performance (feedback) is one of the most important sources of reinforcement for the trainee.[17] Studies have shown feedback to be especially important when training goals are designed to develop social interaction skills. Immediate, regular feedback, for example, has been proved to result in a higher level of self-insight and improved problem-solving abilities in leadership training programs.[18]

Learning Theory and Training Programs

In addition to the guidelines already presented in this chapter, other generalizations concerning the optimum conditions for the operation of training programs have been identified. Several of these generalizations are presented below with some brief explanatory comments.

1. It is important that the training program be planned in a logical manner so that each succeeding step builds upon the previous one the probability of success increases because the trainee encounters the steps in sequence. The best course for changing behavior is to bring about the transition through a progression of small, orderly steps.[19]

2. The previous experience of the individual trainee affects his further learning experiences. New material is related to his previous knowledge. New behavior is formulated using existing foundations as a basis.[20]

3. Training in one activity can be transferred to another if there are similar components and principles. Once a general principle has been learned, all problems

[16]L. Miller, *The Use of Knowledge of Results in Improving the Performance of Hourly Operators*, New York: Behavioral Research Service, General Electric Company, 1965, as quoted by Bass and Vaughn, *op. cit.*, p. 25.

[17]Bass and Vaughn, op. cit., p. 25.

[18]Ewart E. Smith and Stanford S. Knight, "Effects of Feedback on Insight and Problem Solving Efficiency in Training Groups," *Journal of Applied Psychology*, Volume 43, Number 3 (June 1959), pp. 209–211.

[19]Bass and Vaughn, *op. cit.*, p. 62, and Odiorne, *op. cit.*, p. 263.

[20]John H. Proctor and William M. Thornton, *Training: A Handbook for Line Managers*, New York: American Management Association, 1961, p. 45.

of a given class can be solved as they are presented. A manager trained in the techniques of contingency leadership theory, for example, may be capable of analyzing a wide variety of motivational problems and developing solutions to them on the basis of his knowledge of a few basic principles.[21]

4.   Not everyone agrees on this next point, but many training experts feel that training that involves understanding complex problems and discovering new alternative solutions can be achieved best when the environment is relaxed and free of anxiety and the trainees are not under any immediate pressure to produce.[22] This may be interpreted to suggest that training in interpersonal relations skills should be begun in off-the-job, informal settings rather than while the trainee is still on the job trying to be productive.

5.   Learning is accomplished through impressions received and interpreted by the senses. Learning new skills is accomplished through seeing, hearing, and doing things.[23] The use of a variety of training methods that appeal to a number of senses and that provide the opportunity for personal experience provides an advantage over single-appeal techniques.

6.   The differences in abilities, backgrounds, experiences, readiness to learn, and a number of additional factors cause individual trainees to acquire new knowledge, skills, and attitudes at differing rates of speed. Training programs necessarily must be adapted to the training speeds of the separate trainees.

7.   While no universal explanation can be provided for why it is true, many types of learning are characterized by **learning curves** that contain upward spurts (breakthroughs in the acquisition of knowledge and skills) followed by plateaus when little or no learning is apparent. The plateaus in turn are followed by further upward advancements.[24]

Each of these generalizations presents a specific, unique insight into the proper conditions and environment in which the training process may appropriately take place. Each generalization contributes helpful information for the manager-trainer who wishes to aid in the development of his peers or subordinates. Momentarily, the implications of these principles for trainees will be reviewed, but first an important challenge to training for better interpersonal relations must be confronted.

[21]*Ibid.*, p. 46, and Bass and Vaughn, *op. cit.*, p. 40.

[22]Bass and Vaughn, *op. cit.*, p. 63.

[23]William J. McLarney, *Management Training: Cases and Principles*, Fourth Edition, Homewood, Illinois: Richard D. Irwin, Incorporated, p. 411.

[24]Bass and Vaughn, *op. cit.*, pp. 45–49, and Dale Yoder, *Personnel Management and Industrial Relations*, Fifth Edition, Englewood Cliffs, New Jersey: Prentice-Hall, Inc., 1962, p. 404.

Can Interpersonal
Actions Be Modified?

Before we go overboard in the pursuit of training program techniques that can optimize the learning of improved interpersonal relations, it seems fair to consider a challenge that is sometimes thrown out by skeptics regarding the potential effectiveness of these training programs. Often heard comments include statements such as: "You don't change people's behavior by formalized training." "People are born with the ability to relate well to other people. Some people can and some people can't. Training is wasted upon those who can't." Training is possible with operative skills, but you can't train for social skills."

These comments emphasize an important truth—a training program for improvement of interpersonal skills may be brilliantly conceived and planned and still be a failure. Training programs can impart the necessary knowledge to the trainee, but without the cooperation of some personal and experiential-environmental factors, the changes in behavior may never occur. In the first place, the prospective ~~trainee must be capable and personally willing to make the alteration in his behavior~~. Personal ability and willingness to alter interpersonal behavior are functions of several factors. A certain level of intelligence (ability to comprehend and react to situations) is necessary to make social adjustments. A degree of what Rokeach calls the open belief system is also essential for changes in behavior to result through a training effort.[25] ~~Open-mindedness~~ basically is the characteristic possessed by some individuals that ~~allows~~ them ~~to receive, digest, and accept innovative ideas from external sources~~. From behavioral observations, it is apparent that not every individual is equally open-minded.

In addition, the training program will be more likely to succeed if the individual personal goals seem compatible with the rewards promised through successful performance following the training program. If the trainee can envision the personal desirability of the promised rewards, he will, of course, be more favorably disposed to attempt to complete the training and modify his performance.

Experiential-environmental factors also have a significant influence upon the potential effectiveness of the training program. As was stated in Chapter 3, institutions such as the family, religion, education, and so forth, have a large role in the formation of the value systems, role perceptions, and behavior norms of the individual. If the training program asks the trainee to make alterations in his

[25]Milton Rokeach, *The Open and Closed Mind,* New York: Basic Books, Incorporated, 1960, pp. 55–56.

behavior that are consistent with the patterns established by his experiential-environmental background, he will probably be inclined to make the adjustment. If, however, the training program calls for behavior inconsistent with these background factors, the probability of success is extremely limited.

The ~~formal organization~~ through its structure and authority hierarchy will have ~~many influences upon the success of interpersonal training~~ programs. (See Chapter 5 for more discussion of this.) On the one hand, the formal organization will contribute to the need for training in that it structures the working relationships of employees. People are forced to work with other people. Where problems develop because of authority relationships, poor communication, personality variances, and the like, the need for interpersonal skills to contend with the differences will become particularly obvious. As a result, the trainee in a strained position may be especially receptive to training assistance.

The ~~reward and support structure~~ of the formal organization will also be an ~~influence upon the prospective trainee~~. If the rewards offered by the organization are substantial, the trainee may decide to take the request for changed behavior seriously. If the rewards offered are insignificant and unrelated to his own goals, little attention may be given to the training opportunity. (The concepts involved in positive and negative motivation presented in Chapter 10 apply to training as well as to other types of action.)

The ~~superior of the trainees~~ (regardless of their level in the formal organization) ~~will also be influential in determining whether or not a training program will be successful~~. Support from the top of the organization downward must be present if trainees are to give serious consideration to reshaping their behavior.[26] Of particular importance is the behavior of superiors themselves. Subordinate trainees tend to emulate the behavioral patterns of their superiors. In a very real sense, trainees learn from the examples exhibited by their superiors.

~~Informal work groups~~ (Chapter 6) have a direct bearing upon acceptance or rejection of new behavior patterns because they have an important role in shaping the behavior norms of all individuals within the group. Any change in performance may be compatible with or complementary to the norms already established, or it may be contrary to the existing norms. Those that are compatible stand a much greater chance of being adopted by trainees. If the informal work team becomes convinced that a change in behavior is beneficial to its members, it may encourage the change through social endorsement.

[26]See Erwin K. Taylor, "Review of Developing Executive Skills," *Personnel Psychology*, Volume 11, Number 4, (Winter 1958), pp. 605–609, for additional discussion of the importance of top-down support.

FIGURE 21.2   Factors that influence worker behavior

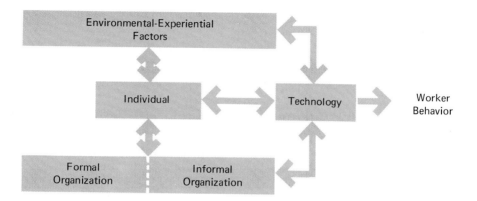

Technology (Chapter 4) creates needs for training as it forces realignments of work groups—sometimes forcing greater teamwork and at other times resulting in reduced socialization opportunities. Technology may in many other ways also be a stimulus for change.

As can be seen, there are a number of individual and environmental influences that may help determine whether training results in a significant change in the trainee's behavior. As early chapters revealed, worker behavior is a combination of interactions between the individual, environmental-experiential factors, the formal organizational structure, the informal organization, and technology (see Figure 21.2); behavior can be changed through the proper interaction of these forces with the training program. The result of this new set of interactions is a new set of behavior patterns (Figure 21.3).

FIGURE 21.3   Factors that encourage new worker behavior

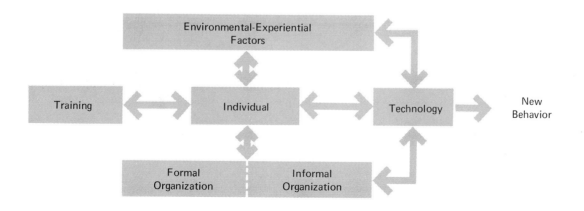

In reviewing the original question, it appears possible that training can result in changed behavior if the supporting conditions are conducive to change. It is conceivable, however, that a well-planned and executed training program might not result in the desired behavioral change if personal and experiential-environmental conditions are restrictive.

Improving the Effectiveness of Training

From these generalizations and findings concerning learning theory and training program effectiveness come several suggestions for the manager or professional trainer who is attempting to develop and improve the interpersonal skills of one or more individuals.

1. ~~Outline specific training objectives~~ on the basis of the type of performance needed in order to achieve organizational goals and objectives. An audit of personal needs compared with operational requirements will help to determine the specific training needs of individual employees. Out of this evaluation should come a well-defined set of performance standards toward which each trainee should be directed.

2. ~~Attempt to determine if the trainee has the intelligence, maturity, and motivation to successfully complete the training program~~. If difficiencies are noted in these areas, the training may need to be postponed or cancelled unless improvements are noted.

3. ~~Help the trainee see the need for training by making him aware of the personal benefits~~ he can achieve through better performance. Help him to discover the rewards and satisfactions that will come his way through changes in his behavior.

4. ~~Plan the training program~~ so that it is ~~related to the trainee's previous experiences and background~~. Use his background as a foundation for new development and new behavior.

5. If possible, ~~plan the training program~~ so that it ~~progresses in small steps,~~ each step building upon the preceding ones. These progressions, of course, may need revision as the program unfolds, but make certain there is an orderly plan of revision, if needed.

6. Attempt to create organizational conditions (formally and informally) that are conducive to a good learning environment. Attempt to relate newly expected behavior norms with existing formal and informal norms. Make clear why changes are needed. Remove distractions from the training environment. Underwrite off-the-job training and practice, if necessary, to provide the proper training environment. Get the support (and correct behavior) of upper levels of management before applying training at lower levels.

7. If appropriate, select a combination of training methods so that variety is permitted and as many of the senses as possible are utilized.

8.   Recognize that not all trainees progress at the same rate. Be flexible in allowing different rates of movement in the training program.

9.   If possible, get the personal involvement or active participation of the trainee in the training program. Provide him with the opportunity to practice the newly needed behavior norms.

10.   As the trainee acquires new knowledge, skills, or attitudes and applies them in job situations, be certain that he is significantly rewarded for his efforts to practice the changed behavior.

11.   Provide the trainee with regular, constructive feedback concerning his progress in training and implementation of the newly acquired abilities.

12.   Provide personal assistance to the trainee when he encounters learning obstacles.

The support of the superiors to the trainees during and following the formal phases of training is particularly important to the successful completion of the training program. Superiors set the example for the desired behavior and serve as the primary source for rewards and feedback as the trainee matures in his new behavior patterns.

Selection of Training Techniques

The success of a behavioral learning experience is dependent upon the selection of the appropriate training techniques through which the new behavior can be conveyed, the motivation to change can be provided, and the skills for implementation can be developed. Some training techniques have emphasized the importance of acquiring new behavior through hearing or after observing the actions of others (through lectures, movies, and other forms of observation). More recent learning theory has encouraged the utilization of training techniques that allow the trainee to benefit from the experiences of others and to make behavioral changes on the basis of his own experiences as well. In the next few pages, some currently used training techniques for interpersonal relations are described. An evaluation of the effectiveness of each technique is also presented.

The Lecture Method.   One of the most traditional of all training methods is the lecture technique. Individuals with even a minimum of formal education have normally been exposed to a significantly heavy dose of lectures in which the teacher presents basic points of knowledge and information to be absorbed by the listeners and to be acted upon in a positive fashion. In the work environment, the lecturer may be the training specialist, the formal superior, or other individuals with information to be imparted to one or more trainees. The lecture method makes it possible to convey a significant amount of information to one or several trainees in a minimum amount of time. Usually, the lecture hits the highlights or major points of emphasis in the discussion topic. Lectures tend to be impersonal if they are given to several individuals simultaneously and no provision is made for questions and feedback.

Coaching.   When coaching is used, the trainer is usually the immediate superior of the employee-trainee. The coach-trainee relationship becomes a continuing one between the two individuals. Some mutually agreed upon goals are established at the beginning of the training period, and the coach helps the trainee live up to those goals through periodic reviews of the trainee's progress and by suggesting modifications in his behavior where needed.

> Coaching . . . will work well if the coach provides a good model with whom the trainee can identify; if both can be open with each other; if the coach accepts his responsibilities fully; and if he provides the trainee with recognition of his improvement and suitable rewards.[27]

The coach must be careful to avoid being too dominant in the performance process, so that the trainee can experience things for himself and does not become completely dependent upon the coach for decisions.

Conferences as Training Techniques.   As the term suggests, in **conferences,** the participating individuals "confer" to discuss points of common interest to each other. Conferences may be used as a group process to modify attitudes and behavior, or they may be used simply as an exchange of information and knowledge among several individuals. Frequently, when conferences are used as a training device, decisions are expected from the participating group, and the process of deriving the decision and the group support of the decision are expected to be influential in encouraging individual participants to modify their behavior.

The success of conferences as training techniques is heavily dependent upon the size of the conference team, the commonality of interest in the training topic being discussed, and the skill of the trainer in leading the group to decisions and action. The size of the group must be small enough to allow each individual to participate and to become personally involved in the deliberations of the group. The training issue must involve a problem or need each individual is currently

---

[27]Harry Levinson, "A Psychologist Looks at Executive Development," *Harvard Business Review,* Volume 40, Number 5 (September–October 1962), pp. 69–75.

facing or interest in the conference results will wane. The leader must be skilled at drawing out ideas, at helping the group to reach conclusions, and at encouraging participation from all individuals.

The Case Study Method and Role Playing. "The case study is based upon the belief that managerial competence can best be attained through the study, contemplation, and discussion of concrete cases. . . ."[28] The **case** is a set of data (real or fictional) that present issues and problems calling for solutions or actions on the part of the trainee. The case study is primarily useful as a training technique for supervisors (as opposed to nonsupervisors) and is especially valuable as a technique for developing decision-making skills and for broadening the perspective of the trainee. He is forced to develop a problem-solving rationale that will be transferrable to problems he faces in the performance of his own supervisory duties. In utilizing the case study method, the trainer is often encouraged to request a specific set of actions from the trainee, including the following steps. The trainee should:

1. Master the facts and become acquainted with the content of the case
2. Define the objectives sought in dealing with the issues in the case
3. Identify the problems in the case and uncover their probable causes
4. Develop alternative courses of action
5. Screen the alternatives using the objectives stated in step 2 as the criteria
6. Select the alternative that is most in keeping with the stated objectives
7. Define the controls needed to make the action effective
8. Role play the action to test its effectiveness and find conditions that may limit it[29]

Role playing used separately or in connection with the case study is important in revising attitudes and in developing interactional skills. Typically, the trainee is presented with a situation or a problem and is asked to act out solutions to the problem as he thinks individuals involved in the situation might. Role playing normally involves a number of people with each one playing a role in the training environment. (See Figure 21.4 for an assessment of the differences between role playing and the case study method.)

Role playing is especially useful in providing new insight and in presenting the trainee with opportunities to develop interactional skills. Unless the trainer

[28]Bass and Vaughn, *op. cit.*, p. 99.
[29]Odiorne, *op. cit.*, p. 283.

FIGURE 21.4   Comparison of the case-study and role-playing methods as training devices

Case study	Role playing
1. Presents a problem for discussion	1. Places the problem in a lifelike setting
2. Derives problems from previous events	2. Involves problems with ongoing processes
3. Typically deals with problems involving others	3. Typically deals with problems involving the participants themselves
4. Deals with emotional and attitudinal aspects in an intellectual frame of reference	4. Deals with emotional and attitudinal aspects in an experiential frame of reference
5. Emphasizes the importance of facts	5. Emphasizes the importance of feelings
6. Typically involves discussion from a psychological position outside the problem situation	6. Deals with participants who are psychologically inside the problem situation
7. Facilitates intellectual involvement	7. Makes for emotional involvement
8. Furnishes practice in analysis of problems	8. Provides practice in interpersonal skills
9. Provides for development of ideas and hypotheses	9. Provides for testing ideas and hypotheses
10. Trains in the exercise of judgment	10. Trains in emotional control
11. Defines the action or solution	11. Provides for execution of the action or solution
12. Involves action the consequences of which are usually undetermined	12. Involves continuous feedback

Source: B.M. Bass and J.A. Vaughn, *Training in Industry: The Management of Learning,*
© 1966 by Wadsworth Publishing Company. Reprinted by permission of the publisher,
Brooks/Cole Publishing Company, Monterey, California and Tavistock Publications, Ltd.

engages in coaching or unless someone else states the criteria for behavior, however, role playing may not adhere well to the objectives of the training program and the reinforcement of the desired behavior may be somewhat lacking. In other words, it is conceivable that the practice the trainee gets in interpersonal relations could be faulty.[30]

[30]McGehee and Thayer, *op. cit.,* p. 203.

~~Laboratory Training.~~   Laboratory training is known by several names including sensitivity training, T-group training, action training, and so forth. The basic pattern of **laboratory training** is to ~~organize trainees into small groups in which interaction will occur regularly throughout the training program~~. The trainees in some laboratory settings may be given cases, role playing situations, or other training assignments as a springboard for group interaction.

In its more unstructured form, the training may be completely open, normally evolving into a discussion of each participant's attitudes, reactions, and other behavioral patterns. In each type of laboratory training, the participants are encouraged to be introspective and at the same time to be more empathetic toward the feelings of others. Some of the specific aims of laboratory training are to provide:

1.   An increased awareness of and sensitivity to emotional reactions and expressions in oneself and others

2.   A greater ability to perceive and to learn from the consequences of one's action through attention to feelings—one's own and others'

3.   A clarification and development of personal values and goals consonant with a democratic and scientific approach to problems of social and personal decision and action

4.   Development of concepts and theoretical insights that will serve as tools in linking personal values, goals, and intentions to actions that are consistent with these inner factors and with the situation requirements

5.   Achievement of greater behavioral effectiveness in transactions with one's various environments[31]

The effects of laboratory training have raised a considerable amount of controversy. There are many who view laboratory training as one of the most effective methods of changing attitudes and ultimately modifying behavior. Many managers and academicians, however, raise serious questions concerning the desirability of the results that emerge from this type of training.[32] Mosvick suggests that T-group training, when applied to technical professional (scientists, engineers, etc.), is often less effective as a training method than more conventional methods such as the lecture approach and conferences.[33] House notes that in addition to the desired effects of T-group training (better consideration of others,

[31]Kenneth D. Benne, Leland P. Bradford, and R. Lippitt, "The Laboratory Method," in L. P. Bradford, J. R. Gibb, and K. D. Benne, *T-Group Theory and Laboratory Method*, New York: John Wiley & Sons, Inc., 1964, pp. 16–17.

[32]See Odiorne, *op. cit.*, pp. 50–64, for a serious indictment of sensitivity training, for example.

[33]Roger K. Mosvick, "Human Relations Training for Scientists, Technicians, and Engineers: A Review of Relevant Experimental Evaluations," *Personnel Psychology*, Volume 24, Number 2 (Summer 1971), pp. 275–292.

improved communication, a higher level of sensitivity, and the like), T-group training may also have destructive influences. He states that:

> . . . T-group training is not only capable of inducing anxiety, but it is very likely to do so. . . . The anxiety may have an unrewarding effect, such as causing the people to be highly frustrated, unsettled, and upset.[34]

In other cases, high levels of depression, rejections, and other disruptive influences have been noted in some of the participants. Some of the conclusions drawn from the House study (and others) suggest that when laboratory training is used, it is extremely important that the leader-trainer be carefully selected on the basis of his ability to lead effectively so that emotional situations can be translated into constructive rather than destructive consequences. Also, participants for laboratory training should be selected for their emotional stability and their tolerance for anxiety.[35]

Programmed Instruction. This training technique has been used only to a very limited degree with interpersonal skill training. It is a means of imparting knowledge in a self-instruction environment quickly and methodically. A bit of information is given to the trainee in a written program or by machine; the trainee is given a question or situation to utilize the information given; and the trainee instantly receives feedback (and sometimes rewards or penalties) on the basis of how well he has learned and can use the information given in the program. Programmed instruction is simple to administer and has other advantages, as will be seen momentarily. It has not been explored freely for its potential in reshaping organizational behavior.

Simulation. **Simulation** as a training technique is, as its name suggests, the duplication of organizational situations in a learning environment. It is a mock-up of the real thing. This technique has long been used to develop technical skills and has more recently come into its own for developing interpersonal skills. Bass and Vaughn suggest the following procedures for using simulation in behavioral training:

> 1.   The essential characteristics of a real-life organization or activity are abstracted and presented as a case—not to be studied and analyzed as in the usual case method, but to be experienced by the trainee as a realistic, life-like circumstance.

---

[34]Robert J. House, "T-Group Training: Good or Bad?" *Business Horizons,* Volume 12, Number 6 (December 1969), p. 73.

[35]*Ibid.,* p. 77.

2.   Trainees are asked to assume various roles in the circumstance and to solve the problems facing them. They are asked to be themselves—*not* to act.

3.   A simulation often involves a telescoping or compressing of time and events; a single hour may be equated with a month or a quarter of a year in real life, and many events are experienced in a relatively brief period of time.

4.   Trainees are required to make decisions that have a real effect in the simulation and about which they receive rapid feedback.

5.   The simulation is followed by a critique of what went on during the exercise.[36]

Other Training Techniques.   Business games, the utilization of film instruction, reading programs, and various other devices have also been utilized for the development and training of individuals for improved interpersonal relations.

The Effectiveness of Training Techniques

A major concern in the selection of training techniques to fit training program needs, of course, is how effective the techniques are in accomplishing their goals of modifying skills, attitudes, and ultimate behavior. One way of predicting the potential success of training techniques is to compare them against a list of desirable results drawn from the guidelines and generalizations presented earlier in this chapter. In Figure 21.5, each of the major techniques of training is evaluated on its potential for meeting the training program criteria.

The evaluations in Figure 21.5 reveal that each technique has its own strengths and weaknesses. The success of several of the programs is directly dependent upon the abilities and actions of the trainer in seeing that important phases of the program are conducted to meet the necessary requirements. In another attempt to evaluate the effectiveness of training programs (see Figure 21.6), training directors were asked to evaluate nine training techniques on their effectiveness in achieving knowledge acquisition, changing attitudes, providing problem-solving skills, developing interpersonal skills, gaining participant acceptance, and achieving knowlege retention.[37] A score of five was the highest score possible on each item, and a score of one indicated the least effective techniques. Programmed instruction was judged to be the most useful technique where knowledge acquisition

[36]Bernard M. Bass and James A. Vaughn, *Training In Industry: The Management of Learning,* Copyright © 1966 by Wadsworth Publishing Company, Inc. Reprinted by permission of the publisher, Brooks/Cole Publishing Company, Monterey, California.

[37]Stephen J. Carroll, Jr., Frank T. Paine, and John J. Ivancevich, "The Relative Effectiveness of Training Methods," *Personnel Psychology,* Volume 25, Number 3 (Autumn, 1972), pp. 495–509.

FIGURE 21.5   Evaluation of different types of training programs

QUESTIONS

1. Does this technique develop its training objectives on the basis of an organizational, operations, and man analysis? In other words, is the technique oriented to the specific needs of trainees?

2. Does this training technique help the trainee to see the benefits he may achieve by completing the training this technique concentrates upon?

3. Does this training technique attempt to relate itself to the previous experiences (background) of the trainee?

4. Does this technique progress through small, carefully planned steps or progressions to its completion?

5. Does this technique attempt to influence the organizational conditions in which the trainee lives and works?

6. Does this technique utilize a variety of the senses as it works?

7. Does this technique make allowances for individual rates of learning?

8. Does this technique get the personal involvement (participation) of the trainee in the process?

9. Does the technique provide for rewards as new behavior results?

10. Does the technique provide for regular, constructive feedback to the trainee?

11. Does the technique provide assistance to the worker when he encounters obstacles?

TYPE OF PROGRAM							
Lecture	Coaching	Conference	Case study	Role playing	Simulation	Laboratory training	Programmed instruction
possibly	yes	possibly	possibly	normally yes	possibly	many say no	possibly
not particularly	somewhat	somewhat	yes	yes	yes	yes	somewhat
not necessarily	possibly	possibly	not necessarily	not necessarily	not necessarily	yes	not necessarily
not necessarily	possibly	not necessarily	possibly	not necessarily	not necessarily	not necessarily	yes
not particularly	not particularly	not particularly	not particularly	not particularly	not particularly	possibly	no
possibly	possibly	possibly	not necessarily	yes	possibly	yes	no
no	yes	no	somewhat	somewhat	yes	somewhat	yes
no	yes	yes	yes	yes	yes	yes	yes
not necessarily	yes, possibly	possibly	possibly	possibly	possibly	possibly	yes
no	yes	possibly	possibly	yes	possibly	yes	yes
no	yes	yes	not necessarily	not necessarily	possibly	possibly	possibly

FIGURE 21.6 Ratings of training directors on effectiveness of alternative training methods for various training objectives

Training Method	Knowledge Acquisition		Changing Attitudes		Problem-Solving Skills		Interpersonal Skills		Participant Acceptance		Knowledge Retention	
	Mean	Mean rank	Mean	Mean rank	Mean	Mean rank	Mean	Mean rank	Mean	Mean rank	Mean	Mean rank
Case study	3.56[b]	2	3.43[d]	4	3.69[b]	1	3.02[d]	4	3.80[d]	2	3.48[e]	2
Conference (discussion) method	3.33[d]	3	3.54[d]	3	3.26[e]	4	3.21[d]	3	4.16[a]	1	3.32[f]	5
Lecture (with questions)	2.53	9	2.20	8	2.00	9	1.90	8	2.74	8	2.49	8
Business games	3.00	6	2.73[f]	5	3.58[b]	2	2.50[e]	5	3.78[d]	3	3.26[f]	6
Movie films	3.16[g]	4	2.50[f]	6	2.24[g]	7	2.19[g]	6	3.44[g]	5	2.67[h]	7
Programmed instruction	4.03[a]	1	2.22[h]	7	2.56[f]	6	2.11[g]	7	3.28[g]	7	3.74[a]	1
Role playing	2.93	7	3.56[d]	2	3.27[e]	3	3.68[b]	2	3.56[e]	4	3.37[f]	4
Sensitivity training (T group)	2.77	8	3.96[a]	1	2.98[e]	5	3.95[b]	1	3.33[g]	6	3.44[f]	3
Television lecture	3.10[g]	5	1.99	9	2.01	8	1.81	9	2.74	9	2.47	9

[a] More effective than methods ranked 2 to 9 for this objective at .01 level of significance.
[b] More effective than methods ranked 3 to 9 for this objective at .01 level of significance.
[c] More effective than methods ranked 4 to 9 for this objective at .01 level of significance.
[d] More effective than methods ranked 5 to 9 for this objective at .01 level of significance.
[e] More effective than methods ranked 6 to 9 for this objective at .01 level of significance.
[f] More effective than methods ranked 7 to 9 for this objective at .01 level of significance.
[g] More effective than methods ranked 8 to 9 for this objective at .01 level of significance.
[h] More effective than method ranked 9 for this objective at .01 level of significance.

Source: Stephen J. Carroll, Jr., Frank T. Paine, and John J. Ivancevich, "The Effectiveness of Training Methods," *Personnel Psychology*, Volume 25, Number 3 (Autumn 1972), p. 498.

and knowledge retention were important. In the behavioral areas of training, sensitivity training (laboratory training) ranked highest on changing attitudes and developing interpersonal skills. The case study method led in the problem-solving skill category, and the conference method was said to be most effective in gaining participant acceptance.

Organizational Development

Beginning in the mid-1940s, training programs began to take on a different perspective in many organizations. Instead of concentrating on skill development in operational matters (how to manage financial problems, marketing matters, and other technical problems), many management experts began to suggest that the way to optimize successful performance and decision making in organizations was to first change the interactional attitudes and habits of the individuals who compose the organization. This change of attitudes and habits was called a change in organizational climate. Following the change, the members of the organization would be in a frame of mind to solve problems, confront conflict, formulate policies, and handle operational matters more effectively. In other words, this trend gave (and continues to give) the first priority to change in interpersonal interaction. Through improvement in interpersonal reactions, it would become possible to achieve the potentials of the organization and its individual members. The trend to emphasize improved interpersonal relations as a means of organizational optimization has come to be known as organizational development—a concept that has acquired a large amount of support in management circles.

Some authors suggest that a general model for the implementation of organizational development might be as follows:

1. Plan the change processes—done primarily by trained consultants (behavioral scientists) advising the client (top management) who approves the program

2. Change the attitudes and habits of individuals (the way people treat one another)

3. Change the group climate or culture (the collective attitudes and habits of individuals)

4. Work out new structures such as (a) subgoals (products, types of patient care, allocation of budget money), (b) who does what (a new specialization pattern), and (c) who has final authority over whom

5. ~~Solve day-to-day problems~~ involving (a) new demands from outside the organization and (b) new discoveries or demands from inside the organization.[38]

There are several items unique to the organizational development concept. The focal point of attention with organizational development is at the top of the management hierarchy (compared to the selective treatment of the other training approaches), and this approach views the organization as a total system. Managerial role behavior is considered a significant variable. Learning is primarily on-the-job. The interventionist (trainer) or initiator of changed behavior is known as a **change agent.** The change agent often is someone outside of the organization who has expertise in interpersonal interaction development. He determines the techniques to be used initially in starting the analysis and interaction of organizational development. He may suggest many of the techniques mentioned earlier in this chapter—laboratory training, role playing, and so forth—as methods for changing attitudes and behavior.

Once the program of development has begun, organization members become highly active in investigating their own attitudes and habits and in relating to the attitudes and habits of others. McGregor has suggested that organizational members as a team need to raise questions such as: In our day-to-day work—

1.   Do we trust each other? or do we suspect each other?

2.   Do we have genuine concern for each other, or is it every man for himself?

3.   Do we communicate openly our true feelings and thoughts, or are we guarded and cautious?

4.   Do we listen to each other, or do we act on our own?

5.   Do we accept conflicts and work them through, or do we deny, avoid, or suppress conflicts?

6.   Does the team utilize the abilities, knowledge, and experience of each member, or does the team ignore the capabilities of some?

7.   Does everyone understand and feel committed to work objectives, or do some fail to understand them or feel negative toward them?[39]

As the organizational members diagnose their own attitudes and feelings (and those of others), they give each other feedback and then project techniques to combat deficiencies that become obvious in their interpersonal relations. This

[38]David R. Hampton, Charles E. Summer, and Ross A. Webber, *Organizational Behavior and the Practice of Management,* Revised Edition, Glenview, Illinois: Scott, Foresman and Company, 1973, p. 850.

[39]Douglas McGregor, *The Professional Manager,* New York: McGraw-Hill Book Company, 1967, pp. 173-174.

process is known as the **diagnosis-feedback-action planning cycle.**[40] The cycle becomes a continuous one so that interpersonal attitudes and feelings are constantly under review.

The change in personal habits and attitudes affects the group's collective habits and attitudes of the group culture, as it is sometimes known. As the habits and attitudes of the group are developed and integrated, the organizational members become more capable of dealing adequately with structural, technical, and operational problems within the organization. One of the weaknesses identified in our earlier discussions of training methods was the inability of most training devices to have much effect on the working environment in which the trainee labors daily. The organizational development philosophy is to attack the environmental climate as a forerunner to actually calling for the action plan. In this way, organizational development gives significant attention to the surroundings in which work takes place.

In summarizing the differences between organizational development and more traditional programs of change or behavior modification, French and Bell suggest that organizational development contains more of:

1.   An emphasis, although not exclusively so, on group and organizational processes in contrast to substantive content

2.   An emphasis on the work team as the key unit for learning more effective modes of organizational behavior

3.   An emphasis on collaborative management of work team culture

4.   An emphasis on the management of the culture of the total system and total system ramifications

5.   The use of the action research model[41]

6.   The use of a behavioral scientist change agent or catalyst

7.   A view of the change effort as an ongoing process[42]

Summary

Beginning with the concepts of learning theory, to management responsibilities for training programs, to individual training techniques, to organizational development, this chapter has covered a large

[40]Hampton, Summer, and Webber, *op. cit.,* p. 857.

[41]French and Bell define action research as the process of tentatively diagnosing problems; gathering, analyzing, and exploring data; and planning and taking action. These activities involve all work team members.

[42]Wendell L. French and Cecil H. Bell, Jr., *Organizational Development,* Englewood Cliffs, New Jersey: Prentice-Hall, Inc., 1973, pp. 19–20.

territory. Perhaps the simplified message of the chapter is this: Armed with a knowledge of how people learn, the strengths and weaknesses of the different programs, and the latest concepts available, trainers and supervisors can devise programs that can effectively result in interpersonal behavior modification. Concentration on support programs involving rewards, feedback, and the reshaping of the organizational climate will further enhance the probabilities of success of training programs and improvement in interpersonal relations.

Questions to consider after reading Chapter 21

1. Is it true that old workers can't learn new behavior patterns and work habits? What problems do older workers have in changing their behavior that young, new employees may not have?

2. Why do so many managers object to the use of sensitivity training upon themselves and their subordinates?

3. Is it really possible to change an individual's behavior as a result of training? In addition to training, what other factors influence behavioral changes?

4. Why do many authors insist that training should be procedural, moving from one steppingstone to another?

5. Should open-minded individuals be more capable of adopting new attitudes and behavioral patterns than closed-minded individuals? Explain your answer. What clues does this suggest for managers and trainers as they lead training programs?

6. "Two training techniques are better than one." What is the meaning of this statement? Is the statement valid?

7. What are the basic differences (if any) between training and organizational development?

8. What makes organizational development particularly effective in so many situations?

The following cases at the back of the book contain problems related to Chapter 21:

Ben Stockton

Mark Williams

H. Gerald Pretzler

Edith Capp and Janet Turner

Earl Fornette

Bentley Cantrell

Billy Snyder

Walt Gladberry

Abigail Spiegal and Trudy Pennington

Additional readings

Andrews, John D. W., "Interpersonal Challenge: A Source of Growth in Laboratory Training," *Journal of Applied Behavioral Science,* Volume 9, Number 4 (July–August 1973), pp. 514–533.

Argyris, Chris, *Management and Organizational Development,* New York: McGraw-Hill Book Company, 1971.

Beckhard, Richard, *Organization Development: Strategies and Models,* Reading, Massachusetts: Addison-Wesley Publishing Company, 1969.

Bennis, Warren G., *Organization Development: Its Nature, Origins, and Prospects,* Reading, Massachusetts: Addison-Wesley Publishing Company, 1969.

Bienvenu, Bernard J., *New Priorities in Training,* New York: American Management Association, 1969.

Blake, Robert R., and Jane S. Mouton, *Building a Dynamic Corporation through Grid Organization Development,* Reading, Massachusetts: Addison-Wesley Publishing Company, 1969.

Bowers, David G., "O D Techniques and Their Results in 23 Organizations: The Michigan ICL Study," *Journal of Applied Behavioral Science,* Volume 9, Number 1 (January–February 1973), pp. 21–43.

Craig, Robert L., and Lester R. Bittel, editors, *Training and Development Handbook,* New York: McGraw-Hill Book Company, 1967.

Dalton, Gene W., Paul R. Lawrence, and Larry E. Greiner, editors, *Organizational Change and Development,* Homewood, Illinois: Richard D. Irwin, Inc., 1970.

French, Wendell, "Organization Development Objectives, Assumptions, and Strategies," *California Management Review,* Volume 12, Number 2 (Winter 1969), pp. 23–34.

Gellerman, Saul W., "Developing Managers without Management Development," *The Conference Board Record,* Volume 10, Number 7 (July 1973), pp. 32–37.

Hall, Jay, and Martha S. Williams, "Group Dynamics Training and Improved Decision Making," *Journal of Applied Behavioral Science,* Volume 6, Number 1 (January–February 1970), pp. 39–68.

Ivancevich, John M., "A Study of a Cognitive Training Program: Trainer Styles and Group Development," *The Academy of Management Journal,* Volume 17, Number 3 (September 1974), pp. 428–439.

Kegan, David L., and Albert H. Rubenstein, "Trust, Effectiveness, and Organizational Development: A Field Study in Research and Development," *Journal of Applied Behavioral Science,* Volume 9, Number 4 (July–August 1973), pp. 498–513.

O'Meara, J. Roger, "Going to School Becomes Part of the Job," *The Conference Board Record,* Volume 7, Number 9 (September 1970), pp. 51–56.

Otto, Calvin P., and Rollin O. Glaser, *The Management of Training,* Reading, Massachusetts: Addison-Wesley Publishing Company, 1970.

SECTION IV

TODAY'S
ISSUES
AND
TOMORROW'S
CHALLENGES

One of the most interesting, challenging aspects of managing is the fact that employees, the work environment, and the conditions outside of the work organization are constantly changing. No manager can feel secure in depending upon yesterday's knowledge, yesterday's techniques, and yesterday's data. New issues, new demands, new problems, and new techniques are constantly arising.

The three chapters in this section discuss current and future trends and issues of concern to students of management. In Chapter 22, recent data concerning the composition and characteristics of the work force, the conditions and environment of the labor force, and other recent facts are presented. Chapter 23 focuses upon four major problems that are becoming increasingly important managerial concerns even though they have existed in earlier years. Chapter 24 brings out the crystal ball and looks to future events, conditions, and responsibilities. From every indication, tomorrow's managers will have an abundance of new concerns as well as several continuing ones.

Chapter 22

The American Work Force

Questions to consider before reading chapter 22

Several generalizations concerning trends in today's work force have been suggested by various authors. Fourteen such generalizations are listed below. Before you read the chapter, give yourself a test and indicate which of the hypotheses you believe are true and which ones you believe are false. After you have read the chapter, review your answers to determine which ones are valid statements.

True	False	
_____ •	_____	1. If the work force is analyzed on the basis of structure by age categories, it can be readily discovered that the work force is becoming younger.
_____ •	_____	2. The trend toward a more youthful work force is expected to continue for several years into the future.
_____ •	_____	3. Women are entering the labor force in larger numbers than has previously been true and compose a larger percentage of the work force than before.
_____ •	_____	4. Blacks and other minority groups are increasing in numbers and percentages of the total work force.
_____ •	_____	5. The number of scheduled work hours of the average employee is decreasing.
_____	_____ •	6. The number of days per week worked by the typical employee has decreased in recent years.
_____	_____ •	7. The level of individual worker productivity (output per man hour) is steadily increasing on an annual basis.
_____	_____ •	8. The level of formal education attained by individual members of the work force has risen progressively so that today's work force has a level of formal

educational attainment superior to that of any previous
work force.

_____ _____ 9. The level of formal educational achievement
influences the career opportunities of the average
worker.

_____ _____ 10. The level of formal educational attainment
achieved by the worker tends to be an important determinant of the income level of the worker.

_____ _____ 11. The income level of workers in all occupational
classifications has increased in recent years.

_____ _____ 12. Employment levels (numbers of workers employed) in all industries (including those with agricultural bases) have progressed steadily upward.

_____ _____ 13. White-collar workers are increasing numerically
and as a percentage of the work force, while blue-
collar workers are decreasing in both categories. In
other words, the labor force is becoming a white-collar
group rather than a blue-collar body.

_____ _____ 14. The work force has become an urban-centered
group of city dwellers.

There are a number of characteristics and traits of the work force that have
important impacts upon managerial attitudes and actions. Several specific
characteristics concerning the work force's composition have been forwarded by
other authors. Some of these have been supported by research data, while others
have not. In the questions preceding this chapter several frequently heard hypotheses were presented. It is now time to investigate the validity of these hypotheses.

Analysis of the Hypotheses

Test Hypothesis No. 1 If the work force is analyzed on the basis of structure by age
categories, it can be readily discovered that the work force is
becoming younger.

The maturation of the children born in the post–World War II baby boom has
called attention to the fact that this group is now old enough to become a signifi-

cant part of the labor force. This group of young people has had an impact upon business operations and managerial thinking that exceeds the impact of any previously known group of young people. Organizations have been encouraged to think young, to modify organizational practices, to be accommodative to the younger members of the work force, and to become more flexible and adaptive to meet the changing structure of the work force. The position has been forwarded that the ~~younger part of the work force~~, particularly ~~individuals in their twenties or below, has come to make up almost a majority of the work force.~~

   The truth of the matter concerning the age composition of the work force is that *there are more young people from 16 to 24 years of age (in numbers and percentages) in the work force than has been true in other modern work forces. At the same time, there are also large increases in the number and percentage of workers in the upper middle-age categories (45 to 64 years of age), and all age categories showed an increase in the number of workers participating in the work force* (as Figure 22.1 illustrates). While the total labor force

FIGURE 22.1   Composition of total civilian work force by age, 1950–1972 (in thousands)

Year	Total Labor Force	Age category							
		16–17	18–19	20–24	25–34	35–44	45–54	55–64	65 and over
1950	62,208	1,658	2,558	7,307	14,619	13,954	11,444	7,633	3,038
1960	69,628	2,095	2,746	6,703	14,383	16,270	14,852	9,386	3,194
1970	82,715	3,132	4,114	10,583	17,009	16,431	16,948	11,277	3,220
1972*	86,542	3,398	4,625	12,010	18,725	16,346	16,970	11,362	3,107
Percentage comparison index of the 1972 figure using 1950 as the base year	139.2	204.9	180.8	164.4	127.4	117.1	148.3	148.8	102.3

*Includes population adjustments not present in other years.

Source: "Civilian Labor Force, by Sex, Color, and Age, 1947-1972,"U.S. Department of Labor, *Handbook of Labor Statistics, 1973*, Bulletin 1790, Washington, D.C.: U.S. Government Printing Office, pp. 33-36.

increased 23,334,000 (an index of 139.2) between 1950 and 1972, the 16 to 17, 18 to 19, and 20 to 24 year age classifications of the 1972 labor force surpassed a comparative index of 160 or more over the 1950 base year. The 45–54 and 55–64 age categories closely approached the 150 index also. Only the group of workers who were 65 years of age or older came near to being the same numerically in both the 1950 and 1972 time periods.

An investigation of the work force by comparing the percentage of workers falling into the separate age categories reveals a similar result. In the period between 1950 and 1973 the percentage of workers falling into every age category except the 25–34, the 35–44, and the 65 and over categories increased (see Figure 22.2). These figures are based upon the total (military and civilian) labor force, while the figures in Figure 22.1 were drawn from the civilian labor force only.

Using the data shown in Figures 22.1 and 22.2 as a basis, it can be said that the labor force is getting younger in terms of the increase in numbers and percentages of workers who are 24 years of age or younger. It must also be noted, however, that workers in several segments of the work force are increasing numerically and in percentages also. Only the above-65 worker group and to some extent the younger middle-aged categories of workers show signs of tapering off or decreasing.

Test Hypothesis No. 2   The trend toward a more youthful work force is expected to continue for several years into the future.

The data analyzed in considering the accuracy of the first hypothesis have already revealed a fallacy in the belief that the labor force is only getting younger. In reality, the work force is growing in some of the older categories also. However, many managers and economists still believe that the trend toward youthfulness in the labor force will continue through the years until the work force becomes extremely young.

Many predictions of the future age composition of the work force estimate that the age segments that will grow the most during the remainder of the twentieth century will be the middle-age categories rather than the younger segments. One prediction suggests that in the year 2000 approximately 23 percent of the total population of the United States will be from 35 to 49 years of age compared with 17 percent in the same age classification in 1972. This growth rate is by far the largest population increase for any age group. Only the 65 and above age group is also expected to show an increase as a percentage of the population, and the increase for this group is expected to be only a single percentage point. The 19 year and below age group is expected to show a noticeable decrease in percentage

FIGURE 22.2   Percentage distribution of the labor force by age, 1950—1973

Year	Total	Age category						
		16—19	20—24	25—34	35—44	45—54	55—64	65 and over
1950	100.0	7.1	12.4	23.7	22.1	18.0	12.0	4.8
1960	100.0	7.3	10.6	20.9	23.1	20.7	13.0	4.4
1970	100.0	8.9	14.3	20.6	19.5	19.8	13.1	3.7
1973	100.0	9.7	15.0	22.7	18.4	18.7	12.3	3.3

Source: U.S. Bureau of Labor Statistics, Employment and Earnings, monthly, as presented in
The Statistical Abstract of the United States, 1974, 95th Edition, Washington, D.C.:
Department of Commerce, Bureau of the Census, p. 337.

of the population (down from 37 to 31 percent). Other age groups are expected
to vary only slightly as percentages of the total population.[1]

Population rates alone, however, do not indicate the full measure of participation in the work force. In a given year, 60 percent of the total population
between the ages of 20 to 24 may be in the work force, and 70 percent of the
individuals between the ages of 35 to 44 may be working. These figures fluctuate
from year to year. Family responsibilities, health factors, the pursuit of additional
formal education, and many other factors may be determinants of the rate of
participation in the work force.

Using the combined gauges of population estimates and expected participation
rates for the different age categories of workers, it has been predicted that the
largest increases from both numerical and percentage points of view will occur
in the age categories of workers 25 to 34 and 35 to 44 years of age. Actual numerical losses are expected in the workers in the 16 to 19 and 45 to 54 age classifications by 1985 (see Figure 22.3).

~~Predictors indicate that the growth areas of the future lie particularly within some of the
middle-age categories and that decreases (in percentages and numerically) may occur in some
younger segments of the work force~~. The heaviest concentrations of workers will exist in
the ranks of those who are between the ages of 25 and 44. The trend in growth

[1]"Population Slowdown—What It Means to the U.S.," *U.S. News and World Report,* Volume 73,
Number 26, December 25, 1973, pp. 59–62.

FIGURE 22.3   Estimates of the structure of the labor force by age segment, 1972 to 1985 (in thousands)

Age category	Estimate of number of workers in category, 1972	Estimate of number of workers in category, 1985	Percentage increase or decrease between 1972 and 1985
16–19	8,367	7,165	−13.3
20–24	13,132	15,019	+13.6
25–34	19,331	29,739	+53.1
35–44	16,668	23,177	+39.1
45–54	17,023	16,281	−5.5
55–64	11,365	12,929	+13.8
65 and over	3,146	3,401	+8.1

Source: U.S. Bureau of Labor Statistics, Special Labor Force Report, Labor Force Projections to 1985 as presented in *The Statistical Abstract of the United States, 1973*, 94th Edition, Washington, D.C.: Department of Commerce, Bureau of the Census, p. 220.

will shift from the youth movement to a more diversified growth pattern with emphasis on the middle-age segments.

Test Hypothesis No. 3 Women are entering the labor force in larger numbers than has previously been true and compose a larger percentage of the work force than before.

This hypothesis appears to be true in all respects. In 1950 approximately three out of every ten workers were women. *By the 1970s women have increased in numbers employed so that nearly* ~~four out of every ten workers (38.5 percent) are women,~~ *for a total of 33,277,000 women working in business and industry* (see Figure 22.4). The quality and content of jobs are not investigated here but will be considered in Chapter 23.

Increases in the number of women employed have occurred particularly in the younger age categories (women 24 years of age or younger) and the categories of women 45 years of age and above.[2] It is highly predictable that women in the

[2]"Civilian Labor Force by Sex, Color, and Age, 1947–1972," U.S. Department of Labor, *Handbook of Labor Statistics, 1973*, Bulletin 1790, Washington, D.C.: U.S. Government Printing Office, pp. 33–36.

FIGURE 22.4   Structure of the civilian labor force by sex, 1950-1972 (in thousands)

Year	Total labor force	Number of men	Percentage of the labor force	Number of women	Percentage of the labor force
1950	62,208	43,819	70.4	18,389	29.6
1960	69,628	46,388	66.6	23,240	33.4
1970	82,715	51,195	61.9	31,420	38.1
1972	86,542	53,265	61.5	33,277	38.5

Source: "Civilian Labor Force By Sex, Color, and Age, 1947-1972," U.S. Department of Labor, *Handbook of Labor Statistics, 1973*, Bulletin 1790, Washington, D.C.: U.S. Government Printing Office, pp. 33-36.

25 to 44 age classifications have not entered the work force in such large numbers because of their responsibilities toward their families. Apparently more married women work before children come into the home and following the completion of the more exacting parental obligations related to having young children.

Test Hypothesis No. 4 Blacks and other minority groups are increasing in numbers and percentages of the total work force.

This hypothesis is an extension of other generalizations based upon the assumption that minority groups on the basis of race are participating in the labor force more fully in ways similar to the increase in participation by women. Data available (see Figure 22.5) suggest that while the number of blacks and other nonwhite workers has increased in the last twenty years (up from 6,824,000 to 9,584,000), the percentage of the labor force made up of minority races has increased only in a minimal way (up from 10.7 percent in 1954 to 11.3 percent in the latest figures). Blacks and other minority ethnic groups composed 14.7 percent of the total population in 1970.

On the basis of available statistics, *the number of blacks and other minority race groups in the labor force has increased in recent years, and the percentage of blacks and other nonwhites as a part of the total work force has increased slightly.*

FIGURE 22.5   Structure of the civilian work force by color, 1954—1972 (in thousands)

Year	Total labor force	Number of white workers	Percentage of the total labor force	Number of black workers and workers of other races	Percentage of the total labor force
1954*	63,643	56,817	89.3	6,824	10.7
1960	69,628	61,913	88.9	7,714	11.1
1970	82,715	73,518	88.9	9,197	11.1
1972**	86,542	76,958	88.7	9,584	11.3

* 1954 was the first year the *Current Population Survey* began to keep employment data by color.

**Includes some population adjustments not found in other years.

Source: "Civilian Labor Force by Sex, Color, and Age, 1947-1972," U.S. Department of Labor, *Handbook of Labor Statistics, 1973*, Bulletin 1790, Washington, D.C.: U.S. Government Printing Office, pp. 33-36.

Test Hypothesis No. 5 The number of scheduled work hours of the average employee is decreasing.

When the most recent data available concerning the work hours of plant workers and office personnel were compared with the scheduled work hours of the same groups of workers ten years earlier, it was revealed that workers in the most recent survey (1969–1970) available were scheduled to work only twelve minutes less than their counterparts of the 1959–1960 era (see Figure 22.6). In 1969–1970 the average plant worker was scheduled for 40.3 hours of labor per week (down from 40.5 in 1959–1960), and the typical office worker was scheduled for 38.8 hours of work (down from 39.0 in 1959–1960).

Workers in the retail trades (both plant and office) showed the greatest decrease in hours worked, while plant workers in the manufacturing industry showed an actual increase of one-tenth of an hour (six minutes) of scheduled work. These statistics appear to indicate that the working conditions affecting time schedules have had little impact upon most workers. The average worker's scheduled work hours have changed little in the past decade. It should be noted that several labor

FIGURE 22.6   Hours worked by plant and office workers, 1959–1970

Average scheduled weekly hours	All industries	Manufacturing	Transportation, communication, and other public utilities	Industry Division		Finance, insurance, and real estate	Selected services
				Wholesale trade	Retail trade		
Plant Workers							
1959–60	40.5	40.3	40.3	41.2	41.2		41.8
1961–62	40.4	40.1	40.3	41.0	41.0		41.5
1963–64	40.4	40.2	40.3	40.9	40.9		41.1
1965–66	40.5	40.4	40.3	40.9	40.6		40.9
1967–68	40.5	40.4	40.3	40.8	40.5		40.6
1969–70	40.3	40.4	40.2	40.6	40.2		40.5
Office workers							
1959–60	39.0	39.4	39.2	39.3	39.6	37.9	38.6
1961–62	38.9	39.4	39.2	39.2	39.5	37.9	38.5
1963–64	38.9	39.3	39.1	39.1	39.4	37.9	38.5
1965–66	38.9	39.4	39.1	39.1	39.4	38.0	38.6
1967–68	38.9	39.4	39.1	39.1	39.3	38.0	38.5
1969–70	38.8	39.3	39.0	39.0	39.2	37.9	38.4

Source: "Scheduled Weekly Hours (By Shift) Percent of Plant and Office Workers by Weekly Work Schedule, All Metropolitan Areas, by Industry Division, 1959–1970," U.S. Department of Labor, *Handbook of Labor Statistics, 1973*, Bulletin 1790, Washington, D.C.: U.S. Government Printing Office, p. 173.

agreements in recent years have called for shorter work weeks for employees, but the effect of these agreements apparently has had little impact upon the hours of the typical worker. In some cases, the number of hours of overtime worked has, no doubt, increased. The impact of the severe 1974–1976 recession upon hours worked is not yet clear, but a further decrease of hours worked is likely, at least temporarily.

Test Hypothesis No. 6   The number of days per week worked by the typical employee has decreased in recent years.

The motivating force behind this hypothesis is the recent emphasis upon the four-day work week in many quarters. In many instances both management and labor have been willing to experiment with the reduction of worker days by the scheduling of longer work periods—usually ten hours per day—so that the worker can have a longer weekend or the equivalent. Other benefits expected to be gained for the organization through revised work day schedules are less absenteeism, less overtime, and less time lost at the beginning and the end of each work shift.

One source has estimated that from 1,800 to 4,000 companies in the United States are now using revised work week schedules including the four-day work week, the three-day work week, and other variations.[3] Work week revisions are known to have occurred among workers in office situations, in plant manufacturing, in hospitals, among police and fire workers, for some civil service workers, and in other types of employment. In many companies the reactions of both management and the worker have been favorable. In other situations the longer work days involved in the modification have resulted in problems of keeping important functions manned continuously and have created problems of increased fatigue and monotony for many workers. Unions have frequently opposed the principle of the worker's being expected to work more than an eight-hour day.

In summary, it appears that more and more organizations (affecting increasing numbers of people) are experimenting with the four-day work week or some variation of a revised work day schedule. The reactions to the effects of fewer days with longer hours have been mixed, with some favorable results and some negative consequences.

Test Hypothesis No. 7   The level of individual worker productivity (output per man hour) is steadily increasing on an annual basis.

This hypothesis appears to be generally true (for all private industries with a nonagricultural base). Using 1967 as the base year, surveys have shown that *output per man hour has*

---

[3]Riva Poor, Poor's Workweek Letter, as quoted by *U.S. News and World Report,* Volume 73, Number 19 (November 6, 1972), p. 104.

almost doubled in private, nonagricultural industries in the period of time beginning with 1950 and extending through 1972 (see Figure 22.7).

The increase in productivity can be attributed to many factors. The skill levels and performance competencies of many workers have increased as a result of additional training and education. Improved managerial action has resulted in better planning and coordination. Technological advances have provided better equipment, materials, and expertise. The end product of many factors has been a higher level of worker productivity.

In a movement somewhat counter to the general trend, it should be noted that in 1974 the level of productivity for each worker began to decline. Many economists feel this to be a temporary reaction to fuel and other supply problems. The trend deserves to be watched, however, to determine its real significance.

Test Hypothesis No. 8 **The level of formal education attained by individual members of the work force has risen progressively so that today's work force has a level of formal educational attainment superior to that of any previous work force.**

The evidence available tends to support this hypothesis fully. The median number of school years completed by all individuals in the total population rose from 10.6 years to 12.3 years

FIGURE 22.7   Indexes of output per man hour in the private economy from 1950 to 1973 (1967=100)

INDUSTRY	Output per man hour			
	1950	1960	1970	1973 (est.)
All private industries	59.7	78.2	104.3	116.1
Manufacturing	64.4	79.9	108.0	127.5
Other nonfarm industries	65.0	80.3	103.4	115.5

Source: "Economic Report of the President," February 1974, as reported in *The Statistical Abstract of the United States, 1974*, 95th Edition, Washington, D.C.: Department of Commerce, Bureau of the Census, p. 357.

in the period of time between 1960 and 1973 (see Figure 22.8). This suggests that the average individual (who is 25 years of age or older) has attained at least the equivalent of a high school diploma and has picked up a few additional months of formal education. The 1973 figures show an increase in the percentage of individuals who have completed four years of high school, the percentage of individuals who have attained one to three years of college training, and the individuals who have received four or more years of college-level education. The lower levels of educational attainment (elementary levels, etc.) all decreased in percentages of the population. If the level of educational attainment is considered along the lines of race, whites have increased their level of formal education over the twelve-year period to a median of 12.3 years (from 10.9 years), and blacks have upped the educational level to a median of 10.6 years (from 8.2 years).

FIGURE 22.8   Years of formal education completed, by race and sex, 1960 and 1973

Year, Race, and Sex	Persons 25 years old and over (thousands)	Percent of population completing							Median school years completed
		Elementary School			High School		College		
		0–4 years	5–8 years	8 years	1–3 years	4 years	1–3 years	4 or more years	
1960, all races	**99,438**	**8.3**	**13.8**	**17.5**	**19.2**	**24.6**	**8.8**	**7.7**	**10.6**
White	89,581	6.7	12.8	18.1	19.3	25.8	9.3	8.1	10.9
Male	43,259	7.4	13.7	18.4	18.9	22.2	9.1	10.3	10.7
Female	46,322	6.0	11.9	17.8	19.6	29.2	9.5	6.0	11.2
Negro	9,054	23.8	24.2	12.9	19.0	12.9	4.1	3.1	8.2
Male	4,240	28.3	23.9	12.3	17.3	11.3	4.1	2.8	7.7
Female	4,814	19.8	24.5	13.4	20.5	14.3	4.1	3.3	8.6
1973, all races	**112,866**	**4.5**	**8.0**	**11.4**	**16.3**	**35.8**	**11.4**	**12.6**	**12.3**
White	100,818	3.6	7.2	11.6	15.7	37.0	11.8	13.1	12.3
Male	47,645	3.9	7.5	11.7	14.8	32.8	12.5	16.8	12.4
Female	53,173	3.4	6.9	11.5	16.5	40.7	11.1	9.9	12.3
Negro	10,585	12.6	14.8	10.1	23.2	25.8	7.5	6.0	10.6
Male	4,711	14.9	15.3	10.8	20.9	25.2	7.1	5.9	10.3
Female	5,874	10.7	14.5	9.6	25.1	26.3	7.8	6.0	10.8

Source: U.S. Bureau of the Census, *U.S. Census of Population, 1960*, Volume 1, and *Current Population Reports*, Series P–20, as presented in *The Statistical Abstract of the United States, 1974*, 95th Edition, Washington, D.C.: Department of Commerce, Bureau of the Census, p. 116

FIGURE 22.9   Years of formal education completed, by age, 1973

| Age | Population (thousands) | Percent of population completing | | | | | | | Median school years completed |
| | | Elementary School | | | High School | | College | | |
		0–4 years	5–7 years	8 years	1–3 years	4 years	1–3 years	4 or more years	
25–29	15,220	1.0	2.5	3.4	13.0	43.9	17.4	19.0	12.7
30–34	12,573	1.5	3.2	4.4	15.4	43.9	14.4	17.2	12.6
35–44	22,461	2.4	5.1	6.1	17.0	42.1	12.2	15.1	12.5
45–54	23,449	3.4	7.1	10.0	17.8	39.3	11.0	11.4	12.3
55 and over	39,163	8.7	13.8	20.6	16.6	24.5	7.8	7.9	10.7

Source: U.S. Bureau of the Census, *U.S. Census of Population, 1960,* Volume I, and *Current Population Reports*, Series P-20, as presented in *The Statistical Abstract of the United States, 1974*, 95th Edition, Washington, D.C.: Department of Commerce, Bureau of the Census, p. 117.

If educational achievement is considered by sex and race, it can be noted that white men and women have almost the same median levels of attainment (12.4 and 12.3), although the percentage of white males having college training is higher than the percentage of women in the same category. The median level of attainment for blacks is slightly higher for women (10.8 years) than for men (10.3 years). Also, the younger adults in the total population have higher levels of educational attainment than do their older counterparts. Of the population 25 years of age or above, the 25 to 29 year age group has a median education of 12.7 years for the highest level. The 55 years and over group has the lowest median level of 10.7 years (see Figure 22.9). It should be recognized that these figures include the total population and not just the labor force, but the figures indicate an increase in the level of educational attainment by all segments of the population.

Test Hypothesis No. 9 The level of formal educational achievement influences the career opportunities of the average worker.

Behind this hypothesis is the assumption that the level of formal educational attainment will increase the job and promotional opportunities of the worker. It is assumed that increased educational training will make it possible for the individual to perform work tasks more adequately and capably as a result of expanded knowledge and skills. Formal education is expected to improve the ability to comprehend and to act. For example, it has been stated that at least four years of formal education are necessary for a worker to be able to read routine job instructions and to align his performance with the demands of the instructions. Formal education, it is believed, better prepares the worker for job performance and therefore improves the opportunities that will become available to him in his work career.

*The enhancement of work careers takes two forms—the initial opportunities for employment and promotions based upon merit or good performance. In both of these measures formal education appears to improve the worker's opportunit*ies. Of initial job opportunities, the industry practice of specifying job requirements in terms of earned high school diplomas or college degrees has become almost universal. In fact, so much weight has been placed upon the level of educational attainment that some civil rights efforts have been directed toward the establishment of recruiting and selection programs more directly on the basis of job needs and less emphatically upon the basis of educational achievement. Also, the *Griggs* v. *Duke Power Company* court decision has altered the use of some educational specifications for hiring. Company recruiting practices have placed such a premium on educational attainment that many overqualified workers have been sought out and hired for simplistic, undemanding jobs.

As another gauge of the effects of educational levels upon job opportunities, a U.S. Department of Labor study has revealed that individuals with five years or less of schooling tend to spend their work lives in positions as operators, service personnel, farmers, laborers, craftsmen, and clerical and sales personnel in that order (see Figure 22.10). High school graduates work as sales and clerical employees, operators, craftsmen, service personnel, managers and proprietors, and professional and technical workers in order of importance. The overwhelming majority of college graduates go into professional and technical positions, with the remaining graduates performing managerial and proprietory work or clerical and sales responsibilities.[4] *On the basis of these findings, it would appear that job opportunities are closely related to formal educational attainment. The higher-status, often more responsible jobs appear to go to the more educated worker.*

In another study it was shown that workers with more education were considered more promotable than workers with limited educational backgrounds.[5] *The effect of these research findings supports the hypothesis that educational attainment is an occupational asset.*

[4]U.S. Department of Labor, *Monthly Labor Review,* Volume 93, Number 10 (October 1970), p. 15.
[5]Fred Luthans, James Walker, and Richard M. Hodgetts, "Evidence on the Validity of Management Education," *Academy of Management Journal,* Volume 12, Number 4 (December 1969), pp. 451–457.

FIGURE 22.10   Occupations of workers according to levels of education attained

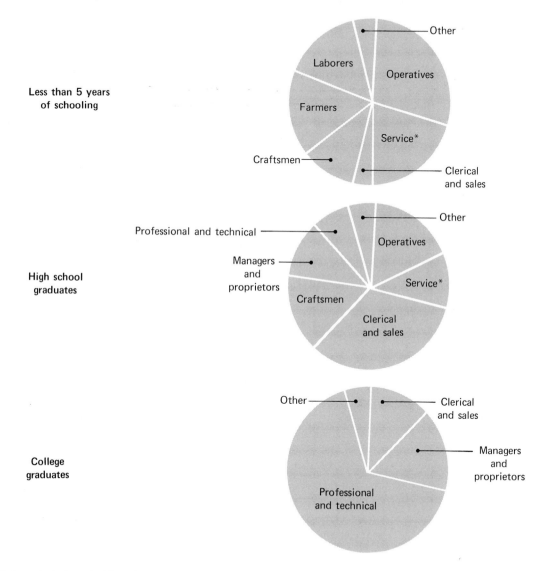

*Includes private household workers.

Source: U.S. Department of Labor, *Monthly Labor Review*, Volume 93, Number 10
(October 1970), p. 15.

Test Hypothesis No. 10   The level of formal educational attainment achieved by the worker tends to be an important determinant of the income level of the worker.

Because the level of educational attainment improves occupational and promotional opportunities, it would appear reasonable to assume that the level of formal educational achievement also enhances the income or earnings of the more educated worker. This hypothesis appears to be true. In a U.S. Bureau of the Census study, ~~income levels for workers increased in a direct relationship with increases in the number of years of formal education achieved by the workers.~~ The following educational level categories and their corresponding mean average incomes were discovered in this 1971 study:

1.   The worker with less than eight years of education averages $5,950 in earnings annually

2.   The worker with eight years of formal schooling has a mean income of $7,407

3.   The mean average for the worker with one to three years of high school is $8,966

4.   The worker with a high school diploma (four years of high school) averages earnings of $10,751

5.   The worker with one to three years of college receives an average of $12,022 each year

6.   The average annual earnings of the worker with four or more years of college is $16,698[6]

Findings of other studies of the U.S. Department of Labor confirm these findings and indicate that the relationship between higher educational attainment and a higher income level definitely exists.[7]

Test Hypothesis No. 11   The income level of workers in all occupational classifications has increased in recent years.

While many workers may feel that their own personal incomes have not increased as much as they should, ~~the generalization that the income level of workers throughout the work force has increased appears to be basically true.~~ It has been estimated that the hourly income (before taxes) of the average worker increased from $2.09 in 1960

---

[6]A U.S. Bureau of the Census study presented in *U.S. News and World Report*, Volume 73, Number 25 (December 18, 1972), p. 93.

[7]See "Percentage Distribution of Families by Income Levels by Years of School Completed, Race of Head 1963–1970," U.S. Department of Labor, *Handbook of Labor Statistics, 1972*, Bulletin 1735, Washington, D.C.: U.S. Government Printing Office, p. 399.

FIGURE 22.11   Hourly and weekly earnings in private industry, by industry group, 1960 to 1974

Industry group	1960	1965	1970	April 1974
Gross Hourly Earnings				
Total	**$2.09**	**$2.45**	**$3.22**	**$4.07**
Manufacturing	2.26	2.61	3.36	4.24
Mining	2.61	2.92	3.84	5.05
Contract construction	3.08	3.70	5.25	6.77
Transportation and public utilities	(NA)	3.03	3.85	5.27
Wholesale trade	2.24	2.61	3.44	4.37
Retail trade	1.52	1.82	2.44	3.01
Finance, insurance, and real estate	2.02	2.39	3.08	3.76
Services	(NA)	2.05	2.81	3.56
Gross Weekly Earnings				
Total	**$80.67**	**$95.06**	**$119.46**	**$148.00**
Manufacturing	89.72	107.53	133.73	167.00
Mining	105.44	123.52	163.97	219.00
Contract construction	113.04	138.38	196.35	243.00
Transportation and public utilities	(NA)	125.14	155.93	209.00
Wholesale trade	90.72	106.49	137.60	169.00
Retail trade	57.76	66.61	82.47	98.00
Finance, insurance, and real estate	75.14	88.91	113.34	138.00
Services	(NA)	73.60	96.66	120.00

Source: U.S. Bureau of Labor Statistics, *The Statistical Abstract of the United States, 1973*, 94th Edition, Washington, D.C.: Department of Commerce, Bureau of the Census, p. 241, and *The Statistical Abstract of the United States, 1974*, 95th Edition, p. 358.

to $4.07 in 1974 (see Figure 22.11). The total weekly earnings (before taxes) for the average worker increased from $80.67 to $148.00 in the same time period. Substantial wage increases are noticeable in *all industries* included in the survey by the Bureau of Labor Statistics.

The wage increases were in excess of simple cost-of-living adjustments. Workers in all private nonagricultural and manufacturing industries showed significant gains in spendable earnings in excess of cost-of-living increases and inflationary dollar effects.[8]

[8]See the Economic Report of the President 1972 as reported in Table No. 371, "Average Weekly Earnings, Gross and Spendable, in Current and 1967 Dollars, Total Private Nonagricultural and Manufacturing Industries: 1955 to 1972," as shown in *The Statistical Abstract of the United States, 1972*, 93rd Edition, Washington, D.C.: Department of Commerce, Bureau of the Census, p. 233.

Test Hypothesis No. 12   Employment levels (numbers of workers employed) in all industries (including those with agricultural and nonagricultural bases) have progressed steadily upward.

This hypothesis is based upon the assumption that the general prosperity of the post-World War II years coupled with the technological innovations of a scientific era have encouraged and fostered growth and consequent increased employment in all industries. *While it is true that employment in most industries has increased rapidly, a few industries have not shared in this growth. On a purely numerical basis, the numbers of individuals employed in mining* (see Figure 22.12) *and in agriculture*[9] *have decreased significantly.* As a percentage of the total nonagricultural labor force, employment in manufacturing, transportation and public utilities, and construction has also decreased. In other words, these industries have increased in numerical positions available for employment but have not kept pace with the more rapid expansion of industries such as the wholesale and retail trades, government employment, service industries, and the finance, insurance, and real estate group. In particular, employment by the government and in service industries has grown phenomenally. The increasing amount of mechanization and automation has, no doubt, taken a toll on the agricultural and mining industries as perhaps on others also.

Test Hypothesis No. 13   White-collar workers are increasing numerically and as a percentage of the work force, while blue-collar workers are decreasing in both categories. In other words, the labor force is becoming a white-collar group rather than a blue-collar body.

The implication behind this hypothesis is that working conditions and responsibilities relating to the work force have improved so that more and more workers are involved in white-collar jobs and fewer workers are employed in the blue-collar ranks. White-collar jobs include those filled by professional and technical workers, managers and administrators, sales workers, and clerical workers. Blue-collar workers include craftsmen, operatives, and other nonfarm laborers.

The truth of the matter is that workers in all nonagricultural occupational classifications have increased numerically over the period of years between 1950 and 1973 (workers in white-collar, blue-collar, and service categories). *On a percentage basis, white-collar*

[9]U.S. Bureau of Labor Statistics, "Employed Persons by Major Occupation Group and Sex, 1950 to 1974," *The Statistical Abstract of the United States, 1974,* 95th Edition, Washington, D.C.: Department of Commerce, Bureau of the Census, p. 350.

FIGURE 22.12   Number of employees in nonagricultural establishments, 1950 to 1974, with percentages by industry (in thousands)

Year	Total nonagricultural labor force	Manufacturing	Wholesale and retail trade	Government	Services	Transportation and public utilities	Finance, insurance, and real estate	Construction	Mining
1950	45,222	15,241	9,836	6,026	5,382	4,034	1,919	2,333	901
1960	54,234	16,796	11,391	8,353	7,423	4,004	2,669	2,885	712
1970	70,616	19,369	14,922	12,535	11,630	4,504	3,690	3,345	622
1974*	76,678	19,785	16,398	14,280	13,294	4,636	4,120	3,513	652
Numerical increase or decrease from 1950 to 1974		+	+	+	+	+	+	+	–
Percentages of nonagricultural labor force									
1950	100.0	33.7	20.8	13.3	11.9	8.9	4.2	5.2	2.0
1960	100.0	31.0	21.0	15.4	13.7	7.4	4.9	5.3	1.3
1970	100.0	27.4	21.1	17.8	16.5	6.4	5.2	4.7	0.9
1974*	100.0	25.8	21.4	18.6	17.3	6.0	5.4	4.6	0.9
Percentage of nonagricultural labor force increase or decrease from 1970 to 1974		–	+	+	+	–	+	–	–

* Preliminary figures.

Source: U.S. Bureau of Labor Statistics, *Employment and Earnings*, as presented in *The Statistical Abstract of the United States, 1974*, 95th Edition, Washington, D.C.: Department of Commerce, Bureau of the Census, p. 345.

workers have increased significantly, and service personnel have also garnered a larger percentage of the total work force (see Figure 22.13 for additional information). Blue-collar workers have decreased as a percentage of the work force from 39.1 percent in 1950 to 34.2 percent in 1974. Farm workers decreased in both numerical and percentage categories.

As a summary of these figures, white-collar workers have come to compose almost one-half of the total work force (48.8 percent) with 41,590,000 workers performing tasks or working under conditions that qualify them for membership in the white-collar ranks.

Test Hypothesis No. 14   The work force has become an urban-centered group of city dwellers.

A recognizable trend in the American society has been the trend of residential movement away from the farms and rural areas to the cities and towns (or urban areas). At the beginning of the era of mechanization (described in Chapter 4), most of the population of the United States was located in rural areas. The pattern of living continues to change so that in 1950, 62.5 percent of the total U.S. population lived in urban areas; by 1960, 66.7 percent dwelled in the cities and towns; and in 1970, 68.6 percent of the people lived in the urban areas.[10] ~~The American population appears to be continually centralizing itself in urban population centers.~~

These figures may not be totally characteristic of the work force, because they are drawn from the total population. However, the data represent a general trend that has an impact upon the work force (see Chapter 3 for a discussion of rural-urban residence as it affects individual behavior).

The Correct Facts Concerning the Labor Force

On the basis of the data presented in this chapter, the following generalizations can be made concerning the structure and characteristics of the work force and the resulting effects.

FACT NO. 1   There are more young people (below the age of 25) in numbers and as a percentage of the work force than has previously been true of any modern

---

[10]Population by Residence and Race, 1950–1970," in *The Statistical Abstract of the United States, 1974, op. cit.,* p. 17.

FIGURE 22.13 Employment by occupational group, 1950 to 1974 (in thousands)

Year	Total		White-collar		Blue-collar		Service workers		Farm workers	
	Number	Percentage	Number	Percentage	Number	Percentage	Number	Percentage	Number	Percentage
1950	59,648	100.0	22,373	37.5	23,336	39.1	6,535	11.0	7,408	12.4
1960	65,778	100.0	28,522	43.3	24,057	36.6	8,349	12.7	5,395	8.1
1970	78,627	100.0	37,997	48.3*	27,791	35.3	9,712	12.4	3,126	3.9
1974	85,192	100.0	41,590	48.8*	29,182	34.2	11,353	13.3	3,066	3.6

* The percentage figures do not equal 100.0 percent as a result of rounding.

Source: U.S. Bureau of the Census, *Population Reports*, Series P-50, and U.S. Bureau of Labor Statistics, *Employment and Earnings* as presented in *The Statistical Abstract of the United States, 1974*, 95th Edition, Washington, D.C.: Department of Commerce, Bureau of the Census, p. 350.

work force. However, there are also increases (numerically and in percentages) in workers in the upper middle-age categories (45 to 64), and there are numerical increases in all age categories over previous numbers of participants.

FACT No. 2   Trends in the age categories affecting the labor force indicate that the move toward a more youthful labor force will modify itself in the coming years so that the growth area of the future will be particularly in the number of workers in the middle-age categories.

FACT No. 3   Women are becoming a more active part of the labor force. At the present time almost two out of five (nearly 40 percent) workers are women.

FACT No. 4   The percentage of the labor force composed of blacks and other minority race groups has increased slightly in recent years. Approximately 11.3 percent of the labor force comes from the ranks of blacks and other non-white races.

FACT No. 5   The number of hours worked by the average employee has decreased only slightly in recent years. The typical employee is scheduled to work only twelve minutes less each week, according to recent surveys, than the same employee was expected to work in a given week ten years earlier.

FACT No. 6   More organizations are changing the work days of their employees to conform to a four-day work week or some other modification of the traditional five-day work week. The organizations with a five-day work week continue to be in the majority, however.

FACT No. 7   The level of individual worker productivity (output per man hour) has generally increased on an annual basis. Some recent dips have been noted, however.

FACT No. 8   The level of formal education attained by individual members of the work force has risen progressively so that today's work force has a level of formal education superior to that of any previous work force.

FACT No. 9   The higher the level of formal education attained by the worker, the more job choices and promotional opportunities he will tend to have.

FACT No. 10   There appears to be a direct relationship between the level of formal education achieved by a worker and the income level he can expect to attain. The better-educated worker tends to have an income level higher than the lesser-educated employee.

FACT No. 11   The income level of workers in all occupational classifications has increased in recent years.

FACT No. 12   Employment patterns within industries have changed significantly in recent years. In particular, the number and percentage of workers in the wholesale and retail trade, the government, service industries, and the finance-real estate-insurance group have increased. Employment levels have decreased noticeably in the agricultural and mining industries.

FACT No. 13   Almost one-half of the total labor force is employed in white-collar jobs. The number and percentage of service workers has increased also. The number of blue-collar workers is still increasing, but blue-collar workers compose a smaller percentage of the total labor force than was previously true.

FACT No. 14   The work force has become an urban-centered group of city dwellers. Seven out of every ten American citizens now live in an urban center. (The percentage of workers employed in business and industry living in the urban areas is probably higher than the figure for the total population.)

Summary

The figures describing the work force provide insight into the structure and environment in which the worker of today lives and labors. The data also reveal many traits and characteristics of the laborer himself.

An analysis of the data provides many clues related to the current interests, issues, and problems confronting today's worker. Each worker who reviews this material will, no doubt, compare his own characteristics and circumstances against those presented as an overview of the work force. Each manager will compare the structure, trends, conditions, and characteristics with those of the workers whom he supervises personally.

The data presented in this chapter should facilitate the comprehension and analysis of the following chapters, because the profile of the work force outlines many important attributes upon which current and future management issues are based. Some of these issues are considered in chapters 23 and 24.

The following cases at the back of the book contain problems related to Chapter 23:

Ben Stockton

Mark Williams

Stanley Lowell

Billy Snyder

Susan Swanson

Walt Gladberry

Chapter 23

Meeting Today's Challenges

A case to consider before reading chapter 23

ELLEN CRENSHAW– A DISSATISFIED BANKER

Ellen Crenshaw has been employed by Third State Bank since her graduation from State University five years ago. At State University she received a degree in general business and came to work for the bank in its management training program. The program, which lasted for one year, gave her an exposure to all phases of the bank's operation. From the training program she was assigned to the bookkeeping and records department as the assistant manager. Two years ago she was promoted to manager of the same department.

Several complaints and dissatisfactions have been building up in her mind since she completed the training program four years ago, but she has been reluctant to mention them. Her feelings have become so strong, however, that she has now sought out her supervisor, Parker Ferrell, assistant vice president for bank operations, and is telling him several things she finds disturbing about her job with the bank. The following statements are a part of her conversation with Mr. Ferrell.

I don't know about everyone's salary here at the bank, but I do know that my salary and some other women's salaries are somewhat lower than many of the men's salaries. I know for a fact that some of the male college graduates hired for the training program last month are being paid only a few dollars per month less than what I'm now being paid, and I have five years of working experience with the bank. ~~The pay scale seems to be unfair to women.~~

It also seems to me that women are treated unfairly when job assignments are given out. Women always seem to get the secretarial, clerical, routine jobs while the men get the more exciting, prestigious jobs. I think men believe all women enjoy routine work, but it just isn't true. Some women may, but I for one would enjoy something that challenges my abilities more fully.

That brings me to another point. I think women are being bypassed for promotions to better jobs. I've applied for a transfer to the personal loan department and to the savings department on two different occasions, but I was turned down and the jobs were given to men just coming out of the training program. I was given no reasons for the rejection of my requests except that I was needed in my present position.

While I'm complaining, I'll get another gripe out in the open. A dual behavior standard exists around here. Men are given many freedoms that women are being denied. For example, there are a few areas where no employee is permitted to smoke (for safety reasons). However, all men are permitted to smoke at their desks. Women, on the other hand, are discouraged from smoking anywhere except in the women's lounge. I think this is unfair.

The other complaint that I have is that the bank's policy toward what employees may wear to work is too restrictive for both women and men. If a man is in something other than a dark brown, blue, or black suit and similarly subdued tie, he is considered out of uniform. If a woman wears something other than a drab knee-length dress she too is out of uniform. These restrictions are stifling and overdone, I believe.

Questions about the Ellen Crenshaw case

1. Which of Ellen Crenshaw's complaints on the surface appear to be valid if they are true? Why? Which ones (if any) are not reasonable? Why?

2. How widespread in the working world are complaints similar to Ellen's? Support your answer.

3. What misconceptions does the case reveal in the attitudes many people have toward women at work?

4. If Mr. Ferrell uses the correct counseling techniques, what will his attitude and comments be during the conversation with Ellen?

5. If these complaints reveal the situation in the bank as it really is, what steps should the bank take to correct the problems? Please be specific.

6. Besides women, what other "minority" groups have been heard to voice similar complaints?

As long as people have been joined together in collective efforts to produce goods and services while achieving their own personal goals, there have been interpersonal problems that have hindered the full achievement of these objectives. Managers of enterprises have found themselves confronted with problems of motivation, cooperation, control, and other fundamental difficulties. Some of these problems appear to be almost perpetual in nature, while others rise and fall in relation to changing conditions (social, demographic, economic, political, workers' attitudes and values, etc.).

This chapter concerns itself with some of the more recent problems and issues related to the management of interpersonal relations. These contemporary issues provide the latest challenges to the wits and skills of today's managers. The procedure used in the chapter is that of identifying the issues, discovering the underlying causes, and presenting managerial solutions whenever possible. Specifically, this chapter addresses itself to issues related to the generation gap (age differentials and their related effects), the position of women in the work force, the problems experienced by minority races, and the newly exhibited rejection by some workers of several traditional organizational factors and methods of operation.

The Generation Gap

It may appear unusual to classify the issue of generation gaps as a contemporary problem, because there have been discussions and debates through the years concerning the differences between young "whippersnappers" and old "fuddy-duddies." In other words, there have been traditional misunderstandings and disagreements between the chronologically young and old through the ages. The factor that makes this issue something more than a continuation of traditional misgivings is the spreading belief that the values and behavior of young workers in the labor force (and youth everywhere) are becoming more widely separated from the values of the older workers. This conceptualization was kindled by articles that pointed out the shift in behavior patterns of students in the 1960s and early 1970s to activist positions compared with the passivity of previous generations of students.[1] A general feeling has grown that the values or ideological systems of the young have made a marked move away from the ideological position of older individuals, particularly in recent years. This position is expressed in the following quotation.

[1]Richard Flacks, "The Liberated Generation: An Exploration of the Roots of Student Protest," *Journal of Social Issues,* Volume 23, Number 3 (July 1967), pp. 52–57, and William D. Watts and D. N. Whittaker, "Free Speech Advocates at Berkeley," *Journal of Applied Behavioral Science,* Volume 2 Number 1 (1962), pp. 42–43.

The older generation, industrial man, lives by the values of the system of free enterprise: success, comfort, security, status-striving, competition, power, money, role-playing, the quest for distraction. The younger generation, post industrial man, believes in establishing a personal identity, authentic relations between man and man, more decentralization politically, communally, and socially, less alienation, social and Christian values, organization for social change, the exploitation of science, technology, and affluence to improve the conditions of man rather than for profit, cooperation and mutual aid, etc.[2]

Another author stresses the differences between generations by saying that today's youth differ from those of previous generations in several important areas.

1.   There is now more concern about basic values, not just different values, but values *per se*.

2.   Action is more important. Not only are values more salient, but there is strong emphasis on behaving in accord with one's values. . . . Values are not trusted unless they are backed by action. . . .

3.   Personal integrity, honesty, openness, and realness are more important. . . .

4.   Many of the "new culture" values are humanistic (relating to personal development, intellectual and emotional growth). . . .

5.   Related to the humanistic and value orientation is a concern for the ultimate social value of one's work. Not only is the intrinsic meaning and challenge of a job important, but also the consequences of one's work are important to youth.

6.   The definition of legitimate authority is changing. Authority based upon age or position is less highly regarded. The authority of one's expertise, personal style, personal connections, or accomplishments carries much more weight with today's youth.[3]

A concern expressed by many businessmen has been the fear of incompatibility between the workers of different age groups as they are required to work together. In addition, it has been suggested that the more individualistic goals of the young may cause a serious revision of organizational goals and methods of operation. The fear has been expressed that these innovations may distract from the purposes and functions of the productive organization.

It is now essential to put assessments of youthful ideologies and managerial fears into perspective. It seems apparent that the values of the young have changed to a degree from the values of young people in previous generations.

[2]Henry Winthrop, "The Alienation of Post Industrial Man," *Midwest Quarterly*, Volume 9, Number 2 (January 1968), p. 123.

[3]Douglas T. Hall, "Potential for Career Growth," *Personnel Administration*, Volume 34, Number 3 (May–June 1971), pp. 18–19.

However, *the values of people of all ages have been modified in recent years* so that there has been an increased interest in action, in establishing and supporting a personal identity, in utilizing the principles of decentralization and delegation, in achieving satisfaction and meaning through work, in the dignity of the individual, and in the encouragement of more attention to humanistic and social values. In a recent study in the banking industry for example, it was shown that the values of employees under thirty years of age were little different from the values of workers in older age categories.[4] Other studies may not support this thesis to the same magnitude, but the point is well taken that the differences may be less than originally expected.

As was discussed in Chapter 3, values are the product of a number of factors involving social institutions and groupings and personal conditions and circumstances. One author has pointed out that the social class of the family is an important determinant of values in relation to ideology toward work, for example.[5] As the values relating to family, friends, religion, education, the government, and other social factors change, so will the values of individuals be transformed. The role of youth in instigating changing values should not be underestimated in this context. There is little doubt that the impatience of young workers with traditional habits and abuses has provided some of the impetus for change. The increased number of young workers (see Chapter 22) has caused this problem to gain greater attention.

Because values are not always consistent with behavioral actions and norms, it is appropriate to observe that younger people do not always act in the same manner as older people and vice versa. Differences may occur as a result of differences in perception of roles, differences in personal needs and desires, differences in levels of responsibilities, and variations of other types. The older worker in a position of high responsibility with a previous record of conservative actions, nearing retirement may act cautiously to protect his seniority and his reputation, while a younger worker with little organizational responsibility, with few family obligations, and with a desire to be active may pursue organizational causes that foster change and risk taking. Many of the values of the two work groups concerning individuality, human dignity, the use of authority, etc. may be similar, but personal needs and conditions may be different.

[4]William Slaughter, III, *A Study of Personal Value Systems of Managers in the Banking Industry as Related to Age and Position,* an unpublished doctoral dissertation, Louisiana State University, Baton Rouge, Louisiana, 1973.

[5]Peter L. Berger, in a speech to the American Association of State Colleges and Universities, Washington, D.C., November 13, 1972, as quoted in *U.S. News and World Report,* Volume 73, Number 23 (December 4, 1972), p. 56.

Dealing with Problems based upon Age Differentiation.   A beginning point in the handling of anticipated problems of worker incompatibilities based upon age differences is the recognition that the values of the young and the old may not be so far apart as was originally expected. Many values are commonly held regardless of the ages of the individuals involved. Another key to the resolution of strife and jealousies may be the realization of the unique needs, desires, and perceptions of individuals as a result of backgrounds, work experiences, family responsibilities, educational qualifications, and the provision of outlets and means of attainment for these personal goals and needs. This attention is deserved whatever the age of the individual may be.

A potential source of conflict may lie in the restlessness of younger members of the work force in relation to the performance of menial tasks and duties lacking in responsibility. These tasks in particular seem to be relegated to the newer employees of organizations. On the other side of the issue, the senior employees may be fearful of losing their authority and rights and may even believe they will be displaced by the younger workers. An ~~effort should be made to help older workers be productive and secure while encouraging younger workers through granting greater responsibility and authority.~~

Many of the problems and fears based upon age can be overcome by involving older and younger workers in cooperative tasks so that they can come to know and understand the values, needs, and desires of each other. Training and educational programs incorporating role playing, case analyses, and group conferences may also prove a beneficial means of attitudinal change and may improve the probabilities of worker compatibility.

Women in the Work Force

Before World War II women were a distinctly small part of the total work force in the United States. Even in the postwar era of 1950, women accounted for only 29.6 percent of all laborers. This figure has steadily risen until in 1973 one governmental accounting showed 38.5 percent of all workers were women.[6] Just as the complexion of the work force has changed, so the interests and roles of women have changed. Anderson and Tersine suggest that the working woman today is a new woman largely because of the effects of: (1) Title VII of the 1964 Civil Rights Act providing equality for women in the work force; (2) technological developments such as the "pill," electrical home appliances, and other advances

[6]"Civilian Labor Force By Sex, Color, and Age, 1947–1972," U.S. Department of Labor, *Handbook of Labor Statistics, 1973*, Bulletin 1790, Washington, D.C.: U.S. Government Printing Office, pp. 33–36.

that have made it possible for women to spend more time outside the home; and (3) the impetus of the women's liberation movement, which has encouraged a new set of norms, values, and roles.[7] ~~This "new" woman often is dissatisfied with her status in business.~~ She frequently has ~~complained about discrimination~~ in hiring practices, promotion policies, assignment of menial tasks as opposed to important decision-making duties, inequitable wage policies, lack of acceptance in social circles by her male counterparts, and other acts of discrimination. The ~~Equal Employment Opportunity Commission~~ of the federal government indicates that complaints received by the commission on the basis of ~~sex discrimination increased from 2,003 in 1967 to 10,436 in 1972~~ and now are the number two source of discriminatory complaints received by the commission.[8] (Discrimination because of race is the number one factor.)

A review of the statistics presented in Figure 23.1 will verify that many of the complaints have foundations based upon fact. Inequities appear in wages and

FIGURE 23.1   Facts and figures concerning men and women in the work force, 1972

Area of comparison	Men	Women
Percentage of total labor force	About 60	About 40
Median annual income for full-time employees	$8,966	$5,323
Percentage of workers who are:		
Clerks	6.7	33.9
Professional and technical workers	13.7	14.5
Managers and proprietors	14.6	5.0
Unemployed	4.2	5.5

Source: Reprinted by permission from *Time,* © Time, Inc., Volume 99, Number 12 (March 20, 1972), p. 81.

[7]Rolph E. Anderson and Richard J. Tersine, "Our Working Women," *Business Horizons,* Volume 16, Number 1 (February 1973), p. 56.

[8]"Job Rights for Women—the Drive Speeds Up," *U.S. News and World Report,* Volume 73, Number 24 (December 11, 1972), p. 90.

salaries, assignments to managerial responsibilities and assignments of other types of work, as well as some areas not included in the table. Surveys indicate that in the case of wages and salaries, the inequities have increased in recent years rather than decreased. In 1970 the average woman worker took home only 59 percent of the wages paid to similarly employed men, while in 1955 she was earning 64 percent of her male counterpart's salary.[9] Also, the percentage of women in managerial and proprietary positions has decreased slightly since 1960.

The causes of the ~~problems women face~~ in connection with ~~lower wages, fewer challenging job assignments and managerial positions, and lack of social acceptance at work are complex in nature~~. To a degree, the problems are a part of the traditional value system of business and industry. Traditionally, the top priorities for salaries and job positions were given to individuals who were the breadwinners for families, and this was thought to be a man's responsibility. Men had always held the positions of management and supervision. Even in educational circles, women were not encouraged to train for important career positions.[10]

Many stereotypes have been a hindrance to women's progress also. Often women have been categorized as too emotional and too easily disturbed to be qualified for positions of major responsibility.[11] Men have often expressed the attitude that "a woman's place is in the home." It has been rumored that women enjoy repetitive, monotonous tasks to a higher degree than do men. It has been said that women are less ambitious than men and are less desirous of responsibility than men. Some have indicated that women worked only for "mad money" or for social reasons, and that economic necessity was not a cause that forced women to work. In addition, it has been revealed that many men would prefer to work under the supervision of men rather than women.

Married women, of course, have always assumed many responsibilities for their families, especially where there were preschool children involved. Many husbands have been reluctant to endorse a work career for their wives that would require them to be away from home for long intervals. These situations have led to the general belief that the absenteeism rates for women are much higher than are the absenteeism rates for men and that career lengths are much shorter for women than for men. The effect of the many barriers and stereotypes has been that most women have had to strive harder to achieve progress at work than have men.

[9]"Slow Gains at Work, *Time Magazine,* Volume 99, Number 12 (March 20, 1972), p. 81.

[10]Lawrence C. Hackamack and Alan B. Solid, "The Woman Executive," *Business Horizons,* Volume 15, Number 2 (April 1972), p. 92.

[11]*Loc. cit.*

Data collected in recent years have clarified some of the stereotypes and dispelled many of the misconceptions regarding women at work. Absenteeism, for example, has been discovered to be only slightly higher for women (5.9 days per year) than for men (5.2 days per year).[12] The assumption that a woman's work career is a brief and passing fancy has also been destroyed, because it has been discovered that the work life (length of time in the work force) for the average working woman is twenty-five years.[13] This length of time, although shorter than the average worked by men, is quite sufficient to justify the training costs and skill developments necessary to prepare women for work careers.

In a study performed by the Institute for Social Research at the University of Michigan it was discovered that:

1.   Approximately one-third of all working women are the sole support of themselves and their families; 40 percent are the sole or major wage earner. *Therefore, many women do work out of economic necessity.*

2.   About 57 percent of the female work force would continue to work even if no economic necessity existed. More married women would not work if the economic necessity did not exist than would be true of single women. *Work careers are important to most women for reasons other than money.*

3.   Women hold down a higher proportion of repetitive, monotonous jobs than do men, *but they gain no more satisfaction from the intellectually undemanding tasks than do men. Boring jobs are equally unattractive for both sexes.*

4.   Women feel that promotions are just as important as men think promotions are, but fewer women than men expect that any opportunities will come along for them to be advanced. *The lack of opportunity for promotions has conditioned women to expect less.*

5.   *Women are less concerned about freedom of movement and freedom of authority on the job than are men.* Women tend to prefer to have responsibilities defined in more detail than do men.

6.   Good working conditions (good hours, pleasant physical surroundings, convenient travel to and from work) *are slightly more important to women than they are to men.*

7.   *The importance of having friendly, helpful co-workers is slightly greater for women than for men.*

8.   Women are as concerned about opportunities for self-actualization (opportunities to excel, to find challenging work, etc.) *as are men.*[14]

[12]Anderson and Tersine, *op. cit.*, p. 57.

[13]Hackamack and Solid, *op. cit.*, p. 90.

[14]From a study by Joan E. Crowley, Teresa E. Levitin, and Robert P. Quinn entitled "Facts and Fictions about the American Working Woman," reported in the *ISR Newsletter*, Volume 1, Number 16 (Autumn 1972), pp. 4–5, published by the Institute of Social Research, the University of Michigan.

These findings illustrate that many of the generalizations made about women at work have not been based upon fact. It is expected that some additional stereotypes will be dispelled as future research is conducted. At the same time, the data identify some unique differences in the preferences of women and in the way in which they approach their work.

Solutions to Problems Facing Women.   Because traditional practices and stereotyped impressions are prominent as causes of many of the problems of working women, improvement and correction must involve solutions that will change these practices and impressions. Inequitable practices, in particular, must give way to decisions made upon merit and fairness rather than on the basis of yesterday's habits. From several sources, the following steps to an approach for improvement have been drawn.

1.   Top management of the organization must commit itself fully to the objective of identifying and upgrading qualified personnel, regardless of sex. This commitment should be spelled out in a policy statement circulated to all employees.

2.   Ordinarily, it is beneficial to assign an individual to the task of directing this program of pursuing equality and fairness for everyone.

3.   Policies on recruitment, selection, placement, and promotion of women (or other minorities) should be reviewed to uncover and eliminate any implicit discrimination.

4.   An organizational audit should be conducted in which the status of women in the existing structure is identified. The qualifications of women, the involvement of women in training programs, the percentage of women in the different hierarchical levels, and other pertinent data should be uncovered. Where inequities are found, specific targets for improvement should be established in terms of how much money, authority, etc. will be provided to correct the problems, and a time sequence should be determined. Without these specifications, the program for improvement will lag.[15]

5.   The attitudes and stereotypes existing about men and women working must be discovered and action to achieve change should be initiated where it is necessary. This is a particularly critical phase since so many misconceptions seem to exist. The use of mixed task forces, sensitivity training, role playing, educational lectures, and simple communication processes can do much to sweep away the misgivings that the sexes may have about each other.

6.   Continuous monitorings and adjustments will be necessary to keep the program relevant and responsive to organizational and individual employee needs. Adaptive, flexible leadership should be applied to meet the needs of individuals as they arise.

[15]M. Barbara Boyle, "Equal Opportunity for Women in Small Business," *Harvard Business Review,* Volume 51, Number 3 (May–June 1973), p. 92.

7. ~~Throughout the program, the emphasis should be placed on ability to perform rather than upon irrelevant variables such as sex.~~[16]

While not all organizations may have been unfair and discriminatory in the treatment of women employees, many have been. Statistics indicate that in many organizations there is significant room for improvement.

An interesting twist to the move toward more equitable treatment of individuals regardless of their sex has been the number of new positions and benefits that have been achieved by men as well. Reports indicate that positions are opening to men (as airline stewards, telephone operators, and the like) in areas previously open only to women.[17] Retirement age has been equalized in some situations so that men can now retire at age fifty-five or after twenty-five years of experience just as women previously had been allowed to do.[18] The avenue for improvement appears to be a two-way street, as it should be.

Minority Races in the Work Force

As women have encountered problems as a minority sex, so have blacks and other nonwhites encountered difficulties as minority races in the work force. The ~~problems of racial minorities involve inequities in wages and salaries, slower promotional advancements, social ostracism, difficulties in gaining entrance to union membership,~~ and ~~other negative consequences.~~ These grievances parallel the grievances of women in several respects.

Data collected tend to verify that there are inequities in salaries received, managerial promotions gained, level of employment attained, and in other quantifiable areas (see Figure 23.2). ~~Blacks and other nonwhites make up only 11.3 percent of the total labor force~~ in comparison with the fact that they represent 14.7 percent of the total population. ~~Unemployment among ethnic minorities is 7.0 percent, while it is only 1.4 percent for white worke~~rs. The median income for the black family is $5,359, while it stands at $8,936 for whites. The salary differences are further illustrated by the fact that the black worker with a high school diploma averages lower earnings than the white worker with only eight years of elementary schooling. Fewer than one out of every ten professionals comes from the ranks of minority groups, and ~~only about 3 percent of the individuals holding managerial positions are of minority background~~s. The data in Figure 23.2 indicate

[16]A majority of these points were presented by Anderson and Tersine, *op. cit.*, pp. 61–62.
[17]See, for example, "Labor Letter," *Wall Street Journal*, June 6, 1972, p. 1.
[18]"Job Rights for Women—the Drive Speeds Up," *op. cit.*, p. 91.

FIGURE 23.2   Facts and figures concerning white and black workers
in the work force, 1970

Area of comparison	Black workers	White workers
Percentage of the total U.S. population	14.7*	85.3
Percentage of the labor force	11.3*	88.7
Median family income	$5,359	$8,936
Percentage earning below poverty level ($3,553 for a nonfarm family of four)	29	8
Per capita income	$1,348	$2,616
Overall unemployment	7.0*	1.4
Number of professional workers	692,000*	10,031,000
Increase in professional jobs in the 1960s	109	41
Number of managerial workers	254,000*	7,721,000
Increase in managerial jobs in the 1960s	43	12

*Includes blacks and other nonwhite ethnic groups.

Source: Reprinted by permission from *Time,* © Time, Inc., Volume 95, Number 13
(April 6, 1970), p. 94.

that the gains by minority groups in professional and managerial employment
have greatly accelerated in the last decade.

The natural question to follow these statistics is, To what can the differentials
in money, job responsibilities, social acceptability, and employment opportunities
be attributed? The answer is difficult to supply but must include consideration
of these factors—the effects of race cultures on interaction and development,
traditional organizational perceptions of the roles and norms for individuals, the
protective nature of the group in power, and the skill and knowledge requirements of industry. In some way, each of these factors may contribute to the
description of the condition of ethnic minorities in business organizations.

In Chapter 3 it was stated that the racial background of individuals: (1) determines the language (or at least some of the idioms) used by its members; (2) has

an impact upon the religious affiliations and involvements of its people; (3) creates a separate set of behavior patterns to differentiate its members from those of other races; (4) provides a source of mutual affiliation and support; (5) establishes a common culture and set of traditions; and (6) unifies the feelings of solidarity and uniqueness among its members. While there has been an increased blending of racial cultures and traditions in recent years, it is not unusual to discover that differences still exist in cultural systems as a result of race identifications. People naturally tend to be drawn together by common interests and means of communicating. The characteristics of uniqueness that have encouraged unity among racial groups have also tended to keep interactions between groups with different backgrounds at a reduced level. As a result, some social isolation and ostracism has occurred among workers of varying backgrounds.

Work organizations in the American economy traditionally have been oriented toward the white male. It has been the white male worker who has filled the ranks of the professionals, the white-collar group, and the managerial positions. These positions traditionally were viewed as jobs to be manned continually by individuals of similar backgrounds. The traditional images and perceptions made it easy to search in the ranks of white males when jobs in these categories opened up and to overlook individuals from other ethnic groups, the opposite sex, or individuals who were in other ways differentiated from the previous norms. If a job that has always been filled by a white male, age fifty or above, with a college degree, trained in a particular discipline, becomes open, the traditional logic has been to attempt to duplicate the same characteristics when searching for a replacement.

Another factor bearing upon the continuation of traditional occupational and managerial patterns has been the natural inclination of individuals holding the reins of the power structure to seek to continue their roles of leadership and power. Those who are the "ins" look with concern on the erosion of their power into the hands of the "outs." Those out of power desire to gain control and influence to reverse the trends that have operated to their disadvantage. This struggle for power, of course, has been the source of much conflict.

Another factor that has influenced the hiring, promotion, and rewarding of workers is the fact that the basis for many decisions must be related to skill and knowledge requirements, and for various reasons, not all individuals have come to the work force with equal preparation. This disequilibrium may be attributed to the continuation of traditional organizational orientation, which has not encouraged groups from minority backgrounds to train for positions dominated by others. Whatever the reasons, those of minority ethnic backgrounds frequently have been at a disadvantage in filling job skill requirements.

Resolving problems of ethnic differences.   To some extent, the approach to improving the status of ethnic minorities in industry is similar to the plan illustrated for working women. ~~Objectives for identifying and upgrading all personnel must be established. Any policies for hiring, selecting, placing, and promoting individuals that contain discriminatory practices should be eliminated.~~ ~~Organizational audi~~ts should be conducted to ~~discover qualifications,~~ ~~needs, promotional attributes, and other pertinent data without overlooking *anyone* in the organization.~~ Where discriminatory practices are discovered, specific action should be taken to correct the inequities.

One of the major problems mentioned earlier was the differences in cultural backgrounds and the social cohesiveness of race groups. Because cultures cannot be altered overnight (many would argue that they shouldn't change anyway) and groups with common interests and traits continue to be cohesive, steps must be taken to improve the level of understanding and cooperation between individuals of different backgrounds. If there are communication barriers, common symbols must be found. If there are ideological misconceptions, they may be overcome through increased interaction. The use of mixed task forces, sensitivity training, and role playing suggested in Chapter 21 may help remove barriers to understanding and cooperation.

If the main barrier to improvement lies in the lack of preparation and skill development, educational and training processes can eliminate many of the difficulties. More individuals from minority backgrounds may be attracted to training opportunities if the doors to jobs, promotions, and salaries are opened with some assurance. One of the main efforts to improve the skill level and employment opportunities of disadvantaged individuals has been the nationwide effort to hire and train the "hard-core unemployed"—individuals who have never held a steady work position. In many cases, the government through its JOBS (Job Opportunities for the Business Sector) program has worked with the National Alliance for Businessmen to attempt to attract and retain previously unemployed people into permanent, productive work positions.

Statistics reveal varying degrees of success for the efforts to hire, train, and retain the hard-core unemployed. One study showed that the retention rate in companies using only informal training programs was but 39 percent with a 57 percent rate of retention for companies with formal training programs.[19] Formal training programs used personal counselors, remedial education, supervisory assistance, help with transportation problems, instruction concerning on-the-job

---

[19]Robert C. Sedwick and Donald J. Bodwell, "The Hard Core Employee—Key to High Retention," *Personnel Journal,* Volume 50, Number 12 (December 1971), p. 950.

and off-the-job problems, and many other tools to attempt to increase retention and performance ratios. The most helpful determinant of success, however, appears to be the dedicated personal attention of one or more individuals toward making the program work. Without the genuine support and involvement of influential personnel, programs of enlistment and instruction appear only moderately successful at best.[20]

Rejection of Traditional Organizational Methods

An issue somewhat different from the three previous subjects is the trend toward an increased rejection by some workers of the traditional values, goals, and methods of operation of business organizations. To illustrate the point, newspaper headlines once told the story of the shutdown of an automobile assembly line by a handful of workers who were disgruntled by the actions of their foreman.[21] By controlling the electrical power sources of the assembly line, the workers stopped all production until they successfully pressured upper levels of management to fire their boss. *This incident illustrates the disillusionment some workers feel about the traditional formal authority structure.* The pressures for decision making at the bottom of the organization are increasing.

The same story revealed in an interview with the successful workers that they lacked confidence in the ability of the union grievance process to provide a just solution to their problems. *Unions as a traditional institution have come under attack* from many sources.

In recent contract negotiations, workers have stressed the desire to alter work routines, to have a choice in whether overtime will be worked or not, to choose work schedules, and to see that other changes are made in work patterns. The flexibility required to meet these demands would drastically affect the method of operation in many organizations. These are a few examples of the changes being called for by some workers.

It is not the purpose of this discussion to decide on the appropriateness of the changes in attitudes that are occurring, for that is a decision individual managers must face. It would appear, however, that a danger exists when workers begin to pull in many different directions on an individual basis. A degree of centralized authority is essential if coordination and integration of effort is to be achieved.

---

[20]*Ibid.*, p. 952.
[21]Reported by the Associated Press news service, July 29, 1973.

The role of the manager in the face of a rejection of traditional methods and values has many facets. The manager must analyze the changes in terms of legitimacy—Is there a reasonable cause for the change in attitude and for the corresponding actions? The manager must unify the efforts of individuals and guide them cooperatively toward common goals. The management must research the suitability of old and new methods of operation.

A most important approach to administering individual worker demands and needs is the utilization of the adaptive approach to leadership promoted in earlier chapters of this book. This technique permits the manager to discover and provide for the needs of individual workers while utilizing the amount of authority necessary to get cohesion and unity. In situations where workers are qualified, where the task allows it, and where the organization structure permits it, a large amount of delegation and participation can take place. Where these factors are not conducive to delegation, centralized action may be taken. The careful cultivation of good communication networks is also essential to the proper handling of this problem. Adequate upward, downward, and horizontal communication goes a long way in resolving these internal difficulties.

Training and educational techniques such as role playing and sensitivity training that force managers and workers to broaden their perspectives are also useful.

Summary

The problems and issues analyzed in this chapter are only a part of a large array of puzzlements present in business organizations. Earlier chapters reviewed problems created by organizationally imposed factors (see chapters 5 and 17), and the problems of specific workers were presented and solutions sought in chapters 15, 16, and 17. Chapter 24 will consider problems that lurk in the future.

The solutions to the more complex problems are often evasive. Some common patterns of organizational and interpersonal problems have been uncovered, however.

1.   Problems are seldom resolved unless there is a recognition from those with power to correct the problem that the problem does exist.

2.   The course of improvement begins with the personal commitment of managers and workers alike to resolve existing difficulties. Research mentioned in earlier chapters illustrated the importance of participation and involvement from all knowledgeable and interested parties.

3.   Progress is infrequently achieved unless specific goals, plans, or targets for improvement are formulated.

4.   The pursuit of fair, equitable treatment for all employees is not only demanded by law, but in the long run it is the most productive, dignity-preserving method of operating a business.

5.   *Some problems cannot be solved with routine amounts of effort, but call for extraordinary energies and abilities to be perceptive and understanding.*

In line with these proposals, a spirit of optimism exists that the problems that divide people at work can be overcome.

Questions to consider after reading Chapter 23

1.   Besides the stereotypes mentioned concerning women at work, what other images and impressions are frequently heard? How accurate are these stereotypes?

2.   What stereotypes do women commonly hold toward men in the work force? What is the accuracy of these perceptions?

3.   Consider and analyze the statement in this chapter that the values of younger and older workers are not as widely separated as would be originally expected.

4.   The study reported in this chapter that indicated the minimal amount of differences in the attitudes of the young and older was conducted in the banking industry. Might the choice of industry have an effect on the research findings? How?

5.   In what additional ways may groups divided on the basis of age, sex, or race be coordinated and unified?

6.   Perform role-playing situations in which you put yourself into the role of a member of the work force who is of a different age, sex, or race than you. What differences do these variables make on your outlook?

7.   Is there any justification for paying less money to workers performing the same jobs where there are differences in age, sex, or race? Discuss.

8.   Consider the statement made in the chapter that the majorities in power tend to wish to continue their dominance and control over the minorities. Do you agree with this statement?

9.   Why do some individuals reject the traditional operational goals and procedures of industry?

The following cases at the back of the book contain problems related to Chapter 23:

> Mark Williams
> Stanley Lowell
> Susan Swanson
> Walt Gladberry
> Abigail Spiegal and Trudy Pennington

Additional readings

Argyris, Chris, "Today's Problems with Tomorrow's Organizations," *Journal of Management Studies,* Volume 4, Number 1 (February 1967), pp. 31–55.

Boldgett, Timothy B., "Borderline Black—Revisited," *Harvard Business Review,* Volume 50, Number 2 (March–April 1972), pp. 132–139.

Ginzberg, Eli, "Paycheck and Apron—Revolution and Womanpower," *Industrial Relations,* Volume 7, Number 3 (May 1968), pp. 193–203.

Goodman, Richard A., "A Hidden Issue in Minority Employment," *California Management Review,* Volume 11, Number 4, pp. 27–30.

Heneman, Herbert G., "The Relationship between Age and Motivation To Perform the Job," *Industrial Gerontology,* Winter 1973, pp. 30–36.

Luthans, Fred, "The Impact of the Civil Rights Act on Employment Policies and Programs," *Labour Law Journal,* Volume 19, Number 6 (June 1968), pp. 323–328.

McGuire, Joseph W., *Contemporary Management: Issues and Viewpoints,* Englewood Cliffs, New Jersey: Prentice-Hall, Inc., 1974.

Peskin, Dean B., "Building Groundwork for Affirmative Action E.E.O. Program," *Personnel Journal,* Volume 48, Number 2 (February 1969), pp. 130–138.

Schneider, B. V. H., *The Older Worker,* Berkeley: University of California Institute of Industrial Relations, 1962.

Weisskoff, Francine B., "Women's Place in the Labor Market," *American Economic Review,* Volume 62, Number 2 (May 1972), pp. 161–165.

Chapter 24

Managing in
the Future

Interpersonal relations are the lifeblood of every organization. ~~People interacting together shape the direction organizations will go and influence how rapidly and effectively an organization will attain its goals~~. The last few chapters in particular have provided us with insight into trends and problems that are unique to today's organizations in the American economy. Chapters throughout the book have presented important concepts and responsibilities for managing in all types of situations. Now it is time to consider the responsibilities that will confront tomorrow's managers.

Before the issues that will concern the manager of the future can be reviewed in full, it is important to analyze the assumptions upon which managing in the future is based. Several sets of ideas are presented in the next few pages. While these assumptions may not be infallible, they will provide a frame of reference for viewing the future. Every manager or student of management will need to decide which assumptions are acceptable and which will become a part of his own approach to managing.

Publics to be Served

Today's managers are accountable to several publics. In these days of increasing professional management, managers must provide a reasonable return on investment for the ~~owners~~ and *stockholders* of every profit-seeking organization. Managers must provide *employees* not only with the opportunity to ~~earn reasonable wages~~ and ~~salaries but also~~ the ~~opportunity to realize the fulfillment of other personal~~ ambitions. Managers have obligations to conform to the expectations of ~~government agencies~~ and to meet the expectations of laws and regulations. As ~~unions~~ win the right to represent parts of the work force, managers have the responsibility to work with unions for the mutual attainment of other goals. Managers have a responsibility to provide ~~customers~~ with products or services suited to their needs and demands. There is the additional responsibility of being a good citizen in the community at large. In more recent days the social responsibility of managers—the responsibility to protect and improve the conditions under which *the total society lives*—has been given even further emphasis as a management obligation. There are, no doubt, other publics toward whom many managers have responsibilities. At the same time, each manager brings to the organization his own private goals and needs. Some of these needs and goals may, at times, conflict directly with the goals and expectations of the publics he is supposed to serve.

From all indications, a manager's responsibilities toward each of these publics will continue to be strong in the future. Some authors even predict that some publics will increase their pressures and demands. It is anticipated that society as a whole will seek more social responsibility from organizations, and these demands must be considered by managers. Already there have been demands for improved environmental conditions, improved employment conditions, industrial cooperation in lifting the economic status of underprivileged individuals, and a host of additional responses. It seems probable that these demands for social responsibility will widen in scope and the cries will become more vocal.

As the composition of society becomes more complex and organizations themselves become more complicated, it seems a certainty that governmental influences will have a stronger impact upon managerial and organizational actions.[1] Governmental pressures may take the form of new laws, regulations, and guidelines. In addition, governmental agencies may provide financial and educational assistance to organizations so that the two can work together as a team to overcome many problems and to achieve improvement on a number of frontiers.

New demands will be forthcoming from the other publics, too. In a few paragraphs, we will be looking at employees and their demands, but before we do there is an important point that needs to be made. Every practicing manager must be attuned to his responsibilities toward all publics simultaneously. While this book gives emphasis to the employees who make up the organization, no manager can give exclusive attention to this group. The manager's concern for his employee responsibilities must be tempered by his responsibilities toward others. The same generalization can be made for those who would put social responsibility head and shoulders above all other management responsibilities. This is an important duty *along with* the manager's other obligations. Ideally, managers can make an effort to maximize the achievement of responsibilities to all publics.

This discussion of management's responsibilities puts one other point in

---

[1] John M. Bergey and Robert C. Slover, "Administration in the 1980's," *SAM Advanced Management Journal,* Volume 34, Number 2 (April 1969), p. 32, and Warren Bennis, *Beyond Bureaucracy,* New York: McGraw-Hill Book Company, 1973, p. 10.

proper perspective. ~~A manager's role includes responsibilities for developing, rewarding, and utilizing human resources and responsibilities for attaining organizational objectives~~. Managers must strive to attain many goals. Managers' responsibilities are truly multiple in nature.

Interpersonal Relations

People at work and their interpersonal relations are the primary concern of this book. In Section I, a model to illustrate many of the basic components was presented. It is appropriate now to review some of the components and to discuss assumptions concerning their future (see Figure 24.1).

The Individual and Environmental-Experiential Factors.   From an interpersonal point of view, the individual is and will be the basic unit of activity. Individual human beings supply the knowledge, skills, and much of the energy utilized in today's organizations. As we look now to the future, what assumptions can be made about interests, demands, and behavior patterns of future employees? Will tomorrow's employees be similar to or different from today's workers?

It is the position of this author that most of the concepts and characteristics described in Chapter 2 can be expected to remain relatively constant into the future. Each individual human being will continue to have needs, drives, and expectations. ~~Pleasure will continue to be more attractive~~ (in most instances) than pain, although each may influence behavior significantly. The human organism will seek an equilibrium in internal and external relationships. Normal individuals will have a capacity to plan and to act rationally, although they will not always do so, because of emotional and social effects. The other concepts involving individual human nature suggested in the model also will continue to be prevalent.

Regardless of the time period in question, it seems apparent that no two people are identical in their goals, ambitions, strengths, and weaknesses. ~~People at work are needing, goal-seeking, human individuals~~. While general classifications of human needs have been identified (as was done in Chapter 7), individuals differ in the urgency of those needs and in the way they prefer to have their needs met. People who affiliate themselves with today's organizations commit themselves to work expecting to fulfill many of their own personal objectives. This is not only true of today's worker, it will also be true of tomorrow's employee. In fact, many individuals affiliated with organizations in the future may expect even more from their employment relationship. Bennis has suggested, for example, that the increased level of education and mobility will change the values people have

FIGURE 24.1   Model of worker behavior and its determinants

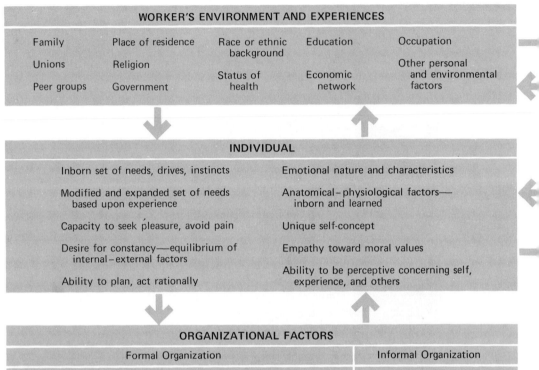

TECHNOLOGICAL FACTORS

Provide new products and services

Increase capacity to provide
  manufactured goods

Decrease labor costs

Affect the level of employment

Change many production and
  communication processes

Have a significant impact upon the
  lives of workers within the
  business enterprise

Demand more of managers

Alter manpower policies and practices

Modify union—management relations

ACTION
or
BEHAVIOR

toward work. "~~People will be more intellectually committed to their jobs and will probably require more involvement, participation, and autonomy in their work~~."[2]

The ~~educational level of the work force is expected to continue to rise~~. The work force will become more diverse in backgrounds, age concentrations, nationality mixes, and ideological philosophies (although these may be less diverse than many have previously predicted). Groups previously considered to be ~~minorities of the work force will increas~~e in numbers and percentages, and ~~their demands will become more vocal~~. It is assumed that many workers will be blessed with an abundance of leisure time as work patterns change. More and ~~more employees will be retiring at an earlier age than has been true previously~~.[3] ~~Managers will face a wide variety of demands from employees~~.

Changes in the institutions of society—the family unit, religion, education, the government, and organized labor, for example—are likely to occur. The effect of these changes will be significant. The specific nature and direction of the changes stretch the imagination, but they will have a definite impact upon people at work.

The relative health of the economy will also be a future influencing factor. The supply of energy resources, for example, has already become an important element in the lives of most employees and employers. The rise and fall of inflationary levels has cast an additional element of uncertainty into the picture. The oversupply of unskilled labor, the undersupply of skilled labor in some areas, and the overeducation of some workers for the jobs available will continue to result in organizational stresses. The uncertainty of competitive forces will also continue in the future.

~~Social affiliation~~s, ~~both formal and informal~~, will ~~continue to have a heavy influence upon the attitudes and behavior of people at work~~ (see chapters 3 and 6). Because people are normally socially oriented, the attitudes and values of organizational peer groups, family members, off-the-job friends, and others to whom they may socially relate will weigh heavily upon their perceptions and actions. On the basis of these predictions, the job of managing may become more challenging and more variable than has been true in previous years. Stereotyped perceptions of individuals in the work force and the related actions toward them will become increasingly unsatisfactory.

There is also hope for a greater understanding of individual human behavior and environmental-experiential influences for planned behavioral changes. The

[2]Bennis, *ibid.*, p. 11.
[3]U. Vincent Manion, "Why Employees Retire Early," *Personnel Journal,* Volume 51, Number 3 (March 1972), p. 183.

writings of Berne[4] and Harris[5] suggest that individuals must not necessarily consider themselves totally at the mercy of environment and experience. These authors, in fact, state that individuals can deliberately redirect their own behavior if they are willing to pursue change adequately. The influences of environment and experience, it is suggested, are forces to be reckoned with, but they are not of necessity repressive or totally inhibiting. The concepts of transactional analysis suggest other trends for the future.

Human nature may remain, therefore, somewhat constant, but human behavior will remain variable. The variations will be related to a number of important influences.

Organizations of the Future

Predictions concerning the characteristics of organizations in which tomorrow's employee will work usually emphasize the tendency toward larger, more complex, more interrelated structurings of people.[6] Because ~~many organizations will be large and complex~~, there will also be a danger that organizations will become more impersonal and more dehumanizing. This may occur at a time in which some individuals are looking to their employers with even higher levels of expectation.

Many organizations, realizing the impact of size and the importance of the human element, will ~~decentralize decision-making and other activities~~. It will be imperative in tomorrow's organizations that employees be able to recognize a common set of objectives, plans, and goals so that they can contribute collectively toward mutually beneficial goals.[7] High-level managers will need to devote more of their time to integrative decision making to unite the efforts of all organizational members.[8]

Intentionally structured roles and authority relationships will continue to be important, although they will not always follow traditional lines. Filley and House suggest that while line and line-staff authority patterns will continue, dual hierarchies, ~~matrix structures (a form of dual supervision where individuals receive both administrative and technical guidance)~~, functional organizations, and

[4]Eric Berne, *Transactional Analysis in Psychotherapy*, New York: Grove Press, 1961.

[5]Thomas A. Harris, *I'm O.K., You're O.K.*, New York: Harper & Row, Publishers, 1967.

[6]See William Simon, "Management in the Future," *Conference Board Record*, Volume 10, Number 3 (March 1973), p. 44, for additional discussions of this.

[7]Harold Koontz, "Management and Challenges of the Future," *SAM Advanced Mangement Journal*, Volume 33, Number 1 (January 1968), pp. 21–30, discusses these and other related points in detail.

[8]Simon, *op. cit.*, p. 45.

tactical units will also occur more frequently.[9] There is a fairly general agreement that organizations will need to become more flexible in nature.

Almost everyone agrees that organizations will undergo significant changes, sometimes arising within the boundaries of the organization but often necessitated by forces from the outside. Many authors also feel that there will be more multinational involvement in tomorrow's organizations.

~~Technology~~ (see Chapter 4) ~~will continue to have a strong impact~~ upon organizations and individuals. Discoveries and innovations will result in new pressures for change. Technology will result in changes in objectives of organizations and methods and procedures to achieve those objectives. Skill requirements will be altered as a result of technology. Interpersonal relationships of employees will undergo change caused by technology. In some instances technology will cause workers and their tasks to become more interrelated, while in others there will be tendencies toward separation and even social isolation. Computer technology may result in the reshaping of a number of organizational roles and will have a particularly significant impact on decision making. These changes further indicate the challenge that lies ahead for tomorrow's managers.

Managing in the Future

Just as the managers of today cannot be considered infallible, tomorrow's managers should not be expected to perform perfectly either. As long as managers are human beings, they will be subject to their own mental and physical limitations, to their own philosophical commitments, to their own biases and prejudices, and to pressures from many directions. Tomorrow's managers, however, should be able to profit from the increasing body of knowledge and experiences of yesterday's and today's managers. As a result, we have every reason to expect tomorrow's managers to serve more effectively, more constructively than did their predecessors.

The ~~manager of tomorrow~~, regardless of his organizational level and position and regardless of the type of organization, ~~will be more knowledgeable about people, organizations, and the total environment.~~ Bergey and Slover state:

> The future manager will be better grounded in social sciences, world affairs, and the humanities in general. He will effectively integrate the techniques of information technology with the human resources available to him.[10]

[9]Alan C. Filley and Robert J. House, *Managerial Process and Organizational Behavior*, Glenview, Illinois: Scott, Foresman and Company, 1969, pp. 487–488.

[10]Bergey and Slover, *op. cit.*, p. 31.

Professionalism among the ranks of managers will continue to be on the increase. More and more managers throughout the hierarchy of organizations will receive formalized educational training in managerial techniques and responsibilities. A recent study by Davis[11] also indicates a significant level of interest in a certified management classification similar to those now existing for Certified Public Accountants and Certified Life Underwriters. All signs lead to a more educationally prepared manager for tomorrow's organizations.

The organizational level in which each manager serves, of course, will affect the type of managerial skills needed. Managers at the tops of organizations may need conceptual, analytical, and decision-making abilities more than would other managers, for example. First-line supervisors may need technical skills and interpersonal leadership abilities more keenly than will top-level managers. Middle-level managers may need a blend of the above skills in addition to coordinative abilities.

All managers, regardless of their levels, will find beneficial the development and utilization of skills and abilities in interpersonal relations. This book has recommended a flexible, contingency approach to leadership and other interpersonal interactions. The implementation of this concept should be an asset to every practicing manager.

Utilization of contingency leadership will require that ~~tomorrow's manager have the ability to be perceptive toward himself; his superiors, colleagues,~~ and ~~subordinates;~~ his employing organization—its goals, resources, etc.; and many additional elements. It will be a requisite that tomorrow's manager ~~be sensitive and empathetic to the people; events~~, and ~~objects~~ that surround him. Because change most certainly will occur, the manager must be perceptive in discerning changes in knowledge, attitudes, behavior, value systems, need levels, technical requirements, and a multiplicity of additional factors. He must have the ability to pierce the surface of things to get to the real heart of each situation. As the size of organizations increases, he must have the ability to be personal in an impersonal atmosphere.

Because the manager will be constantly encountering change, it will be exceedingly helpful if he is open-minded and receptive to new ideas and new operational techniques—particularly to innovations resulting from the endeavors of others. The personal attributes of patience and tolerance will be invaluable tools.

The skill, ability, and desire to apply the concepts discussed in the chapter on conflict (particularly those dealing with the 9,9 approach to conflict) will be

[11]Herbert J. Davis, *Professional Certification in Management with Emphasis on Academic and Practitioner Opinion: An Interpretative Analysis*, unpublished doctoral disseration, Louisiana State University, Baton Rouge, Louisiana, 1974.

almost a must for tomorrow's manager. The astute manager will be capable of perceiving some types of interpersonal conflict before they arise and, as a result, can take steps either to relieve the tensions that are building or to channel them in positive directions. If tomorrow's manager can learn to distinguish between potentially constructive and threateningly dangerous conflict, he will know how to respond more capably. He will learn not to be afraid of every cloud of conflict that arises and will be courageous and optimistic when healthy conflict results from the interactions of people.

In several of the chapters in this book, the problems of employees have been identified. Numerous specific types were revealed and solutions suggested. In truth, the discussions initiated thought on only a few of types of problems that may develop. One of the essential skills for the successful manager of the future will be the ability to perceive problems, diagnose causes, and work with the appropriate individuals to see that good solutions are found. In most instances it will not be necessary for the manager to make all decisions himself. In fact, more and more it appears that the strength of tomorrow's organizational leader will be to help others make decisions for themselves. This type of leader will know how to lead group efforts, how to counsel with individuals, and how to be a good listener.

Whenever it becomes necessary, the manager will need the skill and the courage to make decisions himself. There will be times when he must be individually decisive. There will even be times when he must take stands that are unpopular. Some of his decisions may be unpopular because they must consider long-range effects as well as short-range benefits. Other decisions may not be well received by employees because they give recognition to other publics to whom the organization is responsible (sometimes at the expense of employee benefits). The manager, however, must remember his total obligations.

The manager of the future ~~will benefit from the ability to be objective in making decisions that affect others~~. Objectivity implies that an individual is capable of ~~looking at issues and problems~~ without ~~allowing prejudices, biases, or emotions to obstruct reality~~. If the manager is objective, he is capable of viewing matters as they really are, not as he or someone else wishes they were. Being objective does not mean that the manager can have no personal feelings of his own as he works, but it does suggest that he be aware of his own feelings and keep them under control. This ability, of course, has been valuable for managers throughout the ages, but it will take on additional usefulness in future.

The work environment in organizations of the future will be much more pleasant and more productive if managers place an emphasis on positive motivation—on helping people achieve personal goals while striving toward organizational objectives. This environment induces employees to be productive because they wish to work and not because they are forced to perform.[12] At the same time, however, the manager should not avoid the use of negative motivational techniques when they may be beneficial.

Concluding Challenge

~~Good managerial practice sets off a chain of positive responses.~~ Good management sets the example for others. ~~Sound managerial actions inspire, motivate, encourage,~~ and s~~timulate positive reactio~~ns. Good managers *seek out* actions that are necessary and *do* them. Herein lies the challenge to every student of management: ~~to pursue what is right and beneficial and to follow knowledge with actio~~n.

The concepts presented in this book represent the contributions of a number of authors in addition to the unique contributions of this author. Concepts presented should be weighed carefully, accepted if they appear sound, and applied as opportunities permit. Initiative should be exercised in their implementation so that organizational goals and personal goals of employees can be achieved more fully.

The concepts represent, in the author's judgment, the best knowledge available at this point in time. New findings will be forthcoming regularly; so it will be important for all eyes and ears to keep attuned to innovative concepts as they present themselves. We must all keep our minds open to future developments.

The challenges of managing are exciting and rewarding. Equipped with the right knowledge and skills, managing can also be pleasant and fulfilling.

Questions to consider after reading Chapter 24

1. What other publics, institutions, or external factors besides those mentioned in the chapter are likely to influence managerial responsibilities in the future?

2. Is it possible for a manager to overemphasize the importance of his responsibilities toward the employees he supervises?

3. Some authors have said that employees will expect even more of their employers in the future than they have sought in the past. Why would anyone make this statement? Do you agree or disagree with it? Support your answer.

4. Does it seem accurate to say that organizations of the future will need to be more flexible? Why or why not? How can organizations be made more flexible?

5. How can tomorrow's manager better prepare himself for the fulfillment of his responsibilities?

[12]Koontz, *op. cit.,* pp. 21–22, stresses the value of this.

6. Review the major concepts presented in this book. Which of them can you support and adopt? Which are philosophically compatible with your frame of reference? If there are incompatibilities, which needs revision? You must decide this for yourself.

**The following cases at the back of the book
contain problems related to Chapter 24:**

> Mark Williams
>
> Stanley Lowell
>
> Edith Capp and Janet Turner
>
> Billy Snyder
>
> Susan Swanson
>
> Grace Lanham
>
> Abigail Spiegal and Trudy Pennington

Additional Readings

Bell, Daniel, editor, *Toward the Year 2000: Work in Progress,* Boston: Houghton Mifflin Company, 1968.

Boulding, Kenneth E., *The Meaning of the Twentieth Century,* New York: Harper & Row, Publishers, 1965.

Bremer, Otto A., "Is Business the Source of New Social Values?" *Harvard Business Review,* Volume 49, Number 6 (November–December 1971), pp. 121–126.

Cassell, Frank H., "The Politics of Public-Private Management," *M.S.U. Business Topics,* Volume 19, Number 3 (Summer 1972), pp. 7–18.

Harman, W., "The Nature of Our Changing Society," in John M. Thomas and Warren G. Bennis, editors, *Management of Conflict and Change,* Baltimore: Penguin Books, 1972, pp. 43–91.

Jun, Jong S., and William B. Storm, Tomorrow's Organizations, Glenview, Illinois: Scott, Foresman and Company, 1973.

Katz, Daniel, and Basil S. Georgopoulos, "Organizations in a Changing World," *Journal of Applied Behavioral Science,* Volume 7, Number 3 (May–June 1971), pp. 342–370.

Kuin, Pieter, "The Magic of Multinational Management," *Harvard Business Review,* Volume 50, Number 6 (November–December 1972), pp. 89–97.

McAdam, Terry, "How To Put Corporate Responsibility into Practice," in Max S. Wortman and Fred Luthans, editors, *Emerging Concepts in Management,* Revised Edition, New York: The Macmillan Company, 1975.

Management 2000, Hamilton, New York: American Foundation for Management Research, 1968.

Myers, Charles A., "Management Decisions for the Next Decade," *Industrial Management Review,* Volume 10, Number 1 (Fall 1968), pp. 31–40.

Steiner, George A., "Social Policies for Business," *California Management Review,* Volume 15, Number 2 (Winter 1972), pp. 17–24.

Toffler, Alvin, *Future Shock,* New York: Random House, 1970.

ADDITIONAL CASES

Ben Stockton-A Manager without Authority

The events in this case took place in the dining hall in which approximately 150 varsity athletes from a major state university eat their meals regularly. The dining hall is under the general supervision of Lex Smedling, age forty-five, who has held the job since his graduation from the same university a number of years earlier. Smedling has a staff of twelve full-time workers (cooks, dishwashers, etc.) who report directly to him. In addition, he has a graduate student reporting to him to whom he has given the assignment of seeing that the prepared meals are served and that the dining area is kept properly cleaned. The student supervisor normally serves a one-year appointment and then moves on as he graduates from the university. The student supervisor is responsible for the performance of seventeen student assistants (mostly undergraduates) who do the manual work involved in serving the meals and in keeping the area clean. Smedling hires the graduate supervisor and the student assistants at the beginning of the school year or whenever vacancies in the staff occur. Otherwise, he gives the graduate supervisor a complete free rein to direct the student workers as he wishes.

This year's graduate supervisor is Ben Stockton. He was hired for the job a few weeks prior to the beginning of the fall schedule of athletic activities. He received only a minimum of instructions from Smedling. He was told,

> Keep everything in order. We're a nonprofit organization; so we don't have to cut corners on expenses. We do have a budget to operate within, but it's a generous one. Organize your workers as you wish. The dining hall service and cleaning operations are yours to handle as you wish. Make up your policies and procedures as you need them.

Ben began the year's work by calling the seventeen student workers together to make job assignments. He gave each one of them specific duties for each meal. He asked all seventeen of them to show up for work for every meal. He requested each worker to arrive for work thirty minutes in advance of the serving time and remain until all athletes had been fed and the dining area had been thoroughly cleaned. The student workers would receive their own meals free (this was the only compensation the students received for their performance).

After Ben had been working about a week, he discovered that some of the workers were coming to work late and leaving early. Some were performing their jobs very poorly. Ben's analysis of the seventeen workers under his jurisdiction was that four of them just wanted free food without working, seven were generally apathetic, and six were conscientious workers. Ben issued verbal warnings to the workers coming in late. These warnings had no effect; so Ben decided to get permission from Mr. Smedling to take more severe action.

Ben soon learned that he did not have the support of his superiors. He realized that he had a great amount of responsibility and very little authority. For example, Mr. Smedling said that he would talk to the tardy workers, but he never did. Mr. Smedling also indicated that he had no intention of firing the workers coming in late, and he did not want Ben to fire them either. Ben was faced with the responsibility of correcting the behavior of his subordinates without any power to make or enforce threats.

At this point Ben was completely frustrated. In deciding what he should do, Ben considered three alternatives. The first was to resign. The second alternative was to maintain the status quo and tolerate the inefficiencies and ineffectiveness. The third was to attempt to make the group under him as efficient and effective as possible without any help from higher authorities. Ben chose the third alternative.

In planning his strategy for achieving effectiveness without help from his superiors, Ben felt that there were four actions he could take that would be helpful. First, Ben decided that he would reevaluate his own policies and design them so that they would be beneficial to the student workers whenever possible. One illustration of this effort was the realignment of work schedules so that only the number of workers absolutely required to serve the meal and clean the dining hall had to work at each meal. Also, fewer workers would be assigned to weekend duties and other slack times. All of the workers, of course, would still be allowed to eat every meal at the dining hall. This action was much appreciated by the workers and received a very favorable response. This tactic did not solve all problems, however. Some of the workers continued their poor performance.

Ben then instituted his ~~second~~ strategy. He ~~decided~~ to ~~use pressure on~~ the ~~work~~ers and ~~apply some~~ authority he ~~didn't really have~~. Since all of the workers ate at the dining hall about half hour before regular mealtime, Ben felt that this would be the best time to start using this pressure. He approached the group as a whole and ~~informed them~~ that their ~~work was inadequate~~. Ben stated that if things continued like they were going now, he himself, along with all of the student workers would be fired. He then stated that according to his analysis, there were ~~four workers that were really making~~ the ~~group look bad~~.

Ben approached these four workers and in a calm but loud enough voice so that all of the workers could hear, he informed them that he would like to receive their resignations. He calmly stated that their work was far below acceptable standards and that this was causing the work burden to be shifted to the other workers. Ben stated that it was unfair to the good workers to keep subsidizing the inefficient workers. He added that if these four workers desired to discuss this matter further, they could do so after work.

After work, all four of these workers approached Ben and stated that they would like to keep their jobs. They each gave reasons why they wanted and needed their jobs. Ben then explained that he was responsible for the efficiency of their work and couldn't risk keeping them if the quality of their work did not improve. He reminded them that he himself would lose his job if the workers under him did not do an adequate job. All four of the workers asked for another chance. They promised to do a good job in the future if they were allowed to stay. Ben stressed the fact that what he did was ~~based on work~~ performance ~~only~~ and was nothing personal. Ben gave each worker a ~~friendly handshake~~ and told them that he would not hold any grudges based on past performance. They would be judged only on future performance.

Ben's third step was to ~~form work teams~~. He made sure that each team was composed of good, mediocre, and bad workers. There were an equal number of good workers in each group. All future assignments were made by group rather than by individual whenever possible. Ben made it clear that he was holding the group responsible for performance rather than individuals. Anytime there was a ~~complaint about work performanc~~e, Ben would ~~call~~ the ~~entire group~~ into his office and inform them of the deficiency. He reminded them that if this situation continued, their group would probably not be retained when contracts were renewed next semester.

Finally, Ben decided that it would be helpful in getting a good response from his workers if they saw that he was willing to do his part to contribute to successful performance. ~~He frequently worked side by side with~~ the ~~students~~. He volunteered to take over many of the less desirable tasks. He substituted for some workers when they needed time off. He hoped that this effort would show his personal interest in them and that they would respond accordingly.

Questions about the Ben Stockton case

1.   What impact did the formal organization (its structure, objectives, etc.) have upon Ben Stockton and the way he performed his job?

2.   Does it matter that this organization was a nonprofit organization?

3.   What kind of authority did Ben try to develop over the group in the absense of formal top-down authority?

4.   Evaluate the leadership-supervisory actions of Lex Smedling. (What were his strengths and weaknesses?) What effect did Smedling's actions have upon Stockton and his job?

5.   In the long run, how successful do you expect the following strategies will be?

    a.   the realignment of policies so that they will be more beneficial to the workers

    b.   the application of authority that Ben does not have

    c.   the utilization of teams to accomplish tasks

    d.   the technique in which Ben works side-by-side and frequently substitutes for the workers

6.   Evaluate Stockton's overall performance as a supervisor. What has he done well? What has he done poorly?

7.   If Stockton could start the year over again, what advice would you give him?

Mark Williams–Director of Dissident Employees

The ~~Montgomery Construction Company~~ is the prime subcontractor on the Clear Springs nuclear generating station. The generating station, being built by the Greater Eastern Gas and Electric Company, is considered of major importance in meeting the future electrical needs of a portion of the New England area. The ~~project~~ is also of great importance to Montgomery Construction because it ~~insures~~ a ~~minimum~~ of ~~two years' work at a time~~ when ~~area construction~~ is ~~generally~~ in a ~~depressed state~~.

In ~~charge~~ of the ~~project~~ for Montgomery is ~~Mark Williams~~. Williams, who is now ~~thirty years of age, joined Montgomery seven years ago~~ on completion of his ~~B.S. in electrical engineering~~ at the University of Maryland. Although Williams has supervised several minor jobs in the past, this is his ~~first chance~~ at a ~~really important~~ ~~project~~. He feels that the confidence expressed in his ability by the allocation of this project may mean future advancement if he does his work well.

The Montgomery Company is now ~~six months into~~ the ~~project~~, and Williams is ~~encountering~~ a ~~morale problem~~. The problem is characterized by the division of workers into two seemingly hostile groups. The attitudes and positions of each group can be seen by considering the circumstances and feelings of two very different workers—Tom Beyer and Robert Tipton.

~~Tom Beyer~~ is ~~fifty years of age~~. Following graduation from high school, Beyer joined the navy. It was in the navy, during the five years of World War II in which Beyer served, that he received his first electronics training. In 1946, following his discharge, he joined the New England Electrical Workers Union as an apprentice. Four years later, in 1950 he was granted full status as an electrician. In the following years ~~Beyer has~~ worked ~~on almost all~~ of the ~~major projects~~ in the New

515

England area. He takes great pride in his work. Often he points to a construction project of years past and tells a story that occurred during its building.

Robert Tipton is a twenty-four-year-old inner-city dweller from an impoverished background. At the end of the tenth grade, as the oldest of eight brothers and sisters, he was forced to drop out of school to help support the family. Because of his lack of education, Tipton quickly went through a succession of menial jobs and spent most of his time unemployed. Two years ago, as a part of the JOBS program, Tipton was enrolled in a special trade program to learn electronics. Shortly thereafter he was admitted into the union's apprenticeship program. Last year under a plan to bring more minorities into the construction trades, Tipton was admitted as a full journeyman. The Clear Springs job is Tipton's first as a journeyman.

During the first six months of work, Williams has used two different forms of supervision on Beyer and Tipton even though they frequently work side by side performing similar tasks. Williams has been very general in his direction of Beyer. Williams feels that Beyer, with his vast storehouse of knowledge and his long experience, can be entrusted with a job and can be left to perform it in the best way possible. Williams has been heard to say that he is almost in awe of the skill with which Beyer performs his work.

On the other hand, Tipton has been given close supervision. As Williams explains it, several factors have caused him to watch Tipton more closely. This is the first major job on which Tipton has worked. As such he can be expected to make mistakes through his lack of experience. Secondly, Williams feels that he needs to be near to give the encouragement and support needed by Tipton to build up his confidence in himself. Also, close supervision seems appropriate for Tipton because he is one of the first workers to achieve full status under the new training program, and management is very interested in his development as a means of evaluating the success of the program.

The other workers tend to identify with either Beyer or Tipton. The older, more established workers are treated by Williams in much the same way that he handles Beyer. The workers under the new program are all handled similarly to the supervision given to Tipton.

Williams's differential treatment is being interpreted in very different ways by each group of workers. Beyer and his group feel that Williams's actions are just another example of management's practice of ignoring the problems of the good, steady worker while pampering some special-privilege group. They believe that Williams's close attention to the newer workers is also a result of Tipton and his friends' inadequacies and incompetencies. Beyer and colleagues say that Tipton and friends are not fully prepared for the important responsibilities being given to them. The Beyer-type group believes that the assignment of important jobs to the Tipton-type group is "a real crime because in a tight labor market well-qualified men are being forced to live on unemployment while those incompetents are being nursed along. Those guys should still be apprentices."

Tipton and his co-workers see the controversy in quite another light. To them, the close supervision they are receiving while others work under freer supervision, is another form of discrimination. It is apparent to Tipton and others that Williams is watching them so that he can find an excuse to get them off the job at the first opportunity. It seems to them that Williams is always present when one of them (the Tipton group) makes a mistake, but Williams never seems to notice errors made by the Beyer group. Also, just having Williams watching them so closely makes Tipton and his friends overly nervous. "Who wouldn't make mistakes with someone watching over your shoulder and questioning every move you make?"

Under these conditions, Williams is facing a serious morale problem. Productivity is down, costs are climbing, and the project is slipping behind schedule. To Williams a successful project and subsequent promotions appear to be in definite jeopardy unless something is done soon.

Questions about the Mark Williams case

1. Mark Williams is applying a leadership approach to the old-line workers that is quite different from the approach he is using with the younger, inexperienced workers. Is this dual-style approach wise or unwise in this situation? Why?

2. Is the fact that the young workers are from an underprivileged, economically depressed background a factor in the dissention that occurs? Why or why not?

3. Would it make any difference in this case if the younger workers were from an ethnic minority group? Why or why not?

4. Now that Mark Williams has encountered so many difficulties, what actions would be advisable on his part?

5. What actions could have been taken to avoid these difficulties by the Montgomery Construction Company and other companies in a similar position?

Stanley Lowell–A Leader with a Generation Gap Problem

Business at Rainbow Sporting Goods Manufacturers has been booming since the day some five years ago when the decision was made to diversify the company's products into areas other than the long-established line of fishing equipment. For more than fifteen years, Rainbow had been satisfied with the role of being one of the leading fishing tackle manufacturers. The company's products were recognized throughout the States for their quality and workmanship. At the time, Rainbow's business was steady but volume was not great.

Five years ago Rainbow's management obtained new patents for golfing and tennis equipment and enlarged their activities rather extensively to begin manufacturing many new products. Several of the new items were an instant success. As a result, many new employees had to be added, to meet the flood of orders that arrived. Business continues to be strong, and the company is constantly looking for new products to manufacture.

In the days when Rainbow's emphasis was strictly on fishing equipment, the work force was small and manager-worker relations were excellent. Company policies were liberal and vacation time, sick leave, and other benefits were flexible to fit workers' needs. A profit-sharing plan was developed that gave workers a small share of company profits at the end of each year. A retirement program was established in which the company put up a small amount of money each year for workers who had been with the company fifteen years or more and remained until age sixty-five. Employees were required to put 4 percent of their weekly earnings into the retirement program. If an employee left the company before retirement, he got back his contributions with interest but did not get any of the money contributed by the company. This arrangement seemed satisfactory to most of the employees.

Rainbow has always shown a sincere interest in the welfare of its employees. During the years before expansion, no effort was ever made by the company's employees to form a union. Even in more recent years, interest in unionization has continued at a very low level.

However, a major problem is now facing Rainbow's managers. There appears to be a deep and widening gap between the older, long-time employees of Rainbow and the younger employees who have been newly hired. The differences between the groups appeared to be minor at first but now have become rather serious.

The labor force at Rainbow is unique in that there are very few people currently employed who are in the thirty-five to fifty-year age category. Almost all of the workers who were with the company before diversification are now above fifty years of age. Turnover in pre-expansion days was always low, and the steady, nonincreasing rate of business provided little room for hiring of new workers. When the expansion began, most of the new workers hired were in their twenties.

The underlying problem precipitating the conflict between the two age groups appears to be based upon differing interests and job demands. Most of the older workers are in positions of responsibility and are working in skilled and semi-skilled positions. Because of their nearness to retirement, the company's program of retirement benefits is especially important to the older workers. The younger workers for the most part are in nonsupervisory positions, and many fill semi-skilled or unskilled positions. The younger set has made known the importance of more money needed for immediate purchasing power.

No one seems capable of explaining how the rift between the younger and the older workers really began. In the early stages, it was noticed that the two groups rarely mixed during work breaks or lunch hours. Very little after-work socializing was enjoyed by the separate groups. Gradually cooperation on jobs began to decline. Young workers would do no more than the letter of the law required when working with older workers and vice versa. Casual name-calling gave way to serious verbal abuse. Two or three fights have been rumored between members of the two groups after work hours. Two weeks ago more than one-half the younger workers staged a half-day walkout to protest the promotion of one of the older nonsupervisory workers to a supervisory post. The younger workers felt that one of their group had been entitled to the position. In handing out penalties for the walkout, management stripped one day's earnings from the participating workers' salaries and warned each one that he would be fired for further similar actions.

Immediately following the walkout, Luke Cowpar, who is general manager of
Rainbow, had a conference with Stanley Lowell, personnel manager, and gave
Lowell the responsibility for investigating the division among workers and ~~report-
ing a list of recommendations~~ to ~~resolve the problem~~. Cowpar gave Lowell three
weeks to prepare and submit his proposals.

Lowell had prided himself on his close rapport with the workers. He had always
practiced an open-door policy and had attempted to mix with the workers as
much as possible. In the weeks prior to the assignment from Cowpar, however,
Lowell had been unable to get much information from any of the workers about
their hostilities toward each other. The ~~older workers typically stated that "the
young Turks were out to get their jobs"~~ and otherwise made unreasonable
demands of them. The ~~younger workers~~ said that th~~eir seniors~~ were st~~anding~~ in
the ~~way of progress~~ and ~~had little interest in their welfare~~. Beyond these rather
broad generalizations, most workers were reluctant to discuss specific details.

Lowell felt that because of his lack of information and knowledge on the subject, he must spend whatever time was available the first week after receiving the
assignment attempting to identify more of the underlying problems through
personal conversations with as many of the workers as he could talk with. He
anticipated that he would form a committee representing different factions, which
would meet early in the second week to help him formulate recommendations to
be prepared and forwarded to Cowpar sometime before the deadline.

During the first week, Lowell was busy with many other matters but managed
to find time to speak at length with twenty or more workers of different ranks,
responsibilities, and ages. Lowell could sense the tension that existed as he talked
with each worker. While some were still reluctant to discuss the matter, Lowell
concluded that the main issues on the minds of the ~~young workers were a desire
for greater immediate income with less emphasis on retirement benefits~~, a d~~esire~~
for gr~~eater~~ responsibility and ~~more challenging assignments~~, and a d~~esire~~ to ~~see
merit stressed~~ as the bas~~is for promotion~~s rather than ~~seniority~~. Y~~ounger~~ wo~~rkers~~
generally ~~felt~~ that the c~~ompany~~ e~~mphasi~~zed the ~~older~~ wo~~rkers~~ at the ~~expense~~ of
the y~~ounger ones~~. They felt that management was insensitive to and unconcerned
with them. The older workers had become their enemy—the aggressor who
received all of the breaks.

Older workers tended to express the belief that the y~~ounger workers were
expecting too much too soon~~. They ~~felt~~ entitled to a c~~ertain amount~~ of pr~~ivileged
treatment~~ as a result of their long, devoted efforts for the company. ~~Each~~ of the
senior employees ~~indicated~~ a k~~een~~ inter~~est~~ in an e~~ven stronger retirement pro-
gram~~. The present income level was fairly satisfactory to most of them. The
y~~ounger workers~~ were viewed as a ~~threat~~ to ~~their security~~.

At the end of the week, Lowell realized that the workers were far apart in their ideas, and he hoped that a committee might establish grounds for a better mutual understanding and might also be able to develop some recommendations to help management cope with existing problems. With this in mind, Lowell selected ~~seven worke~~rs on a representative basis and called a meeting for two o'clock the following Tuesday. The seven workers selected were:

Troy Levy, head of the Maintenance Department, age ~~56~~

Johnny Cafferty, tool and die maker, age ~~59~~

Sloan Broussard, foreman in the Fishing Equipment Section, age ~~50~~

Ralph Hansard, assistant accountant, age ~~39~~

Max Efurd, foreman in the Golf Equipment Section, age 31

Joanne Webcott, assembly section worker, age 24

Scottie McBee, forklift operator, age 28

Lowell sent each of the workers a memorandum informing him of the assignment and waited for Tuesday to arrive. (See Exhibit I for a copy of the memorandum.) When the workers arrived at the meeting the following week, Lowell introduced everyone and tried to establish a friendly rapport. Reactions were courteous but restrained. Lowell then began to explain the predicament of the company as he saw it and the role of the committee in making recommendations to the general manager. After a few questions, he reiterated the proposed agenda and suggested that the full discussion begin. The following illustrates the course of the conversation in committee:

Lowell: The first item for close inspection is the company retirement program and related employee benefits. In my brief survey last week, I noted a wide difference of opinion among workers bases largely along age lines. The older workers all appeared satisfied with the existing program. Some wanted even more. Most of the younger people thought we were doing too much. What are your opinions and suggestions on what we should do?

Levy: (after a brief moment of silence) This is a topic you ~~learn to appreciate more as you draw nearer to retirement~~. I know I probably once shared the attitudes of many of you younger people but, with nine years left, some security in years after retirement has gotten very important to me. If you people were in our shoes, I think you would feel the same way.

Efurd: We don't doubt that retirement is important to you, but that's the whole problem. ~~Everything that is important to you gets taken care of.~~ Things that are important to those of us who were hired within the last few years

EXHIBIT I

Memorandum to Special Committee Members

TO: Committee Members Levy, Cafferty, Broussard, Hansard,
           Efurd, Webcott, and McBee

FROM: Stanley Lovell, Personnel Manager

SUBJECT: Special Committee Meeting to Discuss Employee Problems and
           Opinions

As all of you are quite aware, our company has experienced some problems
with differences of opinion between older and younger members of our work
force. Hostilities in recent days have served to point out the severity of these
problems. Mr. Cowpar, our general manager, has requested that I study the
factors which are contributing to existing differences of opinion and make
recommendations for solving these problems. I'm asking your help in doing
this.

You and the other six people listed above are being assigned to a special task
force committee to meet with me next Tuesday at 2 o'clock to discuss the
causes of our internal differences and to prepare recommendations to go to
Mr. Cowpar. The meeting time has been cleared with your superior so that
you can be free to attend.

In my preliminary research, I have identified some areas which I would like
for us to discuss specifically. Please be prepared to share your comments on
each of these topics as well as other factors which you believe are important.
Our agenda for the meeting will be as follows:

1. Our company retirement program and other benefits
2. Promotion policies
3. Assignment of responsibility to workers
4. Other contributing problem areas; and
5. Solutions to problems

I look forward to hearing your opinions and recommendations.

                                                              Stanley Lovell

	always get swept under the rug. I know that I speak for myself and most of the people in my department when I say that what we would prefer ~~would be to take home more money each mon~~th and have less money go into some of these benefit programs that are not too urgent for us.
WEBCOTT:	I'll second what Max has just said. Speaking as the only woman in this group, I'd like to say that money put into retirement and a lot of these other benefits is money wasted so far as I'm concerned. Don't forget, there are quite a few women working at this place, and most of those who work here are married and are t~~rying to supplement the family incom~~e and ~~bring in a little extra cash.~~ There are some exceptions, of course. Most of us are depending on our husbands' retirement programs or social security to take care of us when the time comes.
CAFFERTY:	Don't forget that m~~ost of the men around here are married~~ and have ~~families who depend upon their retirement program~~ when their time comes, too.
LOWELL:	May I remind you, Joanne, that the money you put in now will be returned to you if you should leave the company in a few years, or even in a few months. You're not losing any of the money you put into the retirement program in the long run.
WEBCOTT:	You're missing the point. ~~I need the money now~~, not when I quit! I would even go further by saying that I wish the company would pay me directly rather than diverting its own funds into retirement programs, insurance benefits, and that kind of thing.
BROUSSARD:	You're overlooking the fact that most other companies have the same type of program we have here. We've got to keep this up to be competitive.
McBEE:	Just because other companies do certain things is no basis for this company's decisions. I've got a friend working over at Bloomfield Corporation, and he tells me that they are experimenting with some kind of program that gives them an option on whether to participate in things like retirement programs or to take the money home with them each week. That's what I'd like to see this company do.
LEVY:	That program just won't work. Everyone has to contribute or there won't be enough funds to keep the plan working. ~~It takes a lot of money to meet the obligations of this~~ program.
EFURD:	You see, that's just what I was talking about a moment ago! This ~~organization is run for the benefit of the older workers!~~
LEVY:	I don't see how you can say that. You're making a good salary, and so is everybody else who works around here.
McBEE:	Man, you don't know what you're talking about. ~~I make so little that my wife has had to go to work to help support our family,~~ and lots of people around here make a lot less than I do.

And so the conversation went. At five o'clock the group was still discussing the retirement plan and other benefit programs. Hostility had erupted several times. No solutions were in view. Lowell closed the meeting by saying that he believed the workers on each side had learned more about the problems of their fellow workers, and he appealed for unity. He announced another meeting for two o'clock on Thursday, at which time promotions and job responsibilities would be discussed before considering recommendations.

The Thursday meeting turned out to be more of the same rather hostile discussion. After two hours of conversation, it became obvious to Lowell that no consensus of ideas was possible. He thanked the group for their efforts, requested their future efforts to cooperate, and indicated that he might be calling on their help again before submitting his report to Cowpar.

After everyone has left the conference room Lowell has stayed behind to ponder his next actions. He has only a little more than a week to prepare his recommendations, and he is almost as far from a solution now as he was in the beginning.

Questions about the Stanley Lowell case

1. What were the basic issues that divided the younger workers from the older workers and vice versa? Were these valid issues?

2. Do the younger workers and the older workers have any interests in common? Please explain your answer.

3. Mr. Lowell had thought that the use of group information gathering and decision making would unify the workers rather than divide them. Was he wrong in his assessment? Why or why not?

4. Constructively criticize and evaluate Mr. Lowell's handling of the group decision-making process from beginning to end.

5. What advice should be given to Mr. Lowell as the time for decisions and recommendations draws near without any obvious decisions having been reached?

6. Evaluate the policies of the Rainbow Company. Are the policies fair and equitable to everyone? Is the logic behind their usage correct? Are changes in policies necessary and appropriate? If so, what should the changes be?

7. Assign class members to the respective positions and role play the group's first session as it was, then as it should have been.

H. Gerald Pretzler - The Weekend Weatherman

H. Gerald Pretzler is a twenty-four-year-old student of journalism at a small state university. In addition to his academic studies, Gerald is the weekend weatherman for Station KAAA-TV, an affiliate of a major network in a moderately large western city.

KAAA-TV has evening news at six o'clock and ten o'clock seven days a week, including a five-minute presentation of the weather. A major part of Gerald's job is to present the weather segment for the shows on Saturday and Sunday. He uses many color charts and visual aids while he is on camera. Gerald enjoys being before the cameras and does an excellent job with the weather news. He spends more than the usual amount of time preparing his weather script, rehearsing his presentation, and grooming himself for the appearance. His screen appearances come across to the audience very effectively. In fact, Pretzler is the only reporter at the station who regularly receives fan mail. His mail comes in large quantities, usually from teenage girls who "think he is divine."

Appearances on the weather show are only a part of Pretzler's duties. In addition he must tape certain spot advertisements for showing at later times. If he must make a personal appearance before the cameras for these advertisements, his performance is good. When no personal appearance is required, his performance could best be called "sloppy." Obviously Gerald likes being before the cameras.

Also among Gerald's duties is the responsibility to monitor the station's programs during the evening hours to make live advertisements and station identifications. He is never on camera for these announcements, and his performance of these duties is usually worse than sloppy. He is supposed to read a script to accompany pictures or filmed sequences being shown for sponsoring companies. It is obvious to the television viewers watching these ads that the announcer (Gerald) has not proofed the script before reading it to the audience. He makes many errors while reading these scripts, frequently mispronouncing sponsor's names, bungling product details, and mumbling through important information. Many sponsors have complained about Gerald's poor announcing, so that the station has found it necessary to provide free reruns of many advertisements—an action that is proving quite expensive to the station.

In general, all off-the-camera work by Pretzler has been lacking. The station manager, Bill Ecklund, has orally reprimanded Pretzler on frequent occasions for his mistakes. He has also commended him for his good weather show. Ecklund frequently has gone over the expected preparation and work routines with Pretzler. Gerald has been told of the complaints that have been made and has had it made clear that definite improvements in his announcing are expected.

Yesterday was Sunday—one of Pretzler's days to work. He did an excellent job of the six o'clock weather and then fell into his usually weak announcing routine. His worst blunder came at 8:15 when he was running a picture sequence of automobiles for a commercial. The automobiles were Oldsmobiles, and the sponsor was Werner Oldsmobile. The script that Pretzler read, however, was for a sequence on Fords for Mason Ford Company. Apparently Pretzler did not even discover his mistake until a call came from the station manager, who was watching at home. Ecklund told Pretzler to rerun the ad correctly for the Oldsmobile company, to shape up his performance for the rest of the evening, and to be in his office at nine o'clock in the morning. Ecklund's words were sharp and to the point.

This morning (Monday) as Ecklund arrives at his office, there is a note waiting for him to return a call to Carl Werner, president of Werner Oldsmobile. When Ecklund returns the call, Mr. Werner informs him that the incident of the past evening is causing him to cancel Werner's $12,000 advertising contract with the station.

In about thirty minutes Gerald Pretzler should be arriving at the station manager's office.

Questions about the H. Gerald Pretzler case

1. Why does Pretzler do some things so well and other things so poorly?

2. What were Pretzler's goals for his weekend job? What personal goals does Pretzler have for the future?

3. Evaluate the earlier actions of Ecklund as Pretzler's superior.

4.   What might Ecklund have done to motivate Pretzler to do a better, more conscientious job?

5.   Relate the control process to this case. What phases of the control process were handled correctly and which phases were mishandled?

6.   What actions are appropriate by Ecklund as he prepares for his meeting with Pretzler? How should he handle the meeting? What action should he take? Use role playing to illustrate what should be done.

Edith Capp and Janet Turner – Consultants Who Can't Work Together

Resource Service, Incorporated, is a consulting and training enterprise established about thirty years ago to provide professional organizations, civic associations, and other groups with educationally related services. Organizations with varied backgrounds ranging from medical associations to scouting groups, to united fund associations, to mental health associations, and including other groups draw upon the services of R.S.I. In particular, R.S.I. helps the groups to plan and implement educational activities related to program development, office training, and the recruitment and training of volunteer workers.

R.S.I. has a number of field offices throughout the United States. An area director oversees a number of field offices, and a staff director is responsible for the operation of each individual field office. In this particular case Edgar Jarvis, age fifty-two, is the area director. He has been with the firm for twenty-five years, and served as a staff director for ten of those years, until his promotion to area director only a few months ago.

Problems exist within one of the field offices in Jarvis's jurisdiction. The field office staff is composed of five professional people (all college graduates) and two secretaries who have all had considerable experience with Resource Service, Inc. Professional employees in the field office staff include the following (see Exhibit I for the organization chart):

JAY PEPPER: Staff director, age thirty-eight, was promoted to staff director two weeks ago when the previous staff director, Dennis Sharp, after twenty years experience as staff director in this office, accepted a position with another firm in another state. Previously Jay Pepper had held the position now occupied by Wilbur Powell, who was employed only a week

528

EXHIBIT I   Organization chart for Resource Service, Inc.

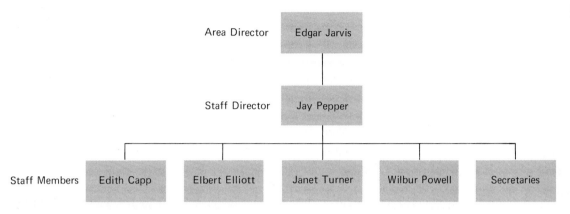

ago. Jay Pepper has worked in this office fifteen years and has had an excellent working relationship with all staff members. It was logical that he be named staff director as a result of his experience with the different phases of work in Resource Service and his experience as Sharp's right-hand man. Pepper, as staff director, also works on consulting projects with clients served by his organization.

EDITH CAPP: Age ~~sixty-three~~, has been with Resource Service ~~twenty-two years~~ and is ~~considered outstanding in her work~~. She has proved to be of much assistance to new staff members in helping them adjust to organizational expectations and work experiences. Edith has worked in two other field offices with Resource Service and left each office to advance to others with outstanding recommendations. She has advanced because she is ~~willing to accept large amounts of responsibility~~. She has been rewarded through good salaries and regular promotions. It is easy for her to move because she is not married and has no family.

ELBERT ELLIOTT: Age thirty-three, has been with Resource Service eleven years, has worked in one other field office, and is considered by his fellow workers to be a very dependable and progressive employee.

JANET TURNER: Age ~~twenty-eight~~, has been with Resource Service ~~eight years~~ and has been a ~~staff member in this field office two years~~, having had experience six years in another field office. Janet has been interested in her work and has ~~done a fine job with the responsibilities assigned her~~. It should be noted that she also was highly respected by her fellow workers in her first work experience with Resource Service.

WILBUR POWELL: Age ~~twenty-four~~, has been with Resource Service one week. He was employed by the company just after finishing college with a degree in sociology. He was employed to fill the vacancy left by Pepper when he was promoted.

Weekly informal staff conferences are held by the staff director to review the work being done by the field office and to dicuss future projects. Staff members (in various combinations) sometimes work together on projects and at other times work individually and separately. The ~~weekly staff conferences serve as a mea~~ns ~~of keeping all staff members informed of the work being conducted by the entire~~ sta~~ff~~. In addition, the staff meetings are used to allocate new projects and to formulate teams for the new assignments.

Although Edith Capp and Janet Turner have always worked on projects with all combinations of other staff members, they never volunteer to accept a project together or to work together in combination with other members. They ~~only~~ ~~work together when~~ they are s~~pecifically assigne~~d to do so by the staff director. They ~~never give credit to each oth~~er for work that has been completed satisfactorily nor do they appear to recognize each other's talents. They ~~discuss projects~~ of mutual interest ~~only when~~ it is a~~bsolutely necessary. Generally~~, they i~~gnore~~ ~~each~~ other as ~~much~~ as ~~possible~~. They have been known to ~~get~~ into a~~rguments~~ ~~when forced~~ to ~~work~~ together. The previous staff director, Dennis Sharp, was aware of the problem but did nothing to alter it. He avoided a confrontation by not assigning the two to work together except in unusual situations. Each woman complained to Sharp about the other one at different times, but he simply listened and told them to be patient.

Jay Pepper, as one of their colleagues, was also aware of the women's problems. However, Jay wanted to stay on good terms with each of them; so he listened and asked them to be more tolerant of each other, but did nothing more. On a few occasions he did offer advice, but it was never accepted. Pepper and the other staff members ~~all knew~~ that the ~~staff would have benefited from a closer~~, better ~~working relationship between Edith and Janet.~~ Each of the women had special abilities that would have been useful in several assignments, but there was a reluctance to call on their talents.

Just before Dennis Sharp left the staff for his new job, both Edith and Janet discussed in confidence with Edgar Jarvis, the area director, some of their concerns about each other. Neither knew the other had talked with him. The following information was revealed to Jarvis to the best of his recollection.

Edith Capp: Edith ~~did not feel~~ that ~~Janet was willing to work as hard~~ as other staff members on project loads. She felt that Janet was ~~not as professionally capa-~~ ~~ble~~ as she should be for the position she holds. She thought Janet ~~exhibited a~~ ~~noncooperative attitude~~, and was ~~not interested in receiving advice~~ or ~~assistance~~ ~~from others on~~ the staff. Edith felt Janet had a ~~poor attitude about her wor~~k, and ~~only did what was required of her~~ in order to get by. She felt that in staff meetings Janet was not being fair in what she generally reported she had accomplished.

Edith, however, ~~expressed willingness to work on joint assignments with Janet~~, but ~~felt that Janet would not meet the standards expected nor would she cooperate~~. Edith had decided it was not worth the effort to try to improve their relationship, feeling that no cooperation would be received from Janet.

Janet Turner: Janet felt that ~~Edith often tried to interfere with her work~~ and was ~~always trying to make her look bad~~. She knew Edith had successfully handled her work load, but did not want to work jointly with Edith. ~~Janet preferred not having any association with Edith~~. When assigned joint work with Edith, she would discuss the project no more than was absolutely necessary and would do no more than was required to complete her responsibility. When there were joint assignments, little conversation and interaction with Edith had taken place—in fact no more than necessary. Janet was not willing or interested in making an attempt to improve their relationship and felt that the best practice was for each to keep her distance and try not to become further involved.

It should be noted that there were no apparent problems or conditions outside the work situation that either Edith or Janet brought to the work situation that could have created conflict between them at work. No complaints had been made regarding either Edith or Janet on past working relationships by other organizations, firms, or groups with which they worked.

Edgar Jarvis, only a few days after he had promoted Jay Pepper, mentioned to Pepper that he was aware of the relationship between Edith and Janet. He suggested that Jay try to correct the situation because he felt it had already gone too far. Jay Pepper indicated that he was aware of the situation and had already given thought to the problem and planned to work on it in the very near future.

Questions about the Edith Capp and Janet Turner Case

1. On the basis of the information supplied in this case, why don't the two women work together more effectively?

2. What additional information might be helpful in deciding what to do about handling the problem between these two women?

3. What actions should be taken by Mr. Pepper in resolving conflict between the women as he assumes his new duties as staff director?

4. Should Pepper have done more to help the women resolve their difficulties when he was one of their colleagues (before he became staff director)? If so, what could he have done?

5. Both of the women discussed their problems with the area director, Edgar Jarvis. What should Jarvis have done about their conflict?

6. What type of leadership and supervision was exhibited by the first staff director, Dennis Sharp?

7. List and analyze communication problems that exist in this case. How can communication be improved?

8. What additional problems are presented in this case?

Earl Fornette – An Independent Supervisor

The products of Columbia Corporation are well known to housewives and farmers alike, for Columbia concentrates its product efforts on these two markets. The corporation has two divisions—one specializing in consumer household products and the other manufacturing or processing agricultural goods. Consumer products made by Columbia include cosmetics, medical supplies, household sprays (deodorants, cleansers, etc.), protective floor and furniture coatings, and other related products. The agricultural division produces commercial fertilizers, veterinary medicines, insecticides, and additives for animal food products.

The major production plants for the two divisions are located side by side in the outskirts of a large midwestern community. Even though they are near each other, the two plants are operated on an almost totally independent basis. In addition to having their production activities completely separated, their in-plant service and supporting activities, such as maintenance, storage, and purchasing, are also operated independently of each other. The top official of each plant (the plant manager) reports to the corporate vice president. As such, the corporate vice president is the only formal link between the two plants. There is some informal cooperation between the two plants, but this is minimal. Also, promotions and transfers sometimes occur between the two plants when personnel in one plant are suited for jobs in the other plant.

As was mentioned previously, each plant has its own maintenance division. Each maintenance division has the responsibility for keeping the physical plant operational and in an excellent state of repair as well as for keeping most of the processing and manufacturing machinery functioning well. The Maintenance Department of the Consumer Products plant is rather large, averaging about forty employees on a continuing basis. Most of the personnel in the Maintenance Department are highly specialized workers. In addition to supervisory personnel, the department is composed of pipefitters, carpenters, electricians, heating and refrigeration experts, and other skilled personnel. Exhibit I shows the organization structure of the Maintenance Department.

The superintendent of maintenance in the Consumer Division is Larry Donlevy. He has been with Columbia for almost fifteen years. When he received his bachelor's degree in mechanical engineering from a nearby university, he was hired and put to work in the Equipment and Machinery Design Section of the Agricultural Division. Because he showed management potential, he was transferred after two years to the position of supervisor in the Maintenance Department of the agricultural plant. Four years later he was promoted to assistant superintendent of maintenance. When the job of superintendent of maintenance in the Consumer Division became vacant five years ago, Donlevy was selected and transferred.

As superintendent of maintenance in the Consumer Division, Donlevy is responsible for seeing that production inefficiencies because of plant or equipment inadequacies are held to a minimum. He has the responsibility for both preventive and corrective maintenance as well as emergency repairs. Donlevy spends most of his time planning and overseeing preventive maintenance projects as well as handling the paperwork of the department. When he has long-range maintenance plans completed and they have been reviewed by the appropriate production personnel, it is Donlevy's practice to turn them over to his assistant, Earl Fornette, to be carried out. He delegates the job of implementing the plans almost completely to Fornette.

When requests for routine maintenance and emergency maintenance come in, Donlevy sometimes participates in some phase of the planning. For the most part, however, routine and emergency maintenance are Fornette's concerns. Donlevy calls Fornette "my chief executioner . . . . When it's time to get work out of the fellows, that's Earl's job. He knows how to deal with them. I just make plans and let Earl see they are carried out."

Earl Fornette is one of the most respected employees at Columbia. At age sixty, he's been with the company for nearly thirty-five years. He's not an educated man in the sense of formal schooling, having quit school when he was in the tenth grade. He came to work for Columbia as a carpenter after knocking around in the construction business. After eighteen years with Columbia, he worked his way up to assistant superintendent of maintenance—the job he's held since that time. Physically and mentally he's very strong. From every indication, he should be able to keep up his work pace through the five remaining years until his retirement.

He feels quite satisfied and secure in his job, with no ambitions for any other job. He dislikes paperwork intensely; as a result, he has never wanted the job of superintendent, which calls for a large amount of paper handling.

Fornette has a strong rapport with the foremen, the carpenters, pipefitters, etc., in his department. He also has endeared himself to many management personnel outside the Maintenance Department. Perhaps the people least pleased with Fornette are the two supervisors who work under him. Their reasons will be reviewed momentarily.

The causes of strong rapport between Fornette and the first-line foremen and their subordinates lie in the identification he has with them. Since he came up

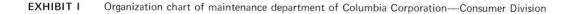

EXHIBIT I   Organization chart of maintenance department of Columbia Corporation—Consumer Division

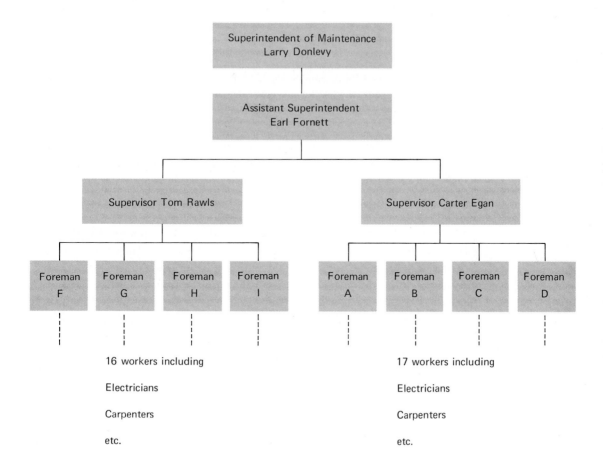

through the ranks, he understands them and talks their language. They, like he, are for the most part uneducated. While some of them (the foremen and workers) have high school diplomas, that is the extent of their education. Fornette takes an extremely personal interest in each of them. He talks with them frequently. They go to his office to ask his advice on problems, including personal matters as well as job difficulties.

Fornette's compassion and concern for the workers are coupled with an attitude of expectation from them. He expects them to perform their jobs well, and he tells them so. If they let him down, he's quick to remind them of their responsibilities. Because he treats them well and shows respect for them, the first-level foremen and their men do their best for Fornette.

Managers in the Production Department and throughout the plant have a great respect for Fornette because he's helped them out of tight situations many times. Several years ago, for example, a part of the plant was flooded because of excessive rains in the area. Fornette almost single-handedly took over and got things cleaned up and operating again in an amazing time—just forty-eight hours—in time for production to begin again to meet an important shipment deadline. Numerous occasions could be cited when Fornette has personally taken charge of emergency repair problems and has worked for continuing periods of thirty-six hours or more until the problems have been resolved and production returned to normal.

As mentioned earlier, perhaps the people who are least pleased with Fornette are the two supervisors who work immediately beneath him—Tom Rawls and Carter Egan. Both men are well trained and qualified for their jobs. Rawls holds a degree in electrical engineering; Egan has a degree in mechanical engineering. Both had brief work experience with other companies before they were hired by Columbia for jobs in the Production Department. After a few years in Production, each was transferred to Maintenance as a supervisor. Rawls has been in his present position three years, and Egan has held his job for two years.

It is the duty of each maintenance supervisor to schedule precisely the jobs assigned to him and his men by the assistant superintendent, to requisition materials and equipment, to delegate assignments to individual foremen, to assign appropriate helpers to the foremen, and to give other appropriate instruction and supervision to the foremen and their work teams. The workers (the carpenters, pipefitters, etc.) do not continually work under the supervision of the same foreman. As a foreman is given a job assignment (for example, as he is assigned to replace all broken windows in the plant), he is given the personnel to complete the job. Thus, the workers and their foreman handle the task until it is completed, then each one is assigned to another project where he is needed. The supervisor makes these assignments and coordinates all work projects. The foreman is the boss when a task group is working together. When their task is

completed, the group is divided to work on other maintenance projects. The foreman may have a new group to supervise, and the individual workers may have
a new foreman to serve as boss for the new job. Changes continue as jobs are
completed and new ones present themselves.

The problems the supervisors have with Fornette can be illustrated by the
following examples:

EXAMPLE 1:   As has already been stated, the workers frequently choose to go to Fornette with their problems (both work and personal) and with their complaints and gripes. For the most part, Fornette attempts to help them if he
can. He seldom consults with their supervisor or the appropriate foreman.
Where work problems are involved, Fornette has the habit of failing to
communicate the suggestions made and the actions he has taken to the
proper managerial personnel. He is quite independent in his actions, not
so much because he intends to be but because that is the way he has
always operated without being challenged. As a result, supervisors and
foremen frequently are left in the dark about promises and instructions
given by Fornette directly to the workers.

EXAMPLE 2:   Another typical illustration of the Fornette way shows his quick temper.
On a recent day it was discovered that vandals had thrown rocks through
some windows during the previous night. At one o'clock Fornette came
by and told Egan to be sure that his men had the job finished before the
end of the shift (three o'clock) because it was going to rain and water
damage to equipment and materials could result. "Get your men right on
it," he said. Egan agreed and promised to get the job done.

Fifteen minutes later Fornette came back by and "blew a fuse" when
he saw that the carpenters were still occupied with another job and had
not gotten around to the window repairs. "I thought I told you to get the
men on those windows. Do you want me to get them or are you going to
do it?"

"I'll take care of it," was Egan's response as he walked toward the
carpenters in question. Fornette stormed off without giving Egan a chance
to explain that the carpenters were just about to finish another job so he
had allowed them to complete the task. By the time Egan reached them to
get them started on the windows, they had finished the other job and were
ready to begin.

EXAMPLE 3:   The policy on vacations at Columbia states that all workers with ten years
or more of seniority in the company are entitled to four weeks' annual
vacation. All of the foremen in the Maintenance Department have been
with the company for more than ten years and are, therefore, entitled to
four weeks off. In implementing the policy, the Maintenance Department
has the following additional policies:

a. Request for vacation time off shall be made for each year before the
beginning of that calendar year (January 1). At that time a schedule will
be made up by each supervisor for those workers under his jurisdiction.

Any change of schedule thereafter will come through the supervisor and shall not jeopardize the vacation time previously assigned to other workers.

b.   When a foreman is off on vacation, he shall be replaced by a worker from the ranks as a temporary foreman. The temporary foreman will be selected jointly by the supervisor and the foreman going on vacation. Upon the foreman's return from vacation, the temporary foreman shall go back to his nonforeman status.

c.   No more than two foremen shall be on vacation at the same time in the section under a single supervisor. It is important not to have too many temporary, inexperienced foremen in charge at one time.

In accordance with departmental policies, Supervisor Egan denied Foreman A's May 15 request to change his vacation time from the previously established dates running from May 24 through June 21 to new ones beginning June 1 and continuing to June 28. Even though only one week would be involved in the adjustment, two other foremen had vacations beginning June 22. A change would mean three temporary foremen would be working, and only two permanent foremen would be present that week. Egan explained his reasons for turning down the request to Foreman A. Foreman A was not satisfied and went to Fornette without Egan's knowledge. Fornette approved the change and later told Egan everything "would be okay."

EXAMPLE 4:   The workers in the Maintenance Department tend to be "pack rats" by nature. In their preventive maintenance in particular they frequently save parts and whole units they think they might be able to use sometime in the future. When Electrician A in Egan's section asked what he should do with an old light fixture just replaced, that he thought still had some life in it, Egan told him to scrap it and throw it away. He explained that for bookkeeping, storage, and tax reasons, discarding it was the best policy. Some weeks later Egan discovered the light fixture hidden away under some old cartons in the storage room. When he confronted Electrician A with the light fixture, Electrician A said, "Earl [Fornette] thought it would be a good idea to keep it." Egan could easily picture the conversation that must have gone on between Fornette and Electrician A.

Questions about the Earl Fornette case

1.   Identify Larry Donlevy's leadership-supervisory style. What specific strengths did he show? What weaknesses did he reveal?

2.   Identify Earl Fornette's leadership-supervisory style and abilities. What specific strengths and weaknesses did he show?

3.   What were the effects of Fornette's actions revealed in each of the examples? Who was helped, and who was hurt? How?

4.   Discuss Carter Egan's actions and abilities.

5.   What evidence exists to indicate that there is an informal organization at Columbia Corporation? What are the goals and objectives of the informal organization?

6.   What communication inadequacies does this case illustrate? How can they be corrected?

7.   As a supervisor, what actions did Egan have a right to expect from Donlevy? from Fornette? from his own subordinates?

8.   Evaluate the organization structure at Columbia. What are the strong points and the weaknesses of the formal authority relationships?

9.   What advice should be given to Egan as he ponders a course of action?

Bentley Cantrell – The Reluctant Administrator*

Fairfields Nursing Home is a well-respected facility established primarily to provide medical attention to the elderly and to other invalid or semi-invalid persons. The home is owned by five businessmen, and one of the men, Lewis Starrker, serves as full-time administrator. The patients or their relatives pay rather sizeable fees monthly for the continuing care provided. The service and attention given by the home is considered by most to be excellent.

In the early years, the home was rather small, and the administrative problems were few. As the capacity of the home was increased and the volume of patients began to grow, the duties of the administrator grew too large for Starrker to handle. About five years ago an assistant administrator was hired and given the duties of overseeing the business office, building and grounds maintenance, and laundry and housekeeping activities. Complete authority was given to the assistant administrator over these activities. In addition, the assistant administrator was designated to serve in the full capacity of the administrator when the administrator was away from the home. In this event, *all* workers were under his jurisdiction.

About a year ago the position of assistant administrator became vacant, and Bentley Cantrell was hired to fill the position. The duties of the assistant administrator remain basically identical to the responsibilities outlined five years ago. (See Exhibit 1 for the current organization chart.) Cantrell is well qualified for his position. He has a bachelor's degree in management with a good foundation in accounting. For two years before coming to Fairfields Nursing Home he was office manager in a hospital where he supervised purchasing, receiving and delivery,

*Some of the material for this case was provided by Winborn E. Davis.

EXHIBIT I Organization chart for Fairfields Nursing Home

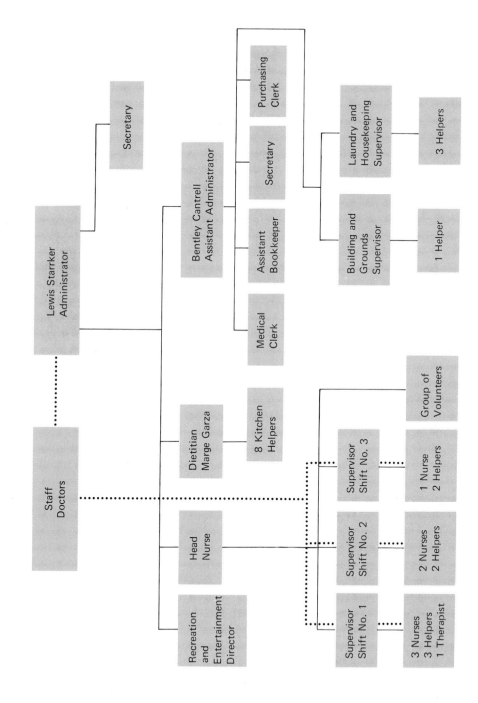

and payroll and bookkeeping. On occasion he also worked on problems of the physical plant of the hospital and its upkeep.

Mr. Starrker is somewhat disappointed in Cantrell's performance over the past year. Cantrell knows how the work should be done, and he gets along with the employees; but he fails to handle problems promptly. He puts off telling his subordinates what to do and is especially reluctant to correct them when they make a mistake. The reluctance to act apparently cannot be explained by ignorance, because when Starrker confronts Cantrell with the need for action, Cantrell always proposes a good solution. However, when Cantrell is instructed to move ahead, he expresses doubt that the supervisors and employees beneath him will be able to follow his instructions. Many times he elects to do a job himself rather than direct his subordinates to handle it.

Starrker can recall many actions on the part of Cantrell that concern him. A few examples are shown below.

EXAMPLE 1:   Two of the workers in laundry and housekeeping strongly disagreed with the actions of the supervisor. Much conflict in the department was rumored throughout the home. Cantrell took no action, and both of the workers (who previously had good work records) quit their jobs. Even after their resignations, Cantrell said nothing to the supervisor about the hassle.

EXAMPLE 2:   When government regulations called for new but routine quarterly reports, Cantrell delayed action on submitting them until the day before the deadline so that he could personally fill out the reports. They were simple and nontechnical and were well within the capabilities of the assistant bookkeeper.

As usual, Cantrell was pushed into action only by the deadline. He is always just ahead of deadlines, if he meets them at all. His activities seem to press him to keep ahead of essential tasks only. Other things remain undone.

EXAMPLE 3:   The railing by the steps at the front entrance to the home has been broken for three weeks. No activity to repair the railing is apparent, and the safety of all who enter from the front is at stake. If anyone should be injured as a result of the home's negligence, a lawsuit would no doubt be likely.

Questions about the Bentley Cantrell case

1. To what may Cantrell's reluctance to act be attributed?

2. Evaluate Starrker's actions toward Cantrell up to the present time. What leadership style has Starrker exhibited?

3. What should Cantrell's actions have been in each of the examples shown in the case?

4. Evaluate the control process as it has been applied to Cantrell.

5. What, if any, disciplinary action is appropriate? Please explain.

6. What leadership-supervisory actions should now be taken by Starrker?

Billy Snyder – The Worker Who Does What He's Told *

Marge Garza, dietitian in charge of the kitchen and all food services at Fairfields Nursing Home, supervises the activities of eight employees.** One of these workers is Billy Snyder, a twenty-five-year-old from an economically and educationally depressed background. Personnel records show that Billy quit school in the eighth grade, that he is not married, and that he lives in a poverty-bound section of town. Little else is known about him.

Billy is the clean-up man and dishwasher. He serves as bus boy, empties dishes, runs the automatic dishwasher, and cleans the kitchen floors. His work is adequate, but Billy does only what he is told and nothing more. Everything is accomplished in a mechanical, uninspired manner. When Billy's assigned tasks are finished, he sits down or goes to the washroom for a smoke.

Marge cannot understand why Billy is not more interested in his work. It appears that he wants only to finish each job and get his check on payday. Marge has attempted to show an interest in Billy's work and to engage him in conversation, but there has been little to praise him about. Billy seldom smiles and usually responds to queries with the fewest words possible.

The dietitian feels that she simply cannot get through to Billy. Other kitchen workers do not feel that Billy is a part of the group. Billy's attitude affects morale even though he doesn't create trouble for anyone.

Questions about the Billy Snyder case

1. What are Billy Snyder's expectations from his work?

*Winborn E. Davis provided the basic material for this case.
**The organization structure and other pertinent background details are provided in the Bentley Cantrell case, which immediately precedes this case.

2. Should Mrs. Garza attempt to expand Billy's job expectations?

3. What incentives and opportunities might be appealing to Billy?

4. Why is Billy not a part of the work "group"? Can this situation be changed?

5. What additional advice seems appropriate for Mrs. Garza?

Kurt Browning-A New Manager Who Asserted Himself

Kingsridge Electric Company is a full-line electrical appliances sales and service store located in a midwestern city of approximately 120,000 population. Founded by Daniel Kingsridge almost thirty-five years ago, the company has a record of quality performance in selling and servicing medium- to high-priced electrical appliances ranging from transistor radios to stoves, refrigerators, and air-conditioning units.

Daniel Kingsridge has been the active manager of his company throughout the years until about six months ago when his health began to deteriorate. Now at age sixty-five, Mr. Kingsridge of necessity has had to begin turning certain managerial duties over to his subordinates. About two weeks ago, he called Kurt Browning, his sales manager, and told him that he was to become assistant manager for the entire company, effective immediately. At the time Kingsridge made these comments to Browning. (At least, this is the way Browning remembers it.)

Kurt, from here on it appears that I will only come to the office two or three hours a day. Your job will be to run the business as if it were your own. I'll come in to sign checks, give some instructions, meet with manufacturing representatives from appliance companies to see what new merchandise they have to sell us, and a few things like that.

You will have total responsibility for sales activities. Also, everyone will report to you, and that includes the boys in repairs and services and the girls in the office, too. In fact, they should come to you always before they talk to me about their problems.

We'll put Ed Chromer in charge of floor sales, and Rick Loftis will head up the repairs group.

All of this came as somewhat of a surprise to Browning, although he was elated at the opportunity to step in and assume the guiding role for the company. Kurt at thirty-three has been with the company for eight years. He went to college for three years, majoring in marketing. Before his senior year he dropped out of school to join the navy for a four-year tour. Upon discharge he came to work for Kingsridge as a salesman and worked his way up to become the unofficial head of floor sales activities. He proved himself to be aggressive, energetic, and creative.

While no formal organization chart was presented by Mr. Kingsridge in their recent discussion, Browning pictured things to be as shown in Exhibit I.

At the time of the discussion two weeks ago, Kingsridge mentioned nothing about a change in office arrangements or desks; so Browning assumed there would be no changes. Since then no moves have been made. Browning continues to work at his old desk located in the middle of the sales floor. The only "office" in the store is an 18′ × 22′ space at the back of the sales floor, separated from the sales

EXHIBIT I   Unofficial organization chart for Kingsridge Electric

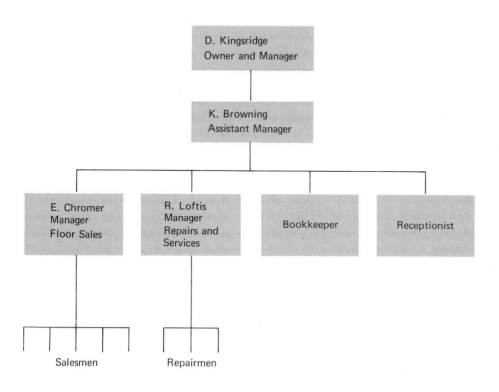

area by only a long counter. Kingsridge, the bookkeeper, and the secretary-receptionist have desks behind the counter.

The past two weeks have been busy ones for Browning. While much of his time has been devoted to setting internal matters in order after a period of neglect by Mr. Kingsridge as a result of illness, Browning has taken the initiative in sales programs. He has been exploring new advertising techniques and media not previously used by the company. One of the fruits of his efforts is a contract he placed on Mr. Kingsridge's desk yesterday afternoon for signing. The memo submitted with the contract is shown in Exhibit II.

When Mr. Kingsridge came into the office this morning he spent a few minutes talking to various employees, then he began reviewing the materials awaiting him on his desk. Almost immediately he called Browning back to his desk. Their discussion was a one-way conversation with Mr. Kingsridge doing all the talking.

> I don't know what the real meaning of this contract is, but I'm choosing to ignore it. There are at least three things wrong. First, I don't wish to commit funds in advance to a campaign that has undetermined potential. Second, our company has an image of quality and respect. Spot advertising that pounds away at our customers just isn't in our best interests. And third, you know as well as I do what kind of appeal Station WXXX has. It's for kids, and they play nothing but that terrible music that's loud and noisy. Advertising on a station like that does nothing for our image of a quality company.
>
> I want you to assert yourself in your new responsibilities but this contract just isn't what we need. Let's forget the whole matter. From now on, be more careful what you do.

Browning was rather stunned by the force of Mr. Kingsridge's comments and said little. He returned to his desk to decide what to do or say. Browning feels that he had good reason for submitting the contract. In addition to saving money on advertising, this approach would help reach the youth–young adult market, which buys more than 50 percent of all the radios, phonographs, and portable television sets sold by Kingsridge. According to a recent market survey, more than 60 percent of the age 15–23 market listen to Station WXXX sometime during each day. The station appears to be an excellent medium for communicating with the young.

More important, however, Browning is concerned about his own job, his role in the company, his relationship to his boss, and his role with his "subordinates." The furor created by the contract leads him to believe that he has mistakenly acted with initiative, but he's not certain where he's gone wrong.

EXHIBIT II   Memo to Mr. Kingsridge

To: D. W. Kingsridge

From: K. L. Browning

Subject: Advertising Contract with Radio Station WXXX

I am submitting the following contract for your signature. As you can see, the contract calls for 300 spot advertisements with WXXX over a period of the next six months. Each advertisement is for a period of 30 seconds and will be designed and used as we specify. By entering into the contract and prepaying 50 percent of the total amount of $1800, we can save ourselves $600. The normal cost of a 30-second advertisement on WXXX is $8, but by entering into the contract and paying in part ahead of time, we receive a $2 discount for each spot. I anticipate that we can use the spots particularly to increase our sales to the youth and young adult markets.

Questions about the Kurt Browning case

1.   Evaluate the supervisory styles and abilities of Mr. Kingsridge. Give specific examples to support your evaluation.

2.   Immediately upon receiving his new assignment, what should Browning have done? Role play the conversation, remembering to ask questions Browning should have asked.

3.   What are the objectives of Kingsridge Electric as Mr. Kingsridge sees them? as Mr. Browning views them?

4.   Some changes took place in this case. What effects should Browning have anticipated for Mr. Kingsridge? for the other employees? What steps should Browning have taken to smooth the way for change?

5.   Review and evaluate Browning's actions in planning the advertising contract. Was he justified in his actions? Did he make mistakes?

6.   What solutions are now available to Browning? Which are the most desirable? Role play the conversation Browning might initiate with Mr. Kingsridge after Mr. Kingsridge's outburst.

7.   How does this case illustrate the effects of the formal organization on the performance of members of the organization?

Susan Swanson—The Unhappy Secretary*

When Susan Swanson ~~graduated~~ from ~~Western State University~~ ~~five years ago~~, she entered the business world with eagerness and enthusiasm. Just four years earlier, ~~she~~ had ~~decided~~ to go to college just long enough to take a ~~two-year~~ ~~secretarial~~ course. By the time she finished that program she had ~~decided to~~ ~~obtain~~ a ~~degree~~ in ~~secretarial science~~. The courses she took and her working experience at college ~~led~~ her to ~~believe~~ that the ~~secretary~~ ~~played~~ an ~~important role~~ in ~~business~~ and ~~industry~~. Courses in office administration, administrative planning, and organizational policy in addition to secretarial skills courses had broadened her understanding of workings of business organizations.

She ~~worked~~ in an ~~office~~ on ~~campus~~ ~~throughout~~ the ~~four years~~ she was in college and while there ~~formulated~~ ~~many~~ of her ~~concepts~~ about what ~~secretaries could~~ ~~do~~. The administrator in the office was a dynamic person who was involved in many projects. He used his chief assistant as a genuine "executive secretary" by involving her in the projects from their inception and by giving her considerable responsibility for other matters. She was literally his "girl Friday." Susan, while not the administrator's chief assistant until the ~~last few~~ months of ~~her~~ ~~college career,~~ was ~~given~~ ~~much~~ responsibility. When the full-time secretary resigned and moved to another city about the time Susan graduated, Susan was asked to take over the work until another full-time secretary could be found.

It was with this background that Susan began her work as a graduate secretary five years ago. This fall, however, she is back in school at Western State taking courses ~~to become~~ ~~certified to teach~~. She has become completely disillusioned

*This case was prepared by Professor Doris B. Bentley of the University of Southwestern Louisiana.

with the opportunities of the secretary and particularly has become dissatisfied with the way executives use their secretaries.

During registration Susan encountered one of her former business professors. He was interested in knowing why Susan had come back to school. When Susan told him briefly what caused her to come back, the professor asked Susan to write down in detail the facts about the jobs she had held since she graduated. The professor believed that analysis of Susan's case might prove revealing and helpful to both educators and businessmen. Perhaps the result would be better education and better utilization of future secretarial graduates. About a week later, Susan had completed her outline and comments on the four jobs she had held as a secretary and brought them to the professor. She presented the following summary with her reactions.

Job 1: ~~Secretary,~~
Religious Charities Center (student aide ~~1966–1970,~~ full-time June–September 1970) ~~Salary: $200~~

This is the job I had while I was in college. The job consisted of ~~sorting~~ and ~~opening all~~ incoming mail (keeping a summary list on hand of all mail received when the boss, Rev. Simon, was out of town; he always called and wanted to know exactly what was received and the contents of letters). I ~~kept~~ a ~~small set~~ of ~~books~~ (including Rev. Simon's personal checkbook), ~~took a large~~ volume of ~~dictation,~~ ~~did some typing,~~ ~~exten~~sively used the ~~Dictaphone,~~ ~~arranged committee meetings~~ (calling individual members, gathering information pertinent to those meetings, typing agenda), ~~took~~ mi~~nutes~~ of ~~board~~ ~~meetings,~~ ~~scheduled~~ appointments, ~~arranged "tennis matches,"~~ ~~coord~~inated ~~alumni~~ and parent ~~appeal~~ mailings, and planned and ~~prepared~~ ~~booklets~~ for the Young People's Club and the Church Guild. I was required to ~~act as~~ "~~hostess~~" to ~~various~~ ~~civic~~ ~~leaders~~ and ~~business~~ ~~asso~~ciates who would come in for coffee or to attend meetings. ~~This job was grand.~~ I had the op~~portu~~nity to ~~use~~ ~~every~~ ~~skill~~ and k~~nowledge~~ ~~I~~ had ac~~quired~~—and more.

Job 2: ~~Receptionist-PBX Operator~~
Graley-Craddock Drilling Contractors, Inc. Oil Center, Oil City (October ~~1970~~–January ~~1971~~) Salary: ~~$325~~ (~~best I could find~~)

Duties: ~~Answering~~ the ~~phone~~ and ~~placing calls~~ for ~~four~~ ~~small companies~~; ~~very~~ ~~little~~ typing; ~~practically~~ ~~no~~ ~~shorthand~~; ~~very dull!~~ Everybody in the Oil Center wanted experienced secretaries. My degree and experience with Rev. Simon didn't seem to be helpful.

Job 3: ~~Stenographer~~
Co-Op Petroleum Corporation Accounting Department, Contract Section
(~~February 1971-February 1972~~) Salary: ~~$410~~

In this job, I reported to Mr. J. L. Truett, the senior clerk. He, in turn, reported to Mr. L. D. Moyle, head of the Contract Section. His boss was Mr. E. D. Goddard, the division accountant. ~~No shorthand~~ was ~~called for~~ in this job even though it was called a stenographic position. It was my ~~duty~~ to ~~help~~ in the ~~processing~~ of ~~all contracts~~ entered into by the company. I ~~typed each contract~~ along with an accompanying form letter (which was actually a letter of transmittal summarizing the terms of the contract to Co-Op's General Office in Tulsa). I ~~also typed~~ the forms ~~for~~ in~~surance records~~, ~~forms for rental~~ payments, and ~~certain cards~~ for ~~filing~~. All of the above were ~~typed from penciled-in~~ information ~~worked up by Mr. Truett~~. Once a month I ~~checked records for~~ expiring ~~contracts~~ and ~~hand-cancelled~~ all of the above papers.

When each contract was completed and assembled, the contract and the transmittal letter were taken to Mr. Moyle for his signature. ~~I was rarely allowed to take the finished materials to Mr. Moyle~~. The senior clerk always did this. When I did have the opportunity to do so, ~~I asked about~~ the ~~possibilities~~ of his letting me ~~work up some~~ of ~~these form letters~~ for the easier contracts on my own (it would involve reading the contract and summarizing terms). He said he ~~would prefer letting~~ the ~~senior clerk handle~~ that for now and perhaps when we were "caught up," we might try it. ~~After one year~~ I was called in by Mr. Goddard, the division accountant, for a review; and at that time I ~~again requested~~ that ~~they allow me~~ to ~~use a little~~ of ~~my own~~ intelli~~gence. I also asked~~ about the ~~possibility~~ of the ~~senior clerk's~~ dictating ~~some~~ of this ~~information to me~~. His answer was that contract work was so voluminous that we could not take time to do this, nor should I spend too much time reading through the contracts. We would continue to handle all procedures the same way. There were always at least twenty or twenty-five contracts waiting to be typed. It was quite voluminous, with no end in sight.

I had ~~no complaints about the salary~~. It was the ~~lack of "secretarial" work~~, the ~~fact~~ that I ~~had no~~ o~~pportunity~~ to ~~use my initiative~~ or intelli~~gence~~, that bothered me. There was no possibility of decreasing the volume so that I could even try anything else. I ~~explained~~ to Mr. Goddard ~~what type~~ of j~~ob I was interested~~ in (based on some of my experience with Rev. Simon and also our secretarial training). He said that I would not find this at Co-Op or at any major company. I ~~asked~~ Mr. Goddard ~~to consider me~~ for a ~~transfer~~ to ~~another department~~ with Co-Op where I might ~~have more~~ of a ~~stenographic job~~. (My salary was now $430, increased by a cost-of-living raise.) He ~~agreed~~ to ~~let me transfer~~ with a promotion into a position that could be elevated into the secretarial line. In March 1972, I transferred to the Exploration Department to work for the district exploration superintendent as a senior steno—starting salary, $500.

Job 4: ~~Senior~~ Stenographer
Co-Op Petroleum Corporation Exploration Department, Geological Section ~~(March 1972–August 1975)~~ ~~Salary: $500~~

The job consisted of ~~learning more forms~~—but different ones. There was ~~practically no dictation~~. I was ~~secretary~~ primarily to the ~~district~~ exploration ~~superintendent~~, the ~~district geologist~~, and the ~~operations geologist~~ as well as to the twenty-two geologists under them. My ~~responsibilities to~~ the ~~DES~~ were ~~answering his~~ telephone, ~~handling~~ his ~~mail~~, ~~cleaning his desk~~ and ~~ash~~ trays, and ~~serving coffee "in china cups"~~ at committee meetings (A.M. and P.M.). I ~~received dictation~~ from him ~~about six times~~ in ~~three years!~~ My ~~responsibilities to~~ the ~~DG~~ were ~~basically~~ the ~~same~~ as above.

Responsibilities to operations geologist (and twenty-two geologists) included the following: ~~some~~ ~~dictation~~, ~~mostly~~ ~~typing from~~ their ~~notes~~; ~~setting up well files~~; ~~filing~~ a ~~tremendous~~ amount of ~~materials~~; ~~making~~ ~~travel~~ arrangements; ~~ordering supplies~~; and ~~taking well~~ reports ~~from other~~ companies (drilling information). Most of this work filtered through the operations geologist.

The ~~biggest project~~ involved in this ~~job~~ was ~~assembling~~ a ~~geological memorandum~~. This was about the ~~only aspect~~ of the ~~job~~ that I ~~could see some challenge in~~ and ~~was allowed~~ to ~~handle entirely~~ on ~~my own~~—mainly because the men didn't know the proper assembling and mailing procedure. Each memorandum consisted of several typed legal pages pertaining to the geological prospect and related maps. I assigned a company number to the memo, typed the text (not from dictation but from written material), labeled the maps, prepared transmittal form, and sent all of it to Co-Op's General Office in Tulsa. It was necessary to know exactly and be able to follow the company's procedure of transmitting these memos. Memos were written only at sale time, which was usually two or three times a year.

Because the operations geologist position was a rotating position, I ~~had a new sub-boss~~ about ~~every six months~~. ~~Each time~~ a ~~new~~ person came in ~~I~~ acquired a ~~little more~~ responsibility—mostly ~~because I was stationary~~ and ~~knew the procedure~~. They relied on me to help them. Each new operations geologist would ~~delegate a little more~~ responsibility; ~~some~~ allowed ~~me~~ to write ~~routine letters~~; ~~gradually~~ I ~~began writing~~ and ~~signing routine letters~~ for the ~~district geologist~~, ~~Mr. Lahaye~~.

When a ~~company reorganization occurred~~, our district was reduced to nine geologists. The ~~critical factor~~ here was the ~~termination~~ of the ~~operations geologist~~

~~position~~ and the creation of a ~~district clerk's position~~. This man was to serve as right-hand man to the district exploration superintendent much as the operations geologist did. What a problem this created for me! ~~I believe~~ that ~~everyth~~ing that ~~this man did could have been handled by~~ a ~~competent secretary~~.

I ~~asked~~ at ~~this time that some~~ of th~~ese~~ ~~responsibilities~~ be ~~given to me~~. The district clerk's responsibilities included keeping a chart on currently drilling wells and reporting this daily to the DES; handling as many requests for information calls for the district geologist as possible; providing drilling information to other companies who were our partners; checking with different geologists in our district to determine what prospects they wanted to present in the DES's daily committee meeting; and working up the agenda for that committee. The district clerk sat in on committee meetings and took notes. If these items were scheduled for presentation in the higher committee (division level), he would take care of getting this on the agenda. If approved here, he would prepare our portion of Co-Op's Division Committee Minutes. This is where I came in. Hooray! ~~I was allowed to type from his penciled copy!~~

When geologists needed well cost estimates, the district clerk had the responsibility of contacting the appropriate engineer and obtaining the information. The district clerk was responsible for filing all required information with the U.S. Geological Survey. These requests came across my desk first. I gave them to him, he worked up and gathered the information, and I typed the transmittal letter. You can see the ~~overlapping~~ ~~responsibilities~~ of ~~my job and his~~. ~~At one time~~ or another ~~in the changeover from one operatio~~ns geologist ~~to another~~ and then to ~~the clerk, I handled all of these duties~~; but they were never delegated to me as full responsibilities. ~~My job was most interesting and challenging at these times.~~ There was ~~no revision~~ of ~~responsibilities~~ as a ~~result~~ of ~~my pleas~~ for ~~more~~ respon~~sibility~~.

With s~~everal~~ ~~cost-of-living~~ raises and m~~erit increases~~ over the years, I had reached a salary of ~~$650~~ and the ~~title~~ of "~~secretary~~." My main f~~unctio~~ns were ~~reduce~~d to te~~lephone service~~, c~~offee service~~, and cl~~eaning service~~. I did, however, have the possibility of increased salary with yearly cost-of-living raises—usually 5 percent, and Co-Op always gave these. Also, merit raises to qualify me for the senior secretary category were possible. I don't know what the ceiling was on this. Job advancement opportunities were practically none as far as I could see.

I had conversations with the DES and the DG after I decided I did not want this to be my future in spite of the good salary. In the conversations with the district superintendent, I asked that he and the district geologist attempt some method of including me in their district organization in a more meaningful way. I did not expect them to explain geology to me but to keep me informed of meetings (time and place) so that I might inform others who called me for such information. Also, I ~~asked~~ that they ~~introduce~~ ~~me~~ to ~~people~~ from the ~~outside~~ ~~who came~~ into the ~~office~~ so that I ~~might~~ ~~make~~ the ~~office~~ ~~run~~ a ~~little~~ ~~more smoothly~~. ~~I asked~~ to be ~~allowed~~ to ~~handle~~ the ~~committee~~ items (I felt this was essential to my knowing what our own district personnel were doing and to help them with many calls that it was not necessary for them to handle). ~~I requested specific~~ ~~responsibility~~ for ~~such things~~ that ~~came across my desk first~~ (U.S. Geological requests, etc.). These things could be handled upon receipt. There were no visible results from this conversation. Mr. Smitten determined that I had a "hang-up on serving coffee." (I do!)

I had basically the same conversation with the DG. Mr. Lahaye was much more informal, and I felt that I got through to him a little better. I told him I needed someone to "go to bat for me." His remarks were, "Susan, I know you are capable of handling a bigger job. I feel sure you could handle this district clerk's job, but this ~~company is just not structured so that a woman can grow~~ and develop along with an organization. You are somewhat of a unique person in that you are capable and willing to grow with a job. Most women don't want to do this." He further stated that he could not tell me what the DES expected of his secretary but that it would ~~never be any other way.~~ He felt that I was wanting a job that women who have worked all their lives finally progress into. ~~I tried to tell him~~ that ~~my degree~~ had ~~prepared me~~ to ~~step into~~ ~~one~~ of ~~those jobs right now.~~ He ~~felt~~ ~~I~~ was just ~~impatient~~ and ~~possibly~~ was ~~expecting too much from~~ a ~~work~~ situation. Maybe I should consider another line of work.

I talked again with the DES. He said he would not recommend me for a transfer to another department, and ~~I~~ was to ~~learn~~ to ~~like~~ ~~my~~ job as it was ~~or resign.~~ I pondered all of this and decided that ~~Mr. Goddard~~ may ~~have been~~ right ~~after all,~~ ~~I would~~ never ~~find~~ ~~what~~ I ~~wanted~~ at ~~Co-Op or any major oil company.~~ I knew my future if I remained in the job would be to continue along just as everything was. The ~~division-level~~ ~~jobs~~ were ~~even~~ less ~~challenging.~~ The ~~higher~~ the ~~management~~ ~~level,~~ the ~~less~~ the ~~secretaries~~ ~~had to do~~ unless you got a special kind of boss. Mr. Smitten, the DES, felt that with the attitude I had about certain secretarial functions (serving coffee), I would ultimately be happier doing something else.

If there is no place in a major oil company for the kind of work I felt capable of doing, I must be in the wrong field. I resigned and am now enrolled in college again to certify in the teaching field.

Questions about the Susan Swanson case

1. Why did Susan find Job 1 so interesting and rewarding?

2. What was Susan looking for in her subsequent jobs that she did not find? Why couldn't she find what she wanted? What were her motives?

3.   What are the problems that develop when overqualified people are hired for unde-manding jobs?

4.   In her last job, Miss Swanson was making more money than she probably could make as a starting teacher in the local school system. What does her decision illustrate about the importance of money as a motivator?

5.   What could Susan's supervisors have done to make her work more satisfactory to her and more productive for the oil company? What would have challenged and interested her?

6.   Evaluate the leadership styles and techniques of each of Miss Swanson's bosses.

7.   Did Susan make any mistakes that may have contributed to her own problems?

Grace Lanham-An Office Manager Who Consulted Her Workers

With the exception of the work done by the general manager's personal secretary and the receptionist-secretary in the Personnel Department, all of the secretarial-stenographical work at the Hyde Company, a printing company, is performed by a secretarial pool composed of ~~six secretaries~~ and ~~an office manager~~. The ~~office manager receives~~ the ~~work~~ from each ~~executive~~ and ~~distributes~~ it to one of the secretaries to be performed.

Business in the secretarial pool is usually brisk. As a result, the typewriting machines and other related equipment receive a good amount of wear. It is time to replace each of the typewriters in the pool. Three weeks ago, the Purchasing Department asked Grace Lanham, the Office Manager, what typewriter she would recommend for purchase for herself and the six women in her department. She in turn asked the women in the department what typewriter they would prefer. She told them to collectively select the electric typewriter they thought would be best, and she would recommend the one they chose.

The women eagerly busied themselves in getting information about available typewriters. They selected typewriter models from four different companies and asked for demonstrations from each of the companies. Following the demonstrations they debated the differences in keyboard formations, marginal adjustments, warranty and service contracts, and other factors that seemed important. After many hours of discussion the women, by mutual consent, ranked the typewriters in order of preference.

The Hathaway Model 2100A was ranked first. The Burex Model 1336 was made the second choice. The women agreed upon the Harbound Model K97 as the third choice. Fourth preference was given to the Bowenwrite Model 555. The women's selections in order of preference were given to Mrs. Lanham.

Two days following the decision by the women, one of them (Kay Brinker) was assigned to type some purchase orders for the Purchasing Department. Among the purchase orders she found an order for ~~seven typewriters, Model K27~~, from the Harbound Typewriter Company. It was obvious to Kay that all of the hard work she and the other women had done to select a typewriter had been ignored. Within minutes Kay had informed the other women of her discovery. She was careful to avoid saying anything to Mrs. Lanham, however.

Questions about the Grace Lanham case

1. What leadership style did Mrs. Lanham use? Was this style appropriate?

2. What personal needs were appealed to when women were given the opportunity to make the typewriter decision?

3. What evidence is there in this case that an informal organization exists?

4. What are the merits of group decision making in a situation like this? What are the disadvantages?

5. What will the women's reaction be if nothing is done by Mrs. Lanham at the end of the case?

6. What actions should Mrs. Lanham take? Support your answer. Role play conversations Mrs. Lanham might have with her superiors. With the women in the typing pool.

7. How could these problems have been avoided satisfactorily?

Bill Caden-The Consultant Who Loses His Office

Travers and Associates is an old firm, established more than thirty years ago by Clay Travers to provide professional consulting services to business and industry. Mr. Travers was formerly with a large automobile manufacturing company in Detroit. In fact, he began his consulting services in Detroit but moved his offices to Chicago shortly after beginning his new work because most of his clients seemed to be in that area. The head quarters office remains in Chicago today, but the scope of the firm's operations has increased considerably. Branch offices now operate in New York, Atlanta, and Los Angeles. Men from each of these offices travel around the United States and throughout the world performing research on a variety of subjects and giving advice to a variety of companies.

The original intent of the Travers firm was to concentrate on manpower and organizational problems of businesses. However, one of the first people Travers hired to help in consulting and research was a young man with a chemical engineering degree as well as some industrial management experience. As a result of the young man's interests and capabilities, the Travers company began providing assistance to companies with technical problems, including very specific problems requiring mathematical, chemical, and engineering knowledge of a high degree. Most of the consultants with technical backgrounds in these areas work out of the Chicago office, but each of the regional offices has a few of these technical experts.

Each branch office is staffed with a number of general consultants who are trained and experienced in all phases of management. Also, every office has statistical experts who utilize computers and other quantitative means to aid in finding answers and solutions to the needs of businesses. Every office has large computer facilities. Each office is staffed by several social scientists—psychologists, sociologists, and others with expertise aiding in industrial research and consulting.

Each branch is headed by a vice president and general manager who is also a major partner in the overall firm. The vice president and general manager serves as the public relations officer for the branch office. When someone in industry needs consulting or research help, the vice president is the one who first talks with the person needing help. The vice president and general manager determines whether the Travers firm is capable of providing the assistance needed and quotes the fee that will be asked for services rendered. If mutual agreement is reached, the vice president and general manager gives the assignment to one of the consultants or researchers in his office. Occasionally, he may choose to handle the project himself.

The vice president and general manager holds all authority and responsibility for the operation and success of the branch office under his guidance. Ted McMorris, the vice president of the Los Angeles branch office (the office of primary interest in this case) has chosen to give much of the responsibility for internal matters to one of the consultants or researchers on a rotating basis. Every two years, McMorris selects one of his chief consultants and gives him the title of office manager. This means that the person assigned for the two-year period performs, in addition to his normal duties, the responsibilities of seeing that all personnel have the supplies, manpower, facilities, and so forth needed by them to do their jobs. He settles intra-office disputes, assigns offices and floor space, reviews personnel policies, inspects the office facilities for cleanliness, and performs any other duties delegated to him by McMorris. After two years, someone else is selected by McMorris and is given the assignment. McMorris has always felt that two years was as long as he could ask any of his associates to fill the job, since it means taking away some of the time they would otherwise spend pursuing their particular specialties. Actually, the job seldom has been allowed by those assigned to it to interfere with their own activities. Most of the personnel in the branch office are professionals anyway and seem to prefer a minimum of supervision. Terry Reardon, a psychologist, is currently acting as office manager. In two weeks, Trenton Merriweather, a statistical expert, will assume the job for the coming two-year period. Merriweather holds a doctorate in business administration from a large state university, had ten years of industrial experience before coming to work with Travers, and has been with Travers for eight years. He began in Chicago and came to Los Angeles five years ago.

The physical plant of the Los Angeles office makes employees in other Travers branches envious because the Los Angeles branch occupies the entire third floor of a beautiful, new building. It is excellently equipped with a library, research laboratory, and large conference room. Travers and Associates occupied the floor when the building was opened two years ago.

Every full-time researcher or consultant of permanent status with Travers has an office of his own with carpeting, draperies, paintings, and other trim. As can be seen in Exhibit I, the executive offices are on the outer walls, and each has a view of the surrounding office district. Also on the outer wall are the computer facilities,

EXHIBIT I   Floor Plan of Travers' Los Angeles Office

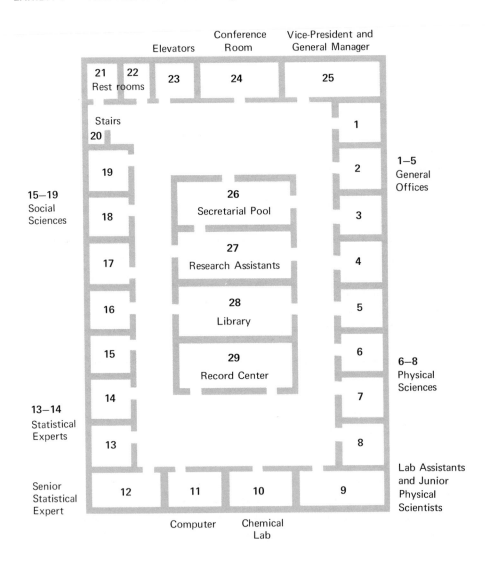

the chemical lab, and a larger office that many junior researchers share. The internal section is divided into three large rooms. The secretarial pool occupies one room; the library and record center fills the second room; and the third room is well filled with research assistants and lower-level executives.

Most of the full-time executive consultants and researchers (those with separate offices) are highly trained professionals. Many of them have doctorates, and all of them have outstanding experience backgrounds.

One of the active younger consultants for Travers is Bill Caden, an organizational communications expert. He is trained and knowledgeable in technical phases of communication (the use of television circuits for training purposes, etc.) through the electrical engineering degree he holds, and he is also an interpersonal communication expert as a result of training received while working on his master's degree in communication and through six years of business experience in which he was primarily a communication troubleshooter for a large manufacturer. In addition to his consulting work, he is taking three hours of course work a semester at a local university toward a Ph.D. in communications. He is considered highly qualified by those who have worked with him.

When Caden came to work for Travers three years ago, his status with the company was not clearly established. It was assumed by Travers executives and by Caden that his employment was semipermanent. Caden could work for Travers until he got his Ph.D. When his doctorate was completed, both parties (the Travers officials and Caden) would review the situation to determine if permanent status was desirable.

Caden quickly adapted to his new work and became very involved in consulting and research. The pursuit of his doctorate became somewhat secondary to him as he devoted more and more time to his consulting duties.

Before Travers moved to the new office facility two years ago, Caden had been located in an office with a senior consultant and a research assistant. Quarters were rather crowded at the time, and everyone (with a few exceptions) shared offices.

When Travers moved to the new building, all of the outer offices but one were filled with executives, senior consultants, or researchers, or with laboratories and other predesigned areas. Room 5 was not assigned to anyone, so the room was given to Caden even though his status was indefinite. Caden was quite pleased with his selection for the office. He brought in green plants and a fish aquarium "to decorate up the place a little."

That was two years ago. The Los Angeles office of Travers has flourished and is growing bigger. A few permanent personnel have been transferred or have left the company. All who left have been replaced. One or two of the replacements have been young like Caden. In fact, one is working on his Ph.D. in psychology in a manner similar to Caden's. In other words, he's taking a course or two each semester. Each replacement has been given the office vacated by the person replaced.

The time has come for additions to the staff, since the volume of requests for consulting and research services has increased greatly. One addition has already been signed. He is Dr. Randolph Kenminger, a noted author and a former faculty member at a Big Ten school. His specialty is communication, but he can handle most managerial consulting assignments. He is one of the best known, most highly respected individuals in his field.

Two weeks ago, Trenton Merriweather (incoming office manager) came into Caden's office, and the following conversation was held.

MERRIWEATHER: Bill, I had hoped Terry [Reardon] would do this, but he said that since I was taking over for him in a few weeks, it was my job. So here goes. How soon do you think you can move over to Room 27?

CADEN: (Jokingly) I'm pretty fast on my feet. What did you have in mind?

MERRIWEATHER: I don't think you understand. With Dr. Kenminger coming in soon, we'll be needing this office space for him. As you know, all of our private offices are filled. We couldn't very well expect him to share an office with someone, could we?

CADEN: (After some moments of silence) No, we couldn't expect that, but I don't see why he should get this office and move me over in the bullpen with mostly just the research assistants. After all, Snowden over in social sciences has been here less time than I have. Why not give him that office?

MERRIWEATHER: We established a floor plan when we moved into this building giving general staff, which includes you, a certain number of offices, physical scientists a certain number, statisticians a certain number, and so forth. We plan to keep the number consistent. Kenminger is considered a member of the general staff. With as much prestige as he carries, we must do our best to keep him happy. This office seems the best place for him. Anyway, things aren't so bad over in 27, are they?

CADEN: I suppose not.

MERRIWEATHER: Good. We'll give you four or five days to get things ready; then we'll help you move over.

The conversation left Caden shaken and disappointed. Were they trying to tell him something around here that he had failed to recognize? He had come to think of himself as a key individual to the firm. In the back of his mind, he had hoped they might ask him to stay permanently. Now he was reasonably certain they were suggesting that he should prepare to leave when he completed his doctorate.

It was clear that he was temporary and expendable. Maybe he should quit being so conscientious at work and hurry his doctorate and get out of here.

Questions about the Bill Caden case

1. Draw the organization chart to describe the Los Angeles office of Travers and Associates.

2. Does the organization structure contribute in any way to the problems that have developed in this case? Why or why not?

3. What are the underlying causes of the problems in this case? Please be specific.

4. What are Bill Caden's personal goals and values that have made his work at Travers so attractive? Which of these goals are now being threatened?

5. Analyze the way in which Bill was requested to change offices. What (if anything) was wrong with the way in which the change was requested? How could the resentment that developed have been avoided?

6. What concepts of motivation, human needs, leadership, organizational structure, and organizational change are illustrated by this case?

7. What important lessons should the perceptive student of management learn from this case?

8. Role play the discussion that took place between Merriweather and Caden at the end of the case.

Richard Jameson-The Guard Who Worked Labor Day

The Tripoli Chemical Company uses petroleum as the basis for most of the products it manufactures or processes. The petroleum is refined, compounds are added, and the finished products are sold to other industries for their use or are retailed to individual families for use in private homes. Tripoli is the major employer in a south Texas community of 35,000 people. Because of the nature of the production process, the company operates on a continuous basis, utilizing shift rotations to keep the plant operating at all times.

Tripoli has been unionized for several years. The union contract spells out many important guidelines for management action. Through the collective bargaining process, it has been determined that employees of the company shall have eight paid holidays each year in addition to vacations. The contract specifies the rate of pay for employees who have to work on holidays and also outlines the procedures to be followed in determining who will have to work. Seniority is a primary factor in determining who must work if work is required during holidays.

Of course, many people are not covered by the collective bargaining agreement; all managerial and some nonmanagerial personnel are exempted. Company policy provides that all of these people shall also have eight paid holidays insofar as is possible according to production schedules. A different policy is applied to the determination of which exempt-status personnel will be required to work when needed during holidays. Policy states that:

Because of the continuing process of the company's products, it will be necessary to have some personnel work on paid holidays. Management shall follow the policy of rotating assignments so that no employee shall be in a position of having to work more than two or three holidays each year except by the employee's choice or under extreme emergency situations. As much as is possible, assignments for holidays shall be made taking into consideration the desires of the workers.

One group of workers not covered in collective bargaining and therefore subject to the company policy stated above is the security force. The security force at Tripoli is rather large considering the fact that three gates must be manned sixteen hours a day, five days a week, with an additional gate remaining open twenty-four hours a day every day of the week. Incoming and outgoing traffic are both checked. Several watchmen are employed for security purposes, particularly for night shifts. Lanier Whyte is the superintendent of all security activities and makes all work assignments in connection with security as well as performing other supervisory duties.

Last Labor Day, Tripoli was expecting to receive several shipments of materials and supplies as well as anticipating the completion of a large shipment of its own to be transported by tank trucks. It was decided that in addition to the one twenty-four-hour gate, another gate would necessarily be kept open on the 7:00 A.M. to 3:00 P.M. shift. Four security men would be needed to keep the appropriate gates open—three would have eight-hour shifts on the main gate, and one would keep the auxiliary gate for the eight hours specified. Richard Jameson was designated to keep the auxiliary gate from 7:00 until 3:00.

Jameson became upset when on August 15 he received the notice of his assignment by memorandum. He called Whyte immediately and told him that he had plans for a trip with his family that weekend and that forcing him to work Labor Day would completely disrupt the plans. He also implied that Whyte was showing favoritism by not requiring certain other individuals to work instead.

Whyte's response was factual and somewhat pointed. Every security officer had worked one or both of the last two paid holidays with the exception of six men. Two of these men had made personal requests for the day off prior to the making up of the assignment list. The other four men, including Jameson, were the ones whose names appeared on the assignment sheet. Jameson had made no request. This would be only the second holiday Jameson had worked in the past ten months. Therefore, it seemed appropriate for Jameson to work Labor Day.

Jameson still was not satisfied. During the days prior to the Labor Day holiday, he continued to pester Whyte whenever possible, asking him to get another worker to substitute for him. Whyte stuck to his position, saying that it was only fair that Jameson work his own turn. No other worker volunteered to exchange places with Jameson.

Jameson worked Labor Day, although he complained to everyone about the unfairness of it all. It is now two days after Labor Day, and the effects of the assignment seem to be lingering with Jameson. Whyte has seen Jameson only twice, but on both occasions it was obvious that he was bitter and discontented. He scarcely acknowledged Whyte's presence and answered only questions specifically directed to him. The end-of-shift reports filed by Jameson for the last several days had all been sloppy, incomplete, and vague. All of this reminded Whyte of the fact that Jameson had a tendency to be temperamental if things weren't going his way.

Word has gotten back to Whyte from two different sources that Jameson's work the last few days had not been up to standard. Drivers going through the gate manned by Jameson have told Whyte that Jameson was rather rude to them. Some of Jameson's fellow security workers have told Whyte that Jameson has been spreading stories about Whyte's acts of favoritism toward some of the security officers at his (Jameson's) expense. The effect of Jameson's action was to stir up some uneasiness among many of the workers with whom he had contact. Whyte is concerned about Jameson's attitude as well as his actions.

Questions about the Richard Jameson case

1. What are the underlying causes of the problems that have developed in this case?

2. Does Mr. Jameson have a legitimate complaint concerning the Labor Day work schedule? Why or why not?

3. Evaluate Mr. Whyte's actions up to this point. What has he done well? What has he handled poorly? Explain your answers.

4. What actions (if any) should be taken by Mr. Whyte now?

5. What concepts of managing people can be learned by analyzing this case?

6. Role play conversations Mr. Whyte might have with Mr. Jameson.

Walt Gladberry –
The Thin-Skinned Trainee

Eastern Oil Company hires a large number of college graduates annually for positions ranging from field representatives (sales) to managerial positions in the offices of the national headquarters in New York or in one of the divisional offices throughout the eastern United States. The main products of Eastern Oil (a subsidiary of a larger corporation) are gasoline, oil, and related products sold to industrial concerns as well as to private customers.

When Eastern hires a new college graduate with no previous experience for any managerial position other than the highly technical (engineering, for example) or some office positions (secretarial mostly), the new graduate goes into a year-long training program. During this year, the trainee spends one month in a general orientation program, then three months each in three departmental offices (sales, marketing research, personnel, real estate, and so forth) at the central office or in divisional offices and finally, two months working in a service station and/or touring the country doing promotional work with newly opened service stations. The rotation to different jobs is designed to broaden the experience and outlook of the trainee; the two-month duty in the service station (doing the work of an attendant) is included to develop customer awareness as well as to familiarize the trainee with operations at the local level. Eastern believes the last two months are extremely valuable in determining the final suitability of the trainee for a career with the company.

Eastern operates a service station in a New Jersey city that serves strictly as a training station for management trainees. A station manager, selected because of his knowledge of the company's service and sales goals and his teaching abilities, heads the operation. Three shift managers, each responsible for an eight-hour

EXHIBIT I   Organization structure of training station

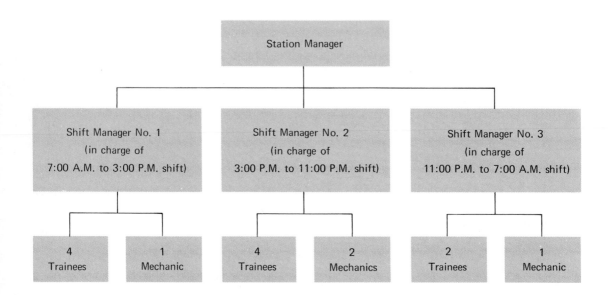

shift daily, report to the station manager. They, too, have been selected because of their knowledge and training skills. The trainees are each assigned to a shift and report to one of the shift managers during the two months they are at the station. In addition, at least one permanent mechanic works regularly under each shift manager. The training station's organization structure is shown in Exhibit I.

Clifford Spann, Shift Manager No. 2, has just indicated to Arland Brannon, the station manager, that he has a problem with one of the trainees reporting to him. The trainee (Walt Gladberry) has been at the station for about three weeks now. He's in the final phases of his training with Eastern, having come to the company straight out of Northern State University with a B.B.A. received almost a year ago. He made a very favorable impression upon those who supervised him in the earlier phases of his training. Generally speaking, Spann also has been positively impressed with Gladberry's performance. Gladberry has shown himself to be very conscientious; he's a very hard worker. Courtesy to the customer is also in the forefront of this thinking.

Gladberry's problem is that he lacks the ability to take criticism, even when it is needed and worded in a positive manner. To illustrate, when Spann sits down to talk to Gladberry about the weekly performance evaluation (required in the training program) that he has made on him, Gladberry grows tense. If any criticism is offered, Gladberry seems bitter and may not speak to Spann for hours at a time. He appears insulted and hurt.

Gladberry also appears quite sensitive to the comments of the other trainees working with him. While they think highly of him, if they tease him, he tends to think they are making fun of him unduly.

Supervisor Spann is especially concerned because he needs to find an approach whereby he can make some suggestions to Gladberry without having him feel insulted. He's also concerned about Gladberry's managerial potential if he continues to maintain such a "thin skin."

Questions about the Walt Gladberry case

1. To what may the tensions and resentment during the evaluations of Gladberry's performance be attributed?

2. What concepts concerning motivation, control, disciplinary action, leadership, and training are illustrated in this case?

3. What kind of future does Gladberry appear to have with Eastern Oil? Is he an employee worth trying to keep?

4. What should be done by Gladberry's superiors to help him and to reduce the tensions that have developed?

5. Evaluate the purposes, goals, and design of the training program at Eastern Oil? Is this type of training desirable? Why or why not?

6. Role play a performance evaluation session between Spann and Gladberry. Attempt to overcome the problems that have occurred in previous evaluations. Assume that Gladberry's performance is generally acceptable but that he needs a little instruction in one area.

7. Role play a situation in which Spann and Gladberry handle the problem of Gladberry's "thin skin."

Abigail Spiegal and Trudy Pennington–Overheard in the Coffee Room

Glen Garrison, assistant manager of Altman's Family Department Store, is on his way to the employees' coffee room when he suddenly pauses to listen to a conversation taking place inside the coffee room. From the voices and the line of talk, he discerns that the two women talking are Abigail Spiegal, a long-time employee of the store who works as a sales clerk in ladies' formal wear, and Trudy Pennington, a young college student recently hired to work as a part-time cashier. The women are unaware that there are supervisors within hearing distance of their conversation. Mrs. Spiegal is saying:

> Honey, you're new at this store, so let me tell you a few things for your own benefit. I've been noticing the way you work in the few days that you've been here, and I think you're ~~working entirely too hard~~. You're ~~too much of an eager beaver~~. I think you should quit working so hard and ~~take life easy~~. They [the managers] will never know the difference.
>
> Let me tell you what I mean. Yesterday afternoon when we weren't very busy, I noticed you started looking for odd jobs to do to keep yourself occupied. You straightened up the shelves behind your counter, and then you went over to the shoe department and helped them sort out some invoices while you waited for your own job to pick up. ~~You shouldn't do things like that!~~ If Mr. Petrie [the manager] and Mr. Garrison should see you doing things like that, they would begin to expect you to do extra things all the time. The longer you work here, the more you'll come to protect yourself from extra work. You've got enough to take care of with your own job. Besides, for no more money than you're making, management is getting all it's entitled to if you just take care of your cashiering.

The thing for you to do is to learn how to look busy even when you're not. Call somebody on the phone, or hide a good book somewhere, or do something else to make yourself look occupied when you have spare time. Life's too short to wear yourself out slaving for Altman's Department Store.

Mr. Garrison could hear Miss Pennington's response:

Gee, I hadn't thought of it like that, Abigail. I see what you mean. From now on, I'll try to be more careful. I probably have been taking my work too seriously.

Mr. Garrison hesitates outside the door to the coffee room, deliberating what his next action should be.

Questions about the Abigail Spiegal and Trudy Pennington case

1.   What will be the effect of Mrs. Spiegal's actions upon the attitude and behavior of Trudy Pennington? On the other employees of Altman's?

2.   What are Mrs. Spiegal's personal work needs and expectations? In keeping with these needs, why does she find it necessary to give instruction to Trudy Pennington?

3.   What are the formal organizational goals of Altman's Family Department Store as seen through the eyes of management (you may need to make up a list of goals and objectives)? Are the formal organizational goals the same as the goals of the informal organization?

4.   What actions should Mr. Garrison take? Explain your answer in detail.

5.   Role play the conversation Mrs. Spiegal's boss might have with her. Also role play the conversation that might occur between Trudy Pennington and her boss.

Alan Purdy–A Section Head Getting the Cold Shoulder

During these past two weeks, Alan Purdy, head of the data processing section at Lighting Falls National Bank, has begun to hate going to work each day. Work once was a pleasure to Alan, but in recent days he has begun to suspect that he has either bad breath or a contagious disease or something worse. His subordinates formerly confided in him and talked frequently about things of personal interest. They gave him free cooperation in their work and were loyal to him. His colleagues had always been enjoyable, and he had been able to engage in mutual joking and other congenial conversations. He had a respect for them, and they seemed to return the admiration. Something changed about two weeks ago, and Alan has been unable to understand what happened.

In recent days Purdy has been lucky to get a nod out of his fellow workers in response to his greetings or questions. Everyone, including some of his superiors , has given him a cold shoulder. Purdy has noted more absences in his department in the past few days than he can recall in years. Departmental efficiency appears to be suffering, also.

Purdy has questioned his subordinates to determine if they are encountering job problems, and they have brushed away his inquires with noncommittal answers. When Alan asked Vic Sanger, an assistant cashier who also is his closest friend at the bank, if he knew why everyone was responding to him so indifferently, Sanger honestly admitted that he knew of no reason for it. Sanger agreed with Purdy that a boycott seemingly was being conducted against him. Sanger also felt that some of his own work associates were giving him a rather cool reaction.

The truth of the matter is, the workers believe that Alan Purdy is a primary cause of the bank's new policy on shorter coffee break hours and closer regulation of the time involved. About two weeks ago, new regulations were established that restricted employees to the bank premises while taking their coffee breaks. Guidelines were established restricting break periods to fifteen minutes in the morning and afternoon. Supervisors were required to enforce the break regulations with disciplinary action whenever necessary.

The policy came from the office of Edward Hunter, vice president of personnel. Hunter's personal secretary, Elaine Roberts, typed the memorandum concerning the new policy from dictation given to her by Mr. Hunter immediately following a long visit between Hunter and Purdy. The meeting was held in Hunter's office and appeared to be the culmination of a long series of meetings in recent weeks between the two men. Miss Roberts assumed that the two were engaged in discussions about coffee break abuses, and the new policy was the result. She passed her ideas along to some other secretaries, and the word spread.

What Miss Roberts did not know was that Alan Purdy had nothing to do with the policy on coffee break restrictions. His meetings with Mr. Hunter were on the subject of more complete personnel data records through the use of computers.

Questions about the Alan Purdy case

1. What characteristics of informal organizations are illustrated by this case?

2. Suppose Purdy discovers the truth—that Elaine Roberts started the false rumor that has led to his rejection. What should he do? Support your answer in detail.

3. What action, if any, should be directed toward Elaine Roberts?

4. What concepts should the student of management learn from this case in addition to the points already discussed?

Index